The Deliberations
of the Council of Four
(March 24–June 28, 1919)

VOLUME II

Lt. Paul Mantoux, with the cross of Knight of the Legion of Honor.
(Courtesy of Jacques Mantoux)

The Deliberations of the Council of Four (March 24–June 28, 1919)

NOTES OF THE OFFICIAL INTERPRETER

PAUL MANTOUX

II

From the Delivery of the Peace Terms to the German Delegation to the Signing of the Treaty of Versailles

SUPPLEMENTARY VOLUME TO THE PAPERS OF WOODROW WILSON

Translated and Edited by

ARTHUR S. LINK

With the Assistance of MANFRED F. BOEMEKE

PRINCETON UNIVERSITY PRESS

PRINCETON, NEW JERSEY

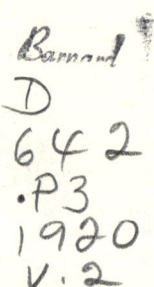

This is Volume II of two volumes

Copyright © 1992 by Princeton University Press
Published by Princeton University Press, 41 William Street,
Princeton, New Jersey 08540
In the United Kingdom: Princeton University Press, Oxford

All Rights Reserved

Library of Congress Cataloging-in-Publication Data

Paris Peace Conference (1919-1920)
   [Délibérations du Conseil des Quatre, 24 mars-28 juin 1919. English]
   The deliberations of the Council of Four (March 24-June 28, 1919) / notes of the official interpreter, Paul Mantoux; translated and edited by Arthur S. Link with the assistance of Manfred F. Boemeke.
   p.   cm.
   Translation of: Les délibérations du Conseil des Quatre, 24 mars-28 juin 1919.
   Includes bibliographical references and index.
   Contents: v. 1. To the delivery to the German Delegation of the preliminaries of peace — v. 2. From the delivery of the peace terms to the German Delegation to the signing of the Treaty of Versailles.
   ISBN 0-691-04793-6 (set : alk. paper)
   1. World War, 1914–1918—Peace—Sources. 2. World War, 1914–1918—Diplomatic history—Sources. I. Mantoux, Paul, 1877–1956.
II. Link, Arthur Stanley. III. Boemeke, Manfred F. (Manfred Franz) IV. Title.
D642.P3 1920
940.3′141—dc20   90-28089 CIP

Publication of this book has been aided by a grant from the Woodrow Wilson Foundation

This book has been composed in Melior Typefaces

Princeton University Press books are printed on acid-free paper,
and meet the guidelines for permanence and durability of the
Committee on Production Guidelines for Book Longevity of the
Council on Library Resources

Printed in the United States of America by Princeton University Press,
Princeton, New Jersey

10 9 8 7 6 5 4 3 2 1

Contents

VOLUME II

Abbreviations — ix

LXVIII. May 8, 1919, 11 A.M.	3
LXIX. May 9, 1919, 11:30 A.M.	9
LXX. May 9, 1919, 4 P.M.	12
LXXI. May 10, 1919, 11 A.M.	18
LXXII. May 10, 1919, 3 P.M.	29
LXXIII. May 10, 1919, 4 P.M.	32
LXXIV. May 11, 1919, NOON	36
LXXV. May 12, 1919, 11 A.M.	42
LXXVI. May 12, 1919, 3:30 P.M.	48
LXXVII. May 13, 1919, 4 P.M.	49
LXXVIII. May 14, 1919, 11 A.M.	60
LXXIX. May 14, 1919, 4 P.M.	69
LXXX. May 15, 1919, 11 A.M.	73
LXXXI. May 17, 1919, 11 A.M.	83
LXXXII. May 17, 1919, 4 P.M.	92
LXXXIII. May 19, 1919, 11 A.M.	100
LXXXIV. May 19, 1919, 4:30 P.M.	109
LXXXV. May 20, 1919, 11 A.M.	120
LXXXVI. May 21, 1919, 11 A.M.	125
LXXXVII. May 21, 1919, 4 P.M.	141
LXXXVIII. May 22, 1919, 11 A.M.	160
LXXXIX. May 22, 1919, NOON	165
XC. May 22, 1919, 4:15 P.M.	168
XCI. May 23, 1919, 11 A.M.	178
XCII. May 23, 1919, 4 P.M.	186
XCIII. May 24, 1919, 11 A.M.	195
XCIV. May 24, 1919, 4 P.M.	200
XCV. May 26, 1919, 11 A.M.	206
XCVI. May 26, 1919, 3:30 P.M.	211
XCVII. May 26, 1919, 4 P.M.	214
XCVIII. May 27, 1919, NOON	228
XCIX. May 27, 1919, 4 P.M.	233
C. May 28, 1919, 11:45 A.M.	235
CI. May 28, 1919, 4:30 P.M.	240

CII. May 29, 1919, NOON	249
CIII. May 30, 1919, 4 P.M.	254
CIV. May 31, 1919, 5:30 P.M.	264
CV. June 2, 1919, 4 P.M.	268
CVI. June 3, 1919, 4 P.M.	278
CVII. June 4, 1919, 11:30 A.M.	293
CVIII. June 4, 1919, 4 P.M.	298
CIX. June 5, 1919, 11 A.M.	307
CX. June 5, 1919, 4 P.M.	314
CXI. June 6, 1919, 11 A.M.	323
CXII. June 6, 1919, 4 P.M.	329
CXIII. June 7, 1919, 11 A.M.	334
CXIV. June 7, 1919, 4 P.M.	338
CXV. June 9, 1919, 11 A.M.	349
CXVI. June 10, 1919, 11 A.M.	362
CXVII. June 10, 1919, 4 P.M.	375
CXVIII. June 11, 1919, 11 A.M.	382
CXIX. June 11, 1919, 4 P.M.	385
CXX. June 12, 1919, 11 A.M.	401
CXXI. June 12, 1919, 4 P.M.	417
CXXII. June 13, 1919, 11 A.M.	425
CXXIII. June 13, 1919, 4 P.M.	437
CXXIV. June 13, 1919, 5 P.M.	442
CXXIVA. June 14, 1919, 11 A.M.	449
CXXV. June 14, 1919, 4:30 P.M.	450
CXXVI. June 16, 1919, 11 A.M.	459
CXXVII. June 16, 1919, 4 P.M.	461
CXXVIII. June 16, 1919, 6:30 P.M.	472
CXXIX. June 17, 1919, NOON	476
CXXX. June 17, 1919, 3 P.M.	478
CXXXI. June 17, 1919, 4 P.M.	481
CXXXII. June 20, 1919, 5 P.M.	493
CXXXIII. June 21, 1919, 11 A.M.	503
CXXXIV. June 21, 1919, 4 P.M.	507
CXXXV. June 22, 1919, 7:20 P.M.	512
CXXXVI. June 23, 1919, 9 A.M.	519
CXXXVII. June 23, 1919, 11 A.M.	520
CXXXVIII. June 23, 1919, 4 P.M.	528
CXXXIX. June 24, 1919, 11 A.M.	533
CXL. June 25, 1919, 11 A.M.	538
CXLI. June 25, 1919, 4 P.M.	546
CXLII. June 26, 1919, 11 A.M.	557
CXLIII. June 26, 1919, 4 P.M.	565

CXLIV. June 27, 1919, 11 A.M. 575
CXLV. June 27, 1919, 4 P.M. 578
CXLVI. June 28, 1919, 10:30 A.M. 586
CXLVII. June 28, 1919, 11:15 A.M. 592
CXLVIII. June 28, 1919, 4:15 P.M. 598
CXLVIIIA. June 28, 1919, 5:30 P.M. 603

Dramatis Personae 607
Sources and Works Cited 628
Index 633

Abbreviations

EMH	Edward Mandell House
FR 1919, Russia	*Papers Relating to the Foreign Relations of the United States, 1919, Russia*
PPC	*Papers Relating to the Foreign Relations of the United States, The Paris Peace Conference, 1919*
PWW	Arthur S. Link et al., eds., *The Papers of Woodrow Wilson*, 65 vols. to date (Princeton, N. J., 1966-)
WW	Woodrow Wilson

The Deliberations
of the Council of Four
(March 24–June 28, 1919)

VOLUME II

LXVIII

Conversation between President Wilson and MM. Clemenceau, Lloyd George, Orlando, and Baron Sonnino*

MAY 8, 1919, 11 A.M.

M. Clemenceau. I have been wondering whether there is any reason to reply to what Count Brockdorff-Rantzau seemed to ask when he spoke of the establishment of commissions on responsibilities and about the text of the treaty as we have written it.[1] On the first point, I propose to reply that we ourselves have determined the method of investigation of everything that concerns responsibilities, and, on the second point, that our decision to admit only written documents excludes any possibility of mixed commissions to consider the clauses of the treaty.

Mr. Lloyd George. If we allowed verbal discussions between our experts and the German experts, for example on the question of reparation, we would never see the end of it.

—*M. Clemenceau's proposals are adopted.*

President Wilson. I had a list of questions about boundaries sent to me—those upon which our experts agree, and those on which there are still decisions to be taken.[2]

There is agreement on the boundaries of Austria, Hungary, and Bulgaria.

The borders of Czechoslovakia have been fixed, except around Teschen and on some points of the Hungarian side.

The boundaries of Yugoslavia are settled except on the Italian side.

Nothing on the boundary between Belgium and Holland: naturally, since that is not within the purview of the conference.

Nothing has been decided about the Polish borders adjoining the Baltic countries, Russia, the Ukraine; on the Czechoslovak side, the question of Teschen remains to be settled, as I have already noted.

*H., *PPC*, V, 510ff.

[1] In his speech at the Plenary Session on May 7, Brockdorff-Rantzau said, among other things, that the measure of guilt of all participants could only be determined by impartial inquiry by a neutral commission and that the principal questions raised by the preliminary peace treaty should be referred to "special Commissions of experts." *PWW*, Vol. 58, pp. 515-16.

[2] S. E. Mezes to WW, May 5, 1919, Wilson Papers, Library of Congress.

Nothing has been decided about Russia's boundaries, or those which will have to be established inside the former Russian Empire.

Likewise, for Albania.

On the other hand, it may happen that our experts agree on a boundary, but that the peoples concerned do not.

Mr. Lloyd George. Since the question of borders are on the whole settled for both countries we wish to attend to first—Austria and Hungary—the most pressing thing is to request from our technical advisers:

> (1) a report on the disarmament of Austria, which can be modeled on the text relating to Germany;
>
> (2) a report on the indemnities and reparations owed by Austria;
>
> (3) a draft of financial clauses relative to Austria.

The same work could be done for Hungary.

M. Orlando. Following a discussion amongst ourselves, the Reparation Commission has already taken up the question of reparations owed by Austria and Hungary.

Mr. Lloyd George. I am going to inquire about that. In that case, it would only be necessary to continue the work begun. Who will summon the military experts to study the plan for Austria's disarmament?

M. Clemenceau. I'll do it.

Mr. Lloyd George. The resolution I have before me proposes to entrust that study to Marshal Foch and his experts. But Marshal Foch has ideas on disarmament which are not our own, and he holds them very strongly. I believe it is preferable to entrust this study to our military representatives at Versailles.

—*This proposal is adopted.*

Mr. Lloyd George. I suppose that we are now going to discuss amongst ourselves the bases of the peace with Austria such as it is now established—the former Duchy of Austria, if you prefer. This will simply consist of fixing the boundaries of this state and determining its status.

President Wilson. I fear that, if we treat separately the question of Austria and that of the other states born of the dissolution of the Austro-Hungarian monarchy, we will subsequently find ourselves in a difficult situation for imposing the execution of our terms. Let me explain.

If you wish to impose your will upon all these states, you must preserve the power which enables you either to grant or to refuse them peace. If, for instance, you determine today the boundary between Austria and the Yugoslavs, and Austria accepts it, that is not enough. The Yugoslavs must also accept it, and they won't do so until they, too, have signed the peace.

Mr. Lloyd George. I don't want to delay the solution of problems which are ripe for solution because others need more time. The boundaries of Yugoslavia can be fixed only when the question of the Adriatic has been settled. Given the current agitation on that issue, I believe it is preferable to wait and to settle the Austrian questions in the meantime.

President Wilson. The way to get out of this difficulty might be the following: we would ask Austria to acknowledge all the boundaries of her neighbors in advance. We will say in the treaty that the Austrian state agrees to acknowledge the boundaries of all the states of the former Austro-Hungarian monarchy, such as they will be approved by the League of Nations. The same stipulation will subsequently be inserted in the other treaties.

Mr. Lloyd George. I don't think we should mention the League of Nations here; we must say: "the Allied and Associated Powers."

President Wilson. I agree. The important thing is to preserve our authority; without that, we will never be able to settle the still more delicate question of the boundaries of Russia. Let us remember that we will have to determine, for example, the boundaries between Poland and the Ukraine.

Mr. Lloyd George. As for the Ukraine, everything I have learned shows me that it is an actual creation of Germany. M. Bark, the former Finance Minister of the Russian Empire, whom I met yesterday, told me that he himself was born in the Ukraine, and that no one had ever seriously thought of this area otherwise than as a part of Russia.

President Wilson. I don't completely agree with you. I believe a true desire for autonomy exists in the Ukraine.

Mr. Lloyd George. For autonomy, agreed; but as for a complete separation from Russia, I think it is a temporary movement.

President Wilson. Concerning the states of the former Austro-Hungarian monarchy, can't we ask the Council of Foreign Ministers to present us with recommendations on the boundaries already settled by the experts?

Baron Sonnino. Do you mean the boundaries between the small states?

Mr. Lloyd George. And the part of the Italian boundary upon which agreement has been reached.

Baron Sonnino. I will point out that the boundary between Austria and the Yugoslavs is not fixed, and that that question concerns Italy, because a railway which connects Trieste to Vienna is involved. The question is whether it should not pass from Italian territory to Austrian territory without crossing any part of Yugoslavia: that can be done easily.

—*The question of boundaries is referred to the Council of Foreign Ministers.*

President Wilson. And the question of responsibilities? Do you intend to raise the question with Austria as with Germany?

Mr. Lloyd George. It doesn't arise concerning the Emperor Charles: he wasn't there when war was declared, and his responsibility is nil.

President Wilson. Do we wish to extend to Austria the system of prosecution for individual crimes against international law?

M. Orlando. We can produce a great number of cases which render these prosecutions necessary.

Baron Sonnino. What was done by Austrian submarines must also be mentioned.

President Wilson. The difficulty is to determine which crimes were committed by German submarines and which are to be imputed to Austrian submarines.

Mr. Lloyd George. In any case, some orders had to have been given by Austrian authorities to the submarines, and the authors of these orders must be punished for organizing piracy.

Sir Maurice Hankey. I remind you that the Commission on Railways and Navigable Waterways had to draw up a special draft of its conclusions in order to insert them in the treaty with Germany. A similar draft for the treaty with Austria will be necessary.

—*The Commission on Ports, Railways, and Navigable Waterways will receive instructions to this effect.*

Mr. Lloyd George. We have already spoken of the total strength of the army of occupation on the left bank of the Rhine. It is a question, above all else, of avoiding an excessive financial charge which would weigh heavily on the total sum of reparations. I propose to have this question studied by a commission.

President Wilson. I don't know whether this commission should be named immediately, because we couldn't find an excuse for not placing Marshal Foch on it. He isn't exactly in the state of mind required to contemplate a reduction in the occupation forces.

Mr. Lloyd George. I accept the postponement proposed by President Wilson: surgeons say it is better to operate on patients when they do not have a fever. That applies perhaps also to the case of Fiume.

M. Orlando. Perhaps.

President Wilson. Colonel Hankey tells me that a plan already exists, prepared by Generals Wilson, Weygand, and Bliss, on a question relating to the occupation army; but it deals with relations with the German population in the occupied zone.

M. Clemenceau. The best thing is to refer this question and that of the total strength of the occupation army to the Supreme War Council.

—This proposal is adopted.

Mr. Lloyd George. I return to what M. Clemenceau said earlier about Brockdorff-Rantzau's statements: I am not sure that he specifically asked for the establishment of mixed commissions.

President Wilson. The sentence he used can be interpreted both ways.

M. Clemenceau. In this case, it is best to say nothing to him and let him do whatever he wants.

Sir Maurice Hankey. The Supreme Economic Council requests that a decision be taken on the question of raw materials. As long as that question is not resolved—says the council's message—there will be no real hope of peace for Europe.

Mr. Lloyd George. This question especially concerns the United States and Great Britain, which together hold the greatest part of the indispensable raw materials; furthermore, it is linked to the question of credits in America. We are loaded with the burden of a rather considerable debt to the United States. The question of credits must be settled, regardless of the difficulties raised by the treasuries; for, if Europe doesn't obtain these raw materials, she will find herself in a position worse, in certain respects, than that of wartime.

President Wilson. The difficulty for the American Treasury lies in providing the guarantee that is asked of it for the German bonds.

Mr. Lloyd George. Without stressing this argument too much, I could tell you that the United States, having been neutral during the first two years of the war, made enormous profits—and this is not a reproach, for the same thing would have happened to us if we had remained neutral. But it seems to me possible and indispensable that the United States guarantee these bonds.

President Wilson. The difficulty is that we will only be able to do so through taxation, which would fall in great part on persons who derived no profit from the war.

Mr. Lloyd George. If we could renounce all debts owed us by our allies, provided you cancel our own, I assure you we would accept, although the balance would be unfavorable to us. It is absolutely necessary for us to deal with this question without delay.

—*The members of the Supreme Economic Council are convoked for tomorrow, Friday, May 9, at 10:30.*

Mr. Lloyd George reads aloud a document proving that the Germans are not carrying out the delivery of their ships in Spanish ports, as they are required to do by the terms of the Armistice.

President Wilson. Why take up our time with this business when we approach the signing of the treaty which will deliver all these ships to us?

M. Clemenceau. I think it is essential to require the execution of the Armistice Agreement and to pursue it right up to the signing of the treaty, all the more so since we greatly need the ships which the Germans are taking so long to give up.

President Wilson. What I want is not to multiply the points of friction and irritation if we can avoid it.

—*After an exchange of observations, it is decided that Admiral Wemyss will be charged with admonishing the German government about the nonexecution of the clauses of the Armistice relative to the delivery of enemy ships in neutral ports. If these admonitions are not followed by results, the Admiral should immediately report to the Supreme Council of the heads of governments.*

LXIX

Conversation between President Wilson and MM. Clemenceau, Lloyd George, and Orlando*

MAY 9, 1919, 11:30 A.M.

—The members of the Inter-Allied Supreme Economic Council are introduced.

Lord Robert Cecil. Our great problem is to put Europe back to work. Unemployment is growing everywhere, above all in the new states. To confine ourselves to feeding this unemployed population would have practically no effect from a political point of view: if they are fed and out of work, they will be even more disposed to revolt than if they were in the most extreme distress. It is therefore essential to restart their industries, and that can't be done without providing raw materials to countries which lack them.

Take Poland for example: her principal industry is the textile industry of Lodz. The equipment in the spinning mills is in perfect condition; but not one machine is in operation because there is no cotton, as well as no credit to buy it abroad. Poland doesn't have the means of payment, since her exports have completely stopped. Her agriculture itself suffers, because agricultural workers, inadequately clothed, can't go to the fields, and they are inadequately clothed because the textile industry has stopped.

The great problem is knowing how to provide the necessary credits. Personally, I wouldn't underwrite a scheme which would tend to open large credits to the Polish government without any control on our part; for the Polish government could use them to fight the Ukrainians rather than to nourish industry.

The problem is thus twofold: the credit must be found, and its proper use must be assured.

What is certain is that, if nothing is done, we will find ourselves faced with chaos and anarchy. What is true of Poland is equally true, in different circumstances, of many other countries, Germany first of all.

The first thing to do is to reestablish peace. I myself regretted that we did not deem it possible to lift the blockade before the

*H., PPC, V, 521ff.

signing of the treaty. The maintenance of the blockade prolongs distrust and instability. The phenomenon that faces us is to a great extent psychological: the depression is such that, even in cases where credits, English or American, have been placed at the disposal of the Poles, they have been little used, because of that inertia which has its root in the circumstances and conditions of life.

Mr. Lloyd George. Isn't the question of prices one of the factors in this situation? Don't merchants fear, by buying at current rates, to be ruined by a drop in prices?

Lord Robert Cecil. Here are our proposals: it is necessary, in the first place, to make an effort to find the essential credits; in the second place, it will be necessary both to prepare openly for the complete renewal of the blockade if the treaty is not signed, and to announce publicly that, from the signing of the peace, the blockade will be lifted.

I am not in position to say what must be done to find the credits that Europe needs. But I call your attention to the situation concerning the provisioning of Germany. We promised to supply Germany with 350,000 tons of foodstuffs a month until the harvest, and we have approximately succeeded. Not only did we deliver all that the Germans were able to pay for immediately, but considerable quantities were also provided without payment and without our knowing how this payment would take place. The Germans had always said that whatever gold and stocks remained to them were insufficient to guarantee these payments. We counted on a revival of German exports; but all efforts in this direction have failed. As a result, with sixty-eight million pounds sterling having been appropriated to send foodstuffs to Germany, payments made do not exceed 39.5 million.

Mr. Lloyd George. Will Germany hold until the harvest?

Mr. Hoover. By using the means of credit she has in the Argentine Republic, it would suffice to find seven million pounds to assure her victualing until harvest time.

Lord Robert Cecil. We have been informed that German securities are clandestinely leaving the country; a certain amount, it appears, has been removed by airplanes. The situation, such as we ascertain it, is serious, for, obviously, we cannot undertake to feed Germany for nothing.

Mr. Norman Davis. The German government is continuing its requisitioning of securities: it has requisitioned twelve million pounds sterling during the last three months. But the question is whether these securities are negotiable; they include a rather large number of Chinese securities.

Mr. Lloyd George. I have been told that the Germans owned a significant part of the Brazilian debt; but perhaps they have already disposed of it.

President Wilson. All we have just heard persuades me that we cannot take a decision today. We need to be advised by specialists. I propose to establish a committee immediately, on which each power will be represented by two experts instructed to study and propose the appropriate methods to insure to the countries now in urgent need of raw materials and foreign credits the help they desperately need.

Mr. Hoover. We must add: "and of foodstuffs."

President Wilson. We will say then: "in urgent need of raw materials, foodstuffs, and the corresponding credits."

Mr. Lloyd George. I accept this proposal. It is the only way out.

M. Clemenceau. I also accept it.

—*President Wilson's proposal is adopted.*

President Wilson. I think that the members of the Economic Council will be able to constitute this commission themselves. They are aware of the urgency of the problem.

Lord Robert Cecil. What is you decision about the blockade?

M. Clemenceau. It would be very good to announce that the blockade will be lifted upon the signing of the peace; by doing that, we will only make our intentions public. But I ask that Bolshevik Russia be left apart.

—*M. Clemenceau's proposal is adopted.*

—*The members of the Economic Council withdraw.*

—*Mr. James Brown Scott, member of the Drafting Committee, is introduced.*

President Wilson. Mr. Brown Scott comes to explain his view of a change in Article 430 to which our attention has been called.

Mr. James Brown Scott. The change is a minor one. The Drafting Committee has written:

"In the event that * * * the Reparation Commission finds that Germany has not observed all or part of the obligations imposed upon her by the present treaty, all or part of the zones specified in Article 429 would be reoccupied immediately by the forces of the Allied and Associated Powers."

President Wilson. The intention of the heads of governments was that the reoccupation would take place if the Germans refused to execute the provisions of the treaty, but not if they were prevented, for such or such a reason, from carrying them out.

Mr. Lloyd George. There is a big difference between "not executing" and "refusing to execute."

President Wilson. Furthermore, our intention was obviously to tie this stipulation to those which relate to reparation. We meant that, if the Germans refuse to carry out a part of the program of reparation, the consequence will be the renewal of the military occupation. Perhaps we should have stated it more clearly.

Mr. James Brown Scott. I think that it is not too late to make this change. The Germans will have no reason to complain about it, since it is to their advantage.

President Wilson. This rectification must be made without delay, and the Germans must be informed of it.

Mr. Lloyd George. I ask that the new text be submitted to us first.

Mr. James Brown Scott. We will draft it in the afternoon.

President Wilson. I propose also to write "may be immediately reoccupied" instead of "would be immediately reoccupied."

Mr. James Brown Scott. The original text said "will reoccupy."

President Wilson. Does anyone object to this change?

M. Clemenceau. The meaning is not the same.

President Wilson. The decision always remains in our hands. We will have the right to do what we deem best.

M. Clemenceau. Isn't it the same if we leave "will reoccupy"? In my opinion, if this is the original wording, we should let it stand.

—*The original wording is kept.*

LXX

Conversation between President Wilson and MM. Clemenceau, Lloyd George, and Orlando*

MAY 9, 1919, 4 P.M.

President Wilson. A question which troubles me is that, during the time necessary for the execution of the military clauses—which, by the way, must not exceed three months—it will certainly be necessary to maintain a larger occupation army on the left bank of the Rhine than later on. My military advisers tell me that, dur-

*H., *PPC*, V, 526ff.

ing this period, that is until the end of September, we must leave thirty divisions on the left bank of the Rhine. That will compel me, in July, August, and September, to delay the embarkation of American troops for the United States; for if it should continue at the same pace, we would drop below the contingent which guarantees our contribution to the common effort.

This is a first disadvantage, from our point of view. But here is a second one: our transports will remain unused for three months and the tonnage they represent can be of no service, because it is impossible to use these ships as cargo ships, barring their complete refitting, which would be followed by a reverse refitting when the transportation of troops would be resumed.

Mr. Lloyd George. General Robertson is a little alarmed by the speed with which the evacuation of American troops is taking place.

President Wilson. We are sending about 300,000 men a month back to America, and this number can be increased.

Mr. Lloyd George. General Robertson is alarmed about this because of possible contingencies: I ask myself what troops we might need for an occupation of Berlin. It is necessary, of course, to calculate the strength required to hold the lines of communication. What is the approximate distance between Berlin and the Rhine?

M. Mantoux. About 300 miles.

Mr. Lloyd George. The coast is nearer.

M. Mantoux. Much nearer: 200 miles at most.

Mr. Lloyd George. That question should be studied.

THE SITUATION IN RUSSIA

President Wilson. I have to talk to you about a rather embarrassing problem for the American government—Siberia. When we first attempted to send food to the Russian people, the Allies agreed to send to the first revolutionary government of Russia an American, Mr. Stevens, who was placed at the head of a commission entrusted, above all, with insuring the operation of the Trans-Siberian Railway.[1] Since then, American troops have policed the railroad between the Pacific and Irkutsk.

---

[1] The American government had sent a commission headed by a veteran American engineer, John Frank Stevens, to Russia in June 1917 to assist in the rehabilitation of Russian railroads. Stevens was followed by a large group of engineers organized as the Russian Railway Service Corps. Arriving at the time of the Bolshevik Revolution, they went to Japan to await developments. Stevens

Our government has no confidence in Admiral Kolchak, who is supported by France and England. Kolchak's partisans are irritated by the presence of the American soldiers, whom they view as neutrals because of their attitude. This attitude, moreover, makes an impression upon the peasants, who regard the United States as the democracy *par excellence* and conclude from America's refusal to declare itself in favor of Kolchak that the latter does not deserve to be supported.

The Cossacks are clearly hostile towards us, and the Japanese could ask for nothing better than to see a collision between the Americans and the Cossacks take place. In these circumstances, we must either support Kolchak and reinforce our occupation army or withdraw totally. But if we increase our numbers, Japan will do the same. When we went to Siberia, we had reached an agreement with Japan to send equal forces there. In fact, we sent 9,000 men and Japan 12,000. But, little by little, she increased their number and brought them up to 70,000 men.

Mr. Lloyd George. She has promised to reduce them to 30,000.

President Wilson. Even if 30,000 Japanese remain in Siberia, the number is all out of proportion to our own. If we confine ourselves to guarding the line as we have done so far, exposing American soldiers to difficulties with Kolchak's partisans, I fear incidents. If, on the other hand, we reinforce the troops who guard the railroad, I fear a coalition between the Cossacks and the Japanese against us.

I am obliged to take an immediate decision. We have received a note on this subject from Admiral Kolchak's Minister of Foreign Affairs, who complains about the attitude of the Americans.[2]

—President Wilson reads the note aloud and adds: in short, we should either cooperate with Kolchak or withdraw.

---

and the corps returned to Siberia in the spring of 1918. After long and labored negotiations with Japan (Japan and the United States had meanwhile sent troops to Siberia), the United States secured an agreement from the Japanese (and the British and French) in January 1919 which placed the Trans-Siberian Railway and the Chinese Eastern Railway under the general control of an inter-Allied committee headed by a Russian, General Dmitrii L. Horvath, and responsibility for the operation of these railway systems on Stevens and his corps. See Betty Miller Unterberger, *America's Siberian Expedition, 1918-1920: A Study of National Policy* (Durham, N. C., 1956), *passim*.

[2] Wilson was here paraphrasing a telegram from the commander of the United States forces in Siberia, Maj. Gen. William Sidney Graves, with a message from Jean (John, Ivan) Sookine, Kolchak's Foreign Minister. See T. H. Bliss to WW, May 9, 1919, with Enclosure, printed in *PWW*, Vol. 58, pp. 568-71.

Mr. Lloyd George. This question is connected to another, vaster one: it is becoming necessary for us to agree upon a common policy in Russia. According to our information, Admiral Kolchak is rapidly advancing west of the Urals, and that seems to prove that either the Bolsheviks no longer have the strength to resist, or that they are completely lacking in means of transport. What is the latest news?

Sir Maurice Hankey. The latest telegrams show that Admiral Kolchak is sending forces in the direction of Archangel and towards the southwest at one and the same time.

President Wilson. For myself, I have always been of opinion that we should withdraw from Russia and let the Russians settle their own affairs themselves.

Mr. Lloyd George. I suggest hearing M. Chaikovskii, the head of the Archangel government. He is, as I have already said to you, a liberal of truly advanced ideas, and he believes that, by intervening in time, we can impose terms of government on Kolchak.

President Wilson. We will be able to obtain promises from him: but then, how will we compel him to keep them?

Mr. Lloyd George. The fact that Bolshevism will have finally failed because it encountered the opposition of the world will be a lesson for Kolchak. Besides, he will be much more in our hands than the Bolsheviks could ever be, because the Bolsheviks fed off the country like a worm on a leaf, but now only the ribs remain. The Russian government, whatever it is, won't be able to acquire locomotives without us, won't be able to acquire rolling stock: now, without locomotives, it could never govern Russia.

M. Bark, the former Finance Minister of the Russian Empire, with whom I very recently had a conversation, says that Kolchak is a rather upright soldier, for whom there are no grounds for distrust. He also disputes the charge that Denikin is, as it has been said, a Germanophile, although he had as chief of staff an obviously czarist and militaristic schemer. Kolchak is not only a man whom we can trust, but he is surrounded by young men who, before the revolution and at its outset, had taken an advanced position. I think we can impose conditions upon Kolchak if we do it now. I make a complete distinction between Kolchak and a man like Iudenich, who is in Finland and is threatening Petrograd: the latter belongs to the old Russia.

President Wilson. What conclusion should I draw with respect to keeping American troops in Siberia?

Mr. Lloyd George. I believe it is better to postpone your decision until we have determined our policy in Russia. You might inform your representatives that we are first studying the overall question.

President Wilson. What they fear is precisely the danger of the *status quo*.

Mr. Lloyd George. It isn't a question of prolonging it; we will take a decision as soon as possible.

President Wilson. We certainly have the right to ask Kolchak what his intentions are.

Mr. Lloyd George. His program is rather vague.

President Wilson. He will have to be asked for precise details.

Mr. Lloyd George. First on the agrarian question: he must be asked whether he is really determined not to take back the land from the peasants.

President Wilson. According to the information I have received from a man who knows Russia and her present situation very well, the peasants seized land at will and haphazardly. The present distribution is the result of violence and has created new inequalities. It would obviously be necessary, in all justice, to regularize the operation and, in many cases, to redistribute lands; but it must be acknowledged that this would not be easy.

Mr. Lloyd George. It is necessary to resign oneself to some irregularities in this kind of revolution: the same occurred at the time of the French Revolution. After the agrarian question, the second question which should be raised would be that of the Constituent Assembly. We must compel Kolchak to convene a truly representative Constituent Assembly.

M. Clemenceau. I agree with you completely.

President Wilson. When will we hear M. Chaikovskii?

Mr. Lloyd George. The sooner the better.

President Wilson. I don't wish to run the risk of a collision between the American troops and the Cossacks of Siberia.

Mr. Lloyd George. We will have to take another decision: should our troops in Archangel go to meet Kolchak?

President Wilson. The American troops in Archangel are not very reliable.

Mr. Lloyd George. If Admiral Kolchak can join us, it is the end of Bolshevism: that will prove its irremediable weakness, and, to the degree that we advance southwards, a very large number of Russians will rally to us. If Kolchak is on the point of succeeding, now is the time to impose our terms on him and to deal with him.

President Wilson. It is always dangerous to interfere in foreign revolutions.

Mr. Lloyd George. Here, it is the Russians who are acting; we will only support them.
President Wilson. You have more experience than we in far-flung expeditions. You have an officer corps which has a long tradition in this respect. As for ourselves, except in the Philippines, we have never had the same reasons to act at a great distance, and the American officer remains first and foremost a civilian.

In accordance with your request, I am postponing my decision on the subject of Siberia.

M. Clemenceau. We have given the Supreme War Council the order to prepare a report on the measures to be taken if the Germans refuse to sign the treaty.[3] The Italian representative said that he had received no instructions to this effect. I instructed the council to set to work without waiting for him.
M. Orlando. This is a misunderstanding, for I told General Cavallero to participate in that meeting.
Mr. Lloyd George. I would like our military experts to tell us also what the occupation of Berlin would involve.
M. Clemenceau. If pressure must be applied on the Germans, I will propose to occupy Frankfurt and Berlin. We already occupy the suburbs of Frankfurt.
Mr. Lloyd George. Frankfurt is less important.
M. Clemenceau. It is one of the centers of German wealth.
Mr. Lloyd George. The important thing is to persuade the Junkers that they are beaten; they still don't perhaps understand this enough, and Count Brockdorff-Rantzau's speech has convinced me that it must be rammed into their heads.
President Wilson. I think I discern a difference of attitude between Brockdorff-Rantzau and his colleagues. The others represent the common people of Germany better.
M. Clemenceau. Marshal Foch would have to be consulted on this question.
Mr. Lloyd George. Can't you consult Marshal Pétain?
M. Clemenceau. That is impossible, in view of the position we have given to Foch. We will hear him, and, having heard him, we will do as we please.
President Wilson. We have taken care previously, in questions of this kind, to consult our military advisers in Versailles.

[3] See the notes of meeting XXIV, April 8, 1919, 11 a.m. The reports of the military and naval representatives on the Supreme War Council are printed in *PWW*, Vol. 58, pp. 579–84. The military measures proposed are discussed in detail in the next meeting of the Council of Four.

M. Clemenceau. Very well; then this new question should be referred to them.

President Wilson. But I don't think we can avoid consulting Marshal Foch.

M. Clemenceau. In that case, he should be spoken to directly. If we ask him to prepare a written report, Weygand's influence will be felt too much.

President Wilson. General Weygand is always tempted to ask for more men than are strictly necessary.

M. Clemenceau. It is a trait common to all military men.

Mr. Lloyd George. If we take this course, another question arises: should the Poles march upon Breslau, or perhaps Berlin? Berlin is not far from Poland.

M. Clemenceau. I will summon Marshal Foch for tomorrow morning, and you will ask him questions.

President Wilson. Can't we see M. Chaikovskii and Marshal Foch tomorrow?

Mr. Lloyd George. I think we can see them both in the morning.

LXXI

Conversation between President Wilson and MM. Clemenceau, Lloyd George, and Orlando*

MAY 10, 1919, 11 A.M.

—Marshal Foch and General Weygand are introduced.

M. Clemenceau (*to President Wilson*). The note from the German delegation[1] must be answered; I propose to do it in five lines.

*H., *PPC*, V, 537ff. MM. Lloyd George and Orlando are not present at the beginning of the meeting.

[1] U. K. C. von Brockdorff-Rantzau to G. Clemenceau, May 9, 1919, *PPC*, V, 563. Brockdorff enclosed a lengthy German plan, or program, of a league of nations (printed in *ibid.*, VI, 765-78). He also asked one question in regard to the Covenant of the League included in the peace treaty presented to Germany: "In the meantime it [the German peace delegation] begs to call attention to the discrepancy lying in the fact, that Germany is called upon to sign the statute of the League of Nations, as an inherent part of the Treaty-draft handed over to us, on the other hand, however, is not mentioned among the states which are invited to join the League of Nations. The German Peace Delegation begs to inquire whether, and if so under what circumstances, such invitation is intended."

President Wilson. The terms of that note are so general that I don't see exactly how it should be answered. The Germans are complaining that we don't provide for their admission into the League of Nations: we can only refer them to the article of the Covenant which deals precisely with that question and where it is said that the League is open to all nations that govern themselves under a democratic form of government.[2] We have to wait and see what the real character of the German government is, and other articles of the Covenant of the League of Nations leave no doubt as to the terms under which a new member can be admitted.

M. Clemenceau. They must be told that the good conduct of a people is the essential condition of their admission.

President Wilson. The Covenant says it expressly.

M. Clemenceau. Do you want to draft this reply?

President Wilson. I'll take care of it.

M. Clemenceau. We have a decision to take on the evacuation of Corfu, which the Greeks request. We are ready to withdraw the French troops; the British government asks nothing better than to withdraw its troops. But the Italians must do the same. I will put this question to M. Orlando right away.

President Wilson. Have you learned anything new about the state of mind of the Germans?

M. Clemenceau. I think that the negotiation will have its ups and downs, but that they will sign in the end.

Marshal Foch. When they have made their counterproposals, in two weeks, and you have answered, they are capable of declaring that it is impossible for them to take a decision without referring it back to their government.

President Wilson. The impression of the Germans is that I am ready to favor a compromise. What shall I do to persuade them that I consider as just the peace terms that we have prepared amongst ourselves, and that I have no intention of favoring them?

M. Clemenceau. You can do it by an interview.

—Mr. Lloyd George enters.

M. Clemenceau. We have summoned you, Marshal, because we are

---

[2] Here Wilson for the first time makes the mistake that he would make many times during the coming months. Article I of the Covenant (concerning membership) said only that "fully self-governing" states, dominions, and colonies were eligible for membership, provided they gave guarantees of fulfilling their international obligations and obligations under the Covenant and would accept the League's regulations concerning their military and naval forces. The adopted version of the Covenant is printed in *PWW*, Vol. 58, pp. 188-99.

compelled to anticipate the case that the Germans might refuse to sign:[3] we have to ask you, after the study which we commissioned you to make on the question, what your means of action would be.

Marshal Foch. On April 24, I had a meeting with the commanders in chief of the Armies of the Northeast, that is, the French, American, British, and Belgian armies.[4] We calculated the total of our available manpower. The result of this calculation is that, during the entire month of May, we could dispose of at least forty divisions to operate on the Rhine front, to which five divisions of cavalry must be added. To put all these divisions in a state of readiness, we would have to be notified a week in advance; this is the time necessary for recalling men on leave and special duty.

When the time comes, the action would naturally be organized according to the objective to be attained. Faced with a government which refused to sign the peace, it would be necessary to strike at the seat of that government, that is to say, to reach Weimar and Berlin. It is true that we might find ourselves in a murky situation: the German government can, without actually refusing to talk, declare that it has to appeal to the people by plebiscite, or use all kinds of dilatory tactics. I am envisaging here only the case of an open resistance; we must suppress it wherever it takes place and reduce the German government to our mercy.

To do that, we must follow the shortest route and use the most powerful forces we can marshal. The shortest route starts from the course of the Rhine between Cologne and Mainz; the forces are the forty-five divisions I just mentioned. By starting from the Rhine between Cologne and Mainz and marching on Weimar and Berlin, we would put ourselves in an advantageous zone of operations; for the two flanks of the army of operations are covered,

[3] Brockdorff-Rantzau had sent the following note to Clemenceau on May 9:

"The German Peace Delegation has finished the first perusal of the Peace Conditions which have been handed over to them. They have had to realise that on essential points the basis of the Peace of Right, agreed upon between the belligerents, has been abandoned. They were not prepared to find that the promise, explicitly given to the German People and the whole of mankind, is in this way to be rendered illusory.

"The draft of the treaty contains demands which no nation could endure, moreover, our experts hold that many of them could not possibly be carried out.

"The German Peace Delegation will substantiate these statements in detail and transmit to the allied and Associated Governments their observations and their material continuously." *Ibid.*, Vol. 59, p. 13, n. 5.

[4] That is, Gen. Henri-Philippe Pétain, Gen. John Joseph Pershing, Gen. Sir William Robert Robertson, and Lt. Gen. Baron Augustin-Michel Du Faing d'Aigremont.

on the left by the Lippe, on the right by the Main. By advancing in that direction, we could induce the German government to capitulate even before having reached its operational center. Indeed, towards the north, the immediate occupation of the Ruhr Basin would considerably reduce its economic and financial resources; towards the south, a march parallel to the Main would cut off northern Germany from Bavaria and allow us to hold out our hand to the Czechs, thus depriving Germany of a large stretch of territory.

This plan is easy to execute and without danger; it can yield results without being pushed to its end; if that happened, its effect would be the final destruction of the German government.

M. Clemenceau. You anticipate the cooperation of the Czechoslovaks?

Marshal Foch. We can carry out a combined operation.

Mr. Lloyd George. How many troops do they have?

General Weygand. Few, for the time being, because the three full divisions they have ready for action are on the Hungarian front. But there are a number of brigades in Bohemia that are incomplete or not formed into divisions.

Marshal Foch. Another advantage of the plan I have just explained is that, if we stop en route, we will find a line of defense on the Weser parallel and similar to that of the Rhine, which gives us a good waiting position.

President Wilson. Are there any German forts along the way?

Marshal Foch. None.

Mr. Lloyd George. Can you expect anything from the Poles?

Marshal Foch. Obviously, as soon as it is possible for them to organize themselves.

Mr. Lloyd George. Aren't there Polish troops in Posen?

Marshal Foch. Yes; they belong to an army other than General Haller's.

President Wilson. How many troops do you think the Germans can line up?

Marshal Foch. None. There are still 450,000 men in Germany who nominally make up part of the army and who are perhaps in uniform; but they are disorganized and disarmed. The military force of Germany, at present, is nil.

Mr. Lloyd George. Is an action against Berlin through Stettin possible?

Marshal Foch. The difficulty of finding tonnage can be added to that of transporting heavy artillery.

In short, on the condition that we are notified a week in advance, we can launch a coordinated attack on a front of 180 kilometers; it can go wherever it chooses, between protected flanks; its first results will be the occupation of the Ruhr and the detachment of Bavaria from northern Germany.

M. Clemenceau. Does the occupation of the Ruhr not present dangers because of the density of the working-class population in that region?

Marshal Foch. We will have enough machine guns so that this population won't stir.

General Weygand. Perhaps the most difficult problem will be victualing this population, of which we will have to take charge.

M. Clemenceau. You tell us that you will need a week's notice. Since it is up to us to give you this notice, and since we can find ourselves compelled to act quickly, can't you, as of today, take the necessary measures to shorten this period?

Mr. Lloyd George. If furloughs were denied as of now, the Germans would know about it, and this might not have a bad effect. Couldn't we take some measures which would be known and make an impression in Cologne and Mainz?

Marshal Foch. I myself can go to the Rhine front to inspect the troops, and I can, at the same time, take some measures to shorten the period of preparation.

General Weygand. Since the principal danger we have to fear is seeing the Germans empty the railroads by withdrawing personnel and rolling stock, we are preparing a certain amount of cavalry and trucks to move the troops ahead a great distance very rapidly. By thus capturing the junctions of the railroads by surprise, we will paralyze the enemy's resistance, and that can be done within a few hours of receiving an order from you.

Marshal Foch. A few troops, kept constantly ready, and a certain number of lorries will be enough to carry out a surprise of great consequence.

M. Clemenceau. How will you proceed?

Marshal Foch. I will ask that each of the Allied armies have two or three divisions at readiness and prepared to march at the first signal.

M. Clemenceau. When will your program of action be ready?

General Weygand. Tomorrow.

M. Clemenceau. So far as we are concerned, we surely don't have to anticipate an action of this kind before ten or twelve days.

Mr. Lloyd George. After the last document received from the German delegation, wouldn't it be well to make a few preparations openly? What encourages the Germans to attempt obstructionary tactics is their belief that we will not use extreme measures.

M. Clemenceau. They are saying so in their conversations, according to what is reported to us. They think that France is incapable of taking action, and they see the Americans leaving.

Mr. Lloyd George. I favor doing something visible now, perhaps by advancing our cavalry.

Marshal Foch. My cavalry is what I have the least of. It would be better for me to make a trip to the front, to which we would give a certain air of mystery, which would in itself provoke comment.

President Wilson. You mean a secret trip, with carefully arranged leaks?

Marshal Foch. Leaks always occur.

I will tell each of the army commanders to keep two divisions continuously ready for action.

Mr. Lloyd George. When will you leave?

Marshal Foch. At the beginning of next week.

M. Clemenceau. I suggest Monday.

—*This proposal is adopted.*

Mr. Lloyd George. This little demonstration will be useful, given the general attitude of the Germans. The reason I would like to make an impression upon them without losing a moment is that they are in the process of determining their course of action, and we shouldn't wait until they have come to a decision.

Marshal Foch. Monday is May 12, and the period of time given to the German plenipotentiaries to present their observations on the text of the treaty only expires on the twenty-second.

M. Clemenceau. We have already received two notes from them.

Marshal Foch. You'll receive many more; but all I mean to say is that we still have time.

M. Clemenceau. You should leave as soon as possible in order to produce the impression we wish.

Mr. Lloyd George. All the more so since the Germans are rather slow to understand. If you leave on Monday, the Germans will need a few days to realize what is being prepared, and it would be dangerous to wait until they have dug themselves in.

M. Clemenceau. I agree completely. Since President Wilson and M. Orlando agree with us, your departure will take place on Monday.

—Marshal Foch and General Weygand withdraw.

M. Clemenceau (*to Mr. Lloyd George*). Have you received copies of the German notes?*

Mr. Lloyd George. No; I would ask you to give them to me. Don't you think the Germans are beginning to make a show of refusing?

M. Clemenceau. They'll have to give in to reason in the end.

Mr. Lloyd George. I fear they may not do so before we have given our armies the order to advance.

M. Clemenceau. Our armies won't have to go very far.

I waited for the arrival of M. Orlando to ask him the following question: the Greek government asks that Allied troops evacuate the island of Corfu; the French and English governments are ready to give them satisfaction. Is it the same with the Italian government

M. Orlando. Certainly.

—*The evacuation of Corfu by the Allied armies is decided.*

President Wilson. Here is the text we have received of Article 430, whose wording, as you recall, has been changed twice:[5]

"If, during the occupation or after the expiration of the fifteen years provided above, the Reparation Commission finds that Germany refuses to execute all or part of the obligations imposed upon her in Chapter VIII of the treaty (Reparation), all or part of the territories indicated in Article 429 will be reoccupied immediately by the armies of the Allied and Associated Powers."

M. Clemenceau. Is this a new draft?

President Wilson. No, it is a return to our original text, or to be more exact, the precise draft of the decision taken here amongst ourselves.

M. Clemenceau. Allow me to compare the two texts carefully, and I'll give you the reply.

—President Wilson proposes the text of a reply to the first German note:[6]

In reply to the observations of a general nature presented by the German plenipotentiaries, it will suffice to say that we have formulated the peace terms on the basis of principles laid down before the conclusion of the Armistice. The German plenipotentiaries must not expect us to consent to make any fundamental changes; we can only consider such

---

*H., *PPC*, V, 541ff.

[5] For the first version of this article submitted by the Drafting Committee and the discussion about it, see the notes of LXIX, May 9, 1919, 11:30 a.m.

[6] Actually, to the note quoted in n. 3 above. The text of Wilson's proposed reply is printed in *PWW*, Vol. 59, p. 12.

or such a suggestion of a practical nature that the German plenipotentiaries may have to present to us.

Mr. Lloyd George. We have summoned M. Chaikovskii. Before we hear him, I would like to inform you of a report forwarded to me by the Russian Red Cross. It indicates that the strength of the Bolsheviks is declining rapidly. A new bourgeoisie was born out of the revolution, and, like the acquirers of state properties in France, it now wishes to return to a stable order.

—M. Chaikovskii is introduced.*

President Wilson. We are eager to hear you and to consult you on the policy to be followed in Russia. The information we are receiving indicates that the power of the Bolsheviks is threatened: Admiral Kolchak may succeed in overthrowing them and in taking their place. Whether it is his government or any other one that is to be established in Russia, we wish to give our support only to a government which will commit itself to maintaining in Russia a truly democratic political system and a land policy which leaves the land in the hands of the peasants.

M. Chaikovskii. I have received a telegram from M. Sazonov, which contains the public declaration made by the government of General Denikin;[7] he promises the convocation of the Constituent Assembly, agrarian reform, and very comprehensive labor legislation. Admiral Kolchak made a declaration of the same kind earlier.[8]

*H., PPC, V, 544.

[7] Chaikovskii at this point submitted a telegram from Anatolii Anatolievich Neratov, former Deputy Foreign Minister of Russia and now a foreign-policy adviser to General Denikin, to Sergei Dmitrievich Sazonov of May 5, 1919. It quoted the text of a declaration sent by Denikin to the chiefs of the Allied military missions in southern Russia on April 23, 1919, with the request that it be transmitted to the heads of their respective governments. In addition to the points mentioned by Chaikovskii below, Denikin's program included the suppression of Bolshevik anarchy and the restoration of order in Russia; the reconstruction of the Russian army and of a united Russia; universal suffrage; the institution of a decentralized administration through regional autonomy and a large measure of local self-government; and the guarantee of complete civil and religious liberty. Denikin's declaration is printed in PPC, V, 551-52.

[8] Chaikovskii here referred to the letter which he, Prince Georgii Evgen'evich L'vov, Vasilii Alekseevich Maklakov, and Sazonov had addressed to Clemenceau on April 15, 1919 (printed in FR 1919, Russia, pp. 332-33). They wrote on behalf of the "Unified Governments," that is, the anti-Bolshevik regimes headed by Admiral Kolchak, General Denikin, and Chaikovskii, which all nominally recognized the leadership of Kolchak. The Unified Governments, they wrote, had no intention of restoring the monarchy or of taking land away from the peas-

President Wilson. That declaration[9] is conceived in much too general terms. There are, for example, agrarian laws without any details. This kind of commitment is not good enough for us.

M. Chaikovskii. Admiral Kolchak's government is sometimes accused of reactionary designs: its character is completely misunderstood. It depends on the Siberian people, and Siberia is a democratic country, because there are no great estates, and the real power is in the hands of the peasants. This is why Admiral Kolchak's government, even if it had other tendencies, would be compelled to follow a democratic policy.

I won't say that it is altogether the same for Denikin. Southern Russia was a region of great estates, where the presence of Denikin's troops has prevented them from disappearing entirely. Denikin, much more than Kolchak, is surrounded by officers of the old regime.

President Wilson. Which of the two is the stronger?

M. Chaikovskii. Kolchak, by far.

One of the most critical questions appearing today is that of the small nationalities of Russia. The forced centralization imposed by czarism and the treatment they suffered or are afraid of suffering under the Bolshevik regime have created amongst all these small nationalities a kind of independence fever. But if we consider their situation and resources coolly, especially from an economic point of view, one wonders whether independence is a desirable solution for them. The states which they would form would remain very weak economically and, as a result, would surely fall once again under the domination of a more powerful neighbor. That neighbor could be Germany.

I had a conversation recently with the representatives of Estonia, who admitted this danger. They asked me to negotiate with Russia on a clean slate, disregarding previous relations. I told them that their main port, Reval, was a creation of Russia and would not exist without the expenditures made by the Russian

---

ants. The purposes of the "national movement" of these governments were to reestablish national unity and to "found the regeneration of Russia upon the solid basis of a democratic organization." "It is for the Russian people themselves," they declared, "to decide their destiny by means of a Constituent Assembly elected freely and under legal conditions. As soon as the Bolshevist tyranny is crushed and the Russian people can freely express their will, we will proceed with the elections and the present governments will turn over their power into the hands of the National Assembly." They appealed for "aid" from the Allies to secure these ends.

[9] That is, the declaration summarized in n. 8.

government. They finally told me: "If you treat us as equals, we are ready to draw closer to you."
Mr. Lloyd George. What do they mean by that?
M. Chaikovskii. They ask not to be considered as compulsory members of the Russian state. They want to be left a voice in deciding their fate and their local institutions. They have sent a telegram to Estonia, asking for an answer from their government; it has not yet arrived.
Mr. Lloyd George. So Estonia has representatives in Paris?
M. Chaikovskii. She has two.[10]
Mr. Lloyd George. And Lithuania?
M. Chaikovskii. She is also represented here.[11]
Mr. Lloyd George. Is Admiral Kolchak represented in Paris?
M. Chaikovskii. I am authorized to speak for him, as is Prince L'vov.
Mr. Lloyd George. Who is representing General Denikin here?
M. Chaikovskii. His Minister of Foreign Affairs[12] is here. His government is, moreover, very complicated.

I have tried to convince all these little groups that only two things matter: the first is to defeat the enemy; the second is to establish for each of them a rational organization of power, whose first principle is a well-defined separation between civil and military power. This is where they are all at fault, and, at Archangel, we have had much to do in order to settle this question satisfactorily.
Mr. Lloyd George. I shall tell you what worries me a little about Kolchak: it concerns, in the latest news I have received about him, the policy of a certain Rinov[13] against representative institutions.
M. Chaikovskii. I don't know who this Rinov is. But I can tell you that Kolchak is very sympathetic to the *zemstvos* and to representative institutions in general.

[10] The chief representatives of the provisional government of Estonia in Paris were Jaan Poska, the Foreign Minister, and Ants (or Antoine) Piip.

[11] The leader of the Lithuanian delegation in Paris was Augustinas Voldemaras, the Minister of Foreign Affairs in the Lithuanian nationalist government. For other members of the delegation, see Alfred E. Senn, *The Emergence of Modern Lithuania* (Westport, Conn., 1975), pp. 89-91, 239.

[12] That is, Sazonov, who was in Paris in the joint capacity of chief diplomatic representative of Denikin's government and Foreign Minister of Kolchak's government.

[13] That is, Gen. Pavel Pavlovich Ivanov-Rinov, former czarist army officer, at this time the nominal commander in chief of anti-Bolshevik forces in eastern Siberia. The remark about his "policy" presumably referred to his harsh and brutal tactics in suppressing all opposition in the area of his military operations.

President Wilson. He can be sympathetic to the local assemblies which support him and prove hostile towards the others.

M. Chaikovskii. I know he is thus accused, and I don't think the accusation is justified. All my life, I have played an important role in the Russian cooperative movement; I am in touch today with the members of the cooperatives of the milk industry in Siberia. Now, I know they all support Kolchak. The government in Siberia, as I have already told you, is democratic by necessity.

Mr. Lloyd George. I received another report this morning which tells me that, as Kolchak advances, troubles erupt in his wake. The Bolsheviks are having some success in eastern Siberia. Doesn't this mean that people believe that, if Kolchak succeeds, the ultimate goal of his entourage would be a return to the past? Isn't it believed that this is what the Allies wish to help him to do?

M. Chaikovskii. What is the date of this piece of news? I will reply to you that we hear rumors of this kind constantly. Kolchak is constantly denounced by the opposition as the perpetrator of the *coup d'état* which brought him to power. Now, the truth is that this *coup d'état* was carried out by others—not by him—who then offered him power and asked him to accept it for reason of public safety.

Mr. Lloyd George. What are Kolchak's origins?

M. Chaikovskii. As an admiral he fought very bravely with the Sevastopol flotilla.

Mr. Lloyd George. So I recall; but I mean: what are his personal origins?

M. Chaikovskii. I believe he is a nobleman.

Mr. Lloyd George. What do you think of his entourage?

M. Chaikovskii. The majority is made up of people who took part in the revolution, for example Mikhailov, son of a well-known Social Revolutionary, who himself participated, with the Social Revolutionary party, in the beginnings of the revolution. As for me, I take my stand only from the point of view of the national interest of Russia. I belong to the Social Revolutionary party, and I don't wish to set myself up as a judge or arbiter of that party. The question at hand is solely a question of national interest.

Mr. Lloyd George. Our preoccupation is to do nothing which might help in the triumph of a militaristic or autocratic regime.

Who is Iudenich?

M. Chaikovskii. A general who had success during the war, especially in the Caucasus. At present, he is in Finland, ready to act, but he doesn't want to do so with the Russian reactionaries in Finland.

Mr. Lloyd George. If we help him march on Petrograd, will he be disposed towards Russian democracy?
M. Chaikovskii. I am convinced of it.
M. Orlando. Isn't a federal system being contemplated in Russia? Do you believe that liberty, in so large a country, is compatible with unity?
M. Chaikovskii. What I can say is that the return of autocracy is absolutely impossible. The belief on which it was based is dead; no one talks of it as if it was a possibility. Nonetheless, there are people who think that the country is in such a state of disorder that a provisional authoritarian regime will be necessary to reestablish order. The right-wing Cadets, for example, want a constitutional monarchy.
Mr. Lloyd George. Whom would they choose as sovereign?
M. Chaikovskii. They don't have a pretender. I don't know whether a constitutional monarchy will be established; but what I can tell you is that it would end in a republic, and a federal republic at that. I never had the slightest doubt of that. In 1907, when I was giving lectures in Chicago, I was asked the question: "What is Russia's future?" I answered: "In ten years, she will be a republic." Since they were surprised and raised the objection that the Russian people were backward and illiterate, I replied: "It is not only Latin and Greek that make republicans."

LXXII

Conversation between President Wilson, MM. Clemenceau, Lloyd George, Vénisélos, and Generals Sir Henry Wilson and Bliss*

MAY 10, 1919, 3 P.M.

Mr. Lloyd George. We must arrange the landing at Smyrna. The best thing is for French or English marine light infantrymen to land first, with the order to turn over the forts to the Greek troops as soon as they appear.
President Wilson. The Turks and the Italians must be informed in advance.

*H., *PPC*, V, 553ff.

Sir Henry Wilson. The Turks must be informed, in principle, by Admiral Calthorpe,[1] since it involves a measure taken in execution of the armistice convention.

General Bliss. Not only the Turks, but also the Italians must be warned in advance; otherwise we are going off into the unknown.

M. Vénisélos. If you notify the Italians now, they will notify the Turks; it would be better to let Admiral Calthorpe take care of it himself at the appropriate moment.

Sir Henry Wilson. In that case, I think the Italians will try to participate in the landing.

Mr. Lloyd George. It would be a serious matter to let them occupy the forts.

President Wilson. If the English admiral only talked with the Turks, the danger is that he could find himself face to face with an Italian commander who will ask what they intend to do and who will, moreover, be acting without orders.

Mr. Lloyd George. Doesn't Admiral Calthorpe have authority over the Italian ships in his waters?

Sir Henry Wilson. If the Italians happen to have a battalion of infantry at hand and say to us, "We're going to help you," how will we answer them?

Mr. Lloyd George. Admiral Calthorpe would reply that he has no instructions to that effect.

General Bliss. The Italian commander, if he has received no instructions either, will think himself compelled to land—to make doubly sure.

Mr. Lloyd George. The Italians must be notified as of Monday. The landing can't take place before Wednesday morning; the Italian admiral will be notified Tuesday.

M. Vénisélos. If Admiral Calthorpe, as commander of the Allied naval forces in the Aegean Sea, proceeds to the spot himself, the Italian commander won't do anything without his consent. Everything will go well, provided the French and English troops occupy the forts immediately.

Mr. Lloyd George. Do you consider it essential that Admiral Calthorpe be present?

President Wilson. I think so.

M. Vénisélos. I received a dispatch from our representative in Constantinople,[2] who had a conversation with Admiral Calthorpe. If

---

[1] That is, Adm. Sir Somerset Arthur Gough-Calthorpe, commander in chief of Allied naval forces in the eastern Mediterranean and British High Commissioner at Constantinople.

[2] Efthymios Kanellopoulos.

the latter went to Smyrna now, there would be no one to take his place in Constantinople since Admiral Seymour is for the moment in the Black Sea.

Mr. Lloyd George. I think it important for Admiral Calthorpe to go in person to Smyrna. The Turks, in these circumstances, will make no difficulties. Admiral Seymour should be immediately recalled to Constantinople, and he should notify the Ottoman government.

M. Clemenceau. I can only approve of this method.

President Wilson. As for the Italians, we'll notify them right here.

Mr. Lloyd George. Next Monday.

President Wilson. And Admiral Calthorpe will inform the Turks twelve hours before the landing.

Mr. Lloyd George. As soon as the Italians know about it, they will immediately warn the Turks. Doesn't M. Vénisélos think that the Italians and the Turks are working together?

M. Vénisélos. Yes; the Italians are also hand in glove with the Bulgarians.

Mr. Lloyd George. The important thing regarding the Turks is to show the French and English flags in the Smyrna roadstead.

Sir Henry Wilson. It is necessary not to act without notifying the Turks in time. It is always dangerous to appear before a fort and to demand its surrender. With soldiers like the Turks, we have every chance of being fired upon.

Mr. Lloyd George. They must be given enough time to receive the order to hand over the forts.

M. Vénisélos. This is why I would ask them to surrender the forts thirty-six hours in advance; if we invoke the terms of the armistice, they will make no difficulty. Twelve hours later, that is twenty-four hours before the landing, I would notify them of the arrival of the troops.

M. Clemenceau. I would like Admiral de Bon to take part in this conversation, and I am going to have him called.

Mr. Lloyd George. It may not be necessary to land many men. Are the forts of Smyrna very large?

Sir Henry Wilson. No; a garrison of twenty men is enough to guard each of these forts.

—Admiral de Bon is introduced.

—*After consultation, it is decided that the Turks will be notified Monday morning, the Italian government Monday evening, and the time of the landing will be communicated to the Turks Tuesday morning, twenty-four hours before the operation.*

Mr. Lloyd George. How many French troops can you deploy on the spot?

Admiral de Bon. We can provide between 300 and 400 marine light infantry.

Mr. Lloyd George. That is enough.

Admiral de Bon. If Admiral Calthorpe leaves Constantinople, Admiral Amet, who is there, could take charge of communicating with the Turks.

Sir Henry Wilson. Will you ask the Italians to refrain from landing troops?

Mr. Lloyd George. No, we will only ask them to place their landing troops under the orders of Admiral Calthorpe.

LXXIII

Conversation between President Wilson and MM. Clemenceau, Lloyd George, and Orlando*

MAY 10, 1919, 4 P.M.

—President Wilson reads aloud the reply he has prepared to the note from the German plenipotentiaries.[1]

M. Clemenceau. When shall we publish it?

Mr. Lloyd George. It should be given to the newspapers this eve-

*H., PPC, V, 559ff.

[1] According to Hankey, Wilson read replies to the two notes, as follows:

(1) "The receipt of the German programme of a League of Nations is acknowledged. The programme will be referred to the appropriate Committee of the Allied and Associated Powers. The German plenipotentiaries will find upon a re-examination of the Covenant of the League of Nations that the matter of the admission of additional Member States has not been overlooked but is explicitly provided for in the second paragraph of Article I."

(2) "The Representatives of the Allied and Associated Powers have received the statement of objections of the German plenipotentiaries to the Draft Conditions of Peace.

"In reply they wish to remind the German Delegation that they have formed the Terms of the Treaty with constant thought of the principles upon which the Armistice and the negotiations for peace were proposed. They can admit no discussion of their right to insist upon the Terms of the Peace substantially as drafted. They can consider only such practical suggestions as the German plenipotentiaries may have to submit." Printed in PWW, Vol. 59, p. 28.

ning. I am told that the Germans have already published the text of their note and that it has appeared in the Swiss newspapers.

—*This proposal is adopted.*

M. Clemenceau. I have a report to submit to you from our admirals regarding action to be taken to guarantee order in Schleswig during the period preceding the first plebiscite. All our admirals are in agreement.

Mr. Lloyd George. This could take place only after the signing of the peace.

M. Clemenceau. No doubt. The admirals ask to which nationality the command of this small expedition will belong.

Mr. Lloyd George. Why concern ourselves with this question right now?

President Wilson. There is nothing pressing about it.

M. Clemenceau. I agree. We can postpone it.

President Wilson. I have received a memorandum from the Ministers of Foreign Affairs to the Supreme Council, informing us that decisions concerning the borders of Hungary and Austria have been taken, which remain to be approved by us. We can't study them without a map.

Mr. Lloyd George. The best thing is for each of us to have time to study these proposals.

President Wilson. It is only a matter of borders upon which our experts already agree.

Mr. Lloyd George. What is your impression of M. Chaikovskii?

President Wilson. Good. But he didn't answer our questions as clearly as I would have liked.

I see in all these governments, once constituted, a general tendency towards the right. That is rather human. From what M. Chaikovskii said, I didn't get a very clear impression of Denikin, nor of his entourage.

If we decide to support Kolchak and Denikin, the public opinion of the entire world wouldn't be able to understand if we were to abandon them afterwards, even if they later behaved as reactionaries. That is what I am afraid of and what causes me to hesitate to commit myself.

Mr. Lloyd George. On the other hand, we can't lose contact with the Russians; the consequences of that would be serious. We must inform ourselves at all costs. There is an English officer with Kolchak; he is a member of the English Parliament, a member of the Labour party, John Ward. He is very hostile to the Bolsheviks.

President Wilson. I have a very intelligent representative in Tokyo: he is our Ambassador, Mr. Morris, who was once my student.

Mr. Lloyd George. I don't believe it would be worth the trouble to ask General Knox's opinion; he's an excellent soldier, but he's only a soldier.

President Wilson. I have confidence in Morris. He was born in Philadelphia, which might be considered the center of the least advanced opinion in the United States. There is a kind of very conservative aristocracy there, and Morris, who grew up in the midst of it, has fought against these tendencies all his life.

Mr. Lloyd George. The man who matters to us is Kolchak; we must know whether we can or cannot count on him. A practical question arises immediately: that of knowing if we should march to meet him near Kotlas. We must know who he is at all costs.

M. Clemenceau. Do you have the means to do it in due time?

President Wilson. I can get information from Morris within a week.

Mr. Lloyd George. I believe we ought to send him a wire, and we could ask him to get in touch with John Ward, who must be in Vladivostok.

Sir Maurice Hankey. We also have an officer in Siberia, Johnson, who is a former editor of the *Westminster Gazette*.

Mr. Lloyd George. It might be worthwhile to consult him. It is useless to consult Knox, except on military questions.

President Wilson. And on the subject of Denikin, how do we inform ourselves?

M. Clemenceau. It isn't easy.

Mr. Lloyd George. General Milne has seen Denikin; but he also could only give us a soldier's opinion.

President Wilson. If Kolchak's intentions are such as M. Chaikovskii described to us, all is well; but I am not certain of it.

Mr. Lloyd George. In any case, you may be certain that it will be a general who will prevail and make himself master of Russia. If it isn't Kolchak, it will be a leader of the Bolshevik troops.

President Wilson. The Russian Bonaparte would find himself in a very different situation from that of Napoleon, who had behind him an organized country, with stable elements, despite the revolution. In Russia, there is only an amorphous and anarchic mass of peasants.

Sir Maurice Hankey. Lord Cunliffe writes that the Reparation Commission cannot continue its work without the Four taking a decision about the financial responsibility of the newly established powers.

President Wilson. I believe it would be unfair to ask Poland to participate in reparations. But the other states formed out of the dissolution of Austria-Hungary have to assume their part of the financial responsibilities.

Mr. Lloyd George. We are free regarding these powers; we are not bound by the terms which we have imposed on Germany, and I believe it would be undesirable to apply in this case the same categories concerning reparation which we provided in the treaty with Germany. The best thing would be to establish definite sums which each of these states would have to pay.

President Wilson. Establishing them on a moderate scale.

Mr. Lloyd George. That is my opinion.

M. Clemenceau. I also believe it essential not to deal with these powers at all as we are dealing with Germany.

President Wilson. It will be rather difficult to establish the sums to be paid. Is it better to begin by determining all that Austria-Hungary should and can pay, and to make the allocation afterwards, or would it be better to determine immediately what is due in turn from each one?

Mr. Lloyd George. The more precise we can be about the figures, the better. We would have done it with Germany if that had been possible. The best thing to do is to ask the commission of experts to which Lord Cunliffe belongs to present us with a practical proposal.

President Wilson. They should be asked what, in their opinion, the whole of the Austro-Hungarian territories will be able to pay, and if possible, to indicate the division amongst the different states.

M. Orlando. This raises very complex technical questions. Concerning war debts, there will be some states exempted and some states that will remain encumbered: whence endless repercussions. The experts alone can give us an opinion.

The best thing to do is to declare that everyone except Poland will be liable, to determine their joint capacity to pay, and to leave to the experts the task of determining the division and the means of payment. That must be done, not only in our own interest, but so that the Germans can't tell us that we are asking them to pay everything and forgetting the responsibility of their allies.

Mr. Lloyd George. We have another justification. After all, we ourselves have contracted enormous debts to carry on a war which liberated all these peoples, and often against themselves; they must participate in the costs of their own liberation.

The inquiry could be extended to Poland, for whom we will reserve to ourselves the right of special treatment.

President Wilson. Not only has Poland been the victim of all her neighbors, but she has been particularly stricken by the war, and there can be no question, in any case, of making her pay the Austrian war debt.

Mr. Lloyd George. By no means, but only a part of the burden which we ourselves carry after having liberated Poland.

Sir Maurice Hankey. The commission charged with studying the financial responsibility of Austria-Hungary requests authorization to consult the Czechoslovaks.

—*This authorization is granted.*

LXXIV

Conversation between President Wilson and MM. Clemenceau, Balfour, and Vénisélos*

MAY 11, 1919, NOON

Mr. Balfour. I see that there has been an indiscretion in Constantinople and that the Turks have been informed—from what it appears, by our own representatives—of our intentions regarding Smyrna. I am very annoyed about it.

M. Clemenceau. I have to ask you to delay our action for forty-eight hours; we must, indeed, be careful about our position regarding the Italians. We will tell them that we were compelled to take a decision in their absence, but that we wish to talk to them about it before it goes into effect.

I took the time to review the Treaty of London and the agreement of Saint-Jean de Maurienne. Mr. Lloyd George said the other day that the promise to give Smyrna to Italy was contingent on Italian participation in England's military action in the Near East; now, I don't find one word about that in the convention of Saint-Jean de Maurienne. Mr. Lloyd George's memory has betrayed him. I am well aware that, by the Treaty of London, the Italians committed themselves to declare war immediately against our enemies and that they only declared war against Germany after thirteen months and against Turkey after eighteen months.

*Does not appear in H.

Mr. Balfour. The Treaty of London provided compensations for Italy in case we ourselves made acquisitions in the Near East.

M. Clemenceau. The Italians shouldn't be given the opportunity to say that, after having refused them Fiume, which had not been promised to them, we are refusing them Smyrna after having promised it to them.

—Mr. Balfour rereads the Treaty of London (*summary*):

In case of acquisitions by the powers in the eastern Mediterranean, Italy will receive compensation in the province of Adalia, where her interests are already recognized by the Allied Powers, and, if the Ottoman Empire should be divided, Italy would have the right to occupy certain specified territories.

Mr. Balfour. I had many conversations on this subject in London— with Marquis Imperiali, M. Paul Cambon, and the Russian Chargé d'Affaires.[1] It was a question of defining that obligation more precisely. Such was the situation when I left for America.[2] In my absence, the Italians demanded a solution instantly. I had shown my opposition to their pretentions towards Smyrna; at Saint-Jean de Maurienne, Mr. Lloyd George, no doubt for valid reasons, promised it to them. Indeed, the other day he said that it was in exchange for a promise of cooperation in Asia; but, as M. Clemenceau has said, his memory deceived him.

What we can say is that that promise does not bind us, because it depended upon the consent of Russia, and that that consent was never given.

President Wilson. Whatever our position might be from a purely legal point of view, I don't see how we can morally justify the cession of Smyrna to Italy.

Sir Maurice Hankey. The document issuing from the negotiation at Saint-Jean de Maurienne is rather obscure; but there is no doubt that it was signed under the condition of the consent of Russia.

M. Clemenceau. That's what we can say to the Italians.

President Wilson. I am not inclined to let the Italians do what they want in that part of the world. I distrust their intentions. If I published in America all that we know about their activity and intrigues, it would cause their infernal machine to hang fire.

M. Clemenceau. In any case, I ask you to delay our action in Smyrna. I insist, furthermore, that our troops land together. I

---

[1] Konstantin Dmitrievich Nabokov.

[2] That is, when he embarked upon the so-called Balfour mission to the United States in April 1917.

agree with you about not letting the Italians occupy the forts; but if they didn't land with us and you, we would put ourselves in a bad position. I propose that the French, English, and Italians land at the same time, with a mutual promise to reembark when the Greeks come to take their place.

President Wilson. The Italians can oppose us on this point.

M. Clemenceau. We must expect resistance on their part. It is better that it take place now, when we will be speaking to them about it.

President Wilson. Are you firmly of opinion that Smyrna must go to the Greeks?

M. Clemenceau. Yes; I only ask you to delay our operation in Smyrna for at least twenty-four hours. We'll tell the Italians that we were compelled to take this decision in their absence. If they ask us why we did it, we'll tell them that we were given disturbing information about the danger run by the Greek elements and that we couldn't wait for their return.

Mr. Balfour. That won't get us out of our difficulty, for they will ask the question: "Will you leave Smyrna to the Greeks?"

M. Clemenceau. For my part, I am ready to give it to them; but there is no reason to say so before the time when we will be taking general decisions about the fate of the Ottoman territories.

M. Vénisélos. I have just received a dispatch from the commander of our warship outside Smyrna. He reports that the Italian battleship *Regina Elena* has landed workmen at Scala Nuova who have fitted out the jetties and landing stages in anticipation of a landing. Three hundred sailors, along with officers, landed next; but two days later, they reembarked, after a kind of inspection of the coast. Landings of this type seem to indicate designs upon Smyrna. The Treaty of London, as far as I can tell, promised the Italians Adalia. But when we speak of Adalia, we exclude Smyrna; otherwise all of the south of Asia Minor would go to the Italians.

As for the conference of Saint-Jean de Maurienne, M. Ribot explained to me what took place there: the heads of the Allied governments were assembled there in order to discuss the letter from the Austrian Emperor to Prince Sixtus of Bourbon,[3] and not to discuss Asiatic questions. Mr. Lloyd George suddenly revealed to M. Ribot that he had decided to offer Smyrna to Italy, in order

---

[3] About this, the so-called Sixtus affair, see Arthur J. May, *The Passing of the Hapsburg Monarchy, 1914-1918*, 2 vols. (Philadelphia, 1966), I, 486-91; II, 630-36.

to incline the Italian government towards the idea of a separate peace with Austria. Thus, that offer of Smyrna to Italy wasn't the result of negotiations; it was made by English initiative to Baron Sonnino, who naturally accepted it, and who, moreover, objected to the idea of a separate peace with Austria.

The Italians have already made landings, not only at Adalia, but at Marmaris; they seem to be preparing to do the same near Smyrna.

A commission, as you will recall, attempted to settle the Greek question in Asia Minor by determining the ethnographic boundaries. In the calculation of ethnic majorities, I had proposed to include the people of the islands with those of the peninsula. But that proposal was rejected. As a result, the Greek majority has diminished or disappeared in certain regions; this is why the country to the south of Smyrna was not assigned to us in the report of the commission. But if that area should be placed under a European mandate, we will ask that this mandate be entrusted to us, at least for a period of ten years. It must not be given to Italy: she would still have another very long stretch of coast in the south of Anatolia, along with large territories in the interior, including the *vilayet* of Konya.

President Wilson. But if Italy should keep the Dodecanese, wouldn't it be better for the neighboring continental region to be placed under the same government? For my part, that's not what I want.

M. Vénisélos. I really hope that the Dodecanese won't be left to Italy. There is not even there, as in Dalmatia, an Italian population of 4 per cent. These islands are entirely Greek and have always been so for three thousand years. I must say that, in a conversation I had some time ago with M. Orlando, he told me: "The Dodecanese and Smyrna will revert to you, but when we have settled our own affairs in the Adriatic."

To return to the planned landing, I have had information from two telegrams from the English naval attaché in Athens, which indicate that Admiral Calthorpe will take over the forts with English and French contingents. The landing of the Greeks will only take place later, after an understanding with Italy.

President Wilson. The Italians won't fail to ask why they shouldn't land also.

M. Vénisélos. I think that all will go well if Admiral Calthorpe is present in person.

M. Clemenceau. I will remind you that we are not dealing with a purely military affair. It would be a great mistake to proceed to an act of sheer force without having first spoken to the Italians about it.

M. Vénisélos. It isn't an act of war; it is only a police operation.

M. Clemenceau. You don't dispose of the forces of the Entente. You have the right to give your opinion, and I have the right to give mine. My responsibility is too great in this affair for me to accept the least unnecessary risk.

M. Vénisélos. Wouldn't it be best to tell Admiral Calthorpe to summon the Turks to surrender the forts, and to warn you immediately if the Turks refuse?

M. Clemenceau. Impossible: that would be the worst of all. Do you see us asking the Turks for permission to occupy the forts and exposing ourselves to their refusal?

Mr. Balfour. What had been proposed concerning the Italians was that they land at the same time as the French and English, but that they occupy the docks and customhouses, whilst the French and English would occupy the forts.

President Wilson. If really necessary, we could say that the Italians made a landing without notifying us, and that we have the right to do the same.

M. Clemenceau. That can be a good argument in the conversation that we will have with them; but that conversation has yet to be held.

Mr. Balfour. I should recall that this question touches on two considerable problems which give me much anxiety—mandates in Asia Minor and the Italian situation. The Italians, without any doubt, are behaving very badly. But unless we wish to break with them, we will have to accommodate ourselves to some of their ways.

Their state of mind is very singular. Yesterday, at the Quai d'Orsay, we were discussing the southern frontier of Austria. Baron Sonnino, at a time when a proposal was being made which was in no way contrary to Italian interests, cried out: "The atmosphere here appears completely hostile to Italy!" Believe me: regarding them, we are like a man who walks on very thin ice. It might possibly end in conflict, but we must do nothing to precipitate it. This business about Smyrna, in the minds of the Italians, will be tied to the Adriatic business, like what we were discussing yesterday, about the railroad from Trieste to Villach. We can be forced into a conflict; but unless you mean to provoke it yourselves, do what M. Clemenceau asks, speak first to the Italians. We will see if that conversation produces an explosion.

President Wilson. I myself am ready to explode; I will soon be compelled to speak. Everywhere, the Italians are creating dangers for peace by the injustice of their claims. If their case was publicly exposed in its crudity, the entire world would abandon them. I have always said that I reserved my right to appeal to my country.

Mr. Balfour. A policy of conciliation is necessary, at least until the signing of the peace treaty with Germany.

President Wilson. The Germans are already reckoning on our break with Italy.

Mr. Balfour. That would create the most painful situation.

President Wilson. We must speak to them tomorrow.

Mr. Balfour. What was the origin of our decision? Were the Greeks the first to speak to us about their fears of massacres in Asia Minor?

M. Vénisélos. No, I was consulted when the discussion had already begun. Like you, I had received disturbing information about the situation in Asia Minor; I said that it was inconceivable that Greek troops should remain inactive in Macedonia whilst the Turks were massacring Greek populations in Asia.

Mr. Balfour. Don't you fear that, if we land at Smyrna, it would only provoke massacres in other parts of the country?

M. Vénisélos. No; the Turks respect force.

Mr. Balfour. I am not going back on the decision taken; the question is how to carry it out.

President Wilson. Isn't it best to send Admiral Calthorpe to Smyrna and tell him to observe and await orders?

Mr. Balfour. What change in our earlier decision does M. Clemenceau propose?

M. Clemenceau. I ask that we wait twenty-four hours.

President Wilson. I suggest that we send Admiral Calthorpe there without delay, whilst postponing the execution by twenty-four hours.

M. Clemenceau. I see nothing wrong with that.

M. Vénisélos. Meanwhile, the fleet could stop at Chios.

M. Clemenceau. Why stop it halfway? I would prefer that it wait twenty-four hours in the roadstead of Smyrna.

—Mr. Balfour reads aloud an outline of a telegram drawn up along the lines indicated, addressed to Admiral Calthorpe.

Mr. Balfour. There are other questions to be settled. M. Clemenceau has informed us that he sees a problem in the French occupying the forts alone, on account of diplomatic reasons. Do the heads of governments wish to change their resolution to this effect?

—*This modification is adopted.*

M. Clemenceau. I believe that we will not be able to land more than two hundred men.

Mr. Balfour. Is it quite certain that the Turks will not fire?

M. Clemenceau. I fear nothing on that score.

M. Vénisélos. Care should be taken to indicate that the Italians must not land troops in numbers greater than your own; otherwise they will seize the opportunity to play the dominant role and put themselves in command.

Mr. Balfour. As a matter of fact, they are already in a position to land more men than we, and they will do so in the absence of an express agreement.

LXXV

Conversation between President Wilson and MM. Clemenceau, Lloyd George, and Orlando*

MAY 12, 1919, 11 A.M.

M. Clemenceau. We have received a new note from Count Brockdorff-Rantzau:[1] the Germans tell us that they can do better than

*H., *PPC*, V, 565ff.

[1] U. K. C. von Brockdorff-Rantzau to G. Clemenceau, May 10, 1919, printed in *PPC*, V, 571-72.

Brockdorff enclosed a draft of an international agreement on labor law (not included with this document but printed in *ibid.*, VI, 774-78). He made three general comments on the labor provisions of Section XIII of the draft peace treaty. First, he noted that Section XIII "only partly realised in principle" the "demands for social justice repeatedly raised ... by the working classes of all nations." Second, he declared that the German delegation deemed it necessary that all nations should participate in the labor agreement, even if they did not belong to the League of Nations. Third, he suggested that representatives of the national trade union organizations of all the contracting powers "should be summoned to a conference at Versailles to discuss and take decisions on international Labour Law" before the conclusion of the peace conference. The proceedings of this labor conference should be based upon the resolutions adopted by the International Trade Unions Conference held in Bern, February 5-9, 1919.

we concerning labor legislation; that, moreover, a certain number of our stipulations are unnecessary, given the superiority of existing legislation in Germany. They request the execution of the resolutions of the syndicalist conference of Bern; they propose that a new international conference of syndicalist organizations take place in Versailles and speak a great deal about fraternity amongst the working classes of all countries.

Mr. Lloyd George. That is rather adroit.

M. Clemenceau. I have written a reply that I can read to you.

—Reading of the reply.[2]

Mr. Lloyd George. We must take a decision on the financial responsibility of the states of Austria-Hungary, as well as of Poland. We agreed to exempt Poland but added that the other states should pay their share of reparations.

M. Orlando. The question of reparations owed by the component parts of the Austro-Hungarian Empire raises the important problem of the merchant tonnage of the Adriatic: here, we can't apply the same provisions as for German tonnage. Germany, in handing over the ships to you—for which she will have to compensate the owners—is meeting an obligation of the German Empire. But in Austria, the empire has disappeared; the ships belong to each of the component parts of the former Austro-Hungarian monarchy.

---

[2] "PRELIMINARY DRAFT OF A REPLY TO HERR BROCKDORFF-RANTZAU," May 12, 1919, printed in *ibid.*, V, 573.

The draft responded in turn to the points raised by Brockdorff. First, it noted that Article 427 of the draft peace treaty indicated clearly that the enumeration of principles in Section XIII was not inclusive. "The purpose of the organisation set up by that part of the Treaty," it continued, "is that it should pursue the constant development of the International Labour Regime. All the necessary improvements will be brought about through that organisation."

In response to Brockdorff's second point, the draft responded as follows: "The Labour Convention has been inserted in the Treaty of Peace and Germany will therefore be called on to sign it. In the future, the right of your country to participate in the organisation created by Article 387 will be determined by the situation of Germany in respect of the League of Nations, that situation being defined by Article I of the Treaty and by the reply sent on May 10th by the Allied and Associated Governments to your letter dated 9th of the same month."

On the third point, the draft said that it had "not been thought necessary" to summon a labor conference at Versailles. The conclusions of the "Syndical Conference at Berne" had been studied "with the closest attention," and representatives of the "Syndicates" had participated in the preparation of the articles of the peace treaty relating to labor. Moreover, the proposed program of the first session of the International Labor Conference, to be held at Washington as soon as the peace treaty came into force, already comprised "the majority of the questions raised at the Syndical Conference at Berne."

The ships which make up the merchant fleet of the Adriatic are today either Italian or Yugoslav, and the interested parties, Italians and Yugoslavs, are solidly together in this: if you take the ships belonging either to one or the other, you are condemning the Adriatic ports to death. I hope there will be an exception made to the principle which was laid down for the case of Germany.

M. Clemenceau. Who has these ships?

M. Orlando. At the moment, they are sequestered in the hands of the Allies; the question now is their future ownership. If they were withdrawn from the Adriatic, it would be the ruin of the cities, Italian as well as Yugoslav, which live on maritime commerce.

Mr. Lloyd George. Does M. Orlando mean that Italy would receive at one and the same time her share of the German merchant fleet and all of the Adriatic fleet, which would be subtracted from the total to be divided amongst the Allies? This would be singularly unjust to France and England.

M. Orlando. These Austrian ships, if they are left to us, do not represent an increase in Italian tonnage; they won't make up for the losses we have suffered. Their economic purpose is special: they are attached to the cities to which they belong. To tell Italy that the possession of Austrian ships will compensate for the losses she suffered at sea would not be fair. Italy is acquiring the maritime territories to which these ships belong, whose life is tied to their possession: thus they don't add to the merchant fleet of Italy as it was before the war.

Mr. Lloyd George. I accept this view if Italy renounces her claim to her share of the German ships. Despite the fact that it was we who bore the entire weight of the battle against Germany at sea, we have conceded Italy's right to participate in reparations; but if the entire Adriatic fleet must be reserved for the Italians, that changes the terms of the problem. I find that inconceivable: it was we who held the North Sea at the cost of an enormous effort; we could also tell you that we are reserving for ourselves a share of the German fleet; we could also tell you that the German ships are indispensable to the commerce of the North Sea.

M. Orlando. I regret the impression I have just made upon Mr. Lloyd George. I am convinced that my request is fair. Italy will have the city of Trieste; Trieste is essentially a port. If you give us Trieste and remove her ships from that city, she is ruined.

Regarding Alsace-Lorraine, didn't we concede that its territory, although until now part of the German Empire, would not contribute to the reparation of damages? It is a principle whose justice we all acknowledged. Didn't we say, in particular, that amongst the ships of the Rhine, those which provide river services to Alsace would belong to it by right? We are asking the question in the same way for Trieste. Trieste must come to Italy along with its merchant fleet; if you take it away, Trieste is ruined.

M. Clemenceau. The case of the ships of the Rhine is altogether different: we claimed only 20 per cent of them, and as reparation for the barges which the Germans took from us in the north of France.

M. Orlando. In the case of Germany, the replacement, ton for ton, applies to the ships belonging to German nationals. In the treaty with Austria, it should be said that it applies to ships belonging to Austrian nationals. It is natural that ships belonging to enemies, that is, to inhabitants of German Austria and Hungary, should be the common property of the Allies. But the ships of Trieste, an Italian city, must be Italian.

President Wilson. They will be Italian and Trieste will be an Italian city, but only after the conclusion of peace.

M. Clemenceau. For the moment, we are obliged to treat all these territories as part of the Austro-Hungarian monarchy.

M. Orlando. I see what will happen in practice: it will be impossible for Italy to receive compensation for her lost ships.

Mr. Lloyd George. That argument is very difficult to support. Hundreds of thousands of tons of the British merchant fleet were sunk carrying coal, food, ammunition to Italy, and we shouldn't have the right to participate in the distribution of the Austro-Hungarian fleet in the Adriatic—and the only ships of which a part would be left to us would be those of the Yugoslavs?

President Wilson. No, for those are becoming Serbian, and if M. Orlando's argument is accepted, these ships will remain with the Yugoslav state.

Mr. Lloyd George. I couldn't present such a proposal to the British Parliament.

M. Orlando. Since it will be very necessary for Trieste to recover the ships which it needs, which are the basis of its commercial life, Italy will remain without reparation for her lost tonnage.

M. Clemenceau. Legally, Trieste is an enemy city until the peace.

Mr. Lloyd George. The passage from England to Italy was one of the most dangerous that our ships had to make during the war: by helping Italy, we lost a very great number of them. Don't believe that Trieste will be ruined if the ships in the Adriatic are distributed amongst us: if commerce continues to flow from the interior towards Trieste, ships of every flag will seek it out.

M. Clemenceau. There is no question, moreover, of taking all these ships for ourselves: in a division of the Adriatic fleet, Italy will obviously have the largest part.

M. Orlando. Will you allow me the right to forgo our participation in the distribution of the German fleet so we can reserve the tonnage of the Adriatic for ourselves?

Mr. Lloyd George. We may choose amongst three principles. The first is to ask each of our enemies to make good the losses which it caused. The second is to place in a common pool all the tonnage which our enemies will deliver to us then and divide it in proportion to losses. The third would be to leave the Austrian ships to Italy, whilst leaving the German ships to England and France. But we can't apply two of these arrangements at one and the same time.

M. Orlando. The least I can ask is that Italy have the commercial fleet of Trieste.

President Wilson. What proportion of all the ships does this fleet represent?

Mr. Lloyd George. If M. Orlando means: "Supposing that Italy had a right, in the general distribution, to one hundred ships of three thousand tons each, she will take them first from the fleet of Trieste," that is an acceptable proposal, one which can in any case be discussed.

—President Wilson reads aloud the letter from the German delegation on labor legislation.

Mr. Lloyd George. It seems desirable to me to see to it that working conditions are regulated in the same way in Germany as in our countries. We will thus avoid unfortunate competition and outbidding.

President Wilson. We will be doing nothing contrary to the interest of the Germans by imposing the eight-hour day on them; for, in America, we have found that it yields better results than the ten-hour day.

Mr. Lloyd George. It is necessary to differentiate: I don't believe that is equally true of all trades.

President Wilson. It is also necessary to act so as to avoid giving the impression to the working class in our own countries that we are being unfair to German workers.

Mr. Lloyd George. I propose that the German note be referred to our experts on labor legislation, I mean Messrs. Barnes, Colliard, Robinson, and an Italian expert.

M. Orlando. I'll send you M. Cabrini.

—*The German note is referred to a commission thus composed.*

M. Clemenceau. We must now bring M. Orlando up to date about what we propose to do at Smyrna. During the absence of the Italian delegates, the Greeks warned us of the imminence of new massacres, which made a landing at Smyrna necessary: we have agreed to it in principle. Greek ships have assembled, at Kavalla, I believe. We would like the matter to take place as quietly as possible. There is no question of occupying or of partitioning territory in Asia Minor, but only of protecting the population.

Admiral Calthorpe has received orders to go to Smyrna. There will be a landing in which French, English, and Italian marines are to participate. Aren't there six or seven Italian ships outside Smyrna?

M. Orlando. There are only two.

M. Clemenceau. Our information and that of the English nearly agree: some say six, others seven. I fear that M. Orlando is not well informed.

M. Orlando. No doubt they included some small torpedo boats.

M. Clemenceau. In the landing, we would not like the different Allied armies to be represented by unequal contingents; the number of Italians, English, and French must be about the same.

Everything is ready; but we didn't want to give orders without first consulting the Italian government.

M. Orlando. The landing would be carried out by the Greeks, French, English, and Italians?

M. Clemenceau. The Greeks will indeed land. They ask to protect the Greek populations of Asia Minor against massacres. We have about two hundred marines there, and the English have about as many.

President Wilson. I should point out that it is not the Greeks who are asking for the occupation of Smyrna.

M. Clemenceau. That's right; they only called the danger of massacres to our attention. Our great desire is to avoid conflict: it is with this end in mind that Admiral Calthorpe was sent to Smyrna in person. There hasn't been any landing yet.

According to our reports, Italian troops landed for two days at Scala Nuova, but reembarked.

It is important to show a united front and, after having occupied the city, we will then leave the Greeks to guard it.

Mr. Lloyd George. We will occupy the forts until a Greek garrison comes to replace our troops.

M. Clemenceau. The Turks haven't been warned yet.

M. Orlando. Allow me to postpone my answer until this afternoon; I need to see Baron Sonnino on this matter.

Mr. Lloyd George. We have learned that there were three Italian landings: one at Marmaris, one at Scala Nuova, one at Budrum. What is their objective?

M. Orlando. That is exactly why I wish to see Baron Sonnino.

Mr. Lloyd George. I will point out that these different points surround Smyrna.

LXXVI

Conversation between President Wilson and MM. Clemenceau, Lloyd George, and Orlando, and Baron Sonnino*

MAY 12, 1919, 3:30 P.M.

President Wilson. Our Italian colleagues are going to inform us of their decision about the operation at Smyrna.

M. Orlando. We accept it in principle; but why not leave the landing troops of the three powers at Smyrna? If France sends two hundred men and Great Britain and Italy do the same, we would withdraw them only when a final decision has been taken on the fate of that region.

President Wilson. Actually, the figure of two hundred men appears to have been exaggerated, given the troops available.

Mr. Lloyd George. We only have fifty marines to land.

M. Clemenceau. I don't see any advantage in staying at Smyrna after the arrival of the Greeks.

Baron Sonnino. That will give an international character to the occupation.

M. Clemenceau. We say to you: today Smyrna belongs to no one; it is not a question of determining the fate of that city, but of carrying out a temporary operation, with a well-defined objective. I would see great difficulties in leaving French, English, and Italian troops under the command of a Greek general.

President Wilson. Is it desirable to leave these handfuls of men there?

Mr. Lloyd George. Every minute we receive information which in-

*H., PPC, V, 576-78.

dicates the urgency of the operation. According to the latest news, the Turks have fired upon the Greek quarter without any provocation and killed a number of inhabitants.

President Wilson. It doesn't seem advisable to me to prolong the common occupation.

M. Orlando. If you have objections, I don't insist.

Mr. Lloyd George. All that remains is to warn the Turks.

M. Clemenceau. So the question is settled amongst us.

LXXVII

Conversation between President Wilson and MM. Clemenceau and Lloyd George*

MAY 13, 1919, 4 P.M.

Mr. Lloyd George. Have you read Scheidemann's speech to the German National Assembly?[1] It can serve as a preface to the sign-

*H., *PPC*, V, 579ff.

[1] Philipp Scheidemann had made an impassioned attack on the proposed peace treaty in a speech before the German National Assembly on May 12. "This treaty," he said, "is in the view of the Imperial German Government, unacceptable, so unacceptable that I am unable to believe that this earth could bear such a document without a cry issuing from millions and millions of throats in all lands, without distinction to party. Away with this murderous scheme!" He appealed for national unity in the face of the threat to Germany's existence occasioned by the treaty. "Let me speak without tactical considerations," he continued. "The thing which is at the basis of our discussion is this thick volume in which 100 sentences begin 'Germany renounces.' This dreadful and murderous volume by which confession of our own unworthiness, our consent to pitiless disruption, our agreement to helotry and slavery, are to be extorted—this book must not become the future code of law."

Scheidemann also attacked Wilson by name. "The world," he declared, "has once again lost an illusion. The nations have in this period, which is so poor in ideals, again lost a belief. What name on thousands of bloody battlefields, in thousands of trenches, in orphan families, and among the despairing and abandoned has been mentioned during these four years with more devotion and belief than the name of Wilson? Today the picture of the peace bringer as the world pictured him is paling beside the dark forms of our jailors." Continuing with this metaphor, he asserted that, if the treaty was accepted, Germany would become a prison camp, with her sixty million inhabitants at hard labor for the benefit of the Allies. The treaty would destroy Germany's international commerce and her domestic economy. Without her mercantile fleet and without the raw materials formerly obtained from such territories as Upper Silesia, Alsace-

ing of the treaty as well as to the refusal to sign. In it, I notice attacks on President Wilson, which will help to make him popular in other countries of Europe.

Scheidemann, like all those who have expressed German opinion up to now, protests especially against the economic losses imposed on Germany, against the cession of coal mines and potash deposits; he protests against the arrangement anticipated for the Saar Basin and, above all, about the cession of Upper Silesia to Poland.

There is no doubt that the change of their eastern border especially affects the Germans; they shudder at the thought of seeing their compatriots placed under the domination of a people whom they consider inferior. With the French, they at least feel that they are amongst equals; but they don't hide their contempt for the Poles.

ITALIAN QUESTIONS

President Wilson. We are assembled today to study together the Italian questions and to seek their solution. I have a proposal to make, which I know will be accepted by the Yugoslavs: it comes down to instituting a plebiscite along the entire coast of the Adriatic.

If we take the Italian boundary, starting from the North, I will propose first to give Italy the Sexten Valley, which, it is true, contains three or four thousand Germans, but whose possession by

---

Lorraine, and the Saar Valley, Germany could not hope to meet the monetary demands of the Allies. "What," he asked, "is a people to do which is confronted by the command that it is responsible for all losses and all damages that its enemies suffered in the war? What is a people to do which is to have no voice in fixing its obligations?"

In contrast to this angry rhetoric, Scheidemann expressed one hopeful note. "We have made counter-proposals," he said, "and shall make still more. With your consent we regard it as our sacred task to come to negotiations. Here and there insight and the common obligations of humanity are beginning to make themselves felt in neutral countries; in Italy and in Great Britain, above all, too. This is a comfort for us in this last fearful flaming up of the policy of the mailed fist—and in socialistic France voices are being heard whereby historians one day will measure the state of humanity after four years of murder."

The above summary and quotations are taken from the extensive extracts printed in the *New York Times*, May 14, 1919. The full text is printed in Germany. Nationalversammlung. *Verhandlungen der Verfassunggebenden Deutschen Nationalversammlung, Stenographische Berichte*, Vol. 327 (Berlin, 1920), pp. 1082-84.

Italy would close off one of the last open doors for invasion across the Alps.

The question of the tunnels of Tarvis was raised in the Council of Foreign Ministers. The solution proposed would give one of the tunnels, with the city of Tarvis, to the Italians; the station at Assling would belong to the Yugoslavs, and Villach would remain with the Austrians. Thus, the branches of the railroad would be fairly equitably divided.

In Istria, the border would follow the crest of the mountains; it would be considerably to the west of the line indicated by the Treaty of London. This, moreover, is drawn by the Italians according to a broad interpretation of the treaty. The treaty says indeed that the boundary must follow the line of the watershed; but since many rivers in this region flow eastward by an underground course, the Italians have determined the boundary line, not according to the point of origin of each stream, but according to the point where it appears on the surface.

Since the island of Cherso blocks the harbor of Fiume absolutely, I am of opinion to leave it to the Yugoslavs, but to give Italy a group of islands further south, whose population is Italian by majority.

In Dalmatia—on the islands as well as on the mainland—there would be a plebiscite, and Italy could claim any part of this territory, small or large, whose population voted for her.

As for the city of Fiume, the Italians have often spoken of the possibility of replacing its port with an equivalent port for the Yugoslavs—that of Buccari, which is a very good natural port, although too closely squeezed by mountains. I will propose that the population of Fiume be asked the following question: "Does the city of Fiume wish to attach itself to Italy, once Italy has built an equivalent port at Buccari for the use of the Yugoslavs?"

Mr. Lloyd George. That would be telling the inhabitants of Fiume: "As soon as you become Italians, you will cease to exist, and your commerce will pass to a neighboring city."

President Wilson. Italy herself offered to create a port at Buccari.

M. Clemenceau. Yes, but with the idea of acquiring Dalmatia. I may be mistaken, but that's how I understood her intention.

Mr. Lloyd George. I don't know exactly what they're looking for in Fiume.

M. Clemenceau. They want above all to save face; they don't know how to get out of the situation in which they have placed themselves.

President Wilson. It is also possible that the capitalists of Trieste want Fiume to be Italian in order to ruin its competition at will.

Mr. Lloyd George. That is Landru's policy:[2] to possess in order to kill.

President Wilson. The Italians tell us: "These lands are Italian." In this case, they can't refuse to ask them to express their will by a plebiscite. If it was possible, moreover, to delay that solution—not to settle it by the terms of the peace treaty—perhaps that would be better.

M. Clemenceau. I fear that's impossible. The monstrosity must be confronted resolutely. We must force the Italians to look at a reasonable solution of the Fiume question. We must know what they want in Dalmatia; it seems that Zara, Sebenico, and the islands are what interests them most.

President Wilson. I cannot depart from the principle of free choice: it is impossible for me to hand over a population to Italy without its consent.

M. Clemenceau. As for us, the Treaty of London binds us.

President Wilson. If you give Fiume to the Italians, how can you give them Dalmatia?

Mr. Lloyd George. That would obviously be impossible; if they want Fiume, which is outside the Treaty of London, they must abandon Dalmatia.

In a conversation I had with M. Pašić, it seemed to me that he did not particularly care about Fiume, and that in the end he would leave it to the Italians, if they renounced Dalmatia.

President Wilson. That is not M. Trumbić's position.

Mr. Lloyd George. That's possible: M. Pašić is a Serb and M. Trumbić a Croat.

M. Clemenceau. It would be most dangerous for the Italians to renounce Fiume whilst claiming Dalmatia.

---

[2] Henri-Désiré Landru, formerly known to French police as a petty criminal convicted several times of forgery and fraud, had been arrested in Paris on April 12, 1919, and charged with the murder of several women. The lengthy investigation which ensued suggested that Landru had murdered by unknown means at least ten women and the adolescent son of one of them and had probably disposed of their bodies by dismembering and burning them. His lure was to hold out to them the prospect of marriage, and his motive was to secure their money and valuable possessions. Despite the fact that none of the bodies was ever found whole or in part, Landru was ultimately convicted on the basis of circumstantial evidence and guillotined on February 25, 1922. By May 1919, the case had already become a *cause célèbre*, as successive revelations appeared in the newspapers. For a detailed study of Landru's career, see Dennis Bardens, *The Ladykiller: The Life of Landru, the French Blue-beard* (London, 1972).

President Wilson. I don't believe that you would run this risk, because Italian public opinion is especially excited on the Fiume question. I am informed about the allegedly popular vote in Fiume in favor of union with Italy; it is the result of the action of a small group of people. I have information on the subject from two sources, Italian and Yugoslav; both clearly reveal action taken by a group of individuals seizing power on their own authority. Here is what the Yugoslavs say: the proclamation of the independence of Fiume, at the time of the armistice, was the act of about ten people, who proclaimed themselves "the Italian Council of the City of Fiume." On October 29, after the Austrians had left the city, the National Croatian Council, in session at Agram, declared that Fiume was an integral part of Croatia. But at the same time the "Italian Council of Fiume" proclaimed that the city was Italian. This council was in no way representative. The Italian occupation followed on November 17, and, since then, no opportunity has been given to popular opinion to express itself freely. Admiral Buller, the American admiral who first visited that area, confirms for us that the Council of Fiume was formed solely by the Italian fraction of the population, and all witnesses agree on this point. This council worked in the most arbitrary fashion to italianize the city, imposing the Italian language in the schools, on signs, arresting and deporting inhabitants of Croatian nationality, etc.

I propose nevertheless to act as if we didn't contest the Italian leaning of Fiume, and to tell the Italians: "As soon as you have built the port at Buccari, you may take possession of the city of Fiume if it solemnly renews by plebiscite the expression of its will to be united to Italy." As for you, gentlemen, this solution will free you from the Treaty of London.

Mr. Lloyd George. Yesterday, I had an interesting conversation with the Aga Khan, an extraordinary character, whom I can only compare to Monte Cristo. He is a man of rare intelligence, without peer amongst the Mohammedans of India; he possesses an immense fortune, acquired by selling advance tickets to Paradise. He knows all languages and all countries, discusses competently French and English political questions, criticizes certain articles of the treaty, particularly those concerning the eastern boundary of Germany. He also spoke to me about Fiume, which he knows, and he said to me: "Whatever the exact proportion of the different elements of the population in Fiume, the city is certainly Italian, not only in its appearance, but in its commerce and in all its ruling forces." This same personage naturally spoke to me about oriental questions, and he advises us to listen to the Mohammedans of his country before settling the Turkish question. We don't realize enough all that Turkey represents for the Mohammedans of India.

President Wilson. I recently glanced at an article in the *Contemporary Review*[3] which shows that there is some agitation in India because the Mohammedans are worried about Turkey's fate.

Mr. Lloyd George. We are now having difficulties with Afghanistan; the Afghans are not very dangerous, because they are lost if they leave their mountains. But we have intercepted messages between them and the Bolsheviks. I believe we must take account of this danger and hear the Mohammedans.

President Wilson. Returning to Fiume, I can tell you that one of our officers, from whom I have recently received a report, thinks, like the Aga Khan, that Fiume is really more an Italian city. But he adds: "If I were the Italian government and I seized Fiume, I would begin by making the Italians there leave in order to replace them with real Italians."

Mr. Lloyd George. There is something to be said in Italy's favor. For her, the great question is the question of national pride. It seems to the Italians that they are not quite being treated as equals.

Let us take the question of mandates, in particular. We concur in thinking that certain backward nations should, in their own best interest, be administered by those who have attained the highest degree of culture and administrative experience. When it is a question of certain parts of Turkey, the United States is asked, despite its natural repugnance to leave its own domain, to assume the mandate. The Japanese must have territories in the Pacific. No one is turning to Italy; offers will have to be made to her, thereby creating an atmosphere that would help us settle the question of Fiume.

As the real representatives of the League of Nations today, we are considering the situation of backward countries, and we think we must do for them what Rome did for us: without the Romans, we would have remained half savages for centuries longer. Can't we ask Italy to participate in this common work? If the Italians haven't always proved themselves superior in the arts of war, I believe they are very well qualified in the arts of peace. Consider what their engineers accomplished in the construction of the most difficult roads across mountainous terrain;

[3] "The Political Situation in India," *The Fortnightly* (not *Contemporary*) *Review*, CXI (May 1919), 742-51.

visualize to yourselves how Italy supports, on relatively infertile land, a population of nearly 40 million inhabitants, who are strong and of a superior type.

Can't we say to the Italians: "You are right, your role has not yet been what it should be?" I believe Italy capable of doing great things in Asia. Her administration is good, and the Greeks themselves acknowledge that the Italians are their superiors in policing mountainous regions. Asia Minor is infested with brigandage; the Italians will know how to eradicate it. If we can't offer them all of Anatolia, we can at least propose that they establish order and undertake the development of a part of that region. Where the Turks made a wilderness, the Italians can build roads, railways, irrigate the soil, and cultivate it. They can even populate these territories; it shouldn't be forgotten that their emigration before the war was several hundred thousand men each year.

In speaking of these questions to them as soon as we meet them again face to face, we'll put them in a better state of mind. Moreover, we have to keep the promise made, in signing the Treaty of London, to grant them colonial compensation to balance our own acquisitions. They expect to receive British Somaliland from us. It is true that our colonists are resisting and saying that Berbera is indispensable to us. The French colonials undoubtedly say the same thing about Djibouti. It is up to us to play a part by acting in commond accord. It seems there is coal and petroleum in Somaliland; this is precisely what Italy lacks, and, as for ourselves, we have enough.

These are the questions which I would like to settle before taking up the difficult problem of Fiume.

President Wilson. It seems to me that this starts on the right foot. We would give a mandate to Italy in southern Anatolia. Greece would receive complete ownership of Smyrna and the territory upon which our experts agree, along with the Dodecanese, and I propose to institute a mandate of the League of Nations, which would be entrusted to Greece, for the rest of the *vilayet* of Aydin.

Mr. Lloyd George. Northern Anatolia remains. If the United States accepts the mandate for Armenia, I will propose to give the mandate for northern Anatolia to France. If the American Congress rejects the idea of the mandate in Armenia, then I would give all of Anatolia to Italy, with France having the Armenian mandate.

M. Clemenceau. Is it possible to forecast what the American Senate will do?

President Wilson. I believe it will accept the undertaking. I will remind you, furthermore, that we are told from different sides that what the Turks wish above all else is not to have their territory divided; they will accept a superior authority on condition that it is a single one.

M. Clemenceau. You will find no one who is in a position to give all this large country the development it needs.

President Wilson. I believe we can administer and develop fairly completely the southern part and confine ourselves, in the rest of the country, to playing the role of counselors.

M. Clemenceau. It is very difficult to establish a line between those two roles.

I consider it as given that the Americans will accept the mandate in Constantinople.

Mr. Lloyd George. I hope so, whatever the solution to the other questions may be. If the Italians are established in southern Anatolia, they would have to be given the port of Makri if they cannot have that of Mersina. Greek jurisdiction would extend south of the region of Smyrna but would stop before the harbor of Makri.

M. Clemenceau. The Greeks don't have much administrative capability. I covered the entire Peloponnese without seeing a single road. I don't wish to say anything against them, but these are the facts.

President Wilson. The Greeks haven't yet been treated as a modern nation. By showing them our confidence, we will give them the ambition to do well.

M. Clemenceau. Greece is still a country where the women till the soil whilst the men smoke their pipes. I believe, though, that something can be done with these people.

President Wilson. Can't we say of races, as of men, that we elevate them when we set them to great tasks?

M. Clemenceau. Their men, with a very few rare exceptions, are mediocre and don't know a word of their ancient history: I remember that they asked me to explain it to them!

President Wilson. If you were able, in the offers which might be made to Italy in the name of the League of Nations, to add that of Somaliland, that would help in the solutions we desire.

Mr. Lloyd George. My intention is to give Greece the island of Cyprus also.

M. Clemenceau. Don't forget that, according to the Treaty of Berlin, you need my authorization for that.

Mr. Lloyd George. I hope you'll give it to me.

President Wilson. If you can make this gift to Greece, it will be a great thing.

Mr. Lloyd George. That would dispel the atmosphere of covetousness and greed whose impression should be feared. Regarding the Turks, I don't have any scruples towards them; they have no rights over a country which they were only able to turn into a desert.

President Wilson. All we owe the Turkish population is the right to live and the guarantee of a good administration. I don't know the Turks directly. But all witnesses agree in representing them as a docile people, against whom no reproach can be made so long as they are not granted the fatal gift of command. It is often repeated that the Turk is a gentleman; he will obey without difficulty the power which serves him as a guide.

Mr. Lloyd George. According to the plans that have been made, Armenia will be very extensive.

M. Clemenceau. Its administration will be an arduous task for the Americans; unfortunately, it is a country where massacre is a chronic disease.

President Wilson. At this very moment, the Turks are interning a great number of Armenians, many of whom are dying of hunger. I have been given some horrible details.[4]

Mr. Lloyd George. It would be good to publish them in America; that would help your public to understand why the United States must assume the responsibility of the mandate. The Turk, when he has the slightest degree of power, is a brute. Whatever the difficulties we may encounter from the Mohammedans of India, we must put an end to the Turkish regime.

M. Clemenceau. The most pressing matter for us is to agree on what shall be reserved to Italy.

President Wilson. I would consent to put Makri in the zone of the Italian mandate; but, as for the rest of the *vilayet* of Aydin, I still think that the mandate must be given to Greece.

Mr. Lloyd George. The question is which administration the Turks will best put up with.

M. Clemenceau. On that score, there is no doubt: it is the Italian administration.

President Wilson. What I fear is putting a power of superior administrative capability in immediate contact with the Greek zone. I would like the entire zone of southwestern Anatolia to be treated

---

[4] In Avetis Aharonian to WW, May 10, 1919, cited in *PWW*, Vol. 59, p. 104.

as a geographical entity. If the Turks feel that they have before them, not only the Greeks, but a great international administration of which the Greeks are the mandatories, they won't oppose them.

Sir Maurice Hankey. I can testify that, around Saloniki, whose environs were very dangerous under Turkish rule, the Greeks have reestablished order perfectly.

Mr. Lloyd George. Could the port of Makri be connected easily to an existing railway? According to the map, that appears to be rather difficult. Furthermore, these coasts don't offer any natural port all the way to Mersina. Adalia cost a fair amount of money and is worthless from the maritime point of view.

M. Clemenceau. Couldn't we give Scala Nuova to the Italians?

President Wilson. In that case, a large part of the *vilayet* of Aydin would be taken away from Greece. Even Makri should not be given to the Italians.

Mr. Lloyd George. They must have Makri if they don't have Mersina, and a port is essential to them for their warships. In this regard, Marmaris would be excellent. What interests the Italians most is Heraclea,[5] on the other side of the peninsula; they have neither coal nor any other fuel, and they would like to have the mines of Heraclea.

M. Clemenceau. But these mines are French.

Mr. Lloyd George. The Italians say that they are part Italian and part German, and that, if the German share passed into their hands, they would occupy a preponderant position. I don't know if there is any great harm in giving them these German shares; they could thus make use of these mines, which would not prevent France from having the mandate for northern Anatolia. The output from the mines of Heraclea is not, by the way, very substantial: 600,000 tons, and the quality of the coal is mediocre.

President Wilson. Regarding the Adriatic, you already know my proposals.

Mr. Lloyd George. Will you undertake to speak to the Italians about the Adriatic, whilst we will make them our offers in Asia?

President Wilson. Do we all agree about the mandate to be entrusted to Greece?

Mr. Lloyd George. I fear that the Greeks fail to hold these Mohammedan populations of the *vilayet* of Aydin well in hand. They are reputed to be rather intractable.

[5] Heraclea Pontica, the ancient name of Eregli, a port on the Black Sea some 120 miles from the Bosporus. It is in Zonguldak Province, an important coal-mining region.

M. Clemenceau. In Crete, the largest part of the Turkish population has remained there since the island became Greek, and the two populations live side by side, without mutual complaints; I don't think there is anything to fear.

—Mr. Nicolson is introduced and receives the necessary instructions for the preparation of a map of the mandates in Asia Minor.

President Wilson. The important thing is for us to agree on the proposals to make to Italy—and on the proposals which will relieve us of the Treaty of London.

Mr. Lloyd George. The best thing is to treat the problem as a whole. I will study the question of Somaliland; I had a conversation this morning with Lord Milner on the subject. I must say that he is making strong objections.

President Wilson. If France took the initiative by offering the part of Somaliland which she owns, on the condition that England do the same, that would undoubtedly help you overcome Lord Milner's resistance.

M. Clemenceau. What is Lord Milner's argument?

Mr. Lloyd George. He says: "We are in Aden. If the Italians are across from us on the African coast, Aden loses its value." He adds that the garrison of Aden is fed by what comes from Berbera. I answered him that the Italians are at least as good gardeners as we, and that they'll send us their vegetables.

M. Clemenceau. Can't we settle the Bulgarian questions tomorrow? Everything seems ready.

President Wilson. The United States is not at war with Bulgaria, but I will join in your discussion. Concerning the Turks, are we going to receive them or take a decision here and communicate it to them through a commission?

Mr. Lloyd George. That remains to be seen. When will you hear the Mohammedans from India? I can have an important Mohammedan personality, who lives in London, come here. I will also summon the Maharaja of Bikaner and the advisers who surround him. The Maharaja himself is not Mohammedan, but he represents the sixty million Mohammedans who live in India, and the effect in India will be excellent if they learn that the Four heard the men charged with speaking in their name.

M. Clemenceau. When can you have them brought here?

Mr. Lloyd George. Thursday or Friday.

President Wilson. What is the agenda for tomorrow?

Sir Maurice Hankey. You will have to study the military conventions relating to the occupied territories on the left bank of the Rhine, the report of the Commission on Ports, Waterways, and Railways about Austria, and the questions relating to Bulgaria.

Mr. Lloyd George. Can't we refer the Bulgarian questions to the Ministers of Foreign Affairs? If they reach agreement, we will only have to approve.

—*This proposal is adopted.*

Sir Maurice Hankey. There is also a Serbian note, in which Serbia asks to participate in reparations for a sum of two billion francs.

Mr. Lloyd George. She is not as demanding as Belgium, but I don't know if she has a right to anything at all, given her territorial acquisitions.

M. Clemenceau. Indeed, Serbia is acquiring large territories free of debt.

President Wilson. You recall that the question has already been raised, but that we concluded that it was a question of debit and credit; it is an account to be established.

Mr. Lloyd George. It must therefore be referred to our financial experts.

—*This proposal is adopted.*

LXXVIII

Conversation between President Wilson and MM. Clemenceau, Lloyd George, and Orlando*

MAY 14, 1919, 11 A.M.

—M. Crespi, president of the Commission on the International Regime of Ports, Waterways, and Railways, Sir Hubert Llewellyn Smith, and Messrs. Claveille and De Martino, members of this commission, are introduced.

President Wilson. The floor belongs to M. Crespi, who is going to present the conclusions of the commission on ways of communication regarding the treaty with Austria.

*H., PPC, V, 589ff.

Mr. Lloyd George. We should confine ourselves to studying the points we are not agreed upon.

M. Crespi. Our commission did nothing more than adapt the terms provided for Germany to the case of Austria. The Italian delegation is opposed to having the arrangement, which provides for the revision of a certain number of clauses at the expiration of a period of five years, apply to Article 26 of the treaty with Austria (corresponding to Article 45 of the treaty with Germany), which relates to the rates of the railroads serving the Adriatic ports.

M. De Martino. It is a question of retaining the prewar rates of the railway lines which serve the Adriatic ports. This question is unconnected to the political solution of the problems which arise concerning this coast.

Before the war, Austrian and Hungarian rates favored the transport of merchandise from the entire monarchy towards those ports which served as its outlets. Today, Austria-Hungary has disappeared and has been replaced by several small states. The danger is that, in the aftermath of war, the established order of railroad rates will be followed by a sort of anarchy. It will be a long time before an agreement is reached over rates amongst all the states involved in the transportation system and those which will control the ports. Not only will the solution be delayed by technical complications, but it can also be imperiled by the ill will of any one of the participants. Furthermore, we know how Germany always favored her ports; we know the special rates which she created in the past and which she can still establish on rivers and railways to divert normal transportation in directions she has chosen. If there is no agreement on railroad rates in the territories of the former Austro-Hungarian monarchy, Germany will not fail to profit from it, to the detriment of the Adriatic ports. Our duty is to prevent a danger that we foresee.

One clause of the treaty stipulates the retention of the prewar rates on the lines which lead to the Adriatic ports: it is a stipulation of defense and justice. But if this clause is subject to obligatory revision after a period of five years, the consequences will be deplorable for trade, which needs to be able to look ahead a certain distance.

The clause, as it stands now, is to everyone's advantage. We are ready to grant reciprocity on our railways. But the limit of five years is contrary to the objective which the commission on ways of communication has held in view in all its work, namely, the protection of natural thoroughfares against artificial and unjustifiable deviations.

Mr. Lloyd George. Do you propose to make this system permanent?

M. De Martino. I propose only to exclude the article mentioned from the terms set forth in Article 61.

President Wilson. The procedure for revision is the same as that proposed for other clauses: it is the League of Nations which has to decide if there are grounds for carrying it out.

Mr. Lloyd George. All I have to say is that, if a stipulation of this kind was imposed upon our railways, it would drive them to bankruptcy, for the increase in salaries and in costs of all kinds makes an increase in rates absolutely necessary.

M. De Martino. What we want is the maintenance, not of the rates such as they were, but of the proportionate relationship between these rates and those of other lines.

Mr. Lloyd George. I fear that the intervention of the League of Nations might be a little too formal a procedure, which, by its very difficulty, would allow exceptional rates to be perpetuated.

M. De Martino. Within the commission, I have already replied to the same objection, voiced by a British representative, that it is essentially a question of retaining a certain proportionate relationship between the rates of these lines and other rates.

Mr. Lloyd George. Yes, but as soon as the increase in rates becomes necessary for legitimate reasons, I fear that the amendment which you propose makes it possible to oppose it.

M. Claveille. I took part in the discussion, and I will merely repeat what I said. I am in favor of the insertion of Article 45, which provides for the retention of the system favorable to the Adriatic ports. We cannot allow a complete upheaval of communications and a diversion of transportation to the detriment of the Adriatic ports to occur as a result of the political changes which have taken place in Austria-Hungary. On the other hand, it is not possible to prevent indefinitely an increase in rates, which is necessary in this area as in our own. But, as M. De Martino says, it is a question of proportionality.

Everywhere, rates fall into three categories: general rates, special rates—that is, set for certain goods—and export rates. If the general rates increase, the special rates and the export rates will also increase; Italy accepts this. On the other hand, it appears impossible to establish this system without a time limit. For other articles of the convention, we have accepted revision by the League of Nations at the end of five years, or continuation on the express condition of reciprocity. If, after five years, the League of Nations judges revision to be useful, I don't think that any obstacle ought to be raised against it. All we wish to do—and what we will obtain with the proposed clauses—is to prevent an unjustifiable diversion of trade.

M. Orlando. We can accept the situation as M. Claveille presents it. We don't request the elimination of Article 61, which, by the way, allows revision, not at the end of five years, but immediately, if the League of Nations so desires; what we reject is compulsory revision at the end of five years.

M. Claveille. Nothing in Article 61A says that this revision is compulsory. Five years is given as the earliest possible time when it can take place. Since you accept the system of reciprocity as an alternative, I don't see what you are risking. The useful aspect of this article is that it assures you the continuation of a privileged system for five years.

President Wilson. Article 61, which provides for revision by the League of Nations without any time limit, applies not to rates, but to administrative questions.

M. Orlando. I propose that the article stand as is, with the indication of a time limit; but instead of five years, we would ask that this limit be extended to ten years. Trade needs time to plan and to develop.

President Wilson. Article 61A doesn't say that the system will necessarily be changed at the end of five years, but only that it can be after five years.

M. Claveille. I agree with this observation. What we wanted was to insure complete stability for five years, and, thereafter, to leave the task of judging to the League of Nations. We can assume that the Council of the League of Nations, which will be composed of leading statesmen of the powers represented here, will prove itself wise and reasonable. I am persuaded that Italy is risking nothing in accepting the text as it is.

M. Orlando. After these explanations, we won't insist further.

Mr. Lloyd George. I now want to raise a question of principle. Austria and Hungary are becoming purely continental countries without ports. Here are the articles which protect the interests of the Adriatic ports: have we made provisions to protect Austria and Hungary from any attempt to close off their access to the sea?

M. Claveille. In the present treaty, there is no guarantee to Austria and Hungary for the use of the ports; but in the general convention on ways of communication, which our commission has prepared, we had exactly this type of case in mind. It would obviously be absurd and contrary to our intentions to prevent Austria from having access to the sea. In the treaty with Germany, we inserted a clause in which the German government accepts in advance the general convention on ways of communication. It is obvious that one of the principal objectives of this convention will be to guarantee access to the sea to those countries which have no coastline.

M. Orlando. What has just been said corresponds to my thoughts. I am entirely of opinion that these countries must receive guarantees. That can be done when we sign the general agreement on the system of ways of communication.

Mr. Lloyd George. The completion of a convention of this kind might require much time, and it involves a question which affects Austria and Hungary in a vital way. They can fear, if they have a dispute with any one of their neighbors, finding themselves cut off from the sea, and, if we refer them to the general convention, they can reply that that provides them with no immediate security.

President Wilson. On the other hand, the Austrians and Hungarians can ask us what the terms provided in this general convention will be.

Mr. Lloyd George. It appears to me absolutely necessary that there be an indication in the treaty with Austria.

President Wilson. That is also the opinion of the American delegation.

Mr. Lloyd George. The commission must be instructed to draft a clause to that effect.

M. Crespi. I can submit a text to you. Moreover, it will suffice to refer to the article which, in the treaty with Germany, relates to the freedom of communications guaranteed to the Czechoslovaks.

Mr. Lloyd George. If we agree on the principle, there is no difficulty, the wording can be left to the commission.

—The members of the commission on ways of communication withdraw.

—The representatives of the Inter-Allied Supreme Economic Council are introduced.*

—Lord Robert Cecil reads aloud a memorandum[1] pointing out the easing of the blockade since the Armistice and announcing the intention of the Allied and Associated governments to lift the blockade entirely as soon as the peace treaty is signed.

Lord Robert Cecil. This is intended to show the Germans what they have to lose if they refuse to sign the treaty. I propose, in con-

*H., PPC, V, 599ff.

[1] Cecil actually read two memoranda. They are printed in PPC, V, 601-604.

formity with your intentions, to point out at the same time that, if the signing is refused, the blockade will be reimposed in all its severity, and the governments might, as of now, open negotiations with the neutrals in order to prepare for the eventual tightening of the blockade. That would show the Germans that we are ready to act and indeed could help us avoid having to act.

Mr. Lloyd George. Can we write that the blockade will be lifted as soon as the treaty is signed? Ratification must follow the signing. What would happen if the German Assembly refused to ratify?

Mr. McCormick. We can write that the blockade will be suspended from the moment of signing.

Mr. Lloyd George. I believe that the Germans must be given a reason to conclude promptly, and, for that, suspension is not desirable.

M. Clemenceau. There will be no state of peace as long as our parliaments, as well as the enemy's, have not accepted the treaty.

President Wilson. We could write: "as soon as Germany has formally accepted the peace treaty."

Mr. Lloyd George. That formula seems satisfactory to me.

President Wilson. In my opinion, what will produce the most useful effect, in case the Germans refuse to sign, is military occupation. The German people mustn't be reduced to despair by famine. That could only throw the country into anarchy and create the greatest difficulties for our occupation troops themselves. In addition, it would not be a very edifying spectacle for the entire world. We must keep in mind that economic sanctions constitute a much more terrible punishment than a simple military occupation and could not be used in all their rigor without offending the moral sentiment of humanity. They must only be resorted to in an extreme situation.

M. Clemenceau. I prefer to use them rather than to have our soldiers killed.

Mr. Lloyd George. If we are obliged to exercise pressure on Germany, it won't have to last very long. At this very moment, Germany is frightened by the idea of signing the treaty; the press is campaigning against signing; Scheidemann says: "I don't want to sign." Haase says: "We must sign, but I won't take responsibility for it." A military occupation accompanied by no other means of pressure could perhaps only prolong the difficulty; there are people in Germany who want an occupation because they fear for their property. If this terrible threat of the blockade were made against the German nation, she would crowd around Scheidemann to tell him with one voice: "Sign! Sign! Sign!"

President Wilson. I should recall that, in fact, the United States has never recognized the existing system of blockade, because it doesn't conform to the provisions of international law.

Lord Robert Cecil. Germany having no more fleet, it will be easy for us to make the blockade effective, which will satisfy your objections. Besides, what matters most just now is the threat, whether or not the blockade is effective.

—*The memorandum presented by Lord Robert Cecil is approved.*

Lord Robert Cecil. I have another question to raise. What should our conduct be towards the states to which we provide supplies and which flout our authority? This is true of Poland, which continues, despite us, to fight the Ukrainians at Lemberg; it is true of Serbia, which, at the very moment that she requests our coal, holds back the wheat of the Banat and prevents its shipment to the coast.

President Wilson. On that, I believe we should give carte blanche to the Economic Council; it is only natural to use the means at our disposal to cause our just decisions to be respected.

M. Orlando.* I have two questions about wording to submit to you. As to the responsibilities of Austria, it goes without saying that the clause of the German treaty relating to the Kaiser is inapplicable here; but we have recognized individual responsibility for crimes against international law. The Drafting Committee has raised the question of whether we can request the prosecution of criminals who are today nationals of states other than Austria or Hungary, strictly speaking. Isn't it sufficient that they be presumed guilty of crimes committed whilst they belonged to the Austro-Hungarian army for the article in question to be applicable in their cases?

President Wilson. The difficulty is that we can't compel Austria to turn over men who are no longer under her jurisdiction.

M. Orlando. I recognize the difficulty; but we must seek ways to obviate it. It wouldn't be fair for a submarine commander, because he was born in Bohemia, not to be punishable, whilst he would be had he been born in Vienna.

—*It is agreed that this question will be sent back to the committee.*

M. Orlando. I also wish to raise the question of languages. The treaty with Germany has been written in French and English. When it comes to Austria, whose principal adversary was Italy, it seems fair that the Italian language be used concurrently with the other two.

*H., *PPC*, V, 605ff.

M. Clemenceau. I don't object to that.
Mr. Lloyd George and **President Wilson.** Neither do we.

—*M. Orlando's proposal is adopted.*

Mr. Lloyd George. My attention has been drawn to an odd lapse in the wording of the peace treaty. The text of the article relating to the trial of the Emperor of Germany states: "The court will consist of four judges, appointed respectively by each of the five great powers. * * * " Obviously, this article must be revised.

—M. Clemenceau reads aloud the reply to the German note on labor legislation.[2]

Mr. Lloyd George. There may be cause to study whether Germany could not be allowed to participate in the International Labour Organization before entering the League of Nations as a full member.
President Wilson. I don't remember well enough the conditions upon which one can enter this organization to state my position.
Mr. Lloyd George. We can decide simply to place this question under study.
M. Clemenceau. I have received three new communications from the German delegation.[3] The first declares that the economic losses imposed on Germany won't allow her to live. The second refuses to acknowledge the responsibility of Germany for the origins of the war. The third protests against our assertion that we applied the principles of the Armistice and dwells upon the violations of right which the treaty has in store in Poland, in the Saar Basin, etc.
Mr. Lloyd George. The best thing would be to refer these three notes to a committee to prepare the replies.
President Wilson. I have received two memoranda from China.[4] The first expresses the desire to see the treaties between China and Japan abrogated; the second requests that all foreign troops be withdrawn from Chinese territory and that foreign postal services, consular rights, etc., be terminated. Mr. Lansing proposes

[2] G. N. Barnes, "Copy of Draft Letter to the German Delegation," printed in *ibid.*, pp. 610-12. The first three sections of this draft were very similar to the three sections of the preliminary draft reply summarized in LXXV, n. 2. However, the new draft included a fourth section which pointed out deficiencies in the draft agreement on labor law which Brockdorff-Rantzau had submitted (see *ibid.*, n. 1), which were in fact covered by the labor clauses of the preliminary peace treaty.
[3] They are summarized in *PPC*, V, 612-13. Clemenceau summarizes them well.
[4] See V. K. W. Koo to WW, April 17, 1919, n. 1, *PWW*, Vol. 57, p. 431, and J. C. Grew to G. F. Close, April 25, 1919, n. 1, *ibid.*, Vol. 58, p. 137.

to reply that these questions will be raised before the League of Nations as soon as it is established.

—*MM. Clemenceau and Lloyd George approve.*

Mr. Lloyd George. The permanent office of the Socialist Conference of Bern requests a meeting with us on the peace terms. I replied to Mr. Henderson, who presented this request to me, that, since the peace terms had been communicated to the Germans, this interview would serve no purpose and that, besides, M. Clemenceau, as President of our conference, had already had the opportunity to inform the delegation from Bern. The best thing would be to reiterate this reply in the name of the conference through the intermediary of the Secretary-General.

—*This proposal is adopted.*

President Wilson. I have to speak to you about Luxembourg. We asked the Luxemburgers to postpone their plebiscite. Their government is sending us a communication[5] stating that the chamber has unanimously voted a resolution which expresses the population's sentiment favoring the right of Luxembourg to self-determination in complete freedom. The government of Luxembourg asks to send a delegation to confer with us, and to proceed to the plebiscite immediately afterwards.

M. Clemenceau. This letter was addressed to you?

President Wilson. Yes, because it was forwarded by the American commander of the army of occupation.

Mr. Lloyd George. I don't see how we could refuse to hear the Luxemburgers.

M. Clemenceau. I share this sentiment completely.

Mr. Lloyd George. It will be necessary for the Belgians to be present.

President Wilson. On the other hand, I have received a telegram from Luxembourg indicating that the chamber has decided to start discussing the question of the economic referendum immediately. The clerical majority seeks an early decision, which would confront us with a *fait accompli*. At the same time, they are slowing down the negotiations with Belgium. If the French government doesn't declare that it doesn't want an economic union with Luxembourg, the vote will go along these lines; if France makes that declaration, the result will be the maintenance of the *status quo*, and probably the reestablishment of relations

---

[5] E. Reuter to WW, May 6, 1919, Wilson Papers, Library of Congress.

with Germany. Such appears to be the scheme of the Luxembourg clerical party.

LXXIX

Conversation between President Wilson and MM. Clemenceau and Lloyd George*

MAY 14, 1919, 4 P.M.

—M. Clemenceau reads aloud an intercepted telegram from Count Brockdorff-Rantzau to the German government: Count Brockdorff-Rantzau approves of the tenor of the speeches of Herr Scheidemann and of the President of the National Assembly;[1] the protests against the treaty, in the Assembly and in the press, will second the efforts of the delegation, which seeks to induce the adversaries of Germany to grant her an acceptable peace.

President Wilson. This shows they are bluffing. Brockdorff writes to Scheidemann: "Go on and play your part, I will play mine." In my opinion, that is rather reassuring, for it doesn't indicate the will to refuse to sign.

Mr. Lloyd George. At the same time, one of the words of that dispatch indicates fear of the military occupation that would follow a refusal.

President Wilson. We could now study the map of Asia Minor and agree finally on the assignment of mandates. The territory assigned finally to Greece would be extended a bit to the south and would include the lower valley of the Meander.[2] If we had wanted, at first, to leave the valley of the Meander to the Turks, it was to give them access to the Aegean Sea. But we no longer have that concern.

Mr. Lloyd George. Doesn't the projected boundary for the region of the Italian mandate give the port of Mersina to Italy?

President Wilson. No, but it would give them Marmaris.

*H., *PPC*, V, 614ff.

[1] Konstantin Fehrenbach. For a summary of his remarks, see Luckau, *The German Delegation at the Paris Peace Conference*, p. 100. The full text appears in *Verhandlungen*, Vol. 327, pp. 1110-11.

[2] That is, the Menderes River.

—Examination of the documents concerning the ports of Asia Minor provided by Lt. Col. Sir Maurice Hankey.

President Wilson. I see that Marmaris is an excellent port, especially for the navy, but with little communication with the interior. Makri, which we spoke about the other day, was already the site chosen by an Italian company as the terminus for a railroad. I ask myself if it wouldn't be better to give the Italians Makri, without Marmaris. The position of Marmaris dominates the island of Rhodes too much.

Mr. Lloyd George. Our intention the other day was to assign Makri to Italy, and not Marmaris.

—President Wilson rereads a series of proposals:[3] (1) establishment of a League of Nations mandate over Constantinople and the Straits; (2) annexation to Greece of the region in Asia Minor surrounding Smyrna, including the lower valley of the Meander; (3) division of the Turkish territory proper among three distinct mandates: (a) a Greek mandate in the vicinity of the region of Smyrna (*vilayet* of Aydin); (b) an Italian mandate over southern Anatolia, up to the desert region; (c) a French mandate for northern and central Anatolia.

—Another memorandum fixes the boundaries of Armenia and gives more precise details on the mandate for Constantinople.

Mr. Lloyd George. The question of the spheres of military occupation in Asia remains to be settled. We must come to an agreement directly on this subject; the French and English Foreign Ministers will never agree.

M. Clemenceau. I am always being accused of making too many concessions to you.

Mr. Lloyd George. This question must be handled by two trustworthy persons.

M. Clemenceau. I suggest M. Tardieu to you.

Mr. Lloyd George. Do you want him to talk with Sir Henry Wilson?

M. Clemenceau. That suits me perfectly.

President Wilson. The right that each power will have to withdraw from the Reparation Commission was anticipated at the time of the discussion of the preliminaries, but it was forgotten in the final draft. The only way to make up for this omission is to sign an agreement amongst ourselves.

What had been proposed was that, in order to withdraw, each power would be obligated to give notice, twelve months in advance, and to confirm it after six months.

---

[3] They were embodied in two memoranda which are printed in *PWW*, Vol. 59, pp. 146-47.

Mr. Lloyd George. Why not insert this clause into the treaty?

M. Clemenceau. It is a matter amongst ourselves; the signature of the Germans is not necessary.

Mr. Lloyd George. The fate of the Germans will depend largely on the decisions of that commission. I favor introducing this amendment, like all those which might be necessary, when we reply to the written observations of the Germans and decide upon the final text.

—(Adopted.)

Sir Maurice Hankey. The Drafting Committee asks whether it is necessary to reproduce the Covenant of the League of Nations and the texts relating to labor legislation in the treaty with Austria. Lord Robert Cecil believes so.

President Wilson. I hope it will be done and that, according to M. Clemenceau's suggestion, Austria will be invited to join the League of Nations. Italy hasn't yet been consulted on this question; but it must be done.

Do we, the Four, have the right to place Austria on the list of powers that can be admitted to the League of Nations? That is the question I ask.

Mr. Lloyd George. We have decided nothing about the nature of the mandates to be established in Anatolia.

President Wilson. I thought we had agreed to establish mandates of a different character in the northern part and in the southern part?

M. Clemenceau. I seemed to understand that the role that you wanted to give us was that of advisers and, as for myself, I have no desire to make this country a French colony.

President Wilson. These two territories together will make up Turkey, and Mohammedan sentiment must be taken into account. What the Mohammedans want, especially the Turks themselves, is that a single Turkish state remain. We have projected three classes of mandates: those appropriate for nations on the verge of being ready for independence, who need only friendly advice; those which must be established in countries which need to be administered by others more advanced than themselves; and, finally, mandates for dependent populations, which have to be guided from every point of view.

M. Clemenceau. What differences do you see between the northern and southern parts of Anatolia?

President Wilson. The northern part is more purely Turkish; there is a Greek element in the South.

Mr. Lloyd George. That element is not substantial. In my opinion, the best thing is to establish a very mild mandate in both these regions.

President Wilson. If we treat them in the same way, it becomes rather awkward to separate them.

Mr. Lloyd George. If the capital is in the North, both the French and the Italians will have to deal with the Turkish government, which will be established in the territory of one of the two mandates.

M. Clemenceau. What would be the type of mandate entrusted to Italy?

President Wilson. The same as for you, since the difference between the two regions is not very great.

Mr. Lloyd George. Our advisers point out the difficulty of dividing these regions. On the other hand, we are confronted with the established presence of the Italians in southern Anatolia, where they obtained certain concessions from the Turks. In short, it is a question of perpetuating a regime to which the Turks are quite accustomed, since they left their railroads, customs, etc., in the hands of foreigners.

President Wilson. It is impossible to divide this mandate between two powers without a clear political separation between the two territories. It must not be forgotten, besides, that the mandate system, from the economic point of view, will call for equal rights for all nations. What we want is to avoid even the appearance of dividing the spoils amongst ourselves. Our goal is to help the populations in question to develop their resources. But a political division is of capital importance if we wish to avoid clashes and conflicts.

Mr. Lloyd George. Would it not be best to maintain the Sultan in Constantinople, with nominal authority over both parts of Anatolia? If the Sultan was in Brusa,[4] that would create a difficult situation for the Italians, who would have to govern a country whose sovereign would be in a territory under French administration.

President Wilson. That is impossible; the southern region must be clearly separated.

M. Clemenceau. But if you give a governor to southern Anatolia, who will appoint him?

Mr. Lloyd George. The Sultan.

M. Clemenceau. That would make trouble between ourselves and Italy. I would much prefer that all of Anatolia became an inde-

---

[4] That is, Bursa, in Bursa Province in northwestern Turkey, fifty-five miles south of Istanbul. Bursa was at times spelled Brusa or Brussa.

pendent state rather than to see it become a source of perpetual quarrels between the Italians and ourselves.

President Wilson. Are the Turks incapable of electing a governor themselves?

Mr. Lloyd George. It is difficult.

M. Clemenceau. We could establish a territory for a prince of the Sultan's family in the South. But, in any case, I wish to avoid all complications with Italy.

President Wilson. We could ask the Italians themselves to choose a Turkish prince, who would be established in southern Anatolia, in a position analogous to that of the Khedive of Egypt before the war.

M. Clemenceau. There may be some difference between these populations; the real Turks are in the center and the North.

—Sir Maurice Hankey points out another question of wording: it concerns the obligation imposed on Austria to acknowledge the boundaries of the new states in advance. The Drafting Committee understands that the intention of the governments is to indicate all the frontiers of these states in the treaty with Austria, for instance, those of Rumania, although this country has no direct contact with Austria.

President Wilson. Yes, if we manage to determine them in time. Otherwise, we would indicate in the treaty with Austria only the boundaries between these new states and Austria herself, whilst imposing a general obligation on Austria to acknowledge the boundaries which will be determined later for the new states.

LXXX

Conversation between President Wilson and MM. Clemenceau, Lloyd George, Orlando, and several members of the Supreme War Council*

MAY 15, 1919, 11 A.M.

President Wilson. Concerning the future military forces of Austria, are there any points on which our military advisers don't agree?[1]

*H., *PPC*, V, 627ff.

[1] The Four had before them two reports, both dated May 13, 1919, on the mil-

Mr. Lloyd George. I would like to raise a question of principle which concerns not only Austria and Hungary, but all the small states of central and eastern Europe. If we allow them to raise large armies, the entire League of Nations won't suffice to maintain peace amongst them. They will want to fight each other, and the danger for Austria is seeing her neighbors take advantage of her weakness. It is already difficult, at the present time, to prevent them from throwing themselves upon each other, and we have succeeded neither in the case of the Poles and the Czechs, nor in the case of the Poles and the Ukrainians. I hope we are going to lay down the principle of general disarmament in all these states. Hence the importance of the decision which we will take today concerning Austria.

Of the two proposals between which our military advisers are divided, I prefer the American proposal, which rejects the idea of one-year service and imposes a professional army upon Austria. Compulsory short-term military service would give all these countries large armies which Germany could use later on for her own ends; what is the point of limiting Germany's armaments if we leave her the means to draw soldiers from elsewhere? That is why I support the American proposal. The war has shown that one-year service is sufficient to form armies capable of fighting; the Americans proved it, and so did we. A system must be found which can be applied to all the small states.

President Wilson. We always intended to limit the armaments of all these nations.

M. Clemenceau. Regarding Austria, what I ask is that we be guided by the same principle as for Germany. Austria must keep only a gendarmerie.

President Wilson. How is the figure of 40,000 men proposed by the military experts to be justified?

M. Clemenceau. It isn't justified. If Germany, with 60 million inhabitants, has an army of only 100,000 men, why should Austria, with 7 or 8 million, have 40,000 men?

---

itary, naval, and aerial clauses of the peace treaties with Austria and Hungary. The report limited the total number of effectives and reservists in the Austrian army to 40,000 and those in the Hungarian army to 45,000. The major disagreement among the experts concerned the way in which these forces were to be recruited. While the American and British advisers proposed to abolish compulsory military service in Austria and Hungary and to permit only voluntary enlistment, the French and Italian experts recommended that the Austrian and Hungarian armies be organized on the basis of one-year compulsory service. For the reports, see PPC, V, 639-67.

Mr. Lloyd George. I insist on the principle of recruitment by voluntary enlistment, as we are imposing it upon Germany.

M. Clemenceau. I am in complete agreement with you.

M. Orlando. I agree with what Mr. Lloyd George has just said. Without alluding to any one people in particular, it is obvious that one of the most dreaded causes of war in the Europe of tomorrow will be the bellicose spirit of the small nations of central and eastern Europe. Today is the most favorable time to impose a general limitation upon them. We are going to present to Austria the terms which she will have to sign; we must take advantage of this to say whether the other countries born of the dissolution of Austria-Hungary will themselves have only limited armaments.

On the choice between an army recruited by compulsory military service and a professional army, a difference of opinion has appeared amongst our experts—between the Americans and the English on one side, and the French and the Italians on the other. But I have just seen M. Clemenceau accept the Anglo-American proposal; Italy, if she holds to the opinion of her military advisers, would thus remain alone.

I have no difficulty in explaining our point of view. I have already done so before the Commission on the League of Nations. The only reason for our opposition is that Italy can have no professional army; her tradition is against it. She can only form her army by compulsory military service. What we might fear, from the political point of view, is the contagious effect of a system which is not only traditional in England and the United States, but which we are now imposing on Germany and the other enemy states. The fact that conscription will have disappeared in all these countries could create in Italy a movement against compulsory military service, which we could not abolish without placing the army itself in danger.

Moreover, since we have already agreed upon the terms to be imposed on Germany, and since it is a matter of applying the same principle to Austria, the Italian government doesn't maintain its opposition.

As for the figure of 40,000 men, General Cavallero says that it was proposed by the British representative, and that the Italian representative agreed to it. It is obviously a maximum figure. For economic reasons, given the high costs of a professional army, it will perhaps be difficult for Austria to maintain 40,000 men in active service. If this figure is left as it is, it will only impose a limit on very probably a lesser effort.

Mr. Lloyd George. I can't understand these figures of 40,000 men for Austria and 45,000 men for Hungary. It is obviously too many, in relation to what we left to Germany.

Maj. Gen. Sackville-West. Forty thousand men provide only a notably inferior contingent of fighting troops: three divisions of infantry and one of cavalry—that yields hardly 15,000 combat troops; that is not too many to guard the frontiers against incursions and to maintain order in the interior. It is not enough to give Austria an offensive power, nor to protect her against possible enemies which will surround her.

President Wilson. How do you arrive at this figure of 15,000 combat troops?

Maj. Gen. Sackville-West. All the services, schools, etc., must be taken into account. At the most, one arrives at three divisions of 6,000 combat troops—20,000 men with cavalry.

President Wilson. But the same reasoning applies then to the 100,000 men which we have left to Germany?

Maj. Gen. Sackville-West. Yes, but the proportion of the services is less, because there is a certain irreducible base.

President Wilson. How many combat troops will the Germans have out of 100,000 troops?

Maj. Gen. Sackville-West. About 60,000.

M. Clemenceau. I am radically opposed to the commission's figure. We decided to leave 100,000 men to Germany. If we allowed Austria 40,000, what would we reply to the Germans if they should tell us that they don't have enough? You recall that Marshal Foch proposed to leave 200,000 men to Germany, recruited by one-year obligatory service. We preferred to give Germany only 100,000 soldiers, and 100,000 professional soldiers.

We speak of schools; I would point out that their importance is considerably reduced in an army of professionals who serve for many years.

It is natural that we should consult the military in such a matter. But their business is to make war. We make peace. What we want is to give Austria a gendarmerie to maintain order. Like Mr. Lloyd George, I think that the figure of 40,000 would be disproportionate; no one would understand, and the Germans would take advantage of it to protest against the decision which we took regarding them. This is what I would not accept.

Like Mr. Lloyd George, like President Wilson, I wish to make a true peace. For that, our first duty is to disarm the aggressor peoples—that is, Germany and Austria—first of all. It was Austria which first declared war, and she refused the arbitration which was offered to her. There is no foreign country which I know better than Austria, where I went every year for a very long time. The Austrians are the exact opposite of a bellicose people; but they are docile and let themselves be led along by others who are more violent. We have seen the effects of that. We must take into consideration the proposals submitted to us by our military advisers, but we should, above all, keep our eyes fixed upon our goal, which is that of a long-term policy. I don't mean by that that the contingent of Austrian troops must be reduced by a mathematical proportion in relation to the German army; but I think that 15,000 men would be enough for Austria. It is a country which has no great industrial centers, outside Vienna; her population is quiet, and internal order is easy to maintain. We should set a final number reasonably proportional to that of Germany.

President Wilson. It is fair, nonetheless, to observe that, according to General Sackville-West, the proportion of combat troops in Germany and in Austria would not be 4 to 10, but 15 to 60.

Mr. Lloyd George. That would still make one quarter. The population of Austria is, at most, one seventh of the German population. How many combat troops would she have if we left her an army of 25,000 men?

Maj. Gen. Sackville-West. 13,000.

Mr. Lloyd George. And if she had 20,000 men?

Maj. Gen. Sackville-West. Eleven thousand or 12,000 combat troops.

President Wilson. One might wonder, seeing how small the number of combat troops is in relation to the nominal effectives, if the 200,000 men of whom Marshal Foch spoke wouldn't be necessary to maintain order in a large country like Germany.

M. Clemenceau. That is a change which I am not ready to grant. For Austria, I think that 15,000 men in all would be enough.

M. Orlando. We all think that Austria doesn't need 40,000 men. To determine the exact figure, we must send the question back to the military experts. It is a question of calculating, not only the number of men, but of units, the proportion of the services, and these are questions which we cannot answer. What we must tell the military experts is that they have to arrive at a total figure of between 15,000 and 20,000 men. At the same time, we will consign to them the study of a general plan of disarmament for the states formed out of the former Austro-Hungarian territories. We all agree on the principle; it is a question of seeing how we can realize it. M. Clemenceau rightly said that Europe was threatened by the aggressive spirit of Germany and Austria; but Austria was not only German Austria.

M. Clemenceau. Who then represented the spirit of aggression in Austria? Was it the Bohemians and the Poles? Most of them had to fight for Austria, as did the people of Alsace and Lorraine for Germany. Vienna is the center of the intrigues which set Europe on fire. I know this Austrian world well: it was two or three dozen Junkers, always the same ones, who threw Austria into the arms of Germany and who are responsible for Austrian policy during the prewar years. Every year, when I passed through Vienna, I campaigned against the German influence. These people always answered me: "Germany is too strong, and we have to follow." In the final analysis, all these people fought for what they believed to be their own interest—for a strong authority and the security of their property.

M. Orlando. Vienna may have been the center of the intrigues against peace; but Vienna itself was a synthesis of the Austro-Hungarian Empire. From the French point of view, the threat came above all from a certain part of Austria-Hungary; but we are obliged to consider the question from a wider perspective, because we were the immediate neighbors of Austria-Hungary. Regarding reparations, we have decided that all the former subjects of the Austro-Hungarian Empire would be treated as enemies; we must follow the same principle in the military clauses.

M. Clemenceau. I have another preoccupation—Hungary. I have said that the Austrians are poor warriors. But the Hungarians are fighters; they provide soldiers of the first quality. We won't be able to avoid granting Hungary the same treatment as Austria, and Hungary will draw Austria into her military orbit. Will it be said that Austria needs to be fortified against new peoples who will wish her harm? That is not my opinion, and it is not Mr. Lloyd George's opinion. Austria mustn't be allowed to arm herself against other peoples, no more than these peoples should be allowed to arm themselves against her.

I know the mental reservations of part of the Italian press, which doesn't hesitate to say these days that Italy should draw closer to Germany.

M. Orlando. I agree with you completely; it is right to reduce the Austrian forces as much as possible; it is right to reduce the Hungarian forces. We know better than anyone that the Hungarians are first-rate soldiers. I don't want the peoples of Austria-Hungary to be fighting amongst themselves.

As for the Italian newspapers of which M. Clemenceau spoke, at this moment they are campaigning against me. Their policy corresponds in no way to that of the government. If I had any influence over them, the first use I would make of it would be to stop their attacks against myself.

Mr. Lloyd George. I propose to have the question of the disarmament of these small nations studied by the Supreme War Council. It is hardly worthwhile to rid ourselves of one unprovoked assault in order to remain exposed to another. If Austria has only 15,000 men, that must be enough for her—on condition that equivalent reductions are imposed upon her neighbors. Without that, Bohemia could, through compulsory military service, raise a million men, and the Czech soldiers have already proved their worth. Rumania would have between one and two million men, and the Rumanians have already shown that they know how to take advantage of circumstances; for, with Bulgaria scarcely defeated, they advanced into the Dobruja.

Vienna has undoubtedly been the center of dangerous intrigues; but what made most trouble in Europe were the struggles in the Balkans. If Yugoslavia and Bohemia each have a million men, Rumania one and a half million at least, Greece 600,000 or 800,000, it is a terrible force which is gathering. Germany, and perhaps Russia tomorrow, will be able to draw resources from it. Europe can find itself threatened by new conflicts, from which America herself won't escape, bound as she will be by her entry into the League of Nations. A solid guarantee against the bellicose spirit of these small nations is necessary. We know that the oppressed easily become the oppressors. If they have a large army and their neighbors have a small one, they will brutalize them; some will seek revenge against Vienna, others against the Bulgarians or the Hungarians.

Italy, of course, has the right to choose the system of recruitment which suits her. But she also must want to reduce her military force. If she has turbulent neighbors next door who can muster one million men, she will be forced to keep her present system of recruitment and to be able, as the case may be, to arm three or four million men. This reduction has to be carried out universally, and it must be done before the peace.

M. Clemenceau. In order to do that, it will be necessary to adopt a point of view which is not strictly the military point of view.

Mr. Lloyd George. This question will come back to us after study by the military experts.

President Wilson. I don't believe that we can establish the final figure for the Austrian army before this entire question has been studied.

M. Clemenceau. I will point out the special difficulty present in the case of Poland. She must be given the means to defend herself on the Russian side.

President Wilson. No doubt; but the important thing is to study the question as a whole.

Mr. Lloyd George. And in that way to avoid the return of complications in which we might risk getting involved. Austria-Hungary didn't leave behind only the present Austria and the present Hungary.

Sir Henry Wilson. What will be the basis of our study?

Mr. Lloyd George. Take as your basis the terms we are imposing on Germany, and take into consideration the special case of Poland.

M. Clemenceau. Do you think, as I do, that the basis adopted for Germany should be applied everywhere?

Mr. Lloyd George. Yes.

President Wilson. Whilst taking into account the technical necessities which prevent us from applying a mathematical proportion.

M. Clemenceau. This is what I said myself. But Germany must be prevented from being able to use one of our decisions to claim more than we wish to grant her.

Mr. Lloyd George. The Germans must also be prevented from finding soldiers outside their boundaries. Yesterday, they had the Hungarians with them; in future, they could seek auxiliaries amongst the Slavic populations.

M. Clemenceau. In any case, it is necessary to begin with Austria, since the Austrians are here, and it is with them that we will first negotiate. Moreover, the question which arises for several other states is subordinate to the future status of Russia, which is a formidable unknown quantity in the whole problem.

Mr. Lloyd George. Austria will tell you: "I accept, if I am told what forces will surround me."

M. Clemenceau. The Polish question will be difficult to settle if we want to do it right now.

Mr. Lloyd George. Our experts must study the problem in its entirety.

President Wilson. About the naval clauses, Admiral Benson made two observations;[2] I remember the second. It is a question of the

---

[2] See W. S. Benson to WW, May 16, 1919, printed in *PWW*, Vol. 59, pp. 197-98.

MAY 15, 1919   **81**

ban on manufacturing any naval matériel for foreigners. It doesn't seem reasonable to me to keep this clause.

Mr. Lloyd George. We are imposing it upon Germany.

President Wilson. Yes, but Germany has coasts and could, on this pretext, manufacture for herself.

Mr. Lloyd George. Without this pretext, Austria could manufacture for Germany.

President Wilson. Can't we eliminate this clause?

Admiral de Bon. We want the ban imposed upon Austria to be the same as that on Germany; our goal is to prevent the Austrians from working for the Germans. Austrian artillery is excellent, and we don't want it to become artillery for export.

President Wilson. But is the factory where this artillery is manufactured in Austria? I thought it was in Bohemia.

M. Orlando. The famous Skoda plant is in Bohemia.

Admiral de Bon. Yes; but it worked from plans coming from Austria.

President Wilson. This clause refers to manufacture, not designs.

Mr. Lloyd George. The danger is that the Austrians would say that they are manufacturing for Chile or Ecuador, when, in reality, they would be working for Germany.

President Wilson. The treaty reduces the number of their arms manufactures to one only.

M. Clemenceau. I believe we should impose the same conditions upon Austria as upon Germany.

M. Orlando. I also fear that they will manufacture for the Germans.

Admiral de Bon. War matériel changes. The article which forbids them from having more than one plant of a certain kind doesn't provide for establishments of another kind which new technology would allow to be built.

Admiral Thaon de Revel. During the war, factories of all kinds were very quickly transformed for the production of war matériel.

Mr. Lloyd George. That's perfectly true. One of our best war factories had manufactured gramophones before.

President Wilson. I can't consent to this article. It is a small thing. But it is not worthy of the great settlement we wish to establish. I thought I understood that we wanted to treat Austria differently from Germany, in order to detach her from German interests. This little question offers us an opportunity to favor her.

Mr. Lloyd George. I must say that, if the President of the United States had raised this question when it was a matter of the matériel of the land forces, I would have opposed him, because it would have been more important. Whatever naval matériel Austria can, in fact, produce isn't very formidable, and I can agree with him.

M. Clemenceau. Admiral de Bon's argument seems strong to me; why give our enemies arms against us? We are formulating decisions here, and we seem to believe that they will be obeyed. I ask that it be written down in the minutes that I am convinced that they won't be obeyed. America will be far away. The enemy states, knowing that we won't declare war on them over trifles, will seek by every means to escape the stipulations we will have imposed upon them.

Every day, I have seen the precautions which we proposed eliminated as useless and superfluous. Lacking proof to the contrary, I stand by my opinion. It is said to be a question here of a very small matter; it is not a very small matter to protect the life and security of peoples. Admiral de Bon and Admiral Thaon de Revel have formally declared that Austria will be able to manufacture for the Germans; if she does, I declare that it will be against my will.

President Wilson. Unfortunately, my naval experts are not present, and it wouldn't be right on my part to insist without having heard them again. I will, nevertheless, recall that we have reduced the German navy to very modest proportions, that Germany cannot build warships without our knowing about it. Do you see a great danger in the naval matériel that she can draw from Austria? I must say, speaking as the layman that I am, it is impossible for me to see it.

My only preoccupation is to avoid a hypercritical method of making peace. We want Austria to be able to live industrially. The industries tied to the life of this country are now in another country, Czechoslovakia. That is all I have to say, and we can postpone our decision until I have seen Admiral Benson again.

Mr. Lloyd George. I have just learned with profound regret that Admiral de Bon, appointed to a high command in the Mediterranean, will no longer attend these meetings. In the name of the British delegation, I wish to say how much we regret his departure, and how much we owe to his tact, common sense, and high competence.

President Wilson. Although I have worked for a much shorter time with Admiral de Bon, I have always been pleased by his frankness, open-mindedness, and courtesy in discussion.

M. Orlando. I wish to join in this praise. Admiral de Bon has won the esteem of us all.

Admiral de Bon. I am proud to leave with the expression of your esteem.

President Wilson. The last article—fifty—provides for an investigation into the military situation of Austria if the League of Nations deems it necessary. I would prefer a formula which would not compel Austria to respond to an inquiry ordered by the League of Nations, and which could be worded in milder terms.

Mr. Lloyd George. Before the war, we offered to open all our naval shipyards to the Germans if they would allow us to visit theirs; Germany refused. I don't see how anyone, if he is acting in good faith, has the right to be offended by a request for an investigation.

President Wilson. Do you accept in principle the change which I am suggesting?

Mr. Lloyd George. I don't see any problem in it.

M. Clemenceau. Nor do I.

LXXXI

Conversation between President Wilson and MM. Clemenceau, Lloyd George, and Orlando*

MAY 17, 1919, 11 A.M.

Mr. Lloyd George. I learn that the Italians have just landed 500 men at Scala Nuova without our having been notified. This is an unacceptable manner of acting, and we must tell them explicitly that it is impossible to negotiate with them in these circumstances; we cannot discuss their war aims as long as their troops have not reembarked. They tried, the other day, to convince us that France had anticipated this kind of operation by landing troops at Heraclea; but no comparison is possible.

M. Clemenceau. I knew nothing about the landing at Heraclea, which was done on the initiative of General Franchet d'Esperey.

President Wilson. It is possible that the landing at Scala Nuova was equally due to the initiative of the Italian military.

Mr. Lloyd George. I suspect an action of M. Sonnino here.

*H., PPC, V, 668ff. M. Orlando not present at the beginning of the meeting.

I must, on the other hand, call to your attention a memorandum which Mr. Balfour has just given me on the subject of Asia Minor.[1] He deems a division of properly Turkish territories to be impracticable and thinks that they must be placed under a single mandate.

M. Clemenceau. I don't wish it from my viewpoint.

President Wilson. In my opinion, what can justify the partition is the presence of Greek elements in southern Anatolia, whilst the North is purely Turkish.

Mr. Lloyd George. This division of Turkey will set the entire Mohammedan world against us.

—M. Orlando is introduced.

M. Clemenceau. The question of the publication of the treaty arises more urgently than ever. The Germans have begun to publish articles of the treaty in their newspapers. People here are beginning to complain strongly. President Wilson and I think we should publish it; but we have awaited Mr. Lloyd George's return in order to take a decision.

Mr. Lloyd George. What hampers me is that I just told Mr. Bonar Law to refuse publication, which is demanded by members of the British Parliament.

M. Clemenceau. What will happen is that our newspapers and yours will publish the articles of the treaty by borrowing them from German sources.

Mr. Lloyd George. My constant concern is to avoid anything that could prevent a reasonable concession on our part, or a change for the better judged necesssary. Once the text is published, people will not fail to say that it is weakness and betrayal if we change one line.

President Wilson. We can say that there is this difference between ourselves and the Germans—that it is we who are the authors of the treaty, and that, consequently, our responsibility is not the same.

---

[1] Balfour's memorandum, printed in *PWW*, Vol. 59, pp. 209-12, was a powerfully reasoned argument against any sort of partition of, or two mandates for, Turkey proper—"that great block of Anatolia lying west of the meridian of Constantinople." Under Balfour's plan, Turkey would remain an undivided state, with the seat of the Sultan at Bursa or Konia. The main problem at this point, Balfour said, was how to mollify the Italians "at the smallest cost to mankind." That might be done by finding some "privileged position" for them in southern Anatolia and by confirming an arrangement that Italy had made with Turkey before the war for concessions in the area of Adalia. The proposal, Balfour concluded, was a bad one from many points of view, but it was worthy of serious consideration.

Mr. Lloyd George. Have the Germans really published the actual text of the treaty?

M. Clemenceau. They have published a certain number of articles.

Mr. Lloyd George. And when must they give us their answer?

M. Clemenceau. Wednesday or Thursday.

Mr. Lloyd George. Do you think it necessary to publish anything before that time? Besides, it would take at least two days to reprint it.

M. Clemenceau. I agree to wait until the beginning of next week to take this decision.

Mr. Lloyd George. Yesterday, I said to some Welsh troops, whom I was visiting: "If the Germans refuse to sign the treaty, are we going to lose the entire outcome of the war? Will you hesitate to reply by marching on Berlin?" They all shouted: "No!"

M. Clemenceau. Following the communication of the Germans concerning the clothing they asked us to provide for their prisoners when they are released, you asked me to bring you information on what France could do. I submit to you a document showing what we have by way of serviceable German uniforms.[2]

Mr. Lloyd George. The German prisoners whom I saw yesterday in the north of France appeared well fed to me. According to our officers, they are working hard. They were dressed in uniforms of every color, which evidently had come from home.

M. Clemenceau. I communicate a new note to you from the Germans regarding the Saar Basin.[3]

[2] Gen. H. M. C. E. Alby to G. Clemenceau, May 16, 1919, printed in *PPC*, V, 682-83. Alby, the chief of the French General Staff, reported that the total supply of clothing available for German prisoners consisted of 2,000 pairs of trousers, 7,200 sweaters, 800 cloaks, 500 "Horse buckets [blankets?]," and "a wagon load of boots, half boots, and lace boots."

[3] The Four actually had before them two notes from Brockdorff-Rantzau on this matter. Brockdorff's first note, dated May 13, 1919, is printed in *ibid.*, pp. 817-20. The "new note," dated May 16, 1919, is printed in *ibid.*, pp. 820-22. The first note was mainly a protest against the separation of the Saar Valley from Germany. It also claimed that it was unlikely that Germany would have the gold to buy back the Saar mines even if a plebiscite at the end of fifteen years went in favor of reunion to Germany, and that, therefore, the Saar region would remain under French control in spite of the wish of the population. "There is in modern history," Brockdorff wrote, "no example of a civilised Power binding another to subject its own nationals to a foreign domination as the equivalent of a sum in gold."

The second note included a proposal by German experts to guarantee from German sources the coal that France would need in compensation for her production lost on account of German destruction of French mines. Details could be worked out by negotiations between French and German experts, and the Germans were willing to give all guarantees for their satisfactory execution.

President Wilson. The situation in Poland deserves particular attention. I have been told that M. Paderewski attempted, when he arrived in Warsaw, to prevent the dispatch of General Haller's troops to Lemberg. The Diet refused and confirmed the General's orders. M. Paderewski tendered his resignation, which was refused. In short, M. Paderewski attempted to keep the promise that he made to us, and the Diet stood in his way. If these facts are correct, we must inform the Poles that they have to conform to the instructions of the conference or renounce our support and recall their plenipotentiaries.

Mr. Lloyd George. I think we must verify the facts and, if necessary, act in the way you suggest. I received a very emphatic letter from General Botha on this subject; he thinks we should order the Supreme Economic Council to stop supplies to Poland if that country resists, and he adds: "If we stand with our arms crossed, our inertia will discredit the conference and ruin in advance the authority of the League of Nations." Besides, in the fight against the Ukraine, Poland is playing the role of a relatively strong state attacking a weaker country.

President Wilson. I agree with you; but what are our means of coercion?

Mr. Lloyd George. We have the economic weapon.

President Wilson. It is powerful. But is General Botha not exaggerating when he writes that the resistance of the Poles to our injunctions is enough to discredit the League of Nations in advance?

Mr. Lloyd George. I don't see how the League of Nations could have more authority tomorrow than we ourselves have today when we are united, with our armies and our fleets still ready for action.

President Wilson. I admit it; but it is also necessary to take the present world into account, with no question having yet received its final solution and turmoil still widespread.

Couldn't we stop the dispatch of General Haller's troops to Poland?

M. Clemenceau. That would be possible.

Mr. Lloyd George. My great wish is to help M. Paderewski, who is doing his best to follow our advice. We must speak strongly to the Poles and tell them that, if they don't listen, they mustn't count on our help. I would point out that the treaty with Germany hasn't yet been signed; we know the opposition the Germans will make to any change of their eastern borders, and, because of that, Poland's fate is in our hands.

President Wilson. We mustn't do anything against M. Paderewski.

Mr. Lloyd George. No; we must support him, by sternly warning the Diet and the nation.

President Wilson. For that, the best thing would be for us to speak to President Piłsudski.

Mr. Lloyd George. I believe that this show of force will strengthen M. Paderewski at a critical moment, by proving to the Poles that in all he told them, his only objective was to bring them into agreement with us.

M. Clemenceau. I communicate to you a document relating to the supply of war matériel to small states,[4] concerning which it may be necessary to call a meeting amongst our experts.

—*It is decided that a meeting will take place between MM. Loucheur and Layton, advised by an Italian representative, who will inform the governments about the facts and recommend to them measures to be taken.*

Mr. Lloyd George. The most pressing thing is to know the situation. Moreover, this question is connected with that of the future disarmament of the small powers.

M. Clemenceau. The difficulty of this disarmament is that we must avoid the bitterness of people who will come to tell us: "You liberate us, and then you make it impossible for us to defend ourselves."

[4] W. T. Layton, "NOTE ON THE SUPPLY OF ARMAMENTS TO THE NEW STATES OF CENTRAL AND EASTERN EUROPE," printed in *ibid.*, pp. 683-84. Layton declared that, at present, "certain quantities" of munitions were being allocated to various nations by France on the instructions of Marshal Foch. The British War Office, however, had refused even to entertain applications for small arms in view of negotiations among the Allies for the signature of an arms convention forbidding the sale of surplus stocks of small arms. The results of the current unregulated situation were likely to be that some of the new states would become militarily much stronger than others and that many of them would dissipate their financial credits in the competitive purchase of munitions at the expense of the raw materials needed to reestablish their industries. Presumably, in time, the League of Nations would deal with the question of "rationing the Armaments allowed to the various States of Europe." Meanwhile, Layton made the following recommendations:

"(a) That the Heads of States should be asked to formulate an interim policy to govern both the scale of equipment and the means by which armament is to be provided for the new States of Europe—having regard to the disarmament terms to be imposed on enemy powers and—

"(b) That the Allied and Associated Governments should undertake not to make any sales or allocations of munitions except on the authorisation of an Inter-Allied Commission to be set up with the duty of seeing that the policy laid down in (I)[a] is adhered to."

Mr. Lloyd George. Their disarmament could be ordered by the League of Nations and not by the conference.

President Wilson. What we must do is to compel them to accept the plan for disarmament which will be drawn up by the League of Nations.

M. Clemenceau. Would it not be better to avoid the word "disarmament?"

President Wilson. It is used in the Covenant of the League of Nations.

Mr. Lloyd George. It seems urgent to me, furthermore, to take a definite stand against the inclination of the military of every country to extend or even reinforce present armaments. Field Marshal Haig gave a speech along these lines, and I don't need to recall the precedents.

M. Clemenceau. We shall indeed have to resist these tendencies.

President Wilson. Public opinion will help us here.

President Wilson. Yesterday I received a visit from MM. Kramář and Beneš, who came to talk to me about the question of Teschen. M. Beneš gave an excellent explanation and presented the arguments of the Czechoslovaks with great clarity and moderation. He remarks that the importance of Teschen for Bohemia comes, not only from its coal mines, but also from the fact that communication between Bohemia and Slovakia can only be assured by a line across this territory. Furthermore, the Teschen district is included within the historical borders of the Kingdom of Bohemia. The difficulty, from the Polish side, is that the question of Teschen is a party question, and it has become almost impossible for M. Paderewski to accept a compromise. Mr. Hoover informs me that coal production in the Teschen Basin is suffering greatly from the uncertainty in which the people find themselves about the fate that is in store for them.

Another question we have to settle is that of the rights of minorities in Poland.[5] You recall that the point upon which our experts did not agree concerned the Sabbath.[6] The article not yet

---

[5] The Supreme Council now turned to consideration of the second report of the Committee on New States, dated May 13, 1919. It is printed in *PWW*, Vol. 59, pp. 180-83.

[6] It read as follows: "Jews shall not be compelled to perform any act which constitutes violation of their Sabbath nor shall they be placed under any disability by reason of their refusal to attend courts of law or to perform any legal business on their Sabbath.

"Poland hereby declares its intention to refrain from ordering or permitting elections, whether general or local, to be held on a Saturday, nor will registration

settled would stipulate that Jews could not be forced to do anything contrary to the observance of the Sabbath and that elections could not be held on a Saturday.

Mr. Lloyd George. The Jews form an important minority in Poland; but I couldn't have an article that would seem to give them a special privilege. The first part of the article is unobjectionable; as for the second, it could be said that, by adopting it, we would be giving Saturday rest an inviolable character which would not be given even to Sunday.

M. Orlando. In Italy, as in France, elections take place on Sunday so that workers and employees can vote.

Mr. Lloyd George. It must be acknowledged that there is a great deal of anti-Semitism in Poland, and that one must obviously fear schemes that would tend practically to exclude the Jews from the electorate.

—Mr. Headlam-Morley is introduced.

Mr. Headlam-Morley. The article in question was drafted after consultation with the representatives of Jews of moderate opinion, like Mr. Lucien Wolf, and with impartial experts such as Mr. Namier; they all agree that this clause is extremely important for the Jews. Lacking any protection such as is provided in this article, the Jews of Poland will be persecuted on account of the Sabbath.

As for the question of voting, we refused to grant the Jews of Poland the special political status they asked, but we must do everything possible to prevent them from being deprived of their political rights. To that end, it is absolutely necessary that elections do not take place on Saturday. One may wonder if it is necessary to insert this stipulation into the treaty, or if it should be mentioned in an exchange of notes between the powers and Poland.

President Wilson. Mr. Miller says that this will make Saturday a more sacred day than Sunday.

Mr. Lloyd George. It would perhaps be enough to say that, if elections take place on a Saturday, arrangements must be made to allow the Jews to cast their votes on another day.

Mr. Headlam-Morley. Perhaps it would be enough to discuss this question directly with the Poles.

President Wilson. I don't think so. We must not repeat what oc-

---

for electoral or other purposes be compelled to be performed on a Saturday." Ibid., p. 179, n. 4.

curred in Rumania, where the right granted to all Rumanian citizens was later refused to Jews, on the pretext that they weren't citizens. Moreover, the word "Sabbath" is often used in English to refer to Sunday; it must be clearly specified that it is a question of the Jewish Sabbath, that is, Saturday.

Personally, I am nearly converted to the second paragraph, that is, to the stipulation regarding the day for elections. I am moved to adopt it, not only by a feeling of good will towards the Jews, but by the certainty of the danger which the unjust treatment of Jews is creating in different parts of Europe. The role of the Jews in the Bolshevik movement is undoubtedly due to the oppression that their race has suffered for so long. Persecutions prevent patriotic feelings from being born and provoke the spirit of revolt. Unless we bring some remedy to the situation of the Jews, it will remain a danger for the world.

Mr. Lloyd George. This difficulty will exist in Poland until the Poles become intelligent enough to turn their Jews to account, as the Germans do.

President Wilson. I am told that M. Dmowski is violently anti-Semitic.

Mr. Headlam-Morley. He has even been suspected of inciting violence against Jews.

Mr. Lloyd George. The question should be brought before the Polish government and discussed with M. Paderewski.

President Wilson. We must begin by asking our committee to get in touch with the representatives of Poland at the conference, and, at the same time, for us to communicate with the Polish government in Warsaw.

—MM. Lloyd George and Clemenceau express their agreement.

Mr. Headlam-Morley. For the moment, according to the terms of the Covenant, only states can address their complaints to the League of Nations. Can't this right be granted to the representatives of minorities? The clause of the Covenant, if it stands as it is, could have this drawback, that the Germans of Poland, if they found themselves persecuted, might appeal to the League of Nations through the intermediary of Germany.

Mr. Lloyd George. The principle laid down by the governments is that a communication made to the League of Nations by any state, on the subject of an act which it judges to constitute a threat to peace, cannot be considered as an unfriendly act to another state. If they are persecuted, the Jews of Poland will find a member state of the League of Nations to take up their cause. I thus believe that the text such as it stands will suffice for all real needs.

We cannot allow propagandist associations and societies from all over the world to flood the League of Nations with their complaints. The Jews, in particular, are very litigious, and, as we know all too well, unfortunately, the treaty will not make anti-Semitism disappear from Poland overnight. If the Jews of Poland could address the League of Nations directly, there would be ceaseless incidents.

Mr. Headlam-Morley. With your assent, our committee will now take up the question of minorities in the Czechoslovak areas.

President Wilson. One question remaining in suspense is that of the representation of Montenegro in the negotiations with Austria. Every time I complain to the Serbs about their behavior towards Montenegro, they reply to me that the King of Montenegro is a scoundrel. If this fact is admitted, it is still true that the Serbs have acted brutally towards Montenegro, arrested some important people, etc., and that adds to our uncertainty about the part that we must take.

—Reading of a letter from the delegates of the great powers especially entrusted with the questions relating to international labor legislation.[7] This letter asks that Germany be admitted to the International Labour Organization after the Washington conference.

M. Clemenceau. I make no objection.

Mr. Lloyd George. I believe it is good to open these prospects to German workers.

President Wilson. It is best to leave the decision to the Washington conference itself.

—This proposal is adopted.

[7] G. N. Barnes et al. to P. E. Dutasta, May 15, 1919, printed in PPC, V, 684-85. The committee recommended that Germany should enjoy "early participation" in the International Labour Organization, even if she was not allowed initially to join the League of Nations. This was advisable to insure that Germany would be under the same obligations to organized labor as the other advanced industrial countries. The committee suggested that Germany not be admitted to the labor organization in time to attend the initial conference in Washington, since her presence there might create confusion and dissension. However, she should be admitted to membership immediately after the Washington conference and should be entitled to a place on the governing body of the organization.

LXXXII

Conversation between President Wilson and MM. Clemenceau, Lloyd George, and Orlando*

MAY 17, 1919, 4 P.M.

—M. Clemenceau reads aloud a note to the Italian government about the landing of Italian troops at Scala Nuova.[1]

Mr. Lloyd George. We must say to the Italian government that it is inadmissible for one of us to act thus without consulting the others.

M. Clemenceau. Furthermore, we have information about the supplies of ammunition which are at this very moment being given to Austria by the Italians. An entire train has gone through, conducted by a former officer of the Austrian army. This news was sent to us by the Serbs; but we have information of the same kind from a French source. We have sent General Humbert there to

---

*H., *PPC*, V, 686ff. M. Orlando not present at the beginning of the meeting.

[1] Its text (printed in *PWW*, Vol. 59, pp. 225-26) follows:
"The President of the United States and the Prime Ministers of France and Great Britain have been told that Italian troops have occupied Scala Nuova, landing sailors and marines, taking charge of the customs house, and hoisting the Italian colours. They would be very much obliged if the Prime Minister of Italy would inform them as to whether this statement is correct and if so as to the reasons which have influenced him in taking this action without giving his colleagues any previous intimation of the intentions of the Italian Government. They are the more anxious as this landing has been preceded by other landings at Adalia, Marmarice and Budrum about which they have also not been consulted. They would point out that they have never taken any action in Turkey without previous consultation with their Italian colleague. In the case of the recent Greek landing at Smyrna they discussed the proposal with him before orders were given for a single Greek detachment to leave the shores of Greece and Signor Orlando himself agreed to the expedition and to a joint Allied landing to secure the forts. They also feel bound to express their astonishment at the action of the Italian authorities, if it is true, in view of the fact that M. Clemenceau had informed Signor Orlando on Thursday last that, in the opinion of the majority of his colleagues on the Council of Four, Scala Nuova ought not to be included in an Italian sphere of influence in Asia Minor. They would be much obliged if Signor Orlando could give them full information in regard to this matter as they feel it is impossible for the Council of Four to attempt to deal with the problems of the near East if one of its members persistently takes action on its own account without previously consulting the other members.
"17 May, 1919."

report about all that; it is better to wait until we are in full possession of the facts.

Mr. Lloyd George. The Italians have lost their heads.

President Wilson. However, they can't expect to defy all of Europe.

Mr. Lloyd George. And America.

They are ready to send troops everywhere in Turkey, now that there are no more enemies to face there. They didn't display such eagerness when I asked them to collaborate in our expedition. Baron Sonnino certainly spoke of sending some officers to Palestine; but it was above all in order to keep an eye on the French expeditionary force.

M. Clemenceau. What will you do about the Holy Places?

Mr. Lloyd George. An international agreement is necessary. Sir Mark Sykes was working on it when he died; he was a Catholic and, for that reason, better suited to understand some aspects of the question.

—M. Orlando is introduced.

President Wilson. We'll explain our difficulty to M. Orlando.

M. Clemenceau. You are going to receive a note in which the French, British, and American governments will inform you of the disturbing impression produced by the landing of Italian troops at Scala Nuova without our having been notified. In an earlier discussion, we asked that you refrain from landings in that region. Not only was there a landing, but Italian troops seized the customhouses and planted the Italian flag.

There had already been landings at Marmaris, Budrum, and Makri. If each of us did the same, it would become impossible for us to come to an understanding. When we contemplated a landing at Smyrna, we acted only after you were notified and asked to collaborate with us.

You will receive our communication in writing.

M. Orlando. When you announced the intention to carry out a landing at Smyrna, Mr. Lloyd George asked me for an explanation of the Italian landing which had taken place at Scala Nuova. I told him that I had not been informed, and that is the absolute truth. I added that I would speak to M. Sonnino about it. M. Sonnino explained to me that local disorders had provoked our landings—which were, moreover, only temporary. I went with M. Sonnino to see Mr. Lloyd George. Then I heard no more about this question of landings.

I will communicate what you have just told me to M. Sonnino, and we will consider the matter.

Mr. Lloyd George. It is a question of the landing which took place on the fourteenth. There was a first landing at Scala Nuova; your men worked to repair the jetty, then reembarked. But, on the fourteenth, a second landing, undoubtedly prepared by the first, took place. This time, 500 men landed; they seized the customhouse and hoisted the Italian flag. At Marmaris, only the Italian fleet appeared. This is a serious landing.

What lends gravity to this incident is that—although I don't favor assigning Scala Nuova to Italy—no decision has been taken; whilst we debate, you land without warning us. That makes it very difficult for us to settle the questions pending in Asia Minor or wherever it might be. Imagine if, during the course of a discussion which involved her, France forestalled our decision with a landing; that would create an equally disturbing impression. What I regret is that you should seem to be prejudging our decisions precisely at the moment when our discussions were taking a favorable turn. We will all do our utmost to give Italy satisfaction; but nothing could be more unfavorable to the result we are seeking than acts whose objective appears to be that of forcing our decisions.

M. Orlando. I understand the feeling Mr. Lloyd George has just expressed, if our action is interpreted in the way he has just done. I affirm that we did not have the intention that he ascribes to us. I believed, moreover, that he wished to speak of the earlier landings, and I state that, as for the landing of the fourteenth, I am completely ignorant of the facts. I believed it was a simple repetition of what had taken place earlier and not an important landing, such as the one of which you speak.

We have no intention of prejudging the decisions of the conference; it is a duty which applies to us as it does to the representatives of the other powers. I will read the document that you are communicating to me and will take the necessary measures.

Mr. Lloyd George. We took great care to leave Scala Nuova outside the zone which is to be occupied by Greek troops, although that area is one of those which might subsequently be assigned to Greece. We thought it would not be fair to let the Greeks establish themselves there before a decision had been reached, with Italy taking part with us in the discussion. I only ask that you observe the same restraint.

—Mr. E. S. Montagu, Secretary of State for India, and the representatives of Mohammedan India are introduced.*

*H., *PPC*, V, 688ff.

Mr. Montagu. I thank you for being willing to hear the Mohammedans of India. The solution to the Turkish problem now being contemplated constitutes, from the Mohammedan point of view, a serious danger to future peace. The government of India insisted especially that this point of view be presented to you by Indians, and there are here not only Mohammedans, but also Brahmins, who, on this question, sympathize with Islam.

I introduce to you first the Aga Khan, who is a descendant of the Prophet and the President of the Moslem League of India.

The Aga Khan. There are seventy million Mohammedans in India, and, if the border areas, like Baluchistan, which are linked to the Indian Empire, are counted, this figure increases to seventy-five million. Their feeling regarding Turkey is shared by the Hindus, that is to say, by the inhabitants of India who are not of the Mohammedan religion.

The fall of Turkey is due primarily to the effort of the Indian Empire. Throughout the war, the Indians were convinced that this war in which they were taking part was a crusade for a moral principle, for an ideal of justice, and for this very reason, we think that Asia Minor, which is the homeland of the Turkish race, as well as Constantinople and Thrace, must remain in the hands of the Turks. We are appealing to France and England, whose interests are so closely bound to those of Islam; we are appealing to President Wilson, we are invoking his Fourteen Points. We ask that the principles for which we also fought be applied here.

We will insist in particular on two points. We ask that the Turkish people be admitted to the League of Nations; it would not be just to punish future generations for the mistakes made by our contemporaries. We also ask that the Turks be protected against reprisals which certain abuses in the past might provoke.

In northeastern Asia Minor and as far as the Caucasus, all the populations of the East are mixed. Whatever form of government is established in what is known as Armenia, it must insure complete equality amongst the races and safeguards against persecutions of which Mohammedans, as well as Christians, could be victims.

Such are the observations which we have to make and about which seventy million men feel more strongly than I can express.

Mr. Montagu. I am anxious that the heads of governments take account of the moral position of the Sultan as Caliph, that is, as the spiritual authority recognized throughout the Moslem world.

The Aga Khan. The Indian soldiers, who fought in Mesopotamia and Palestine, fought against the Turks all day, and then, in the evening, when it was time for prayer, prayed for the Caliph. No one has suggested taking Berlin away from Germany or Vienna from Austria; why take his capital away from the Sultan?

Mr. Aftab Ahmed Khan. The seventy million Mohammedans occupy a special place in the British Empire. As British subjects, they took full part in the fight for the great cause of the Empire and of the Allies. They are concerned about the fate of the last great Mohammedan state, which must remain independent. We are told that Constantinople will cease to be Turkish, that Asia Minor will be divided between France, Italy, and Greece, whereas Mesopotamia, Syria, and Palestine will be placed under non-Mohammedan governments.

In the month of January 1918, Mr. Lloyd George, defining England's war aims, declared that the Turks would retain their national existence. He also said that the Allies were not fighting to deprive Turkey either of her capital or of the countries in Asia Minor inhabited by the Turkish race. These words penetrated deeply into the hearts of Mohammedans, and nothing can erase them. The conference has sought the triumph of the principle of nationality everywhere; it must apply this same principle to Turkey.

It is a question not only of the future of the Caliphate, but of the future of the Turkish race. The establishment of a foreign domination over Turkey would be seriously resented by all the Mohammedans. Their impression would be that the conference is animated by a spirit hostile to Islam. They see no reason why, when the Germans, Austrians, and Bulgarians keep their capitals, the Turks are losing Constantinople, where Sultans have reigned for nearly five centuries. We ask independence for them and admission to the League of Nations.

Regarding Turkish sovereignty, if countries are inhabited by other races, we'll consider it fair to apply the principle of self-determination to them. We ask that this principle be applied also to Mohammedans, and that they be protected, not only against foreign domination, but also against foreign exploitation. At the same time, we are in favor of all measures which aim at insuring them the benefits of modern education and progress. The Mohammedans will respect any organization which the League of Nations might establish to inspect the countries in which they live.

I am appealing most earnestly to your consciences in asking you to consider these claims. The future relations of India and the British Empire depend upon your answer, and also the attitude of the entire Mohammedan world, whose discontent would have the most dangerous consequences.

Mr. Yusuf Ali. I have studied the indigenous press of India closely for a long time now, and I am struck by the fact that what most interests Indian opinion is what is taking place in the Mohammedan countries affected by the war and the future of these countries. There is no doubt that the Indian subjects of the British Crown had to make a great military effort to carry out their loyal duty and that they have the right to be heard.

From the ethnographic point of view, it must not be forgotten that there is an element of Turkish race and tradition amongst the Mohammedans of India. The language of the Mohammedans of India, which the Europeans designate with the name Hindustani, is called "Urdu," which means in Turkish, "the language of the camp." When Captain Hawkins visited the Mogul Jahangir, the common language used at the court of the Great Mogul was Turkish. Amongst other elements, its presence is still felt. From the religious point of view, the bond existing between Mohammedans is stronger than that which unites the members of any other religion. The disappearance of the last great Mohammedan power would open up formidable questions for whose solution the world is not prepared.

Certain statements have been made, certain commitments have been taken; we must consider them as the Mohammedans of India have understood them, and they have always assumed that the general settlement which would follow the peace would not exclude the possibility of an independent life for Turkey. As for the Caliphate, if we consider it from a practical point of view, leaving aside history and theology, it remains a spiritual power whose influence extends over all the Mohammedan population of India, for whom any prospect of intellectual and moral progress would be compromised if their feelings about the Caliphate were violently offended.

Mr. Lloyd George. Is the Caliphate hereditary?

Mr. Yusuf Ali. It is in fact. Theoretically, it is elective.

We are now in the midst of great plans full of promise for the future of India, for which a rather wide measure of free government is being contemplated. If, for external reasons, Indians should be, in the end, deprived of their legitimate role as citizens of the British Empire, it would be a great calamity.

It seems that Europe sometimes forgets Islam and all that it represents. It is our duty to say that it still exists, and that, if its interests and feelings are neglected, it will be a source of great dangers in the future. The Mohammedans of India ask that Turkey keep Thrace, Constantinople, and Anatolia, and that guarantees be given to the Mohammedans in the other parts of western Asia, along with the prospect of being admitted in the near future to the League of Nations.

The Maharajah of Bikaner. The Indians who are not of the Mohammedan religion sympathize with their Mohammedan compatriots and, as the representative of the Indian princes, I must recall that the first of these princes is a Mohammedan whose authority was used to support the King-Emperor and the Allies.

We can only advise in the most explicit manner against any partition of Turkey proper, as well as against any solution which would drive the Turks from Constantinople. The loyalty of the Mohammedans of India has proved unshakable; they fought for the Allies throughout the world—in France, in Mesopotamia, in East Africa, in Shantung. Despite their respect for the spiritual authority of the Caliph, for whom they prayed every day, they fought and defeated the Ottoman Empire.

It is with a full sense of my responsibility that I call your attention to the danger of disorder and hatred which this question contains, not only for India, but for the entire world.

Lord Sinha. It has already been said that the Mohammedans of India number seventy million; that is more than one fifth of the population of that great country. The Mohammedan Indians constitute the most warlike elements of the peninsula; they provided the greatest part of the armies thanks to whom it was possible to defeat the Turks. Rumors of the dismemberment of Turkey are causing much anxiety in India. The Mohammedans of India are wondering today whether they were not led by false promises to fight against the leader of their religion and against their religion itself—which, if I am permitted to say so here, has retained for them more reality and force than many other religions for other peoples.

It is a subject which deserves your most serious reflection. The consequences will cause India herself to suffer; but the danger will not extend to India alone. We ask you not to treat the Turks more harshly or less justly than any other of your enemies.

Mr. Montagu. There is a real threat to the peace of the world. A few days ago, I saw an American who had been a prisoner of the Bolsheviks in Tashkent and who had returned to Europe after a perilous journey. He had been struck by the attitude of the Mohammedans towards the Allies since the Armistice; the feeling amongst them was that the conference was taking sides against Islam.

I have no need to recall the recent events which have occurred in Egypt and Afghanistan. In the Punjab, Hindu agitators, stirred up by the Bolsheviks, provoked the populations to revolt. Now, the mosques were opened to them to preach sedition; it is unprecedented that the mosques should thus be opened to preachers and orators who did not themselves belong to the Mohammedan religion.

The causes of this state of mind are what is being heard about the fate of Constantinople, rumors of the landing of Italian and Greek troops in Asia Minor; it is the idea that Saint Sophia will cease to be a mosque and will become once again a Christian church. Hence the impression that the world war has, in the final analysis, become a war against Islam, and that the peace is being made against Mohammedan interests. It would be dangerous to allow such a state of mind to continue.

Mr. Lloyd George. However, the Mohammedans must surely know that the war was fought primarily amongst Christians?

Mr. Montagu. They have the impression that, at the peace conference, the Turks are being treated less favorably than other enemies.

President Wilson. It has been asked that the League of Nations be open to Mohammedan powers. That presents no difficulty; but we have laid down one general condition for admission to the League of Nations: it is that the country which wishes to enter it possess a truly democratic government. In the case of Germany, for example, she will have to prove that her democratic government is firmly and solidly established and that her state of mind has changed. We will never raise any opposition to the admission of a government constituted as we ask and which proves itself capable of keeping its commitments.

The Aga Khan. Precisely; the preoccupation of the Mohammedans is that Turkey be a state which governs itself.

President Wilson. The idea upon which the system of mandates rests is not that of permanent domination. It is a question of helping countries which are not themselves in a position to defend their own interests and to prepare them to govern themselves. The countries under mandate are candidates for full admission to the League of Nations.

The Aga Khan. Democratic ideas are mixed with the very principles of our religion. What we ask is that you leave the door open to the Mohammedan states.

Mr. Yusuf Ali. We fear that the arrangements which are being made will delay the entry of Turkey into the League of Nations.

President Wilson. In Asia Minor, the difficulty of the problem stems from the mixture and conflicts of the races.

The Aga Khan. Isn't it the same in Macedonia? There, however, you sought a solution which would leave nations their full independence.

—Mr. Montagu and the representatives of the Mohammedans of India withdraw.

Mr. Lloyd George. I conclude that it is impossible to divide Turkey proper. We would run too great a risk of throwing disorder into the Mohammedan world. It isn't England alone which would be threatened by this danger, but she is more particularly bound by the declarations and promises made, and, as it is she who fought Turkey, her responsibility is more direct.

I am trying to find out how it would be possible to leave the Sultan in Constantinople without placing him under the tutelage of any particular mandatory.

M. Clemenceau. In any case, he must not be left the forts of the Straits.

Mr. Lloyd George. No; but appearances must be kept up by leaving him in his capital.

LXXXIII

Conversation between President Wilson and MM. Clemenceau and Lloyd George*

MAY 19, 1919, 11 A.M.

—Marshal Foch and General Weygand are introduced.

M. Clemenceau. I asked Marshal Foch to come and give us an account of his trip on the Rhine.

Marshal Foch. I visited the Allied armies. The French occupy the southern region, around Mainz; they are ready to march, with eighteen divisions, of which three are in the Belgian zone and three are cavalry divisions. Some soldiers are on leave; but the numbers are sufficient for the order to advance to be given at any

*H., PPC, V, 702ff.

moment. The morale of the commanders is such that they are ready whenever we want. Nothing is lacking in the way of ammunition or means of transport.

To the left of the French zone, around Koblenz, is the American army. Until May 27, this army consists of three infantry divisions, the First, Second, and Third. After May 27, the Third Division will withdraw, so that the American army of occupation will be reduced to two divisions. If absolutely necessary, until May 27, we can have at our disposal the Fourth and Fifth American divisions, whose transport is to begin on the twentieth or twenty-first; it would suffice to countermand their departure.

The American troops are in perfect condition. Their numbers, artillery, ammunition, sanitary provisions are satisfactory. Despite that, given the reduced number of their divisions, I offered them a division of French cavalry, which would assure their junction with the British army.

What will be insufficient are the numbers.

President Wilson. Are our divisions not 27,000 men?

Mr. Lloyd George. But are the ranks at full strength?

M. Clemenceau. The ranks are at full strength; but the American divisions have not remained what they were at the beginning. The battalions have from 800 to 900 men, instead of 1,000; there are twelve battalions to a division.

Mr. Lloyd George. During the war, we calculated that an American division represented 16,000 riflemen and machine-gunners.

Marshal Foch. Today, it does not represent more than 11,000.

The British army at Cologne still consists of ten divisions; but it is in process of redeployment and could march only after a warning of seven days. Indeed, they have just recalled officers who had seen action; they are replacing them with new officers. This change is not completed. Certain complements, cavalry, motorized guns, are below strength. If you call the attention of General Wilson to this situation, we can make the necessary arrangements together.

Mr. Lloyd George. Mr. Winston Churchill is here; if he is notified about what is missing, he will put things in order.

Marshal Foch. The Belgian army, which occupies the northern sector of the occupation zone, has six infantry divisions and one cavalry division on the ready. It is supported by the three French divisions in Belgium. The Belgian army is in excellent condition; it was lacking a few trucks, which were provided by the French.

If we consider everything, what seems to be most urgent is to put the British army in a state of readiness. When we have transferred a cavalry division to the American zone, we will be completely ready. That could take eight, ten, fifteen days, according to the speed of preparations of the British army. The only shortage we have to fear comes from the withdrawal of the American troops. It is important for me to know how far it will go.

At the same time that we are assembling the armies of the Rhine, the Polish army of General Haller continues to make good progress in moving to Poland across German territory. One hundred and ninety-two trains have passed through, each of which carried a battalion, a battery, and supplies. There still remain about a hundred units; at the rate of six trains per day, seventeen or eighteen more days will be needed for the entire Polish army to pass through. Thus, in little more than a fortnight, there will be in Poland a Polish army, very well trained and officered, and entirely new.

M. Clemenceau. Does it contain French officers?

Marshal Foch. At least 600. It is a splendid army, entirely new and well placed for action.

As for the Czechs, we have been led to hope that they could send three divisions in the direction of Nuremberg, in the event that our troops, coming from Mainz, should march eastwards along the valley of the Main.

My conclusion, reservations aside, is that it is not in our interest to rush an offensive as long as the transport of the Polish troops has not been completed; the first measure the Germans would take would be to block their passage.

That is all I have to say about my trip from the military point of view.

Dr. Heim, the Bavarian deputy who requested to come to French headquarters, announced his visit the day before yesterday. Today, he will meet one of my officers in Luxembourg. This officer has instructions to listen to him, without making any commitment.

Mr. Lloyd George. What is the earliest possible date when our armies could effectively move forward?

Marshal Foch. Theoretically, in a week, on condition that the decision be taken today. I recall that the British army asks to be notified a week in advance.

M. Clemenceau. When the time comes, it will be necessary to act without delay.

Mr. Lloyd George. If we are required to send an ultimatum, it is very important that it be followed by instantaneous action, and for that, everything must be ready. Let Marshal Foch and Mr. Winston Churchill get together today so that everything can be put in order; I suppose we should give the Germans, after next Thursday, five more days to sign. In this case, would our troops be ready to march without delay? Any appearance of hesitation would be fatal.

Marshal Foch. They will be ready if the order is given this very day.

Mr. Lloyd George. The Germans must not be allowed to think that we are hesitating. Make all the necessary arrangements with Mr. Winston Churchill.

—Marshal Foch and General Weygand withdraw.

Mr. Lloyd George.* I have news about the state of opinion in Berlin. Demonstrations took place against England. A crowd demonstrated in front of the Adlon Hotel, the seat of the Allied missions. There are, it seems, very few troops in the western part of Germany. Depression is profound and—something which seems to indicate that the Germans will sign, despite certain hesitations—they don't seem ready to risk an offensive against Poland. They know that that would immediately cause the renewal of general war. Such is the information given to me.

M. Clemenceau. It is rather encouraging.

President Wilson. I would like to return to the question of Poland and the Ukraine. We sent a qualified person[1] there, who saw M. Paderewski. Upon his return, the latter discovered that new operations were being prepared against the Ukrainians; he stated to his government that that was contrary to the commitments he had undertaken to the conference, and that, unless the orders were canceled, he would tender his resignation. But the reports reaching Warsaw about the atrocities committed by the Ukrainians in Galicia have so inflamed public opinion that a strong movement has developed in favor of the advance of the Polish army.

M. Paderewski once again stressed to the Diet the necessity of keeping the promises made to the Allies, at the same time asking that the independence of Lithuania be respected, and that eastern Galicia be united with Poland only under an autonomous regime. The situation in Warsaw is certainly dangerous. Public opinion is very agitated, and to all the nationalist excitement are added threats of a general postal and railroad strike.

We have a choice between two policies: we must either yield on certain points to Polish public opinion in order to insure that

*H., *PPC*, V, 705ff.

[1] Hugh Simons Gibson, United States Minister to Poland, whose report of his confidential talk with Paderewski is printed in *PWW*, Vol. 59, pp. 263-65.

Paderewski, whom we trust, remains in power, or else adhere firmly to the principles we have established, but at the risk of seeing Paderewski fall. There is no question that the account of atrocities committed by the Ukrainians has produced a deep impression. M. Paderewski warns us that total intransigence on our part would result in a revolution in Poland and, to begin with, the fall of his government. He doesn't seem hopeful that we will be able to impose a change of attitude upon either the Diet or the Polish people.

Mr. Lloyd George. I conclude that definite facts exist nowhere; we are on shifting sands. If what we are told about the Ukrainian atrocities is true, that changes the entire basis of our decision. I propose to take this question immediately before the commission presided over by General Botha;[2] the General is a man of great common sense. What we need first is to know the real facts.

M. Clemenceau. I second this proposal. The best thing is to transmit the report that President Wilson has just received to the commission.

Mr. Lloyd George. Have you seen the telegram from Lenin?[3] He also accuses Denikin's troops of atrocities. I fear that, in fact, atrocities have taken place on both sides.

Also, what can we make of Kolchak's victories? By refusing the ceasefire requested as a condition for victualing, Lenin gives the impression that it is he who is advancing.

President Wilson. The same uncertainty about Hungary. We are receiving reports of the unpopularity of the dictatorship of the proletariat.[4] The execution of so-called socialist measures has given rise to all kinds of abuses and individual violence. Béla Kun, personally, is attempting to exercise a moderating influence; but he isn't succeeding. The advance of the Rumanians, moreover, tied his hands by making it impossible for him to move closer to more moderate elements and, when the Rumanians were stopped, the result of this temporary victory of the Budapest government was a renewal of the terror.

This government, obviously, doesn't represent Hungary, and it would be unwarrantable to invite it to conclude peace in the name of the Hungarian people. I have been warned, at the same

---

[2] The Inter-Allied Commission for the Negotiation of an Armistice between Poland and the Ukraine, about which, see XVI, n. 1. About its report, see LXXXVII, n. 2.

[3] Lenin's reply to the Nansen proposal, about which see LXXXV.

[4] See the memorandum by Philip Marshal Brown printed in *PWW*, Vol. 59, pp. 239-40.

time, that Italian intrigues extend into Hungary. The conclusion of my representative is that the only way to settle the Hungarian question is by military intervention. There would be no resistance; Béla Kun himself is ready to obey the orders of the Entente if they are imposed upon him. The French troops in Belgrade can proceed with the occupation if they are ordered to do so. As soon as the occupation has taken place, we are advised to send a political mission to Budapest, with a man like General Smuts at its head, in order to insure the establishment of a stable government.

M. Clemenceau. It appears to me difficult to occupy Budapest. What will we be asked to occupy next? It isn't the first time we have been invited to occupy such or such a part of Europe. In any case, Rumanians would have to be sent there; I don't want to put only Frenchmen there.

President Wilson. I would have confidence only in a French occupation. The Rumanians have direct claims to make good against the Hungarians. I fear their presence would provoke the hostility of the people.

M. Clemenceau. General Franchet d'Esperey has been asking me for a long time to occupy Budapest; I have always refused. I am willing to study the question; but I call to your attention that neither the American nor the British army can help us.

Mr. Lloyd George. That is why I don't think I have the right to insist.

President Wilson. We should perhaps already have come to this decision.

Mr. Lloyd George. We never wanted to do it.

M. Clemenceau. What we can do in Budapest depends a great deal on what we will have to do on the German side.

A telegram intercepted between Versailles and Berlin indicates that the German delegation is preparing other notes and will undoubtedly ask us for a delay. I think we should grant them a few days.

Mr. Lloyd George. Certainly, within reasonable limits.

President Wilson. If the Germans request a delay, it is a rather good sign. People who want to refuse do not need a delay.

M. Clemenceau. My latest information is that Brockdorff-Rantzau would rather not sign if he found someone to replace him; if he doesn't succeed, he will sign himself.

Mr. Lloyd George. If I was in his place, I would not like to sign a treaty which will deliver to foreigners all the colonies, the entire merchant fleet of my country.

President Wilson. We must return to the question of Smyrna.

Mr. Lloyd George. Yesterday, I had a strange visit from M. Orlando. He came unaccompanied by Count Aldrovandi, which is significant; for Count Aldrovandi is M. Sonnino's man. He showed me the proposals which the Italians had made to Mr. Miller of the American delegation,[5] and he ended by asking for a mandate over all of Asia Minor. I answered that there was absolutely nothing doing on that basis. In the end, he let it be known that he was not much worried about Asia Minor; Italy would only be interested in it if she were refused Fiume. I asked him: "Would you prefer Fiume to a mandate in Asia Minor?" He replied: "Yes."— "And you would abandon any claim to Asia Minor if you had Fiume?"—"Possibly." He asks if we couldn't leave Fiume to Italy on the condition that she build a port for the Yugoslavs.

I believe that to put the Italians in Asia Minor would be to introduce a source of trouble there. You have heard the Mohammedans; their feeling towards the Italians is a feeling of contempt. It is not for me to say whether or not this is justified. But placing the Turks under Italian control would give no satisfactory result, and the Mohammedan world would be in a state of revolt. If necessary, I am not afraid to change my opinion and to suggest solutions different from those which I have contemplated up to now.

President Wilson. Nor am I, provided we reach a fair solution.

Mr. Lloyd George. The presence of the Italians in Asia Minor would create difficulties for us in Mesopotamia, for America in Armenia, and for France in Syria. Furthermore, I deem it impossible to divide the lands that are properly Turkish.

President Wilson. What struck me in our recent conversation with the Mohammedans of India is the feeling they attach to the sovereignty of Turkey. I am forced to remind myself that I, myself, used this word in the Fourteen Points, and that these have become a kind of treaty which binds us.

Mr. Lloyd George. Yes, but towards Germany.

President Wilson. We can't do otherwise than apply the same principles everywhere.

There is obviously a very strong feeling amongst the Mohammedans in favor of preserving the sovereignty of the Caliph. It

---

[5] During the past few days, Orlando, Sonnino, and Di Cellere had been carrying on talks with David Hunter Miller, George Louis Beer, Douglas Wilson Johnson, and Colonel House. The main upshot of these talks was a solution of the Adriatic problem proposed by Miller but not accepted by the Italians or President Wilson. See Albrecht-Carrié, *Italy at the Paris Peace Conference*, pp. 167-83.

appeared to me that, if soldiers of the Mohammedan religion had thought that they were doing anything other than breaking the alliance between Germany and Turkey, they would undoubtedly have refused to fight. They were not unaware that we wished to eliminate Mohammedan control over the Greek populations; but they would not have accepted our using them to deprive a purely Mohammedan country of its independence. Besides, promises have been made.

Mr. Lloyd George. I acknowledge that I made some.

President Wilson. It could be said that, since I wrote the Fourteen Points, the situation has changed radically; but what does not change is the essential principles upon which we were agreed.

Can't we find a way to leave to Turkey her sovereignty over Anatolia, entrusting only one of the great powers with giving her advice in certain matters, such as finance, economic development, perhaps international relations? The French government could be designated for this task. I even wonder whether the Sultan couldn't continue to reside in Constantinople, without having sovereign rights over that city, but somewhat as the Pope resides in Rome. There is no reason for the mandatory power to be in conflict with the representative in the same city of the power which would help the Sultan govern his Anatolian domain; the spheres of activity would be absolutely separate.

Mr. Lloyd George. I have been asking myself the same question for twenty-four hours.

President Wilson. We would give the Sultan part of Constantinople in order to establish his residence there, and his kingdom would be outside it, at a short distance.

Mr. Lloyd George. I would entrust the task of guiding the Turks in financial and economic matters to the French; but I believe that they should not interfere at all in the government of Turkey, for that would raise the Mohammedan world against them and us.

M. Clemenceau. A mandate of this kind would have to be drawn up with the utmost care. To keep the Turkish government is fine; but government by the Turks has always meant massacres from time to time.

President Wilson. This time we will only leave them subjects of the Turkish race.

Mr. Lloyd George. The organization of the gendarmerie could be assigned to France. But it would be a serious mistake to try and divide Anatolia into spheres of influence.

M. Clemenceau. The best thing is to try to draft a text.

Mr. Lloyd George. We have large interests in near eastern affairs.

Lord Curzon is here, and I shall consult him. I must say that he is completely hostile to the idea of leaving the Turks in Constantinople.

President Wilson. At the end of our conversation with the Mohammedans, I recall that the word "mandate" was mentioned, and the Mohammedan delegates pricked up their ears. If we give France the role that we have just described, I would propose to entrust her with a mandate without calling it by that name; the French will be "advisers" of the Turkish state, without responsibility to the League of Nations. The treaty which would establish this situation would place narrower limits on it than those of a mandate.

Mr. Lloyd George. If France assumes the mandate for all of Anatolia, that will necessarily involve a new study of the question of mandates in the entire territory of the former Ottoman Empire.

President Wilson. Italy again raises the question of her compensations in tonnage.[6]

Mr. Lloyd George. She could only obtain what she asks at the expense of the British Empire, which lost more than a million tons on the way to Italy whilst sending that country what was absolutely essential to it.

President Wilson. About all the Italian questions, here is what I would say to M. Orlando. He must make the Italians understand that it is not in their country's interest to fall out with the United States. Any well-defined territorial unit in the Adriatic which expresses by vote its will to belong to Italy will become Italian with my full consent. How could the Italians refuse this proposal without placing in doubt what they have repeated so many times about the Italian character of these territories?

Mr. Lloyd George. If the Italians are excluded from Asia Minor, it will be worthwhile to leave aside part of what we said earlier on the Adriatic question.

President Wilson. Whatever the fate of Anatolia may be, I could not consent to any solution which would turn an alien people over to a great power against its will.

Mr. Lloyd George. What I will propose could only be done through an understanding with the Yugoslavs. It must be admitted that Fiume is, in many respects, an Italian city. If the Yugoslavs agree to having another port constructed for them with the right, in the

---

[6] The transition here was not nearly so abrupt as the Mantoux text would indicate. Actually, Wilson reintroduced the question of Fiume and said that he had heard that the Italians and Yugoslav shipping people were getting together on the question of shipping in the Adriatic. *PWW*, Vol. 59, p. 260.

meantime, to use the port of Fiume, and if we promise possession of Fiume to Italy, we can, in this way, lead her to renounce Dalmatia, which the Treaty of London gives her, and Asia Minor, where her presence would be a danger for everyone. If we obtained this result through an arrangement which the Yugoslavs would accept, I don't see what your objection could be.

President Wilson. An American proposal along these lines has already been made.[7] But I don't see how Italian capital could be used in this unselfish work of building the port of Buccari. Didn't you notice the nature of the Italian argument against recruitment by voluntary enlistment? In France, it can truly be said that compulsory military service is embedded in national tradition. But what the Italians are telling us is that, if they had to be content with a volunteer army, they would have none at all—no doubt because they would not pay their soldiers enough.

Mr. Lloyd George. In Asia Minor, Great Britain claims nothing for herself; but it is essential to world peace not to admit the Italians there; that would cause difficulties all around them, particularly in Armenia.

[7] In the so-called Miller proposal. However, according to Hankey, Wilson also pointed out that the latest American proposal "had not been to hand Fiume to the Italians but to have a plebiscite if the Italians had constructed a port at Buccari. This, of course, was subject to the people of Fiume still desiring to become Italian." Ibid., p. 261. See also the memorandum by D. W. Johnson printed in ibid., pp. 589-91.

LXXXIV

Conversation between President Wilson, MM. Clemenceau, Lloyd George, and Vénisélos, and Baron Sonnino*

MAY 19, 1919, 4:30 P.M.

President Wilson (to Baron Sonnino). Do you know about the letter which we addressed to M. Orlando about the landing at Scala Nuova?

Baron Sonnino. Yes; we are bringing you our reply.[1]

*H., PPC, V, 716ff.

[1] V. E. Orlando to WW [et al.], May 18, 1919, PWW, Vol. 59, pp. 250-51. It read as follows:

"The landings of Italian Troops in Asia Minor, concerning which the Presi-

President Wilson. What struck us is that this landing was not warranted.

Baron Sonnino. I came to discuss this question before the leaders of the principal powers; but I wasn't prepared for a discussion that would take place before someone else.

M. Vénisélos. In these circumstances, I offer to withdraw.

—M. Vénisélos withdraws.

President Wilson. I take the liberty of observing that M. Vénisélos is, as much as ourselves, a member of the peace conference.

Baron Sonnino. Undoubtedly; but I am not speaking here in my own name. You addressed yourselves to our Prime Minister; I bring you his reply. I don't think other persons involved in the question should participate in the discussion amongst the great

---

dent of the United States and the Premiers of France and Great Britain have asked for information, were determined by imperative reasons of public order and carried out without giving rise to any conflicts such as occurred in [the] case of the Greek landing at Smyrna.

"For nearly a month before the Italian occupation, the province of Adalia has been a prey to anarchy. The further occupations are purely military in character, as are the others effected by the Allied Powers in Turkey, and will in no way affect the ultimate decision as to the final disposal of the various territories belonging to the Ottoman Empire.

"Furthermore, and although the final settlement of those territories is not now in question, the Italian Prime Minister cannot but draw the attention of the Prime Ministers of France and Great Britain to the provision of article 9 of the Treaty of London of April 26th, 1915, and the rights which, on the basis of this article, were recognized to Italy.

"As to the remark that such action was taken without previous consultation with his colleagues, Signor Orlando wishes to point out in his turn that the very cause and the conditions of such landings made any previous consultation impossible. On the other hand it was entirely without Signor Orlando's knowledge that Greece was invited to participate with her troops in the occupation of Smyrna. This action prejudiced 'de facto' if not 'de jure' the final settlement to be arrived at in the case of this city, concerning which and in accordance with the wishes of the Allied Powers there had been—between the Italian and Greek Governments—conversations which were still pending and showed all the conciliatory spirit by which the Italian Government was animated in the matter.

"Likewise no previous notice was given to the Italian Premier of the occupation of Heraclea by French forces.

"The Italian Prime Minister wishes to assure the President of the United States and the Premiers of France and Great Britain that he is no less anxious than they are to arrive to a friendly understanding with his colleagues for the final settlement of the Mediterranean problem in a way which, by fulfilling in their letter and their spirit the agreements which determined Italy's entrance into the war, may give Italy, also on this point, the satisfaction the Italian people rightly expect."

powers. If you later wish for clarification of certain points, it will be only natural to ask M. Vénisélos to participate in the conversation.

We have already talked about the situation in Smyrna. But during our absence, on May 6, you invited M. Vénisélos to prepare troops for a landing.

President Wilson. Your delegation had, indeed, returned to Rome.

Baron Sonnino. We had earlier had a general discussion about the Greek questions, without reaching a conclusion.

Mr. Lloyd George. The new development was the threat of a massacre of the Greeks in Asia Minor. Italian interests in this region are less than English interests, whereas a large part of the population is Greek, and Greeks were being killed every day in the streets of Smyrna.

Baron Sonnino. I am not disputing the facts.

M. Clemenceau. The Italians complained about a French landing at Heraclea. I had a lengthy inquiry made to find out why our troops—one company—had carried out this landing. I had not given any orders; the Foreign Ministry knew nothing. It was the commander in chief at Constantinople who acted, and he did so at the request of the Turkish government, because the mines of Heraclea supply Constantinople with coal, and it was a question of insuring order in that mining region. I am ready to withdraw the troops immediately if the conference so desires. Italy reproached us for this landing; she would do better to explain herself concerning the landing at Scala Nuova.

Baron Sonnino. What took place at Heraclea is an instance of a landing made without prior notice to the Allies.

M. Clemenceau. It was the Turks who requested it.

President Wilson. The note which you are delivering to me in the name of the Italian government doesn't explain your reasons for landing 2,000 men at Scala Nuova.

Baron Sonnino. The justification was the disturbances, the massacres which were taking place in that region. I recall, moreover, that Scala Nuova, in the agreement of 1917,[2] was part of the territories reserved to Italy. We are not at present claiming these territories as our own. We were in the midst of negotiating on this subject with M. Vénisélos when the events occurred.

Mr. Lloyd George. You never sought to take part in expeditions in this region during the course of the war.

Baron Sonnino. We indeed requested to participate in operations in the Near East; but you did not wish it.

[2] That is, the agreement of Saint-Jean de Maurienne.

Mr. Lloyd George. You offered a few Abyssinians. It was the British army which did everything in the Near East.

Baron Sonnino. We had the entire Austrian army on our hands.

Mr. Lloyd George. And we had two million men in France.

President Wilson. From the American point of view, the only thing to consider is the present situation. You speak of disturbances; were there any in Marmaris, in Makri, before your landings? I am not saying that your intention is to anticipate the decisions that the conference will take, but, in fact, you are anticipating them.

Baron Sonnino. We only want order to be maintained. I am told, furthermore, that the Greeks are in Aydin.

M. Clemenceau. We have no such information.

President Wilson. We wished to treat you courteously by inviting you to come and discuss this question with us this afternoon. Why do you object to the presence of M. Vénisélos, whom we brought here precisely because we wanted to give you the opportunity to explain yourself to him?

Baron Sonnino. We have already had to negotiate with M. Vénisélos ourselves. When the negotiations were interrupted, he acted without consulting us.

Mr. Lloyd George. Excuse me, Greece consulted us; it was Italy which did not do so. Unless Italy removes her troops from Scala Nuova, I will no longer concern myself with her interests in the Near East. This landing took place at a time when we were discussing here the future fate of this region. It seemed that Scala Nuova should revert to Greece; but no decision had been taken; whereupon, your landing took place. I cannot conceive of a more regrettable proceeding.

Baron Sonnino. Scala Nuova and Smyrna are mentioned in the agreement of 1917.

Mr. Lloyd George. That agreement was contingent upon the consent of Russia. Now, immediately afterwards, Russia moved away from us and the United States joined our side. Mr. Balfour has long since notified you that the convention was not valid without the consent of Russia.

Baron Sonnino. France considers herself bound.

M. Clemenceau. M. Pichon never said so.

Baron Sonnino. The Treaty of London mentions the province of Adalia.

President Wilson. In order to include Scala Nuova in the province of Adalia, the latter would have to be extended a little beyond its present boundaries. But I must say that the government of the United States doesn't recognize the right of any one of our governments to turn Greek populations over to Italy, regardless of any agreements that might have been made. At this time, we are trying to settle the fate of the world by basing ourselves upon principles which we accepted in common.

Mr. Lloyd George. In the eventuality that mandates should be established over these different countries, commissions would be entrusted with seeing which mandatory is most acceptable to the people concerned.

Baron Sonnino. We would make no objection to an inquiry of that kind.

President Wilson. In these circumstances, do you see a difficulty in withdrawing your troops?

Baron Sonnino. Must we make them leave tomorrow? And if the consequence is disorder and massacre?

President Wilson. You haven't proved that there were disorders in Scala Nuova.

Mr. Lloyd George. If there were any, why should that concern Italy especially?

Baron Sonnino. Italy's interests in the eastern Mediterranean have been recognized by you, and, moreover, we are occupying the island of Rhodes, which is opposite this coast.

President Wilson. The island of Rhodes has never been ceded to you.

Baron Sonnino. We have been occupying it since 1912. Why ask us for a withdrawal which would incite an upheaval of public opinion in Italy?

President Wilson. We have asked you, not for an evacuation, but for an explanation; you haven't given us one. There were disorders in Adalia, but nowhere else.

Baron Sonnino. If we sent our troops to Marmaris, it is because it is the only spot on that coast where a fleet can be stationed. Besides, what harm have we done to anyone?

Mr. Lloyd George. If you see it that way, we ourselves could land wherever we pleased.

Baron Sonnino. As far as France and England are concerned, there was a convention amongst us.

Mr. Lloyd George. Execution of the convention of 1917 was to depend upon the effort Italy would make to cooperate with us in the Near East.

Baron Sonnino. That is inaccurate. No such stipulation was made. Only a general effort was asked of us, which we carried out wherever we could.

Mr. Lloyd George. It was the condition of that convention.

Baron Sonnino. There was no such thing in the convention.

Mr. Lloyd George. In our conversation in Saint-Jean de Maurienne, I insisted upon this fact, that everything we were proposing depended upon the aid Italy would give us to put Turkey out of action.

President Wilson. All that we are asking of Baron Sonnino today is to provide us with a justification for the landings which have been made.

Mr. Lloyd George. There were no disorders in Scala Nuova. You have only sought a pretext for maintaining your pretentions in that region. You are occupying this place at the very same moment when we are discussing its future fate, and you are doing so without notifying us, when we are holding daily meetings.

President Wilson. It might be helpful now to bring M. Vénisélos in.

—M. Vénisélos is introduced.

President Wilson. We would like to question you about the development of the current situation in Smyrna.

M. Vénisélos. I will recall that, in January 1915, a communication from Sir Edward Grey, on behalf of the French, British, and Russian governments, informed me that, if Greece came to the aid of the Serbs, the Allied governments were ready to grant her important territorial concessions in the western part of Asia Minor. No more definite promises were made.

I asked for nothing more. Moreover, when as of the month of August, I made known my desire to cooperate with the Allied Powers, I asked for nothing. When we foresaw the duty of coming to Serbia's aid against Bulgaria, we asked for nothing from her either, although we anticipated the possibility of a substantial enlargement of the Serbian state.

In February 1915, I was compelled by the opposition of the King to resign, and I was replaced by M. Gounaris. The governments of the Entente negotiated with M. Gounaris with a view to obtaining the cooperation of Greece. M. Gounaris asked then for details about the promises made the previous winter, and the *vilayet* of Aydin was mentioned.

Mr. Lloyd George. I think that M. Vénisélos misunderstands the question that we asked him: it is only a matter of the present, and the question is whether there are grounds for sending Greek troops into the interior of Asia Minor.

President Wilson. I think they should be sent into the entire *vilayet* of Smyrna and be able to make use of the railroad from Smyrna to Aydin.

M. Vénisélos. In addition to the first division landed, I have sent there two infantry regiments and 500 gendarmes, whose presence has been made necessary by a strike of the Turkish gendarmerie. I think the Greek military authorities have the men they need to assure order in the interior of the province. It will be necessary for one regiment to be distributed amongst the chief towns of the different *sanjaks*. Besides, a telegram which I have just received tells me that, in certain areas, the Turks themselves have hoisted the Greek flag and called for our troops, not because they wish to see us installed in the country, but because they fear complete disorder. The two regiments which I just mentioned have not yet landed, but they are en route.
Mr. Lloyd George. Who is responsible for order in the interior?
M. Vénisélos. The Turkish authorities. I have no exact information on what is happening there.
Mr. Lloyd George. You have sent no troops to Aydin?
M. Vénisélos. Not to my knowledge.
M. Clemenceau. Are you sure there are no Greek troops in Aydin?
M. Vénisélos. I gave only a general order, and news reaches me only about twelve hours later. My instructions expressly stated that Greek troops are not to be sent towards areas occupied by Italian troops and that no troops should go south and east of Aydin.
President Wilson. Wouldn't it be best to await the development of events before making more extensive plans for occupation? We will always be ready to listen to you; if you have a reason to act, notify us, and we will take the necessary decisions.
M. Vénisélos. I am ready to give the order not to send troops far from the coast. But if there are massacres, I will ask not to be compelled to wait for a decision to be taken here. Our command must be able to act with the authorization of Admiral Calthorpe, who is in the roadstead of Smyrna. If it is necessary to wait for a telegram to reach Paris, to inform you, and to wait for a decision to be taken and for a reply to be sent to Asia Minor, this reply will arrive too late to avoid a massacre. Nothing, moreover, would be done without the consent of the Admiral, and, at the same time, Greek troops would avoid coming into contact with Italian troops.
President Wilson. The proposition seems good to me, provided Admiral Calthorpe is on the spot near Smyrna.
Mr. Lloyd George. It would be better to say "the Admiral commanding the Allied fleet."

President Wilson. Shouldn't the use of the railroad between Smyrna and Aydin be subject to the same conditions?

M. Vénisélos. Yes, as well as that of the other line, from Smyrna into the interior.

—*M. Vénisélos' proposal is adopted.*

M. Vénisélos. Three hundred thousand inhabitants of the western coast of Asia Minor have sought refuge in Greece at various times since 1914, when that population was threatened by Turkish brutality. It would be well to be able to repatriate them before winter, in time for the agricultural work in that region. If it was possible for us to occupy the entire coastal region between Ayasalouk and Ayvalik, to insure order there, this population could be repatriated in the coming months. In short, it is a question of the *sanjak* of Smyrna as far as Aydin in the south, and of the *caza* of Ayvalik.

M. Clemenceau. Where are these refugees?

M. Vénisélos. There are 70,000 of them in Mitylene and 60,000 in Macedonia; there are some in Samos, in Chios, and in all the islands in the Aegean Sea, as well as in continental Greece. A certain number of Greeks who live in the interior of Anatolia also ask to be repatriated to the coast.

M. Clemenceau. I can only approve your proposal.

President Wilson. It is entirely reasonable.

M. Vénisélos. Outside the coastal region, no occupation will take place without the Admiral commanding the Allied fleet being consulted.

—*M. Vénisélos withdraws.*

President Wilson. Have you formed an opinion on the German note relating to general responsibility for damages?[3] At the time of the

---

[3] U. K. C. von Brockdorff-Rantzau to G. Clemenceau, May 13, 1919, which read as follows (*PWW*, Vol. 59, p. 274):

"In the draft of a Peace Treaty submitted to the German Delegates, Part VIII, concerning Reparation, begins with Article 231, which reads as follows:

" 'The Allied and Associated Governments affirm and Germany accepts the responsibility of Germany and her Allies for causing all the loss and damage to which the Allied and Associated Governments and their nationals have been subjected as a consequence of the war imposed upon them by the aggression of Germany and her Allies.'

"Now the obligation to make reparation has been accepted by Germany by virtue of the note from Secretary of State Lansing of November 5, 1918, independently of the question of responsibility for the war. The German Delegation cannot admit that there could arise, out of a responsibility incurred by the former

Armistice, the Germans acknowledged their responsibility for damages caused by Germany's aggression by land, by sea, and in the air. Today, they continue to declare that it was not they who caused the war. This attitude is unbelievable.

Mr. Lloyd George. It shows that Germany is still in the hands of her former officials, or hasn't yet got rid of them.

President Wilson. Or at least Germany allows them to speak in her name.

Baron Sonnino. Since M. Vénisélos, in what he has just asked of you, indicates Ayvalik on one side and Aydin on the other as the boundaries of the Greek occupation, I will ask you if I may consider that things will remain *in statu quo* to the south of Aydin and Ayasalouk.

President Wilson. I don't admit the legitimacy of the occupation of Scala Nuova by the Italian forces.

Baron Sonnino. Since they are there, and the presence of Greeks and Turks would be of such a nature as to create serious incidents, is it not better to leave things as they are?

President Wilson. If it keeps its troops at Scala Nuova, the Italian government must assume sole responsibility for it; I don't want to clothe it with my approval.

Mr. Lloyd George. My position is exactly the same.

M. Clemenceau. Mine as well.

Mr. Lloyd George. This is a matter of a decision taken by the Italian government without consulting us. You made a dangerous move at a time when we were doing our very best to meet Italy's wishes

---

German Government in regard to the origin of the world war, any right for the Allied and Associated Powers to be indemnified by Germany for losses suffered during the war. The representatives of the Allied and Associated States have moreover declared several times that the German people should not be held responsible for the faults committed by their Government.

"The German people did not will the war and would never have undertaken a war of aggression. They have always remained convinced that this war was for them a defensive war.

"The German Delegates also do not share the views of the Allied and Associated Governments in regard to the origin of the war. They cannot consider the former German Government as the party which was solely or chiefly to blame for this war. The draft Treaty of Peace transmitted (by you) contains no facts in support of this view; no proof on the subject is furnished therein. The German Delegates therefore beg (you) to be so good as to communicate to them the Report of the Commission set up by the Allied and Associated Governments for the purpose of establishing the responsibility of the authors of the war.

"Pray accept, Mr. President, the assurances of my high consideration. (Signed) BROCKDORFF-RANTZAU."

in Asia Minor. You tried to prejudge the question. It seems to me certain that M. Orlando knew nothing; the head of the Italian government was not consulted.

Baron Sonnino. It is important that the limits of Greek action be clearly specified.

President Wilson. Do you want to reserve to yourselves the right to intervene south of the line you indicate, without consulting the Allies?

Baron Sonnino. I want to see the rights accorded to Greece clearly defined.

Mr. Lloyd George. It is necessary to add that, in future, no one—neither the Italians, nor the French, nor the English, nor the Americans, nor the Greeks—must land anywhere, whether it be to the north or to the south of Aydin, without the consent of the powers.

—President Wilson reads aloud the text of the reply to the German note on responsibility for damages.

—*This text is approved, with a few amendments.*[4]

Mr. Lloyd George. Where are we on the question of the clothing which the Germans ask for their prisoners?

M. Clemenceau. I saw some German prisoners yesterday, and I found them better dressed than I was.

Mr. Lloyd George. At this very moment, we are lacking 200,000 civilian suits for our demobilized soldiers. All the German prisoners in England are very adequately clothed. We don't have any stock of civilian clothing at our disposal. Colonel Kisch suggests that, upon their departure, these prisoners be given English uniforms, which would be altered in such a way as to remove their military look; but I don't like this idea very much. The simplest thing is to tell the Germans that we don't have the means to satisfy them, which is true.

President Wilson. We can say that we will do everything possible, but that we don't have enough clothing for our own demobilized soldiers.

Mr. Lloyd George. This week, we have to take up the Russian question.

---

[4] It pointed out that Germany, in signing the Armistice Agreement on November 5, 1918, had not only promised to make reparation for all damages caused by German aggression but had also implicitly but clearly "recognised" its responsibility for the war. The letter also said that the documents requested by Brockdorff-Rantzau were of "an internal character" and could not be transmitted to him. *Ibid.*, pp. 275-76.

President Wilson. I have instructed the State Department to enter into direct communication with Admiral Kolchak and to ask him a certain number of questions, notably about his intentions concerning the Constituent Assembly and the agrarian system.[5]

Baron Sonnino. Hasn't he already made a statement?

President Wilson. Yes, but it is inadequate, because the terms are too vague. Furthermore, I have read a document which was delivered to me here and which bears, amongst other signatures, that of Kerensky; his is not the one which adds most to the authority of this document.[6] What it contains agrees with the information which has already been communicated to us. The signatories reveal a certain distrust of the governments of Omsk, Archangel, and the Don; they hope that none of them will be recognized by us as the government of all Russia; they propose to ask for identical assurances about the convening of the Constituent Assembly and the fundamental nature of the regime. That seemed very reasonable to me. We can recognize none of these governments as the government of Russia, and we must bind them to a procedure which will lead to the formation of a regular democratic government. If they resist, we can break off relations with them.

Mr. Lloyd George. It is we who are supplying them with arms and ammunition.

Baron Sonnino. I am told they are ready to take commitments.

Mr. Lloyd George. The obscure point is the attitude of Denikin, who is, moreover, advancing and seems to be on the verge of overrunning the Bolshevik zone which still separates him from Kolchak.

Sir Maurice Hankey. Will the reply to the German note about reparations be published?

M. Clemenceau. Only after the Germans have received it.

Sir Maurice Hankey. In the draft of Article 232, a difference between the French text and the English text has appeared. The English text stipulates that reparations are owed to each of the Allied Powers only for the period during which it was a belligerent. This stipulation was forgotten in the French text.

---

[5] Wilson, on May 14, had instructed the State Department to ask Ambassador Morris to go to Omsk to obtain from the Kolchak government official assurances with regard to the future governmental regime, the methods to be used in setting it up, the reform of land tenure, universal suffrage, and a new constituent assembly. Morris should learn as definitively as possible "the influences that Kolchak is under." WW to F. L. Polk, May 14, 1919, *ibid.*, p. 148. See also WW to J. P. Tumulty, May 16, 1919, *ibid.*, p. 189.

[6] A. F. Kerenskii *et al.* to WW, May 14, 1919, *ibid.*, pp. 150-56.

M. Clemenceau. It must obviously be restored.

Baron Sonnino. Concerning Poland, when did she become a belligerent?

President Wilson. Poland has never been recognized as one of the Allied and Associated Powers, except very recently.

Baron Sonnino. Then she has no right to reparations? That is a bit hard.

Mr. Lloyd George. In fact, two thirds of the inhabitants of Poland contributed, voluntarily or by force, to inflicting the damages upon us for which we are asking reparation.

President Wilson. Annex I clearly limits the right to reparation to the Allied and Associated Powers.

M. Clemenceau. Thus it is agreed that we will restore to the French text the words which limit the right of each power to the period during which it was in a state of war with Germany.

LXXXV

Conversation between President Wilson and MM. Clemenceau, Lloyd George, and Orlando*

MAY 20, 1919, 11 A.M.

—Consideration of the reply to the German note[1] on the economic consequences of the losses of German territories, the cession of the merchant fleet, etc., stipulated in the peace treaty.

Mr. Lloyd George. We must strengthen this document[2] and redraft it in such a way as to make an impression on German public opinion. The German delegation complains that Germany in the future won't possess what is necessary for her economic life. We must show that England and Italy can only live by imports.

*H., *PPC*, V, 732ff.

[1] U. K. C. von Brockdorff-Rantzau to G. Clemenceau, May 13, 1919, *PWW*, Vol. 59, pp. 305-307. This was in fact the preliminary German commentary on the economic impact on Germany should the provisional peace terms be imposed upon her.

[2] Printed in *ibid.*, pp. 307-309. It answered the German note point by point and assured the Germans that the Allied and Associated Powers had no intention to destroy Germany's economic life.

M. Orlando. Of the raw materials necessary to Italy, only one seventh was carried by Italian boats before the war. Today, that proportion has fallen to one fourteenth.

Mr. Lloyd George. We have to ask the facts of the specialists and then entrust the drafting to someone who is capable of reaching German opinion.

—After an exchange of observations, the drafting of the text is entrusted to Lord Curzon, who will be assisted by Captain Clement Jones.

Mr. Lloyd George. I have learned about an interview by Herr Dernburg, former German Colonial Secretary. The result seems to be that, for the moment, the Germans are not inclined to sign; Herr Dernburg says they would like to do it, but that they will not be able to do it. Moreover, he complains of imaginary wrongs, for example, the assessment by an Allied commission of the taxes which the Germans will have to pay. There is nothing of the kind in the treaty; it is simply stated that we will have the right to assure ourselves that Germany is taxing her population on a basis at least equal to our own. The Germans also fear that, within twenty or thirty years, the Reparation Commission could impose new obligations upon them which it would be impossible to foresee. Above all, they want to know exactly what they must expect.

President Wilson. We have said that the Reparation Commission will make known definitively the total sum of our demands in 1921.

Mr. Lloyd George. Herr Dernburg says again that Germany cannot accept obligations which she could have barely met when she was still in all her power and prosperity. The present stipulations would turn the Germans into an enslaved people, working for other peoples. Germany cannot sign in these circumstances.

There are also some words about the occupation army, the charge for which is considered too heavy. That question also concerns us, and we agree on a reduction of the occupation forces.

President Wilson. I have been told that the French government intends to send some Senegalese to the left bank of the Rhine. Is this true?

M. Clemenceau. There is exactly one Senegalese battalion there; but I intend to withdraw it, and, like you, I think that it would be a grave mistake to have black troops occupy the left bank of the Rhine.

M. Orlando. On the subject of the change of Article 232, which was a question in our last meeting, I don't know if my colleagues are aware that the commission charged to study the same question for Austria-Hungary unanimously voted for a certain American amendment. Did you know about it when you discussed it yesterday? I think the members of the commission should be questioned about it.

President Wilson. I vaguely recall something of this kind. The amendment in question was proposed by Mr. Dulles, who was thinking, above all, about our losses at the time of the torpedoing of the *Lusitania*. At that time, we were of course not belligerents.

Mr. Lloyd George. But Mr. Dulles is not a member of the commission?

President Wilson. No, but he is one of our legal advisers.

Mr. Lloyd George. I don't think there is anything to change in the decision we took yesterday.

—*The decision is affirmed.*

—Reading of Lenin's reply to the Nansen proposal for the victualing of Russia:[3] Lenin won't accept the terms of a cease-fire. Lord Robert Cecil, after consultation with the Supreme Economic Council, advises the governments to choose between two policies:[4] they must either crush the Bolsheviks or impose provisional boundaries upon the different belligerent groups of Russia and send them supplies on the condition that a Constituent Assembly will be convened immediately. In all events, they must try not to mix the two policies.

Mr. Lloyd George. What do you think of these two documents?

M. Clemenceau. I don't see how we could change our present position. It is obvious that the power of the Bolsheviks is on the decline. If the Nansen plan, based exclusively on a humanitarian concern, is rejected by them, there is nothing else to do.

President Wilson. Lenin says that we want to prevent him from defending himself. But all that we asked of him is to cease all offensive action. What he could say is that we are granting Kolchak and Denikin material support and that we should order them to stop fighting.

M. Clemenceau. You can instruct them as you like—that's not what will stop them. What means of action do we have?

President Wilson. We can stop sending them arms.

[3] It is printed as an Enclosure with H. C. Hoover to WW, May 16, 1919, *ibid.*, pp. 193-97.

[4] Actually, this commentary on the Bolshevik reply to the Nansen proposal was prepared by Lord Robert Cecil, Hoover, and Bernardo Attolico. See *PPC*, V, 743, 747-48.

M. Clemenceau. If we stop sending arms to Kolchak and Denikin, that will not stop Lenin.

President Wilson. Can't we try moral arguments to sway Lenin?

M. Clemenceau. I have no hope of this kind.

President Wilson. I no longer regret as much as I did several months ago not having a policy in Russia; it seems to me impossible to define one in such circumstances.

Mr. Lloyd George. On the one hand, we have violent and unscrupulous revolutionaries; on the other, people who claim to act in the interest of order, but whose intentions we suspect. Nevertheless, we have the duty not to abandon those whom we needed when it was a matter of reconstituting the eastern front in some way, and public opinion would not forgive us for abandoning them when we no longer need them.

President Wilson. We ought to send them a formal summons to pledge themselves to convene the Constituent Assembly. That is what I had intended to do regarding Kolchak, in order to make the position of the government of the United States very clear. Why shouldn't Mr. Balfour draft a dispatch along these lines in the name of the Allied and Associated governments?

Mr. Lloyd George. I don't know whether Mr. Balfour is the ideal drafter for such a dispatch. I would like to give a frankly democratic coloring to it.

President Wilson. It is necessary to ask precise questions and to demand precise commitments. We know very well that it is impossible to convene the Constituent Assembly on short notice. But what the document I mentioned to you yesterday,[5] and which is signed by Kerenskii, Avksentiev, and some others, recommends, is to demand from all the Russian governments the promise of the convocation of the Constituent Assembly, and, meanwhile, the immediate meeting of local assemblies, elected by universal suffrage, which could form amongst themselves a central body of delegates to discuss the general interests of Russia.

In short, it is a question of asking from each one of these groups the assurance that it is ready to unite with the others to reconstitute the Russian Republic. In the meantime, each of them will guarantee the existence of a local regime based on individual liberty and universal suffrage.

Mr. Lloyd George. I have only one objection to make: this prolongs the division of Russia. Be assured that, if Kolchak reached Mos-

---

[5] About which, see LXXXIV, n. 6.

cow, the civil war would end immediately, and the convocation of a National Assembly of all Russia would become possible.

President Wilson. Will Denikin rally to it?

Mr. Lloyd George. I think so. His chief of staff is a reactionary; but he himself does not appear to have bad intentions. As for Kolchak, he is only a soldier and nothing more.

President Wilson. Soldiers most often have very simple ideas about politics.

Mr. Lloyd George. Nothing is more true: look at Marshal Foch.

—Mr. Philip Kerr is introduced and receives instructions to prepare the draft of the dispatch to be sent to the different governments in Russia.

Mr. Lloyd George. We will also have to study the question of the Baltic countries. The complete independence of these countries would result in cutting Russia off from the sea.

President Wilson. I have received a letter from Mr. Hoover about the Baltic provinces.[6] From the economic point of view, he considers that it would be easy to restore the situation if order was insured. He proposes to protect the Baltic coast with Allied naval forces and to establish close contact between the mission for economic aid and the naval authorities. The present situation in these countries is terrible.

Mr. Lloyd George. But how can we count on these peoples? At one time, we sought to give arms to them to fight against the Bolsheviks; but we abandoned that, because we found too few people whom we could trust.

Sir Maurice Hankey. The Serbs have sent a note asking for two billion francs' indemnity, under the heading of reparation. The opinion of the experts is against it.[7]

Mr. Lloyd George. The note of the experts appears to me rather poorly drafted; it will have to be changed.

[6] H. C. Hoover to WW, May 9, 1919, *PWW*, Vol. 58, pp. 594-95.

[7] See N. P. Pašić to G. Clemenceau, May 9, 1919, and "Memorandum on the Request of the Serbian Delegation . . . ," both printed in *PPC*, V, 751-53. While the memorandum stated that Serbia's demands were exorbitant and "inadmissible," it also pointed out that Serbia had suffered serious material and economic damages and deserved prompt assistance. The principal suggestion of the memorandum was that the Allies should immediately create a credit for Serbia of up to £5 million pounds "from the first sums realised out of the German reparation."

LXXXVI

Conversation between President Wilson and MM. Clemenceau and Lloyd George*

MAY 21, 1919, 11 A.M.

M. Clemenceau. We have received a communication from the German delegation requesting a delay in the delivery of its observations on the peace treaty, but without indicating a time limit.

President Wilson (*after the reading of the note*). That request doesn't seem unreasonable: it tries only to obtain time to complete the draft in question.

M. Clemenceau. Yes, but without specifying the time required. If we gave our consent under these conditions, it would create an impression which I don't wish to see made.

Mr. Lloyd George. Can't we ask the Germans through Colonel Henry when they can be ready? When we have this information, we can fix a time limit for them.

M. Clemenceau. I can send M. Cambon to them.

Mr. Lloyd George. It is better not to do the thing in an official manner, and to try only to find out what they want.

M. Clemenceau. I am going to summon Colonel Henry.

—General Alby is introduced.

M. Clemenceau. General Alby is going to inform you about the news he is receiving about Poland.

General Alby. We have received a telegram from Prague indicating that the Poles are advancing into the region of Przemysl and that the Galician populations are fleeing before them into the Carpathians. The Ukrainians have asked the Czechs to help them against the Polish invasion; but the Czechs have no troops available. The situation of the Ukrainians is critical, for they have been fighting the Bolsheviks for several months and are being attacked by the Poles from the rear.

Mr. Lloyd George. What the Poles are doing is a flagrant violation of commitments taken; they are only helping the Bolsheviks to crush the independence movement of the Ukrainian people.

President Wilson. Mr. Hoover advises us to warn the Poles that, if they don't cease their aggression, we will cut off supplies.

Mr. Lloyd George. Sir Esme Howard, who is a great friend of Po-

*H., PPC, V, 754ff.

land, comes to the same conclusion and makes the same recommendation to me.

M. Clemenceau. Haven't we already decided to give a warning to the Poles?

Mr. Lloyd George. All these small nations are at this moment heading straight towards their own perdition if they conduct themselves as Poland is doing. It will come to pass that we will judge them as did the Prussians and the Russians; we will conclude that they have no right to exist. After having been so oppressed, the Poles think only of oppressing others. Their attitude is the same as that of the Catholic Irish towards Ulster.

President Wilson. We are forgetting one fact: it is that the boundaries are not yet defined; we must fix them and then say that, whoever crosses them, is against us. As long as that hasn't been done, the uncertainty in which these peoples find themselves is enough to explain the incidents which are taking place.

Mr. Lloyd George. We could stop them by refusing them ammunition and supplies.

President Wilson. But where would you stop them? That's the point.

Mr. Lloyd George. We have already fixed a boundary between the Poles and the Ukrainians which should have marked the separation between their troops during the armistice which we wanted to impose upon them. For the moment, it is impossible to determine the ethnographic boundary; but it appears certain that the Poles don't constitute more than one sixth of the population in the contested territories.

President Wilson. Isn't Lemberg a Polish city?

Mr. Lloyd George. Yes, but surrounded by Ukrainian countryside, like Thorn, which is a German city in the midst of Polish territories.

M. Clemenceau. General Botha and his colleagues on the Commission on Polish Affairs must be seen on this subject.

President Wilson. Here is a letter from Lord Robert Cecil in reply to the plan for the League of Nations offered by the German delegation;[1] he shows that the Covenant upon which we agreed is more practical than the German proposal.

Mr. Lloyd George. I haven't seen with my own eyes the German document concerning the League of Nations.

President Wilson. It is a document which they presented upon their arrival.

---

[1] About the German note, see LXXI, n. 1; for the text of Cecil's draft reply, which is paraphrased below, see *PPC,* V, 767-69.

Mr. Lloyd George. I remember it; but I haven't seen it again since then.

—President Wilson reads aloud the memorandum prepared by Lord Robert Cecil (*summary*):

The bureau of mediation proposed by the Germans will not have the necessary authority to stop conflicts; the function they wish to give it properly belongs to the Council of the League of Nations. Impartial commissions of inquiry could play a useful role; but the text adopted by the Allied and Associated Powers in no way excludes the use of such commissions.

The German plan for the creation of an International Court of Justice will be submitted to the League of Nations. The League of Nations Commission has studied closely the question of compulsory arbitration; after having studied all the possibilities, it did not think it possible to establish a system of this kind.

The suggestion contained in the German document, according to which the costs of future wars would fall upon whoever had broken the Covenant of the League of Nations, appears excellent, and we will adopt it all the more willingly since it comes from Germany. The German delegation declares itself in favor of disarmament: we could not wish for anything better.

As for sanctions for nonobservance of commitments taken by members of the League of Nations, we think that the promptest and most efficient means will be economic pressure, and we prefer it to the means suggested by the Germans.

Mr. Lloyd George. I rather like the tone of this reply.
President Wilson. It discusses the issues and gives our reasons.
Mr. Lloyd George. We will have to resume our discussion on Asia Minor; I have a proposal to make on the fate of Turkey. In the absence of M. Orlando, we will do well also to study the Adriatic question; M. Orlando agrees with me about that.
President Wilson. The Italians know that we are perhaps more indulgent towards them when they are not here.
Mr. Lloyd George. They know, in any case, that it is easier for us to debate freely amongst ourselves and to oppose each other's views, if there are reasons for it.

—Mr. Lloyd George presents a plan for the Adriatic and Asia Minor to his colleagues.[2]
—Colonel Henry is introduced.

M. Clemenceau (*to Colonel Henry*). The Germans tell us that they

---

[2] It is printed as an appendix to these notes.

cannot be ready to answer us concerning the treaty as a whole within the allowed time of two weeks, and they request an extension for it, without, however, specifying any date.[3] Ask them what extra time they themselves would propose, so that we may have a basis upon which to take our decision.

—Colonel Henry withdraws.

Mr. Lloyd George. I first explain the reasons for the proposals relating to Asia Minor, the text of which I have just given to you.

The Mohammedan world is agitated; you know our difficulties in Egypt; Afghanistan is in a state of war with us. During the war, we raised more than a million men in India, almost all Mohammedans; it is they who, although supported by white troops, bore almost the entire weight of the struggle against Turkey. The Mohammedan world doesn't forget that.

The partition of the strictly Turkish portion of Asia Minor would be unjust and impolitic. After reflection, the British government cannot support it; the cabinet has taken a formal decision on this subject. We must not treat Turkey as Poland was treated a century and a half ago. Will it be said that Turkey doesn't know how to govern herself? As much could have been said of Poland.

To the extent that the Turks are a domineering people, establishing their government over other races, we have the right to say to them: "It is over." But if Smyrna and its region, if Armenia, if Constantinople cease to be part of the Turkish Empire, the remainder of Anatolia contains a population of which the Turkish element forms 95 per cent. This purely Turkish part cannot be cut in two without great dangers. I will recall what happened recently in India, when Bengal was divided into two administrative zones. It was only a question of a purely internal measure,

---

[3] U. K. C. von Brockdorff-Rantzau to G. Clemenceau, May 20, 1919, printed in *PPC*, V, 767. Brockdorff-Rantzau stated that the German delegation intended to submit to the peace conference during "the next days" communications, or notes, on the following subjects: the "territorial question in the East," Alsace-Lorraine, the occupied territories, the "extent and discharge of the obligation undertaken by Germany in view of reparation," the "further practical treatment of the questions of Labour Law," and the "treatment of German private property in enemy countries." In addition, a "syllabus" was being prepared "of the observations which the German Government are called for by the Draft of the Treaty of Peace in its detailed provisions." Since these problems were complicated and required much discussion with experts both in Paris and Berlin, it might not be possible to meet the time limit of fifteen days from May 7 set by the Allies. The German delegation therefore requested that the requisite time be granted for more detailed exposition.

yet it caused grave difficulties for years, because Bengal would not hear of being divided.

If you divide Turkish Anatolia, what will you do with the different parts? The Italians would establish themselves in the South, the French in the North. But if the Sultan resides in Brusa, in the French zone, he will be in the hands of the French, and French influence will inevitably be felt in the affairs of the northern region. Conflicts between French and Italians would surely ensue.

M. Clemenceau acknowledges this; that is why he would prefer to create two distinct states, one of which would have its center at Brusa, the other at Konia. But of the two sovereigns, which would be Caliph? How could we justify that partition in the eyes of the inhabitants and of the Mohammedan world? We are dealing here with a homogeneous population, which we could not divide in two without creating constant agitation. The British delegation cannot accept such an arrangement. The mandate over Turkey must be placed in the hands of a single power: such is the conclusion we have reached.

In Constantinople, in Armenia, in Syria, in Mesopotamia, the European nations must take charge of administration, because these areas, where the Turks are not the majority, have been poorly governed by them. In Anatolia, they will govern themselves; it is enough to be at their side, to guide them in the administration of their finances, and to insure the protection of the minorities who will remain alongside the Turks.

The solution which seems best to us is to entrust this role to the United States. Its intervention is the one which the Mohammedan world will best accept, because of its history as a country of liberty, and also because it has no history as a Mohammedan power. The Mohammedans are afraid that the Algerian regime will be extended to Turkey; they have suspicions of the same nature with respect to England.

I see another reason against the assignment of this mandate to France. If France is established in that region, Italy will have the right to complain; her impression will be that France is becoming the only great Mediterranean power, and that she herself is almost excluded from the Mediterranean. If Italy receives nothing in Asia Minor, placing France there would put the Italian government in an untenable position. I don't see any solution other than to entrust the task of advising the Turkish government to the United States. If the United States doesn't think that it can accept, I would maintain the regime currently in existence in Anatolia.

Indeed, the presence of the Americans in Constantinople and in Armenia, of the French in Syria, will exercise constant influence and pressure upon the Turkish government and will make it impossible for it to fall back into the abuses of the past. Moreover, only Turks, or very nearly so, will be governed in Anatolia. Let us not forget that the Turkish regime, such as it is, already tolerates in rather wide measure intervention and advice from foreigners. The Ottoman debt is administered by an international organization under French presidency: that administration must be maintained. An entire system of concessions for public works to foreign enterprises already exists and must continue.

I don't believe, moreover, that we should exaggerate the importance of the interests we might have in these concessions during the period just beginning; for none of us will have capital to invest in these countries for quite a long time, with the exception perhaps of America. France will have almost all of the Cameroons and Togoland in which to develop her enterprises, and I propose to assign to her immediately a provisional mandate over Syria, until we have received the report of the commission which should serve to justify the final distribution of mandates in western Asia.

I believe that neither we nor France could undertake the development of a large country like Anatolia at the present time; the United States can do it.

Such are the views which I wished to present to you, after consultation with my colleagues. I have presented you with a series of different proposals; I admit that I vacillated very much. I have reached the conclusion that any solution other than this one will create difficulties for France and the world. We can't divide Anatolia, and I don't see how, if this country were placed under a French mandate, we could extricate ourselves vis-à-vis Italy. America is thus the only power to whom we can appeal; as long as Russia is not in a position to shoulder her share of the burden, I think that the country which will supervise the administration of Anatolia must also administer the Caucasian regions. Furthermore, if Italy is excluded from Asia Minor, I see such an advantage for the peace of the world that that deserves an effort on our part to impose our solution in the Adriatic upon the Yugoslavs.

President Wilson. We must not contradict ourselves. You are on solid ground in Asia Minor when you say that you don't have the right to divide a homogeneous population. But how would it be possible to give Italy compensation in the Adriatic against the wish of the peoples involved? The only acceptable procedure appears to me to be the consultation of these peoples by a plebiscite. In this way, all Italian groups, wherever they really exist, will be able to unite with the mother country. But, in fact, everywhere a poll has been taken, the result has been unfavorable to Italy. I have a report on Lissa which shows that even that island, which we wished to leave to the Italians, would prefer to be made part of the Yugoslav state.

Italy should begin by evacuating all that area and then leave it to the disposition of the League of Nations. Fiume, provisionally, would be a free city under the protection of the League of Nations for a period determined by the time necessary for the creation of a Yugoslav port at Buccari at Italy's expense. At the end of that period, the population of Fiume would be consulted and would decide itself on the city's fate. With respect to the remaining contested territories, plebiscites would determine, commune by commune, what should be Italian and what should stay with the Yugoslavs. This procedure would be absolutely consistent with our principles.

Similarly, if doubts arose on the subject of the Polish character of certain parts of Upper Silesia, the only way of knowing what the final decision should be is to consult the people. All told, it would be a question of ascertaining, not what the race and the language of the people are, but under which regime they prefer to live.

In Asia Minor, it seems to me, as it does to you, impossible to divide the purely Turkish area. I would fear nonetheless extending Turkish domination as far as the coast which faces the islands of the Dodecanese; the Turks haven't reconciled themselves to having lost these islands, and we must see to it that future conflicts are avoided.

What was said the other day by the Mohammedans of India made an impression upon me, as upon you, and I also believe it necessary to leave the government of all Anatolia to the Turks. What I myself suggested the day after that meeting was not, moreover, unrelated to what Mr. Lloyd George has just set forth. I proposed to grant Turkish Anatolia its independence by giving the Sultan a residence in Constantinople. That independence of the Turks carries with it, moreover, the assistance and advice of a western power, with clearly defined functions. I add, that, if America had the mandate over Constantinople and another power was the mandatory in Anatolia, I am convinced that there would be no friction to fear.

Mr. Lloyd George. There is much to be said in favor of an arrangement which would leave the Sultan in Constantinople, but aren't you afraid to see an independent sovereign, surrounded by his court and guard, in the zone which you would administer?

President Wilson. I have doubts about the wisdom of a policy which would place Anatolia under any mandate whatsoever.

Mr. Lloyd George. If the Sultan is in Constantinople and you have no power over him—since he will be governing that large neighboring region from Constantinople—that will place you in an impossible situation.

President Wilson. I believe he will necessarily submit to the influence of the power which will administer Armenia, on the one side, and the Straits, on the other.

The men whom I designated to be part of the commission of inquiry in Syria[4] have long been asking me to leave, and I authorized them to go.

M. Clemenceau. Concerning Syria, if things go against me, I cannot accept. It was said that the zone of occupation in Ottoman Asia would be determined after a conversation between General Sir Henry Wilson and M. Tardieu. They did indeed meet; General Wilson could reach no agreement with M. Tardieu on the occupation of Syria. He told him that he had no instructions. You promised me the settlement of this question. France cannot allow herself to be treated this way.

Mr. Lloyd George. What do you mean?

M. Clemenceau. When I went to London last autumn, I said to you: "Let me know what you want in Asia, in order to eliminate any cause for misunderstanding between us." You said to me: "We want Mosul, which the Sykes-Picot Treaty places in the French zone of influence." I promised you that I would take care of the matter, and I have done it, despite the opposition of the Quai d'Orsay.

You then promised me to evacuate Syria, which was to be occupied by French troops; the boundary of the zones of occupation was to be fixed at Versailles; but Lord Milner brought everything to a halt, and things have remained at an impasse. You also promised me a meeting with Faisal, which never took place.

Then I received maps from you dividing Syria in a way which we never accepted and which appears unacceptable to us. A little later, it was decided that the United States would have a mandate over Armenia and, to give them satisfaction, it was proposed that Cilicia be included in the Armenian mandate instead of being joined to Syria. I accepted without difficulty.

---

[4] That is, Charles Richard Crane and Henry Churchill King.

I have thus abandoned Mosul and Cilicia; I made the concessions you asked of me without hesitation, because you told me that, afterwards, no difficulty would remain. But I won't accept what you propose today: my government would be overthrown the next day, and even I would vote against it.

Mr. Lloyd George. You accuse me of having gone back on my word: I am still waiting to know in what particular I have done so.

M. Clemenceau. A few days ago, you promised me to study the question of the zones of occupation in Syria without delay; we designated M. Tardieu and General Wilson to settle that question between them. At the end of three days, General Wilson said: "I have no instructions; I must know how the boundaries of Syria are to be fixed."

I believed that, in ceding Mosul to you, in agreeing that part of Syria be taken in order to let a railroad pass through it, and that Cilicia be joined to Armenia, I might have the right to some compensation. It was then that you came up with the idea of the mandate in northern Anatolia entrusted to France. Then all of Anatolia was offered to us. I am not saying, indeed, that you took any commitment towards us. I listened to these proposals. Yesterday, we were discussing a French mandate which extended over all Anatolia, and today, France is ousted.

I believe that all of that comes from your conversations with Lord Curzon. Lord Curzon is a charming man and very able, but he is hostile to France. Everything I have just heard [from you] he said in London, where someone took note of it before coming to tell it to you here.

You are taking Mosul, Cilicia, part of Syria from France in order to let a railroad run through, and you exclude her from Anatolia after having almost promised it to her. That seems to me a bit thick.

My constant policy has been to preserve the union of France with Great Britain and America. In order to do so, I have made greater concessions than I at first would have thought possible. I am glad I made them. That is what I was explaining this very morning to a delegation from the Right, which came to make certain recriminations against me. I explained to them that our relations with England and the United States should be determined, not only by the immense service that these two countries rendered us during the war, but by the necessary solidarity between them and us after the conclusion of peace.

You say that France mustn't be in Asia Minor because that would displease Italy: do you think there is no public opinion in

France? France is, moreover, of all Europe, the country with the greatest economic and financial interests in Turkey—and here she is thrown out to please first the Mohammedans, and then Italy.

I, too, was impressed by what the representatives of Islam said; I make allowance for their feelings, I respect their religion, I think that we must do something for them. But is it not a fact that the Turks have always proved themselves incapable, not only of governing other peoples, but of governing themselves? Both assumptions of Lord Curzon seem to me equally dangerous. I don't see the Turks governing themselves without great problems. As for the idea of introducing America into our disputes—of placing her between the English and French by installing her in all of Asia Minor—I don't believe that is the way to avoid dangerous frictions. I don't know what the Americans will think of the proposal, but French sentiment would be wounded, in spite of our profound sympathy for America.

The United States did a great deal in this war; she came to help us deal the last blow, the decisive blow, and we are deeply grateful to her. But if our people got the idea that the English placed the Americans in Asia in order to chase out the French, that will create a frame of mind which, for my part, I would dread.

I am the least colonialist of all the French; I can't be accused of having excessive ambitions in this respect. If this decision was taken, I wouldn't do what our Italian colleagues did, I would not leave the conference, but I would leave the government.

I didn't have the least idea of that proposal, so I am speaking without a moment's warning. My intention is not to plot against you with the Italians; but I could not prevent public feeling from joining Italian public sentiment and turning against you: that could create great difficulties in the world.

Aside from general political considerations in Syria, there are sentimental considerations. Note that I do not doubt for an instant that American administration in Asia Minor would be an excellent thing; it would perhaps even be better than the administration of that country by any other nation. But you can't wipe out all the results of the past at one fell swoop—traditions and interests accumulated over centuries; beware of the reaction that that could produce in the French mind.

If I haven't spoken with enough composure, please excuse me. I have no proposal to make. We have agreements concerning Syria; we will hold to them if that is necessary. But what is necessary above all else is an arrangement which gives satisfaction to everyone. If Asia eludes us, I will not, on that account, forget the past which binds us, I will continue to do my duty for the peace of the world and to my country. But think about what you wish to impose upon us, and think it over twice.

Mr. Lloyd George. I don't think France has the right to complain about the fidelity of Great Britain: she has very recently given proofs of it. If M. Clemenceau consented to sacrifices on certain claims, it was because England has promised to come to the aid of France if she is attacked.

M. Clemenceau. Did I not allude to that?

Mr. Lloyd George. British public opinion willingly offers to place the entire strength of Great Britain at the disposal of France if the latter is in danger. To say that we haven't kept our word is without justification, and such a manner of speaking would make all discussion impossible.

Since Syria had been promised to France and Mesopotamia to Great Britain [in the Sykes-Picot Treaty] I did indeed ask you in London to have Mosul transferred to the British zone, and you consented to it. I will observe that, in the memorandum which I read to you earlier, the first line recalls that Syria will be placed under French mandate.

With a view to making our demobilization possible, I proposed that the occupation of Turkish Asia be divided between us. Upon my return from London, President Wilson proposed to send a commission of inquiry to Syria; he named his experts. I named mine; they remained here because the French government hasn't appointed its own. I don't say that M. Clemenceau has broken his word to us. It is the French who, for the moment, have not carried out their part of the contract. If there is a breach of promise, it is on the part of the French government, which is not carrying out a common decision.

General Wilson, you say, stated to M. Tardieu that, in order to establish zones of occupation, it would be necessary first to know the boundaries. But General Wilson sent you a map which gives the occupation of all of Syria to the French army. Is that a breach of promise? I think that M. Clemenceau should take back what he has said. M. Tardieu can say that he could not agree with the General; but there is no breach of promise there.

I hear talk of a railroad that must cross Syria; it is a question of transporting petroleum, of which half must go to France. As for Anatolia, I never heard it said, until these last days, that France had territorial claims in that region. To suggest that we didn't keep our word in that region is truly intolerable. We held a discussion amongst ourselves which originated in our desire to settle the Italian question. M. Clemenceau suggested a division of Anatolia; it then appeared to us that that division would lead to serious difficulties.

M. Clemenceau has just said that France holds first place in Asia Minor from an economic point of view. As for external commerce, England stands first; before the war, Germany came second and France third, far behind the other two. It is true that there is French money in the railroads of the Levant, including the Baghdad railroad; but the latter crosses territories which will necessarily be placed under different administrations. I don't believe that French public opinion demands Anatolia or would be surprised if Anatolia was not placed under the control of France. I have read only one article on the subject—in the newspaper Le Temps—and, since the conclusion dealt with concessions to be made to Italy, I concluded from it that that article was only a piece of Italian propaganda.

As for the treaty concerning Syria, its stipulations were contingent, in principle, on common military action. General Foch drew up a plan in 1917. The question was raised upon the assumption of power by M. Clemenceau, who was amongst those least favorable to this plan. It was England alone who made all the efforts required for the execution of the Sykes-Picot Treaty, even though it had been understood that the action would be made in common.

M. Clemenceau. Was there ever a written convention concerning our military cooperation?

Mr. Lloyd George. No; but we had to refrain from landing at Alexandretta,[5] because it was pointed out to us that this port was in the French zone. A plan for a landing at Tripoli[6] was also set aside for the same reason.

Our views on Anatolia are those of a great near eastern power which has experience in the Near East. It is that experience which guides Lord Curzon, and not hostile feelings towards France, which you wrongly attribute to him. It is in the common interest that I arrived at the conclusion that an American mandate had to be established in Anatolia. M. Clemenceau suggests that that proposal is made only to evict France: I don't understand why he raises a suspicion of this kind against a power which has done so much and which is ready to do so much for France.

[5] Or Iskenderun, Turkey.
[6] Tripoli in Lebanon, not in Libya.

President Wilson. I believe our decision must be postponed. Great questions have been raised, and I would view with the greatest apprehension the grave differences they could create.

I have to say without further delay that it will be very difficult for the United States to assume the mission which you propose to it. It has no direct interests in Anatolia; it has invested no capital there. We could only accept the role you offer us as a burden and against sharp opposition from American public opinion. We desire absolutely nothing in Asia Minor. We desire only two things: agreement amongst the great powers and the peace of the world. Our duty is to find a plan which establishes order in Asia Minor and helps to maintain order in the Mohammedan world.

My mind isn't yet made up. I still study the question; but it appears to me impossible for America to accept this mandate. She will take the Armenian mandate for humanitarian reasons. Americans have already sent missionaries, money, and relief societies to Armenia. American public opinion is interested in Armenia. But I don't believe I could present plans to Congress like the one just laid out. That is enough to rule out America as a possible mandatory in Anatolia.

But we must help in the solution. The conviction I have come to is that it is impossible to divide Anatolia and that the Sultan should remain in Constantinople, if that is possible. If, however, his presence in Constantinople causes too many complications, it will be necessary for him to settle either in Brusa or in Konia. Another point upon which I insist is that the Turks must not be placed too close to the Dodecanese.

The only point upon which there is a divergence of opinion between us is Anatolia. Yesterday, I suggested that Anatolia should not be placed under a mandate of the League of Nations, but that we should only place alongside the Turkish government a power which will give it advice on matters of finance, economic matters, and the organization of the police. France already occupies that position concerning the debt; in my opinion, the same role has to be assigned to her in the other fields.

Perhaps we have the impression today of a greater disagreement than actually exists. I hope M. Clemenceau will not misunderstand what I said with respect to my representatives on the commission of inquiry on Syria; they have remained here without doing anything for some time; today they must either go to Syria or return to America.

M. Clemenceau. I am ready to send my representatives to Syria as soon as the relief of the occupation troops has begun. But I find it useless to send a commission to Syria to make an inquiry under the dictatorship of General Allenby. That is why I arranged this meeting between General Wilson and M. Tardieu. General Wilson said that he didn't know the boundaries of Syria; M. Tardieu could only reply that the question was in the hands of the heads of governments. For the moment, we only have to fix the boundaries of the occupation zone.

Mr. Lloyd George. You received a map from us several days ago. If you don't agree with us on the boundaries indicated on that map, there is nothing to be done, and I warn you that I am going to give instructions that the negotiations regarding the railroad which you mentioned earlier are to be halted immediately. The French will do what they like. If they consider our attitude to be a breach of promise, we will go our way without worrying further. I have done everything I could to meet the wishes of the French in Syria, and that has only led to an accusation of a breach of faith. I declare that I will make no further effort in that direction. I feel that M. Clemenceau should apologize for having made that accusation against us.

M. Clemenceau. Don't wait for apologies on my part. But I wish it to be noted that I am ready to discuss the boundaries of the military occupation in Syria this very day.

{ A P P E N D I X }[7]

SCHEME FOR THE SETTLEMENT OF ITALIAN CLAIMS

Fiume

(1) On the signature of peace with Austria, Fiume to be held provisionally in trust by the League of Nations pending the construction of a harbour for Yugo-Slavia at Italian expense.

On the completion by Italy of a harbour on the Adriatic which shall be deemed by the Council of the League of Nations to provide a satisfactory substitute to Fiume with sufficient anchorage, wharfage, and railway facilities and connected by a practicable line of railway with the railway system of Yugo-Slavia—Fiume to be handed over to the sovereignty of Italy. Italy to allow railway facilities within Fiume itself should this be necessary in order to provide railway connection.

---

[7] Printed in *PPC*, V, 769-71.

Dalmatia

(2) Italy to resign all claims on the mainland of Dalmatia.

The Islands

(3) Italy to have the Island of Cherso when Fiume is handed over to her. Italy to have immediately on the signature of the Treaty of Peace with Austria in full sovereignty those islands south of Cherso in which the Italian nationality preponderates including the island of Lissa.

MAY 21, 1919.

SCHEME FOR SETTLEMENT IN THE TURKISH EMPIRE

Constantinople and the Straits

(1) The United States of America to have a full mandate over Constantinople and The Straits of the Dardanelles and Bosphorus.

Asia Minor

(2) *First Alternative*: The United States of America to have a light mandate over the whole of Anatolia. The Sultan of Turkey and the Government to remain at Constantinople.

Second alternative: If the United States of America cannot accept a mandate over the whole of Anatolia this region to remain subject to the sovereignty of the Sultan of Turkey without a mandatory.

(3) In either alternative provision to be made for access from Anatolia to the Mediterranean, Sea of Marmora, and Black Sea.

Smyrna

(4) The portion of the vilayet of Aidin proposed by the Greek Commission to be united with Greece in full sovereignty. No mandate to be given to Greece over any more extended zone.

Armenia and Cilicia

(5) The United States of America to have a full mandate over Armenia and Cilicia.

Caucasus

(6) The mandate for Armenia to include a provisional mandate

over Russian Armenia, Azerbaijan, and the whole Caucasus region pending a solution of the Russian problem.

Syria

(7) France to have a provisional mandate over Syria pending the report of the Commission which is proceeding to the Near East.

Mesopotamia and Palestine

(8) Great Britain to have a provisional mandate over Mesopotamia and Palestine pending the report of the Commission that is proceeding to the Near East.

Arabia

(9) To be independent.

The Holy Places

(10) These arrangements have been made after sympathetic consideration of the just claims of Mohammedans in the interest of the peace and good government of the world. They have been framed with the fullest desire to safeguard the essential interests of the Moslem faith.

The Allied and Associated Governments pledge themselves to leave to Mohammedan Guardianship the Holy Places of the Moslem faith wherever situated and declare that they will not assist or countenance any interference with the present purposes to which any religious edifice is dedicated.

The Allied and Associated Powers state emphatically that they regard the question of the Kaliphate as being one purely for decision by Mohammedans and that they will in no case intervene in the matter.

LXXXVII

Conversation between President Wilson, MM. Clemenceau and Lloyd George, and Baron Sonnino*

MAY 21, 1919, 4 P.M.

—Colonel Henry is introduced.

Colonel Henry. I saw Baron von Lersner. I raised the question with him of the time the German delegation thought it needed to complete its counterproposals. He told me that two weeks would probably be necessary. I asked him whether he could confirm this figure to me; he replied that he would prefer not to mention it to Herr von Brockdorff-Rantzau, because that could create difficulties for the latter with the German government, if this time was later deemed insufficient. He added that the delegation was still preparing six notes on rather secondary subjects, but that it will deliver a "*mémoire*"—he used the French term—to the Allied governments. It probably involves a counter-project to the treaty as a whole.

Baron von Lersner also told me that the German delegation requested authorization to send for a trainload of printers, consisting of five cars and fifteen people, in order to hasten the printing of the *mémoire*. I told him that I would submit this request to the governments.

He spoke earnestly of the effort being made by the German delegation to finish quickly: its work continues every night until one or two o'clock in the morning.

The information that we are receiving indicates: (1) that an order to retreat would be given to all German troops in the case of an advance by the Allies; (2) that another order instructs that all railroad equipment and agricultural machinery be withdrawn one hundred kilometers to the east of the present line of occupation; finally, the banks in Essen are to send their securities and records to Berlin.

President Wilson. The most probable conclusion to draw from this is that the Germans don't intend to sign in the present circumstances. Nonetheless, it seems reasonable to me to grant them a delay.

*H., *PPC*, V, 772ff.

M. Clemenceau. But do you grant them a fortnight?

Mr. Lloyd George. There can be no question of it.

President Wilson. What would you think of ten days?

Mr. Lloyd George. I would give them until Wednesday, the twenty-eighth. As for their train of printers, let them come. After all, one week should be enough, since it is for them a matter of making known their observations, and not of deciding whether or not they will sign.

M. Clemenceau. And then what will you do?

Mr. Lloyd George. We will see what they say.

M. Clemenceau. They will ask for new delays.

Mr. Lloyd George. We will then do whatever we wish. I favor giving them until Wednesday of next week and of granting them their train of printers immediately.

M. Clemenceau. Will you not tell them now that, if they aren't ready next Wednesday, we reserve our entire freedom of action?

President Wilson. I don't agree with this.

Mr. Lloyd George. Is it necessary to do it now? I think that, by giving them an extra week, we are allowing them time to prepare what they have to say.

President Wilson. We can even add: "We hope it will be possible for you to be ready before this date."

Baron Sonnino. If we don't intend to grant them a second delay, it would be better to give them a little longer delay now and to indicate clearly that it will not be extended. If you want to say: "You have until this date, and not a day longer," it is better to give them a few additional days.

President Wilson. We can't act as if the delivery of their document was a pure formality. We ourselves may need time to study it. All we can say without any risk is: "You have until such or such a date to deliver your *mémoire* to us." After study, we will tell them: "You have until such a date to take your decision."

M. Clemenceau. Be prepared for requests for further delays.

President Wilson. I favor giving them a reasonable extension and holding to it.

Mr. Lloyd George. The whole business will only really begin when you have their first reply. It will have to be studied, and it is in order to begin this study as soon as possible that I propose not to grant them more than a week.

President Wilson. When will they have this trainload of printers that they request at their disposal?

M. Clemenceau. Four days are probably necessary.

President Wilson. That will leave them only three days for printing.

Mr. Lloyd George. I think they can have their train Saturday, and that they will have four days for printing.

M. Clemenceau. I will call to your attention that this train has not yet been officially requested.

Mr. Lloyd George. Let's give them until Thursday, the twenty-ninth.

M. Clemenceau. They will undoubtedly ask for another week: an absolute limit must be set.

President Wilson. Give them a week's extension from Thursday.

M. Clemenceau. It is best to fix a date.

President Wilson. Until the evening of the twenty-ninth.

M. Clemenceau. In my reply, I cannot speak of a trainload of printers, since I have not been asked for anything.

President Wilson. Reply to them through the offices of Colonel Henry, who informed us of their wish.

M. Clemenceau. And what will we do after the twenty-ninth?

President Wilson. We have time to think about that; there is nothing to be said for the moment.

—Colonel Henry withdraws.

Baron Sonnino. Our attention has been called to an incipient conflict between the Austrians and the Yugoslavs at the line where they meet: mustn't we do something to stop it?

President Wilson. Unfortunately, the boundary has not yet been completely determined, and this is what is creating an unstable situation.

—The representatives from the Ukraine[1] are introduced.*

President Wilson. We are meeting today about the deplorable conflict going on between the Ukraine and Poland. These gentlemen were summoned here to inform us about this situation from the Ukrainian point of view, and we will be much obliged to them if they would kindly give an explanation of it.

M. Sydorenko. In the name of the Ukrainian delegation, I express the gratitude of our country to the representatives of the great powers for the interest they are showing towards it.

The Ukrainian population is undergoing frightful sufferings. A

*H., *PPC*, V, 775ff.

[1] Gregory Sydorenko, Vasil Paneyko, and two silent members.

deplorable state of war exists between us and Poland, with which we would like to live in fraternal unity. We are doing nothing other than defending the land of our fathers. We stated to the armistice commission that we were ready, on our part, to stop the hostilities completely. We hope the representatives of the Entente will settle the questions which concern us according to the principles of justice and of right which have been formulated by President Wilson and accepted by the Allied powers.

What we most desire is that the armistice be concluded without delay. The commission asked us to make our views known; we have accepted the proposals which have been made to us. Despite this acceptance, we receive news indicating that the Poles are beginning a new expedition against us and invading our territory.

Mr. Lloyd George. What is the attitude of the Ukraine towards the Bolsheviks?

M. Sydorenko. The Ukraine is defending her territory against the Bolshevik bands which are invading and pillaging it, as they are doing, moreover, in their own country. The population is terrorized. But our government, supported by national feeling, is working to maintain law and order. The Bolsheviks are our greatest enemies: without them, we would be assured of order and peace in our country.

Mr. Lloyd George. This means that you are being attacked by the Bolsheviks and the Poles at one and the same time.

M. Sydorenko. That is exactly what is happening.

M. Paneyko. Eastern Galicia and northern Bukovina are inhabited by four million Ukrainians. The Hapsburgs delivered us over to Polish domination. That is why, when the Austro-Hungarian monarchy collapsed, the Ukrainians joyfully greeted this collapse and immediately chased out the Austrian civil servants to win back their national life. The principle of the right of peoples to self-determination should guarantee their independence, as well as the rights of minorities.

Our new state was created on the basis of democratic institutions and with the desire to accomplish all necessary reforms. We don't want to implement these reforms by extreme and violent methods. We want to give land to the peasants, not through confiscation, but through a system of repurchase. The goal of our social policy is to develop small peasant ownership in our country as the most solid foundation of the state.

In spite of the equality of rights guaranteed by us to the Polish elements of the population who live in our territory, the Poles, dreaming of reconstituting their great empire of the past, which stretched from the Baltic to the Black Sea, have attacked us and invaded our country.

The Polish population of the Ukraine lives only in the cities, where the colonies of civil servants are concentrated; in the countryside, it is represented exclusively by the great landowners. The mass of the population is Ukrainian.

Mr. Lloyd George. Is there a profound difference between the Polish language and the Ukrainian language?

M. Paneyko. The Slavic languages are closer to each other than the Latin or Germanic languages are; but Ukrainian and Polish are two very distinct languages, and not two dialects. The same difference exists between Ukrainian and Russian.

President Wilson. Can Poles and Ukrainians understand each other?

M. Paneyko. There were Polish schools in Galicia. That is why the people in the cities generally understand Polish; but this language is neither spoken nor understood in the countryside.

Mr. Lloyd George. Your language is the same as that of southern Russia?

M. Paneyko. It is the same language.

Mr. Lloyd George. What is the religion of the Ukraine: Orthodoxy or Catholicism?

M. Paneyko. In Galicia, it is the Catholics, or rather the Uniates, who dominate; in Bukovina, all the Ukrainian people are of the Orthodox religion.

Mr. Lloyd George. Do the Uniates recognize the supremacy of the Pope?

M. Paneyko. That is the difference between them and the other branches of the Greek Church.

The government of Skoropadskii, which was established by the German military authority, was overthrown by our people as soon as the Germans withdrew. Then a union of a federal nature was established between Galicia and the Ukraine.

Mr. Lloyd George. Suppose that, in the final analysis, it was decided that the Russian part of the Ukraine will receive autonomy within the Russian state: would you prefer to participate in this autonomy or to remain outside Russia?

M. Paneyko. It is difficult to answer. The goal for which free peoples fight in the twentieth century is complete independence. For ourselves, autonomy wouldn't settle the question, but would only delay the solution by creating the same situation amongst us which has caused so many difficulties and conflicts in the Balkans.

Mr. Lloyd George. There is one point upon which the Bolsheviks and the anti-Bolsheviks of Russia agree: they want the Ukraine to remain an integral part of Russia. We haven't taken a decision on this issue; but suppose that the question was asked as I just put it, would you prefer to receive autonomy within Russia or within Poland? After all, a great part of the Ukrainian population gave itself up without resistance to the Bolsheviks.

M. Sydorenko. The Ukrainian people are now completely united. They had been divided by the monarchical governments of Russia and Austria in the interest of those governments. Since their fall, the Ukraine is united, with only one wish—that of complete independence. As for union with Poland, that is inconceivable. There are 40 million Ukrainians and 20 million Poles: to attach the Ukraine to Poland would be an absurdity. As for the Russians, they never ceased to have the same policy towards the Ukraine, which consists of exploiting her in Russia's interest. What we want is the independence of the Ukraine.

Mr. Lloyd George. Whatever the fate of the Ukraine may be, I think I understand that eastern Galicia doesn't wish to be separated from its compatriots in the Russian Ukraine.

The Ukrainian Delegates. No, we wish to be united.

Mr. Lloyd George. The Poles are circulating rumors of atrocities committed by the Ukrainians.

President Wilson. These rumors have reached us only in a rather imprecise form.

Mr. Lloyd George. In any case, I notice that the Ukrainians declare themselves ready to stop the fighting on the line they are now occupying, if the Poles do as much.

M. Paneyko. We have solemnly declared it on several occasions. We are on the defensive. We desire to bring to an end the struggle which the Poles forced upon us and to concentrate our forces for the defense of our country against the Bolsheviks.

Mr. Lloyd George. And will you treat the Poles who are living in your territory fairly?

M. Paneyko. Our legislation guarantees the personal status of the Poles, and a great number have declared themselves satisfied.

Mr. Lloyd George. If the order to end hostilities was sent from here to the Ukrainian troops, would they obey?

M. Paneyko. We can give you explicit assurances on this point.

Our troops are entirely under the control of our government and high command. They are not gangs, but a disciplined army.

Mr. Lloyd George. If you are freed from the Poles, can you fight more strongly against the Bolsheviks?

M. Paneyko. That is what our army wants; but we will ask the Entente to give us officers and matériel. We have the advantage of being in contact with our own people, whilst the Poles and Bolsheviks are in foreign territory.

Mr. Lloyd George. Didn't the Polish attack make the invasion of Galicia by the Bolsheviks possible?

M. Paneyko. In the past, the Galician people had more freedom than the Ukrainians of Russia. This is why the Bolsheviks are afraid of their spirit of independence and are trying to destroy them.

Whilst we were defending our homes against the Bolsheviks, we were attacked from the rear by the Poles. We then had to turn around and, at the moment, the Poles, with the aid that the Entente gave them with other intentions, are invading Galicia and pillaging it. All our country is on fire.

In the name of humanity, we ask that the Allied and Associated Governments stop the Poles with an immediate order. The situation is critical.

—The Ukrainian delegation withdraws.
—The members of the Commission on Polish Affairs are introduced.
—Lt. Col. F. H. Kisch reads aloud the report of the commission.[2]

Mr. Lloyd George. Have the Ukrainians accepted the conclusion of the commission?

Lt. Col. Kisch. Yes.

President Wilson. Were the military authorities consulted on the effects of the armistice that we are proposing?

General Botha. No; we consulted only a Polish general and a Ukrainian colonel.

---

[2] REPORT WITH APPENDICES PRESENTED TO THE SUPREME COUNCIL OF THE PEACE CONFERENCE BY THE INTER-ALLIED COMMISSION FOR THE NEGOTIATION OF AN ARMISTICE BETWEEN POLAND AND THE UKRAINE, May 15, 1919, printed in *PPC*, V, 783-99. The commission reported that it had produced a draft armistice convention between Poland and the Ukraine, as it has been instructed to do, but that conditions demanded by the Polish delegation in Paris raised questions of general policy which were "beyond the competence of the commission." The appendixes to the report included the draft armistice convention and the comments of the Polish and Ukrainian delegations in Paris.

President Wilson. Does the Polish general agree with his government?

General Botha. It seems so.

President Wilson. The line of demarcation requested by the Poles would take them very far towards the east.

General Botha. It gives them, in fact, all of Austrian Galicia.

President Wilson. The problem is knowing the practical means for bringing the Poles to their senses. Their people are very agitated. Paderewski is overwhelmed. General Piłsudski first yielded to our agents, then annulled the order given. The Diet then pushed the new offensive led by General Haller.

Mr. Lloyd George. That is what the news that General Alby provided this morning shows.

Lt. Col. Kisch. We know, furthermore, that the Poles have occupied the city of Belsk.

President Wilson. Our difficulty obviously does not come from the Polish government, which accepts our injunctions, but from the Polish nation, which has truly taken the bit in its teeth. What is General Botha's opinion about the measures to be taken?

General Botha. Our commission didn't take up the political problem in general terms. We concerned ourselves only with stopping the hostilities and with the terms of the armistice.

Mr. Lloyd George. But what is your personal opinion on that question?

General Botha. Hostilities must be stopped at any cost. We have concluded an armistice with Austria, and Poland is renewing the state of war in the Ukraine. The Supreme Council of the Allies must speak to her forcefully and say to her that our governments won't tolerate the prolongation of this struggle. Whether you decide today that eastern Galicia should belong to Poland, or whether, on the contrary, you don't recognize any right for her in that region, it is essential that everyone obey you.

In fact, there are, in eastern Galicia, a million Poles, 700,000 Jews, whom the Poles claim, but who are not Poles in any way, and four million Ukrainians: the conclusion is obvious.

—President Wilson reads aloud the message prepared to be sent to the Polish government;[3] he adds:

You will notice that it is a matter here of a dire warning: we are threatening to starve Poland if she does not obey.

---

[3] It is printed as Appendix I to these notes.

Mr. Lloyd George. And also to stop sending her ammunition; I see no other way to force the Poles to listen to us.

General Botha. For my part, I was very glad when General Haller's troops were sent to Poland. But the Ukrainians tell us that these troops, who should have fought against the Bolsheviks, came to make war on them. We have no reason to provide these people with the means to fight one another.

M. Clemenceau. Do you find the text of the message too strong?

General Botha. No; the Poles don't want to yield an inch; your will must be imposed upon them.

President Wilson. I don't want to take a decision which would result in the starving of women and children and to punish them for mistakes made by politicians. Couldn't we declare that we are stopping all supplies of a military nature for Poland, without speaking of food?

Mr. Lloyd George. I don't know whether the effect will be adequate: that depends on their stores of ammunition.

General Botha. You could announce that you will stop supplies, without further specification.

President Wilson. That is rather dangerous, if we don't know exactly what effect our message and its threat will have. We can't send armies there to reestablish order.

Mr. Lloyd George. We have to know whether halting the shipment of war matériel would be enough to stop the Poles.

General Le Rond. We must consider the arguments that the Poles are stressing. They say that the Ukrainians are incapable of opposing the advance of the Bolsheviks and that Poland's preoccupation is to establish a continuous front as far as Rumania—a front, moreover, on which the Ukrainians would have their place. At present, the area occupied by the Ukraine represents a gap through which communication between Russia and revolutionary Hungary is being established.

If the decision taken by the Allies results in bringing famine back to Poland, if M. Paderewski is overthrown and replaced by an ultranationalist government, you could have both famine and Bolshevism in Poland at the same time. The telegram that you are going to send could thus have considerable consequences. I think you should begin by telling the Poles: "If you don't listen to us, you will have no more munitions," but without mentioning food.

There is something to the idea of a single front between Poland and Rumania. The Ukrainians only indifferently opposed the

Bolsheviks; at the moment, they are proving themselves pretty much incapable of fighting against the Poles. The latter are much more capable than they of stopping the advance of Bolshevism.

General Botha. My personal conclusions are as follows. The Poles are under the protection of the Allied and Associated Powers. We have recognized them; we sent them food, arms, and everything they requested. They are in the process of fighting against a people who have received nothing from us and whose distress, as a result, must be much greater than Poland's.

I believe that it is in Poland's interest to listen to your warnings. It is up to the Supreme Council to settle the question of territorial boundaries. The Bolshevik danger is nothing but a bogey. I don't believe that any nation has the right to crush a smaller nation in order to procure a so-called strategic advantage: that is what Germany did in Belgium. Poland has received our help; it is her duty to listen to us. If you attach importance to the strategic argument, it is better, in any case, to have 60,000 Ukrainians with us than against us.

Whilst you are sitting here in order to make peace, the Poles, with munitions which they are receiving from you, are attacking people who are not our enemies. If they need what we are giving them in order to fight the Bolsheviks, we are ready to continue to give it to them. If they must fight in the Ukraine, let them do it as the Americans and the English fought in France: it is possible to defend a country without forcibly replacing its own government. If we tolerate what Poland is doing today, we ourselves will throw the Ukrainian people into the arms of the Bolsheviks. The Ukrainians accept the armistice exactly as we propose it. We can't tell them: "Go home," without guaranteeing them that we will carry out what has been decided.

President Wilson. My feeling is entirely the same as yours. The doubt which persists in my mind is this. If Paderewski falls and we cut off food supplies to Poland, won't Poland herself become Bolshevik? Paderewski's government is like a dike against disorder, and perhaps the only one possible. That is the risk we are running, given the state of mind of the Polish Diet. If I knew what means to use to avoid this risk, I wouldn't hesitate to use it.

Doctor R. H. Lord. All the members of the Commission on Polish Affairs agree with General Botha; but we fear, indeed, escaping from one catastrophe only to fall into another. For the fall of Paderewski and the disorder which would follow in Poland would be a catastrophe. I believe we can act without going to extremes.

President Wilson. To that end, we must confine ourselves to halting the shipment of war matériel.

Doctor R. H. Lord. At the same time, we must speak very forcefully. Instead of offering our mediation, orders must be given. The commission has communicated its conclusions to the representatives of the Poles and the Ukrainians; but the heads of governments haven't yet spoken. If you yourselves impose the terms of the armistice, I believe they will be accepted.

The difficulty comes from Polish public opinion. A message worded in such a way as to make an impression upon it without provoking it would allow us to wait for the return of M. Paderewski to Paris and the discussion you can have with him.

President Wilson. Will a message of this kind have enough effect?

General Botha. We have waited only too long to use the appropriate language with the Poles. M. Dmowski says openly: "Just let the present situation last a little longer, and we will occupy all the contested territories."

Mr. Lloyd George. I realize that our action has sinned through weakness. How will we impose our terms upon Germany, if Poland, which wouldn't exist without our support, defies us? All that we are told about the fight against Bolshevism is a pretext: the Poles aren't fighting against Bolshevism in Galicia, but for the conquest of the oil wells. Bolshevism can really only be fought with Russian elements.

The Poles believe that the way to fight the Bolsheviks is not to join forces with the Ukrainians against them, but to put down the Ukrainians. Forty million Ukrainians, if they are trod upon, would rise up against us and could create a new Bolshevism when the old one collapses.

We are told: "Warsaw will revolt and overthrow Paderewski if he follows our advice." Poland would thus prove herself incapable of self-government. If she can't accept the advice of the powers to which she owes her independence, I would point out that we haven't yet made peace with Germany: the question of Silesia isn't settled.

I favor sending the message read by President Wilson to Poland without delay. He does not mention specifically the type of supplies that we will stop; the word "supplies" is enough; I believe it will have its effect. At the same time, I propose to send a telegram directly to General Haller in order to tell him that we have heard the rumor of a Polish offensive in Galicia, contrary to our orders. We should ask him only for a reply about the facts, adding that we cannot believe that he wished to act against our intentions.

President Wilson. We could, at the same time, stop the passage of General Haller's army across Germany.

General Le Rond. Instead of sending a telegram directly to General Haller, who only obeys the orders of his governments, wouldn't it be better to send this message to Warsaw?

M. Clemenceau. We must act without delay.

President Wilson. Isn't General Haller's army supposed to be part of the French army?

General Le Rond. It is now part of the Polish army.

M. Clemenceau. It is commanded by French officers, whom we can recall.

Mr. Lloyd George. If this message isn't sent directly to General Haller, he must, in any case, be sent a copy.

President Wilson. I will change my telegram by adding that the Polish state can only be fully established with our consent and that the heads of the Allied and Associated governments accept and support the terms of the armistice proposed by the Commission on Polish Affairs.

M. Clemenceau. You won't speak to them any more of the blockade?

President Wilson. Yes, indeed! What I am proposing is only an addition.

M. Clemenceau. Your text seems a little harsh. I understand the Ukrainians, but I would like to hear what M. Paderewski has to say.

Mr. Lloyd George. The Poles are doing everything required to revive Bolshevism, just at the very time when it is about to die. We have already heard M. Paderewski; the Ukrainians explained themselves to us for the first time today.

M. Clemenceau. You never heard M. Paderewski on the terms of the armistice. When is he coming to Paris?

General Le Rond. He will be here in two days.

M. Clemenceau. In any case, the message that you have prepared must be sent to M. Piłsudski.

President Wilson. And clearly indicate that we, the heads of governments, entirely approve of the terms of the armistice, whilst recalling that the existence of Poland and the determination of her borders depend on us.

Mr. Lloyd George. We have the right to speak in this manner at a time when we are going to have to struggle with the Germans to impose acceptance of their new border on the Polish side upon them.

President Wilson. I will revise the draft of the telegram to the Polish government.

M. Clemenceau. If you wish, I will take care of the telegram to General Piłsudski and to General Haller.

Mr. Lloyd George. The latter will only have the object of asking for information about the rumors which come to us on the matter of the Polish offensive.

President Wilson. Will you send it to General Haller through General Piłsudski?

Mr. Lloyd George. I fear that, in those circumstances, it would never arrive.

M. Clemenceau. I will send it to General Haller through the French liaison officer whom we have placed at his side.

—Reading by President Wilson of the reply, drafted by Lord Curzon, to the note from the German delegation[4] concerning the economic consequences of the peace treaty.*

President Wilson. I favor letting the German experts meet with ours so they may receive an explanation of the economic clauses which they are interpreting erroneously.

M. Clemenceau. They will think that this concession is a sign of weakness.

President Wilson. On the other hand, if the peace isn't signed, it will be a calamity for the entire world. We will have to extend our occupation of Germany; our war expenditures will be prolonged, our peoples will reproach us for not having consented to any reasonable agreement that could have avoided this new effort. If we can clearly show the Germans that the burden imposed upon them is no more than that which will weigh on other nations, that might induce them to sign.

M. Clemenceau. Don't look upon the situation so gloomily: they won't sign; but as soon as our troops are set in motion, they will have the excuse they seek, and they'll sign.

Mr. Lloyd George. I think that the excuse they are seeking is, rather, a concession on our part. Should this concession involve coal, reparations? They will probably make proposals to us. We'll have to study them. But it is better first to await their reply. Let's

*H., *PPC*, V, 800ff.

[4] This reply to the German note, cited in LXXXV, n. 1, is printed as Appendix II to these notes.

not forbid ourselves, however, to give them some explanations when they present their counterproposals to us.

M. Clemenceau. We'll see. In any case, the reply drafted by Lord Curzon seems good to me.

President Wilson. Yes; but it doesn't yield an inch on the treaty. The financial delegates who are gathered at the Château de Villette round Herr Melchior are intelligent men; they represent the element in Germany which would like the recovery of business and desires above all to avoid disorder. They are desperately impatient to see the peace signed, and they will listen to our experts if we put them in touch with them.

You know that our American experts don't believe that the reparation plan provided for by the treaty will yield the results we desire. If our experts can make the Germans understand the powers given to the Reparation Commission, if they can show them that this commission will have the right, in many cases, to make the necessary adjustments, that could help the German delegation to sign.

M. Clemenceau. You are entirely right; but we shouldn't put ourselves in the position of supplicants. The Germans have announced a counterplan: let's wait for it, we will see what it contains and what will have to be done.

Mr. Lloyd George. You will perhaps find it to your advantage to clarify different points through meetings of German and Allied experts.

M. Clemenceau. If it is necessary to take that decision at that time, we'll take it.

President Wilson. It wouldn't be an act of weakness on our part: it is a purely practical question.

Mr. Lloyd George. Like M. Clemenceau, I think it necessary to wait for the German counterproposal; they haven't made one yet, they have confined themselves to criticism, without practical suggestions.

President Wilson. What I fear is discovering, at the end of ten years, that our settlement doesn't work.

—Sir Maurice Hankey reads the text of the telegram to be sent to General Piłsudski and to General Haller.[5]

M. Clemenceau. A few words should be added recalling the com-

---

[5] It asked whether it was true that Haller's army was engaged in operations against the Ukrainians in eastern Galicia. It is printed in *PWW*, Vol. 59, p. 360.

mitment taken by General Haller not to send his troops to the Ukrainian front.

I'll send a copy of this text to General Villemain, who is General Haller's chief of staff, so that he can communicate it to the latter.

{ A P P E N D I X I }[6]

PARIS, MAY 19TH, 1919.

Telegram.

From: The President of the Peace Conference.
To: General Piłsudski, Head of the Polish State.

The Council of the Principal Allied and Associated Powers feel that it is their duty to call the attention of the Government of Poland to facts which are giving them the greatest concern and which may lead to consequences for Poland which the Council would deeply deplore. The boundary between Poland and the Ukraine is under consideration and it is as yet undetermined, and the Council has more than once informed the Polish Government that they would regard any attempt either by Poland or by the Ukrainian authorities to determine it, or to prejudice its determination, by the use of force, as a violation of the whole spirit and an arbitrary interference with the whole purpose of the present Conference of Peace, to which Poland, at least has consented to leave the decision of questions of this very sort. The Council has, therefore, more than once insisted that there should be an armistice on the Ukrainian front, arranged in Paris and under the advice of Council itself. The Polish military authorities, while acquiescing in principle, have in effect insisted upon such conditions as would amount to a settlement of the very questions in controversy, and have continued to use force in maintenance of their claims. This has inevitably made the impression on the minds of the members of the Council that the Polish authorities were in effect, if not in purpose, denying and rejecting the authority of the Conference of Peace. The Council feel it their duty, therefore, in the most friendly spirit but with the most solemn earnestness, to say to the Polish authorities that, if they are not willing to accept the guidance and decisions of the Conference

---

[6] Printed in *ibid.*, pp. 359-60.

of Peace in such matters, the Governments represented in the Council of the Principal Allied and Associated Powers will not be justified in supplying Poland any longer with supplies or assistance of any kind. If it is her deliberate purpose to set at naught the counsel proffered by the Conference, its authority can no longer it is feared be made serviceable to her.

{ A P P E N D I X II }[7]

SUGGESTED REPLY TO GERMAN NOTE ON THE ECONOMIC EFFECT OF THE PEACE TREATY

Redraft by Lord Curzon.

1. The Allied Powers have received and have given careful attention to the report of the Commission appointed by the German Government to examine the economic conditions of the Treaty of Peace.

This Report appears to them to contain a very inadequate presentation of the facts of the case, to be marked in parts by great exaggeration, and to ignore the fundamental considerations arising both out of the incidence and the results of the war, which explain and justify the terms that it is sought to impose.

2. The German Note opens with the statement that the industrial resources of Germany were inadequate before the war for the nourishment of a population of 67 millions, and it argues as though this were the total for which with diminished resources she will still be called upon to provide. This is not the case. The total population of Germany will be reduced by not less than six million persons in the non-German territories which it is proposed to transfer. It is the needs of this smaller aggregate that we are called upon to consider.

3. Complaint is made in the German Note that Germany is required to surrender her merchant tonnage, existing or in course of construction, and that a prior claim is made upon her shipbuilding capacity for a limited term of years. No mention, however, is made of the fact that a considerable portion of the smaller tonnage of Germany is left to her unimpaired; and it seems to have entirely escaped the notice of her spokesmen that the sacrifice of her larger shipping is the inevitable and necessary penalty imposed upon her for the ruthless campaign which, in defi-

[7] Printed in *ibid.*, pp. 362-66.

ance of all law and precedent, she waged during the last two years of the war upon the mercantile shipping of the world. As a partial offset against the 12¾ million tons of shipping sunk, it is proposed to transfer 4 million tons of German shipping. In other words, the shipping which it is proposed to take from Germany constitutes less than one-third of that which was wantonly destroyed. The universal shortage of merchant shipping is the result, not of the terms of peace, but of the action of Germany, and no surprise can reasonably be felt if she is called upon to bear her share—and it is a very moderate share—of a loss for which her own criminal deeds have been responsible.

4. Great stress is laid upon the proposal that on the Eastern side Germany shall be deprived of the Regions specially concentrated to the production of wheat and potatoes. This is true. But the Note fails altogether to observe that there is nothing in the Peace Treaty to prevent either the continued production of these commodities in the areas in question, or their importation into Germany. On the contrary the free admission of the products of the Eastern districts is provided for during a period of five years. Moreover, it is fortunate for Germany that these Regions have lost none of their productivity owing to the ravages of war. They have escaped the shocking fate which was dealt out by the German armies to the corresponding territories in Belgium and France on the West, and Poland, Russia, Roumania and Serbia in the East. There appears to be no reason why their produce should not continue to find a market on German soil.

5. Stress is laid upon the proposed restriction in the import of Phosphates. It is, however, forgotten, that Germany has never produced but has always imported the Phosphates of which she stands in need. Nor is there anything in the terms of peace which will prevent or hinder the importation of phosphates into Germany in the future. Other countries, which do not produce phosphates, are also compelled to import them in common with many other products from the outside; and the only difference in the two situations will arise from the relative degree of wealth or impoverishment in the countries concerned.

6. The German Note makes special complaint of the deprivation of coal, and asserts that nearly one-third of the production of the existing German coal mines will be lost. But it omits to notice that one-fourth of the pre-war consumption of German coal was in the territories which it is now proposed to transfer. Further it fails to take into account the production of Lignite, 80 million tons of which were produced annually in Germany before the war, and none of which is derived from the transferred territories. Neither is any reference made to the fact that the output of coal in the non-transferred districts was rapidly increasing before the war, and that there is no reason to doubt that under proper management there will be a continuing increase in the future.

7. But should not the coal situation be viewed from a different and wider standpoint? It cannot be forgotten that among the most wanton acts of devastation perpetrated by the German armies during the war was the almost complete destruction by her of the coal supplies of Northern France. An entire industry was obliterated with a calculation and a savagery which it will take many years to repair. The result has been a grave and prolonged shortage of coal in Western Europe. There can be no reason in equity why the effect of this shortage should be borne exclusively by the Allied nations who were its victims, or why Germany who deliberately made herself responsible for the deficiency should not to the full limit of her capacity make it good.

8. Stress is also laid upon the hardships alleged to be inflicted upon Germany by the necessity of importing in future iron ores and zinc. It is not understood why Germany should be supposed to suffer from conditions to which other countries contentedly submit. It would appear to be a fundamental fallacy that the political control of a country is essential in order to produce a reasonable share of its products. Such a proposal finds no foundation in economic law or in history.

9. The Allied Powers cannot accept the speculative estimate presented to them in the German Note of the future conditions of German industry as a whole. This estimate appears to them to be characterized and vitiated by palpable exaggerations. No note is taken of the fact that the economic disaster produced by the war is wide-spread, and, indeed, universal. Every country is called upon to suffer. There is no reason why Germany, which was responsible for the war, should not suffer also. She must for this reason realise that her economic, in common with her political and military existence, must be conducted henceforward on a reduced and lower plane. The German Note tabulates and aggravates every contemplated deprivation of material, and endeavours to paint a picture of unrelieved gloom. But it fails, as already mentioned, to make any allowance for the fact that the present population of Germany will be diminished by 6,000,000 and that there will consequently be that less number of people to provide for, to feed and to clothe.

10. Similarly, as regards the population of the future, no reliance can be placed on the data which are contained in the German Note. On the one hand, it is sought to prove that emigration from Germany will be necessary, but that few countries will receive the intending emigrants. On the other hand, it is sought to show that there will be a flood of Germans returning to their native land to live under the conditions which have already been described as intolerable. It would be unwise to attach too much weight to either speculation.

11. Finally, the German Note rashly asserts that the Peace Conditions will "logically bring about the destruction of several millions of persons in Germany," in addition to those who have perished in the war or who are alleged to have lost their lives in consequence of the blockade. Against the war losses of Germany might very fairly be placed the far greater losses which her initiative and conduct of the war have inflicted upon the Allied countries, and which have left an ineffaceable mark upon the manhood of Europe. On the other hand, the figures and the losses alleged to have been caused by the blockade are purely hypothetical. The German estimate of future losses, which, though it is described as logical, appears to be no less fantastic, could be accepted only if the premises upon which it is presumed to rest are accepted also. But they are entirely fallacious. There is not the slightest reason to believe that a population is destined to be permanently disabled because it will be called upon in future to trade across its frontiers instead of producing what it requires from within. A country can both become and can continue to be a great manufacturing country without producing the raw materials of its main industries. Such is the case, for instance, with Great Britain, which imports at least one-half of her food supplies and the great preponderance of her raw materials from abroad. There is no reason whatever why Germany under the new conditions should not build up for herself a position both of stability and prosperity in the European world. Her territories have suffered less than those of any other Continental belligerent state during the war. Indeed, so far as pillage or devastation is concerned, they have not suffered at all. Their remaining and untouched resources, supplemented by the volume of import trade, should be adequate for recovery and development on a modest but sufficient scale.

12. The German reply also ignores the immense relief that will be caused to her people in the struggle for recovery by the enforced reduction of her military armaments in future. Hundreds

of thousands of her inhabitants, who have hitherto been engaged either in training for armies or in producing instruments of destruction, will henceforward be available for peaceful avocations and for increasing the industrial productiveness of the nation. For no boon should Germany be more grateful.

13. But the first condition of any such recuperation would appear to be that Germany should recognise the facts of the present state of the world, which she has been mainly instrumental in creating, and realise that she cannot escape unscathed. The share which she is being called upon to bear of the enormous calamity that has befallen the world has been apportioned by the victorious Powers, not to her deserts, but solely to her ability to bear it. All the nations of Europe are now bearing burdens and suffering from losses which are almost more than they can carry. These burdens and losses have been forced upon them by the aggression of Germany. It is right that Germany, which was responsible for the origin of these calamities, should make them good to the utmost of her capacity. Her hardships will arise not from the conditions of peace, but from the acts of those who provoked and prolonged the war. Those who were responsible for the war cannot escape its just consequences.

Villa Majestic,
Paris
May 21st, 1919.

LXXXVIII

Conversation between President Wilson and MM. Clemenceau and Lloyd George*

MAY 22, 1919, 11 A.M.

THE QUESTION OF SYRIA

—General Sir Henry Wilson is introduced.

M. Clemenceau. I will confine myself to presenting facts. It was the Sykes-Picot Treaty which determined the political atmosphere in Syria. When I went to London last fall, since there were then difficulties between the English and the French, which I do not

*H., *PPC*, V, 807ff.

wish to bring up again, I asked Mr. Lloyd George what his last word was. He told me without hesitation that he wanted Mosul to be included in the British zone of influence; I told him that I was ready to impose this solution on the French Ministry of Foreign Affairs.

A little later, a negotiation took place between M. Bérenger and an English representative who specialized, like him, in petroleum questions, for the establishment of a pipeline from the wells of the interior to the coast of Syria. I don't know much about this negotiation, and I won't speak of it any longer. All I can say is that it is completely distinct from the question of the railroad. It was a question of building an oil pipeline towards Tripoli, in the interest of both buyers and sellers.

Whilst I was in London, Mr. Lloyd George also spoke to me about Palestine, which was supposed in principle to be placed under an international administration. Mr. Lloyd George asked me that Palestine be placed under a British protectorate, with special stipulations regarding the Holy Places. I accepted, with the qualification that the terms concerning the Holy Places be satisfactory to us.

I thought that, after these concessions, everything was settled: the map which I have before me shows me that nothing is settled.

In the Sykes-Picot agreement, an enclave at Haifa was provided for the terminus of a railroad line between the coast of Syria and Mesopotamia. This line was to cross territory administered by France: I am surprised to see that, on this map, the boundary of Palestine extends to the north in such a way as to make the railroad pass entirely through British territory. This isn't the map you showed me in London, and it was on the basis of earlier agreements that I accepted the addition of Mosul to the British zone, the establishment of the British protectorate in Palestine, and, later, the extension of the American mandate over Cilicia, which the Sykes-Picot Treaty assigned to France.

Today, new renunciations are requested of me—after all the concessions I have made—without being negotiated, without even my having been told about them in advance. Why this change? To insure a railroad right of way. I understand very well that England wishes to establish rail communication between Mesopotamia and the Syrian coast. It was anticipated that this railway had to cross territory administered by France; it was what our London agreement provided, and I was ready to subscribe to that solution. But I don't accept the establishment of a boundary which cuts in two the Druse mountain region—one of the areas with which France has the oldest ties of affection—which reduces Syria substantially. I cannot accept this solution.

But the present question is more limited: it is only a question of determining the zones of occupation and, I only want to put my protest on record concerning the final solution.

As for the occupation, we want French troops to occupy all of Syria proper. I won't offer an opinion on the way to accomplish this: I will only say that it must be done in such a way as to avoid any conflict or clash of rightful self-respect. I want this question to be resolved to our mutual satisfaction.

As for sending a commission of inquiry to Syria, I don't want it to take place before the occupation troops have taken their final positions.

Mr. Lloyd George. I would like to know whether the French government requests the complete execution of the Sykes-Picot Treaty, or invokes it only to the extent that this convention can be of use to her in blocking British claims. I recall that, according to this treaty, Damascus, Homs,[1] and Aleppo were to be placed, not in the French zone, but in the Arab state or confederation.

One mustn't be able to refer to the Sykes-Picot Treaty when one desires one thing and to repudiate it when one seeks another. We have all admitted for a long time that this treaty is a bad solution; but if it is admitted that it stands, then France possesses no rights east of Lebanon, she can't plant her flag there, she can't send a single soldier there.

France was invited, on several occasions, to collaborate with us in the conquest of these areas; she refused to do so. All she did was to prevent British troops from landing at Alexandretta, because that city was in the French zone, and the English army certainly had to make a greater effort and undergo heavier losses, because it was impossible for it to use that base, which would have been so serviceable to it. During the entire period when we asked the French to help us carry out the Sykes-Picot Treaty, the French government seemed little disposed to make any effort in that direction. M. Clemenceau himself has told me that this convention is of no value.

M. Clemenceau. The only thing I said was that I didn't think that France could derive any great advantage from it economically.

Mr. Lloyd George. As you know, I had to fight against the Chief of the Imperial General Staff, General Robertson, in order to obtain

---

[1] A communications center on the Damascus-Aleppo road and railroad in central Syria.

the dispatch of troops to the Near East; the General was of the same opinion as M. Clemenceau on this question.

A report was prepared by the Supreme War Council, under the direction of Marshal Foch, with a view to a combined action; but that never took place.

If claims are made on the basis of the Sykes-Picot Treaty, I demand that it be executed in its entirety—and I wonder if you have any right to make claims under it, after having refused to take part in the effort that made its execution possible. If I am answered that France could not act in the Near East because there was too much to do in France, I will remark that the British army also made a considerable effort in France, precisely during the period when we were fighting in the Near East. Our losses, in 1917, whilst General Pétain remained on the defensive and restored order to his army, were 50 per cent higher than those of the French; in 1918 also, we had losses greater than yours.

As for the pipeline, it is essentially an arrangement amongst the groups involved, and I state frankly that I am not committed to it: from the moment M. Clemenceau objects to it, I say that this convention should be annulled. I don't want to help transactions between oil trusts; this one was signed by Mr. Walter Long without my knowledge.

We are reproached for having drawn boundaries on this map different from those which the French had accepted. But the cession of Mosul would be without any value if the line of demarcation across the desert remained as it was. Mosul would be at the mercy of the power which controlled the nearest oases.

As for the immediate decision to be taken, I want to say that, unless the boundary drawn on this map is accepted more or less as it is, I will do nothing before I have received the report of the commission of inquiry. I am ready to accept the verdict of the people themselves; I am equally ready to settle the occupation according to the boundaries indicated on this map, but not otherwise.

M. Clemenceau. You ask me whether I am demanding the execution of the Sykes-Picot agreement. When you asked me for Mosul, you told me: "I am faithful to the treaty; the English government gave its word and won't go back on it: a treaty is a treaty"—and I give my word that Mr. Lloyd George repeated to me several times that he would be faithful to it. He asks me whether this treaty stands. My answer is yes.

Mr. Lloyd George. So you give up Damascus and Aleppo?

M. Clemenceau. When I gave up Mosul, you didn't ask me about the demarcation line across the desert. If you had told me at that time that the cession of Mosul would lead to the yielding of an immense territory, I daresay I would not have agreed to cede Mosul to you.

You assert, furthermore, that the Sykes-Picot Treaty compelled us to participate with you in operations in Turkey: I don't think so. It is perfectly true that I opposed sending troops to far-flung battlefields. When Villers-Cotterêts[2] was threatened, the rest mattered little. You tell us that the British army lost more men than the French army in 1917 and 1918; I won't dispute that, not having the figures at hand. I know too well, and I have always acknowledged it in the most ringing manner, what the English did in France; I assure you that I will be the last not to bear witness of my gratitude to you.

We sent insignificant forces to the Near East, I admit, but they carried our flag. My opinion was and remains that, if the white troops which you sent over there had been thrown against the Germans, the war could have been ended some months earlier.

Today, you confront us with this map: there no longer remains anything of the Skyes-Picot Treaty, contrary to what you told me in London, and the reason is that I began by yielding Mosul to you.

As for the occupation, I don't want to say anything which could provoke a conflict between the military. It is up to you to take your decision. I cannot accept what you present today. You say that you will send your commissioners and that you won't withdraw your troops. Very well. I won't say another word. I think you are wrong; you may think, on your part, that it is I who am wrong. The foremost thought that we have to keep in mind is that of the common interest of the Entente.

What I will tell you frankly is that I will not continue, in any fashion whatsoever, to associate myself with you in that part of the world if mutual commitments are not kept.

You are indignant over the oil convention: I know no more about it than you. It is up to Great Britain to decide what she will do. As for me, I have nothing more to say.

President Wilson. What part do you assign me in this difficult affair? You know my position; I have never admitted or understood the right of France or England to hand these people over to whomever it may be.

Mr. Lloyd George. I accept the decision of the peoples themselves.

[2] In northeastern France near Soissons. It was here that Foch assembled his forces for the Allied offensive that began on July 18, 1918.

President Wilson. We agree on this point, that these people are not capable of governing themselves. They must be helped, in their own interest, by a western power. What we will ask them is which guardianship they prefer.

Mr. Lloyd George. If France doesn't send any commissioners to Syria, we won't send any either. I will accept the decisions of the American commissioners.

Sir Henry Wilson. In these circumstances, France should not continue to send troops to Syria; that could create great difficulties.

Mr. Lloyd George. Certainly; besides, with things remaining in *statu quo*, it is General Allenby who is commander in chief: he'll carry out his responsibilities.

LXXXIX

Conversation between President Wilson and MM. Clemenceau, Lloyd George, Loucheur, Tardieu, Haskins, Sir Eyre Crowe, and Headlam-Morley*

MAY 22, 1919, NOON

THE QUESTION OF THE SAAR

Mr. Lloyd George. Here is the question which we want to resubmit for study by the experts. The German delegates say that, according to the present wording of the treaty, the territory of the Saar would remain with France, even if the people, by plebiscite, pronounced themselves in favor of Germany, in case the latter could not pay back the value of the mines in gold within six months. Thus, for an economic reason, the people would be in actual political servitude.[1] We acknowledge that the German objection is admissible.

President Wilson. At the time of the plebiscite, the people will have to choose between three solutions: annexation to France, return to Germany, or continuation of the arrangement provided for by the treaty. Couldn't we amend the clause in question by

*H., *PPC*, V, 813ff.

[1] The German notes on the Saar are summarized in LXXXI, n. 3.

saying that, if the people vote for return to Germany and Germany is incapable of paying, the arrangement provided by the treaty would be prolonged during the time necessary to insure payment?

M. Tardieu. We have prepared a reply to Count Brockdorff-Rantzau, indicating that, in case the difficulty should arise, the question would be brought before the League of Nations. Our American colleagues proposed the amendment of three lines to this effect, and we don't object to it.

President Wilson. What the Germans fear is not that they will not have the means to pay, but that they will not be able to apply them to that particular object, and they fear the opposition of the Reparation Commission. The necessary amendment must have the effect of forestalling that opposition. It will always be easy to borrow money on the security of the mines themselves, and we can send a special recommendation to that effect to the Reparation Commission.

Mr. Lloyd George. Our reply must clearly show that neither the sovereignty established over this territory nor the right of the people to self-determination depends on a payment made or not.

M. Clemenceau. The new text proposed satisfies you?[2]

Mr. Lloyd George. It is certainly much better than the former one.

Mr. Headlam-Morley. We'll remove the sentence which says that, if Germany doesn't pay in the desired time, sovereignty will pass to France. Even if this eventuality cannot take place, the mere fact of contemplating it would produce a deplorable effect in Germany.

President Wilson. The only question which remains is whether a certain pressure should not be maintained in order to compel the Germans to meet their obligations.

Mr. Lloyd George. In any case, the present wording cannot stand.

President Wilson. It is better to change the wording of the entire paragraph.

Mr. Lloyd George. Certainly, we must have guarantees; but imprisonment for debt is not one we can require.

M. Clemenceau. I think absolutely as you do: we can't make the liberty of a people security for a debt.

M. Tardieu. Couldn't we confine ourselves to saying that the territory won't become German as long as the debt hasn't been paid?

Mr. Lloyd George. It is better that the article should allude exclusively to the ownership of the mines.

M. Clemenceau. I agree.

[2] This text is printed in *PPC*, V, 823-24.

M. Tardieu. We could draw up an amendment indicating that, within one year after the plebiscite, the Reparation Commission will settle the question of payment, if need be, by the liquidation of the mines.

Mr. Lloyd George. Thus the last line would disappear.

M. Tardieu. Yes.

Mr. Lloyd George. It is important to inform the Germans of this amendment.

President Wilson. This is an excellent solution. We would have to change not only the article, but the letter of reply to the German note.

Mr. Lloyd George. It must be clearly stated that it was never our intention to exchange people for gold.

M. Tardieu. We will take up the wording of Paragraphs 1 and 6 again and make the change indicated.

Mr. Lloyd George. We must make use of the concession we are making to the Germans; that could have an effect on German public opinion. They are told that our stipulations concerning the Saar only disguise an annexation; we must seize this opportunity to affirm the contrary. Men who, like Bernstein, are advising the Germans to sign the treaty, will take note of our rectification.

M. Clemenceau. There is another letter in reply to the second German note.[3]

President Wilson. It must be reread in the light of the changes made in the first letter and changed accordingly.

---

[3] Although Mantoux does not record the fact, the Four met at 4 p.m. to examine the redrafts of the replies to the two German notes on the Saar. The revised answer to Brockdorff's note of May 13 denied that the Allied Powers had any intention to transfer peoples from one allegiance to another (quoting the German note) "as though they were but mere things or pawns." The note first commented on the general reasons for the Saar settlement. Most important, it informed the Germans that the Supreme Council had reworded the paragraph of the treaty relating to German recovery of the mines so that if Germany could not pay for the mines in gold, the Reparation Commission could liquidate all or part of the mines in order to recompense France. In any event, sovereignty over the Saar Valley would return to Germany if its inhabitants voted in favor of reunion with that country.

The second revised draft was a note in reply to Brockdorff-Rantzau's note of May 16, 1919. In this revised version, the Four said that the economic arrangements proposed by the German delegation were unworkable and provided none of the guarantees necessary to assure an adequate supply of coal to France.

These notes are printed in *ibid.*, pp. 827-29.

The council decided on May 24, to combine the two notes and send a single reply. The final version is printed in *PWW*, Vol. 59, pp. 458-60.

XC

Conference between President Wilson, MM. Clemenceau, Lloyd George, and Orlando, and the financial experts*

[MAY 22, 1919, 4:15 P.M.]

President Wilson. We have instructed the financial experts to consider the new states formed from the dissolution of the former Austro-Hungarian Empire as being responsible for a portion of the reparations owed by this empire and to calculate, in proportion to territories received, the share of responsibility of each one of them for damages.[1] The experts are of opinion that this system would weigh down these new states with a crushing burden, as heavy as or heavier than that of the countries which suffered most from the war.

Mr. Lloyd George. The Reparation Commission will have the power to grant the necessary reductions.

President Wilson. The greatest difficulty for these new states will be finding credit, which is a good deal more difficult for them than for older and better established states. Some of them are so alarmed at the consequences of such a decision that they are talking about refusing their signature, unless another arrangement is granted them.

From the political point of view, the danger would be to create solidarity between these states and Germany, for they would find themselves with her on the side of the debtors. Furthermore, what we can extract from these new states is very problematic. Their exports will barely suffice to provide them with what is absolutely essential to their economic life. It is less a matter of the impact of what the Reparation Commission can actually decide later on than of the immediate impact of the principle, if we accept it today. If they are responsible as of now for a portion of the debt corresponding to the reparations and uncertain for two years about the amount of that debt, these new states won't be able to find credit and won't know how to manage.

Mr. Lamont. We didn't discuss the principle which was enunciated by the council; we only studied its consequences. Two prob-

*H., PPC, V, 830ff.

[1] The council had before it the reparation clauses of the draft treaty with Austria. They are printed in PPC, V, 836-57.

lems confronted us: that of the credit that must be established for these new states, and, secondly, that of their participation in the reparations owed.

The difficulty stems from the fact that the Reparation Commission will not announce its figures for two years; in the meantime, it will be impossible for these states to find credit, since they won't know the amount of their liability. Moreover, we are afraid that we are creating this difficulty without any practical result.

Mr. Lloyd George. We must ask ourselves, on the one hand, what is right, and, on the other hand, how we can come to the aid of these new states. We have to deal with nations which, voluntarily or not, fought against us. If their freedom was won, it was through the efforts of Great Britain, France, Italy, and the United States. By fighting against the victory which liberated them, they added to their own burden. If they had only remained neutral, that victory could have come a year or two earlier. They provided our enemies, willy-nilly, with three or four million soldiers. During the final period of the war, our propaganda amongst the Czechs and the Yugoslavs produced some rather important results. Nevertheless, the soldiers of Yugoslav nationality fought until the end, and fought very well, in the Austro-Hungarian armies. If they obtained freedom, it was because we won it for them, against themselves.

It would be rather unfair if, after the war, they were in a more favorable condition than we ourselves. Will it be said that a nation of six or seven million cannot compare with a nation of forty million inhabitants and can't be treated in the same way? But we could compare six million Yugoslavs with six million Frenchmen or Italians. Each Italian peasant will have to bear a share of the national debt equal to 300 pounds sterling as a result of the war which liberated the Yugoslavs; it may be that the son of this same peasant who will bear this burden was killed by a Yugoslav soldier in the service of Austria: the latter is free today, thanks to the effort of that Italian peasant—and he will be exempt from all burden? Nothing could be more unjust. If the responsibility of these new peoples is not acknowledged, if they don't shoulder their share of the war costs, those imposed on our populations will be increased by that much more.

It would obviously be an excellent thing for the Yugoslav state or the Czechoslovak state to be born free of all debt. But would that be equally agreeable to the Scottish taxpayer, who, before the war, had never heard of the Yugoslavs? These peoples must assume their share of the burden which the war that granted them their independence left behind it. We all agree to give the Reparation Commission the power to estimate what can be imposed on them without unduly overburdening them.

France and we advanced certain sums to Serbia. Shouldn't the Yugoslavs bear their share of that debt? It isn't Serbia alone, after the frightful losses she suffered, which is our debtor. This question should, moreover, have been clearly raised when we presented our terms to Germany. Will the territories which were part of the former Austro-Hungarian monarchy, and which are today united to Rumania, Poland, or Serbia, have a right to a portion of the reparations owed by Germany to their new fatherlands? That would reduce what should be paid to ourselves, and some of the countries in question are very rich. Bohemia, for example, is one of the best endowed countries of Europe: she has mines and great industries. Transylvania is very rich in forests and ores. Can we admit that these countries should bear no costs, whilst our people will stagger under the weight of their debt? They must assume their fair share of the cost of this great war of liberation, without which they would never have won their freedom. Their present situation is beyond what they could have dreamed of only a few months ago; it is inadmissible that they should throw the whole burden back on us.

President Wilson. It must not be forgotten that this question of reparations is linked to those raised by the financial clauses. According to them, the states in question must assume responsibility for a portion of the prewar Austro-Hungarian debt, and even of the war debt. Under these conditions, these new states will be burdened with a war debt like other countries.

In principle, Mr. Lloyd George is right. But the real question is this: here are new states which cannot live without credit; it is impossible for them to find it if, for two years, they don't know what they owe. It is not a question of exempting them, but of informing them as soon as possible of what they will have to pay, in order to be able to give a basis for absolutely essential credit.

M. Orlando. The decision already taken by the Four on this fundamental question indicated that all parts of the former Austro-Hungarian monarchy had to contribute to the reparation debt: it is that very decision which is being called into question again. All the work done by the experts is disappearing.

Italy, for her part, acknowledged that even the territories which will be annexed to her would bear their share of the Austro-Hungarian debt. But it would be inconceivable for Italy to pay a portion of what is owed by Austria-Hungary, whilst the other states constituted from the fragments of the monarchy paid nothing.

When it was a question of the distribution of the Austro-Hungarian tonnage, Mr. Lloyd George said: "We must consider the ships of Trieste as enemy ships." I accept this point of view. But if the other Austro-Hungarian states are no longer considered as enemies, I request equality of treatment for the areas which concern us.

Let's look at the heart of the matter. Mr. Lloyd George has said with much heat what I myself think. In practice, it is quite possible that these new states can pay nothing. But the question is important from a moral point of view. Can Italy be told that she will emerge from the war overwhelmed with financial obligations, whereas two thirds of what was yesterday still Austria-Hungary would have to pay nothing? That would have such serious consequences that, if one of the states in question threatened not to sign, I request that I be reserved the same right.

President Wilson. This entire discussion is off on the wrong foot, for no one is proposing to exempt the new states, but to determine as soon as possible what each of them must pay.

M. Klotz. It is very difficult to establish absolute figures today. Articles 10 and 14 of our text provide special advantages for these states: no delivery of bonds will be requested of them, as we have demanded of Germany; they shall have no payment to make before 1921; they are guaranteed against any increase in their obligations resulting from the application of the principle of interdependence; the Reparation Commission will have the right to remit all or part of their debt. It can therefore be said that we have tried to favor them. It will be up to the Reparation Commission to grant them all desirable delays and accommodations.

Mr. Lloyd George. The problem is a little different from the German problem; the total of reparations is much less, and the necessary investigations will be much less complicated. Why, in these conditions, provide a period of two years? Can't this work be done in six months? Like M. Klotz, I think that we can't announce even arbitrary figures today; but it would be worth the trouble to make an effort to determine the figures in a shorter period.

President Wilson. We should try as of now to establish a general system of credit into which these new states should enter. Will the Reparation Commission be the same as for German reparations?

Mr. Lloyd George. That seems impossible to me: the Reparation

Commission will already have an overwhelming task; another one must be created for the countries of Austria-Hungary.

President Wilson. It appears difficult to me to create two separate commissions, given the interdependence of the operations which will have to be carried out. But the five members of the Reparation Commission can only give guidance. They will necessarily be surrounded by subcommissions; in these circumstances, it doesn't seem impossible to refer everything involving Austro-Hungarian reparations to them.

Mr. Lloyd George. The idea of a single commission rested upon the premise that everything would be done in the same length of time—two years. If, on the one hand, we have a period of six months, and on the other, a period of two years to fix the debt, two different commissions have to be set up. Not only will the period of time not be the same, but it is essential that we deal with these states in a spirit different from that which will be applied to the German problem.

President Wilson. What I thought was that a special subcommission could be charged with this task.

Mr. Lamont. It is very important to prevent two different commissions from competing in the financial market, where they will have so many operations to carry out. It would be better, indeed, for the Reparation Commission to entrust Austro-Hungarian questions to a special subcommission.

M. Orlando. Undoubtedly, the work of the commission is so extensive that, in any case, it will have to surround itself with a large number of subcommissions; but, like President Wilson, I think that strict coordination is necessary, and that the best thing is to have a single commission, appropriately subdivided.

M. Klotz. Article 3 of our text provides for a single commission. That becomes more difficult if we establish, on the one hand, a period of six months and, on the other, a period of two years. We could decide upon the formation of a special section, entrusted with Austro-Hungarian reparations, which could be established immediately.

President Wilson. In light of the discussion which has just taken place, the experts could themselves work out the details of the desired system.

Mr. Lloyd George. We agree on the principle.

M. Crespi. We ask to return to Article 232. The text proposed for the treaty with Austria is thus worded:

"Not included are the damages sustained by the states which, at the time these damages occurred, were not yet recognized by the majority of the Allied and Associated Governments."

This text is different from the one which was inserted in the German treaty, where the right of each state is limited to the period during which it was belligerent. This text seems preferable to us: certain countries suffered a great deal before they entered the war, and the amendment gives them the right to claim reparation for damages at whatever time they may have taken place.

Mr. Lloyd George. What does M. Crespi request?

M. Crespi. We are satisfied with the text adopted for the Austrian treaty; but we would like it to be substituted, in the German treaty, for the text previously adopted.

Mr. Lloyd George. It doesn't seem to me that this arrangement can be applied to the case of Germany.

M. Orlando. The question raised here is the same as in the treaty with Germany: therefore, the solution must be the same—whichever text you prefer. In the German treaty, there was a discrepancy, which we noticed and corrected, between the French version and the English version. This discrepancy led, when we drafted the Austrian treaty, to the adoption of another text. It is necessary either to put in the German treaty the text which the experts unanimously accepted for the Austrian treaty, or else, on the contrary, to put in the Austrian treaty the text which appears in the German treaty.

Mr. Lloyd George. I have a question to ask. Take the thirteen months during which Italy was not at war with Germany: could she make claims against Germany for that period? That would be the result of the text presented to us. The only reasonable principle is to admit damages for the period during which each power was a belligerent.

M. Orlando. If we introduce the English text into the German treaty, I simply ask that it be transferred as it stands to the treaty with Austria.

To the question raised by Mr. Lloyd George, I will reply: we wanted to base the entire system of reparation on the principle of the interdependence of debts. With respect to the tonnage of the Adriatic, Mr. Lloyd George told us: "We grant you absolute interdependence; you can't, at the same time, claim privileged treatment for the Adriatic." So be it! But in this case, interdependence mustn't be limited. The difficulty of the formula which Mr. Lloyd George prefers is that, for each damage, it would be necessary to determine the moment when it was sustained.

I will point out that it wasn't the Italian delegation which prescribed the text presented to you today. It was all our experts who adopted it unanimously. We could ask them what their motives were: in any case, an exclusively Italian concern did not lead them to it.

M. Crespi. On February 21, 1916, my own factory was bombed by a German airplane, and we were not at war with Germany. Many Italian boats were sunk immediately after the declaration of war on Austria, and we will never know whether by Austrian or German submarines. We took many German prisoners before our declaration of war on Germany: there was belligerence *de facto*.

According to the principle of interdependence, Germany is responsible for all damages committed against any one of us. If the English text proposed for the treaty with Germans is retained, that reduces the extent of interdependence.

Mr. Lloyd George. Looking at it from the point of view of strictest justice, can we ask Germany to repair the damages which a country suffered before it was in a state of war with her? We asked Italy, as soon as she aligned herself on our side, to declare war on Germany. For her own reasons, she declared war on Germany only a year later. During that entire year, she continued to send goods to Germany and to allow goods destined for Germany to pass through her territory, which delayed and reduced the effect of our blockade. Can Italy ask Germany to indemnify her for damages sustained during this period? What would we reply to the objection which the Germans would naturally make to us?

It is probable that, during the year which preceded the declaration of war by Italy, their submarines sank Italian ships: they also sank neutral ships. There is no way of justifying claims for the reparation of damages suffered at a time when Italy was not at war with Germany. That is a position which cannot be defended. We are compelled to impose a rather harsh treaty upon Germany: it must at least be fair and, for myself, I could not defend such a provision.

If you had declared war on Germany at the same time as on Austria, she would today be responsible for all your damages. I regret the losses that M. Crespi suffered; but if you had been certain that Germany sent airplanes to bomb your factories, you would have declared war or, as the neutrals often did, claimed compensation.

Mr. Lamont. It is only fair to say that, concerning Austria, the experts did indeed accept the text which limits the right to reparation, not to the belligerent states, but to the states recognized as such by the Allied and Associated Powers. We thought we understood that the other text had remained in abeyance as a result of a misunderstanding.

Mr. Lloyd George. I hold to the English text of the treaty with Germany, which was approved by the council.

M. Klotz. In that case, it is necessary, in the German treaty, to rewrite the French version on the basis of the English version.

M. Orlando. If that is the way it is to be, I ask only that the same thing be placed in the treaty with Austria as in the treaty with Germany, the right to reparation being limited to the period during which each state was a belligerent.

—*This proposal is adopted.*

M. Klotz. Concerning the merchant marine, we should point out the difference between the treaty with Austria and the treaty with Germany. We asked the Germans to hand over to us their entire merchant fleet, except for half of the ships of less than 1,600 tons and three quarters of the fishing boats. Since Austria is today a continental country without any contact with the sea, she has no need of a merchant fleet.

As for distribution, the French and American delegations agree to recommend a convention that would allow a part of this tonnage, greater than that which would result from a distribution without any priority, to be granted to the Adriatic ports. Since the English delegation objected to this proposal, we ask the heads of governments to decide.

M. Orlando. I leave to the French and American delegates the task of explaining their plan, which I thank them for having put on the table. If the principle which they envisage is accepted, the details of execution can only be determined by the experts.

I couldn't conceive of a worse fate being assigned to the tonnage of the Adriatic—which belongs, in fact, for the most part, to Italians and Yugoslavs—than the one assigned to German tonnage. The Germans are left one half of the ships between 1,000 and 1,600 tons and three fourths of the fishing fleet. In contrast, the tonnage of the Adriatic would be confiscated altogether, fishing boats included, with a view towards a general distribution. Now, this small tonnage of the fishing fleet amounts to a total of 60,000 tons: what is that in relation to the merchant fleet of the world? It would be inhuman and unjustifiable to take the boats away from fishermen of the Adriatic coast, whilst we are not taking those of German fishermen of the Baltic and the North Sea.

You reply that we are dealing with Austria, and that Austria has no more ports. But will the treaty eliminate the existence of the coast and the ports and the sailors and the fishermen? Do you want to consider those people as friends or as enemies? You can say that, as long as the treaty is not signed, they are, legally speaking, enemies. Very well! But then, at least treat them as well as the Boches!

Concerning the small tonnage, its distribution amongst all the Allies is of no interest, whilst it is of vital importance to the fishermen of the Adriatic coast that these boats remain in their hands.

Mr. Lloyd George. I won't insist upon the fishing fleet. We don't want to take it away from those who are using it. If we are especially interested in this question of the distribution of enemy tonnage, it is because of the substantial losses which we suffered. Two countries are particularly concerned in this matter because of their losses in the Mediterranean: they are Great Britain and Greece. Of the ships we lost in the Mediterranean, many were sunk whilst carrying to Italy what was absolutely essential to her. We placed our tonnage at the disposal of the entire world, and we have the right to recover at least a part of the very serious losses we suffered.

But as soon as it is a question of distributing enemy tonnage, requests for exceptions arise from all sides: in favor of the United States, in favor of Brazil, in favor of Portugal, in favor of Italy. The impression would be very unfortunate in Great Britain if the English public could think that our allies, by keeping the greatest part of enemy tonnage for themselves, prevent us from receiving the reparation due to us according to the principle of equity. Concerning the fishing fleet, I have nothing to say. But I hope this council won't accept without more thorough discussion the proposal to withdraw the entire merchant fleet of the Adriatic from the total which will be divided amongst us.

We lost eight million tons due to enemy aggression; all our allies altogether lost three million. Maritime transport is our trade and calling par excellence. I ask that you allow me to consult the Board of Trade on this question. I am ready to make a concession if it is judged possible. The most important thing is to avoid giving British public opinion, which is particularly sensitive on this point, the impression of an unfavorable treatment of England's vital interests.

President Wilson. All that is being proposed now is to discuss what could possibly be done to accommodate the interests of the people of the Adriatic.

Mr. Lloyd George. That discussion is all right with me. I ask only that the greatest possible consideration be given to the losses we suffered, and also to those of Greece.

M. Clemenceau. Were the Greeks belligerents when they sustained those losses?

Mr. Lloyd George. If Greece was not on our side, her merchant fleet was; for, in fact, we had requisitioned it with the approval of M. Vénisélos, whose authority extended over the entire Aegean islands. Greece suffered very heavy losses.

President Wilson. It is thus decided that this question will be sent back to the experts and that Mr. Lloyd George will consult the Board of Trade.

—*This proposal is adopted.*

—*This text submitted by the commission is retained, except with respect to the fishing fleet. An agreement about the distribution of the Austrian merchant fleet will be prepared with the help of the English government.*

Lord Sumner. The Yugoslavs request that everything in the museums, universities, libraries, and archival repositories of Austria, concerning especially the countries of the former Austro-Hungarian monarchy now separated from Austria, be divided amongst them. I replied that this question didn't fall under the heading of reparation. It seems impossible to me to sanction this dislocation before knowing if these new states have enough character of permanence to guarantee the preservation of objects which are of such a kind as to interest the entire world. I would suggest a text which would not impose upon Austria the cession requested by the Yugoslavs, but which would allow friendly negotiations for the cession of objects of local interest.

M. Clemenceau. In the general interest, it is necessary to avoid the dispersal of the incomparable collections in Vienna.

Mr. Lloyd George. If the proposal is limited to objects or documents which are of special interest to each of these countries, I see no objection.

I propose that the reparations owed by Bulgaria be referred to the commission which has just dealt with this question concerning Austria.

—*This proposal is adopted.*

President Wilson. I ask that this commission be authorized to get in touch with the delegation of each of the new states involved.

—*This proposal is adopted.*

XCI

Conversation between President Wilson and MM. Clemenceau, Lloyd George, and Orlando*

MAY 23, 1919, 11 A.M.

M. Clemenceau. I have received two notes from the Germans, including a new one on labor legislation.¹ I don't see the use of beginning this discussion all over again.
Mr. Lloyd George. Have we informed them that we are disposed to admit them to the International Labour Organization fairly soon?
M. Clemenceau. We have.

The second note concerns private property,² and I propose to refer it to the experts.

I have been informed that Japan is going to propose that we recognize the Omsk government. It seems to me that we must go ahead with it.

---

*H., PPC, V, 861ff.

[1] U. K. C. von Brockdorff-Rantzau to G. Clemenceau, May 22, 1919, printed in PPC, V, 869-72. In this comment on the reply of the Allied and Associated governments of May 14, 1919 (LXXV, n. 2), to the German note on international labor legislation of May 10, 1919 (see ibid., n. 1), the German delegation affirmed its opposition to the proposed treaty's provisions for an international labor organization. It repeated its previous request for the convocation of an international labor conference at Versailles as part of the peace negotiations in order to enable the representatives of the workers of all countries to vote on the issues concerning them and to reconcile the labor provisions of the peace treaty with the proposals of the German government and the resolutions adopted by the International Trade Unions Conference in Bern in February 1919.

[2] U. K. C. von Brockdorff-Rantzau to G. Clemenceau, May 22, 1919, printed in PPC, V, pp. 865-69. The German delegation stated that it could not accept in principle the provisions of the preliminary peace treaty which dealt with German private property within the reach of the Allied and Associated governments, since they violated "the most elementary conceptions of a peace of Right." The German delegation claimed that the entire matter involved questions of private law which ought to be excluded from considerations motivated by political power. In particular, the German delegation objected to the provisions of Articles 297 and 298 which stipulated that, whereas all Allied nationals would be entitled to full compensation from Germany for damages caused to them during the war by Germany's enemy alien laws, all measures taken against German private property in enemy countries during the war were to remain legally binding even after the signing of the treaty, and German nationals in enemy countries were denied any claim to compensation.

Mr. Lloyd George. The British government has received the same information.

President Wilson. Does Japan propose to recognize the government of Admiral Kolchak as that of all of Russia? As for me, I couldn't do it.

M. Clemenceau. I think it desirable, in this matter, not to leave the initiative to Japan.

Mr. Lloyd George. The telegram prepared by Mr. Philip Kerr to be sent in our name to Admiral Kolchak is ready, and we can study the text this afternoon.

M. Clemenceau. Another question arises: that of Luxembourg. We prevented Luxembourg from holding a plebiscite on the political question: it appears to be necessary to prevent her also from holding a referendum on the question of economic union with France or Belgium.

President Wilson. In conformity with our decision of the other day, I invited Luxembourg to send us a delegation. I have received no reply yet.

M. Clemenceau. The French government doesn't wish the economic question to be raised in Luxembourg. For if, through a referendum, the people of Luxembourg should declare themselves in favor of economic union with France, we wouldn't want to say yes, because we don't want to do anything which seems contrary to the interests of Belgium, and, on the other hand, it would be very awkward to say no. We thus have only one way out: that is to avoid having the question raised now.

President Wilson. I hoped this delegation would visit us about now.

Mr. Lloyd George. When did you invite them?

President Wilson. Last week.

Mr. Lloyd George. The question concerns the people of Luxembourg themselves; our only policy must be nonintervention.

President Wilson. At the same time, any difficulty with Belgium must be avoided.

Mr. Lloyd George. If Luxembourg adopts a solution which doesn't draw her towards Belgium, it won't be our fault.

M. Clemenceau. Be assured that the Belgians would blame France for it. They are only now beginning to believe us when we tell them that we don't wish to annex Luxembourg. It wouldn't do for this justified impression to be contradicted the very next day. France's prime interest is to maintain her good relations with Belgium. I want a very clear situation; I don't want to appear to be playing a double game.

We could wait two or three days more for the Luxembourg delegation, and, if it doesn't appear, President Wilson could renew his invitation.

Mr. Lloyd George. That is the best thing to do.

M. Clemenceau. We are going to discuss again the question of the future military forces of Austria and the new states of Central Europe.[3] This question is very delicate. I have moved closer to President Wilson's point of view concerning Austria. For all these small nations, the questions of their financial responsibility and the limitation of their military forces are of capital importance. It will be necessary to review closely the wording of the text we agreed upon concerning the military establishment of each of these states. We must avoid leaving them enough forces so that they can misuse them, but, at the same time we must leave them the means to defend their independence.

President Wilson. There is an unknown factor in that part of the world—Russia. Can't we say that, wherever this factor can come into play, military forces sufficient to fend off any eventuality can be maintained?

M. Clemenceau. The most essential thing is not to hasten too much the disarmament of the states of Central Europe. The best thing may be to put this question in the hands of the League of Nations.

President Wilson. The League of Nations won't have the means which we have at our disposal today to impose its will.

Mr. Lloyd George. It can exclude the states which don't obey it: that is a serious sanction for all these small states.

M. Clemenceau. I would like the financial clauses of the Austrian treaty not to be presented to us before a revision in which M. Loucheur has participated. The present text only reproduces those in the treaty with Germany. Now different problems are involved, and they must be taken into account.

M. Orlando. I think it is primarily a question of coordinating the financial clauses with the reparation clauses.

M. Clemenceau. That's it.

—M. Cahen-Salvador and the members of the Inter-Allied Military Council are introduced.*

President Wilson. Is there any question about the clauses of the Austrian treaty relating to prisoners of war?[4] I suppose they are drafted in the same manner as in the German treaty.

*H., PPC, V, 873ff.

[3] For earlier discussion of this matter, see LXXX.

[4] They are printed in PPC, V, 882-85.

The proposed articles stipulate only the return to their homes and hearths of "Austrian" prisoners, in the strict sense of the word. Shouldn't we extend this provision to Yugoslav, Polish, etc., prisoners, who were part of the Austrian army?

M. Cahen-Salvador. The commission assumed that it could only make provision for Austrian prisoners, because it is with Austria that we are dealing, and we cannot deliver prisoners of other nationalities to her. But it appeared impossible to us to propose the repatriation of Austrians without asking the Supreme Council to decide about the immediate repatriation of Yugoslavs, Poles, Czechs, Transylvanians. We present this recommendation to you after having heard the governments concerned, which have unanimously insisted that we should do it. It is at one and the same time a measure of justice and high policy that we urge you to undertake.

The French government has already taken certain steps regarding prisoners belonging to friendly nations. The English have repatriated the prisoners from Schleswig. Those Poles, Czechs, and Yugoslavs who, as our prisoners, didn't volunteer to serve in our armies, were grouped in camps where they received favorable treatment. But they are still prisoners, and it would appear impossible to delay their liberation. The Italian delegation had some scruples about joining in our recommendation, because it thinks that this question is outside the treaty with Austria.

M. Orlando. We all agree on this point, that the question raised is outside the preliminaries of peace with Austria, since it is a question of prisoners who are not of Austrian nationality. In order to understand the Italian point of view, we must distinguish between fact and law.

In fact, Italy didn't wait for this appeal to create very favorable conditions for prisoners of certain nationalities, and even to send them back home. We liberated almost all the Czechs, over 40,000, many Poles, Rumanians, and also some Yugoslavs. Those who are still prisoners enjoy special treatment, as in France. The difficulty which delays their repatriation is, above all, that of transportation. We want to send back as many of these prisoners as possible. Thus, in fact, we spontaneously began what is being asked today, and we will do our best to continue it and to speed it up.

In law, since the liberation of prisoners is linked to the conclusion of peace, it is a question of knowing in each case when there will be peace. For many parts of the former Austro-Hungarian Empire, there will be peace when the boundaries are determined. At that time, legally, the liberation has to take place. That moment cannot be delayed. Failing that, I could not accept the obligation, legally, to liberate these prisoners. I am freeing them in practice; but I could accept an international obligation to do so only when we are at peace with their respective countries. That would, moreover, be practically impossible in a certain number of cases. How can the nationality of certain prisoners be determined before the boundaries are established? Should such and such a prisoner be treated as a Rumanian, or as a Hungarian? As a Yugoslav or as an Austrian?

In conclusion, Italy has already carried out a great deal of repatriation; there is no question that, as soon as the boundaries are fixed, all prisoners without exception have to be set free. But before that time, I could not accept a formal obligation. I have just explained why. If this way of looking at things raises some objection, I ask that the question be discussed amongst the heads of governments.

President Wilson. In any case, we can let these poor devils go home.

M. Orlando. All right, and I accept the recommendation of the commission, which corresponds to what I am already doing. I only state that I can take no commitment which legally binds me.

President Wilson. If, after the Austrians are set free, prisoners belonging to other nationalities were detained, that would create the impression that we wanted to treat them as enemies; that impression would help to increase the dangers of the situation in southeastern Europe.

M. Orlando. I state that I absolutely rule out this possibility. When the Austrian prisoners are repatriated, all others will be as well. The only thing I cannot accept is a formal obligation.

President Wilson. Right now, it is only a matter of our agreeing on a practical measure.

M. Orlando. In that case, we are completely in agreement.

—M. Cahen-Salvador withdraws.

President Wilson. We come to the naval and military clauses.[5]

M. Orlando. It would be helpful to hear a report from our military advisers. I see that, whilst including figures which conform to our last instructions, they declare that they are retaining those

---

[5] The Four were considering at this point a report by the military representatives on the Supreme War Council, dated May 21, 1919, on the strength of the armies to be allowed for Austria, Hungary, Bulgaria, Czechoslovakia, Yugoslavia, Rumania, Poland, and Greece; and drafts of the military and naval clauses of the Austrian peace treaty. They are printed in *ibid.*, pp. 885-95.

which they had earlier proposed. Mustn't they tell us their reasons?

Mr. Lloyd George. They are clearly indicated in the written report they have provided.

President Wilson. I will ask General Bliss to inform us of the considerations that dictated his position.

General Bliss. The first draft was studied by the Four on May 15 and the question was referred back to the military experts. I was then absent; but I agree with my colleagues.

The figures indicated were based on purely military considerations. Your military advisers took into account, for each country, its population figure, geography, the nature of its land or maritime boundaries, the industrial or agricultural occupations of its inhabitants, etc. Each military delegation, taking these different factors into consideration, proposed a coefficient, and, if there was some difference between our figures, it was inconsiderable.

I realize that we are more or less bound by the figure imposed on Germany. What hindered us was precisely that this figure was not determined in conformity with the opinion of the military experts. I recall that the latter unanimously proposed to leave Germany an army of 200,000 men recruited through the system of one-year service: this was Marshal Foch's plan. The Supreme Council rejected this plan and requested a new report; that report proposed the figure of 140,000 men; the representatives of France requested its reduction to 100,000 men.

I remember that Mr. Lloyd George made a statement indicating that it was not without regret that he was departing from the opinion of his military advisers, but that he wished to take into account the legitimate fears of France. It was in these circumstances that the figure was finally reduced to 100,000 men. I have never seen an argument which justifies this figure from the military point of view, and, consequently, my personal judgment cannot be altered.

Acting on the instructions we received on the fifteenth, we calculated the forces which would be left to each of the states of Central Europe, taking as a base the figure of about 15,000 men for Austria, which had been indicated to us. But in this way we arrive at insignificant contingents, and possible disturbances in eastern and central Europe must be anticipated. If they should take place without our having left these countries the means to maintain order themselves, who will do it for them? If the recommendations of your military experts were accepted, the total strength of the armies they would possess would be less than that of the least important of the Allied armies.

I apologize for entering into political considerations; but one cannot disregard this point of view in settling the question. By fixing such low figures for their contingents, you would reduce these states to actual vassalage to the two great continental powers of the Entente: for it is necessary to keep order there, and that can only be done through a French or Italian occupation. I don't believe such a situation would be favorable to world peace; it would lead inevitably to a regrouping of all these states around Germany against the Latins and Anglo-Saxons. This civilization, which we have saved by our efforts, would remain only on the periphery of Europe, where it would run the risk of being one day thrown into the sea. We would then see if the present exaltation over our victory is anything other than the color which rushes to the cheeks of a consumptive sentenced by the doctor. The figures established according to your indications would reduce the peoples of central and eastern Europe to the state of vassals.

Mr. Lloyd George. What does General Bliss propose?

General Bliss. I propose to keep the figure presented by your military experts.

President Wilson. I see that, for Austria, the figure of 15,000 men has been considered as given. For my part, I never accepted it; my figure was 20,000.

Mr. Lloyd George. I even proposed 25,000.

President Wilson. It seems to me that the considerations laid out by General Bliss are important and deserve our serious consideration; no hasty decision should be taken on this question; we must take the time to study it from the political point of view.

M. Clemenceau. I support what President Wilson has just said. I ask that Colonel Hankey give each of us an exact transcript of what General Bliss has just said, so that we can reflect upon it further.

M. Orlando. I agree with you, and what the General has just said has made a great impression upon me.

Mr. Lloyd George. There is no doubt that the Germans will have something to say about the figure of 100,000 men which our preliminary treaty imposes on them: I don't believe they will accept it. Although I myself endorsed it, today I realize, along with General Bliss, that it is a very low figure.

I didn't want to insist upon a higher figure, given the objection made by France; but I now think that 100,000 men to keep order in a country as large as Germany is very little. Since we are undoubtedly going to receive the observations of the Germans in a short time, it is best to wait and consider this entire problem as a whole.

President Wilson. What matters most is that the countries of which we have just spoken be in a position to resist any threat coming from Bolshevik Russia. According to the opinion of our military advisers, the Poles and Rumanians must have the right to keep their troops mobilized under the supervision of the League of Nations as long as the situation in Russia is not clarified.

Mr. Lloyd George. On the other hand, if we allowed all these countries to arm themselves as they liked, the Czechoslovaks could have a million and a half men. The Germans would have only one option: to reach an agreement with them and to try to enlist them against us. An agreement between the Germans and the Slavs is by no means impossible: the Prussians are germanicized Slavs anyway.

President Wilson. Is there any observation on the naval clauses?

Mr. Lloyd George. The only point in abeyance was the question of production of naval matériel in Austria.

President Wilson. It is a question of very little importance; it seems to me useless to impose a vexatious restriction for so little positive result.

Mr. Lloyd George. I admit that I don't hold to this article at all.

M. Clemenceau. Nor do I insist on its retention.

M. Orlando. I agree with you.

President Wilson. Is there any observation on the air clauses?[6]

Mr. Lloyd George. I am bothered by the clause forbidding the manufacture of aviation matériel.

President Wilson. But this clause applies only for a period of six months after the end of hostilities.

Mr. Lloyd George. If that is the case, then I don't insist.

[6] Printed in *ibid.*, pp. 892-95.

XCII

Conversation between President Wilson and MM. Clemenceau, Lloyd George, and Orlando*

MAY 23, 1919, 4 P.M.

Mr. Lloyd George. I have received a copy of a document signed by Marshal Foch—it is dated May 17—which gives some rather interesting news about Germany; it comes from General Dupont. He states that the Germans are undertaking military preparations, that they have reached an agreement, deemed satisfactory by the Berlin government, with the Russian Soviets, with a view to common action. General Dupont's telegram ends by asking the governments to take a decision.

M. Clemenceau. I didn't receive this telegram.

Mr. Lloyd George. It seems rather important to me.

—President Wilson reads the telegram aloud: The German government is resolved not to sign a "peace of violence." An agreement was concluded with the Soviets with a view to an initiative on the Polish front. The German noncommissioned officers who wish to enlist voluntarily to serve in the Russian army should assemble at Königsberg.

M. Clemenceau. This document seems authentic to me; I'll request all the details this evening.

I also have a communication to impart to you. At Spa, General Desticker saw Dr. Heim, that Bavarian deputy of whom we have already spoken.[1] The General gives me an account of their conversation.

—M. Clemenceau reads the report[2] aloud: Dr. Heim advocates the division of Germany into two states. Southwestern Germany, which would include Austria, with a Catholic majority, is the only force that can resist anarchical tendencies.

Concerning reparations, Dr. Heim thinks that the Allies are harboring illusions about what they will be able to obtain from Germany, because the terms imposed upon that country will put a halt to its productive power.

*H., *PPC*, V, 899ff.
[1] See XXXI.
[2] It is printed in *PPC*, V, 906-909.

President Wilson. It is a remarkable document. Like Count Brockdorff, Dr. Heim claims that, if Germany doesn't keep everything currently produced on her own soil, all her industries will shut down. It is a difficult argument to defend.

Mr. Lloyd George. I received a telegram reproducing a conversation with the Lord Mayor of Cologne:[3] Scheidemann, whom he saw recently, has decided to let the Allies renew the offensive and then to sign, after a protest.

It would seem that Germany is going to fall to pieces. That would mean that our terms will not be carried out; on the other hand, Germany would be singularly weakened. We have to choose between these two assumptions.

M. Clemenceau. If Germany goes to pieces, I will do nothing to prevent it.

Mr. Lloyd George. Under these conditions, I believe that Bavaria will not remain with Germany. We may have a decision to take on this subject.

M. Clemenceau. Italian opinion is very heated against France: that is a fact. M. Barrère, who is a very great friend of Italy, sends me dispatches which are unpleasant to read: the *Marseillaise* was hissed in Turin; French officers have been insulted. M. Barrère has lodged a protest to the Italian government. Such a movement cannot develop if the government resolutely opposes it.

One of the most recent dispatches I have received reports that French officers in Milan were insulted in such a way that we cannot, under these conditions, leave French troops in that city. We now have 1,200 French soldiers in Milan. I investigated and was told: Milan is the base for French troops in Italy; if they leave this city, the entire French contingent must be withdrawn from Italy. M. Barrère appears to fear new incidents and insists strongly that the French troops in Milan be recalled immediately.

What should I do? We can easily withdraw them; but then we will be told that we are separating ourselves from Italy. I cannot take it upon myself to risk disgraces like those which just took place.

Even today, a solemn demonstration is taking place in the Chamber and the Senate to celebrate, in a spirit of friendship towards the Italian people, the anniversary of Italy's entry into the war—and this is the answer we are receiving! It is not the fault of our colleague, M. Orlando. But I can assure him that M. Bar-

[3] Konrad Adenauer.

rère isn't a witness prejudiced against Italy. If I leave French troops there, what will happen will happen.

M. Orlando. I sincerely regret not being able to deny that the state of mind in Italy is very troublesome. It is an admission which costs me dearly. The exasperation of Italian public opinion stems in part from war fatigue, in part from the feeling of anxiety produced by the fact that Italy doesn't see the questions which concern her finding a solution, and doesn't perceive what that solution can be. Tension has resulted from all this which, I admit, borders on paranoia; and that is turning against the Italian government itself.

This alarming situation was one of the reasons for my recent trips to the Italian border: I was very concerned about it; I spoke to my colleagues about the action required to remedy it. I am assured that a lull has come in these past few days. I know nothing of the incidents about which M. Clemenceau just spoke. An incident in Genoa was called to my attention; I questioned the prefect of that city, who replied that it was nothing serious. I don't know about the other incidents, and I was not informed of the steps taken by M. Barrère.

M. Clemenceau. M. Barrère telegraphs me precisely in order to alert you, because he fears you may not have been informed of his moves.

M. Orlando. But Count Aldrovandi had likewise received nothing from the Ministry of Foreign Affairs.

M. Clemenceau. That is what M. Barrère feared.

M. Orlando. I will make inquiries and give you an answer immediately. You must understand the regret I feel.

M. Clemenceau. I cannot expose our troops to insults. Should I withdraw them or keep them there? Tell me: we must decide without delay. I would regret to have to withdraw the French soldiers from Milan, because it would then be necessary to withdraw all out troops from Italy.

Mr. Lloyd George. Is it any use leaving French troops in Italy at present?

M. Clemenceau. No; but the consequence of the recall of French troops will be the departure of Italian troops which are still in France, and I fear the effect upon public opinion.

Are there still American troops in Italy?

President Wilson. No.

M. Clemenceau. And English troops?

Mr. Lloyd George. They have almost all been withdrawn.

M. Orlando. Indeed, only a single English brigade remains; I believe only one French brigade remains as well.

M. Clemenceau. I want to do nothing to make the situation worse than it is. Give me your answer as soon as possible.

—Mr. Philip Kerr is introduced and reads aloud the draft message to the government at Omsk,[4] asking Admiral Kolchak and his associates for guarantees concerning political liberty and the social system in Russia, in the event they should take control of the central government.

President Wilson. This message is addressed only to Admiral Kolchak; couldn't that antagonize General Denikin and the government at Archangel?

Mr. Lloyd George. M. Chaikovskii accepts. As for Denikin, he has his dangerous aspects, but I think he will follow the movement.

President Wilson. The question is to know whether, in the event no similar letter is sent to Denikin, this would not contribute to alienating him from Kolchak.

Mr. Lloyd George. We intend to send a copy of this letter to Denikin and another to Chaikovskii.

M. Clemenceau. Amongst the terms that you set, there is one relating to the abolition of conscription, which is indicated as one of the principles accepted in common by our governments. You will understand my objection to this wording, which would not be understood in France: it is better to speak simply of a reduction of military forces.

President Wilson. In fact, the abolition of conscription is not expressly stipulated in the Covenant of the League of Nations.

Mr. Lloyd George. I believe it must be imposed on Russia, and I would fear nothing more than to see Russia raise four or five million men whom Germany could make use of one day.

M. Clemenceau. Do you think there is one word in this document which will prevent that?

President Wilson. Recognition of the Russian debt is mentioned in this message: that can give us the appearance of acting out of concern for money. When Lenin made us an offer of this kind,[5] we reproached him for it as a maneuver aimed at showing that the

---

[4] It is printed as an appendix to these notes.

[5] That is, in his reply to the so-called Prinkipo proposal. See G. V. Chicherin to the Governments of Great Britain, France, Italy, Japan, and the United States, Feb. 4, 1919, printed in FR 1919, Russia, pp. 39-42; summarized in PWW, Vol. 55, p. 163. See also Thompson, Russia, Bolshevism, and the Versailles Peace, pp. 82-130.

bourgeois governments were ready to recognize any regime, provided it guaranteed the payment of the coupons.

Mr. Lloyd George. I will observe that it was Kolchak who offered to recognize the Russian debt; we are only taking note of it.

President Wilson. We must indicate clearly that the entire document constitutes an inseparable set of terms for the recognition of the governments in question.

Mr. Lloyd George. The text does indeed say that we will recognize them only if they provide the guarantees demanded.

President Wilson. It is also necessary to insist upon the creation of free local assemblies in each of the regions which these governments now administer.

Mr. Lloyd George. The text provides for respect for all free local institutions. Is it reasonable to ask for more? Within six weeks, Admiral Kolchak has advanced several hundred kilometers. Can we ask him to hold general elections under such conditions? During the war, when our government did not move about from day to day, as the government of Kolchak is now doing, we judged it impossible to hold elections. If, on the other hand, we believe it necessary to convene an assembly representing the entire Russian nation immediately, I will recall that the old Constituent Assembly was elected less than two years ago by universal suffrage.

President Wilson. Whom exactly did it represent?

Mr. Lloyd George. It represented moderate revolutionaries: that is why the Bolsheviks dissolved it.

M. Clemenceau. The Russians must be given the choice between the convocation of this assembly and the election of a new one.

Mr. Lloyd George. That is what we want. In any case, it is impossible for them to do either before they are in Moscow.

President Wilson. Did not England supply the greater part of arms and ammunition to Kolchak and Denikin? The United States provided nothing, except to the Czechoslovaks.

Mr. Lloyd George. It was indeed Great Britain which provided the greater part of these supplies.

M. Clemenceau. We provided some too, but less than you did.

President Wilson. This statement is sent to Admiral Kolchak in the name of the Allied and Associated Governments. On this particular point, a distinction must be made.

Mr. Lloyd George. The text says that Great Britain has provided 50 million pounds sterling in arms, war matériel, and provisions to the anti-Bolshevik governments. There are people at home who will not like this sentence; but it states the facts.

M. Clemenceau. I would like to see what we ourselves have done. It may be necessary to mention it.

President Wilson. Our role is different. We have only come to the aid of the Czechoslovaks and guarded, in part, the Trans-Siberian Railway.

I rather like this document on the whole. I am trying to see how to associate the American government with your action without increasing the anomaly of its position.

M. Clemenceau. I recall what I said on the subject of conscription.

President Wilson. We could say: "limitation of number of troops and of military organization."

Mr. Lloyd George. Here lies the drawback of being great military nations: conscription has become a dogma with you.

M. Orlando. At home, people accept the obligation imposed by law; but those who make an occupation of military service are scorned.

—*The dispatch as a whole is approved.*

Sir Maurice Hankey. The Secretariat asks to know what part America will take in the negotiation of the treaty with Bulgaria.

President Wilson. The United States is not at war with Bulgaria; but, as a member of the League of Nations, it has to sign the peace treaty with Bulgaria if the Covenant of the League of Nations is included in it.

Mr. Lloyd George. The question of the military forces of the small states of Central Europe has to be reviewed. We must absolutely reach a conclusion on this point in order to deal with Austria.

President Wilson. The observations presented by General Bliss seem to me to have a lot of force.

M. Clemenceau. They confirm my own misgivings when I think of the difficulty of making these small states obey us if we impose too strict limitations upon them.

Mr. Lloyd George. We should, furthermore, watch out for their insubordination. If Germany and Austria are disarmed and left at the mercy of small greedy powers, nothing will be more deplorable. Their ambitions are enormous, and they are stronger today than Prussia was at her beginning.

M. Clemenceau. The question doesn't arise for half of these states.

Mr. Lloyd George. We cannot tell Austria that she will have the army that she wants; for, in that case, we would be compelled to grant the Czechs the same latitude. If Germany only has 100,000 men and Bohemia can raise 1,500,000, Poland two million, we are creating an impossible situation. We must be fair, even to the Germanic peoples.

M. Orlando. It is a serious question, whose solution will have many repercussions. I request time to think it over. The text proposed by the military experts would give the states of Central Europe an army proportionately as strong as Italy's before the war. They propose, for example, to allow Bohemia 50,000 men. Italy, with a population three times greater, had, before the war, 180,000 men. Therefore, these figures are not figures of disarmament. With 50,000 men, Bohemia would have an army equal to half the German army. We mustn't help these states pursue a militaristic policy.

M. Clemenceau. On the other hand, if we disarm them too much, they will perhaps tell us: "You are exposing us to aggression from Italy. * * *." If we have liberated these peoples only to throw them into the arms of Germany, nothing would be more dangerous.

I approve what Mr. Lloyd George said, but I think we mustn't do anything without consulting these states themselves. They are our allies. If we ask them, on the one hand, to participate in reparations, and if, on the other, we should reduce their military strength to an extreme minimum, we will turn them against us. One of our best guarantees against Germany in the future is the presence of the Poles and the Czechoslovaks on her borders.

We will leave Poland troops because of the proximity of Russia; we will leave Rumania troops for the same reason. But do you think Serbia will accept an army reduced to 20,000 men, after all that she has done and all that she has suffered? Do you believe Bohemia will be content, given her position in the center of Europe and threatened from all sides?

I approve what Mr. Lloyd George has said; at the same time, I see the danger that could result from a too rigid application of the principle that he propounds. I don't yet see how we will get out of this.

President Wilson. I have reviewed the figures: by adopting those proposed by the military experts, the total forces of all these states would be about 350,000 men, but it would not be a single force.

M. Clemenceau. You are forgetting that, except for Germany and Austria, on whom we are imposing long-term service, these figures are only those of the annual levies. With 50,000 men per year, Bohemia will have a million in twenty years.

President Wilson. On the other hand, you forget that we intend to limit armaments strictly. What good are a million men if they can't be armed?

Mr. Lloyd George. We found the means to arm our home guard.

M. Clemenceau. There is no possible comparison between a country which has the industrial resources of Great Britain and the small states we are discussing.

{ A P P E N D I X }[6]

DRAFT DESPATCH TO ADMIRAL KOLTCHAK.

(Prepared by Mr. Philip Kerr for consideration at the request of the Principal Allied and Associated Powers, 23rd May, 1919.)

The Allied and Associated Powers feel that the time has come when it is necessary for them once more to make clear the policy they propose to pursue in regard to Russian affairs.

It has always been a cardinal axiom of the Allied and Associated Powers to avoid interference in the internal affairs of Russia. Their original intervention was made for the sole purpose of assisting those elements in Russia which wanted to continue the struggle against German autocracy and to free their country from German rule, and in order to rescue the Czecho-Slovaks from the danger of annihilation at the hands of the Bolshevik forces. Since the signature of the Armistice on November 11th 1918 they have kept forces in various parts of Russia and the British Government have sent munitions and supplies to assist those associated with them to maintain their position to a total value of more than £50,000,000 (?). No sooner, however, did the Peace Conference assemble than they endeavored to bring peace and order to Russia by inviting representatives of all the warring Governments within Russia to meet them in the hope that they might be able to arrange a permanent settlement of Russian problems. This proposal and a later offer to relieve the distress among the suffering millions of Russia broke down through the refusal of the Soviet Government to accept the fundamental condition of suspending hostilities while negotiations or the work of relief was proceeding. They are now being pressed to withdraw their troops and to incur no further expense in Russia on the ground that continued intervention shows no prospect of producing an early settlement of the Russian problem. They are prepared, however, to continue

---

[6] Printed in *PWW*, Vol. 59, pp. 440-42.

their assistance on the lines laid down below, provided they are satisfied that it will help the Russian people to recover control of their own affairs and to enter into peaceful relations with the rest of the world.

The Allied and Associated Governments now wish to declare formally that the object of their policy is to restore peace within Russia by enabling the Russian people to resume control of their own affairs through the instrumentality of a freely elected Constituent Assembly and to restore peace along its frontiers by arranging for the settlement of disputes in regard to the boundaries of the Russian state and its relations with its neighbours through the peaceful arbitration of the League of Nations.

They are convinced by their experiences of the last year that it is not possible to secure self-government or peace for Russia by dealings with the Soviet Government of Moscow. They are therefore disposed to assist the Government of Admiral Koltchak and his Associates with munitions, supplies, food and the help of such as may volunteer for their service, to establish themselves as the government of all Russia, provided they receive from them definite guarantees that their policy has the same end in view as that of the Allied and Associated Powers. With this object they would ask Admiral Koltchak and his Associates whether they will agree to the following as the conditions upon which they accept the continued assistance from the Allied and Associated Powers.

In the first place, that, as soon as they reach Moscow they will summon a Constituent Assembly elected by a free, secret and democratic franchise as the Supreme Legislature for Russia to which the Government of Russia must be responsible, or if at that time order is not sufficiently restored they will summon the Constituent Assembly elected in 1917 to sit until such time as new elections are possible.

Secondly, that throughout the areas which they at present control they will permit free elections in the normal course for all local and legally constituted assemblies such as municipalities, Zemtsvos, etc.

Thirdly, they will countenance no attempt to revive the special privileges of any class or order in Russia. The Allied and Associated Powers have noted with satisfaction the solemn declarations made by Admiral Koltchak and his associates that they have no intention of restoring the former land system. They feel that the principles to be followed in the solution of this and other internal questions must be left to the free decision of the Russian Constituent Assembly; but they wish to be assured that those whom they are prepared to assist stand for the civil and religious liberty of all Russian citizens and will make no attempt to reintroduce the regime which the revolution has destroyed.

Fourthly, that the independence of Finland and Poland be recognised, and that in the event of the frontiers and other relations between Russia and these countries not being settled by agreement, they will be referred to the arbitration of the League of Nations.

Fifthly, that if a solution of the relations between Esthonia, Latvia, Lithuania and the Caucasian and Transcaspian territories and Russia is not speedily reached by agreement the settlement will be made in consultation and co-operation with the League of Nations.

Sixthly, that as soon as a government for Russia has been constituted on a democratic basis, Russia should join the League of Nations and co-operate with the other members in the limitation of armaments and of military organisation throughout the world.

Finally, that they abide by the declaration made by Admiral Koltchak on November 27th 1918 in regard to Russia's national debts.

The Allied and Associated Powers will be glad to learn as soon as possible whether the Government of Admiral Koltchak and his associates are prepared to accept these conditions, and also whether in the event of acceptance they will undertake to form a single government and army command as soon as the military situation makes it possible.

XCIII

Conversation between President Wilson and MM. Clemenceau, Lloyd George, and Orlando*

MAY 24, 1919, 11 A.M.

—M. Tardieu presents the new draft of the article of the preliminaries of peace with Germany relating to the repurchase of the mines of the Saar,[1] in the event that a plebiscite returns all or part of the mining basin to Germany.

*H., PPC, V, 912ff.

[1] It is printed in PWW, Vol. 59, p. 460. It provided means other then payment

—*This new text is accepted.*

—MM. Clémentel, Crespi, Baruch, Sir Hubert Llewellyn Smith, and Alphand are introduced.*

President Wilson. Agreement on the economic clauses of the treaty with Austria[2] seems nearly complete. I give the floor to M. Clémentel to present the questions still pending.

M. Clémentel. In the treaty with Austria, one clause which we accept envisages referring questions of annulment of contracts to mixed tribunals. This clause has no equivalent in the treaty with Germany, although it would have been to our advantage concerning Alsace-Lorraine. It was introduced in the Austrian treaty at the request of the English delegation. If this text is accepted, it seems to us impossible not to modify the text of the treaty with Germany along these lines. The people of Alsace-Lorraine would reproach us for not having secured for them the same guarantees as those which will be accorded the Transylvanians or the people of the Trentino by the treaty with Austria. We would especially request the insertion in the German treaty of a provision as follows:

"Annulled are all exceptional measures taken during the war by Germany with respect to the goods, rights, and interests of former German nationals."

The words "Germany" and "German nationals" replace here the words "Austria-Hungary" and "Austro-Hungarian."

Mr. Lloyd George. No doubt, if we had thought of it in time, this provision would be in the treaty with Germany. The institution of mixed tribunals is to the advantage of the Austrians and would be to the advantage of the Germans. As a consequence, we can propose to insert the article on mixed tribunals, specifying that the annulment of exceptional measures taken during the war against former German nationals will be required as a condition. We can propose this to them; but, in my opinion, we cannot impose it on them. This is an oversight on our part. This oversight is no reason to omit from the Austrian treaty what should have been in the German treaty.

*H., *PPC*, VI, 1ff.

---

in gold for Germany in the repurchase of the mines of the Saar at the end of the fifteen-year period in the event that the inhabitants of the basin voted for reunification to Germany. This new draft of this article was in the combined draft of the reply of the Four on the Saar question, about which, see LXXXIX, n. 3.

[2] They are printed in *PPC*, VI, 5-14.

M. Clémentel. I don't see what prevents us from making reasonable changes in the text of the preliminaries; this text isn't final. Concerning the Saar, we have just introduced an amendment taking the German point of view into account. As long as the treaty is not signed, we have the right to change it, and the proposed change is only fair.

President Wilson. I don't believe it is proper to add to the terms already communicated to the Germans. We had plenty of time for thought.

M. Clemenceau. Do you mean that the only right remaining to us is to make concessions?

Mr. Lloyd George. I don't believe it would be either fair or politic to appear to be raising new demands and create unnecessary irritation amongst the Germans. Besides, I don't know whether what is asked of us is fair: the people of Alsace-Lorraine were German subjects during the war. If there have been sales of goods and buyers in good faith, can we ask for their expropriation?

M. Clemenceau. Is it acknowledged that good faith justifies the possession of a stolen object?

Mr. Lloyd George. It is not a question of theft, but of confiscation in conformity with German law.

President Wilson. The question is whether the German government acted within its legal rights; if it did, we are helpless.

M. Clemenceau. Then don't put this provision in the Austrian treaty.

M. Clémentel. The measures taken against the people of Alsace-Lorraine were often acts of vengeance; they were most often taken against those whose French sympathies were known, against those who had sons in the French army. They amount to actual persecution. If we introduce the provisions in question in the Austrian treaty, we ask that they be added to the German treaty.

M. Orlando. Two questions arise. The first is—these clauses being considered as just—whether it is possible to insert them in the German treaty: in my opinion, there is no difficulty here. Until now, we have only made a draft of the treaty, we have the right to change it: that is what we have just done concerning the Saar—to the advantage of the Germans. It is a question here, not of making our terms harsher, but of correcting an obvious omission. In case it should be thought, on the contrary, impossible to modify the German treaty, that would be no reason to delete justifiable provisions from the treaty with Austria. Measures were taken against nationalities hostile to the Austro-Hungarian state;

it would be unjust to admit that the result of these measures will be maintained.

Concerning contracts, a question of general law is involved. These contracts have as their basis the unity of a state which has crumbled into dust; it is quite possible that, according to public law, many of them can no longer be executed. Providing for their annulment by a mixed tribunal is the best we can do.

I propose, in any case, to keep the text which has been submitted to us in the treaty with Austria; in my opinion, it can be inserted without difficulty in the treaty with Germany.

President Wilson. Who will determine whether the measures taken against the former nationals of Germany and of Austria-Hungary had an exceptional character?

M. Clémentel. The mixed tribunal, if there is any doubt in the matter.

M. Clemenceau. No; the mixed tribunal can only rule about contracts.

M. Alphand. The exceptional measures against the people of Alsace-Lorraine—since Alsace-Lorraine has been mentioned—were taken either in Alsace-Lorraine or in Germany. If they were taken in Alsace-Lorraine, it is easy for us to annul them ourselves. That leaves the measures against the property of the people of Alsace-Lorraine located in Germany; there, jurisdiction will belong to the German authorities, unless we should decide otherwise.

President Wilson. And who will decide in the case of Austria-Hungary?

M. Alphand. The question arises in the same manner as for Alsace-Lorraine.

Mr. Lloyd George. It is clear that, in Alsace-Lorraine, France will have to decide whether or not a measure was of an arbitrary and exceptional character. In Bohemia, it will be the Czechoslovak state.

M. Clemenceau. In that case, is it not best to delete the two lines relating to these exceptional measures?

Mr. Lloyd George. Article 5, relating to contracts, must be kept at any rate.

M. Clémentel. Yes, and reproduced in the German treaty, as the British delegation asks.

M. Orlando. I insist that the two lines relating to the annulment of exceptional measures be kept. It is true that, in restored territories, it is up to us to annul them. But if an Italian from Istria, who was a victim of confiscations, can see his wrong redressed by the Italian government, can this same citizen, if he owns property beyond the new boundary, find himself without any recourse? That would be a contradiction and an injustice. I propose that these questions be brought before mixed tribunals, which will decide whether or not there has been an exceptional measure.

President Wilson. M. Orlando is a jurist: suppose that you yourself were asked to sit on this mixed tribunal; when you are asked this question: "Is such an act an exceptional measure or not?", I don't know what you will answer in many cases. I can already see a large twilight zone where it will be difficult to determine whether we are confronted by acts of vengeance with measures which can be justified by a state of war. The tribunal won't have any sure principle on which to base its decisions. It is a question, indeed, of determining not what was done by a government, but the government's motive in taking its decision. The clause, as it stands, doesn't seem to me to be applicable.

M. Orlando. That is a serious objection; but I will observe that it is the duty of judges, in the majority of cases, to rule on questions as dubious as this one. Very often, moreover, the doubt will not be as great as President Wilson thinks. For instance, when citizens have been prosecuted for sedition and their property has been confiscated, there is no doubt about the cause and the nature of the confiscation.

Mr. Lloyd George. Indeed, it seems to me that this clause is of little interest; for, in the restored territories, the states concerned will be free to act as they see fit.

M. Orlando. This assumes that injustice can be corrected in the restored territories, but that we will renounce any means of correcting it beyond our own borders.

Mr. Lloyd George. You will never redress all wrongs.

M. Clemenceau. If Article 5, which relates to the annulment of contracts by a mixed tribunal, isn't inserted in the German treaty, the provision relating to the annulment of exceptional measures can't be left in the Austrian treaty. What we don't want is to appear to be adding to the German treaty a provision rather favorable to the Germans, without adding its counterpart as well.

Mr. Lloyd George. We are arguing over very little. The main thing is that the damage suffered by the Alsatians in Alsace somehow be redressed; but that is up to you.

—*The provision relating to exceptional measures is deleted from both treaties. The article relating to contracts is retained.*

—*The experts withdraw.*

President Wilson. One of the Americans who collaborated most actively in the solution of the Danzig question calls my attention to an oversight in the draft.[3] Our intention was to establish the state of Danzig ourselves by determining the terms of its existence. The treaty is drawn up in such a way that the state of Danzig is established right away, and that causes us to lose the control that we wanted to establish.

We also forgot to mention that our four governments will themselves work for the conclusion of a treaty between Danzig and Poland: there again, our intervention is essential.

Mr. Lloyd George. We will have the opportunity to change the text relating to Danzig. We can expect the Germans to voice the strongest opposition on this question, and that will allow us to introduce changes in our text.

President Wilson. If the free city of Danzig is established by the very text of the treaty, it won't be bound to us, and nothing can compel it to undertake negotiations with Poland.

—*The Drafting Committee is asked to prepare a modification of the text in order to correct the omission.*

[3] See the memorandum by S. E. Mezes printed in *PWW*, Vol. 59, pp. 456-57.

XCIV

Conversation between President Wilson and MM. Clemenceau, Lloyd George, Orlando, and Viscount Chinda*

MAY 24, 1919, 4 P.M.

President Wilson. We would like to consult the Japanese delegation about the message that we propose to send to Admiral Kolchak. The text of this message was drafted under Mr. Lloyd George's care. We will present it to you in its final form; its substance is as follows.

We fear that Admiral Kolchak, General Denikin, and the Archangel government may be subject to counterrevolutionary influences and that, if they haven't taken any commitments towards us, their victory may result in a reaction which would undoubtedly lead to new disorders and a new revolution. The purpose of

*H., *PPC*, VI, 15ff.

our message is to make known the conditions under which we will continue to support these governments. We ask them:

1) as soon as they arrive in Moscow, to convene a Constituent Assembly, elected by universal suffrage, or, if it appears to them that order has not been sufficiently established to proceed with this election, to recall temporarily the Constituent Assembly of 1917;

2) in their respective territories, these governments must not impede in any way the functioning of regularly elected local assemblies;

3) class privileges abolished by the revolution cannot be restored; the changes introduced by the revolution in the system of landownership must be maintained; the civil and religious liberty of all Russian citizens will be guaranteed: in a word, there must not be, in any way whatever, a return to the old regime.

4) the independence of Finland and Poland will be recognized, as well as the boundaries drawn under the auspices of the League of Nations;

5) the same guarantee will be given to the countries of the Baltic, as well as to the regions of the Caucasus and of the Caspian;

6) as soon as Russia has established her institutions on a democratic basis, she will be received into the League of Nations, with the obligation to cooperate in the general plan for a limitation of armaments;

7) the Russian state will confirm the recognition of the financial obligations already acknowledged by Admiral Kolchak in his declaration of November 27, 1918.[1]

Viscount Chinda. What is the exact meaning of Admiral Kolchak's proclamation? Did he acknowledge only the prewar debts or all those which Russia contracted until the fall of Kerenskii?

Mr. Lloyd George. Admiral Kolchak's proclamation clearly asserts that he will repudiate only the financial transactions of the Soviet government; this covers the obligations contracted by the Kerenskii government. What do you have to say about the draft of the message we have just heard?

Viscount Chinda. I have no objection to make. But is it necessary for me to give you my answer immediately? Baron Makino is absent, and I myself would like to have the time to read this text more closely.

Mr. Lloyd George. It is important that Japan be in agreement with us on this initiative.

Viscount Chinda. I believe my government will agree with you. I

---

[1] For which, see PWW, Vol. 59, p. 462.

have reasons to believe that it takes the same position. The Japanese Ambassadors in London, Washington, Paris, and Rome have just received the following instructions from our government: the provisional government at Omsk has been established for more than six months; it has so far succeeded in the difficult task which it undertook; we recommend today *de facto* recognition of this government, under terms which satisfy the legitimate demands of the Allied governments. We request the guarantee of the Russian debt, including the obligations contracted by the Kerenskii government, and we propose that this question be submitted for discussion to the heads of governments meeting in Paris.

Mr. Lloyd George. For the moment, our policy is simply to set terms. If they are accepted, we can recognize the Omsk government.

Viscount Chinda. Concerning the help to be given to the governments of Russia, I assume that there will be an arrangement amongst us, taking into account the capacity of each government.

Mr. Lloyd George. We would be happy with an arrangement of that kind—for it is certain that the United States would bear the heaviest burden!

President Wilson. It is not I who must be persuaded, but the Congress of the United States, which, until now, has shown itself hostile to the idea of any intervention in Russia. I believe that attitude could change if Admiral Kolchak replies satisfactorily to the questions we are going to ask him.

Viscount Chinda. The prepared text indicates that the only military assistance we could provide will be given by volunteers: given the nature of her military system, it is difficult for Japan to act on this basis.

President Wilson. The sentence of which you speak refers, not to military assistance which might be provided by the governments, but to individual enlistments. We want to avoid having armies intervene in Russia.

Mr. Lloyd George. In England, the feeling against action by any British troops in Russia is growing increasingly stronger. On the other hand, we can allow all individuals who, of their own volition, enlist in the service of one of the Russian governments to provide that kind of individual assistance. Indeed, when we called for volunteers for our occupation force at Archangel, we found many.

President Wilson. All we want is to help Russia help herself. We agree on withdrawing our troops from the Archangel region.

Mr. Lloyd George. Besides, what Russia needs above all is specialists, gunners, aviators, etc.

President Wilson. Our reply to the question put by Viscount Chinda is this: it is not a question of sending regular forces to Russia. I add that this decision does not affect the troops who are guarding the railroad in Siberia. But in order to help Admiral Kolchak in his march westward, we will only provide him with material means, leaving to individuals the right to enlist voluntarily in the Russian armies.

Mr. Lloyd George. It is better not even to mention these volunteers in our dispatch, since their action doesn't depend on the governments.

President Wilson. It is better indeed.

The commission charged with studying the status of the small states wishes to have a Japanese member join it. Does this proposal have your consent?

Viscount Chinda. Certainly.

President Wilson. Furthermore, the Italian representative on the Baltic Commission[2] asks that this commission receive more precise instructions on the future relations of the Baltic countries with Russia. It is indeed perhaps rather urgent to take a clear position on that question. Now is the time to lay down terms for Admiral Kolchak on this subject. After his success, it may be too late. The commission requests authorization to study that question immediately.

M. Clemenceau. That is quite reasonable.

Sir Maurice Hankey. Mr. Hoover proposes to advance ten million pounds to the Baltic states,[3] which would be provided by all of the Allied and Associated Powers.

[2] For the background of the situation in the Baltic area and early Allied policies in that region, see X, n. 5. The Council of Four, on April 28, 1919, had appointed a Commission on Baltic Affairs consisting of Sir Esme Howard, Samuel Eliot Morison, and others. The question raised by the Italian member, Giuseppe Brambilla, was conveyed in E. W. Howard to M. P. A. Hankey, May 24, 1919, about which see PWW, Vol. 59, p. 466, n. 5.

[3] The Council of Foreign Ministers, on May 9, 1919, had appointed a special committee to study the "best means of establishing and maintaining order in the Baltic Provinces and of revictualing." Members of this committee included Allied and American naval leaders, military personnel, and economic experts, notably Hoover and Howard. The committee, in a report submitted to the Foreign Ministers on May 23, said that it believed that the maintenance of order was a necessary condition for the distribution of food in the Baltic countries. It then made the following recommendations: (1) all German troops should be required to withdraw from Latvia and Lithuania as soon as local forces could be organized to replace them; (2) a military mission, under British command, should be

Mr. Lloyd George. Why do that? We are sending arms, ammunition, and supplies directly to them.

President Wilson. Mr. Hoover proposes also that we should take charge of provisioning the Baltic countries invaded by the Bolsheviks, without considering their present political situation.

Mr. Lloyd George. Talking about the ten million pounds, I will observe that we are giving money neither to Admiral Kolchak nor to General Denikin. Admiral Kolchak is at this time seeking a loan in London, and Lord Revelstoke has undertaken to float it. When consulted on this matter, we did nothing other than say that the British government would raise no objection.

Sir Maurice Hankey. Mr. Balfour and M. Pichon also made reservations about the ten million pounds.

—Lt. Col. F. H. Kisch is introduced: he explains the military situation in Russia. Kolchak's army is advancing in the direction of Viatka; but it is drawing back further south. Reserves are arriving at the threatened points. General Denikin is creating a diversion at Tsaritsin. The Bolshevik troops are superior in number, but their morale has fallen greatly. In all the areas they have occupied, the Siberian troops have been well received.

Mr. Lloyd George. In one of his latest radiograms, Lenin speaks of recent successes of the Red armies: where are they occurring?

Lt. Col. F. H. Kisch. Near Samara. The Bolsheviks are rather well organized, but they lack rolling stock and fuel; it is becoming impossible for them to transport rapidly from one point to another.

Mr. Lloyd George. What is your opinion on the situation?

Lt. Col. F. H. Kisch. I believe Admiral Kolchak will take Viatka. In the south, it is possible that the Bolsheviks are still advancing. Once the Siberian troops have arrived in Viatka, the Bolsheviks

---

established in Libau or Reval to advise the governments of Estonia, Latvia, and Lithuania on the organization, equipment, and training of the local forces and on the best means of defending themselves against German and Bolshevik aggression; (3) all volunteers should be recruited in the Scandinavian countries; (4) a credit of ten million pounds sterling should be placed at the disposal of the Baltic states to be used as decided upon by the military and political missions; (5) food, equipment, clothing, arms, munitions, etc., should be provided by the Allied and Associated Powers and should be paid for by the credit mentioned in the previous article; and (6) the political and economic missions should inquire as to what collateral guarantees could be obtained from the Baltic countries to cover the above-mentioned credit. After a lengthy discussion, the Foreign Ministers adopted the committee's recommendations, with the exception of the fourth point, which was referred to the Council of Four. See PPC, IV, 752-57, 762-63.

will undoubtedly withdraw west of the Viatka-Kotlas line, and Kolchak will join the Archangel troops at Kotlas.

Mr. Lloyd George. How long can that take?

Lt. Col. F. H. Kisch. About two months. Petrograd may fall much earlier, and that would have rather important consequences for lines of communication. It is possible that Vologda will fall before the end of the summer and open direct communication between the Urals and the Baltic.

At the moment, the center of gravity of the Bolsheviks is moving south, where the Ukraine, which they recently captured, offers them a stronghold.

Mr. Lloyd George. The essential question will arise when we have to recognize a government for all Russia.

President Wilson. Our Ambassador in Tokyo, Mr. Morris, is on his way to Omsk; he is to see Admiral Kolchak and form an opinion of him and his entourage.

Mr. Lloyd George. It would be wise to send someone on a similar inquiry to General Denikin. He's a man I fear more than Kolchak. But we only have military people in the vicinity. Denikin is surrounded by good officers, but their methods are brutal: they shot 15,000 Bolsheviks after having taken them prisoners. But it was probably in retaliation for acts of the same kind.

President Wilson. What does M. Chaikovskii say about General Denikin?

Mr. Lloyd George. He says that he is purely a soldier. On the other hand, Lukovsky, his chief of staff, seems suspect to us.

Viscount Chinda. Then I will submit the text of this dispatch to Marquis Saionji and Baron Makino, and I'll give you their reply Monday.

XCV

Conversation between President Wilson and MM. Clemenceau, Lloyd George, and Orlando*

MAY 26, 1919, 11 A.M.

—M. Clemenceau reads aloud a note from the Austrian delegation, which complains about the delay in the opening of the negotiations.[1]

Mr. Lloyd George. We have always thought it was not necessary to deal with the Austrians in the same way as with the Germans. Why not begin to study with them the clauses of the treaty which are ready now? Two major questions—those of reparation and of the military forces of the states of Central Europe—won't be settled for another eight or ten days. But concerning boundaries, economic clauses, waterways, railways, and many other questions, we can present our text right now.

Since the Austro-Hungarian monarchy has fallen to pieces, the Austrian delegates will have no trouble understanding that the section on responsibilities and indictments cannot be drawn up in an instant. But on this question, as on that of the military forces, can't we ask them to appoint experts who will possibly meet with our own?

President Wilson. Concerning the military question, the difficulty is that the discussion is not taking place amongst the experts, who agree amongst themselves, but between the experts and ourselves. Moreover, I admit that we have always deemed it possible to adopt a different procedure towards the Austrians from the one we followed with the Germans.

M. Orlando. Wouldn't it be better to try to settle the questions still pending in a few days, in order to present a complete text to the Austrians? We must not adopt a procedure which could be misunderstood in Italy. In Italy, the war was essentially a war against Austria. Our feelings towards the various peoples of the Austro-Hungarian monarchy are rather different; but concerning Austria, there can be no doubt: she was our principal enemy. The procedure adopted mustn't give the Italian people the impression that

*H., PPC, VI, 25ff.

[1] It is printed in PPC, VI, 37-38.

the questions which are of capital importance to them appear to be treated here as questions of secondary concern.

Like you, I think we must try to open negotiations quickly, leaving blank, if need be, the figures of the effectives until further notice. But a procedure completely opposite to the one followed with respect to Germany would create an unwelcome impression in Italy, and with no useful result.

Mr. Lloyd George. Italy must, nevertheless, understand the reality of the situation. There is a fundamental difference between Germany and Austria, because Austria-Hungary no longer exists. Suppose Bavaria had not only detached herself from the German Empire, but had sided with us, as the Czechs did; that Saxony had followed her; that two thirds of Germany was today constituted into anti-German states: under those conditions, we could not have proceeded towards Germany as we have. It would, above all, have been impossible to negotiate with the German Empire because it would have fallen into pieces. I ask M. Orlando to acknowledge this essential difference.

M. Orlando asks us if we could not adopt immediately, at least provisionally, a solution to the financial and military questions. That appears impossible to me. A conversation I had with M. Beneš has shown me the very great difficulty of these problems, and if we try to settle them in three or four days, we will settle them badly, and we will suffer the consequences.

I come to the same conclusion as M. Clemenceau: we must go back on our decision of the other day and review these two questions again. That cannot be done in a few days; I hope M. Orlando will understand that.

President Wilson. Mr. Lloyd George is not proposing, moreover, that we engage immediately in a thorough negotiation with Austria on these litigious questions; he is only proposing to invite the Austrians to appoint experts who can present their observations in a preparatory discussion.

Mr. Lloyd George. We can be ready, except with regard to these two questions—reparation and military strength. It seems to me that it would be helpful for the Austrian experts to meet with those of the states formed from the dissolution of Austria-Hungary.

M. Orlando. We decided that our relations with Austria and Hungary would be the relations of victor to vanquished. As we did for the Germans, we must prepare amongst ourselves the peace terms, summon the enemy plenipotentiaries, and hand them our text. Now we are talking about changing this procedure. If it is simply a question of postponing the communication of certain terms, which can only be determined after an agreement has been reached with the nationalities concerned, nothing is easier than to notify the Austrians to this effect. But in order to do that, it is not necessary to institute an entirely new procedure and to admit Austrian experts into the discussion. If you can present a definite proposal to me in writing, I will study it and tell you if I can support it.

M. Clemenceau. I am ready to defer to the wishes of Italy. I have learned at my own expense that, when I do not agree with her, the organization of anti-French and pro-German movements ensues. I wish to preserve the indispensable union amongst us. However, I take the liberty to observe that it is a mistake to speak of a new procedure. When we invited Austria to send her representatives to Saint-Germain, the Italian delegates were absent; it wasn't my fault. It was then that we decided to adopt a position towards the Austrians which was not the same as the one we had taken towards the Germans. I regret that my Italian colleagues were not there to hear us.

What I want is something that puts us all in agreement; I seek a reasonable formula.

Peace with Austria, in certain respects, is more difficult to make than peace with Germany. The dissolution which has taken place, the struggles which are being waged or are dawning on every side, the barbed wire which General Humbert saw stretched between the Yugoslavs and the Italians in Istria—all that explains the difficulty.

President Wilson came here to tell us: "Let us make peace amongst all men." This high ideal unfortunately clashes with rivalries, with century-old hatreds. In order to give each his share, there are terrible problems to be solved. Amongst us, the serious problem of the Adriatic still remains without solution. M. Orlando and I had a long conversation on this subject yesterday. If Italy appeals to the Treaty of London and occupies Dalmatia, any proposal of disarmament presented to the Yugoslavs will seem a bad joke to them.

M. Orlando spoke to me yesterday about the question of the departure of French troops from Italy. What I have to say is that I cannot allow French officers to be insulted in the streets of Italian cities. M. Orlando told me that the facts are not as serious as they were reported to me; but I continue to receive alarming dispatches from M. Barrère, not only about the incidents which I have already mentioned, but about the propaganda which continues in favor of Italy's return to the German alliance.

All this must be stopped. The only way is to settle the litigious questions as soon as possible. That may prove disagreeable. I too have had difficult discussions with Mr. Lloyd George; but I concluded by saying that nothing must nor can separate us. This is not the language being spoken in Italy.

These problems which have to be solved, will we solve them all in a few days? No; it will take weeks. Until then, it will be impossible to say to the Austrians: "Here are all our terms." If M. Orlando agrees with me in all that I have said, we must try to gain time. Whilst we are talking amongst ourselves, conversations amongst the experts, in which the Austrians can participate, will make them be patient.

I don't wish to oppose Italy: she is like a pretty woman, with whom it is better to agree. President Wilson is bound by his word to the right of peoples to self-determination; France and England are bound by the treaty they signed. If M. Orlando wants to discuss matters with a supreme solicitude for maintaining the indispensable union between us, it is necessary, whilst awaiting a solution, to be patient with Austria.

As for the sensitivity of the Italian people, I don't believe we will provoke it by saying: "One part of the treaty is ready; as for the rest, the experts will have to confer." If that leads to difficulties in Italy, I withdraw what I said. But I think nevertheless that it is rather important to avoid having the Austrians return to Vienna discouraged. I ask M. Orlando to help us in assuming this responsibility.

M. Orlando. I thank M. Clemenceau very sincerely; he has spoken with his two usual qualities of frankness and clarity. I won't return to the incidents which took place in Italy or to what was reported to you. There is certainly some difference of opinion between M. Barrère and myself as to the importance of the incidents which have occurred. I can't deny that the present state of mind in Italy is such as to worry us. But one can explain the excitement of Italian opinion without justifying it.

I recall that, in a discussion which took place on this very spot, Mr. Lloyd George said: "If I am not in a position to announce to my country that we have taken a step towards peace, the situation can become serious." This uncertainty has been prolonged for Italy, and that explains her anxiety. What troubles our country is uncertainty over her fate; when it has ceased, you will find Italy just as she was during the war—loyally and sincerely with you. She was hurt, because she thought that her allies and associates were abandoning her after she had taken her share with them of the greatest dangers. The alarming occurrences of today will cease when the anguish which I myself share ceases.

As for myself, I have decided always to remain in the Entente and to run all personal risks for that. I can't be reproached for having taken an intransigent position; I have always made an effort towards conciliation. In a conversation with Colonel House and Mr. Miller, I went as far as to consent to painful renunciations.

I thank M. Clemenceau for his courageous words about the necessity of confronting the problem. But, given the state of public opinion in Italy, why excite it even more by raising a mere question of procedure? If, without any intention of hurting the Italian people, you hurt them indeed, you will have done a poor piece of work. If I have insisted upon the procedure settled with regard to the Austrians, it is for this reason alone.

President Wilson. Hasn't M. Orlando himself indicated the solution? We can tell the Austrians that, in the course of the week, we will present to them the parts of the peace treaty relating to questions which arise exclusively between Austria and the Allied Powers, whilst reserving those which concern other states previously included, in whole or in part, in the Austro-Hungarian monarchy.

Thus, we will discriminate between Austrian questions, strictly speaking, and those which must be tied to a more general settlement. The texts relating to the first can be ready in two or three days; for the others, we need more time.

M. Orlando. You have interpreted my wish very well; I accept this proposal.

Mr. Lloyd George. The sorting out remains to be done.

President Wilson. I don't think it necessary to place anything other than the military clauses and the clauses relating to reparation in the secondary category.

M. Clemenceau. I have received a letter from M. Dutasta whose wording implies that Germany will be admitted to the next international labor conference: that is contrary to our decisions.

President Wilson. Certainly. What was decided was that the international labor conference to take place in Washington will deliberate on the admission of the Germans.

M. Clemenceau. Marshal Foch asks for instructions in order to be prepared for the operations which will occur if the Germans refuse to sign. He says that the tactical changes will require three days.

President Wilson. In that case, it is enough to notify him three days in advance.

M. Clemenceau. The Germans have presented observations in the interest of their religious missions abroad.[2] M. Pichon proposes that a commission be formed to study all extra-European questions.

—*This proposal is adopted.*

[2] It is printed in *ibid.*, pp. 779-80.

XCVI

Conversation between President Wilson and MM. Clemenceau and Lloyd George*

MAY 26, 1919, 3:30 P.M.

Mr. Lloyd George. M. Orlando failed to seize the opportunity which was offered him this morning. I will make him speak.

M. Clemenceau. M. Tardieu has seen M. Crespi: the latter mentioned the desiderata of Italy touching the Tarvis Pass and Albania. If the Italian argument was accepted on these two points, that would help in the solution. As for M. Orlando, he no longer knows where he is. If this course is opened to him, I believe that we can make him move forward.

Mr. Lloyd George. The difficulty is that, when an argument is reached with M. Orlando, he returns to see Baron Sonnino, and we find that nothing has been done. Baron Sonnino has ideas of expansion in Asia.

M. Clemenceau. On this point, I will tell you that I have been notified that the Italians have seized two more points in Asia Minor. If things go on in this way, I don't see where we will go. I will tell M. Orlando today: "You must speak; we have the right to ask you to make known in writing what you want."

I told him in our conversation yesterday: "You failed to inform your Chamber of Deputies that the Italian government, in the Treaty of London, promised Fiume to the Croats, and, because

*Does not appear in H.

we did not wish to embarrass you, the British Prime Minister and I have been unable to explain that to our own parliaments."

M. Orlando must speak now and give us his proposals in writing. We ourselves will reply in writing.

Mr. Lloyd George. Shall we raise the question of Asia Minor at the same time?

M. Clemenceau. That would seem to me more difficult. The public understands nothing about it, and I must tell you that the Greek landing went off rather badly. There were difficulties, people were killed. I fear that the Greeks are behaving a little like the Poles.

Mr. Lloyd George. M. Vénisélos holds his Greeks in hand better than M. Paderewski his Poles. But I fear that the Greek army is worse than the Italian army, and there are also discussions which I do not like amongst our representatives in Constantinople. We must beware of all that.

President Wilson. It is better to separate the question of Asia Minor from the question of the Adriatic. For the peace of the world, I believe Italy must remain outside Asia Minor.

M. Clemenceau. We will repeat that there can be no question of the Treaty of London if Italy insists upon Fiume. The Italians must be compelled to speak: the public knows nothing.

Mr. Lloyd George. Perhaps things would go better if the public knew even less about it.

M. Clemenceau. The French public does not know the facts. The demonstration which has just taken place in both chambers[1]—and which, in my opinion, is helpful—rests upon a complete misunderstanding.

Mr. Lloyd George. Indeed, I believe that here, as at home, they think rather little about Italy.

M. Clemenceau. The only way out is to put the question clearly, and I told M. Orlando to consider the consequences if Italy should break with the United States.

President Wilson. What I fear is that publicity might make a retreat more difficult for the Italian statesmen, because men who are at once weak and obstinate think it impossible to retreat when it becomes known what position they have taken.

---

[1] "On the occasion of the anniversary of the entrance of Italy into the war, the French Chamber of Deputies and Senate today adopted unanimously a resolution asserting the continued fraternity of the two nations, and declaring they would remain united in a just and durable peace. The Government associated itself with the resolution." *New York Times*, May 24, 1919.

Mr. Lloyd George. I am completely reassured regarding the repercussion on British public opinion.

M. Clemenceau. I said to M. Orlando: "You have bought our newspapers." He disputed the fact. I replied to him: "Do you want proof?" I think that all this must be brought into full light.

Mr. Lloyd George. Concerning the treaty with Austria, I favor communicating the parts of the treaty which will be ready next Wednesday to the Austrian delegation. We can't prolong the present state of affairs indefinitely. The British government is divided between Paris and London, and one or another of our ministers is compelled to make the trip each week.

M. Clemenceau. If Italy claims Dalmatia, we'll see what we have to do.

President Wilson. The Italians must realize, furthermore, that they can't have what they want without the consent of the United States. If their only preoccupation is to save their pride, they are throwing themselves into an impasse.

I adhere to the principle that one cannot dispose of peoples without their consent: the Italian government must begin by admitting this as we do. I will say to M. Orlando: "Can you ask the United States, as a member of the League of Nations, to guarantee a boundary of which it disapproves?"

It is absurd to insist upon the execution of the Treaty of London, when Russia, which signed it, is no longer in the ranks of the Allies and when amongst the powers which will make peace tomorrow is the United States, which did not sign the Treaty of London—whilst the enemy against which this treaty was directed, Austria-Hungary, has disappeared!

Mr. Lloyd George. In spite of that, we are bound by our signature. The Italians have taken their part of the mutual commitment: they have lost 500,000 men.

M. Clemenceau. Are you sure of this? M. Pašić told me the other day on this subject, whilst stroking his long beard, "It is in retreats that most men are always lost."

President Wilson. Didn't Italy declare war on Germany a year after the time she had agreed to break with all your enemies?

M. Clemenceau. Should I put the question to M. Orlando?

President Wilson. Yes, but it is better not to ask for anything in writing, for the reason I have just mentioned.

M. Clemenceau. Not yet.

XCVII

Conversation between President Wilson and MM. Clemenceau, Lloyd George, and Orlando*

MAY 26, 1919, 4 P.M.

—The members of the commission charged to study the problem of reparation in the Austrian treaty[1] are introduced. After an exchange of views, it is agreed that the commission should take up the entire question again [with all the states concerned], without taking any earlier decision into account.

—The members of the Commission on National and Religious Minorities[2] are introduced.**[3]

President Wilson. For guarantees to minorities, shall we write the same provisions into the Austrian treaty that we wish to impose on the Poles, Czechs, etc.?

Mr. Headlam-Morley. It would seem very difficult not to impose on the Austrians and Hungarians the same terms as on friendly states, even though the problem of minorities doesn't arise in either Austria or Hungary, under the new boundaries, as it does elsewhere.

President Wilson. Mr. Miller explained to me that the terms relating to the Jews have not been inserted in the Austrian treaty, because the question arises in a totally different way than in Poland.

Mr. Headlam-Morley. Everyone tells me that the situation of the Jews in Poland is quite peculiar to that country.

President Wilson. The experts seem to agree on all points; but what we wish to avoid is the impression that we are imposing terms on friendly states that we have omitted in a treaty with enemies. Can the Poles complain if certain clauses relating to the Jews don't appear in the Austrian treaty?

Mr. Headlam-Morley. I don't think so.

M. Berthelot. There will nevertheless be a question of national mi-

*H., PPC, VI, 43-44.
**H., PPC, VI, 45ff.

[1] Lamont, Tardieu, and Crespi.

[2] Actually, the Committee on New States.

[3] The Four had before them the draft articles on the protection of minorities to be inserted in the peace treaties with Austria and Hungary. They are printed in PWW, Vol. 59, pp. 509-12.

norities in Austria, for about 500,000 Czechs will remain inside that country. As for the Jews, the question arises in a completely different manner than in Poland, where they constitute 14 per cent of the population.

President Wilson. What I mean is this: even if the clauses concerning the Jews are not necessary in the treaty with Austria, isn't it politically desirable to insert them in the treaty anyway, to avoid a complaint on the part of the Poles?

Mr. Headlam-Morley. I have another question to submit to you. In our work, we have treated Austria as a new state. The question must be raised because in the entire treaty, except in the financial clauses, the Austrian Republic has been considered as the heir to the former Austrian Empire. If Austria is a new state, she cannot cede territory to the Yugoslavs, the Czechs, or the Poles.

The former Austria has disappeared from the face of the earth: the present Austrian state doesn't have to be asked to renounce, for example, the Treaty of Algeciras, because that state did not participate in it any more than did the Czech or the Polish states.

President Wilson. What you indicate is true from a historical point of view. But from the legal point of view, hasn't the present Austria succeeded the former Austria?

Mr. Headlam-Morley. German Austria never had supremacy over the Kingdom of Bohemia.

Mr. Lloyd George. All the constituent parts of Austria-Hungary will sign the treaty one after the other.

Mr. Headlam-Morley. The present Austria is only a part of the former empire; she isn't the former empire diminished.

President Wilson. In that case, why are we treating her as an enemy state?

Mr. Headlam-Morley. In fact, she is in that situation. But I insist upon my point of view, because it is important not to let Austria speak in the name of the Germans of Bohemia. She must be told clearly: "You are a new state, and you have no rights over your neighboring states."

President Wilson. In that case, Austria wouldn't have to cede any territories.

Mr. Headlam-Morley. No; she would only have to renounce her union with other nationalities, whose boundaries we would indicate.

Mr. Miller. It seems to me that Austria and Hungary are enemy states, not only in fact, but legally: a state of war exists between us and these states. Like Mr. Headlam-Morley, I think that there exists no successor to Austria-Hungary; the right of Austria to speak for the Germans of Bohemia is inadmissible. The Germans of Bohemia are a minority in another state.

Mr. Headlam-Morley. In asking Austria to renounce her rights over this or that territory, you implicitly recognize those very rights.

Mr. Lloyd George. I recognize that there is much to be said in favor of this argument, which deserves to be studied closely. What would satisfy Mr. Headlam-Morley would be a preamble recalling that the Austro-Hungarian monarchy has ceased to exist by the will of the populations, that the different parts of the Austro-Hungarian Empire are becoming states or are joining pre-existing states, Austria being nothing more than one amongst them. It is a question that must be referred to the experts.

M. Orlando. The problem is important and deserves to be studied closely. I will simply observe that, if we adopt Mr. Headlam-Morley's views, we will depart from what we have done up to now; credentials have always been exchanged without this point of view having been taken into account.

As for the disappearance of the former state of Austria, it is a debatable fact. We were then in the presence of two states, the Austrian state and the Hungarian state, with distinct sovereignties, whose two parliaments made their laws separately. Does the fact that many territories cease to make up part of Austria result in the disappearance of the Austrian state? That is very debatable.

In law, changes in quantity do not change the quality of the object. Germany, deprived of Silesia, of Alsace-Lorraine, of the Saar, of Schleswig, remains Germany. Isn't Austria simply a diminished state?

We have a precedent—Turkey. When European Turkey was reduced to a bit of Thrace, it was a radical amputation; it was never said, however, that Turkey had disappeared. Since 1878, when Serbia became independent and Bulgaria received her autonomy, Turkey has been cut up bit by bit: the Ottoman state has nevertheless survived.

My conclusion is that this question is so serious that it would be dangerous to formulate a conclusion without a very thorough study.

M. Clemenceau. I completely support what M. Orlando has just said.

President Wilson. The difference between the cases which have just been mentioned and that of Austria is greater than M. Orlando appears to believe. Turkey constitutes a single state; the same thing was true of Germany, despite the federal character of her government. But Austria was one of two states, bound to each other by a personal union and by the compromise of 1867, which regulated their relations and established, for questions of common interest, a sort of federal government—the Austro-Hungarian Delegations.

This dual monarchy broke up. Take Bosnia-Herzegovina: I can't remember whether it was assigned to Austria or to the two states at once.

Mr. Headlam-Morley. It was a province of the empire, which belonged jointly to Austria and Hungary.

President Wilson. This complicates the situation even more; for here is a territory which neither of the two states could alone cede to a foreign state. Such a complicated situation is very different from Turkey's or Germany's.

Mr. Lloyd George. M. Orlando has said that, in law, quantity cannot affect quality; but there is a point where quantity involves quality. If you take Alsace-Lorraine and a part of Silesia away from Germany, Germany survives. But Czechoslovakia is going to be a country of thirteen million inhabitants, and Austria will only have eight million. Galicia was also a part of Austria. When one takes three quarters of its territory from a state, can one say that that state survives? If Germany lost Bavaria, Saxony, Württemberg, Hannover, and the Rhenish provinces, would she still be Germany?

There is much to be said for Mr. Headlam-Morley's argument: Austria does not even retain—like the Byzantine Empire when it possessed only Constantinople—the prestige of a center acknowledged as the national center par excellence.

M. Clemenceau. How should the question be presented to the experts?

M. Orlando. Can't we present it to those who are studying the problem of national minorities? It is useless to involve ourselves in a purely academic question.

M. Clemenceau. I will ask that they study it at the same time that they discuss the name that the Austrian state should take. I could not accept the appellation of German Austria.

President Wilson. We could say: "New Austrian State."

Mr. Lloyd George. If the Drafting Committee is too busy to settle that question, we will ask it to appoint legal experts who can deal with it.

—The experts withdraw.

President Wilson. I have received a letter from the Luxembourg government, telling me that it is ready to send a delegation to us and asking at what date it could be received.

Mr. Lloyd George. When will the treaty with Austria be ready?

Sir Maurice Hankey. Not before Saturday, taking into account the time necessary for printing and corrections.

President Wilson. Do you want to summon the Luxemburgers for Wednesday evening?

Mr. Lloyd George. Agreed.

M. Clemenceau. Mustn't the Belgians be present?

Mr. Lloyd George. I believe they must be invited.

Sir Maurice Hankey. So I am to ask the Secretariat to inform the Austrian delegates about the date when the treaty can be communicated to them—towards the end of this week. At the same time, you could invite the Austrian delegation to designate experts who would be consulted on the question of reparation and the military clauses.

President Wilson. The reason why we are dealing with these two questions apart from the rest must be indicated. That reason is the division of Austria-Hungary into several states and the necessity of taking into account the respective rights and interests of these states.

M. Orlando. Why ask the Austrian delegation to name its experts immediately? We can wait a bit. The important thing is to make clear the distinction that warrants the separate treatment of these two questions.

President Wilson. It is easy to show that it is the consequence of the division of the Austro-Hungarian Empire and of the relations which must be anticipated amongst the different states of Central Europe.

—President Wilson reads aloud a memorandum on Carinthia.[4]

[4] D. W. Johnson to the American Commissioners, May 22, 1919, printed in *ibid.*, pp. 406-408. The question at issue was the disposition of the so-called Klagenfurt Basin, an area in Carinthia in southern Austria, which was inhabited by both Slovene and Germanic populations. The Commission on Rumanian and Yugoslav Affairs, on April 6, 1919, had decided that the Klagenfurt Basin should be considered a geographical and economic entity and should not be divided between Austria and Yugoslavia. The commission had recommended that the area be given to Austria, with the stipulation that, after five years, a plebiscite was to be held "in order to afford the inhabitants of the Klagenfurt Basin an opportunity of protesting, should they wish to do so, against inclusion in Austria, and demanding union with Jugo-Slavia." The Council of Foreign Ministers and the Council of Ten approved these recommendations on May 10 and 12, respectively. See *PPC*, IV, 680-81, 696-703; *PWW*, Vol. 59, pp. 60-61.

President Wilson. You remember that we met at the Quai d'Orsay with the Ministers of Foreign Affairs in order to study that question.⁵ On the triangle of Tarvis, we adopted the recommendations of the Foreign Ministers.⁶ Since then, the question of the plebiscite in Klagenfurt has arisen. The insistence of the Yugoslavs has changed the opinion of our experts: they now suggest cutting this district into two parts, the south being given to the Yugoslavs without a plebiscite.

On the Klagenfurt region, I have an interesting report from four Americans who visited this area.⁷ The feeling of the population, they say, is Austrian. Carinthia, whatever the origin of its people, forms a geographic and economic entity. If we put the area to the south of the Drava under the government of the Yugoslavs, with a plebiscite at the end of five years, they fear pressure and frauds that could falsify the popular vote.

Mr. Lloyd George. That means that the triangle should go to Austria?

M. Orlando. I know that there was supposed to be a meeting of the experts today to deliberate on the substance of this question: shouldn't this very interesting document be communicated to them?

M. Clemenceau. We have a document to the contrary, provided by M. Pašić.

M. Orlando. The most urgent thing is to stop the fighting which

---

However, in a meeting with the members of the commission on May 20, 1919, the Yugoslav delegates protested against this decision and argued that, due to the large German-speaking majority in the northern part of the area, a plebiscite in the whole of the Klagenfurt Basin would undoubtedly result in favor of Austria. As an alternative, they proposed to divide the area roughly along ethnographic lines, to award the southern part with its Slovene majority to Yugoslavia outright, and to hold a plebiscite only in the northern half of the basin. As a result, the British, French, and Italian members of the commission reversed their earlier decision and now endorsed the Yugoslav proposal. The American representatives were divided on the question, with Douglas Wilson Johnson favoring the Yugoslav plan and Clive Day and Charles Seymour supporting the earlier solution. See the memorandum by D. W. Johnson cited above; C. Day and C. Seymour to the American Commissioners, May 22, 1919, *ibid.*, pp. 405-406; and the memorandum by Sherman Miles, May 22, 1919, *ibid.*, pp. 403-405.

⁵ At a meeting of the Council of Ten on May 12, 1919, for Hankey's minutes of which, see *ibid.*, pp. 60-64.

⁶ To reserve the question of the attribution of Tarvis and the area known as the Assling Triangle until the boundaries of Yugoslavia had been determined.

⁷ The memorandum by Sherman Miles cited in n. 4 above.

goes on at this moment between the Yugoslav and German populations in that region; it is necessary, as at Lemberg, to seek to impose an armistice. Shouldn't we, as with the Poles and the Ukrainians, give a warning to the two opposing parties?

President Wilson. The American experts had recommended what we had approved together at the Quai d'Orsay; but their opinion has changed.

Mr. Lloyd George. I propose to put the study of this question over until tomorrow.

M. Orlando. But what will you do to stop the hostilities? There is an urgent necessity here.

President Wilson. Make a proposal.

M. Orlando. I will seek a formula with a view to a proposal for an armistice.

President Wilson. My opinion is that one can only stop the hostilities in Carinthia by fixing the boundaries.

M. Clemenceau. Can't we send one dispatch to Agram and another to Vienna?

M. Orlando. The Austrian delegation raises the question urgently; a reply must be given.

M. Clemenceau. The Austrians are indeed making this request; they even insist on having interviews with us. The Secretariat replied by asking them to send a written note.

M. Orlando. It isn't a question of study, but of immediate action.

President Wilson. We can address ourselves to the Austrian and Yugoslav delegations in Paris and demand that they cease hostilities.

Mr. Lloyd George. They will both ask: "Where will you stop us?" It is always the boundary question which is asked.

President Wilson. They must be told: "Stop fighting first."

M. Orlando. That's right. For us, it is a matter of conscience not to allow this situation to be prolonged.

M. Clemenceau. I am willing to try.

Mr. Lloyd George. Can't we form a very small committee, as we have already done in similar cases, to settle the question of the boundary quickly?

M. Orlando. The simplest thing is to hasten the work of the commission which has studied that question thoroughly.

President Wilson. I believe that it should be asked to name a limited subcommission, which will reach conclusions more quickly.

Mr. Lloyd George. And to summon the Austrians and the Yugoslavs.

M. Orlando. Once the boundary has been fixed, the fighting will obviously cease.

President Wilson. The simplest thing is for us to take the question in hand, fix the boundary, and then invite them both to withdraw into their respective territories.

M. Clemenceau. We could hold another meeting with the Foreign Ministers on this subject.

President Wilson. That's it—tomorrow, for example.

M. Clemenceau. We must address a final appeal to our Italian colleague. The seriousness of the situation, fortunately, is not yet extreme. But the Austrians are pressing us, and we shall have, willy-nilly, to take up the litigious questions. Yesterday, when I saw M. Orlando, I showed him the gravity of the situation, for us and for Italy; he acknowledged it with his usual good faith and told me: "If you raise the question, I will make proposals."

We must try to put an end to it, through a conclusive conversation. I beg M. Orlando to cooperate by making proposals which will be what they will be, but which will in any case help us out of this impasse. If he acts with his usual loyalty, I am convinced it will result in immense relief for us all, even at the risk of an unsatisfactory solution. M. Orlando will help us by explaining himself today, if he so wishes.

M. Orlando. For me, it will be a true deliverance; I feel it even more than M. Clemenceau, whom I thank for what he has just said. I feel, even more than he does, the gravity of the situation.

I am asked: "What are your proposals?" When we studied the Italian question together, from the thirteenth to the twentieth of April, the difference became accentuated between what I could call Italy's minimum program and the unanimous opinion of our Allied and Associated colleagues. On the twentieth, I told you: "If Italy is compelled to abandon what she is asking beyond the Treaty of London, she must stand on the Treaty of London, with all its consequences." But this separates the Allies from President Wilson. The Allies told me: "Whatever the merits of the treaty may be, we signed it, we won't deny our signature." President Wilson said: "I don't approve of that treaty, I can't accept its execution."

Hence a very regrettable disagreement. If it is impossible for Italy to reach an honorable compromise, I will be compelled to abide by the text of the treaty. I admit that this is not desirable. I seek a path in the direction of conciliation indicated by Mr.

Lloyd George; I showed it between the twentieth and twenty-third of April, before the public statement of President Wilson, and also in the conversations that I recently had with Colonel House and Mr. Miller. I ardently wish to find a way out of our present situation, a way out that can be accepted by all of us.

If this agreement isn't possible, I am compelled to abide by the Treaty of London.

I recall the proposals that were made by Mr. Lloyd George, the more recent suggestions that came out of my conversation with Colonel House. It is upon these that I resume the conversation. I can say no more. If you don't grant me what these conversations allow me to hope for, nothing more remains to me but the Treaty of London.

President Wilson. Like you, I fear our getting into an impasse. I want to explain very seriously how this question weighs on my mind. We can't go in two opposite directions at once, yet this is what we are trying to do. The Treaty of London was concluded in circumstances which have since changed. I do not allude to the disappearance of Austria-Hungary; but other powers have since entered the war, and world opinion itself has changed.

When the Treaty of London was signed, there existed an alliance, relatively restricted, amongst three great powers, France, Great Britain, and Russia, and two small powers—victims of German aggression—Serbia and Belgium. The Allies at that time wanted to induce Italy to join them: from that came the Treaty of London. The world had not yet understood that this was a question which concerned it and in which its very future was at stake; that was only understood gradually in the United States and in other countries.

Then we saw the danger which threatened the political liberty and national independence of all the countries of the world. When this danger was well understood, everyone wanted to take part in the struggle. It was then that nations completely disinterested in European territorial questions aligned themselves on your side. They entered the struggle enthusiastically, as in a crusade, not for territorial changes, but for the destruction of the intolerable danger of a political and ethnic tyranny which would have held back the progress of the world for a century or more.

Hence a new state of mind: it was no longer a matter of defending only Serbia or Belgium, but all weak states, all suffering minorities. The freedom of the world had not only to be saved, but to be established forever.

It was then that I made my speech on our war aims to the Congress, a few days after the similar speech delivered by Mr. Lloyd George. There is little difference between our statements. My Fourteen Points are represented by five or six in Mr. Lloyd George's speech; but the spirit is the same. For Mr. Lloyd George, as for myself, it was a matter of expressing, not personal ideas, but public feeling concerned, not about territorial claims, but about a policy appropriate for insuring the future of humanity.

You allowed me to speak in your name at the time of the conclusion of the Armistice and to take as its basis the principles I had articulated. These were not yet present in the minds of peoples and statesmen when the Treaty of London was signed. Today, their influence makes itself felt even to the Orient and in the whole world. It was when they were imprinted upon people's minds that the League of Nations became a living ideal, and that those who had first regarded it as an unrealizable dream began to change their opinion.

When we met here, we accepted a common basis for discussion, which excludes the Treaty of London. The Treaty of London is based on the idea of former European policy—that the stronger power has the right to settle the fate of the weaker: from that it follows that France and England had the right to deliver to Italy populations which didn't belong to them. If this idea was maintained today, it would provoke reactions fatal to the peace of the world. If part of the Yugoslav people were delivered to Italy, we would not fail to be told: "That is exactly what, according to you, was never to have taken place." By insisting on the Treaty of London, you would be insisting on the very antithesis of the ideal which threw the people of the United States into the war, and on a principle opposed to that of the new world.

The League of Nations must be the guarantor of the new territorial arrangement of Europe. We would have to ask the Yugoslavs to reduce their army while leaving a great military power like Italy at their side: they would not submit to our decisions; we would have to use force against them, that is to say, begin again what Austria did against Serbia in 1914.

If I want to be able to continue to speak in the name of my fellow countrymen, to be, in some way, their spiritual representative, it is impossible for me to agree that a people can be handed over to foreign domination without their consent. I am ready to accept everything that these people themselves decide. Beyond the line of mountains which encloses Italian territory on the Istrian side, Italy would have everything which the people themselves would grant her by plebiscite.

I also have to observe to M. Orlando, without it being necessary to insist further upon my desire to act as a friend towards Italy, that neither France nor Great Britain can deliver to Italy any territory whatsoever otherwise than by the peace treaty: if one of the signatures which must appear at the bottom of this treaty is refused, the conclusion will remain in abeyance, and you will find yourselves once again in an impasse.

The Italian orators and statesmen have always said that their supreme concern was not to abandon their Italian brothers on the other side of the Adriatic. If that is the position they adopt, it is impossible for them to refuse to yield before the result of a plebiscite. The popular will would express itself freely, under the supervision of the League of Nations, of which Italy herself is a member, and which would prevent any fraud or violence.

If we adopt any other solution, we are establishing on the boundaries of Italy a permanent enemy of that country and we are creating again, in the heart of Europe, the difficulties and dangers of which the Balkan peninsula has been the focus for so long. This is not the way to give the world the peace it needs. We must choose between two courses: either abandon the program full of hope that we marked out, or renounce solutions whose time has passed in order to insure greater peace and security to the world than all the former guarantees could ever give.

M. Orlando. I have no difficulty in acknowledging that everything President Wilson has just said is perfectly logical, and that it would also be true, if the argument upon which his system is based could be admitted. He begins, indeed, with the assertion that the Treaty of London is a violation of the principles of justice upon which he wishes to stand. Given these premises, the consequences that he set forth with such eloquence and sincerity must necessarily be admitted.

But I don't accept the premises, I don't admit that the Treaty of London is a violation of justice—the handing over to Italy without any justification of territories and peoples by France, Russia, and England. What was done then resembles what we do here every day. Every day, we have to resolve very complex territorial problems; ethnographic questions are mixed with economic questions; coasts, railroads, mountains must be taken into account: we are trying to find the best way or to avoid the worst. The Treaty of London is only an anticipation of what is being done here every day. This treaty was a compromise, such as we have often made for some weeks.

The result of such compromises is often to introduce diverse elements into the territory of a power. In many cases, it even happens that these elements are more numerous than in the treaty in question. What accentuates this character of compromise is the renunciation by Italy of Fiume and southern Dalmatia—which is, economically, the most important part of Dalmatia, and where at least two cities, Spalato and Trau, are now amongst those claimed by Italian popular sentiment.

Everything that President Wilson said follows logically if one admits his premises; but I cannot agree that the Treaty of London should be condemned, without appeal, as a violation of the right. It is a compromise, which is neither better nor worse than those which we have tried to make concerning Teschen or Temesvar.

There are good compromises, and there are bad ones. Experience has shown that this was a rather bad one, and one must admit it even from the point of view of the Italian claims, since Italy did not receive satisfaction on Fiume. But I am obliged to remark that, if the premises are not accepted, neither are the conclusions.

I know the absolute opposition of President Wilson to the Treaty Of London. It is an agonizing fact that this compromise, whatever its intrinsic value, should lack the approval of a power which has served the entire world and Italy herself so well, that it be rejected by a man whom I respect, and so I say: it is necessary to look for something else.

I regret not being able to accept the plebiscite, and that for several reasons. The first is the delay this procedure would cause, a delay whose first effect would be to prolong the present anxiety. I would prefer to be less completely satisfied and to extricate ourselves quickly from the situation we are in.

The second reason is the complexity of the problem. I cannot deny that, even on our side of the Istrian Alps, inside the frontier which you accept, there is locally a majority of Slavs. Nonetheless, you accepted the decisive argument that here is the natural frontier and line of defense of our country: this consideration applies elsewhere.

In the third place, without wishing to lack respect for other peoples, I sense a difference of mentality and of behavior between Serbs and Italians which corresponds to a difference between the two civilizations. A plebiscite in Yugoslav territory would not take place without intimidation. The Slovene populations, in the territories now occupied by our troops, often show their fear of reprisals by the Serbs, if the latter were to occupy the country later and accuse the inhabitants of having been too favorable towards Italy.

I am ready for a deal. But if I don't find one, what is to be done? I have only this treaty. I appeal to it, not like Shylock, determined to obtain his pound of flesh, but as a compromise which France and England accepted. I myself am not satisfied with it; I would deplore a conflict with the United States. But if I see no other way out, I will be a prisoner of necessity.

President Wilson. I didn't characterize the Treaty of London as anything other than being contrary to the principles that we have sought to apply everywhere in these negotiations. Except where nearly impassable frontiers forced themselves upon us, such as the one drawn by the crests of the Alps, we have followed the boundaries traced by ethnographic affinities, according to the right to self-determination. For example, we had the most decisive strategic and economic reasons for giving Danzig to Poland, with all the necessary ways of access. However, since there were territories around Danzig and further south occupied almost exclusively by a German population, we reached the conclusion that it was not possible to allow material reasons to take first place, and we decided that the fate of this region would be settled by a plebiscite.

I will only propose a plebiscite in the Adriatic area under the strictest supervision of an international authority: under such control, no act of violence or of intimidation could pass unnoticed.

I wish to ask M. Orlando the following question in a friendly way: if I publicly explain to Italy the reasons which I have just given, proposing that, in the region in question, Italy would receive all that the popular vote will accord her, would M. Orlando feel free publicly to refuse such an offer?

M. Orlando. I insist on dispelling all ambiguity. When I spoke of the intimidation of these peoples, I wasn't thinking of everything that could happen at the very time of the vote; I was thinking especially of their fears for the future: those who could be afraid of constituting, after the vote, a minority amongst citizens of the Yugoslav state will be terrified in advance, and their vote will show the effect of it. That would prevent a genuine plebiscite.

You decided upon a plebiscite in Poland; but you limited it to a certain zone, whilst leaving 1,700,000 Germans in Poland without a plebiscite. Now, if all the Italian claims were admitted, and if one accepts the Austrian statistics—whose value you know—

the Slavic elements included within Italian boundaries wouldn't reach half that figure. The example of Poland cannot, therefore, be invoked against Italian claims.

As for the question just raised by President Wilson, here is my reply. I don't want a public discussion; but if it must take place, I would say what I have just said here, emphasizing the same reasons.

President Wilson. I beg M. Orlando, before taking a final decision, to consult his colleagues. He sees where this situation leads us: it will be impossible to carry out the Treaty of London without our assent, and I hope that M. Orlando will spare no pains in seeking a solution.

M. Orlando. When it is a matter of seeking an avenue of conciliation, I never refuse.

M. Clemenceau. I was going to express the same wish as President Wilson. What strikes me is that M. Orlando is not proposing anything. We have as yet received no firm proposal from Italy. Italy asked for Fiume in the name of the right of self-determination, and she also claims Dalmatia, contrary to this principle. Italy requests the execution of the Treaty of London, and she claims Fiume, contrary to the provisions of the treaty.

The latest position taken by Italy, which consists in demanding the execution of the Treaty of London, provides no solution. France and England, if you demand execution of the treaty, will honor their signatures, and then you will have no peace, no solution.

Since the only solution proposed isn't one, and since you haven't yet made any suggestions, we must try another tack. Couldn't we name a small committee of three or four persons who would study your proposals? The first thing to do is to make some. We must carry it through: otherwise we will be both the laughingstock and the danger of the world. Even before concluding the peace we are preparing here, we will have thrown the world into chaos again. If that happens, I at least don't want it to be my fault.

I beg you not to offer us a solution which would be nothing other than a continuation of the war. I do not repudiate the Treaty of London. But the truth of what President Wilson said must be acknowledged. At a certain moment, we caught a glimpse of this great ideal of the liberation of all peoples and, since then, our policy has perforce changed.

We are not—and M. Orlando knows it—enemies of Italy. But I invite Italy to think it over and judge herself; I ask the Italian government and Italian public opinion to do this. We must absolutely find a way out: we don't have the right to plunge humanity back into war. Make some proposals!

M. Orlando. That is what I am doing.

M. Clemenceau. You are proposing the Treaty of London: it isn't a solution, it *means* anarchy, it *means* the resumption of war, and the President of the United States would return to America at moral war with Italy. Make us some proposals that would allow us to strike out on a new course.

Mr. Lloyd George. When there were proposals, it was I who made them.

M. Clemenceau. I am convinced that M. Orlando will respond to our invitation.

XCVIII

Conversation between President Wilson and MM. Clemenceau, Lloyd George, and Orlando*

MAY 27, 1919, NOON.

—The members of the Drafting Committee are introduced.

President Wilson. The Austrians are showing some impatience. That is why we have decided to separate the parts of the treaty which concern only Austria and can be ready soon from those which concern other states of Central Europe, in particular the clauses relating to armaments and reparation.

Would we gain any time by having what is ready typed up?

Mr. James Brown Scott. It will be at least as fast to have it printed.

President Wilson. We can send the Austrians the text in proofs, if required.

Mr. James Brown Scott. I will observe that there are clauses about which we haven't yet received your instructions, notably the economic clauses. Since the articles of the treaty with Germany cannot be transferred without changes to the Austrian treaty, there must be a very careful revision.

President Wilson. Mr. Headlam-Morley said to us that, up to now,

*H., *PPC*, VI, 65ff.

we have treated Austria as if she was the heir of the former Austrian state. In asking her to renounce certain territories, we are admitting that it is she who possessed them.

Mr. Hurst. The case of Austria is that of the onion whose skins one successively peels away.

President Wilson. Mr. Headlam-Morley in fact presents the case differently; he says that Austria must be treated as a new state. If this is so, then we must establish this state and compel it to recognize the existence and boundaries of neighboring states, instead of treating it as if we were dealing with the former Austrian Empire, which we would ask to cede certain territories.

Mr. James Brown Scott. The question is rather difficult. If you consider Austria as a new state, you are not in a state of war with her; as a result, there is no need to sign a peace treaty with her, but a treaty of the same kind as those you are signing with Bohemia and Poland.

President Wilson. We have many reasons to proceed in that manner.

Mr. James Brown Scott. But wouldn't that remove all justification for the articles imposing on Austria, for example, the reduction of her military forces?

President Wilson. Our intention is to impose reductions of the same kind on other states which are not our enemies.

Mr. James Brown Scott. It would follow that Austria would have to be admitted to the League of Nations?

President Wilson. That is our intention.

Mr. James Brown Scott. From the point of view in which our committee must place itself, that would lead to a general revision of the draft.

President Wilson. That revision is undoubtedly necessary. What delay can result from it?

Mr. Hurst. It won't be very great.

President Wilson. It seems to me that we could indicate our position towards Austria in a preamble. We thought that the Drafting Committee, if it does not itself have time to undertake this task, could entrust it to competent persons.

I am told that the economic clauses are based on the old theory of Austria as heir to the Austro-Hungarian monarchy, whereas the financial clauses are based on the new theory. We must, at any rate, agree with ourselves. What we are trying to do is to separate Austria from all her old traditions.

Mr. Lloyd George. What parts of the treaty are ready now?

Mr. James Brown Scott. The Covenant of the League of Nations will be inserted verbatim into the Austrian treaty. The questions of boundaries are settled, except for two or three points.

Mr. Lloyd George. Those points will be settled today.

Mr. James Brown Scott. Certain questions raised by Italy are still pending.

M. Clemenceau. Which ones?

M. Orlando. They concern the clauses called "political," similar to those which have been adopted concerning Alsace-Lorraine. We are ready to discuss them.

Mr. Lloyd George. We must see these clauses today.

Mr. James Brown Scott. Almost all the other political clauses are ready. It may be necessary to take a decision on Vorarlberg.[1]

Mr. Lloyd George. Do the Czechs and the other states concerned know about these clauses? They are of the highest importance to them.

M. Clemenceau. They must see them.

Mr. Lloyd George. I ask that everything necessary be done to get their opinion.

Mr. James Brown Scott. The naval and air clauses are ready; the military questions are reserved. We are ready on the question of prisoners of war.

Have the financial questions been reviewed by the heads of governments?

President Wilson. We will study them this morning.

Mr. James Brown Scott. The economic clauses are in our hands; we will have to review the wording from the legal point of view if Austria is considered as a new state; perhaps there may even be grounds for referring the question to the specialists on economic questions.

We have no indication on the guarantees for execution.

President Wilson. You mean an occupation, like the one contemplated for Germany? We foresee nothing of the kind.

M. Orlando. I ask to consult the military advisers of the Italian government on this point.

M. Clemenceau. We would be grateful if you did so promptly.

Mr. James Brown Scott. I learn that some persons object to the term "German Austria." But the credentials of the Austrian plenipotentiaries, which have been received by your representatives, carry this title.

---

[1] The citizens of Vorarlberg had declared their independence on May 11, 1919, and proclaimed their desire to join the Swiss Confederation as a canton. The Austrians denied the validity of the plebiscite, and the question at this point was whether Vorarlberg would become Swiss or remain with Austria.

M. Clemenceau. Who accepted it?

Mr. James Brown Scott. The Committee on Credentials, M. Cambon.

President Wilson. Does the fact that credentials were accepted without observation prevent us from doing anything now?

Mr. James Brown Scott. No; but it creates a kind of precedent which we would have to break.

M. Clemenceau. I'll see M. Cambon on the subject.

Mr. James Brown Scott. The question of knowing whether Austria should be treated as a new state requires a very careful study.

Mr. Lloyd George. Try to see to it that we are able to transmit the treaty to the Austrian delegates on Thursday.

—The Drafting Committee withdraws.
—The members of the Financial Commission[2] are introduced.

President Wilson. Our Financial Commission was to have heard the observations of the small states of Central Europe on the clauses of the treaty with Austria. I ask Mr. Lamont to report to us what these countries said to the commission.

Mr. Lamont. They provided us with memoranda and a statement in which they protest against all measures which, by placing them on the same footing as the enemy states, would reserve for them the same treatment as for Austria.

M. Beneš told us that the Czechoslovak Republic is ready to assume its share of war costs, provided the word "reparations" is not mentioned. We asked him to provide us with a formula, which we hope to be able to apply to the three other nations involved. That, moreover, would cause the clauses concerning them to be omitted from the treaty with Austria; we shall have to make separate conventions with them.

Mr. Lloyd George. M. Beneš said to me: "We cannot be held responsible for a war which we condemn." I pointed out to him that the new states have to participate in the costs of the war of liberation. He replied to me: "That is different."

M. Crespi. We are ready to follow him in this course. We would also prefer that the peoples in the liberated Italian regions not be treated as enemy peoples.

M. Orlando. These countries don't want to accept responsibility for a war of which they say they are the victims. There is nothing to say to that. I accept this point of view; I accept it especially regarding the Czechs, who were our effective allies during the

[2] Lamont, Tardieu, and Crespi.

war. But if they pay nothing under the heading of reparation, then Trieste shouldn't do so either. As for the contribution to the costs of the war which we will ask from them, Italy has already paid it.

The new states must certainly be granted the satisfaction they ask.

Mr. Lloyd George. The clauses relating to reparation will be drafted in this sense, and we will have to negotiate afterwards with the states concerned.

President Wilson. The principle accepted is that they participate in the costs of the war to which they owe their independence.

Mr. Lloyd George. Apart from that, do we agree on the financial clauses?

M. Loucheur. Mr. Davis has proposed an amendment to us.

President Wilson. It involves giving the Reparation Commission the power to allow exceptions to the principle of the absolute priority of reparation debts. These exceptions might be necessary in order not to ruin the credit of the Austrian state. Are there any objections?

M. Loucheur. Our only objection would be that the admission of such an amendment could tempt the Germans to request the same advantage.

President Wilson. There is a difference between the case of Germany and that of Austria which we will not suffer to be minimized.

M. Loucheur. We have another question. It is the one of the railways of southern Austria.[3] It concerns taking measures to safeguard the interests of the bondholders, since the network is being divided amongst several states.

President Wilson. We cannot insert a clause favoring a particular company in the treaty.

Mr. Lloyd George. If we take this course, the clause will have to be extended to all companies.

M. Orlando. I don't dispute the relevance of the question, but undoubtedly you will also find Allied interests in Germany which have to be protected. If we find it just to insert that clause in the treaty with Austria, similar ones will have to be inserted in the treaty with Germany.

Mr. Lloyd George. Actually, all legitimate interests are protected by Article 6, which certainly extends to bonds. I wouldn't like to

---

[3] The Südbahn, about which there will be more discussion.

protect by a special measure bondholders whose interests could be linked to speculation.
M. Loucheur. There is a misunderstanding here. We are not requesting special protection for special interests. But this company will find its network cut into five pieces by the new boundaries. Will it continue to operate? Will it be forced to disappear? Hence the necessity of a provision such as the one we propose.
President Wilson. Other questions of the same type will arise. It seems to me dangerous to embark upon this course.
M. Loucheur. If the legitimate interests of which we speak are really protected by Article 6, that is enough for us. But I am not at all certain of it.
Mr. Lloyd George. We cannot take the course you propose without danger.

—*The proposal is withdrawn.*

XCIX

Conversation between President Wilson and MM. Clemenceau and Lloyd George*

MAY 27, 1919, 4 P.M.

—General Mordacq and Lt. F. H. Kisch are introduced.

M. Clemenceau. I will ask General Mordacq to explain what delayed the transmission of our telegram to General Haller.[1]
General Mordacq. On May 22, I received from the Prime Minister the text of a telegram which was to be sent, in the name of the Allied and Associated Governments, to General Piłsudski and General Villemain, the latter having to transmit it to General Haller. This telegram was coded and sent to the general in charge of our military mission in Warsaw, General Spier, with the order to transmit it and verify its transmission.

On May 23, General Spier requested that the telegram be repeated; we did so and asked him to acknowledge receipt of it.

On Saturday, the twenty-fourth, he replied that he couldn't de-

*H., *PPC*, VI, 69ff. (See *PPC*, VI, 60-61.)
[1] About which, see LXXXVII, n. 5.

code this telegram. We then discovered that that was true because he was using the key for the month of April. He didn't answer the new telegrams which were sent to him on Sunday. It was only on Monday that we knew that our telegram had been transmitted and communicated.

M. Clemenceau. I have here the telegram in which General Henrys informs me that General Haller is now doing only what he should be doing.

Mr. Lloyd George. Hasn't General Haller sent troops into Galicia?

Lt. Col. Kisch. Some troops in southern Poland have penetrated into northern Galicia; but none were sent to Lemberg.

M. Clemenceau. I am now informed that they have been withdrawn and sent to the German front.

Mr. Lloyd George. It was reported to me that the French Minister in Warsaw[2] told the Polish government that France did not cast an unfavorable eye upon Polish operations against the Ukraine.

M. Clemenceau. General Henrys says that M. Dmowski, according to his own statements, would like this whole affair to be placed in the hands of Marshal Foch; he concludes that the Poles think that they have Marshal Foch behind them. With respect to what you were told about the French Minister, there is a misunderstanding. As for the transmission of the telegram, you see exactly what happened. I don't want it to be thought that this delay occurred through any failure on our part.

Mr. Lloyd George. You remember that Marshal Foch always wanted to send General Haller's troops by way of Lemberg, whereas we insisted that they should pass through Danzig.

M. Clemenceau. The conclusion is that General Haller received our instructions, and that he will not intervene in Galicia.

Mr. Lloyd George. I am satisfied, now that the affair is in your hands; but make your Minister clearly understand that he must put pressure on the Poles to compel them to sign and respect the armistice.

—General Mordacq and Lt. Col. Kisch withdraw.

—The members of the commission entrusted with determining the boundaries of Austria and Yugoslavia are introduced.

President Wilson. It seems to me that I am expressing precisely the conclusions of the commission in saying that the economic boundary of the Klagenfurt Basin is situated further south than

[2] Eugène-Léon Pralon.

its ethnographic frontier. The latter divides the basin into two parts: the southern part, although the majority of the population there is of the Slovene race, is linked geographically and economically to the northern part, whereas it is separated from Slovenia by the barrier of the Karawanken Mountains, whose steepest slope faces south.

With respect to the Istrian Alps, we agreed that they should form the boundary of Italy, despite the Slovene character of the population thus included in Italian territory; the present case seems to appear in the same way. A portion of this population is Slovene; but its fate seems to be determined by geographic and economic factors; it would be a serious mistake to divide the basin, which forms a real entity. The question is whether we will do violence to geographic and economic factors for political reasons, or vice versa.

I am more or less bound by the precedent we created, and I don't want to go back on the decision we took concerning the natural boundary necessary for Italy's defense.

—Conversations with the experts follow.

C

Conversation between President Wilson and MM. Clemenceau, Lloyd George, and Colonel House*

MAY 28, 1919, 11:45 A.M.

M. Clemenceau. The credentials of the Austrian plenipotentiaries are drawn up in the name of the "Republic of German Austria." We haven't yet given our answer; my intention is not to admit that formula.

Mr. Lloyd George. Isn't it necessary to ask their opinion from the neighboring states? They can find, on the contrary, that the word "Austria" by itself would seem to transfer to the new state the titles and the claims of the old one.

Colonel House. Can we say "the New Republic of Austria"?

*H., PPC, VI, 82.

President Wilson. What puts us in a quandary is that the Austrians themselves have designated their state under the name of German Austria.

M. Clemenceau. It remains to be seen whether we will recognize it as such.

Mr. Lloyd George. The best thing is to consult the Slavic states and ask them if they have any objection.

—*It is decided that instructions will be given in this sense.*

Colonel House. I was present at the interview between Mr. Lloyd George and M. Orlando; the latter seems inclined to accept a compromise along the lines indicated by M. Tardieu.[1] Fiume would become the center of a small free state, governed by an international commission, of which two members would be Italian. Italy would abandon the entire coast, except for Zara and Sebenico. It remains to be determined which islands should belong to Italy. M. Orlando asked to consult his colleagues.

Mr. Lloyd George. In this conversation, I pointed out the opposition of the Yugoslavs to the cession of the islands. I insisted with M. Orlando that he demand only the islands absolutely indispensable and whose population is by majority Italian.

With respect to Zara and Sebenico, M. Orlando demands Italian sovereignty. I said to him: "If these two ports are in the hands of Italy, Dalmatia is deprived of her windows on the sea. If you make them free cities, that is another matter." I made him understand that there wasn't the least chance of having either the Yugoslavs or President Wilson accept this compromise if Zara and Sebenico should be Italian.

As for Albania, I believe that that question must be studied without prejudice. There is much to be said in favor of a mandate which could be entrusted to Italy.

Colonel House. Mr. Lloyd George forcefully impressed upon M. Or-

---

[1] That is, the so-called Tardieu Plan. It proposed that Fiume would become an independent state under the League of Nations and would be governed by a commission composed of two Italian representatives and one representative each of Fiume, Yugoslavia, and the League. The city of Fiume would retain the municipal autonomy it had enjoyed under the statute of Maria Theresa and would be a free port. After fifteen years, a plebiscite by commune would decide the permanent status of the area. In addition, the Tardieu Plan gave Zara and Sebenico to Italy; provided that the rest of Dalmatia be neutralized and assigned to Yugoslavia; awarded all the islands, except Pago, to Italy; proposed an Italian mandate over Albania; and gave both Tarvis and the Assling Triangle to Italy. It is printed in *PWW*, Vol. 59, p. 559. See also Albrecht-Carrié, *Italy at the Paris Peace Conference*, pp. 186-91.

lando that it wasn't in Italy's interest to have the Yugoslavs as enemies, with the German population in the Italian Tyrol.

Mr. Lloyd George. I wrote a letter to M. Orlando, in order to represent to him clearly the dangers that Italy can run. Italy can hardly claim people who don't want to be subject to her. No equivalent case can be found anywhere in the present negotiations. That is what Italy doesn't yet admit; but she must admit it. What I fear are the conversations between M. Orlando and Baron Sonnino; without being able to take part in them, and in order that our point of view might at least be represented there, I wrote the letter which I just mentioned.

President Wilson. Yesterday it was difficult to get a clear view on the question of the boundary between Austria and Yugoslavia with all those experts around us.

Mr. Lloyd George. M. Orlando will be here at 4:30. If we first settle the question between ourselves and Italy, all the rest will become easy.

President Wilson. On the other hand, the Italians are continuing to send troops to Asia Minor, despite our warning. What should we do?

Mr. Lloyd George. If that continues, I will say that England dissociates herself from all Italian claims in Asia Minor.

M. Clemenceau. The excitement generated in Italy over the Smyrna affair arises from the fact that M. Orlando never said that he had given his consent to our joint landing.

President Wilson. That's not an honest way to do things.

Mr. Lloyd George. I think that, as far as Asia is concerned, the Treaty of London has been torn up by the Italian landings.

M. Clemenceau. General Humbert, who is returning from the Adriatic, informs me that the Italians have taken possession of Fiume in the name of the King of Italy; he saw with his own eyes the trenches and the barbed wire destined for defense against the Yugoslavs.

President Wilson. If it must come to a conflict there, it is better that it take place quickly; that will disturb world peace less.

M. Clemenceau. We mustn't forget that we will have enough trouble with the Germans in the years to come.

President Wilson. We will not have to fight them militarily.

Mr. Lloyd George. What do you fear from Germany?

M. Clemenceau. She will sign the treaty with the firm intention of not carrying it out. She will overwhelm us with notes and explanations; it will be a perpetual controversy.

I have some interesting news from Germany. A telegram from

Berlin indicates that the Germans are preparing for a renewal of hostilities: in the western region, all able-bodied men have been transported to the interior of the territory, the garrisons have been alerted, etc. Another telegram which comes from Haguenin reports a conversation with Scheidemann. The latter says that after the signing, the German government will resign and be replaced by an Independent Socialist government, incapable of insuring the execution of the treaty, which will compel the Allies to occupy Germany and to administer it themselves.

Regarding Poland, I have a telegram from M. de Saint-Aulaire announcing that the Poles are beginning new offensives in Galicia. The danger is great that the Ukrainians, disappointed by the failure of our intervention, will be thrown into the arms of the Bolsheviks.

President Wilson. An article must be inserted in the Austrian treaty, imposing on Rumania the same obligations with respect to minorities that we are imposing on the Czechoslovaks and on the Poles; this concerns Bukovina in particular.

—*That proposal is adopted.*

Sir Maurice Hankey. You are notified of a request by the Serbs, who are soliciting financial aid.

—*The question is referred to MM. Keynes and Loucheur.*

President Wilson. The Italians request the insertion of certain so-called political clauses in the Austrian treaty.[2] These clauses have been studied by Mr. Lansing. One of them stipulates that the period of option in the redeemed territories will be limited to one year. Mr. Lansing asks that we remove Article 31, which would give Italy the right to organize emigration.

Mr. Lloyd George. The Italians are making this request in order to divert the commerce of Fiume towards Trieste. This clause, as we have already decided for others, should be communicated to the other interested nationalities.

President Wilson. By another article, certain Italian nationals would have the same rights in Austria as the Austrians, without reciprocity. Mr. Lansing proposes to grant them only most-favored-nation treatment.

Several others of these articles must be referred for study to the different competent commissions.

Mr. Lloyd George. A summary of the Austrian treaty will have to be communicated to the Allies. We have prepared one.

[2] A revised version of these draft articles is printed in *PPC*, VI, 223-28.

M. Clemenceau. Send it to M. Dutasta, who will have it translated into French. When do you want it to be read to the delegates of the powers?

Mr. Lloyd George. Couldn't this reading take place tomorrow evening? I don't think that all those who were present when we read the summary of the treaty with Germany have to be summoned this time. Why should Nicaragua and many others hear the summary of the Austrian treaty?

President Wilson. The nations directly involved should be summoned.

Mr. Lloyd George. Assuredly: the Czechs, the Yugoslavs, the Rumanians, the Poles have to be present.

Colonel House. It appears natural to summon all the nations which declared war on Austria-Hungary, as well as the ones formed out of the fragments of the Austro-Hungarian Empire.

Mr. Lloyd George. We can hold a real conference, in such a way as to allow them to ask questions.

M. Clemenceau. It is thus settled for tomorrow.

President Wilson. On the limitation of military forces, have our experts seen the different governments involved?

M. Clemenceau. Wouldn't the simplest thing be to set the figure at 30,000 men for Austria, without trying to determine now the numbers granted to the other states?

Mr. Lloyd George. I fear what can happen if these states have armies much superior to Austria's. I have no great confidence in Rumania or Serbia.

M. Clemenceau. We have the right to grant more substantial numbers to Austria later, if we judge it necessary.

President Wilson. It is better to set up a provisional arrangement as long as the period of uncertainty and disorder continues. It is impossible today, when eastern Europe is in so critical a state, finally to limit the forces of each state.

Mr. Lloyd George. It is these very states which are creating the present difficulties by fighting against one another.

President Wilson. Another question raised by Mr. Lansing is that of the Dobrudja, part of which is obviously Bulgarian. When Mr. Lansing spoke of that at the Quai d'Orsay, they replied to him: "We can't give an enemy territory which, before the war, belonged to a friendly power." It is indeed a problem; but it is necessary not to violate our principle, which requires that each population be attached to the state that it prefers.

CI

Conversation between President Wilson and MM. Clemenceau, Lloyd George, and Orlando*

MAY 28, 1919, 4:30 P.M.

THE QUESTION OF FIUME

Mr. Lloyd George. According to the plan prepared by M. Tardieu, Fiume would be established as a state under the authority of the League of Nations and administered by a council of five members until the plebiscite which, at the end of a period of fifteen years, would determine the final fate of the city and of the district. In short, it is the Saar settlement.

Under such an arrangement, everything depends on the composition of the commission or council. President Wilson proposed this morning a change in the original plan: according to this amendment, the council would be composed of two Italians, two Yugoslavs, a representative of the state of Fiume, and a representative of the League of Nations. Supposing the state of Fiume designated a representative of Yugoslav nationality, the delegate of the League of Nations would then have the deciding vote. I understand that M. Orlando accepts this part of the proposed arrangement.

There remains the question of the islands—those of Dalmatia—and the cities of Zara and Sebenico. The Italians are ready to renounce the Treaty of London if Zara and Sebenico become free ports, placed under Italian sovereignty, or, at the very least, under an Italian mandate; they declare themselves ready to leave almost all the large islands to the Yugoslavs, notably those of Brazza, Lesina, Curzola, Meleda, and, further north, the island of Pago. These are the only ones which have a modest population. All the others, except Cherso, are nothing but rocks. Italy claims Cherso as an integral part of Istria. M. Orlando assures us that the majority of the population of these islands is Italian; but the information available to President Wilson doesn't support Italy's claims.

President Wilson. My judgment is based on an Italian map—that of Marinelli.[1]

*H., *PPC*, VI, 89ff.

[1] Olinto Marinelli, author of an ethnographic map of the frontier zone of

M. Orlando. We demand Cherso and Lussino.

M. Clemenceau. What will be the official language of the state of Fiume?

President Wilson. That is one of the questions which must be settled by the state of Fiume itself.

You know what troubles me in this question of the Adriatic. The government of the United States does not feel it has the right—no more than it admits it for others—to hand over populations to anyone without their consent. What we seek, as I have often repeated, is to apply in this case the same principle that has guided us throughout all these negotiations.

I am ready to accept this proposal as a basis for discussion and to recommend it to the Yugoslavs, whose assent is absolutely essential in reaching a solution. I will try to see if it is possible to obtain a settlement of the question along the lines indicated.

I acknowledge the serious and sincere effort which the Italian government has just made; I admit that it is giving up a very large part of its first claim. Since the question of Fiume is not even raised in the Treaty of London, we are now working on a clean slate. In determining the boundaries of this new state, it seems fair to me to include, not only the island of Veglia, but also that of Cherso. As for the island of Lussino, everyone agrees that its population is Italian.

Do you authorize me to propose to the Yugoslavs the formation of a state of Fiume whose boundary would follow the crest of the mountains in the eastern part of Istria and would include the island of Cherso, whilst Lussino would remain with Italy? In this way, the state of Fiume would be master of the positions commanding the approaches to the port. The northern half of Cherso, at least, is essentially Yugoslav. When we decided upon the establishment of the autonomous state of Danzig, we recognized the necessity of guaranteeing free access to the sea and free use of the railways to all concerned. In the case of Fiume, we must obtain similar guarantees in order to insure access to the port, with the requisite facilities, for all interested nations. Otherwise, the port of Fiume wouldn't be a free port. The state of Fiume will thus have to give these guarantees to all who have an interest in using Fiume as a port.

A satisfactory answer to the questions which I now raise will greatly facilitate my conversation with Yugoslavs.

M. Orlando. I am very glad to see that President Wilson acknowledges the spirit of sacrifice which has motived the Italian govern-

---

northern Italy, about which, see *PWW*, Vol. 57, pp. 270-71.

ment. I hasten to add that, regarding the total freedom of the port of Fiume, the Italian government can make no objection; we will do everything incumbent upon us to insure the complete freedom of the trade of this port. We consider that to be our absolute duty.

As for the territorial questions, I recall that I received a document from M. Tardieu, which had been studied by Mr. Lloyd George and I believe also by M. Clemenceau, if not by President Wilson. I have made every effort to obtain the consent of my colleagues of the Italian delegation to most of the proposals contained in this document. I have telegraphed Rome, and I am awaiting the reply.

Despite the painful effort required of us to take such a decision, I accept the proposed solution, but I accept it as it is. If new concessions are asked of us, I fear that it would be difficult for me to persuade my colleagues. I didn't hesitate to give up nearly all the islands—the three large islands of the south, with Meleda, the only ones of any real importance. I must state that, if we must reduce our claims further, I won't be able to maintain my consent, which is based on M. Tardieu's document. The latter leaves the other islands to us and gives the state of Fiume a boundary slightly different from the one which President Wilson mentioned. Moreover, the question of Zara and Sebenico is still pending. We are ready to give all guarantees for the free use of these ports, and also all guarantees against their use with any offensive goal whatsoever.

In conclusion, I had the first part of M. Tardieu's document accepted, with President Wilson's amendment; I obtained the renunciation of the southern islands. If you ask more from us, I won't reply immediately: "It is impossible," but I foresee the greatest difficulties.

President Wilson. I will only say one word: I will do everything possible to have the proposals we have just heard accepted as the basis for the settlement amongst the states concerned.

—The delegates of Luxembourg and M. Paul Hymans, Foreign Minister of Belgium, are introduced.*

M. Clemenceau. We expressed the desire to hear the representatives of Luxembourg, and we thank you for responding to our invitation. We wish only to hear the freest and most sincere expression of your wishes, according to the principle of self-deter-

*H., *PPC*, VI, 93ff.

mination. No doubt questions will be asked of you once we have heard you; we ask that you reply without any hesitation or reserve.

M. Reuter. I thank M. Clemenceau for his encouraging words. You will understand our emotion in appearing before the representatives of the great Allied and Associated nations as representatives of the Luxembourg people, who respond to your invitation most willingly.

Yesterday, before our departure for Paris, we met with the Luxembourg Chamber of Deputies; we presented to it the program which we proposed to bring here; the Chamber approved it unanimously. We therefore have the right to say that we speak in the name of the people of Luxembourg.

Our people want, above all, to continue their own life, preserving their independence in close friendship with the Allied and Associated Powers. This independence is our most precious treasure, and Luxembourg believes that it hasn't merited being deprived of it. Luxembourg expresses the desire to be admitted amongst the members of the League of Nations and requests to know the terms under which she can be received into it.

We wish to settle freely the form and organization of our internal political form of government, and, in order to give our national status the widest and most democratic basis, we have decided to appeal to our people through a plebiscite. This plebiscite, to be announced soon by a vote of the Chamber, is to put the question about the form of government and the dynasty. The people of Luxembourg hope that the powers will accept the solution which they themselves will have approved by popular vote. Nothing could conform more to the principle of self-determination, which inspires your decisions.

Through the publication of the summary of the peace terms, we learned that the powers envisage the abolition of the stipulations relating to the neutrality of Luxembourg, which Germany violated in 1914. We would like to know what will be the consequences of this decision, in our own interest and in the international interest.

Another question arises for Luxembourg—that of her economic orientation. The conference knows that Luxembourg broke with the German customs union. This rupture necessarily leads to an orientation towards the Entente powers, and our government indicated this at the time of the Armistice. The ideal solution for Luxembourg would be an economic alliance with France as well as with Belgium.

By virtue of the different decisions taken by our Chamber of Deputies, we communicated with the French and Belgian governments, asking them to open negotiations to establish the basis of a union. This solution of the economic problem is seen as the ideal solution by all Luxembourg groups, as much amongst producers as amongst customers.

Several years ago, we established an investigating commission, composed of the most qualified men—industrialists, farmers, specialists of every kind—to study the problems created by the war; it finished its work at the beginning of this year, and its conclusion points in the direction which I just indicated, that is towards an economic alliance with the two countries which are our neighbors.

I must add that the majority of the economic interests of Luxembourg lean particularly towards alliance with France. These conclusions were not reached without some very heated discussions.

We have conveyed our wishes to both the governments of France and Belgium. The Belgian government replied that it was ready to undertake discussions to determine the basis of an agreement. These discussions have been in progress for several weeks now. The French government replied in January that it was taking note of our intention to break with Germany and to join the countries of the Entente, but it added that the general situation did not allow it to begin negotiations. Nonetheless, it promised, when the time came, to study the question in a spirit favorable to our wishes. Since then, we have received no communication from the French government.

The different economic groups of Luxembourg are concerned with this question, notably the labor unions and the farmers' association. They have also concluded—with the exception of a local agricultural society—in favor of an economic union with France. The government was able recently to question the professional groups. The General Confederation of Labor of Luxembourg was invited to make contact with the workers' organizations of the two neighboring countries, in order better to assess the advantages and the disadvantages of the two proposed solutions.

The metallurgical industry, which is our principal industry, thinks that it will find the raw materials in France which twenty years from now will be lacking on our own soil. Furthermore, it is looking for the largest possible market, and that is why it wants an economic union between Luxembourg and France. As for ore,

France unquestionably has the reserves we lack. In the event of an economic union with a country other than France, Luxembourg would request the favor of supplying herself in France, and of doing so under the same conditions as the industry of Lorraine, which is her neighbor and competitor. As for coal, we have noted with satisfaction that the Allied and Associated Powers have provided, in the treaty with Germany, a provision favorable to the Grand Duchy, obliging Germany to provide it with the same amount of coal as before the war. We thank the powers for the good will they have manifested on our behalf. But the duration of this delivery is not specified, nor is the price. Luxembourg has no doubt that the conference will do everything possible to safeguard the interests of the Grand Duchy.

The federation of agricultural shows considers France to be the natural supplier to Luxembourg of potash and seeds. It also observes that the conditions of production in Luxembourg are very similar to those in Lorraine.

The peace treaty provides us with the right to export freely to Germany for a certain number of years. We ask that you impose this same obligation on Germany with respect to our agricultural products. This is a vital question for us during the period of transition which will follow the signing of the treaty.

We continue to hope that it will be possible for us to conclude an economic union with the two neighboring countries; if this solution is deemed to be impossible, we wish to have it unquestionably established towards which side the majority of the economic interests of the country are going to go. According to the proposal of our Council of State, we have introduced a bill to institute a referendum on the economic orientation of Luxembourg. It is a question of establishing beyond possible dispute the side to which the interests of the country carry us, and of thus putting an end to all the controversy which is stirring up public opinion amongst us.

The economic referendum is also proposed in the hope that the expression of the national will will facilitate overtures from the other countries with whom we hope to enter into conversation. We are not unaware of the difficulty of consulting our people on the problem of the economic union when it is still impossible to say on what basis this union will be established. But there is no doubt that the majority of the people are requesting this plebiscite.

What is our practical conclusion? Our mission solicits the friendly support of the peace conference in opening negotiations in both directions, so that the orientation of our country will be determined with full knowledge of the facts, with complete freedom.

We also ask for the reparation of damages which we suffered on account of the German occupation. We hope to be able to address this request more particularly to our future economic associate or associates.

In the name of a small country which has always enjoyed the precious friendship of the powers of the Entente, we express the hope that our claims will be favorably received by you. To use the word which we read in President Wilson's most cordial letter, we hope that you will do your utmost for the people of Luxembourg.

M. Clemenceau. I will gladly say a word in reply to what M. Reuter has just said. After his excellent speech, three main questions come to mind.

M. Reuter is surprised that we have contemplated the abolition of Luxembourg's neutrality. The war revealed that neutrality was insufficient protection, for Luxembourg as well as for Belgium. It is natural that the peace conference thought this question deserved a new study. That is all I can say for the moment.

In the second place, I would be sorry if you thought that the reticence of the French government represented any lack of regard for Luxembourg. I will speak frankly on this subject. We wish to be on the best possible terms with the people and the government of Luxembourg. We know your fellow countrymen well, many of whom live amongst us, and of whom a great number served voluntarily, with the greatest devotion and bravery, in the French army during the present war. In this matter, we express to you our sincere gratitude. But the Luxembourg problem must be seen in the context of general policy. We are and want to be your friends; we also want to be on the best terms with the Belgian people; they threw themselves into battle with a heroism which we must never forget and which made all of us deeply indebted to them. The bonds which were established between Belgium and France during the war must not be loosened; we value the friendship of Belgium highly, and we wish that, in all that pertains to Luxembourg, Belgium should have her word to say. Since the political situation did not appear quite clear to us, we preferred to wait. So you know the reasons for the delay which we asked in regard to your political referendum.

We must be allowed time to settle the general questions to which the Luxembourg question is tied. It would be very regrettable if in Luxembourg public feeling expressed itself ahead of the clarification of the questions and the settling down of opinions.

In the same spirit—I speak here only in the name of the French government—I will ask you for the postponement of the economic referendum. The two questions, economic and political, are closely related. If the plebiscite takes place before we have time to study the whole of the problem, the result could hamper us, and there is no point in asking this question of the Luxembourg people before it has come to maturity.

You must consider our difficulties. After this frightful war, we met here and found ourselves confronted with all the problems; we had, so to speak, all the crimes of history to redress simultaneously. We couldn't begin by settling the questions which concern Luxembourg in particular, and we would have been wrong to do so. As for myself, I am glad that I waited. I feel that the difficulties, the possible misunderstandings, are subsiding.

In speaking of your future economic arrangements, you pointed out the preference for a union with France which manifests itself. You are concerned about bringing France, Belgium, and Luxembourg together. We have deferred our reply up to now. Today, as far as France is concerned, I will tell you that, if you wish to begin a three-way conversation about the economic arrangements of Luxembourg, France is ready. Belgium has already begun these conversations; we are ready to join them if you wish.

M. Hymans. Our conversation with Luxembourg has remained in the economic field.

M. Clemenceau. I don't want to come as an intruder. Since the government of Luxembourg seemed to be reproaching us for not having answered anything since January, I had to reply, and I suggest, if Belgium sees no difficulty, a three-way conversation. Nothing will better establish the union amongst our peoples and yours. In order not to jeopardize your agreement, we waited until now; if you admit us to the conversation, we will be happy to lend our friendship.

The question of Luxembourg is greater than the territory of Luxembourg itself. Northern Frenchmen, Belgians, Luxemburgers are people who have many traits in common: industrious, fully aware of their rights, animated by a spirit of orderly work; if they could work together, the world and the cause of peace will greatly profit.

M. Reuter. In the name of the entire Luxembourg people, the Luxembourg government can only applaud the proposal made by the

Prime Minister of France. Luxemburgers, without exception, will see an economic union between France, Belgium, and Luxembourg as the most advantageous thing for the three countries. Until now, our negotiations with Belgium have taken place to gather information, to look for the possible basis for an accord. Luxembourg views France's participation in this negotiation as a very happy event.

You wish us to postpone both our political referendum and our economic referendum. Since it doesn't seem absolutely necessary to link the two questions, the Luxembourg government would very much like to have the economic referendum to take place as soon as possible, to help towards the general appeasement of public opinion in the Grand Duchy.

M. Clemenceau. Do you accept the postponement which we ask of you?

M. Reuter. We are authorized to do so. Moreover, the Chamber of Deputies of Luxembourg will be informed immediately of your decisions.

M. Clemenceau. It is necessary to delay further, in the interest of all.

M. Hymans. I have listened attentively to the very noble speech of M. Clemenceau about the economic union of the three countries. But the idea is still a bit new to me; it needs to be studied closely, and I can say no more today.

M. Clemenceau. I am only replying to the question raised by M. Reuter; the idea of a three-way accord is one which comes from Luxembourg.

M. Reuter. I have a practical question to raise. I am sure that the Luxembourg Chamber will defer to your desire to see the economic referendum postponed further. But it will want to pass a law regulating the procedure of the referendum; do you see any difficulty in this?

M. Clemenceau. It is your right to do it; you are at home in your country, and we have no intention of interfering in your internal affairs.

CII

Conversation between President Wilson and MM. Clemenceau, LLoyd George, and Orlando*

MAY 29, 1919, NOON.

—M. Jules Cambon is introduced.

M. Cambon. In accordance with your decision, I put the question of the name of the Austrian state to the representatives of the Czechs and the Yugoslavs. Both protest against the use of the words "German Austria." The Czechs, especially, point out that, with such a title, the Austrian state could raise claims to the German populations of Bohemia.

On the other hand, the expression "German Austria" is used in the Constitution of the Austrian Republic; therefore, we face an accomplished fact here.

Mr. Lloyd George. M. Cambon's explanations remove my doubts, and I subscribe to the elimination of the word "German."

M. Clemenceau. How are we going to proceed?

President Wilson. I propose to write in the treaty that we recognize the Austrian state under the title of "Republic of Austria."

Mr. Lloyd George. Isn't it also necessary to indicate that we consider Austria as a new state, and not as the former Austria diminished?

President Wilson. We will write "a new state, under the name of 'Republic of Austria.'"

—(Assent.)

M. Orlando. I want to call your attention to a question of wording. The question is whether or not to strike out the words "such as she was in August 1914," in the reparation chapter and when we define Austria in this report. It is not the purely legal question of whether or not we are dealing with a new state. It is a matter of knowing, with respect to the damages to be redressed, whether we should consider Austria as she was in 1914, or as she is today. That is of great practical importance.

In the German treaty, we had to write "such as she was on August 1, 1914." We ask that this text be reproduced here. If you

*H., PPC, VI, 106ff.

have any doubts, since it concerns a question which entails considerable material consequences, I ask that it be referred to our Reparation Commission.

President Wilson. What compels us to use the most restrictive form is that it is impossible to ask Austria to pay for everything which might be owed to us by others than the present subjects of this state. We won't get any practical result by adding the words "such as she was on August 1, 1914." Suppose that it was a question of compensating for the loss of an English house in Prague. Can the compensation be found amongst Austrian properties sequestered in London? Nothing would be more unfair. Bohemia must provide that compensation.

Mr. Lloyd George. I would like to see the effects of these two versions concerning damages caused by the troops. If Hungarian soldiers destroyed an Italian village, it is clear, in that case, that Austria and Hungry are both responsible. How can we know, in each case, whether the damage was done by Austrian or Croatian troops, or by those of some other nationality?

President Wilson. That is why we cannot impose a general obligation upon Austria alone, as she is constituted today.

M. Orlando. The objection is serious and reveals the necessity of having the effects of this provision verified. Only our legal experts can do it, and the responsibility of the other states formed out of the dissolution of Austria-Hungary must be clearly determined. Otherwise, in the case you just mentioned, an English company that suffered damages in Vienna has a right to compensation, whereas, if the damage had occurred in Prague, this right would vanish. It might be better to strike out the words "such as she was in August 1914," but we must keep the consequences in mind and, if need be, find another solution.

President Wilson. These words can be deleted only after the opinion of the legal experts has been obtained.

Mr. Lloyd George. The question seems to me of very little practical interest, since, whatever provisions we write in the treaty, Austria won't pay.

M. Orlando. We can keep the present draft whilst awaiting the opinion of the experts.

—*This proposal is adopted.*

—M. Mantoux presents notes from M. Kramář on the political clauses of the treaty with Austria and from M. Pašić on the boundary between Austria and Yugoslavia.

—M. Kramář's note is referred to the Drafting Committee. M. Pašić will be able to raise the question in the Plenary Session.

—Sir Maurice Hankey announces that, on the subject of the convention to regulate the occupation of the Rhine region, the Economic Commission proposes to have the question studied by a joint military-economic commission.

President Wilson. This won't do; this question must be studied from the political point of view. I would very much fear the consequences of a solution dictated by the military; I am receiving letters which reveal to me all the dangers which could result from this.[1]

Mr. Lloyd George. It is a very important question for the peace of Europe. In Russia, nothing has contributed more to the popularity of the Bolsheviks than foreign occupation. We must avoid having an occupation irritate the population, exacerbate hatreds, and create a danger for all of Europe.

We can look at the question of the occupation from another point of view. The occupation army must be paid for, and everything that will be spent on this account will be taken from the total of the reparations. We must take into account the fact that an occupation army always costs much more than an army which remains on its own territory.

For these two reasons, I fear we may have agreed too easily on the idea of a prolonged occupation. The period of fifteen years, during which this occupation will continue, is not the dangerous period, for Germany will be powerless for fifteen or twenty years. In my opinion, the entire plan should be sent back for study.

M. Clemenceau. I agree with President Wilson; the question must be looked at from the political point of view; but I cannot agree that we reconsider what has been decided here amongst us.

Mr. Lloyd George. I reserve the right to return to this question. As one of the powers which contributed to the victory, England has the right to participate in the final decision.

President Wilson. In any case, we agree to have the question studied from a point of view other than the purely military one.

M. Clemenceau. I am quite ready to do so; but not to call into question the very principle of the occupation.

Mr. Lloyd George. After all, the peace must be signed. We cannot

---

[1] Wilson read a letter from Pierrepont Burt Noyes, the American representative on the Inter-Allied Rhineland Commission, to him of May 27, 1919. It is printed as an appendix to these notes.

remain in a state which would be neither peace nor war for two or three years. England, at any rate, wouldn't resign herself to that. If France prefers such a state of affairs, that is her business.

President Wilson. A commission must be formed to study the question.

M. Orlando. The German troops which occupied France after the Treaty of Frankfurt played no part in the administration of the country; they only maintained garrisons.

M. Clemenceau. That corresponds to my intentions concerning the occupation of the left bank of the Rhine.

Mr. Lloyd George. We will have to reply to the Germans in the coming days about this question of the army of occupation; its importance will have to be pointed out.

President Wilson. As far as the United States is concerned, it was agreed with M. Clemenceau that our flag would be represented, but that we would not have substantial forces in the occupied zone.

Mr. Lloyd George. From my point of view, the important thing is the total contingent of the occupation army, whatever its composition might be.

President Wilson. It is possible to determine the size of this contingent now, without deciding what each share will be.

M. Clemenceau. I propose to form a commission of four civilians and four military men in order to study the question as a whole.

President Wilson. If, as certain members of the military wish, you established a system of military government in the entire occupation zone and had to guarantee the execution of martial law there, you would need many more troops, much more dispersed, than for an occupation pure and simple, with a civil administrative commission in charge of relations with the German authorities.

Mr. Lloyd George. Are there enough barracks on the left bank of the Rhine to quarter all the occupation troops?

M. Clemenceau. Without any doubt, and I am as opposed as you are to quartering occupation troops on the local inhabitants. Be assured that I won't let the military do so; they are quite ready to govern the country and are already talking about building new huts and barracks everywhere to quarter their troops there. In that matter, I am ready to help you with all my strength.

—*It is decided to form a commission to draft the convention relating to the occupation of the left bank of the Rhine.*[2] *France will be represented*

[2] On the basis of Noyes' skeleton plan.

by Marshal Foch and M. Loucheur; England, by General Sir Henry Wilson and Lord Robert Cecil; Italy, by General Cavallero and Marquis Imperiali. President Wilson will announce later the names of the representatives of the United States on this commission.

{ A P P E N D I X }[3]

Honorable Woodrow Wilson
 President of the United States of America,
  11, Place des Etats-Unis, Paris.

Dear Sir: PARIS, MAY 27, 1919.

After a month spent in the Rhineland as American Commissioner I feel there is a danger that a disastrous mistake will be made. The "Convention" for the government of these territories, as drafted by the military representatives of the Supreme War Council on May eleventh, is more brutal, I believe, than even its authors desire upon second thought. It provides for unendurable oppression of six million people during a period of years.

This "Convention" is not likely to be adopted without great modification. What alarms me, however, is that none of the revisions of this document which I have seen recognise that its basic principle is bad—that the quartering of an enemy army in a country as its master in time of peace and the billeting of troops on the civil population will insure hatred and ultimate disaster.

I have discussed this matter at length with the American Commanders of the Army of Occupation; men who have seen "military occupation" at close range for six months. These Officers emphatically indorse the above statements. They say that an occupying army, even one with the best of intentions, is guilty of outrages and that mutual irritation, in spite of every effort to the contrary, grows apace. Force and more force must inevitably be the history of such occupation long continued.

Forgetting the apparent ambitions of the French and possibly overlooking political limitations, I have sketched below a plan which seems to me the maximum for military domination in the Rhineland after the signing of peace. Our Army Commanders and others who have studied the subject on the ground agree with this programme:

---

[3] Printed in PWW, Vol. 59, pp. 593-94.

SKELETON PLAN.

I. As few troops as possible concentrated in barracks or reserve areas with no "billeting," excepting possibly for officers.

II. Complete self-government for the territory with the exceptions below.

III. A Civil Commission with powers:

(a) To make regulations or change old ones whenever German law or actions—

(1) Threaten the carrying out of Treaty terms, or—
(2) Threaten the comfort or security of troops.

(b) To authorize the army to take control under martial law, either in danger spots or throughout the territory whenever conditions seem to them to make this necessary.

Very truly yours (Signed) P. B. NOYES.
American Delegate, Inter-Allied Rhineland Commission.

CIII

Conversation between President Wilson and MM. Clemenceau, Lloyd George, and Orlando*

MAY 30, 1919, 4 P.M.

President Wilson. The fighting between the Slovenes and Austrians in Carinthia seems to be taking a rather serious turn.

M. Clemenceau. We must stop the Yugoslavs, who are in the process of seizing Klagenfurt.

Furthermore, the Rumanians are advancing and have only just taken the place of the French in Arad; this city is in the zone which will eventually be assigned to Rumania, but I feel that the Rumanians should have waited to replace our occupation troops.

I wonder whether the Greeks shouldn't also be asked not to advance far from Smyrna; they have just occupied Magnesia.

President Wilson. We decided that they could extend their occupation over the entire *sanjak* of Smyrna and as far as Aydin.

M. Orlando. Shouldn't a commission composed of Frenchmen,

*H., PPC, VI, 115ff.

Italians, Englishmen, and Americans be sent to Carinthia in order to come between the combatants?

President Wilson. Yes, but we can send a warning to the Yugoslavs now.

M. Orlando. You can communicate with the delegation in Paris.

President Wilson. We should send them a note to remind them that a resort to arms is a defiance of the authority of the conference.

M. Clemenceau. I am ready to sign that letter.

President Wilson. Mr. Philip Kerr could be asked to draft it.

Mr. Lloyd George. I am going to instruct him to do it immediately.

—Reading of a letter from the Grand Vizier[1] requesting that a Turkish delegation be heard by the conference.

President Wilson. We have received no enemy delegation yet.

Mr. Lloyd George. There is no reason to treat the Turks like the Germans. Is there any objection to hearing them?

President Wilson. No, but the Bulgarians will ask as much from us.

Mr. Lloyd George. Do you see any drawback in that?

President Wilson. I fear that might create a difficulty for us with the Rumanians.

Mr. Lloyd George. At present, I have no decided views on the Bulgarian question.

President Wilson. The Turks will begin by protesting against what we did in Smyrna.

M. Clemenceau. What difference does that make to us?

President Wilson. We mustn't allow ourselves to become engaged in a debate.

M. Orlando. We can always hear them.

President Wilson. Yes, but not in the capacity of plenipotentiaries, given the present inadequacy of our preparation. Why not instead make an inquiry on the spot and ask them what points they wish to make?

M. Clemenceau. We agree to hear them, and that's all.

Mr. Lloyd George. Let them say what they wish; that's no great danger.

—*It is decided to draft a note in reply to the letter from the Grand Vizier.*

Sir Maurice Hankey. The Drafting Committee refers Article 228 of the treaty with Germany to you. It is one of the articles relating to responsibilities and sanctions. The question is whether one

---

[1] Damad Ferid Paşa.

should keep in it the words "by military law." They point out that, in Belgium, a certain number of crimes committed by the military are tried by civil courts. The commission proposes to cut out the word "military"; Mr. Lansing, president of the Commission on Responsibilities, is of that opinion.

President Wilson. I suppose that military law in different countries is more uniform than civil legislation. By eliminating this word, we risk losing the advantages of a more uniform jurisprudence.

M. Clemenceau. I don't think the wording matters; let the commission do what it wishes.

M. Orlando. If Belgium sends her military prisoners at the bar before civil courts, even that is part of military law. There is thus no drawback in keeping the word.

M. Clemenceau. Let us allow Mr. Lansing to settle the question.

Mr. Lloyd George. We'll have to study the whole of the German counterproposals.[2]

President Wilson. I handed them over to my experts, in sections, with a view to a complete study. We'll have to see to what extent we can take these counterproposals into account.

Mr. Lloyd George. I have gathered together my colleagues who are in Paris; opinions are rather diverse. I have summoned a great meeting for Sunday in which several ministers, come from London for the occasion, will take part. In the meantime, our experts are beginning a detailed examination of the counterproposals.

President Wilson. I will also have a meeting on Monday with the American delegation to see whether there is agreement amongst its members.

Mr. Lloyd George. The Germans are advancing certain assertions, notably on the subject of the eastern provinces, which I would like to be able to verify. Perhaps it will be necessary to ask them to send their maps to us.

M. Clemenceau. What is the issue, more specifically?

Mr. Lloyd George. Silesia. It seems that the arguments used by the Germans are not without weight. They say that this area has not been attached to Poland for more than seven hundred years.

President Wilson. Are you very sure of that? In any case, the commission made its decisions, not upon historical grounds, but upon ethnic considerations.

Mr. Lloyd George. The Germans base their argument on elections

---

[2] Brockdorff-Rantzau's letter transmitting "Observations of the German Delegation on the Conditions of Peace" is printed as an appendix to these notes. The cover letter includes the main points of the "Observations," which is printed in PPC, VI, 800-901.

in which the majority of the votes, they say, has gone to German candidates.

From the historical point of view, the main point is that this area has no truly Polish memories. The Commission on Polish Affairs appears to me to have been in a way obsessed by partiality for Poland. I never saw anything so scandalous as the first draft of its report.

President Wilson. You are going too far. In the case of Danzig, you raised an objection to the commission's conclusions because you thought the strategic argument should not take precedence over the ethnographic and linguistic. But the commission, whilst proposing a different conclusion from your own, provided you with the very facts upon which you stand in concluding otherwise, and it didn't seek to hide its reasons from you.

M. Clemenceau. We must see.

—President Wilson reads the text of a reply to the last German note on labor legislation.[3]

—This text is approved.

Mr. Lloyd George. I would like to come back to the telegram sent by M. Clemenceau to General Haller. It seems to me without doubt that the military men directed to transmit our instructions to General Haller have not carried out our orders.

M. Clemenceau. I have the acknowledgement of receipt of my telegrams.

Mr. Lloyd George. I am not speaking of what has taken place these last days, but of the instructions which we gave initially; either General Haller isn't telling the truth, or Marshal Foch didn't let him know, when Polish troops began to leave France, that these troops were only to be used against the Bolsheviks. You recall that Marshal Foch always had in mind sending his troops to Cracow by way of Lemberg, despite our insistence that they pass through Danzig.

M. Clemenceau. I will inquire about that.

—President Wilson reads aloud a report on the situation in the region of Lemberg.[4] This report is not very favorable to the Ukrainians. The atrocities with which the latter have been reproached are true, and the author of the report is surprised that the Polish army, when it advanced

[3] Brockdorff-Rantzau's letter of May 22, 1919, and the proposed reply, dated May 28, 1919, are printed in ibid., pp. 121-26.

[4] It is printed as an enclosure with R. H. Lord to WW, May 29, 1919, PWW, Vol. 59, pp. 596-99.

into Galicia, should have acted with such moderation. The Ukrainians do not seem capable of governing themselves.

Mr. Lloyd George. The author of this report concludes a bit hastily that the Ukrainians should be turned over to the Poles.

President Wilson. At the moment, I am not declaring myself in favor of one or the other. I want to hear what there is to say on both sides.

Mr. Lloyd George. From our point of view, the important thing is the armistice which we stipulated for them and which they refused to carry out. Since their opposition has not been followed by any sanction, they continue to defy our injunctions. I fear that, sooner or later, we will find ourselves dragged into that struggle.

M. Orlando. In the treaty with Austria, there is a point which remains in suspense—the one concerning punishment for war crimes. The criminals who become citizens of a state other than Austria must be covered by a special article. The Drafting Committee has as yet received no communication on this subject yet.

President Wilson. The difficulty lies in finding a satisfactory legal formula when it is a question of men who are today citizens of friendly states, participating in the League of Nations.

M. Orlando. The formula that we propose is simple. It consists of asking each government, itself, to punish the culprits who are within its jurisdiction.

Mr. Lloyd George. That seems quite fair.

M. Clemenceau. I approve this text.[5]

{ A P P E N D I X }[6]

TRANSLATION FROM THE GERMAN.

Mr. President, VERSAILLES, MAY 29TH, 1919.

I have the honour to transmit to you herewith the observations of the German Delegation on the draft Treaty of Peace. We came to Versailles in the expectation of receiving a peace proposal based on the agreed principles. We were firmly resolved to do everything in our power with a view to fulfilling the grave obligations which we had undertaken. We hoped for the peace of justice which had been promised to us. We were aghast when we

---

[5] In fact, the Four signed an agreement to this effect. It is printed in *PPC*, VI, 128-29.

[6] Printed in *PWW*, Vol. 59, pp. 579-84.

read in that document the demands made upon us by the victorious violence of our enemies. The more deeply we penetrate[d] into the spirit of this Treaty, the more convinced we became of the impossibility of carrying it out. The exactions of this Treaty are more than the German people can bear.

With a view to the re-establishment of the Polish State we must renounce indisputably German territory, nearly the whole of the province of West Prussia which is preponderantly German, of Pomerania, Danzig which is German to the core; we must let that ancient Hanse town be transformed into a free State under Polish suzerainty. We must agree that East Prussia shall be amputated from the body of the State, condemned to a lingering death, and robbed of its northern portion including Memel which is purely German. We must renounce Upper Silesia for the benefit of Poland and Czecho-Slovakia, although it has been in close political connexion with Germany for more than 750 years, is instinct with German life and forms the very foundation of industrial life throughout East Germany.

Preponderantly German circles (Kreise) must be ceded to Belgium without sufficient guarantees that the plebiscite, which is only to take place afterwards, will be independent. The purely German district of the Saar must be detached from our Empire and the way must be paved for its subsequent annexation to France, although we owe her debts in coal only, not in men.

For fifteen years Rhenish territory must be occupied, and after these fifteen years the Allies have the power to refuse the restoration of the country; in the interval the Allies can take every measure to sever the economic and moral links with the mother country and finally to misrepresent the wishes of the indigenous population.

Although the exaction of the cost of the war has been expressly renounced, yet Germany, thus cut in pieces and weakened, must declare herself ready in principle to bear all the war expenses of her enemies, which would exceed many times over the total amount of German State and private assets. Meanwhile her enemies demand in excess of the agreed conditions reparation for damage suffered by their civil population, and in this connexion Germany must also go bail for her allies. The sum to be paid is to be fixed by our enemies unilaterally and to admit of subsequent modification and increase. No limit is fixed save the capacity of the German people for payment, determined not by their standard of life but solely by their capacity to meet the demands of their enemies by their labour. The German people would thus be condemned to perpetual slave labour.

In spite of these exorbitant demands, the reconstruction of our economic life is at the same time rendered impossible. We must surrender our merchant fleet. We are to renounce all foreign securities. We are to hand over to our enemies our property in all German enterprises abroad, even in the countries of our allies. Even after the conclusion of peace the enemy States are to have the right of confiscating all German property. No German trader in their countries will be protected from these war measures. We must completely renounce our Colonies, and not even German missionaries shall have the right to follow their calling therein. We must thus renounce the realisation of all our aims in the spheres of politics, economics, and ideas.

Even in internal affairs we are to give up the right of self-determination. The International Reparations Commission receives dictatorial powers over the whole life of our people in economic and cultural matters. Its authority extends far beyond that which the Emperor, the German Federal Council and the Reichstag combined ever possessed within the territory of the Empire. This Commission has unlimited control over the economic life of the State, of communities and of individuals. Further the entire educational and sanitary system depends on it. It can keep the whole German people in mental thraldom. In order to increase the payments due by the thrall, the Commission can hamper measures for the social protection of the German worker.

In other spheres also Germany's sovereignty is abolished. Her chief waterways are subjected to international administration; she must construct in her territory such canals and railways as her enemies wish; she must agree to treaties, the contents of which are unknown to her, to be concluded by her enemies with the new States on the east, even when they concern her own frontiers. The German people is excluded from the League of Nations to which is entrusted all work of common interest to the world.

Thus must a whole people sign the decree for its own proscription, nay, its own death sentence.

Germany knows that she must make sacrifices in order to attain peace. Germany knows that she has, by agreement, undertaken to make these sacrifices and will go in this matter to the utmost limits of her capacity.

1. Germany offers to proceed with her own disarmament in advance of all other peoples, in order to show that she will help to usher in the new era of the peace of Justice. She gives up universal compulsory service and reduces her army to 100,000 men except as regards temporary measures. She even renounces the warships which her enemies are still willing to leave in her hands. She stipulates, however, that she shall be admitted forthwith as a State with equal rights into the League of Nations. She stipulates that a genuine League of Nations shall come into being, embracing all peoples of goodwill, even her enemies of to-day. The League must be inspired by a feeling of responsibility towards mankind and have at its disposal a power to enforce its will sufficiently strong and trusty to protect the frontiers of its members.

2. In territorial questions Germany takes up her position unreservedly on the ground of the Wilson programme. She renounces her sovereign right in Alsace-Lorraine, but wishes a free plebiscite to take place there. She gives up the greater part of the province of Posen, the districts incontestably Polish in population together with the capital. She is prepared to grant to Poland, under international guarantees, free and secure access to the sea by ceding free ports at Danzig, Königsberg and Memel, by an agreement regulating the navigation of the Vistula and by special railway conventions. Germany is prepared to ensure the supply of coal for the economic needs of France, especially from the Saar region, until such time as the French minds [mines] are once more in working order. The preponderantly Danish districts of Sleswig will be given up to Denmark on the basis of a plebiscite. Germany demands that the right of self-determination shall also be respected where the interests of the Germans in Austria and Bohemia are concerned.

She is ready to subject all her colonies to administration by the community of the League of Nations if she is recognised as its mandatory.

3. Germany is prepared to make payments incumbent on her in accordance with the agreed programme of peace up to a maximum sum of 100 milliards of gold marks,—20 milliards by May 1, 1926, and the balance (80 milliards) in annual payments without interest. These payments should in principle be equal to a fixed percentage of the German Imperial and State revenues. The annual payment shall approximate to the former peace Budget. For the first ten years the annual payment shall not exceed one milliard of gold marks a year. The German taxpayer shall not be *less* heavily burdened than the taxpayer of *the most* heavily burdened State among those represented on the Reparation Commission.

Germany presumes in this connexion that she will not have to make any territorial sacrifices beyond those mentioned above and that she will recover her freedom of economic movement at home and abroad.

4. Germany is prepared to devote her entire economic strength to the service of reconstruction. She wishes to cooperate effectively in the reconstruction of the devastated regions of Belgium and Northern France. To make good the loss in production of the destroyed mines in Northern France, up to 20 million tons of coal will be delivered annually for the first five years and up to 8 million tons for the next five years. Germany will facilitate further deliveries of coal to France, Belgium, Italy and Luxemburg.

Germany is moreover prepared to make considerable deliveries of benzol, coal tar and sulphate of ammonia as well as dye-stuffs and medicines.

5. Finally, Germany offers to put her entire merchant tonnage into a pool of the world's shipping, to place at the disposal of her enemies, a part of her freight space as part payment of reparation, and to build for them for a series of years in German yards an amount of tonnage exceeding their demands.

6. In order to replace the river boats destroyed in Belgium and Northern France, Germany offers river craft from her own resources.

7. Germany thinks that she sees an appropriate method for the prompt fulfilment of her obligation to make reparation, by conceding participation in industrial enterprises, especially in coal mines to ensure deliveries of coal.

8. Germany, in accordance with the desires of the workers of the whole world, wishes to see the workers in all countries free and enjoying equal rights. She wishes to ensure to them in the Treaty of Peace the right to take their own decisive part in the settlement of social policy and social protection.

9. The German Delegation again makes its demand for a neutral enquiry into the responsibility for the war and culpable acts in its conduct. An impartial Commission should have the right to investigate on its own responsibility the archives of all the belligerent countries and all the persons who took an important part in the war.

Nothing short of confidence that the question of guilt will be examined dispassionately can put the peoples lately at war with each other in the proper frame of mind for the formation of the League of Nations.

These are only the most important among the proposals which we have to make. As regards other great sacrifices and also as regards the details, the Delegation refers to the accompanying memorandum and the annex thereto.

The time allowed us for the preparation of this memorandum was so short that it was impossible to treat all the questions exhaustively. A fruitful and illuminating negotiation could only take place by means of oral discussion. This treaty of peace is to be the greatest achievement of its kind in all history. There is no precedent for the conduct of such comprehensive negotiations by an exchange of written notes only. The feeling of the peoples who have made such immense sacrifices makes them demand that their fate should be decided by an open, unreserved exchange of ideas on the principle: "Open covenants of peace openly arrived at, after which there shall be no private international understandings of any kind, but diplomacy shall proceed always frankly and in the public view."

Germany is to put her signature to the Treaty laid before her and to carry it out. Even in her mind, Justice is for her too sacred a thing to allow her to stoop to accept conditions which she cannot undertake to carry out. Treaties of Peace signed by the Great Powers have, it is true, in the history of the last decades again and again proclaimed the right of the stronger. But each of these Treaties of Peace has been a factor in originating and prolonging the world-war. Whenever in this war the victor has spoken to the vanquished, at Brest-Litovsk and Bucharest, his words were but the seeds of future discord. The lofty aims which our adversaries first set before themselves in their conduct of the war, the new era of an assured peace of justice, demand a Treaty instinct with a different spirit. Only the cooperation of all nations, a cooperation of hands and spirits can build up a durable peace. We are under no delusions regarding the strength of the hatred and bitterness which this war has engendered; and yet the forces which are at work for an union of mankind are stronger now than ever they were before. The historic task of the Peace Conference of Versailles is to bring about this union.

Accept, Mr. President, the expression of my distinguished consideration.

Brockdorff Rantzau.

CIV

Conversation between President Wilson and MM. Clemenceau, Lloyd George, and Orlando*

MAY 31, 1919, 5:30 P.M.

M. Orlando. The preamble of the treaty with Austria states that the Austro-Hungarian monarchy has ceased to exist through the free movement of peoples. This wording could be offensive in Italy, where they would believe that it diminishes the importance of the Italian victory. I propose to write only that the monarchy has ceased to exist. Moreover, there is no need to say more in a text of this kind.

Mr. Lloyd George. The statement of fact is indeed enough.

M. Orlando. Further on, I read: "The Allied and Associated Powers have recognized the union of certain parts of that empire as an independent and allied state, under the name of 'Kingdom of the Serbs, Croats and Slovenes.'" As a matter of fact, that is not accurate, for Italy has not recognized that state.

Moreover, it seems to me pointless to mention in that passage the states formed out of the debris of Austria-Hungary. In any case, we would have to mention Poland, whose name I don't see.

President Wilson. We wanted to name these states in the preamble, because they are mentioned in the text of the treaty and we insisted on defining them first in some way.

M. Orlando. At any rate, Poland isn't mentioned.

Mr. Lloyd George. From the point of view of the Drafting Committee, there must be a reason for mentioning these states in that place; the best thing is to consult the Drafting Committee on the subject.

M. Clemenceau. What do we decide on the text relating to minorities, about which we are going to hear Rumania's observations? I propose to leave this text as it is.

Mr. Lloyd George. Rumania has no grounds for complaint at the time when we are doubling the extent of her territory.

M. Clemenceau. It was not done by Rumanian soldiers.

Mr. Lloyd George. Without us, part of Rumania would have been lost forever.

M. Clemenceau. Then we will leave the words whose omission M.

*H., PPC, VI, 130ff.

Brătianu requested: "judged necessary by the Principal Allied and Associated Powers."

President Wilson. I believe that these words are necessary and that we must insist upon our right to intervene in the matter.

—The Drafting Committee is introduced.

—M. Orlando presents his objections to the preamble of the treaty with Austria.

M. Fromageot. We have only followed the directions of the Council of Four.

M. Orlando. Do you see an objection to omitting to mention the states formed out of the territories of the Austro-Hungarian monarchy?

M. Fromageot. It is not for me to answer you, for that is a political question.

President Wilson. It seems to me necessary to retain the mention of these states in the preamble, because a certain number of stipulations in the treaty concern them directly. It is true that all the Allied and Associated Powers have not recognized the Yugoslav state; but can't we write: "Considering that a majority of the said Powers have already recognized * * *" etc.?

Concerning Poland, it is true that she is not mentioned; but Mr. Brown Scott reminds me that we haven't yet decided on the fate of Galicia.

M. Orlando. I will observe that the Yugoslav state is not recognized by the majority of the Allied and Associated Powers. In fact, it has only been recognized by the United States.

M. Clemenceau. If we have not recognized the Yugoslavs, it was out of regard for you. But today they are recognized in fact, since we presented their credentials to the German plenipotentiaries, with the name which they themselves give to their state.

M. Orlando. I don't know if that is equivalent to recognition.

M. Clemenceau. We are told that it is. Besides, what does it matter? You will be compelled to recognize them also some day.

—The Drafting Committee withdraws.

—M. Tardieu is introduced.

Mr. Lloyd George. I asked that M. Tardieu be present, because I have already discussed the question about which I have to speak to you with him.

I received a telegram from General Allenby[1] which gives me

---

[1] It is printed in *PPC*, VI, 136-37.

serious news. According to Emir Faisal, the rumor in Damascus is that the commission of inquiry won't come to Syria and that a large French army is going to appear under the command of General Gouraud. A telegram from the Hedjaz says that, if the commission doesn't make its inquiry, and if Syria is given to France, there will be an uprising of all the Mohammedan populations, and that responsibility for the blood shed in the opposition of peoples who don't want to allow themselves to be divided like livestock will fall back on the conference.

General Allenby's commentary on this news from an Arab source is that the situation is very serious and that he personally declines all responsibility. Unless you allow me to reassure Faisal and to tell him that the commission of inquiry is going to Syria, he will raise the Arabs against France and us. The most immediate danger is for the British troops. We must decide without delay whether or not we are sending the commission, and whether I can telegraph the same to General Allenby today. If France doesn't think she can participate in the inquiry, the American commissioners, who have already left, can take charge of it. As for myself, I am ready to leave the matter in their hands. In that case, I shall wire that we are ready to accept their conclusions. The situation is so serious that we must act without delay.

M. Clemenceau. My position is very clear. I am ready to send a mission to Syria when I know that the relief of British troops has begun. I don't believe it is useful to send investigators there to go and see the population as it might have been under the administration of the British occupation.

As for the dispatch of French troops, you know very well that I won't send a single man without being in agreement with you. At this very moment, two or three of our battalions are en route to Cilicia, where we no longer have direct interests, because General Allenby requests us to put them there. As soon as the relief has begun, I agree to send our representatives.

Mr. Lloyd George. Before acting as I am going to do, I thought it my duty to warn you. General Allenby says there will be immediate danger if we withdraw our troops, and Emir Faisal says that the country will revolt if the French make their appearance. I am going to read you the telegram which I propose to send to General Allenby.[2]

---

[2] Printed in *ibid.*, p. 137. The telegram said that, for various reasons, neither the British nor the French government had appointed members of the commission of inquiry. Allenby was instructed to say to the American commissioners when they arrived "that the greatest weight and consideration" would be given by the British government to their advice and recommendations.

M. Clemenceau. Its wording concerns only you.

Mr. Lloyd George. I insist upon informing you of what I am doing.

—Reading of the text of the telegram, which announces the arrival of the commission of inquiry. The American members of that commission are already en route. France has not decided to participate in it.

M. Clemenceau. It should be added: "before the beginning of the relief." I insist that there be no ambiguity. I have nothing else to say.

Mr. Lloyd George. The British commissioners won't be sent to Syria before the French government's. I will add that that commission doesn't have power to take decisions, but only to prepare a report which will be submitted to us.

Will Italy send her commissioners to Syria?

M. Orlando. I will wait for the others.

President Wilson. The American commission has already left.

M. Clemenceau. Mr. Lloyd George has just said that he won't send anyone to Syria if our representatives don't go there.

M. Orlando. I will do the same as you.

M. Clemenceau. Would you please give me the text of the telegram which you received from General Allenby and Emir Faisal?

Mr. Lloyd George. Very well.

President Wilson. I see in the amendments proposed to the treaty with Austria an article on historical properties claimed by the different nationalities. What is its scope?

M. Tardieu. Bohemia, for example, asks not to be required to reimburse Austria for the value of the castle of Prague, which is one of her national properties. Poland likewise requests that her ownership of ancient Polish monuments be acknowledged, as well as that of national forests.

President Wilson. I don't think any of us can oppose that amendment.

CV

Conversation between President Wilson and MM. Clemenceau and Lloyd George*

JUNE 2, 1919, 4 P.M.

President Wilson. Early this afternoon, I consulted my experts on the question of Klagenfurt. It seems that the difficulties come from the Yugoslavs, who want to hold a plebiscite by commune, instead of organizing one for the entire region. In other cases, we have rejected the procedure requested by the Yugoslavs; it seems to me particularly ill-adapted to the Klagenfurt Basin, which forms a geographic and economic unity, since it is completely surrounded by mountains, with a single center for railroads, the city of Klagenfurt.

Mr. Lloyd George. There is a river in the middle of this valley, and a river is not a bad frontier. North of the Drava, the Germans are unquestionably the majority; to the south, the country is Slovene. A plebiscite for the entire region would perhaps give the Yugoslavs a slight majority. Furthermore, I think the American experts believe that the Slavs of the Klagenfurt Basin, who are Wends, are linked by their interests to Austria and would probably vote in favor of the Austrian state.

President Wilson. The interests of these populations do indeed bind them to Austria. Those amongst our experts who visited this country noted that the population, on the whole, wanted to remain with Austria.

Mr. Lloyd George. Can't we hear what the Yugoslavs have to say on this subject?

M. Clemenceau. I think we must. I believe we should hear M. Vesnić.

Mr. Lloyd George. I feel it is my duty to indicate to you the position of the British delegation with respect to the peace treaty. It is difficult. Our public opinion desires peace above all else and doesn't attach excessive importance to the terms of that peace. It wouldn't support a government that would resume the war without the most compelling reasons. That is why I thought I had to invite all my colleagues in the English government who could leave London to come to confer with me.

We have had four meetings. I first consulted the delegation of

*H., PPC, VI, 138ff.

the British Empire. Later, Saturday evening, I had a private conversation with the members of the British cabinet; and finally, on Sunday, we had two large meetings, in which both the members of the government and of our delegation to the conference took part.[1] It seemed useful to me to ask for the opinion of men who, not having had to concern themselves with details of the peace treaty, could see things from a greater distance. Each expressed his opinion, and my colleagues seemed to me to be unanimous on a certain number of points.

They are obviously not disposed, in the event the Germans refuse to sign, to continue the war or to resume the hostilities or the blockade unless certain amendments are made to the treaty. I regret to say that Mr. Barnes, who is the only representative of the labor world in the present government, has written me a letter in which he states that he cannot sign the peace treaty as it is. The South African delegation refuses to sign the peace treaty; General Botha, who is a very moderate man, insists that certain changes be made. All the others think that, if certain provisions of the treaty are not changed, they could agree neither to having the British army advance into Germany nor to having our fleet secure the blockade.

I must point out that the people who participated in this debate represented fairly well the different sections of the British government. There were Conservatives and Unionists, Mr. Barnes, who is a Labour member, representatives of the dominions, and a moderate Liberal, Mr. Fisher, whose statements carried great weight. Before meeting here, they had read all the documents carefully. They are in touch with public opinion in Great Britain which, they say, wants peace and is not particularly interested in the details of the treaty.

Several amongst them were surprised that the Germans, in

---

[1] The three large general meetings were of the leaders of the British government and of the dominions—the so-called British Empire delegation. They took place at the headquarters of the British delegation at the Hôtel Majestic, 21 rue Ninot, on May 30 at 3 p.m., June 1, 11 a.m., and June 1, 5:30 p.m. Minutes of these meetings are printed in M. Dockrill, *British Documents on Foreign Affairs: Reports and Papers from the Foreign Office Confidential Print*, Kenneth Bourne and D. Cameron Watt, general eds., Part II, Series I, Vol. 4 [Frederick, Md., 1989], pp. 91-116.

Members of the cabinet dined with Lloyd George in his apartment in the Hôtel Majestic on the evening of May 31. Discussion lasted until midnight and resumed at breakfast the next morning. For a good account of these discussions, see Lentin, *Lloyd George, Woodrow Wilson and the Guilt of Germany*, pp. 94-95.

their counterproposals, had made such important concessions. These are the views of Mr. Fisher, of Mr. Chamberlain. Lord Robert Cecil also believes that it is absolutely necessary to make serious changes in the treaty. The two Archbishops of York and Canterbury[2] have written to me along the same lines, and they can be considered to be representatives of moderate opinion. These are facts which I am compelled to take into consideration.

Here are the questions which, above all, drew the attention of my colleagues. The first is that of the eastern boundary of Germany; they say that they cannot justify it as we have drawn it. Unless this boundary is changed, they think a march on Berlin could not be justified. On this point, they have the support of our experts. Their opinion is that we cannot determine the fate of Upper Silesia without a plebiscite, since this region has not been part of Poland for several centuries. If the population itself decides by a vote to unite with Poland, it cannot later on be a question of revenge. Imagine what would have happened if Alsace-Lorraine in 1871 had been reunited to Germany by a plebiscite. Personally, I think that the popular vote in Upper Silesia will decide in favor of Poland.

Further north, towards Guhrau and Militsch, there is a territory inhabited by German populations which was assigned to Poland in order to make the boundary coincide with the course of a river. Even further north, towards Schneidemühl, there is a region whose entire population is German, which was assigned to Poland because there is a certain railway line there. There is also something to say on the subject of Memel.

Everyone appeared to be very uneasy over the question of the Saar. There, I took a very strong position, and I believe I persuaded them that we can't go back on what has been decided. I pointed out to them that the people themselves will decide their fate at the end of a period of fifteen years.

Concerning reparation, everyone agrees that we are asking of Germany more than she can ever pay. But what they criticize most is the indefinite and unlimited character of the debt imposed on Germany. I have two suggestions to make on this subject, between which we could choose. I have already discussed them with Mr. Baruch. But before submitting them to the experts, I would like to have the opinion of the heads of governments.

There remains the question of the occupation, to which they

---

[2] The Most Rev. Cosmo Gordon Lang and the Most Rev. Randall Thomas Davidson.

don't want to consent. Since Germany has an army of 100,000 men, is it necessary, they say, to have 200,000 men on the left bank of the Rhine to prevent the Germans from invading France? They say that the occupation is only a means of feeding the French army at Germany's expense. During these fifteen years, Germany cannot be a danger, and it is precisely when she will emerge from her present state of weakness that the occupation troops will be withdrawn. One can understand—whilst rejecting them—Marshal Foch's ideas about the permanent occupation of the bridges of the Rhine; but the arrangement adopted by the treaty doesn't withstand close study. Our military advisers say that it cannot be defended and that it will cost Germany—that is to say, in the end, the Allies—100,000,000 pounds sterling a year, unless France herself assumes the costs. During the first years, this sum is nearly all that Germany will be able to pay.

I have just received a document signed by Messrs. Loucheur, Clémentel, Lord Robert Cecil, etc., in which they acknowledge that Germany will be unable to pay for some years. As soon as she can pay, the expenses of the army of occupation will absorb everything.[3]

Furthermore, the presence of this army on German soil will be a source of irritation and perhaps of dangerous incidents. The experience after 1815, even though France had at that time a government which was on good terms with the Allies, and the experience of 1871 are not such as to encourage us.

Such are the convictions held by my colleagues, who declare that they could not authorize me to sign the treaty unless the terms are changed. Occupation would only create dangers and deprive the Allies of all that they can expect to receive, even for the restoration of the devastated countries of France and Belgium, for at least ten years.

Concerning the League of Nations, they think that, if the Germans show good faith in the execution of the peace treaty, they should be admitted into the League of Nations as soon as possible. This question would have to be studied as early as next year.

On all these points, the persons whom I consulted are unanimous and say that public opinion has been disturbed by the German counterproposals. The Germans did not say: "We refuse to

---

[3] This document was also signed by Norman H. Davis and Bernard M. Baruch. It was drawn up by an informal committee and reviewed the entire question of reparations, postwar credits for France and Great Britain, indeed the entire international economic situation in which western Europe found itself. For a long summary, see *PWW*, Vol. 60, p. 26.

sign." They went very far in their concessions. My colleagues are struck by the criticisms of the Germans concerning the drawing of the eastern boundary of Germany, the indefinite character of the financial obligations imposed on Germany, and the arrangement for the occupation. They are also struck by the great number of what they call pinpricks—minor provisions relating to railroads, the future position of German subjects in Allied countries, etc.

M. Clemenceau. Some of these minor points are not without importance.

President Wilson. The objections which you have just presented to us are of such importance that I will have to convene my delegation tomorrow morning to discuss them with it.

M. Clemenceau. I'll do the same.

President Wilson. I will proceed as Mr. Lloyd George has, that is, I will listen to my colleagues and gather their impressions. On the whole, several of these criticisms seem to me worth studying.

Mr. Lloyd George. Mr. Balfour, Mr. Massey, and I were the only ones to defend the treaty. You must understand the state of mind of our people; they don't have the same military tradition as France. They want to go home and wouldn't cooperate in a renewal of hostilities if the treaty contains anything at all which part of public opinion considered unjustifiable.

M. Clemenceau. I thank Mr. Lloyd George for having presented to us a situation which, in my opinion, is extremely serious; it could not be more so. Like him, I feel the current of public opinion of my country, and I must take it into account. I believe that everyone is anxious to have done. In England, it is thought that the way to succeed is to make concessions. In France, we think it necessary to rush matters. Unfortunately, we know the Germans better than anyone; we think that the more we concede to them, the more they will ask. I believe the route we are taking will lead to peace only over the course of an incalculable number of months—I say "months," not "weeks."

I come to the questions you have raised. With respect to Poland, I won't discuss the boundary details. The delimitation which was submitted to us is undoubtedly not intangible. But it may happen that the ethnographic principle has to yield to other considerations. President Wilson himself admitted it when he thought that, in the Klagenfurt Basin, an incontestably Slovene population should return to Austria.

In Poland, we have not only to redress a historical crime; we must consider this country as the natural barrier between Germany and Russia. In an interview published today by the *Chicago Tribune*, Erzberger recalls that Poland is interposed between Russia and Germany and that, for this reason, she must be weakened as much as possible.[4] The day when Germany will have reestablished her communications with Russia, she will be able to use this country, and it will become possible to resume the march on Paris—says Erzberger—with a much greater chance of success than in 1914.

I believe that you will acknowledge along with me that, if Germany is left free to colonize and exploit Russia, the blood which has flowed for five years will have been spent in vain. I don't want to say any more about this today.

I am leaving aside the question of the Saar, since you are not proposing to change the provisions of the treaty.

Concerning reparations, the position of French public opinion is very clear: it thinks—wrongly—that we have not demanded all that we should have from Germany. France is the country which suffered most from the war, and today she is convinced that we are not demanding enough of Germany. This conviction is expressed in the speeches of eminent and moderate men, such as that of M. Milliès-Lacroix the other day in the Senate, and even that of M. Ribot recently.[5]

I am convinced that we have done what was reasonable; but if I move back one step, I know that I will have a general uprising against me. Can we satisfy justifiable criticisms through a better distribution without stirring up French opinion? I am ready to study it with you. British public opinion doesn't complain that Germany has to give up all her colonies, her entire fleet. That is natural, every people sees things from its own point of view. A no less natural feeling in France will be that the British criticisms focus on continental questions.

Mr. Lloyd George. I can tell you that there is no movement of public opinion in England concerning the colonies; that is a question which interests the dominions much more than ourselves. Never,

---

[4] This was a fraudulent report in the Paris edition of the *Chicago Tribune*, June 1, 1919, of a letter from Matthias Erzberger, leader of the Center (Catholic) party to various German leaders, in which Erzberger allegedly said that the German plan for world domination, including domination of the United States, would begin in eastern Europe. The first step in the plan was to prevent the establishment of a strong Poland.

[5] About Ribot's speech, see *PWW*, Vol. 60, p. 29.

in a public speech, in any resounding article, does this question take first place. The only subject which really preoccupies public opinion, in England as much as in France, is reparation.

M. Clemenceau. I come to the question of the occupation. There is none more difficult or painful for me. At this time, I have to fight every day against generals who go beyond their authority and commit errors that I regret. In this question of the occupation, many people—and, as you know, highly placed ones—believe I have made excessive concessions. One of your arguments hits home: that of the expense. Care must be taken not to diminish, by the expenses of the occupation, the share of our allies in the reparations, and even our own.

As for the necessity of the occupation, the question has not been well put. Germany will not attack France, that is not what we fear. But she will sign the treaty with the intention of not carrying it out, she will raise difficulties on one point, then on another, and, if we don't have the means to impose our will, everything will go bit by bit.

My policy at the conference, as I hope you will acknowledge, is one of close agreement with Great Britain and America. I am not unaware that you have great interests far removed from what most concerns us, I know something of the great American continent and of the immense achievement of the British Empire. Because I have made the entente with England and America the essential foundation of my policy, I am attacked on all sides as weak and incompetent. If I disappeared, you would find yourselves faced with differences even more intractable than those which may separate us today.

There remains the possibility of a final disagreement between us. I don't even want to contemplate it. Let's try to reduce the questions to their narrowest proportions, let's consider only the facts and attempt to see them as they are. If, after that, irreducible points remain between us, I don't know how we will be able to contemplate the future. I don't want to believe that we will have to tell public opinion that we are obliged to break off our negotiations because we are incapable of giving a common reply to the Germans.

Mr. Lloyd George. The preoccupation of the public in England is the same as in France. The only question upon which I am sharply attacked is that of reparation. There are people who demand that Germany pay to the last penny. They also insist on the ships; that is not surprising, since the Germans sank eight million tons of ours.

I must declare that, if Germany said: "I will yield, on the condition that you give me back my colonies," I would be ready to return East Africa to her—on the condition that you did as much with the Cameroons. We have enough colonies; more are a burden for us.

But the question of the occupation is our business. We are ready, as you know, to come to your aid in case of danger.

M. Clemenceau. My dear friend, we have no wish to begin the war again!

Mr. Lloyd George. Since our assistance is assured you, the situation is the same, whether your army is in France or on the Rhine.

M. Clemenceau. I agree to discuss the costs of the occupation, but nothing else.

Mr. Lloyd George. You speak of reducing the questions to their narrowest proportions. I don't think it wise to underrate their seriousness. Our generals believe that a large French army on the Rhine will be a danger for the peace of Europe. A prolonged occupation in peacetime, leaving peoples who hate each other face to face, the risk of seeing the German populations, under foreign domination, lose patience—all that appears to them as a threat for the future. If you and your government conclude that you can make no concessions to us on this point, I will be compelled to return to England and to take the question before Parliament.

No doubt, I should have resisted you more in our previous discussions. I never liked this occupation of fifteen years; but I didn't realize it would provoke such a strong feeling amongst my colleagues. Several of them told me: "It would have been better to ask France to choose between the occupation of the left bank of the Rhine for fifteen years and the British guarantee." The British cabinet is unanimous today in the opinion that the question should have been asked in this manner.

Like you, I think the situation is serious. I knew that a few of my colleagues were inclined to make concessions to Germany; but I didn't think they would be so unanimously of that opinion. Mr. Churchill and Mr. Chamberlain were both very emphatic against Germany, but both declare themselves along these lines. The Lord Chancellor[6] also, and I was surprised by this. Mr. Hughes himself, whose ardor you know, told me that he didn't understand how we could have consented to the occupation arrangement provided by the treaty. It was the same for the representatives of Canada and New Zealand.

---

[6] Frederick Edwin Smith, 1st Earl of Birkenhead.

M. Clemenceau. It is my duty to be frank. I tell you right now, fully conscious of the significance of my words, that I can make no concession on this point; it is an impossibility.

President Wilson. But on the costs of the occupation army?

M. Clemenceau. That I am ready to study. But Mr. Lloyd George just told me: "I will be compelled to take the question before Parliament." I find myself in the same situation. I am ready to offer my resignation and ask the President of the Republic to find someone to negotiate with you on that basis. I won't seek to recriminate.

Mr. Lloyd George. Nor do I recriminate; I reproach you for nothing. I reproach myself for not having stood out more in our previous discussions.

President Wilson (to Mr. Lloyd George). What do you have to propose concerning reparation?

Mr. Lloyd George. I would leave our claim intact, and I wouldn't touch a single one of our categories. But I understand that the Germans want to know how far their obligation extends. M. Loucheur replies to this: "We ourselves don't know what we have lost. We are in the same state of uncertainty as our enemies." I will propose two ways of getting out of this difficulty.

We could accept a commitment on the part of the Germans to repair or restore directly, in a given period, everything they destroyed. At the end of that period, they shall have either repaired or paid. Concerning pensions or sunken ships, and no doubt some other categories, it is possible to set the figures now. Therefore, I will propose to accept Germany's offer to repair the devastation herself within a limited period, adding the figure of what she will have to pay under the other headings.

We could still tell Germany: "You will sign the treaty as it is, and, in three months, you will present us with a figure for the total payments to be made. The figure you have just announced is insufficient; in reality, it doesn't represent more than two billion sterling at current value. If, at the expiration of a period of three months, we cannot agree with you on the figure, then the treaty will remain as it is."

Don't imagine I have told you what you have just heard in order to threaten you; I only wanted to inform you of what I myself have just learned.

M. Clemenceau. If I sensed a game on your part, I would have already told you so, and I would prefer that it was so, for the situation wouldn't be as serious as it is.

I propose to leave things as they are, and for all of us to hold conversations with our technical advisers tomorrow morning. We will see each other again tomorrow in the afternoon.

Mr. Lloyd George. Without M. Orlando?

M. Clemenceau. I believe that would be better. I have some information on his relations with the Austrians which worries me a bit.

Mr. Lloyd George. Considering the state of Italian public opinion, it can't be said that he is wholeheartedly our colleague.

President Wilson. If the Germans had had the good sense to speak like the Austrians, the situation would be better. The Austrians said to us: "We are in your hands; but we are not alone responsible."

M. Clemenceau. What will we say to M. Orlando?

Mr. Lloyd George. That we are consulting our technical experts about the German counterproposals.

President Wilson. We can also ask him to consult his own.

M. Clemenceau. Should I bring the experts on the Polish question to you tomorrow?

Mr. Lloyd George. It is better to begin with a general discussion.

President Wilson. I'll go to the Hôtel Crillon tomorrow, and I will ask my advisers first for their views on the German counterproposals as a whole. Then we will move on to the different problems.

It seems to me a bit awkward to remain two or three days without calling M. Orlando.

M. Clemenceau. However, there are questions we can discuss more freely if he is not present, especially the question of the occupation. But he could undoubtedly participate in the discussion on the boundaries of Poland.

Mr. Lloyd George. The unfortunate thing is that he will connect everything to the questions which concern him, and in that question of the Polish boundary, he will only look for arguments to settle the question of Fiume to his liking.

President Wilson. In any case, he has to participate in our discussion on reparation.

CVI

Conversation between President Wilson and MM. Clemenceau, Lloyd George, and Orlando*

JUNE 3, 1919, 4 P.M.

President Wilson. If you are agreeable, we will begin consideration of the possible changes in the treaty with Germany[1] with the ones relating to Polish questions.

According to the financial clauses, each of the Allied and Associated states has the right to expropriate, as a means of compensation, the property of German subjects found in its own territory. For example, the government of the United States can seize sequestered German properties and use them as compensation for the losses suffered by its nationals in Germany. The difference, if there is any between the two totals, has to go to the common reparation fund.

In our minds, that clause was conceived for the benefit of the belligerents. But we see that Poland can use it to seize the German mines of Silesia by expropriation.

M. Clemenceau. Aren't these mines the property of the Prussian state?

Mr. Lloyd George. I think so; the companies which exploit them do so by virtue of a leased concession.

President Wilson. In any case, I must say that my intention was not to allow the new states to proceed in this manner. I fear that the results may be rather serious.

Mr. Lloyd George. I am of that opinion regarding Silesia; it is a case which cannot be compared to that of Alsace-Lorraine; it is a territory which has not been Polish for several centuries.

President Wilson. Nor can it be said that it was German during that entire period. But it is obvious that a change is necessary. It must be stipulated that Germany will receive the quantities of coal that are necessary for her at the same price as Poland, and that all expropriation will give rise to fair compensation on the part of the Polish state.

*H., PPC, VI, 147ff.

[1] Wilson had had a long and open discussion with all the American commissioners, experts, and advisers in the morning and early afternoon of June 3. A transcript of this discussion is printed in PWW, Vol. 60, pp. 45-71.

Mr. Lloyd George. Why allow expropriation in any manner at all?

President Wilson. You can't prevent any state from making expropriations on its own territory.

Mr. Lloyd George. This is a special case. It must not be forgotten that, in Silesia, the inhabitants of German race and language will constitute one third of the total population.

I also fear that the Poles will use the right of expropriation in order to persecute the Jews.

President Wilson. The right of expropriation is not one of those which we can either confer upon them or refuse them by the treaty; for it is a right that belongs to all states, to expropriate or to requisition properties which are found on their territory—given just compensation.

Mr. Lloyd George. In that case, a portion of the value of the expropriated properties should revert to the reparation fund.

President Wilson. In fact, many of the localities where the coal is consumed will be part of Polish territory from now on. When Germany complains of losing 24 per cent of her coal by the cession of Silesia, she reasons as if Posen has to remain German. What must be said is that Germany will have the right for a certain number of years to receive a definite amount of coal on the same terms as the Polish consumer.

As for the changes to be made in the boundary, Mr. Lloyd George drew our attention to the region of Schneidemühl: that region is sparsely populated, a part of it is composed of marshes, and what influenced the conclusion of our experts is the presence of a railway line.

Mr. Lloyd George. The Highlands of Scotland are also very sparsely populated; but if it was a question of ceding them, under this pretext, to Germany or to Poland, you would have serious difficulties.

President Wilson. The railroad follows the ethnographic line rather closely in the area located further south. Around Schneidemühl, the frontier could be drawn further to the east, where the railroad actually serves German areas and could remain entirely on German territory.

Mr. Lloyd George. I also drew your attention to a small area near the coast which is actually part of Pomerania; but that question is of little importance compared to that of Silesia.

President Wilson. I have thought about the question of Silesia. It appears to me difficult to hold a plebiscite in that region. It would be necessary to begin by making all the German civil servants leave.

Mr. Lloyd George. You don't mean that it would be necessary to expel all petty civil servants?
President Wilson. No, but those who administer the region.
M. Clemenceau. I will recall that mayors in Germany are appointed by the central government.
Mr. Lloyd George. Of course, the main German authorities must disappear before the plebiscite.
President Wilson. The main point is that all of Upper Silesia is in the hands of fifteen or twenty German capitalists; it is from this quarter that all the protests we hear are coming.
M. Clemenceau. That is quite true; it is people like Henckel von Donnersmarck, who passes for the richest man in Germany.
President Wilson. My advisers say that it won't be possible to obtain a truly free and genuine vote from a population which has been so long in a state of vassalage, one which will always fear the consequences should the area remain in the hands of its present masters.
Mr. Lloyd George. I will point out that, in the elections of 1907, despite the feeling to which you refer, the Poles had the majority. The British experts are convinced that a plebiscite would result in Poland's favor; they are advocates of the plebiscite; the point is to prevent the Germans from saying later that, although Polish by race or language, these populations were in the majority attached to Germany—just as the population of Alsace, whose Germanic origin is undeniable, preserved its consciousness of being French.
President Wilson. Opposition to the cession of Upper Silesia doesn't rest on any popular sentiment in Germany; it is a matter of defending the interests of the great German capitalists in Silesia.
Mr. Lloyd George. The German delegation in Versailles doesn't represent the capitalists; it represents a government in which the Socialists are in the majority.
President Wilson. In any case, it is pleading the capitalist cause.
Mr. Lloyd George. No, it speaks for its country. Prussian Poland has been part of Prussia for only 150 years, but Silesia has been detached from Poland for 700 years. All I ask is that the people have the right to speak for themselves on the fate of the region.
President Wilson. Exactly; can they do it?
Mr. Lloyd George. We may have to occupy the territory during the plebiscite.
President Wilson. In that case, the Germans will say that the vote took place under the pressure of our bayonets.

Mr. Lloyd George. That matters little if we ourselves have good reason to think that the vote took place freely. I know what intimidation by great landowners is like; I had some examples of it in Wales, where, moreover, we were able to shake off this yoke without any outside support. In Upper Silesia, the agricultural population, the only one which could be subject to this kind of pressure, is relatively inconsiderable; we have there mainly an industrial population, always difficult to intimidate.

President Wilson. You are reasoning on premises based upon your experience in Great Britain. Here, the problem is entirely different. I have myself lived in a region subject to capitalist influence, and I have worked to destroy it; but I can assure you that even today capitalists still dominate the electorate in Pittsburgh and in the other great industrial centers of America.

Mr. Lloyd George. I can challenge you with figures. In 1912, in the seven districts which concern us, the Polish party received 97,000 votes, against 82,000; this last figure includes the Catholics and the Socialists, who both had Polish voters. That is what took place under a regime of intimidation. You can be sure that it wasn't the Prince of Pless who urged people to vote for the Socialist candidates.

President Wilson. There is a great difference between an election which affected only the domestic politics of Germany and a plebiscite which will decide whether the province should cease to be part of the German state. There is no doubt that, if the separation occurs, capitalist interests will be affected.

Mr. Lloyd George. No one has proclaimed more forcefully than you the principle of self-determination. It means that the fate of peoples must be determined by the people themselves, and not by a Dr. Lord, who thinks he knows better than they what they want. I am doing nothing but adhering to the Fourteen Points; why, after having decided that there would be plebiscites in Danzig, in Klagenfurt, in Fiume, in the Saar Basin, must we rule out that solution in Silesia?

President Wilson. I hold as much as you do to the principle of self-determination. What I want to avoid is having a Polish population being called upon to make a decision under the influence of Germany and the aegis of German officials.

Mr. Lloyd George. That is more or less what M. Orlando says when he asserts that a plebiscite in Dalmatia would be worthless because of the pressure exerted by the Yugoslavs.

President Wilson. I cannot allow you to say that I am not for the right of self-determination. That is absurd. What I want is the true expression of popular sentiment. I am told that the impression gathered these last few days is that we can fear armed resistance in Silesia on the part of the Germans.

Mr. Lloyd George. That is what you would avoid by a plebiscite.

President Wilson. Practically speaking, what do you propose?

Mr. Lloyd George. I propose to act here as in the area of Allenstein, where we have decided that the terms of the plebiscite would be settled by a commission of the League of Nations.

President Wilson. And how will you compel the Germans to carry out what that commission orders?

M. Clemenceau. They will make promises to you, and, if that is enough for you, you will be content.

Mr. Lloyd George. We may have to occupy the disputed territories.

President Wilson. In that case, how do we convince the Germans that our troops aren't there to force the hand of the voters?

Mr. Lloyd George. I would make the German as well as the Polish authorities leave the area, and I would put a small force there, whose task would be to make sure that everything occurs properly. One division would be enough.

President Wilson. That appears rather dangerous to me. What we seek is a genuine plebiscite. What we want to avoid is the suspicion of arbitrary intervention. The presence of troops would furnish the Germans with the best argument.

Mr. Lloyd George. What I want is peace. All the information I receive from Germany, all I have heard said about the German delegation from Versailles, shows that the question of Silesia is the one that most concerns the Germans. It is better to send an American or English division to Upper Silesia than an army to Berlin.

M. Clemenceau. If you have the choice.

Mr. Lloyd George. I am afraid of finding another Moscow in Berlin, that is, of not having anyone before us with whom we can sign the peace.

President Wilson. It is a little late to say all that. The question is whether or not our earlier decisions have been just. If we haven't followed the line indicated by the ethnographic data, we can correct our mistake. But I am not moved by the argument that Germany won't sign unless it can be shown that we have violated our own principles in our provisions. I admit that the Germans may have something to say on the question of Silesia, and I am ready to study the question, but nothing more.

Mr. Lloyd George. I don't admit that it is too late; the text which we have drafted is not an ultimatum, it is not viewed as such by my colleagues in the British government. We have done our best with the data we possess. The Germans present the other side of the problem; we must hear them and see whether there is anything to be changed in our decisions. That is the opinion of the British delegation.

The Germans say: "For 800 years, Silesia has been more or less associated with our national body." How are we to answer them, if not by consulting the people themselves? It goes without saying that it is necessary to insure the independence of the vote. If the Germans don't accept the verdict of the Silesian people, then English soldiers will march on Berlin as resolutely as when they marched to defend France and Belgium. What I want is to feel the English people behind me. I am not subject to the influence of the pacifists; I am thinking about the men who supported me during the entire war and who will still support me if we give heed to their present objections.

President Wilson. We are perhaps less far apart than we appeared to be a moment ago. I am only saying that we don't have to make concessions to the Germans simply because they do not want to sign this or that provision. I am ready to make concessions wherever they show me that they are right and we are wrong. Concerning reparations, for example, if they prove to us that the arrangement we have contemplated will not work, I will reply that I am ready to study the question.

Mr. Lloyd George. There are some intermediary cases. We can make an unimportant concession to the Germans if it leads them to sign. For instance, if I am convinced that a plebiscite will give Upper Silesia to Poland and will facilitate the signing, why not consent to it? This plebiscite will remove any element of doubt about the sentiment of the population.

President Wilson. I am convinced of the importance of the objective which you have in mind; but I fear that the presence of troops would prevent us from attaining it. I wonder whether it would not suffice to prescribe certain guarantees to protect the freedom of the vote, entrusting a commission with verifying whether these guarantees are respected.

M. Clemenceau. I very much fear that, in order to avoid certain difficulties, we are jumping from the frying pan into the fire. The plebiscite is a system very favorable to the expression of the popular will; but Germany's whole history denies a truly free expression of will. If we could say: "Hold a plebiscite," and then go and wash our hands of it, very good. But if we are compelled to occupy the disputed territory, the Germans will hasten to say that the vote isn't free. We will have in peace all the difficulties of war, and we will find ourselves facing a situation perhaps more serious than that of today.

Mr. Lloyd George has no longing to go to Berlin; neither have I. We did not want to have millions of men killed to defend our existence, but we were forced to do so.

We want to know the sentiment of the Poles; be assured that, if they remain under German administration, they won't be able to vote freely, and that, if they vote under a regime of Allied occupation, the protest of the Germans will be as loud as it is today. We will only have preserved and exacerbated the passions which we wanted to extinguish. It is necessary to have the courage to say "No" if we believe we are right. President Wilson has said it very well. I have shown that I myself was not hostile to any concession by accepting a change of the clauses relating to the Saar; I didn't want it to be possible for us to be reproached for having made a people's fate dependent upon the payment of a certain sum of money.

If you undertake to maintain order during the period of the plebiscite, be assured that the Germans, as soon as the arrival of the Americans is announced, will resist; you will have quarrels, if not battles, which will yield a result absolutely contrary to the one you desire. I am of opinion that, apart from the rectifications of the boundary to which President Wilson consents, the best thing is to leave things as they are.

Mr. Lloyd George. If the Germans resist the American troops, why not expect their resistance to the cession of Upper Silesia? The cession would be imposed upon them by the treaty in circumstances in which it would not be difficult for them to resist us.

President Wilson. I refer back to the Fourteen Points. Concerning Poland, they say that she must include all territories inhabited by an indisputably Polish population.[2]

Mr. Lloyd George. That is precisely what the Germans are contesting about Upper Silesia.

M. Clemenceau. German statistics reveal that the great majority of the population in Upper Silesia is Polish.

Mr. Lloyd George. The question is not only one of language, but one of the sentiment of these populations. All I ask is that it be made evident in an undeniable fashion.

---

[2] Point XIII: "An independent Polish state should be erected which should include the territories inhabited by indisputably Polish populations, which should be assured a free and secure access to the sea, and whose political and economic independence and territorial integrity should be guaranteed by international covenant."

President Wilson. We have no doubt about the ethnographic fact. I am completely ready to add something to my earlier statements if it is right or expedient; but what I said in the Fourteen Points does not compel us to order a plebiscite in Upper Silesia.

Mr. Lloyd George. If we were to talk exclusively on the basis of ethnography, Alsace should remain with Germany.

President Wilson. In any case, the Germans would have no right to say that the cession of Upper Silesia is contrary to the Fourteen Points.

Mr. Lloyd George. I don't believe any of us would have thought about Upper Silesia before the commission pointed out to us that this region ought to be considered Polish.

President Wilson. I beg your pardon; I knew perfectly well what was involved. When I received M. Dmowski and M. Paderewski in Washington, I said to them: "It is necessary for us to agree on the definition of Poland." They then showed me a map which evidenced immense pretensions in all directions. I then said to them: "As for myself, Poland must include only the whole of the areas inhabited by Polish populations."

Mr. Lloyd George. We were thinking of historical Poland and not of a region which has been separated from the Polish state for 800 years.

M. Clemenceau. All the Poles who presented their claims to me have mentioned Silesia.

President Wilson. We could hold a plebiscite under the surveillance of an inter-Allied commission. If that commission informs us that things did not proceed correctly, we will have the right to annul the plebiscite.

Mr. Lloyd George. I don't believe the Germans would revolt against an American occupation.

M. Clemenceau. Try it, and you'll see.

President Wilson. They don't like us any more than they like you. Do you favor making the changes indicated in the drawing of the boundary? And holding a plebiscite in Upper Silesia, under conditions to be prescribed by an inter-Allied commission?

Mr. Lloyd George. It is also necessary to stipulate that the Germans will withdraw their troops from Silesia.

President Wilson. Naturally, and the commission will be able, if it deems it necessary, to call upon Allied troops to police the region.

Mr. Lloyd George. We would have to make this latter point clear and to say that the troops in question will be American.

M. Clemenceau. How many will be needed?

Mr. Lloyd George. One division.

President Wilson. We can also stipulate, with respect to German private property, all guarantees which conform to the general dispositions of the treaty.

Mr. Lloyd George. And assure the Germans of the supply of coal which they need.

President Wilson. Yes, under the same terms as for Polish consumers. If we act in that manner, I don't think that we leave any valid objection to the Germans.

Mr. Lloyd George. That is what I would like, in case the Germans should refuse to sign. I must be able to show my colleagues and British public opinion that we are not responsible for this refusal.

—Sir Maurice Hankey is instructed to have Dr. Lord and Mr. Headlam-Morley prepare a text along the lines indicated.

President Wilson. On the question of reparation, I have already indicated my position. It would not be unjust on our part to impose complete reparation upon the Germans; but we have acknowledged that this is impossible. Can't we ask our experts to study the system of payment again? We had decided not to announce any figures for two years, to instruct the Reparation Commission to make the calculations and to determine the mode of payment. The Germans complain, in the first place, of not knowing as of today the totality of the obligations incumbent upon them, and, in the second place, that their entire economic life would be at the mercy of the Reparation Commission for a long period.

Mr. Lloyd George. My opinion is that they are exaggerating.

President Wilson. If we could inform the Germans of our intentions, they would undoubtedly be less frightened. But how do we give them guarantees that the commission, in twenty years, will interpret the treaty as we ourselves are doing today? Can't we convey, without drastically changing our wording, what we intend to do?

Mr. Lloyd George. I believe we have already said it.

President Wilson. Obviously, if it was possible to fix a total sum today, that would singularly alleviate the commission's task.

Mr. Lloyd George. There would still be a great deal left to do in order to calculate annuities, determine the modes of payment, and assure all the necessary operations. The only argument of the Germans which is valid is that, as long as they remain completely uncertain about the obligations incumbent upon them, they can find no outside credit.

President Wilson. You know that the American experts have always been strong advocates of a fixed sum.

Mr. Lloyd George. No question has cost us as much time and work, and we were unable to determine that sum.

President Wilson. It is strange, nonetheless, to see that the Germans are announcing the same figure to which we returned so frequently—five billion pounds sterling. The difference is that for us, it was a question of capital, to which interest had to be added, whereas for them it is the sum total of the payments. Could we not say to them: "We accept the figure that you announce, but as capital, to which the interest will be added?"

M. Clemenceau. M. Loucheur is completely opposed to the idea of fixing the total now.

President Wilson. Didn't Mr. Lloyd George propose yesterday to indicate a fixed sum for a portion of what Germany owes?

Mr. Lloyd George. Yes, but it is impossible to do so for reparation, since we ourselves don't know the totality of what must be repaired.

We might perhaps be able, after a study of three months, to indicate an approximate sum. I must say that I prefer the other system that I proposed: to demand that the Germans repair or restore all that has been destroyed, whatever the value, and besides that, to pay everything for which a total amount can be stated today.

The text of the treaty, by the way, gives the Germans the right to appeal to our governments through the Reparation Commission when they are truly incapable of paying. That is a provision we should emphasize.

M. Clemenceau. I don't think we can profitably push this discussion today; I must consult my specialists.

Mr. Lloyd George. I don't favor putting these questions to a great number of experts who will engage in interminable discussions; they must be brought before three or four carefully chosen men.

In our delegation, opinions are divided. Mr. Keynes adopts a position of great moderation towards the Germans, whilst Lord Sumner and Lord Cunliffe appear very intransigent. Perhaps it will be necessary for me to ask Mr. Bonar Law to come here; he and Mr. Chamberlain would give good advice.

President Wilson. As you know, the American experts are in agreement in principle; any one of them can take care of it. The man who knows best the two questions of reparations and finance is probably Mr. Baruch.

What gives the Germans an argument are the indefinite features of our arrangement.

Mr. Lloyd George. We can reply to that that the losses are also indefinite; do we know what the Allies lost by way of houses, factories, etc.?

M. Clemenceau. The Germans link that question to the one of their admission to the League of Nations.

Mr. Lloyd George. Our military experts make an observation on the clauses relating to the army. They think that, during the period of uncertainty and trouble which Germany is going through, she must be allowed to keep more than 100,000 men under arms.

M. Clemenceau. If they maintain more than 100,000 men today, be sure they will keep them forever.

President Wilson. I don't see any disorder in Germany. German troops are massed on the Polish frontier.

Mr. Lloyd George. Small republics are springing up on all sides— in Hesse, on the Rhine.

President Wilson. Mr. Hoover's agents, entrusted with a task which is in no way political, nevertheless observe what they see and have sent us reports on German opinion. They think that admission to the League of Nations is one of the things that most preoccupies the Germans. When it is a question of knowing whether they will sign the treaty, the question which comes first in importance is that of Silesia; then comes that of the League of Nations.

Mr. Lloyd George. That is also what I am told.

President Wilson. These are simple questions that people understand. Concerning the League of Nations, the Germans ask if we will treat them as pariahs. We agree to admit them to the League when we are convinced that their democratic form of government is durable and genuine.

M. Clemenceau. They want to be in the League of Nations to create difficulties amongst us. I am not against the principle of their admission, and I have accepted without difficulty their impending admission into the International Labour Organization. But we must first assure ourselves that the peace is solidly established, and that Germany respects it.

President Wilson. Can't we give them some assurance for the future?

M. Clemenceau. I would leave the question in the hands of the League of Nations itself.

President Wilson. Certainly, it is the League which pronounces on the admission of its new members. But what we can say today is that we will wait until we are assured of the permanence and genuineness of the democratic government of Germany.

Mr. Lloyd George. It is necessary to give them some hope.

President Wilson. My opinion is that, in our interest, it is better to have the Germans in the League of Nations than outside it.

M. Clemenceau. We must see what proof of good faith they will give in the years following the conclusion of peace.

President Wilson. At present, not only Germany, but Russia and Hungary are outside the League of Nations.

Mr. Lloyd George. I fear Kolchak has suffered a serious setback.

M. Clemenceau. He made a speech in the sense requested.

Mr. Lloyd George. But we haven't received his reply.

M. Clemenceau. I received a telegram indicating that our note reached him and that he is preparing his reply. M. Sazonov is very hostile to the note we sent.

Mr. Lloyd George. I know that, and I had Admiral Kolchak warned that we will withdraw our support from him if he doesn't grant the guarantees demanded.

Mr. Lloyd George. The most difficult questions which remain for us to resolve are those of reparation and the occupation. Must we not begin by replying in general terms to the German counterproposals? I believe that it is necessary to give our reasons. There is no doubt that the German document[3] has made some impression, and we can and must defend ourselves. There are a certain number of points on which we must explain ourselves; for, if the Germans refuse to sign, we must have done everything to insure that our public opinions are behind us. For that, it is necessary to make an appropriate statement to carry conviction.

President Wilson. This statement must be written clearly and without harshness. Couldn't Mr. Balfour take care of it?

Mr. Lloyd George. I have asked Mr. Philip Kerr to present us with a draft. Mr. Balfour might perhaps have toned it down too much.

President Wilson. We have to reply to the inadmissible accusation of having ourselves put aside the principles which we established as the basis of the peace treaty. It is on this point that we must reply first. It is also necessary to prepare a series of replies indicating the concessions we can make.

M. Clemenceau. The text must not be too long. We must conclude by setting a deadline for the Germans for their final reply.

Mr. Lloyd George. If we can come to an agreement on a common

---

[3] That is, "Observations of the German Delegation . . . ," cited in CIII, n. 3.

reply, we can conclude by giving the Germans a period of five or seven days.

President Wilson. If, at the end of the period named, the Germans refuse to sign, will we give them the three days' notice which must precede the end of the Armistice?

M. Clemenceau. No, we should act immediately.

Mr. Lloyd George. The three days will be included in the period granted.

President Wilson. I think they will sign if we make concessions to them on the points indicated.

Mr. Lloyd George. I believe it.

M. Clemenceau. I don't believe it; but the signing will soon come, after a first refusal.

Mr. Lloyd George. In that case, it is not the present German government that will sign; it will be neither Brockdorff nor Scheidemann.

M. Clemenceau. No, but others will sign.

Mr. Lloyd George. It would be a Haase government;[4] that wouldn't be very satisfactory.

Sir Maurice Hankey. The Drafting Committee points out that you have neglected to add to the treaty the article relating to the abolition of the neutralized zones of Savoy and of the Gex district;[5] it proposes to add the article as approved by you to the final text.

—*This proposal is adopted.*

Mr. Lloyd George. There is no news from Turkey?

M. Clemenceau. I have received a new dispatch from the Grand Vizier, which only repeats the first.

Mr. Lloyd George. Have we replied?

M. Clemenceau. We decided to reply through our representatives in Constantinople.

President Wilson. It seems that we proposed plebiscites in Schleswig in a larger area than the Danes themselves request. The Germans note this. It should be easy to settle that question.

Mr. Lloyd George. Undoubtedly.

---

[4] That is, a government of the radical Independent Social Democratic party, led by Hugo Haase.

[5] The French territory of Gex (*pays de Gex*) runs along the Swiss border near Geneva between the towns of Gex and Collonges. "Savoy" in this context really meant the French department of Haute-Savoie, an Alpine area to the south of Lake Geneva. Article 435 of the preliminary peace treaty with Germany dealt with the abolition of the stipulations of treaties of 1815, which had made Haute-Savoie and the Gex district free-trade zones.

Sir Maurice Hankey. I recall the reservations formulated by the Serbian and Rumanian delegations on the subject of the treaty with Austria.[6]

Mr. Lloyd George. What do they mean?

M. Clemenceau. No doubt that they will sign the treaty but not carry it out.

President Wilson. Surely, they can't sign and then refuse to honor their signature.

M. Orlando. That means rather that they won't sign.

M. Clemenceau. They must be asked the question; I will do it in your name.

Sir Maurice Hankey. The council has taken no decision yet on the amendments proposed by the Czechoslovak delegation.[7] The Drafting Committee presents conclusions contrary to these amendments. It must be admitted that it is impossible to take into account today an Austrian nationality other than that of the new state, since the old Austria has ceased to exist.

---

[6] N. P. Pašić to G. Clemenceau, June 1, 1919, and the Rumanian Delegation to [G. Clemenceau], June 2, 1919, printed as Appendixes III(a) and III(b) to Hankey's notes of this meeting in PPC, VI, 163-64. Both letters reserved the "rights" of Yugoslavia and Rumania in regard to the declarations and proposals they had made at the Plenary Session on May 31, 1919. At the Plenary Session, Brătianu had strongly objected to the provision of the Austrian peace treaty that required Rumania to give adequate protection to the rights of minorities within her borders, on the ground that this was an infringement of Rumania's sovereignty. In addition, he declared that Rumania was taking every measure to facilitate transit and trade with other nations, and he proposed several changes in the financial clauses of the Austrian treaty. At the same Plenary Session, Trumbić also objected to the clause relating to Yugoslavia's (or Serbia's) treatment of minorities as an infringement of Yugoslavia's sovereignty. In addition, he requested certain changes in the proposed northern boundary of the new state of Yugoslavia.

Wilson had replied in what Dr. Grayson called "the strongest speech he had made since he came to Europe." "He frankly warned the wrangling representatives of the smaller nations that inasmuch as the big powers would be compelled to guarantee the safety of the world in the future it was essential that they mix in the affairs of the small nations. He told the Roumanian Premier that while he was desirous of meeting the views of the small powers as far as possible, yet it was necessary that religious and political minorities who were included in newly created states but who differed in language and custom from the prevailing majority have their rights upheld by an independent organization such as the League of Nations." Grayson Diary, May 31, 1919, printed in PWW, Vol. 59, p. 626. For the minutes of this Plenary Session, see PPC, III, 394-410. Wilson's speech is printed in PWW, Vol. 59, pp. 628-30.

[7] The Czech delegation had requested certain very specific changes in the political and financial clauses relating to Czechoslovakia in the draft treaty with Austria. See the Drafting Committee's comments on these changes in Appendix IV to Hankey's notes of the present meeting in PPC, VI, 164-67.

Moreover, the Drafting Committee does not think that it is authorized to admit the assertion that the Czechoslovak Republic existed legally before any decision of the Allies, and that it had, consequently, an unconditional freedom of action. For these reasons, it doesn't think it can make the changes proposed without new instructions from the Council of Four.

I have other notes on questions which are pending concerning state properties in the territories reunited to Poland and the division of the prewar debt amongst the states of central Europe.

President Wilson. All that must be studied.

Mr. Lloyd George. Couldn't we appoint two people to do it? For example, M. Tardieu and another delegate of the same competence.

M. Orlando. Why not refer these questions to the meeting of the Foreign Ministers?

M. Clemenceau. There would be no end to it.

M. Orlando. The questions that have just been mentioned are technical questions; but they are also delicate questions, whose solution entails important consequences.

Mr. Lloyd George. The best thing is to refer the study to a small committee.

—*It is decided that this committee will consist of Messrs. Tardieu, Miller, De Martino, and Sir Eyre Crowe.*

Mr. Lloyd George. A serious difficulty arises regarding the contribution to the cost of the war which we are asking of the new states of Central Europe. Italy refuses to pay her share for the liberated regions of the Trentino and Trieste.

M. Orlando. The difficulty stems from the fact that Italy has, in fact, already paid her part.

Mr. Lloyd George. The Czechoslovaks, the Rumanians, the Poles say they won't pay if Italy doesn't pay.

Moreover, we haven't been able to agree on the subject of the distribution of tonnage. In my opinion, there are two ways to proceed. Either Italy must confine her claims to Austria and take no further interest in Germany, or else we must combine all our losses and all means of compensation. We can't accept that Italy should have the right to reparation from Germany if she demands a privileged position vis-à-vis Austria. It is a fundamental difficulty which can only be settled by the heads of governments.

M. Orlando. I ask to study these questions more closely; I am not acquainted with the details.

Mr. Lloyd George. Should we or should we not summon the experts for tomorrow?

M. Orlando. It is better to begin by a discussion with the experts.

Sir Maurice Hankey. The Belgian delegation has heard about the committee which you formed to draft the convention relating to the occupation; it asks to be represented on that committee.

—*After a brief exchange of views, it is decided that Belgium will be invited to make her desiderata known.*

CVII

Conversation among President Wilson, MM. Clemenceau, Lloyd George, and Orlando, and the members of the Reparation and Financial Commissions*

JUNE 4, 1919, 11:30 A.M.

President Wilson. In the text which our commissions are submitting to us,[1] I see that certain states in Central Europe are claiming objects which were taken from them in the eighteenth or nineteenth centuries. That is going back a long way. I have spent my life in universities, and I know how regrettable it is to disperse collections. That is a scholar's objection, and I hope our legal experts will take it into account while studying these claims.

Lord Sumner. We opposed everything which could lead to a dispersal of great collections and accepted only the return to each country of objects of local interest.

President Wilson. I see here an article on the restitution of livestock "removed, seized, or sequestered." The date of the seizure or sequestration is not indicated.

M. Orlando. "During the war" must be added.

Mr. Lloyd George. I regret that this livestock should be removed from a country like Austria, which is today in a state of famine. We must take into account the condition in which Austria finds

*H., *PPC*, VI, 168ff.

[1] The council had before it the draft reparation clauses of the Austrian treaty. This draft is missing.

herself; in any case, we have to see what is the proportion of livestock retaken.

M. Loucheur. The figures indicated here were accepted by Dr. Taylor, who is one of Mr. Hoover's assistants.

Mr. Lamont. We are all struck by the deplorable condition of the people of Vienna. But the livestock concerned would be taken from areas far from Vienna, near Italy, and it is unlikely that it would go to the Viennese in any case.

Mr. McCormick. In addition, what is claimed is only a small proportion of the total. I believe that we cannot refuse to acknowledge the claims of the Italians and Serbs whose livestock was stolen. The removal will take place in agricultural regions which lack nothing.

Mr. Lloyd George. If Dr. Taylor is of that opinion, I have nothing to say.

M. Orlando. The Austrians took 360,000 cows in Italy; we are asking that only 10,000 of them be restored to us.

Mr. Lloyd George. I withdraw my objection.

Mr. Lamont. The Czechoslovaks are asking that a stipulation of the same kind be granted to them. I propose to refer the question back to the legal advisers.

M. Crespi. Concerning historical monuments having belonged once to each of the nations which are recovering their independence, the Poles and the Czechoslovaks asked for the insertion of a clause which was accepted: these monuments must be restored without payment. We have a claim of the same kind to present for the Palazzo Venezia in Rome. Should it be included here or in the territorial clauses?

Mr. Lloyd George. Wasn't the Palazzo Venezia the seat of the Austrian embassy in Rome?

M. Crespi. Of the Austrian embassy to the Vatican, not to the Quirinal, and we agreed about this with the Holy See.

Lord Sumner. This palace, which once belonged to the Republic of Venice, became Austrian at the same time as Venice itself. It is located in the center of Rome. For the Italians, it is a veritable symbol of Austrian domination; in their eyes, its restitution will be a sign of complete liberation. I will recommend that the council give satisfaction to Italian sentiment.

Mr. Lloyd George. The proposed clause goes much further. I fear that a large number of valuable properties which were part of the domain of the former Austrian Empire will pass to these different countries without compensation.

Mr. McCormick. What the Poles and Czechs ask is that their national monuments be given back to them.

President Wilson. The text provides that these properties will be restored without payment, with the approval of the Reparation Commission. Can't we write, instead of "shall be restored," "may be?"

—*This proposal is adopted.*

M. Sergent. In the treaty with Germany, Poland asked for and received restitution of her state forests without payment. This stipulation is included in the territorial clauses. Poland has presented the same claim against Austria, which was accepted in principle; but the article was omitted when the territorial clauses were drafted. Poland asks today that this article be inserted in the financial clauses, in view of the precedent established in the German treaty and the admission of the principle by the principal powers. The Financial Commission can acknowledge Poland's request; but this arrangement would have to be granted to Poland alone. There is a risk of provoking similar claims on the part of other states.

President Wilson. How can this risk be avoided?

M. Sergent. In the German treaty, it is a special clause, aimed only at Poland.

Mr. Lloyd George. Wasn't this clause inserted in the German treaty because the Germans destroyed Polish forests, and by right of compensation?

M. Clemenceau. How can we ask the Poles to pay for these forests if they were once, as I believe, properties of the Polish Crown?

Mr. Lloyd George. If it was only a question of payment, I would have nothing to say. But this question is connected to that of Poland's contribution to the cost of the war of liberation.

M. Clemenceau. You don't insist that she give money to Austria?

Mr. Lloyd George. No, but I insist that she contribute to the cost of the war.

M. Clemenceau. Do these forests represent much monetary value?

M. Klotz. We are told that they represent a value of several billions.

Mr. Lloyd George. The Poles would have nothing of all this without the sacrifices made by other nations, which won their independence for them.

Mr. Lamont. The Poles are relying on the fact that their claims were acknowledged in the treaty with Germany.

Mr. Lloyd George. I propose postponing our decision until we know how far Poland will participate in the cost of the war of liberation. We mustn't forget that she is going to acquire coal mines of considerable value and immense forests.

President Wilson. Mr. Lamont has prepared a report about the contribution which these small powers will provide.

Mr. Lamont. All these powers decided that they would participate in the cost of the war which liberated them. We found a formula which was accepted by the Czechs and which we hope to see accepted by the other states.

Each of the nations involved would begin by making a statement acknowledging the sacrifices made by the great powers for its liberation, and agreeing to participate in the cost of the war; each of them would pay a sum equal to 25 per cent of the total value of Austrian war loans presently placed on its territory. If we can't manage to arrive at this total exactly, we will work on the basis of an estimate, and the proportion will be reduced to 15 per cent.

We estimate that the total quantity of securities for Austro-Hungarian war loans in the liberated territories amounts to around 40 billion crowns. The contribution of the states in question would thus be between six and ten billion crowns.

Mr. Lloyd George. I have two observations to offer. I don't see the reason for this distinction—25 per cent in one case and 15 per cent in the other. It will be very difficult to find out what amount of Austro-Hungarian securities is located today in each of the parts of the former monarchy. We tried to make calculations of this kind for the counties of England, and we never succeeded. I would indicate in both anticipated cases the same proportion of 25 per cent. We shall probably be obliged, in the end, to be satisfied with a more or less rough estimate, basing ourselves upon the relative wealth of each of the countries under consideration.

In the second place, I would like to know how this arrangement can be made to square with a proposal made by M. Orlando. Here are countries, Serbia, Rumania, which are asking for substantial reparations, but which are acquiring large territories. It might be well to open an account of debit and credit and to reduce the assets by the entire amount of the liabilities. It seems to me very important to maintain this principle, which would give more satisfactory results, when it comes to Transylvania and Croatia, than the arrangement indicated by Mr. Lamont. Each of these states will draw all or part of the reparations due it from the territories which it acquires.

Let us suppose that Serbia and Rumania claim one billion pounds sterling in reparations. Serbia is acquiring Croatia, Bosnia, Herzegovina, the Banat, etc. If these territories remained Austrian, they would contribute to the reparations due to Serbia. Let us suppose that the figure for this contribution amounts to 600 million sterling; from 1,000, I deduct 600, 400 remain. It is this difference which Serbia will have the right to claim in the final accounting.

Otherwise, it would be very difficult to collect the sums indicated. As far as Germany is concerned, we can use means of pressure and, if necessary, resume the war. We can't do that to force the Czechoslovaks, the Poles, or the Yugoslavs to pay us. I have enough confidence in the Czechoslovaks, who are serious people and who have business experience; I have less in Serbia or Rumania, and I would rather like to see them collect all or part of what is due them from the very territories which are assigned to them.

M. Loucheur. That is renewing a difficulty which we had trouble surmounting. These states refuse to pay under the heading of reparation; they agree to contribute to the cost of the war, but they don't want to be ranked amongst those who were responsible for it. Furthermore, we must avoid a general bankruptcy of these states.

M. Orlando. It is actually a contribution to the cost of the war which is in question, not reparations.

Mr. Lloyd George. The difficulty is to fix the amount.

M. Orlando. This sum must be fixed by arbitrators.

M. Crespi. The small states refuse all arbitration of this kind.

M. Klotz. But they will simply have to accept it.

CVIII

Conversation between President Wilson
and MM. Clemenceau, Lloyd George,
Orlando, and Vesnić*

JUNE 4, 1919, 4 P.M.

President Wilson. M. Vesnić has expressed the wish to be heard on the Klagenfurt Basin. We ask him to inform us of his government's views.

M. Vesnić. First, I must thank you for having acceded to our request and having postponed the solution of this question; all the points of view have not yet been sufficiently considered. The importance of the problem surpasses that of the boundary between the Kingdom of the Serbs, Croats and Slovenes and the Republic of Austria. In order to prove it, I must recall the origins of the war.

This war was a German war, the conclusion of a long policy whose constant objective was the march of Germanism towards the southeast, towards the Adriatic Sea and towards the Aegean Sea. I don't assert this in order to plead a cause of one day. A professor of the University of Prague, Herr Niederleck,[1] explained this policy very clearly in 1911 and had the courage to denounce it, even though he was an Austrian subject.

In this Germanic push towards the south, the Slovene element was the most exposed; it retreated little by little before the Germans for several centuries. It once occupied the entire territory extending up to Salzburg; the map is still covered with Slovene place names, and to cite only one, the capital of Styria, Graz, is the old Slovene city of Gradetz.

The Germanic push has manifested itself most strongly since the creation of the German Empire and the development of Pan-Germanism. In the region of Klagenfurt, the mixture of both Slovene and German populations is, above all, the result of the systematic work of the last fifty years. The Austrian element not being sufficient, priests were brought from Bavaria and Württem-

*H., PPC, VI, 173ff.

[1] Actually, Lubor Niederle, Professor of Ethnography and Prehistorical Archaeology at the University of Prague and a technical adviser to the Czechoslovak delegation.

berg, receiving their directions from the German *Schulverein*,[2] one of the great organizations of Pan-Germanism. Not only propaganda by the Church took place in these regions, but German influence was also propagated in the schools. In the economic field, expropriations were made at the expense of the Slovenes, as in East Prussia at the expense of the Poles.

In this entire region, political directives came from Berlin rather than Vienna. By the force of things, the population was obliged to yield to this regime, and this is why I hear it said that there are Slovenes who wish today to remain in their former situation. This fact must not impress you. Analogues can be found in other countries which found themselves in the same conditions. In Fogazzaro's book, *Piccolo Mundo Antico*,[3] we see that, in Lombardy, at the time of the Austrian occupation, there were partisans of Austria. The influence of the government, of the police, the competition of interests make these facts inevitable. Not all men have high civic courage. The same thing happened here which can happen and did happen elsewhere; it is a fact to which we must not assign excessive importance.

We had, as you know, the ambition to embrace in our territory a larger part of the Slovene areas. But after a close study, after difficulties experienced in discussion with your specialists, we limited our request to what, according to us, is both unquestionable and absolutely essential to the life of our people. We think we can insist for two reasons—in a Yugoslav interest and in a general interest.

In the first place, the Slovenes form the most exposed part of our people; but until now, they have all been under a single domination. This domination was hard: it was Germanic—that says everything. At least they remained together, they shared the same sufferings and the same hopes. The consequence of the treaty, if it were to remain as it has been prepared, would be to divide this population into four parts, of which one part would go to Serbia, another would remain with Austria, a third with Hungary, whilst a fourth, some 350,000 or 400,000 strong, would pass to Italy.

I understand the necessity that might lead the council of the great powers to separate part of our brothers from us and to have

---

[2] The Allgemeiner Deutscher Schulverein, or German General School Association, founded in Berlin in 1881. Its purpose was to fund and construct German schools for German children living outside the German Empire and to supply them with German books and German-speaking teachers.

[3] Antonio Fogazzaro, *Picolo Mundo Antico: Romanza* (Milan, 1895).

them pass under the administration of an Allied country; but we could not understand a harsh solution concerning us, when it is a matter of negotiating, not with friends, but with enemies. We asked for a plebiscite in order to settle the differences which arose between our Rumanian friends and ourselves; we did the same in order to settle the differences between us and our Italian friends. In these two cases, the solution of a plebiscite was discarded, and today you want to impose it upon us vis-à-vis the enemy. If this decision is maintained, there would remain in the heart of our people an impression which you do not intend and cannot want to create.

But the question has still greater importance if one considers it from a general point of view. Don't harbor any illusions—allow me to say this to you, it is my duty. You are creating a small Austrian state, which you believe you have an interest in treating gently. This state is a German state and will never be anything else. In future, it will have a much stronger tendency than before to ally itself to Germany; despite all the mildness and suavity of his speech at Saint-Germain, Herr Renner said it very clearly in insisting on the right of the Austrian people to self-determination.[4]

What is still more significant is Count von Brockdorff-Rantzau's insistence, in the German reply,[5] upon the right of Austria to self-determination; therefore this question is considered by the German government as a German question.

Today, you can impose solutions which will satisfy the necessities of the moment; but there are forces more powerful than all treaties. You have proclaimed so many times your respect for the right of peoples to self-determination that the time will come when Austria, relying upon what she considers her right, will unite with Germany. You won't be able to prevent her. I don't think that you will make war to forbid that union. Even if you were inclined to do it, you don't know if public opinion would allow you to.

Thus, Austria will join Germany, and Germanism will continue its policy of pushing towards the south, towards the sea, with experience reinforced by misfortune. I don't see why, from now on, you yourselves should smooth the way for this policy, directly by placing Slovene populations under German domina-

---

[4] For Renner's speech on the occasion of the presentation of the preliminary peace terms to the Austrian plenipotentiaries, see PPC, III, 427-30.

[5] That is, in Brockdorff-Rantzau's cover letter to the German "Observations" of May 28, 1919, printed as an appendix to CIII.

tion, and indirectly by giving a small people—ours—a lesson in pessimism, making it believe that its sacrifices in the past were in vain and that, as a consequence, it must be motivated in the future only by its own narrowest interest. I beg you to weigh this situation and to draw the unavoidable conclusions from it.

I represent a small country which does not pretend to give advice to powers greater and more powerful than herself. But one fact is certain: Austria will be treated like a spoiled child by Germany, which will give her all possible cooperation, in order to allow her to play the same part as in the past, that is, that of the instrument of German culture and policy in central and southeastern Europe. Your interest is not to strengthen Austria by making subjects of populations which do not belong to her. On the contrary, it is to strengthen the barrier which will stand in the way of the Germanic push if it threatens us once again.

The boundary we ask for would finally assign to us 60,000 Slovenes and 24,000 Germans—figures borrowed from official Austrian statistics. In the region which this line makes us abandon, there would be 21,000 Slovenes who would remain Austrian subjects. If we take 24,000 Germans and abandon 21,000 Slovenes, the difference is rather small. But if, instead of consulting official Austrian statistics, we refer to ecclesiastical statistics, the figures are quite different: 80,000 Slovenes and a little less than 5,000 Germans.

The ethnographic maps published in Vienna by German geographers give to Slovene populations the territory which we are asking for. I don't see how our friends, with whom we fought as champions of the same cause, could refuse to us today what the testimony of our enemies themselves grants us.

We understand that economic reasons must be taken into account; we are prepared to establish an arrangement that would allow adjacent regions, bound to one another economically, to continue their common life across the frontier. We ask you to grant us the line which we have indicated; in all conscience, I don't think this decision deviates from any of your principles or from the stated aims of the Allies during the war.

In conclusion, we ask you to grant us this reduced line without any other formality. We believe that peace must be established as soon as possible. If, today, you begin a new procedure—a plebiscite—you will only prolong anxiety and agitation and delay the consolidation of our new state.

Mr. Lloyd George. Can you show us on the map where the claimed boundary runs.

President Wilson. It follows the river Gurk, then the line of the lakes.

M. Vesnić. Our request is reinforced by the opinion of your special commission.

President Wilson. Its views have varied.

Mr. Lloyd George. Is the population south of this line Slovene in the very great majority?

M. Vesnić. Yes.

M. Clemenceau. What influenced our judgment was the consideration of the geographical unity of the Klagenfurt Basin.

M. Vesnić. We acknowledge it, and we shall have to offer all facilities for the communications on which its economic life depends.

President Wilson. Geographically, the Klagenfurt Basin is without any doubt a unity. There are no important industrial centers there, and the region is not even independent from the agricultural point of view. Klagenfurt has no large commercial houses but only retail commerce and local markets. A plebiscite which would be held for the entire basin would probably end in a vote in favor of Austria.

M. Vesnić. I don't agree; I have told you where the Germanophile tendencies in that region came from. The result would depend upon the date and the form of the plebiscite.

President Wilson. What I was going to propose is this: after six months, a plebiscite would take place in a region which we will designate as A, south of the line claimed by the Yugoslavs. If this plebiscite decides in favor of union with the Kingdom of the Serbs, Croats and Slovenes, the question is settled for that district. After another period, the plebiscite would take place in zone B, that is, between the line mentioned and the border which you claimed earlier, and which would include all the rest of the basin.

About the desire of this region to continue to live as a unit, we have received contradictory information. The arrangement which I propose would allow the population to decide for itself. If region A votes for union with the Yugoslavs, you have the border that you claim. If region B follows its example, you have the border that you first claimed.

M. Vesnić. This proposal rather puzzles me. We don't see the necessity of forcing us to this vote. We are asking not to be subjected to an unfavorable treatment in comparison to our neighbors, to whom these purely Slovene areas will be assigned without a plebiscite. The Klagenfurt Basin is certainly a mixed region, but one where our enemies themselves acknowledge that the Slovene element is in the majority.

President Wilson. We are faced with similar problems in other areas. In Upper Silesia, we don't doubt that the majority of the population is Polish; we are wondering, however, whether we shouldn't hold a plebiscite.

Mr. Lloyd George. In what way would the plebiscite be unjust?

M. Vesnić. The plebiscite would be impractical. This region has always been the theater of violent racial conflicts; it lies on the route of the great movement of the German race towards the south.

Mr. Lloyd George. I understand your objections to a plebiscite for the entire Klagenfurt Basin, the result of which could be doubtful. But I don't understand your objection to a plebiscite in the southern region, which is purely Slovene.

M. Vesnić. That population is still under the spell of those who dominated it for so long. It has been told many times that the Serbs and Croats are barbarians and that there can be peace and order only under Austrian administration. The same state of mind existed in Lombardy before its liberation.

Mr. Lloyd George. I am convinced that Lombardy, if it had been consulted, would have voted for Italy.

President Wilson. What you are telling me gives me doubts about the desire of this population to join the Yugoslavs.

M. Vesnić. It isn't that; but it can't break away from the influences of its masters. Perhaps a plebiscite by commune would be acceptable.

President Wilson. The danger of this arrangement is fragmentation.

Mr. Lloyd George. There are, no doubt, many Germans in the cities?

M. Vesnić. The Germans everywhere began by taking over the strongest positions, which are the cities.

Mr. Lloyd George. I recall that, in Schleswig, the Danes decided against voting by commune.

M. Vesnić. If you could put the Slovenes outside all German influence for two or three years, the plebiscite would become possible.

President Wilson. We had contemplated a plebiscite in six months so as not to give time for systematic German propaganda to develop. If, on the contrary, you prefer to delay the date of the plebiscite, we can place this area under the administration of an international commission for three years and apply to it a regime similar to that of the Saar Valley. But I would have thought this solution more dangerous than the other, for it allows time for the intrigues of your adversaries. I think that an immediate decision offers you more guarantees.

Our experts have given us a series of reports on this question. Their last conclusions propose a plebiscite in region A, that is, up to the frontier which you ask for, and then, if this plebiscite is in favor of the Yugoslavs, a similar referendum in region B, located further north.[6]

M. Clemenceau. M. Vesnić spoke of delaying the plebiscite by two or three years. President Wilson proposes, in this case, to place the Klagenfurt Basin under the same administration as the Saar Basin. Would this solution be agreeable to M. Vesnić?

M. Vesnić. I cannot answer without having consulted my colleagues. In any case, it would be absolutely necessary to establish an impartial administration in this region.

M. Clemenceau. It would be under the authority of the League of Nations; that is the arrangement that we ourselves have accepted and which satisfies us with regard to the Saar Basin.

Mr. Lloyd George. That means that this region would govern itself, under the auspices of the League of Nations.

M. Clemenceau. I think it is the best solution.

President Wilson. During this period of independence, the inhabitants would certainly manage to find out what they think. The problem arises wherever there are mixed populations that have lived for a long time under foreign domination. We are trying to apply the same fundamental principle everywhere, so that we cannot be reproached for disposing of peoples against their will.

—Mr. Leeper is introduced; he is instructed to draft the text of the proposed decision.

—M. Vesnić withdraws.

President Wilson. We must arrive at a solution concerning the military clauses of the treaty with Austria.*

M. Clemenceau. It is necessary to determine what the strength of the Austrian army will be; but it seems to me impossible at this time to do the same thing for all the new states of Central Europe.

Mr. Lloyd George. I know very well what forces they will have if we allow them to do as they please.

M. Clemenceau. It is not a matter of allowing them to do what they please, but of not hastening the solution too much.

*H., PPC, VI, 182ff.

[6] See D. W. Johnson to WW, June 4, 1919, and its enclosure, printed in PWW, Vol. 60, pp. 121-22.

President Wilson. Like Mr. Lloyd George, I fear these peoples are all motivated by the same spirit of war and conquest. Without fixing the strength of their armies right now, we can tell them that, beyond a fixed date—for example, January 1, 1921—they must commit themselves to accept a stipulated limitation of their forces, the League of Nations having the right to prolong the transition period if circumstances require it.

M. Clemenceau. I believe we will deeply irritate these small states if we fix these figures now. I would rather say that, on a certain date, the League of Nations will study and settle this question.

President Wilson. They will protest more against an indeterminate limitation than against a firm decision.

M. Clemenceau. Have you got in touch with them about this?

President Wilson. No.

M. Clemenceau. I have, with some precautions, and I wasn't very well received.

Mr. Lloyd George. They should be summoned.

M. Clemenceau. I am prepared to do it.

President Wilson. We must summon the Poles, the Czechoslovaks, the Yugoslavs, the Rumanians, and the Greeks. We have to consult them all; for we cannot impose conditions upon them as we have done for Austria, Hungary, and Bulgaria. Perhaps they should be summoned separately; otherwise it will be the Tower of Babel.

M. Clemenceau. Take the Greeks; they are still neighbors of the Turks. The Rumanians are going to continue to fight in their self-defense.

Mr. Lloyd George. We are strongly resolved to impose a very strict limitation of their military strength on the Turks.

M. Clemenceau. It is easier to impose it upon enemies than upon friends. In any case, we cannot fix the figures before having seen the representatives of these states and having consulted them. We will tell them that we intend to limit their effectives.

Mr. Lloyd George. I fear that these small states will become hotbeds of German intrigue.

President Wilson. Today, they are separate pieces of the great machine that Germany used for her designs against the rest of the world. We have the right to insure that they won't be used in a dangerous manner.

These states will obviously put this question to us: "Are you going to limit your own forces?" We will reply: "The League of Nations will prepare a general plan for reduction of armaments." If they reply: "Will you be compelled to accept the decision of the League of Nations?," that will undoubtedly place us in a bit of an awkward position.

M. Clemenceau. In any case, we must wait.

President Wilson. We will hear the statesmen; then, if there is cause, their military experts can talk with ours.

In any case, it appears to me easy to fix the future numbers for Austria. The calculation of our experts is based upon a proportion of four soldiers for 1,000 inhabitants, with a supplement which represents the needs of a large city like Vienna and the necessities of an unstable situation. Thus, we arrived at the figure of 40,000 men, which is higher than that which the proportion of four per 1,000 strictly applied would give.

M. Clemenceau. If Austria has 40,000 men, Germany will ask to have more than 100,000.

Mr. Lloyd George. Why not 30,000?

M. Clemenceau. That was what I was going to propose.

Mr. Lloyd George. The greatest part of the country is agricultural, a fact which precludes great risks of domestic disorder.

President Wilson. Can't we instruct our military advisers to draft this part of the treaty now? It is pointless to enter into the same details as for Germany.

M. Clemenceau. We must simply ask that the Austrian army be, like the German army, a professional army.

President Wilson. And, certainly, to limit war matériel strictly.

Mr. Lloyd George. The important thing is to see to it that Austria cannot create armies which Germany would then use.[7]

—*After a brief exchange of observations, it is decided that M. Paderewski will be heard on the question of the Polish boundary before the drafting of the answer to the German counterproposals.*

[7] The Four decided at this point to instruct the military representatives of the Supreme War Council to redraft the military terms of the Austrian treaty. The strength of the Austrian army was to be limited to 30,000 effectives, and Austria was to be prohibited from manufacturing guns and supplying war matériel to Germany or any other state. The council also agreed to invite the representatives of the central and eastern European states to inform them of the proposed limitations on the size of their respective armies. See *ibid.*, pp. 135-36.

CIX

Conversation between President Wilson and MM. Clemenceau, Lloyd George, and Orlando*

JUNE 5, 1919, 11 A.M.

M. Clemenceau. I transmit to you a report from Marshal Foch on the situation between the Rumanians and Hungarians.[1] I propose that it be studied by the Supreme War Council.

(Assent.)

M. Orlando. I had proposed to refer also to Versailles the question of the conflict between Austrians and Slovenes in Carinthia.
M. Clemenceau. A decision was taken.
President Wilson. We each decided, on a proposal of M. Orlando himself, to send an officer to Carinthia to oversee the armistice negotiations.

—M. Paderewski is introduced.**

President Wilson. At this time, we are studying the whole of the German counterproposals and preparing our reply. We are told that one of the questions which most troubles the Germans is that of Upper Silesia. The memorandum which we have sent you[2] shows the kind of changes we might contemplate in our earlier resolution on this subject. Before taking a decision, we wanted to know your opinion.

What is most important is not the rectifications in detail of the boundary, the aim of which would be to incorporate into Poland as few Germans as possible; it is the question of a plebiscite. We have no doubts about the Polish character of a large majority of the population. But the way in which the question is put by the Germans makes it desirable that a plebiscite, if decided upon, be of a character beyond challenge. Naturally, this plebiscite would take place after the withdrawal of German troops.

---

*H., *PPC*, VI, 180-90.
**H., *ibid*., pp. 191ff.

[1] Foch reported that information had been received that the Hungarians had attacked the Czechs, and that a very serious situation had been created. See *PPC*, VI, 189. There will be much discussion of this problem in following meetings.
[2] It is printed in *ibid*., pp. 186-87.

M. Paderewski. My country's interests are in your hands. I thank you for hearing me. Your plan, as I know it, was wise and fair. It is true that the boundary as it was proposed would include in Polish territory some districts where the majority of the population is German; but, in many other cases, districts with a Polish majority would remain with Germany.

President Wilson. It would be better if we looked at this later on the map. Let us begin with the question of the plebiscite.

M. Paderewski. There are two districts in Upper Silesia where the Polish majority is overwhelming, Gross Wartenberg and Namslau,[3] and one where the majority is German, Leobschütz. The eastern region is mining and industrial; the western region is exclusively agricultural. This western part is under the influence of a Catholic clergy educated in a very pronounced German spirit by the Prince-Bishop of Breslau.[4] From our point of view, the influence of this clergy is very dangerous. Although the Poles are nine tenths of the population amongst these peasants, the expression of their opinion would be strongly affected by the influence of this German clergy. In the eastern part, the worker population is free of this influence and much more independent. There is no doubt that the vote will be in our favor there. But, if this region alone becomes Polish, that will have the great disadvantage of leaving the industry on the border of Upper Silesia exposed to all possible dangers.

Mr. Lloyd George. Where is the most important population, towards the east or towards the west?

M. Paderewski. The East is more heavily populated.

Mr. Lloyd George. In what proportion?

M. Paderewski. In the mining region, there are 900,000 Poles and 400,000 Germans.

Mr. Lloyd George. What is the population of the agricultural area?

M. Paderewski. About half: 600,000 people in all. This is an undoubtedly Polish region which must belong to Poland.

President Wilson. The Germans themselves admit the Polish character of this population.

M. Paderewski. But, at the same time, they claim Upper Silesia in the name of your principles.

Mr. Lloyd George. Can you enlighten us about the question of Memel?

M. Paderewski. It is not a Polish question, but a Lithuanian one.

---

[3] Actually, Paderewski said "Silesia." Both Gross Wartenberg and Namslau were in Lower Silesia.

[4] Adolf Cardinal Bertram.

Memel is without any doubt Lithuanian, and its possession is essential for the life of Lithuania; for it is the only port which serves that country, whose principal resource is the export of lumber. Germany has many ports, and Memel has no German hinterland.

As far as we are concerned, the uncertainty which the treaty leaves in regard to the fate of East Prussia adds to our anxiety.

Mr. Lloyd George. The treaty leaves East Prussia to Germany.

President Wilson. It says nothing about East Prussia, because that province remains German.

M. Paderewski. Tilsit is also a Lithuanian city; but part of the population is Germanized.

Mr. Lloyd George. And the populations of the interior?

M. Paderewski. They are entirely Lithuanian. The Lithuanian people is, moreover, a small people of two million inhabitants.

Mr. Lloyd George. It is as if independence were given to Wales.

M. Paderewski. It is in your interest to do everything to protect Poland: she resisted revolution; she has no internal troubles; her frontier battles are due only to the necessity of defending herself.

Mr. Lloyd George. I don't entirely accept this last assertion.

M. Paderewski. I am prepared to prove it with facts.

Mr. Lloyd George. This very morning, I received a telegram showing that you are continuing to advance in the Ukraine.

M. Paderewski. Galicia is not the Ukraine. The language is the same; but, in reality, Galicia is a region which is under German and Austrian influence. There is no real harmony between Galicians and Ukrainians. The Ukrainians of Galicia are 3,300,000, compared to 800,000 Poles. They have their government, which is not that of the Ukraine, strictly speaking; it was until recently established at Stanislau,[5] whilst Petliura's is at Rovno.

You have asked us to stop the fighting in Galicia. General Bliss, in your name, asked me to agree to an armistice. I accepted it in principle. Negotiations took place. Then I was told to prevent General Haller's troops from taking part in the fighting in Galicia; I did so. During the armistice negotiations, bombing of the open city of Lemberg continued, and many inhabitants were killed by the so-called Ukrainian army.

Upon my arrival in Warsaw, I made known your wishes to the chief of the Polish state.[6] Then I received a telegram from Pavlenko, chief of the Ukrainian forces in Galicia, saying that the

---

[5] About the ephemeral government of the so-called Western Ukrainian National Republic, see PWW, Vol. 58, p. 505, n. 4.

[6] That is, Piłsudski.

Ukrainians were prepared to stop hostilities in order to facilitate the armistice negotiations, which were taking place in Paris, and inviting us to do the same. On May 11, we gave the order to stop the movement of Polish troops.

That decision created a very dangerous situation in our country. When the public was informed of the halting of our troops in Galicia, agitation was such that we thought we were on the eve of a revolution. I then offered my resignation, which was not accepted. Hundreds of public meetings, thousands of protests took place. We found ourselves in a truly dangerous situation.

Moreover, beginning the next day, May 12, the Ukrainians attacked at two new points and renewed the attacks north of Lemberg. We weren't able to hold back our soldiers, who advanced on forced marches, making more than forty kilometers per day, and who retook the contested territory with very little bloodshed. We had 100 men killed or wounded. The population received our troops with open arms. I recall again that it contains one third purely Polish elements.

Mr. Lloyd George. Does Poland claim all of Galicia?

M. Paderewski. She wants to assure it autonomy.

M. Clemenceau. Do you claim Galicia, or don't you claim it?

M. Paderewski. We claim it. It is impossible to draw an ethnographic boundary in these areas. In the center of Galicia, the Ukrainian majority is particularly strong; but further south, the Polish element reappears.

President Wilson (*studying the map*). I would like to look with you at the western border. There is a corner there of Pomerania inhabited by Germans.

M. Paderewski. It is a Germanized area.

President Wilson. Our idea is to rectify the boundary near the coast and, a bit further south, to change the line in such a way as to leave the railway on German territory. Near Militsch, the proposed boundary was drawn especially for topographical reasons; there are purely German populations there.

M. Paderewski. Purely Polish populations are also left inside the German frontier.

Mr. Lloyd George. It goes without saying that, if we change the boundary, we must do it in both directions. If we give the Germans to Germany, all the Poles must be given to Poland.

President Wilson. If the plebiscite took place for all of Upper Silesia at once, could the presence of Germanic elements in the Southwest change the vote?

M. Paderewski. If there must be a plebiscite in Upper Silesia, the vote would have to be taken as in Masuria,[7] that is, by commune. The German communes which you just mentioned would undoubtedly go to the Germans.

Mr. Lloyd George. Why did the proposed border exclude Polish elements?

President Wilson. Our experts undoubtedly wished to preserve administrative units.

Mr. Lloyd George. Or else they were motivated by so-called strategic necessities; we mustn't stop at that. Let us take all of Silesia, and not only Upper Silesia; all together, the majority is German?

M. Paderewski. Yes, although in my youth I met many people in Breslau who spoke Polish.

President Wilson. Will the small changes of the boundary which we contemplate affect many Polish interests?

M. Paderewski. The central region, near Konitz, has some importance because of the railway.

President Wilson. This railway serves above all German territories.

M. Clemenceau. Will you accept a plebiscite after the evacuation of the territory by German troops?

M. Paderewski. If the text of the treaty must undergo such a change, I will be compelled to hand in my resignation. I would be compelled to do so even if important territorial changes were made in what has already been foretold. In that case, I no longer want to have anything to do with politics. My country will become ungovernable. Revolutions take place when peoples no longer have confidence in their leaders. The Poles were told: "Here is what you will have." If, today, they are told something else, they will lose their confidence in me and in you.

Mr. Lloyd George. We did not make promises, strictly speaking. We drafted an outline of a treaty which wasn't an ultimatum, and today we are studying the counterproposals of the Germans, looking to see if it is possible to make reasonable concessions.

Until very recently, Poland was divided, under the heel of her enemies, without the least hope of future independence. Most of the Poles fought, willingly or by force, against the liberty of their country. Now, whatever happens, you have the guarantee of a unified Polish state, with more than twenty million inhabitants. You ask further that you be assigned populations which are not Polish—three and a half million Galicians. All we want—and that is why we propose some changes in the boundary—is not to place populations in Poland which would not be Polish.

---

[7] An area in the southern part of East Prussia.

Don't forget that your liberty was won by the 1,500,000 dead that France lost in this war, by the 800,000 dead of the British Empire, by the 500,000 Italian dead. Your liberty was paid for with the blood of other peoples, and truly, if Poland, in these circumstances, should revolt against our decisions, she would be something quite other than we had hoped.

M. Paderewski. All I meant was that I could not remain in power.

Mr. Lloyd George. We liberated the Poles, the Czechoslovaks, the Yugoslavs, and today we have all the trouble in the world preventing them from oppressing other races. I myself belong to a small nation. I have the warmest and most profound sympathy for small nations which are fighting for their independence, and I am seized with despair when I see them more imperialistic than the great nations themselves.

M. Paderewski. I must protest against these words. The Poles, on every occasion, have fought for the liberty of the world. They are not imperialistic; they wish to oppress no nation and no religion, no more than they wish to impose their language and their traditions. We have always respected the existence of the Lithuanians, the Ukrainians, who, today, with our help, are developing their national individualities. The accusations you bring against us here come from rumors which run through the press. I ask you for permission to read a telegram from one of our bishops, denouncing atrocities committed by Ukrainian bands. (*Reading.*) I will also read you the document in which the Ukrainian government asked Poland to help it to achieve its freedom.

Mr. Lloyd George. What I mean by imperialism is the annexation of populations against their will.

M. Paderewski. We want nothing of the kind.

Mr. Lloyd George. That is not what the news we get says.

M. Paderewski. But we are obliged to defend our oppressed and murdered compatriots.

Mr. Lloyd George. It is impossible for us to know the truth of the facts. The same accusations of violence come to us from both sides.

M. Paderewski. The day I left Warsaw, I saw in the hospital a child of thirteen who had received a bullet in his arm and another in his lung; he was a defender of Lemberg! I saw a girl also wounded whilst defending the city; do you think she was fighting for conquests?

Mr. Lloyd George. I know that Lemberg is a Polish city; but it is surrounded by Ukrainian countryside. Likewise, there are German cities surrounded by Polish populations; we are assigning them to Poland, and in this case, you don't protest.

M. Paderewski. I said a short time ago that there was a Ukrainian district near Lemberg; but beyond that, only Polish districts are found.

—M. Paderewski reads aloud the declaration of the Polish Diet on the right of self-determination, the necessity of establishing a durable peace amongst nationalities and of granting ethnic and religious minorities equal rights.[8]

Poland asks for an understanding with Lithuania, based on the principle of free determination.

Eastern Galicia must be part of the Polish state under an autonomous regime. Poland hopes that the same form of government will be granted to the 1,500,000 Poles who will remain in the territory of the Ukraine.

Mr. Lloyd George. Most of the general principles formulated in this document are excellent; I can only endorse them.

M. Clemenceau. Let me ask you a question about the plebiscite: suppose that it doesn't take place immediately and that, in the interval, Upper Silesia is occupied by American troops; don't you think that the vote would then take place under favorable conditions?

M. Paderewski. Yes, for the eastern part of Silesia. It is not the same for the agricultural part in the West, where the activity of landowners, civil servants, and the clergy continues. Moreover, the Germans are presently using methods of provocation; what they want is a movement which they can repress. Their troops are concentrated on the Polish front and are being reinforced constantly. They amount to 350,000 men.

M. Orlando. Didn't Marshal Foch estimate the other day the entire German forces at 300,000 men?

M. Clemenceau. They are concentrated on the Polish frontier.

M. Paderewski. Moreover, the Germans are ready to mobilize. We have information from Polish soldiers, who unfortunately are still in the service of Germany, since they belong to areas awaiting their liberation. There was a large political meeting recently in Berlin, under the chairmanship of Scheidemann, where the different states of Germany were represented. Scheidemann said that the situation was better, thanks to the secret treaty signed

---

[8] This declaration is printed in *ibid.*, Vol. 60, pp. 166-67.

with Trotsky: he promises his assistance to the German government, on condition that he be sent 3,500 German instructors—which was done.[9]

The generals present at that meeting said that the morale of the rank and file was as good as in 1914, and that mobilization would yield a million men of that quality. As for munitions, many were manufactured recently in Silesia itself, especially asphyxiating gases. Shells filled with these gases were fired during these last days on a Polish village, where there were several victims. This is not yet war strictly speaking; but it can begin any day.

President Wilson. I am very grateful to you for what you have said, and we will take careful account of it in our deliberations.

[9] Insofar as the Editors know, no such meeting took place and no such secret agreement was concluded.

CX

Conversation between President Wilson and MM. Clemenceau, Lloyd George, Orlando, Paderewski, Beneš, Brătianu, Mişu, Vénisélos, and Vesnić*

JUNE 5, 1919, 4 P.M.

President Wilson. When the question of the limitation of Austria's military forces was put to us, it seemed difficult to impose conditions on that power without having studied the corresponding problem for the different states formed out of or enlarged by territories of the former Austro-Hungarian monarchy; it appeared to us necessary to contemplate a system embracing all the states of Central Europe.

We asked for the opinion of our military advisers, who presented to us solutions by adopting, for each of the states concerned, the same theoretical basis.[1] In each case, they took into

*H., PPC, VI, 202ff.

[1] The report of the military representatives on the Supreme War Council on this matter is printed in PPC, V, 885-91. It recommended the following troop strengths for the armies of the central and eastern European states: Czechoslovakia, 50,000; Yugoslavia, 40,000; Rumania, 60,000; Poland, 80,000; Greece, 20,000; Hungary, 45,000; Bulgaria, 20,000.

account the population, extent of the land or sea border, distribution of populations between cities and the countryside, and the presence of large cities and industrial centers making larger forces necessary for the maintenance of order.

The figure they proposed for Austria is 40,000 men; but since we granted Germany a permanent army of only 100,000 men, this figure of 40,000 seemed excessive for a state of eight to nine million inhabitants at most. Figures were also stated for Hungary and Bulgaria, as well as the other states of that part of Europe. But we deemed it impossible to approve these proposals without having consulted you.

We know that there is a difference between the arrangement which will follow the re-establishment of peace and that which must be provided during a period of transition. That is why we thought it would be appropriate, in fixing the figure of effectives for each state, to indicate a date on which this decision would take effect, for example, January 1, 1921. Supposing it might appear that, in a particular case, this time limit is insufficient, the League of Nations would be advised and would have the right to postpone it. We have not forgotten that the conditions of the world today are not—fortunately—the final conditions of the life of nations. We acknowledge that a provisional arrangement must be anticipated.

The general proportion which served as the basis for the calculations of the military experts is that of four soldiers per thousand inhabitants. In the case of Austria, that proportion was exceeded because of the large population of the city of Vienna.

M. Vesnić. The problem which is raised is of the highest importance to us. I must say that the way in which you consider it has surprised us. We respectfully address the following question to you: how could the problem be stated in the same way for allies and for enemies? I confess to you that this would give us the greatest concern.

In the second place, I would see in this manner of dealing with the problem—and I hope that I am wrong in this—a tendency to diminish, if not to nullify, our rights of sovereignty. I must declare formally that one of the principal objectives for which we fought was to obtain for ourselves—small nations—the same sovereignty, the same political rights, the same legal situation, which has always been acknowledged for independent states since there has been any international law. We would be greatly alarmed if, from today on, before the League of Nations had established its authority, we found ourselves compelled to accept an arrangement such as the one you indicate. We would certainly be disavowed by our peoples; we would not obtain ratification of the treaty; and we would find ourselves faced with difficulties which I believe could be avoided if this important and delicate question before us is handled without being tied to the limitation of the armaments of Austria, Hungary, and Bulgaria.

When you limited the troop numbers and armaments of Germany, you did not do so for the other large or small nations which participate with you in the treaty. If nations which fought with you were placed in the position which I anticipate, they would be less favored than the neutral states.

Without insisting further, I must, in the name of the Kingdom of the Serbs, Croats and Slovenes, make every reservation, not only to the application, but to the very principle. If the large powers should take a decision in the sense we fear—and I hope it will not be so—I reserve our right to discuss the proposals which would result from it. It is absolutely essential to safeguard the domestic peace of our states as well as international peace.

M. Vénisélos. The limitation of military forces is one of the great hopes of all our countries, and I trust it is not an unattainable ideal. It would be a great disappointment for all of us if, after the sacrifices imposed on the world by the war, we were obliged to maintain the [present] level of armaments.

But I must acknowledge that what M. Vesnić has just said made a great impression on me. Instead of fixing the strength of our armies for 1921 now, why not wait for the decision of the League of Nations? Such a decision belongs to it. Concerning Greece, I state that she will conform scrupulously to the instructions which the League of Nations will give her.

With this clarification, I support what has just been said by M. Vesnić, and I ask that the question be referred to the Council of the League of Nations.

M. Brătianu. I thank you for having been willing, in examining this question with us, to allow us to express our point of view and the interests of our states in a spirit of complete frankness.

We have as much interest as anyone in the limitation of armaments. The principle has already been accepted by all of us at the same time as the Covenant of the League of Nations, and it is the latter which must take up the question: to settle it outside of it is to settle it only in part.

Words often end by creating concrete situations. You must not attach yourselves too much to that expression, which was found convenient, of states "with limited interests." It is true that there are states with limited influence; but their interests go beyond what can be seen on the map. As far as Rumania is concerned, it would be impossible for her to accept a limitation of her forces which would be calculated solely with respect to Austria. You say that your military experts took into account the situation of each country. But it is not only a matter of knowing if there are cities or industrial populations in a state. You must still consider the nature of its borders, which can be more or less easy to defend, and furthermore, the nature of the neighboring areas which geography or history have imposed upon it.

Rumania's frontier is not yet drawn, and Rumania is not only in a state of war, but in a state of declared war with the Bolsheviks of Russia and with those of Hungary. It is well to disarm the constables, but on the condition of having first disarmed the brigands.

On our eastern frontier, will we have a Ukrainian state or a great Russia? Austria is becoming a secondary power, of which we are not neighbors. For us, tomorrow's problem is the Russian problem. To determine today what the Rumanian army must be, without knowing what Russia will be, what her troop numbers will be and if she will be disposed to accept their limitation—that is impossible. Like my colleagues, I have nothing but sympathy for the principle stated; but its application cannot be immediate, and I side with what has just been said by MM. Vesnić and Vénisélos.

M. Beneš. I am happy that you should give me this opportunity to set forth the point of view of our government. It has already taken decisions which correspond to the ideas of President Wilson and to those who preside over these debates. Both in the general interest and on account of the presence amongst us of a great number of German-speaking compatriots, we have prepared a constitution which will not be without analogy to that of Switzerland. We do the same from the military point of view. Our economic situation lends itself to this arrangement; our people are well prepared for it, and a program of this kind corresponds to the general idea of the limitation of armaments.

I must draw your attention to the facts which lead me, speaking in the name of the Czechoslovak Republic, to the same conclusions as MM. Vesnić, Vénisélos, and Brătianu. The first is the present situation of Central Europe. The question of disarmament can only be raised universally. Today, Russia, the western nations, and the neutrals would remain outside the system. The nations of Central Europe are in a state of agitation and uncertainty which is not without danger; they don't know what will happen from the side of Germany; they know still less what will happen from the side of Russia and in the East. It would be very dangerous to take an action that would aggravate this state of uncertainty and irritation. Through a decision like the one just mentioned, the nations of Central Europe would be placed in a position inferior to that of Holland, Switzerland, or Belgium. The problem must not be localized, for you would not thus obtain stabilization, but just the opposite.

Moreover, you must consider the consequences inside our state of a decision by the conference limiting our military strength. In our country, as in other countries, there is a strong popular movement for total disarmament. Now, we are fighting against the Hungarians; we have differences with the Poles; we don't know what will become of Russia. A decision which would make part of the public believe that the time has come to renounce all military establishment would have very dangerous repercussions on our domestic arrangements.

Only one solution remains. Our government has already prepared a plan of disarmament. We are ready to bring it before the League of Nations when a general discussion is initiated. What would be dangerous is an immediate debate and solution.

M. Paderewski. I insist on saying that, contrary to certain rumors, Poland has no intention of flouting the authority of the peace conference. In this, as in other questions, we rely upon the wisdom and fairness of the conference, and we will accept its decision with a confidence which cannot flag.

From the purely military point of view, our army is not under our orders but under those of Marshal Foch, and I think Marshal Foch would have to be consulted.

We will gladly support all efforts which can be made for the limitation of armaments. Nothing can do more good for our country in the future. On the application of the principle, I associate myself completely with what has been said by the distinguished speakers who preceded me. It is my duty to draw your attention respectfully to the situation of my country. It is even more critical than Rumania's. The Poles are threatened by the Germans, who are not only on the northern and northwestern front, but even on Polish soil. According to the most reliable information, there are now 350,000 German soldiers in Silesia, around the province of Posen, in East Prussia, and in Lithuania. The monster is wounded, but it is not dead.

For the moment, the battles have not begun; there are only skirmishes. But Polish villages are already being bombarded with asphyxiating shells, and Polish peasants have been killed. The future alarms us.

On the other side, we are fighting against the Bolsheviks of Russia and the Ukraine. The authority of the conference does not extend directly to this side. If our forces were limited tomorrow, we would ask the Allied and Associated Powers to assume their responsibilities and to come to help us against the Germans and the Bolsheviks. Will the Bolshevik danger be eliminated, and what part will the powers take in that? As long as this question and the German question are not settled, it is impossible for Poland to limit her military effort.

President Wilson. The precision of the statements I have just heard has impressed me. These statements show that we have before us not only local difficulties, but general ones. That is why I had proposed that the reduction of troop numbers take place only after a certain date, with the possibility of extension if the League of Nations deemed that action necessary. My reflections on this problem will be much aided by the presentation of the various national points of view. I admit that I feel obliged to study this question anew.

Mr. Lloyd George. I will speak in the same sense. What has just been said by the representatives of the different states of Central Europe has made a great impression on me. In a conversation with M. Beneš, he had already convinced me that any attempt to limit troop numbers before the present risks had ended would be most dangerous. But we never thought of an immediate limitation. Here is how the problem presented itself to us.

We are negotiating with Austria, with Hungary. We are, as a matter of fact, reducing them to impotence. We are cutting large pieces out of their territories to make new states. You cannot compare your situation to that of Holland. Serbia's territory is tripled; that of Rumania and her population is more then doubled—and that thanks to our common efforts. The question arises whether we should not regulate the terms of the existence of the new states thus constituted. The same question arose at the time of the negotiations which ended in the Treaty of Berlin. We thought that, after the dismemberment of old states like Austria and Hungary, after having completely disarmed them, we could not leave them at the mercy of their neighbors.

We never wanted to infringe on the sovereignty of friendly states. But when certain of those states double or triple their territory, we wonder on what basis their future existence should be established. The statements which we have just heard have much force; but, without wishing to infringe on the sovereignty of anyone, I call to your attention that, if each state raises armies in proportion to its population, all your states together will have millions of men under arms, and that can create a more dangerous situation than ever.

Moreover, we don't want to impose terms on you that we are not ready to accept ourselves. I can assure you that, after this war, Great Britain will have an army considerably smaller than Rumania's and certainly smaller than Poland's.

M. Clemenceau. If I take the floor, it is not to contradict anyone. The observations of the states of Central Europe seem to me justified on all points, and I believe we are now in agreement.

Although no one has spoken of reducing France's armaments, that is one of the first questions which comes before us. Even if we did not want to make this reduction, we would be forced to it, because of the inclinations of public opinion, as much as by the obligation to concentrate all our resources on the economic effort. You have no spirit of aggression to fear on our part.

M. Vesnić said with much moderation: "The powers which are here are victorious powers, they are your allies, and they would not like to see their forces reduced at the same time as those of Austria and according to the same principle." There is an obvious distinction to be made: we are imposing our terms upon the enemy; we are talking with our friends with a view to a general reduction of armaments. Nothing is more important for permanent peace than to maintain agreement amongst the victorious powers.

Our friends of the states of Central Europe will surely want to help us. If we confine ourselves to saying today: "Let us disarm Austria and put the question of disarmament before our friends and ourselves," I believe that we will have done all that is possible at present. As for myself, I cannot ignore what was said by MM. Brătianu and Paderewski. The Czechoslovaks are today being driven back by the Hungarians. Some time ago, we had the idea of settling matters with Hungary. We questioned the commander in chief of the Army of the East,[2] who presented such a program to us that we were frightened by it. Things then remained in *statu quo*. When we heard word of an advance by the Rumanians, we asked M. Brătianu a question, to which he replied.[3] Now the situation has changed; it is not a matter of taking

[2] That is, Gen. Franchet d'Esperey.
[3] That is, Brătianu denied that the Rumanians were advancing.

an offensive or of stopping it, but of knowing if we will not be compelled to help the Czechoslovaks tomorrow. Hungary is the only enemy state which we have not yet reached. It is possible that, a few days from now, we will have to ask the military experts in Versailles to prepare a plan of action in Hungary for us.

For his part, M. Paderewski gave us a formidable figure, unfortunately rather in agreement with those transmitted to us from elsewhere. There are 300,000 or 350,000 German soldiers on the Polish border. Germany, crushed in the West, has only one idea left: to play her part in the East. If she wins, if she seizes Russia politically and especially economically, she has won the war. Three hundred and fifty thousand Germans in Silesia: they are not there for a parade.

Will the Germans sign the peace treaty? If they sign it, it is not certain that we will obtain the withdrawal of those 350,000 men in a reasonable period of time. Today, the Polish army is one of the guarantees of the signing of the treaty. Three hundred and fifty thousand men are before her—that is to say, before us.

I believe we must all arm or disarm at the same time. During my entire career, I have been the enemy of war. In the name of France, I solemnly take the commitment that she will never provoke new conflicts in Europe; she has made enough sacrifices in the past to want to avoid them. The peaceful spirit of the great English and American democracies is known to you. In view of our peaceful intentions, we must give no advantage whatsoever to the aggressor.

It is impossible that we should not all be agreed on this point: in order to limit armaments, war must be ended; now, it is not certain that peace coincides exactly with the signing of the treaty. The best thing would be to take a mutual commitment today to settle this question when the time comes. When will it come? I am not an advocate of a fixed date. Will we say in one year, in two years? One would be as arbitrary as the other. We don't know what will happen either in Germany or in Hungary. We know still less what will happen in Russia.

In this question of disarmament, the League of Nations must play a big part. When the war has ended, that is to say, when the conquered not only have signed the peace treaty but have given proof that they are doing what they can to carry out its clauses, the question of disarmament can be raised, either in a congress of the powers or before the League of Nations.

As for myself, I have confidence in the League of Nations. If you want to entrust this problem to it, I accept that decision. The war isn't yet over; the Czechoslovaks are fighting, the Poles are fighting, the Rumanians are fighting. When the war is truly over and our peoples are restored to serenity in a peace of liberty and work, it would be advisable for us to meet in order to study together a general plan of disarmament. When I say "we," that can be the League of Nations. I ask the question so that each of us might think about it.

M. Orlando. I have nothing to add. But everyone having taken the floor, I would not like my silence to be interpreted as a sign of any disagreement. Like my colleagues, I think that no one wanted to limit the sovereignty of those who were our associates and companions in our great victory. That has been very well said.

The difficulty of settling the question of disarmament now has not escaped the heads of governments; hence, the proposal to prepare an arrangement which would be applied only beginning in 1921. To think that the date might be too early is to be rather pessimistic about the future. However, it was anticipated that the period could be extended.

For the time being, the problem has been considered on a technical rather than a political basis. Four soldiers per thousand inhabitants—that is approximately Italy's proportion in peacetime. After the war, with the financial difficulties in which we find ourselves, we will considerably reduce that proportion.

The discussion which has just taken place has been useful, although skeptics say that no discussion is ever useful. I heard statements which made a great impression on me. I echo M. Brătianu's argument: "How can one determine the forces of a state if it does not know its boundaries?" I agree with my colleagues, and I thank the heads of governments of Central Europe for their contribution to the study of this serious question.

—MM. Paderewski, Beneš, Brătianu, Mişu, Vénisélos, and Vesnić withdraw.

Mr. Lloyd George. When will we discuss this question? In any case, as for Hungary, I have only agreed to limit her troop numbers on the assumption that those of the neighboring states would be limited at the same time.

M. Clemenceau. At this time, Hungary is attacking Bohemia.

Mr. Lloyd George. We don't know how to act at a distance; our orders are not obeyed.

M. Clemenceau. Concerning the Poles, we thought that General Haller had not respected our instructions, we thought we had

had those instructions sent to him, but it was impossible for me to find any trace of them.

President Wilson. I am thinking about the concentration of Germans on the Polish front.

M. Clemenceau. All these men we have just seen are fighting for their very existence. If England had a revolt in India tomorrow, she would raise armies to put it down.

Mr. Lloyd George. A state compelled to raise an army to face a danger can't adopt an aggressive policy.

M. Orlando. We can ask for a mutual commitment to participate in a plan for disarmament and postpone the debate.

CXI

Conversation between President Wilson and MM. Clemenceau and Lloyd George*

JUNE 6, 1919, 11 A.M.

President Wilson. M. Orlando seems to have misunderstood me. I don't know if Count Aldrovandi conveyed my thought to him correctly. According to a letter which he addresses to me, he believes we are allowing the Italian delegation the right to raise anew the question of the boundary of the state of Fiume after having accepted M. Tardieu's plan.[1] I said nothing of the kind. Likewise concerning the city of Fiume. M. Orlando believes he understood that Fiume would remain an independent city inside the free state. His mind seems to me completely unstable, and one never knows if one has come to an agreement with him.

Mr. Lloyd George. He has stirred up forces that he can no longer control.

President Wilson. The Italians ask that the state of Fiume include the island of Veglia; the Yugoslavs want Veglia to be made part of their state and the frontier to be drawn between Fiume and the suburb of Sušak.[2] The island of Cherso, claimed by the Italians,

*H., PPC, VI, 210ff.

[1] For the same letter, see V. E. Orlando to D. Lloyd George, June 5, 1919, printed in PWW, Vol. 60, pp. 197-98. For a discussion of this latest Italian counterproposal, see Albrecht-Carrié, *Italy at the Paris Peace Conference*, pp. 191-92.

[2] For the Yugoslav counterproposal, which Wilson details well, see *ibid.*, p.

should be made part of the state of Fiume. As for the islands situated along the coast of northern Dalmatia, which the Tardieu plan grants to Italy, the Yugoslavs ask that they be placed under the authority of the League of Nations for a period of five years, at the expiration of which a plebiscite would decide their fate. If we don't accept this last proposal, the Yugoslavs ask that the islands of Lussino and Lissa be assigned to the League of Nations, which will dispose of them as it decides, and which can, consequently, give them to Italy.

As for Zara and Sebenico, the Italians continue to claim them; the Yugoslavs won't hear of their cession to Italy and agree only to grant these cities an autonomous administration under their sovereignty.

If the Yugoslavs insist that they be granted the island of Veglia and the suburb of Sušak immediately, it is in order to be assured of having a port with free access to the sea in the event that the state of Fiume, after fifteen years, should vote for union with Italy. The Italians, on the contrary, would like the island of Veglia to belong to the state of Fiume and for the islands across from Sebenico to be given to them in full sovereignty.

I have before me an Italian map published before the war—that of Marinelli—which would be enough to contradict the Italian argument; it shows that, aside from the southern portion of the island of Cherso and the island of Lussino, there are Italian elements only on some isolated points. What discourages me is that, when Italy has made proposals, they dissolve as soon as one tries to be precise.

I was rather moved by what a Slovene delegation, which I received yesterday, said to me. These Slovenes told me that, despite their repugnance at Austrian domination, under that domination they had the advantage of living together, of preserving their traditions and their common life. "You are liberating us," they said, "and, at the same time, you are cutting us into pieces. It was inevitable that the Italian boundary should include Slovene populations. But now that boundary is going to extend beyond Tarvis. Even now, the powers are considering whether a part of the Slovenes won't remain in Austria."

Mr. Lloyd George. What we are discussing is whether these populations won't be called upon to determine their own fate.

President Wilson. I was struck by their great moderation. They are

---

190. See also the memorandum by D. W. Johnson printed in PWW, Vol. 60, pp. 137-38.

not complaining to us; they are asking that we do everything possible for them.

If I judge according to the Italian press, public opinion in Italy is not much concerned about the Dalmatian islands. Fiume is the essential question for it.

Mr. Lloyd George. I don't know whether Italian public opinion in general is interested in the question of the islands; but be assured that the people of the Adriatic coast of Italy are interested in it. During the entire war, it was almost impossible to have trains pass along that coast. The Austrians, although their fleet was comparatively weak, could at any time come out of the barrier of islands which protected them and destroy the railway.

President Wilson. To tell the truth, the Italians are not afraid of the Yugoslavs on the sea, but of an alliance between them and a naval power. Now, the only naval powers with which the Yugoslavs can ally themselves are France and England.

Mr. Lloyd George. There still remains a power that we are not taking into our calculations—Russia; we don't know what she will become.

President Wilson. If another power is mistress of the Straits, Russia cannot adopt an aggressive policy on the seas.

Mr. Lloyd George. For France, the great danger is the German danger; I believe it is averted for a century. I fear the Slavs much more. The Slav is a force one cannot control; he can be the instrument of the worst tyranny or the bloodiest anarchy, he can become a terrible danger for the world. Moreover, we mustn't forget the ties of race which unite the Slavs of Russia and the Slavs of southeastern Europe. If I were Italian, I wouldn't like to see the Slavs on that coast across from my country; that is what gives force to the last note presented by Baron Sonnino.

President Wilson. What makes the Slav less formidable than the German is that he has not attained the same degree of organization. The German is a perfect cog in a powerful machine. Moreover, an entire generation had prepared him for the present war. Men of my age, who, in their youth, had attended German universities, having returned to Germany a little before the war, came back frightened by the systematic education which had deformed the German mind. History, philosophy, political economy had been fashioned to serve German ambitions. Germany has a more complete system of education than any other country; if Russia was capable of doing as much, she would be irresistible. But she is backward in many respects.

Large industries are necessary in order to create a powerful fleet. Who will provide Russia with warships? We need all our shipyards for years in order to construct merchant ships for ourselves and other countries. With her immense natural resources, Russia is almost as unexploited as China. Her population of *mujiks* is so ignorant that one can only reach it through oral communications; we have had experience in that.

In my opinion, of the dangers which threaten Italy, the most serious would be the discontent of the Slavs.

Mr. Lloyd George. It must be acknowledged that the Italians have made considerable concessions. As a signatory of the Treaty of London, I am happy to see them today content with a few islands which are hardly more than rocks; but the channels between the islands are submarine nests.

Russia won't be in the League of Nations; we have no hold over her. That is why I wanted, in writing to Kolchak, to compel him to abolish compulsory military service. I remember the past. It wasn't only Beaconsfield, it was Gladstone, the man of peace par excellence, who thought himself on the verge of war with Russia. We will see the Slavic danger again: if Russia recovers, she, with her 160 million inhabitants, will have to be reckoned with in Europe. On the other hand, you have in all our countries hundreds of thousands of men whose only profession today is war. There are many in Germany; they will find work in Russia and will be able to provide officers for the formidable numbers which the latter has at her disposal.

We mustn't base all our reasoning on the German danger; we must see beyond that. Italy has good reasons to fear the proximity of the Slavs. If we can satisfy her without giving her any very populated territory, it is worth thinking about.

President Wilson. That means returning to the idea of the strategic frontier.

Mr. Lloyd George. You granted it to her in the Alps.

President Wilson. That is different. The Alps don't constitute only a defense; they give geographical unity to the countries they bound. When it was a matter of the boundaries of Germany, we heard Marshal Foch present arguments which, from the military point of view, no one could answer, and which would have led to bringing the frontier of France to the Rhine. M. Clemenceau wondered if there wasn't ground for establishing a buffer state there. But he acknowledged, along with us, that such a solution would be a danger for peace; France then has not had a strategic frontier.

Mr. Lloyd George. There is a great difference between the annexation of the left bank of the Rhine, which would place millions of Germans inside the French border, and the annexation to Italy of a few rocks.

M. Clemenceau. What do you propose?

Mr. Lloyd George. That we hold to the Tardieu proposal.

M. Clemenceau. What I would like is to be both just and practical.

Mr. Lloyd George. We must also take into account the difficulty of our position as allies of Italy.

President Wilson. Once the Italians raise the question of Fiume, they depart from the Treaty of London. If you give the islands to Italy, the Yugoslavs will say that she is mistress of their coast.

Mr. Lloyd George. During the war, we studied the possibility of making landings on that coast, and we acknowledged that it was impossible; there is no coast more formidably defended by nature.

President Wilson. Without attacking the Yugoslavs, Italy could strangle them. Don't forget that all the proposals of the Italians aim at putting Fiume at their mercy. For example, concerning the railroad, further north, if they were masters of the Assling crossing, that would allow them to divert commerce towards Trieste.

M. Clemenceau. Do the Italians accept the Tardieu proposal?

President Wilson. They make reservations about the boundary of the state of Fiume.

Mr. Lloyd George. That we cannot accept.

President Wilson. I will say frankly that I am not inclined to give the Italians any of these islands without a plebiscite. The proposal of the Yugoslavs to entrust the assignment of these islands to the League of Nations seems reasonable to me.

M. Clemenceau. What do you think about Zara and Sebenico?

President Wilson. The Yugoslavs propose to give them autonomy inside the Yugoslav state. In Sebenico, the Yugoslav population is much larger than the Italian population.

M. Clemenceau. Why not give Zara to Italy?

President Wilson. I see a great disadvantage in establishing the Italians on that coast. It is true that the majority of the population of Zara is Italian. But would you propose to give Milwaukee to the Germans?

Mr. Lloyd George. What I am trying to do is to avoid the impression that Italy is not being well treated. The solution you propose has the disadvantage of giving her nothing.

President Wilson. Unless the plebiscite turns out in her favor. I don't know why M. Orlando comes to see me so often; I have told him the same thing over and over since December.

Mr. Lloyd George. I am sorry to see him in this position; he is a lost man if he is compelled to capitulate.
President Wilson. I regret it also.
M. Clemenceau. For myself, I am ready to take a step in his direction.
President Wilson. According to my experts, the figures for Sebenico are 858 Italians and 9,031 Yugoslavs.
Mr. Lloyd George. It is obvious that Italy has no claim there.
M. Clemenceau. The Italians accept the Tardieu proposal, which gives them the small islands facing northern Dalmatia, along with Zara and Sebenico.
Mr. Lloyd George. I will remind you that they renounce all the large islands, except Cherso. That is going much further than they have ever done. Cherso's population is about 7,000 inhabitants, of whom it is true 5,000 are Yugoslavs.
M. Clemenceau. I would give them Zara and leave Sebenico to the Slavs; I think that will satisfy both.
President Wilson. I don't like establishing Italian sovereignty on that coast. We can propose to make Zara a free city, represented in her foreign relations by Italy.
M. Clemenceau. The Italians would prefer to make it an Italian city.
President Wilson. They also demand a hinterland.
Mr. Lloyd George. That we cannot grant.
M. Clemenceau. I would give them Zara. I don't think they will fight for Sebenico.
President Wilson. What would you think of a proposal which is entirely improvised and which I would not like to have entered into the minutes at present? The free state of Fiume would include the islands of Veglia and Cherso. Cherso closes the bay of Fiume so completely that I would have qualms about putting it in other hands. The islands off central Dalmatia would go to Italy.
M. Clemenceau. Will we make this proposal to them?
President Wilson. I would include in the free state of Fiume the territory on the northern coast, between the line of the Treaty of London and the American line.
M. Clemenceau. You don't favor giving Sušak to the Yugoslavs?
President Wilson. No, that would be a mistake.

—After a study of the map, it is decided to ask the experts to prepare a plan based on the foregoing proposal.

Mr. Lloyd George. I have received a telegram from Constantinople saying that the communication we were to make to the Grand Vizier was made by the French representative alone.[3]

M. Clemenceau. This is contrary to my instructions.

Mr. Lloyd George. Some comments immediately appeared in the Turkish press on the friendship of France. Since then, M. Pichon has sent a telegram of thanks of the President of the Republic to Constantinople in reply to a ceremonial message from the Crown Prince of Turkey.[4]

M. Clemenceau. I said at first that our representative should not discourage the Turks. After the communication we received from them, we decided to send them a reply through our representatives in Constantinople. M. Pichon proposed to me to take this step through the representative of France; I refused.

Mr. Lloyd George. What is most annoying is the telegram from the President of the Republic. Imagine the King of England sending a letter to President Ebert!

M. Clemenceau. What I had ordered was completely different; the President of the Republic had nothing to do with that.

[3] It is printed in PPC, VI, 217-18.
[4] Abdul Medjid Effendi.

CXII

Conversation between President Wilson and MM. Clemenceau, Lloyd George, and Orlando*

JUNE 6, 1919, 4 P.M.

—Mr. Norman H. Davis and M. d'Amelio are introduced.

President Wilson. The Drafting Committee has sent back to us a certain number of clauses of the Austrian treaty, notably the political clauses proposed by the Italian government.[1] One of these clauses relates to the option for Austrian subjects who, in the areas annexed to Italy, would like to retain their nationality; it requires them to transfer their domicile to Austrian territory within one year.

*H., PPC, VI, 219ff.
[1] They are printed in PPC, VI, 223-28.

M. Clemenceau. It is the Bismarckian system; that article was copied from the one of the Treaty of Frankfurt which compelled Alsatians and Lorrainers, if they wished to retain their French nationality, to transfer their domicile to France.

M. d'Amelio. We copied that article from the clauses relating to Czechoslovakia.

M. Clemenceau. In that case, we should come to an understanding with the Czechoslovaks to change their text.

Mr. Lloyd George. I propose to refer the matter to the Foreign Ministers who, with the assistance of the experts, could take a decision.

—*This proposal is adopted.*

M. Mantoux. The Czechoslovaks have obviously asked for the insertion of that article in order to prevent three million persons of German language, living in their territory, from being able to opt for Austrian nationality whilst remaining within the Czechoslovak state, which would constitute a great danger.

M. Clemenceau. That is true; it must be taken into account.

President Wilson. Article 20 of this treaty provides for the restitution, within three months, of rolling stock taken from Italy by the Austro-Hungarian armies, with the option of replacing locomotives and cars with equivalent material, if they can't be identified. I will point out that to adopt that clause would be to admit a principle which has been rejected for other countries and which, if applied universally, would not leave Germany and Austria enough rolling stock for their most pressing needs.

Mr. Lloyd George. In any case, a clause of this kind should not appear under the heading of reparation.

Mr. Davis. The Reparation Commission set it aside; that question, already asked for other countries, had been settled in the negative.

M. Orlando. It is a restitution of stolen objects. Concerning France and Belgium, that restitution was ordered in the Armistice Agreement. But in the Austrian armistice, which was drafted first, that stipulation was forgotten. It is fair that the treaty repair this omission.

President Wilson. The German Armistice fixed the number of locomotives and cars to be delivered, whilst the clause proposed to us has an indefinite character.

Mr. Lloyd George. Above all, it is impossible to make Austria alone responsible; she is now no more than a state of eight million inhabitants, and today the cars involved could be in Croatia, Hungary, or Bohemia. It is fair that Italy recover her rolling stock; but the burden can't be placed on Austria's back alone.

Mr. Davis. The question had already been asked in the same terms by France, Belgium, and Rumania; but our Reparation Commission has discarded the idea of replacement when the rolling stock could not be identified.

Mr. Lloyd George. If one can find the Italian locomotives and cars in all the former Austro-Hungarian Empire, very well; but Austria is only a small part of it today.

M. Clemenceau. What is M. Orlando's immediate conclusion?

M. Orlando. I ask that this question be sent back to the commission; we don't have to settle it today.

President Wilson. But we have the commission's report right in front of us.

Mr. Davis. More correctly, this report is that of the financial group of the commission charged with studying the whole of these clauses. We left aside those which, in our opinion, were properly political clauses.

Mr. Lloyd George. I would propose to M. Orlando to renounce for the moment the second part of Article 20, which provides for replacement in case the rolling stock cannot be recovered. If the information and opinions collected by M. Orlando lead him to raise the question again, that is his option.

M. Orlando. I accept.

—President Wilson reads the clauses to be accepted by Poland as a member of the League of Nations.[2] The right to call the attention of the League to any infringement of the pledges taken for the protection of ethnic or religious minorities must belong to every member of the Council.

President Wilson. Lord Robert Cecil is of opinion that that question falls within the jurisdiction of the future permanent court of international justice. I will call to your attention that this tribunal will only exist if the League of Nations establishes it. The French, English, and Japanese experts would like to limit the jurisdiction of that court to differences between states; the representatives of the United States and of Italy would give it a more extended ju-

---

[2] The Council of Four had before it a report of the Committee on New States presenting a new draft of Article 14 of the proposed treaty between the great powers and Poland for the protection of ethnic and religious minorities in the new Polish Republic. The report, with the proposed article included, is printed in *PWW*, Vol. 60, pp. 223-25.

risdiction, which would allow national or religious minorities to bring their causes directly before it.³

In the first case, the text would be written as follows: "Poland acknowledges that any dispute about the application of these guarantees will have the character of an international dispute and can be brought by one of the members of the Council of the League of Nations before the Court of International Justice."

The matter is critical. You recall how, in our last Plenary Session, the sensitivity of the small nations showed itself; they fear an encroachment upon their sovereignty. If the members of the Council alone have the right to call the League's attention to the application of this clause of the treaty, this intervention becomes the monopoly of a few powers. They will give the appearance of imposing their will on the particulars of the execution as on the very text of the guarantees stipulated by the treaty. Perhaps it is better to leave this right of intervention to all the members of the League.

Here is how I see the thing. The Jews are treated on a footing of perfect equality by the great powers—France, Italy, Great Britain, the United States. Also, it is not on their territory that one finds that Jewish element which can become a danger for the peace of Europe, but in Russia, Rumania, Poland—wherever Jews are persecuted. Under the arrangement that I indicate, if Poland does not keep the promises that we ask her to make, the Rumanian delegate, for example, will have the right to bring it up, or vice versa. Thus, we would avoid the feeling that might be provoked by an intervention contrary in appearance to the principle of equality amongst all nations.

Mr. Lloyd George. I would like to know which of these two arrangements would be accepted most easily by these small countries. Perhaps we ought to ask them.

M. Clemenceau. They are very touchy, and we must be careful of that. They just received a letter from us asking them straight out what their reservations mean.⁴ That is enough for the moment.

You know that M. Brătianu is leaving office.⁵

---

³ The two drafts concerning the jurisdiction of the proposed world court are printed in the report just mentioned.

⁴ About the Yugoslav and Rumanian reservations, see CVI, n. 6. The letter in reply to these communications is missing. However, the Four had instructed Hankey on June 3 to draft a letter to the Rumanian and Yugoslav delegations asking for a "signification" of their communications: "Was the intention not to sign the Treaty, or was it proposed to sign and then not to carry it out?" *PPC*, VI, 160.

⁵ Brătianu left Paris for Bucharest on July 4. He did not resign until September 11 or 12, 1919.

Mr. Lloyd George. I am not too upset by that; I would like to see Take Ionescu here, or another man who takes the western point of view.

President Wilson. In the proposal I made, it is only a matter of giving all the powers the right to place the question before the League of Nations.

Mr. Lloyd George. It is very difficult to judge the domestic affairs of a country other than one's own. But it seems to me that, if I were Rumanian, I would prefer to see a question like this one presented by a great power like France or the United States, rather than by Brazil or Greece. That is the danger we run if all the member states of the League have the right to intervene.

President Wilson. For other powers, the treaty provides the right to intervene amicably, without any other specification. The best thing is to consult the countries concerned.

—*It is agreed that each of the great powers will put the question to one of the nations concerned.*

—President Wilson reads a telegram from Admiral Kolchak in reply to the Allies' demand for guarantees.[6]

(1) As soon as the Bolsheviks are completely vanquished, the Constituent Assembly will be convoked and elections will take place by universal suffrage. It appears impossible to recall the assembly of 1917, "elected under a regime of Bolshevik violence, a majority of whose members are now in the ranks of the Soviets."

Paragraphs 2 and 3 and a part of paragraph 4 have not been transmitted.

The second part of paragraph 4 provides for administrative autonomy for the nationalities of the Caspian area, with appeal to the League of Nations in case of difficulty in the establishment of this regime.

Paragraph 5 lays down the principle that the question of Bessarabia cannot be settled without the ratification of the Russian National Assembly.

Paragraph 6 confirms the commitments taken on November 27, 1918, concerning the payment of the debt.

Paragraph 7 affirms that no return to the prerevolutionary regime is possible, and that the land must remain in the hands of the peasants.

President Wilson. The sentence concerning the impossibility of reestablishing the old regime was transmitted incompletely, so there can be some doubt about it.

---

[6] A. V. Kolchak to G. Clemenceau, June 4, 1919, printed in *PWW*, Vol. 60, pp. 141-44.

M. Clemenceau. We must wait for the complete and correctly transcribed text that we will have tomorrow.

Earlier, we received a telegram relating a conversation with the Admiral[7] which gives us complete satisfaction.

Mr. Lloyd George. However, I don't like his repugnance at the idea of convoking the assembly of 1917; no doubt it was too advanced for him.

[7] This was probably a telegram from Ernest Lloyd Harris, American Consul at Omsk, to Lansing, May 29, 1919, enclosed in Lansing to Wilson, May 30, 1919, printed in *ibid.*, Vol. 59, p. 619, which Wilson might have either read or distributed to his colleagues on the council. Kolchak said, among other things, that, on the question of recognition, "he was not asking such a step on the part of Allied Governments but was leaving this important matter to their best judgment uninfluenced by any statement from him."

CXIII

Conversation between President Wilson and MM. Clemenceau, Lloyd George, and Orlando*

JUNE 7, 1919, 11 A.M.

M. Clemenceau. I asked for information about the telegram which was addressed by the President of the Republic to the Crown Prince of Turkey; it is only a reply to a ceremonial message sent by the latter.

Mr. Lloyd George. We received this same message, and we made no reply. It would certainly have been better if the President of the Republic had abstained. It is the eternal game of the Turks to try to make advances to all of us, to see who will respond, and in what way to try to divide us. Turkey is still an enemy power. (*To M. Orlando*) Did the Italian government receive a communication of the same kind?

M. Orlando. We did indeed receive it; but we confined ourselves to giving our representative in Constantinople instructions to act in concert with yours.

M. Clemenceau. I agree with you completely about the way we should have proceeded. The reply of the President of the Repub-

*H., *PPC*, VI, 232ff.

lic wasn't at all contrary to the Constitution; but I regret it, because it goes against our common policy.

—President Wilson reads aloud a proclamation of Admiral Kolchak:[1] the struggle taking place in Russia is not against the Russian people but against the criminals who oppress them. Amnesty is promised to all who were forced to follow the Bolsheviks against their will. The Constituent Assembly will have absolute freedom in determining the future regime of Russia. Possession of products of the soil will be guaranteed to the cultivators. Workers' organizations will receive all encouragement from the state. The day of victory is near.

President Wilson. It is a fine proclamation.
M. Clemenceau. Excellent.
Mr. Lloyd George. Wouldn't it be helpful to publish it here?
M. Clemenceau. It is better to publish the reply to our telegram; we will have it in full this evening.
Mr. Lloyd George. This will be useful. It will have a happy effect on public opinion. I have just been attacked in the House of Commons for the role attributed to us in Russia.
M. Orlando. I saw M. Brătianu on the subject of the minorities; he is like a madman and says that he won't reply to our last note.
M. Clemenceau. When is he leaving?
M. Orlando. He says that he is going to hand in his resignation, but he doesn't say when.
M. Clemenceau. The truth is that the Rumanians want to leave the Jews in the position they have kept them in up to now. We know how they escaped all their earlier commitments.

—Reading of the proposals of the Serbs for the provisional organization of the Klagenfurt Basin.[2]

First proposal: zone A would be occupied by the Yugoslavs, zone B by the Austrians. Within six months, registers would be opened in these two zones, in which the population would be able to express their wishes concerning the final settlement of their fate.

Second proposal: zone A being occupied by the Yugoslavs and zone B by the Austrians, a plebiscite can be held in each of these zones at the request of the inhabitants.

President Wilson. I don't like these proposals. The first seems to me completely unacceptable. The second places the entire zone

[1] It is printed as an enclosure with R. Lansing to WW, June 5, 1919, *PWW*, Vol. 60, pp. 180-81. Wilson summarizes its main points.

[2] They are printed as an enclosure with M. R. Vesnić to WW, June 6, 1919, *ibid.*, pp. 232-33.

in the hands of the interested powers, since they would occupy the disputed territories from this time on.

Mr. Lloyd George. The Yugoslavs haven't answered the questions that we asked them.

President Wilson. No, it is a counterproposal that we have before us.

Mr. Lloyd George. In every place where we have instituted a plebiscite, we have sought to establish conditions which insure local opinion complete freedom of expression. These proposals would not be such as to guarantee it.

—M. Orlando transmits a report on the situation in Carinthia,[3] where hostilities are continuing between the Yugoslavs and Austrians.

President Wilson. All that we can do for the moment is to call the attention of the Yugoslavs to it and ask for explanations.

Mr. Lloyd George. The same thing is happening there as occurred further south, after the Balkan War: the victorious Bulgarians wanted to take more than their allies wanted to allow them, the others fell upon them: all that is deplorable.

Mr. Lloyd George. Sir Hubert Llewellyn Smith raises the question of an international conference on means of communication; if it is to take place soon, the neutrals have to be summoned.[4] It would seem desirable to take advantage of the facilities offered by the present meeting. In any case, we must settle the clauses to be imposed upon the enemies now.

President Wilson. It seems to me preferable not to set down in an international agreement the terms which we wish to impose upon the enemy.

Mr. Lloyd George. Shouldn't someone—who would not be one of us—have a conversation with the Germans about reparations, the delivery of raw materials, etc.? The Germans are exaggerating the draconian powers attributed to the Reparation Commission:[5] it would be to our advantage to explain these to them.

[3] It is printed in *PPC*, VI, 237-38.

[4] The question was whether to attempt to draw up a convention for the control of international waterways, etc., now, or whether to defer the matter to a conference called by the League of Nations. See *ibid.*, p. 235.

[5] Lloyd George referred most particularly to a memorandum by the financial commission of the German delegation which Brockdorff had sent to Clemenceau on May 29. It discussed in great detail the reasons why the German government could not possibly submit to what it considered the unnecessarily harsh and unjust financial conditions imposed by the Allied and Associated Powers. It argued that the proposed terms would bring about Germany's economic and finan-

President Wilson. I am glad you raised the question. At this time, we are trying, without yielding anything on essential points, to create a situation which makes the signing of the treaty easier. The Germans are reading the treaty in a sense that we haven't wished to give it; that impression can be dispelled by conversations. It would be a great advantage to let one or the other of our experts go to Versailles to talk with Herr Warburg or Herr Melchior and to dispel excessive apprehensions. I see no other way of mitigating the impression which prevails amongst the Germans and which makes it almost impossible for them to sign the treaty.

M. Clemenceau. For myself, I am convinced that they understand very well, but that they are pretending not to understand. They want some conversations: it is in order to try to divide us. If we have good reasons and good explanations to give them, we can do it in writing. After a conversation, they will announce that M. Loucheur said this, whilst Mr. Davis said that—and even if it isn't true, how will we prove it?

Mr. Lloyd George. Couldn't you send M. Loucheur there alone?

M. Clemenceau. Nothing would be more dangerous for him and for us. If, contrary to my opinion, this discussion was admitted, no one should be sent there alone.

---

cial annihilation and condemn the German people to slavery for generations to come, without, at the same time, enabling the Allies to squeeze out of that country the gigantic and altogether fantastic amount of reparations which they were apparently seeking. The memorandum directed its most vehement criticism at the sweeping authority of the Reparation Commission, whose powers to interfere in Germany's domestic affairs were allegedly incomparably greater than even those of the former Emperor. Germany, the memorandum claimed, would cease to be a people and a state and would become "a mere trade concern placed by its creditors in the hands of a receiver, without its being granted so much as the opportunity to prove its willingness to meet its obligations of its own accord." The memorandum then pointed out certain conditions under which the German government would be capable and willing to meet what it regarded as its obligations, and it elaborated in detail on the German counterproposal for the payment of reparations. The memorandum is printed in *ibid.*, pp. 902-17.

CXIV

Conversation between President Wilson and MM. Clemenceau, Lloyd George, and Orlando*

JUNE 7, 1919, 4 P.M.

M. Clemenceau. I am concerned about the situation between the Hungarians and the Czechoslovaks. When the Rumanians crossed the armistice line, we commanded them three times to stop; finally, we succeeded. But as soon as they were rid of the Rumanians, the Hungarians fell upon the Czechoslovaks. They drove them back and now have come very near Pressburg. I propose to telegraph the Hungarians that, if they want us to give them peace, they must stop immediately, otherwise we will use force.

The problem is serious, for the report that we have requested of our military advisers[1] assumes, in case of intervention, a considerable and difficult effort. General Bliss made remarks on this subject[2] which have much weight. We must take this question up without delay.

—Mr. Lloyd George is introduced.

Mr. Lloyd George. On the question of reparation, I learn that there is a divergence of opinion between the American experts, on the

*H., PPC, VI, 240ff. President Wilson and M. Clemenceau are present alone at the beginning of the meeting.

[1] "Joint Note No. 43," June 7, 1919, printed in PWW, Vol. 60, pp. 256-58. In this note, the military representatives on the Supreme War Council stated that the Allied and Associated Powers had to take immediate measures to stop the Hungarians from attacking Czechoslovakia. These measures should include the strengthening of the Czechoslovak army through the shipment of supplies and matériel and the transfer of Czechoslovak troops from Italy to Czechoslovakia. The advisers also recommended that, if necessary, military action be taken against Hungary and that the country be occupied by Rumanian, Serbian, and French troops.

[2] Bliss made a number of reservations to the recommendations of Joint Note No. 43. He pointed out that the occupation of Hungary by Rumanian and Serbian troops might have far-reaching political consequences. He reminded the Four of the previous aggressive behavior of the Rumanians and their repeated defiance of the council's orders to stop their advance into Hungary. If the Rumanians, Bliss concluded, were now to be allowed to occupy large portions of Hungary, they might prove equally recalcitrant if they were later ordered to withdraw. Bliss' memorandum is printed in ibid., pp. 259-60.

JUNE 7, 1919   **339**

one hand, and M. Loucheur, on the other. The Americans insist on fixing a total figure now; M. Loucheur believes that it is impossible; I am rather of his opinion.

President Wilson. It is difficult but desirable to fix a total figure.

Mr. Lloyd George. Of course, but if we fixed it today, the figure would be too high, and the Germans would sign less than ever. It is in their own interest that this figure should not be fixed for several months.

President Wilson. Wouldn't it be possible to take the figure advanced by the Germans themselves, but only accepting it as the amount of their debt in capital—to which interest during the entire period of payment would have to be added?

Mr. Lloyd George. According to M. Loucheur's proposal,[3] the Germans would have three or four months to study with us the extent of the damages and to make their own estimate; as far as possible, they would provide materials and manpower. It is probable that German workers couldn't be used to reconstruct Arras or Rheims; but there are regions now uninhabited where their presence would have no drawbacks. For myself, I am disposed towards M. Loucheur's arrangement.

M. Clemenceau. So am I.

M. Clemenceau (*to Mr. Lloyd George*). I have just explained to the President of the United States the present situation between the Hungarians and Czechoslovaks. As soon as they were rid of the Rumanians, the Hungarians attacked the Czechoslovaks; the latter, insufficiently armed, had to withdraw, and the situation is bad. I proposed to the President to warn the Hungarians that, if they don't stop hostilities immediately, we will use military means. I recommend that General Alby draft a plan and submit it to us.[4]

—(*Assent.*)

---

[3] Loucheur's proposal, of June 5, is printed in Burnett, *Reparation at the Paris Peace Conference*, II, 124-25.

[4] Toward the end of this meeting, the council approved the message drafted by Alby. It stated that the Allied and Associated governments were on the point of summoning representatives of the Hungarian government before the peace conference in order to communicate to them the "proper frontiers" of Hungary. It was at this very moment, however, that the Hungarians had launched "violent and unjustified attacks" against the Czechoslovaks and had invaded Slovakia. After recalling the "firm determination" of the Allies to put an end to all useless hostilities between the Hungarians and their neighbors, the telegram continued:

"In these circumstances, the Government of Buda-Pesth is formally requested to put an end without delay to its attacks on the Czecho-Slovaks, otherwise the

President Wilson. It was agreed that we would come back this morning to the Italian question. I have some scruples about the solution I myself suggested concerning the islands. It is contrary to the principles to which I am attached to hand over to Italy these islands, whose population is Slavic.

Mr. Lloyd George. That population is quite small.

President Wilson. Undoubtedly, but some of them have up to two thousand inhabitants. In any case, it is not an Italian population.

M. Clemenceau. These islands are very sparsely inhabited.

Mr. Lloyd George. Moreover, they are populations of fishermen; it is quite possible that their markets are on the Italian coast.

President Wilson. Here is what we propose.[5] The free state of Fiume would include all the territory located between the line of the Treaty of London and the line drawn by the American experts; it would be governed, during the scheduled period of transition provided for, by a commission named by the League of Nations. Guarantees given to the states of the interior for the free use of the ports would be similar to those we have provided for Danzig. Guarantees would also be given for the complete freedom of residence and commercial establishment in the territory of Fiume. The final fate of that area would be settled at the expiration of a period of fifteen [five] years by a plebiscite taken on the entire territory of the free state, three questions being asked: union to Italy—union to the Yugoslav state—maintenance of the free state.

The islands which face northern Dalmatia would become Italian, as well as Lissa and Lagosta, with the exception of those across from Sebenico. Italy would be able neither to fortify them nor to establish naval bases there, and the same obligations would be imposed upon the Yugoslavs for the islands that would be assigned to them.

Zara would be a free city under the control of the League of Nations, with Italy entrusted with representing her in her external relations. Sebenico would remain with the Yugoslavs.

Mr. Lloyd George. It seems to me that it would be better not to

---

Allied and Associated Governments are absolutely decided to have immediate recourse to extreme measures to oblige Hungary to cease hostilities and to bow to the unshakable will of the Allies to make their injunctions respected.

"A reply to the present telegram should be made within 48 hours." It is printed in PPC, VI, 246-47.

[5] The text of this proposal is printed in *ibid.*, pp. 249-51. The documentary record is silent about the drafting of this proposal. Douglas Wilson Johnson, Wilson's chief adviser on Adriatic questions, was presumably its author.

mention that last stipulation. If Sebenico isn't assigned to the Italians, it goes without saying that it will remain with the Yugoslavs and, taking Italian feeling into account, it is unnecessary to mention it. What has been provided for the railroads of Fiume?

President Wilson. The question of the railroads is settled, as I just said, in the same way as for Danzig.

Mr. Lloyd George. I am not sure that we have yet solved the problem.

M. Clemenceau. We have a chance of succeeding with it. I believe we are obliged to yield a bit more, if the Italians prove reasonable.

Mr. Lloyd George. I don't think you will induce the President to make other concessions. Moreover, the Italians are hardly showing themselves reasonable anywhere.

President Wilson. Are we presenting this text to M. Orlando?

Mr. Lloyd George. Certainly; he is waiting for it.

M. Clemenceau. It is a good thing he is not going to Rome. He is only going to Turin, to speak with the Italian ministers about the domestic situation.

—M. Orlando is introduced.

Mr. Lloyd George. I saw M. Vénisélos and M. Paderewski on the subject of guarantees for the protection of the minorities. The intervention they prefer is that of the Council of the League of Nations. M. Vénisélos spoke with much wisdom. There is one thing that M. Paderewski does not accept: it is to be obliged to subscribe officially to the maintenance of the language of the Polish Jews, which is only a corrupted German dialect. On the question of who will have the right to call the attention of the League of Nations to such or such a legal case, M. Paderewski promised me a written answer. Both take a very different attitude from M. Brătianu's and say: "It is painful for us to think that, if that stipulation is imposed upon us, it is on account of the past behavior of Rumania."

—President Wilson communicates the report of the Commission on Yugoslav Affairs on the organization of the plebiscite in the Klagenfurt Basin.[6] The commission observes that the administration to be established provisionally in this territory, as well as the procedure of the plebiscite, must be envisaged differently, since the plebiscite will take place in six months or three years. In the first place, it is necessary to provide an arrangement of the same kind as in East Prussia and in Schleswig. In

[6] It is printed in *ibid.*, pp. 248-49. Wilson summarizes it well.

the second place, the arrangement should be similar to that of the Saar Basin. If this second solution is adopted, the difficulty will be to find the elements of an administration in the local population, and it would not be without risk to appeal to the Austrians or the Yugoslavs. The commission proposes the appointment of a commission of five members designated by the Principal Allied and Associated Powers, charged to prepare and carry out the plebiscite under the most favorable conditions in both zones A and B. The local administration of zone B would be left provisionally to the Austrian authorities, while the local administration of zone A would be entrusted to the authorities of the Kingdom of Serbs, Croats and Slovenes.

—The Italian delegation proposes that the boundary between the two zones be traced, not from east to west, but from north to south, Klagenfurt being left in the western part. It also asks that the triangle in which the northern exit of the Karawanken tunnel is located, which contains approximately ten kilometers of railroad serving the port of Trieste, should not be included in the same zone as the tunnel.

Mr. Lloyd George. I hope we are not going to reopen this discussion, or we shall never arrive at a decision.

Mr. Lloyd George. I have this instant received news that the Germans are attacking the Estonians, who are moving on Petrograd.

M. Clemenceau. That is significant.

Mr. Lloyd George. Moreover, the Estonians have declared that, if they take Petrograd, it is not in order to turn it over to Russia, but to keep it, and that they are not marching in agreement with Admiral Kolchak. This telegram comes from the admiral who commands our fleet in the Baltic.[7]

M. Orlando. About the Klagenfurt region, I must say that I consider the plebiscite unnecessary, since the commission acknowledges that the majority in zone A is indisputably Yugoslav, whilst in B it is no less certainly Austrian. The commission's plan would allow both sides to occupy the sector where their nationality dominates; since the outcome is certain in advance, it is better to take an immediate decision.

The economic unity of the basin was invoked first in seeking a solution which would place the entire entity under one government. If one divides the basin into two parts, the plebiscite would seem to me unnecessary and in conflict with the precedents we ourselves have created. If, however, the solution proposed by the commission is insisted upon, it is not I who will oppose it.

[7] Rear Adm. Sir Walter Henry Cowan.

As for the small piece of territory about which the Italian delegation makes a reservation, it is a very small piece of land crossed by the railroad from Trieste to Assling. The fate of Assling has been reserved until now; if this territory returns to the Yugoslavs, that reservation becomes ineffective. It is for that reason that our delegation asked that this corner of territory be excluded from the zone of the plebiscite.

President Wilson. I must say to M. Orlando frankly that I went beyond what I would have preferred in order to give Tarvis to Italy, thinking that Villach had to go to Austria and Assling to the Yugoslavs; it is the only fair way to resolve the problem. If both lines which serve Trieste and the two stations of Tarvis and Assling are in Italy's hands, that's not fair.

Mr. Lloyd George. I must say to M. Orlando that it is not certain that zone A will vote for the Yugoslavs. From what we are told, the population is Wendish, and rather inclined towards Austria. Undoubtedly, it will want the basin not to be divided. M. Vesnić is no more in favor of the plebiscite than M. Orlando; but that rather confirms the information received by President Wilson, according to which those people don't want to become Yugoslav.

M. Orlando. In that case, the plebiscite must be organized with all possible guarantees. But the commission's proposal gives immediate administration in zone A to the Yugoslav authorities; that gives no guarantee—very much the contrary—and that does not conform to your instructions.

Mr. Lloyd George. I acknowledge that the argument is good.

President Wilson. This is a proposal by the experts, not instructions given or the decision we will take.

Mr. Lloyd George. The population of the Klagenfurt Basin is a very quiet one. Don't you believe that the commission of the League of Nations and the communal authorities will be able to maintain order?

President Wilson. The commission says that the local authorities are Austrian. Our instructions give full power to the commission to settle the terms of the plebiscite; consequently, it can change the composition of local organizations, if it judges it necessary.

M. Orlando. Can't we maintain our previous resolutions, with this sole change—that the plebiscite will take place in two separate zones?

Mr. Lloyd George. I accept that.

—*The proposal is adopted.*

—Rear Admiral George P. Hope is introduced.

Mr. Lloyd George. Admiral Hope is going to explain the situation in Estonia to you.

Rear Admiral Hope. Admiral Gough,[8] who commands our Division of the Baltic, talked with the Estonian Prime Minister;[9] the latter informed him that the Germans are advancing towards Riga, and that contact between the Germans and the Estonians is imminent. The Estonians don't want to submit to the Germans. They ask that we call upon the latter to evacuate Latvia without delay.

The Germans have already established air communications with the Russian forces in Narva. It is obvious that they intend, with the help of the Germans in the Baltic provinces, to advance eastwards and to crush the Estonians, then to march on Petrograd with Russian elements in order to establish a government of their choice there.

Mr. Lloyd George. I propose that the question be referred to the Naval Council in Versailles, which will compare the information received by each of our governments.

M. Clemenceau. Your sailors are best situated to gather information.

President Wilson. We have to give our military representatives at Spa the order to demand immediate explanations from the Germans; this concerns the execution of the Armistice.

M. Clemenceau. We can do both: act at Spa, and alert the Naval Council at Versailles.

Rear Admiral Hope. Admiral Gough recommends an immediate order to the Germans to halt their movement and to evacuate Latvia. He asks that the Allied high command stay ready to act in case the Germans resist, and to provide the Estonians with the means to hold their ground. The Estonians have already solicited a credit of ten million sterling.

Mr. Lloyd George. I propose to do nothing more than the step just indicated by the President of the United States until we have received a report on this question from our military experts.

President Wilson. According to the Armistice, the Germans were to remain in the Baltic provinces as long as we did not ask them to evacuate that region.

Mr. Lloyd George. We never did it.

Rear Admiral Hope. Admiral Gough thinks precisely that the time has come to do it.

---

[8] Mantoux here and below might have misheard. Hope referred to Lt. Gen. Sir Hubert de la Poer Gough, chief of the Allied mission in the Baltic, stationed at Helsingfors, or Helsinki.

[9] Otto Strandmann.

M. Clemenceau. According to my latest news, the Germans of Estonia were marching against the Poles, and the Poles were asking me to stop them.

Mr. Lloyd George. All that is very confused.

President Wilson. In that case, I no longer understand. I believe we must do nothing before our military advisers in Versailles have compared their respective information.

M. Clemenceau. They know the question, for I have already asked them to study it.

President Wilson. Since this latest news reached us through the English, shouldn't Great Britain get in contact with our military advisers in Versailles?

Mr. Lloyd George. If you wish; but the best thing would be to base our request on a recommendation by the Four.

—Admiral Hope withdraws.

President Wilson. I have at last got the note which I had prepared on the question of Fiume. It is dated yesterday evening, and, to tell the truth, it is only an outline. The only part which was studied in detail is the one relating to the boundary of the free state of Fiume.

I don't have to remind M. Orlando of the great doubts that I have entertained about being a party to a compromise. I don't feel that I am authorized to accept a solution under which, without their consent, populations which are not subject to my government would change sovereignty. At the same time, I took account of the very delicate situation in which my French and English colleagues find themselves, bound as they are by a treaty concluded between their governments and that of Italy before the intervention of the United States. Rather than remain in the impasse we are in, we have formulated proposals that I am going to present to you. They have not yet been communicated to anyone. Before any discussion, I want to place them in the hands of M. Orlando, who will kindly regard them as our common suggestions.

It is quite probable that the people of the United States will think that my participation in this transaction was not warranted, until I succeed—which is not certain—in explaining to them the difficulties in which we found ourselves. What I just said shows M. Orlando that it would be practically impossible for my government to go beyond what we propose today. I beg him to remember that and to make his colleagues understand it thoroughly.

In this statement, part of the boundary specified by the Treaty of London is mentioned: it is what our American experts call "the Italian line of the Treaty of London." You recall that there was in fact a difference of interpretation on the subject of the watershed line, because many rivers of that region run underground.

I hand you this document in order that you may study it at your leisure.

M. Orlando. I thank the President of the United States for the care he has always taken to study this difficult question in depth and conscientiously. As for myself, I will study this plan in the best frame of mind. But in all loyalty, I must say to you that it was already an extraordinary sacrifice for us to accept the proposals formulated by M. Tardieu: they were below our minimum program, and we accepted them only with resignation. They compelled us to very painful renunciations. I am, as you know, a conciliatory spirit, but it is hard to have made such a war as the one we have made without having the door of our house closed today. For me personally, that is very bitter. It was necessary to give the greatest proof of our good will, and we accepted the Tardieu proposal.

On Fiume, we do not obtain satisfaction; that city will be subject to the same control that you are imposing on semibarbarians or on enemies. A highly civilized people, who were victorious with you in such a terrible war, subjected to an arrangement which you judged appropriate for the Pacific Islands and the Saar Basin! To accept that was a very great sacrifice for us. That made us go below our minimum, I assure my colleagues. If the new text—which we will study with all the respect which we owe your suggestions—should lead us still further below the level already attained, I fear it will be impossible for us to accept.

Mr. Lloyd George. What do you mean by "close the door of your house?" Do you mean the islands of the Adriatic?

M. Orlando. I mean the Alps.

Mr. Lloyd George. I did not believe we had done anything to deprive you of the frontier of the Alps.

M. Orlando. I am speaking of the eastern Alps.

M. Clemenceau. Your border will go up to the Brenner.

Mr. Lloyd George. On the side of Istria, the crest of the mountains will belong to Italy.

M. Orlando. No, it will be the boundary of the new state of Fiume, not of the Italian state.

Mr. Lloyd George. I believed the opposite.

M. Orlando. It is a matter of knowing what the line of the Alps is.

For us, that line will be east of the free state of Fiume. Trieste will be left twenty kilometers from the frontier. As it has been drawn, that line is like a scar which cuts the face.

President Wilson. But it was already in the Tardieu document.

M. Orlando. Yes; that shows what sacrifices we are making in accepting it.

Mr. Lloyd George. You said that the mandate system was created for barbaric peoples; the inhabitants of Danzig are not barbarians.

M. Orlando. No, but they are enemies. I am going to study your new text.

—President Wilson reads aloud the reply prepared by the League of Nations Commission to the request of the Germans to be admitted to the League at the time of the signing of the treaty of peace.[10]

The Allied and Associated Powers in no way intend to exclude Germany from the League of Nations; from the time they are convinced that a democratic government is firmly established in Germany and that the German people are animated by a peaceful spirit, they will admit Germany to the League; they hope that that can take place a few months from now.

M. Clemenceau. Ah! That is saying a lot.

President Wilson. In place of these last words, we could put: "in a short time."

M. Clemenceau. We will see about that.

President Wilson (*reading*). From the time of the admission of Germany to the League of Nations, the Allied and Associated Powers commit themselves to submit to the Council of the League, with a view to revision, Chapters IX, X and XII of the peace treaty—financial clauses, economic clauses, clauses relating to means of communication—and a regime of reciprocity will be contemplated.[11]

Mr. Lloyd George. This raises serious questions. It is better to take time to study this document.

President Wilson (*reading*). In reply to the German observations on

---

[10] This draft is printed in *PWW*, Vol. 60, pp. 274-75. Wilson summarizes it below. This document was the work of Colonel House and Lord Robert Cecil.

[11] House and Cecil had slipped in this clause. House claimed that Léon Bourgeois, the French member of the committee, had raised no objection to this clause, since "he did not have the intelligence to see the significance of it." Its obvious meaning was that the financial and economic (but not the reparation) clauses of the treaty would be subject to renegotiation once Germany was admitted to the League. See the Diary of Colonel House, June 8, 1919, printed in *PWW*, Vol. 60, pp. 296-97. House's and Cecil's ploy did not succeed.

general disarmament, it is stated that the Covenant of the League of Nations provides for the general reduction of armaments and also provides for the mutual guarantee of obligations taken in that regard by the members of the League. This question includes that of compulsory military service, which will be one of the subjects of early discussions.

Mr. Lloyd George. I don't know whether this dish is to M. Clemenceau's taste.

M. Clemenceau. I won't find it difficult to digest, because I won't swallow it; Lord Robert Cecil will make peace alone if he wishes.

Mr. Lloyd George. This comes from the League of Nations Commission, that is to say, from M. Léon Bourgeois.

President Wilson (*reading*). The Allies are prepared to grant the guarantees given to national minorities in other countries to the German minorities which will be located outside German territory.

M. Clemenceau. I will read this text attentively, and I will make some annotations.

Mr. Lloyd George. I believe it is quite necessary for the reply to the Germans on this point to be framed in conciliatory terms.

M. Orlando. It is going a bit far to promise our disarmament before that of the Germans is carried out.

President Wilson. Let us take the matter seriously; we have to choose between delivering an ultimatum and making concessions.

M. Clemenceau. I believe we can take a position between ultimatum and capitulation; but this text doesn't represent my position between the two.

Mr. Lloyd George. Certainly the words "in a few months," when it comes to Germany's admission to the League of Nations, go a bit too far.

President Wilson. My opinion has always been that we will restrain the Germans better when they are in the League of Nations than if they remain outside.

M. Clemenceau. You will never restrain them, I know them well.

Mr. Lloyd George. I am prepared to go quite far in the direction indicated.

M. Clemenceau. Lord Robert Cecil is ready to open his arms to the Germans.

President Wilson. I believe that I must defend him; he doesn't deserve this reproach.

M. Clemenceau. I have the greatest respect for him, but I am not obliged to feel the same way.

Mr. Lloyd George. I attach a great importance to this reply. The other main points about which we have to answer the Germans are reparation and the occupation. Nor must we forget what they call the "pinpricks," the detailed clauses which can perhaps be pruned. I propose to take our decision on Monday on the four or five points upon which our reply depends.

M. Clemenceau. I ask that the question which was just brought up be treated in the last place; I will tell you my opinion when I have seen what we are doing about the rest.

Mr. Lloyd George. League of Nations, eastern frontier of Germany, occupation, reparation—we will take up all these subjects from Monday onwards, and we shall decide.

M. Clemenceau. Agreed. On the League of Nations, I insist on making myself well understood. I desire in no way that Germany be excluded from it; I have always been of opinion that she must be admitted to it one day, and I base great hopes on the League of Nations; but I believe the formula to be used in our reply is yet to be found.

CXV

Conversation between President Wilson and MM. Clemenceau, Lloyd George, and Orlando*

JUNE 9, 1919, 11 A.M.

—The members of the Supreme War Council are introduced.

M. Clemenceau. I receive from my best informant in Berlin an account of a conversation with Theodor Wolff, editor of the *Berliner Tageblatt*. He says that Ebert and Scheidemann are adamant about refusing their signature to the treaty unless we make enormous concessions. Theodor Wolff declares himself satisfied about the firmness of these two statesmen.

Mr. Lloyd George. The information I am receiving is a bit different.

M. Clemenceau. You will have no doubts left in a short time. I have learned also that Hungary acknowledged receipt of our telegram ordering her to halt hostilities against the Czechoslovaks.[1]

*H., PPC, VI, 254ff.

[1] About the Hungarian reply, see n. 1 to the next meeting.

President Wilson. I ask the members of the Inter-Allied Military Council to inform us about the military situation in Hungary.[2]

Sir Henry Wilson. It was the Czechs who attacked. Their attack reawakened the military spirit of the Hungarians, who fought the Czechs and are today in Slovakia.

Mr. Lloyd George. I have recent information from an Englishman, arrived from Budapest, and, moreover, very hostile to Béla Kun. He casts all the blame for what happened on the Rumanians. General Franchet d'Esperey established a line at the time of the armistice; despite the injunctions of the commanding general, the Rumanians crossed it. We stopped them on a second line; again, they violated it. At that time, Béla Kun was lost. He was isolated in Budapest. His situation could be compared to that of the Paris Commune immediately before its fall. The advance of the Rumanians aroused Hungarian national feeling and gave Béla Kun an army. In advancing against Hungary, the Czechs threatened the only important mining region which remains in Hungarian territory; that provoked a new surge of national movement.

The witness through whom I know this told me: "It was the Rumanian aggression alone which allowed Béla Kun to rally the nation behind him."

M. Clemenceau. I call your attention to the question raised by President Wilson. What is the real military situation?

Mr. Lloyd George. One word only. I received two telegrams from our military representative in Prague. The first says that the situation is very serious, that the Czechs lack munitions, that Pressburg is threatened, and that Bolshevism is developing in Slovakia. The second says that, at the request of President Masaryk, General Pellé was placed at the head of the Czechoslovak army and that martial law was proclaimed in Pressburg.

—General Belin explains the situation on the map: the Czechs have been pushed back in the southern part of Slovakia and the Hungarians are operating on their left flank and placing themselves between it and the right flank of the Rumanian army.

Mr. Lloyd George. Where are the Rumanians?
General Belin. On the second line fixed since the armistice.
Mr. Lloyd George. That line, in relation to the first, is halfway from Budapest.

[2] The following discussion was based on Joint Note No. 43, about which, see n. 1 to the previous meeting.

M. Clemenceau. Where did the Czech attack take place?

General Belin. North of Budapest.

Mr. Lloyd George. We must be fair even to the Hungarians; they are only defending their country.

General Cavallero. M. Allizé has asked General Segre to give Austro-Hungarian war matériel found in possession of the Italian army to the Czechoslovak government. We consented, whilst reserving the rights of the Italian government to this matériel. The transfer must be assured by the Italian armistice commission.

Mr. Lloyd George. What shall we do about the Hungarians? General Franchet d'Esperey, who represents all of us, first gave the Rumanians the order to halt; that order was not obeyed. The Rumanian attack was followed by a Czechoslovak attack. I propose to halt the sending of all matériel to Rumania until she has obeyed our order. The greater part of all these difficulties comes from the fact that the states which are our friends refuse to follow our instructions. We must put an end to it. Everything that is happening is contrary to the formal orders of the Commander in Chief of the Army of the East. I propose to halt all assistance to the Rumanians until they have given us satisfaction.

M. Clemenceau. The Rumanians halted after our last injunction. It is our military experts who now propose that they advance to extricate the Czechoslovaks.

General Cavallero. According to reliable information that we received several days ago, the Minister of National Defense of the Czechoslovak Republic,[3] on April 27, ordered his troops to cross the armistice line in order to occupy territories which, in his opinion, the Hungarians would have to evacuate following the Rumanian push. It was then that the Czechs advanced under the command of General Hennocque.

M. Clemenceau. Why should the Hungarians have to evacuate this territory?

General Cavallero. It was the probable consequence of the advance of the Rumanians. The movement of the Czechs threatens the Ore Mountains,[4] which are the last resource of Hungary in terms of mines; that explains the energetic resistance of the Hungarians.

Mr. Lloyd George. Should we not see M. Brătianu, and M. Kramář or M. Beneš about this matter?

---

[3] Václav Jaroslav Klofáč.

[4] Mantoux undoubtedly misheard. The Ore Mountains are on the border between Bohemia and Saxony. The Czechs had been advancing toward the Mátra Mountains, a coal mining area, the center of which is Miskolc.

President Wilson. I don't like to play with ammunition dumps; that can produce explosions.

M. Clemenceau. Can't we see them this afternoon, if you think it necessary?

Mr. Lloyd George. After having placed themselves in impossible situations, these gentlemen come to us and say: "Come to our aid!" They are all little brigand peoples who only want to steal territories.

M. Clemenceau. M. Brătianu will say to us: "You left me alone, and I halted at your second injunction."

Mr. Lloyd George. Don't forget that the Hungarians are a proud people and have a great military tradition. Let us summon M. Brătianu.

M. Clemenceau. I prefer that we settle this question amongst ourselves. I've had enough of giving advice.

Mr. Lloyd George. The time has come to impose our orders.

—The members of the Supreme War Council withdraw.

Mr. Lloyd George.* The members of the commission instructed to report on the plebiscite to be held in Upper Silesia disagree about the period of time between the signing of the treaty and the vote. The provisional administration to be established must vary according to whether the period is more or less long. I propose to settle the question here. It is a matter of a political directive to be given and no longer of technical advice. Let us not forget that three of the members of that commission belong to the Commission on Polish Affairs and fear a decision which might go against their earlier recommendation.

President Wilson. Couldn't they be asked to present us with a choice between two arrangements?

Mr. Lloyd George. Yes, and it is we who will decide.

I see here a proposal to expel all the clergy from Silesia; it is impossible, it would set the Catholic Church against us. We must leave the task of deciding what people should be expelled individually to the commission which will be sent to the site to assure the most favorable conditions for the plebiscite.

M. Clemenceau. I don't propose that the clergy be expelled. But we must recognize that their influence will be considerable.

Mr. Lloyd George. It is the same in Ireland, and we don't expel the Irish clergy.

In my opinion, the institution of a plebiscite will allow the Germans to sign the treaty. In a conversation between one of our

*H., *PPC*, VI, 259ff.

officers and Warburg in Versailles, the latter said that one of the questions which moves Germany most was that of the eastern frontier. If a plebiscite takes place, that undoubtedly won't satisfy the Germans, but it appears to me certain that it will deprive them of any pretext for complaint. According to what Warburg said, it is quite necessary that some concessions be made in the chapter on reparation. His interlocutor believes that the Germans will sign if these concessions are made.

The Germans don't know where they are. They resemble a man caught up in a cyclone, who would suddenly be asked: "What price do you ask for your horse?" Moreover, we are a little in the same situation. One of my financial experts[5] has just left us because he finds our terms too hard. We must succeed. We can't restrain any of the other nations as long as we haven't made peace with Germany.

I am told that the Yugoslavs are advancing on Klagenfurt.

Count Aldrovandi. They have just occupied it.

President Wilson. Do you want to reexamine the question of reparation before seeing the experts again?

M. Clemenceau. The most urgent matter is to settle the military question in Hungary. It is all very well to have sent a telegram to the Hungarian government; but we must be ready to act if we don't receive a satisfactory reply, or if we receive none at all.

President Wilson. Why not tell the representatives of Rumania and Bohemia this very day—in my opinion, it is the Rumanians who are the main culprits: "If you don't observe our terms, which alone make possible a settlement of your own affairs, we will refuse you all assistance from this time on?"

Mr. Lloyd George. I think we must do it. If General Franchet d'Esperey was a diplomat, he would compel these people to agree on a line of demarcation, and he would stop them.

M. Clemenceau. At this time, the Hungarians are the victors; would they obey?

Mr. Lloyd George. No doubt they would say: "We will withdraw if the Rumanians, for their part, withdraw to the first line fixed at the time of the armistice."

President Wilson. In any case, it would be madness to allow the Rumanians to advance again; you would never make them pull back.

M. Clemenceau. What will we answer our military men, who are proposing to have the Rumanian army advance?

Mr. Lloyd George. General Sackville-West has just told me, cor-

---

[5] John Maynard Keynes.

rectly: "We were only asked for military advice. As an immediate military solution, the advance of the Rumanians is what is best." However, General Bliss was of another opinion.

President Wilson. General Bliss concedes that, from the purely military point of view, it would be necessary for the Rumanians to advance. But he wonders if the political results would be what we want.

Mr. Lloyd George. Between now and tomorrow, we will see what we have sent as matériel to the Rumanians. It is hardly worthwhile to say to them: "We will stop supplying you," if what we have given them already is sufficient for a rather long time.

Behind all these difficulties, I see the hand of M. Brătianu.

—President Wilson reads aloud the report of the committee entrusted with preparing a reply to the German counterproposals under the heading of reparation.[6]

That reply relates to three main points: (1) the establishment and powers of the Reparation Commission; (2) the setting of a total figure of payments demanded of Germany; (3) the expenses of the occupation army and certain deliveries which the Germans object to.

On the first point, the commission is unanimous; thus there is no reason to linger over it.

Concerning the figure for reparation, the French and English experts think that it cannot be fixed now without danger; for, if it is fixed too high, the Germans will be more frightened than ever, and if it is fixed too low, discontent will be very sharp in France and in England. But all the experts agree in recommending that we consider, within a period of time to be fixed, any proposal made in good faith by the Germans themselves, after a study on site of the damages to be repaired.

On Germany's financial capacity, only hypotheses can be made now. The period of two years fixed by the treaty would correspond to the period during which any calculation could only rest on arbitrary conjectures.

The United States delegation has refused to associate itself with these conclusions; it does not think it enough to indicate the intentions of our governments. It believes it necessary to fix a figure as of today; it proposes the one of 120 billion marks in gold, which would be accepted for practical reasons as the maximum of Germany's capital debt to the Allied and Associated Powers. This immediate specification seems to it absolutely necessary in order to establish the foundations of international credit from now on. At the same time, it proposes to leave Germany the minimum capital which she cannot do without for the recov-

---

[6] It is printed as an appendix to these notes.

ery of her economic activity, in tonnage, gold, and negotiable securities. As for the expenses of the occupation army, the delegates of the United States think it is necessary to make them known in order not to create an impression contrary to our intentions.

The representatives of Great Britain and of France oppose these concessions and think they would be impolitic. The Italian experts agree with the French and English experts on the impossibility of determining now the total debt of Germany, but believe it desirable to be able to fix this sum by common agreement in the near future. In their opinion, the limitation of the expenses of the military occupation must not be settled by the treaty, but by later negotiations amongst the Allied and Associated Powers. The representatives of Japan also think that it is impossible to fix the total sum at present; in the event Germany should keep the capital indispensable for the recovery of business, they especially oppose leaving any ships to her.

Mr. Lloyd George. The most important thing is the question of fixing the total sum. There is much to be said in favor of the idea that all that can be determined now must be; nothing would better help the Germans to decide to sign. What troubles them most is the uncertainty in which they find themselves. The minimum capital which they need in order to resume their economic life also has a very great importance. It is obvious that, if we don't leave them the means to revive their economic activity, that would be as much against our interests as against theirs.

As for fixing the total sum, it is a question I have pondered a great deal, and nothing would be more dangerous. The figure we might set would terrify the Germans, or it would be impossible for M. Clemenceau and me to get public opinion to accept it. Mr. Bonar Law was rather of the opinion of the American delegates; he would have liked to see a figure set down in the treaty, but as soon as one was proposed to him, he drew back.

It is, besides, a question of justice amongst allies. France cannot accept less than the complete reparation of the damages she suffered. I think the estimates made up to the present time are exaggerated; but I may be wrong, perhaps they are below the reality. What I think is that, in three or four months, one can arrive at an estimate, not perfect, but sufficient to give a figure which will not be purely arbitrary.

As for us, I don't see how we could manage to apply our minds to this problem in the midst of all the tasks that burden us. A multitude of questions press upon us from all sides, we are caught up in a whirlwind. Responsible as I am to my compatriots, I can't apply myself enough to this study in order to take responsibility for it. We must have time, and the same information reaches me from the German side: it is better, for them as well, to have a little time ahead of them and then to find themselves faced with a figure reasonably prepared. The period of time which I proposed for the summary inquiry is three months. M. Loucheur would prefer four months. During this period, the devastated regions would be inspected by ourselves and the German experts, and the latter would see to what extent they can undertake reparation in kind. From the time of the signing of the peace treaty, our experts and the German experts will be able to meet.

Moreover, I agree with the Americans in thinking that the sooner the German industrialists start producing again, the better it will be.

President Wilson. I was ready to hold to the treaty as we had written it, whilst only giving the German delegation explanations about its text. But I took it that the English and French governments were disposed to make some concessions in order to induce the Germans to sign. If we want to make concessions, let us make them. What I ask of you is to determine precisely what they have to be. I am not particularly interested in one solution more than another; if you wish, I am entirely prepared to hold to the text purely and simply, whilst explaining it. But a solution must be reached, and soon. I understand the full force of what Mr. Lloyd George has just said; no one knows the true total of the German debt for reparation.

Mr. Lloyd George. Nor Germany's capacity to pay.

President Wilson. Any figure will necessarily be arbitrary. But the Germans want a figure.

Mr. Lloyd George. I am not sure of that.

President Wilson. The only question we have to face is this: will this concession be helpful? If peace is not concluded, or if it is not concluded at an early date, my financial experts fear the gravest consequences. Business the world over cannot be resumed as long as that question isn't settled.

After the signing of the treaty, we will have to study the financial system upon which the commerce of the world can be reestablished; the basis of this system can only be credit. I warn you solemnly that, if you don't leave the Germans the assets necessary to reconstruct their credit, their industries will not start up, and your entire plan for reparation will collapse. America is completely ready to lend its assistance. But the government of the United States cannot lend money to Germany; she can only obtain it from banks, on a commercial basis. The bankers of the United States won't be able to lend without knowing how their money will come back to them, that is to say, without having some idea of the future of German industry and Germany's wealth. If we want to act as practical men, we have no time to lose. We must either renounce reparations and let Germany fall to pieces, or else, with a view to the reparations to be obtained, give Germany the means to get back on her feet.

Mr. Lloyd George. We must put to our experts the question of a study which should last three or four months. The rest leads us to a crowd of details which can only be discussed after the signing of the peace.

President Wilson. I admit that any sum fixed today would be arbitrary. The only argument to be made in favor of the immediate announcement of this sum is that it will provide credit with an absolutely necessary basis. Having this figure in hand, the financial world will know whether Germany can or cannot pay and, as a consequence, will lend or not lend you money on the bonds we are making Germany sign.

Mr. Lloyd George. I agree with you; but it is impossible to fix a figure before the signing of the peace, before our experts have been able to meet with the German experts.

President Wilson. I read you a draft reply prepared by the American experts.[7]

—(*Summary*) The Allied and Associated Powers refuse any discussion on the principle of reparation. But the fears of the Germans are based only on a false interpretation of the treaty. The problem of reparation is so complicated that it can only be settled through long work entrusted to a commission. But the instructions of the latter will prohibit it from doing anything that might impede the industrial and commercial life of a Germany sincerely returned to peace. The commission cannot fix the taxes that the German taxpayer will pay; it must only make sure that the burdens of the latter are no less than those of the taxpayers of Allied countries. The power given to the commission to effect certain changes in the provisions of the treaty has been provided only in the interest of Germany herself, if it is acknowledged that it is truly impossible for her to pay within a certain period. Moreover, Germany has the right herself to appoint a commission which will be constantly in contact with the Reparation Commission.

The sum total of reparation is estimated at approximately 120 billion marks in gold. This figure would be accepted as the maximum, in capi-

---

[7] It is printed as an appendix to the notes of the following meeting.

tal, of what is due by Germany. We take note of Germany's offer to assist in the restoration of the devastated regions by providing manpower.

Mr. Lloyd George. And materials.

President Wilson. On this point, we answer that the Reparation Commission is authorized to accept payments in various kinds.

The Allies are taking care not to ignore the needs of Germany. The commission will receive the formal instruction to take into consideration the necessities of the social and economic life of the German people. That is why the American experts propose that, during a period of two years, Germany keep 30 per cent of her merchant fleet and a certain amount of capital. In particular, it would be stipulated that the first payments will not be made in gold.

During the first year, France would receive only 50 per cent of the coal which is promised her. A special arrangement would settle the provision to Germany of iron ore from Lorraine. The expenses of the occupation army would be fixed at an annual figure of 250 million marks at most.

In conclusion, the German plenipotentiaries have seen in the treaty what we never wanted to put there. The burden that Germany will have to bear will be heavy, but it is determined only by consideration of justice.

Mr. Lloyd George. I rather like the crust and the sauce of this pie, but not the meat.

President Wilson. My dear friend—

M. Clemenceau. I am always a bit afraid when you begin by calling us "my dear friend."

President Wilson. If you prefer: my respected colleague. You must however prepare your stomach for meat that will be able to sustain you.

Mr. Lloyd George. Yes, under one condition: it is that you give me enough of it.

M. Clemenceau. And, especially, I would like to be sure that it will not go into someone else's stomach.

President Wilson. Mr. Lansing asked me the other day: "Have you appointed a commission to examine the concessions to be made to Germany?" I replied: "No, and I told you what I thought about concessions in general. The only question is to know how we can make this treaty workable."

Mr. Lloyd George. I won't go as far as you: I am prepared for any concession that will allow a conclusion, and I believe we can get there without going as far as your experts.

President Wilson. That seems possible to me; we must think about it.

{ A P P E N D I X }[8]

REPORT OF THE REPARATION COMMISSION TO THE SUPREME COUNCIL.

Mr President,   8 JUNE

As directed in your letter dated 4th of June, 1919, the Committee met on June 6 and 7 to draft a reply to the German comments on the reparation clauses contained in the letter of Count Brockdorff-Rantzau dated 29th May, 1919.

They examined particularly the Three principal objections:

1° That the constitution and Powers of the Reparation Commission were objectionable;

2° That the clauses named no fixed sum as the amount of liability of Germany;

3° That they took objections to the deliveries of certain articles and to the cost of the army of occupation.

As to (1°) in pointing out that the comments on the Reparation Commission were founded on misconceptions of the meaning and effect of the clauses, the Delegations were unanimous. As to (2°) and (3°)

I.

The Delegations of France and Great Britain were prepared to concur in a reply to the following effect: (1) that it was impossible to fix the amount of the liability of Germany now, because the damage done was so vast, so various and so recent that it could not yet be calculated correctly; that in matters of such magnitude errors would either gravely prejudice the sufferers or result in serious over-charge against Germany; and they considered that they had no right to resort to mere conjectures in a matter of such vast importance; (2) That the Allied and Associated Powers, through the Commission, would in their own interest be willing to consider any bona fide proposals made by Germany, whereby the amount might be more readily fixed or agreed, or any other useful purpose might be served and that it was competent to Germany to present arguments, evidence or proposals by nominating a commission or otherwise as she may think fit;

---

[8] Printed in *PWW*, Vol. 60, pp. 321-23.

(3°) Further, as to the financial capacity of Germany, at present little more can be done than to hazard a hypothesis. Like all the other belligerent Powers, Germany is still living under an exceptional regime. The rate and extent of her recovery cannot at present be forcasted, but the period mentioned in the Treaty was chosen in order to give time for the national economy to adapt itself to the new situation. The substitution of a sum fixed now by an arbitrary hypothesis for the system established by the treaty after very full and arduous discussion appears to be very undesirable, and to abandon without any sufficient advantage a plan which secured to Germany the opportunity and the right to be heard and to have decision taken in accordance with equity.

The Delegation of the United States declined to concur in such a reply. The proposed American reply does not contemplate any change in the text of the conditions of peace. It should take the form of a statement of intentions of the Allied and Associated Governments with reference to directing the activities of the Commission and indicate the spirit which animates these Governments. The American Delegation believes that a fixed sum should be named now. The U.S. proposal contemplates a reply containing a finding that the total damage under the categories will approximate 120 milliards of marks gold, which, for practical reasons, is accepted as a maximum of Germany's liability. The American delegates have been convinced, not by German arguments, but by current developments, of the soundness of their original view that, in the interest of the *Allies*, Germany's reparation liability should be limited *now* to a definite amount which there is reason to believe Germany can pay. Only in this way can there be secured what the world instantly requires, a new basis of credit. Only under such conditions is it reasonable to expect that Germany will put forward those efforts which are indispensable to create a value behind what are otherwise paper obligations.

II.

The American Delegation believes that definite assurances should be given with reference to (a) the retention by Germany of certain amounts of working capital in the form of ships, gold, and investments abroad; (b) the operation of the coal and chemical options, and the possibility of Germany securing minette ore; (c) the intentions of the Allied and Associated Governments as to the cost of the army of occupation which Germany is to support. The American Delegation expresses its view that vagueness on these subjects will react to produce the contrary impression to what may be desired. Unless, therefore, these subjects are susceptible of specific treatment, they question whether they should be alluded to at all.

On the other hand the Delegations of Great Britain and France oppose themselves to these concessions, not only upon grounds connected with the terms of the proposals themselves, but also because they believe it to be unwise and inopportune for the Allied and Associated Powers to volunteer particular offers under present circumstances, especially as Germany has made no definite offer at all. They think that nothing is to be gained and much may be lost by such an attitude.

III.

1° The Italian Delegation agrees with the English and French Delegations in thinking that it is impossible to fix in a document such as is now in preparation the total amount of Germany's liability.

They believe however that it shall be wise at a future and early date to fix by negotiations with Germany a definite sum.

About Germany's requests concerning the delivery of ships and raw materials the Italian Delegation thinks that it shall belong to the Reparation Commission to take such requests into account in so far as it shall think them equitable, and that the said Commission disposes to that effect of all necessary Powers.

Further they believe that the delimitation of the cost of the army of occupation should be the matter of later negotiations.

2° The Japanese delegation desires it to be reported that they concur in objecting to any sum being fixed, as it is now impossible to fix a sum which will both be accepted by Germany and satisfy the reparations claims in full. Further, they oppose any proposal for the retention of any ships.

CXVI

Conversation between President Wilson and MM. Clemenceau, Lloyd George, and Orlando*

JUNE 10, 1919, 11 A.M.

M. Clemenceau. I have the reply of the Hungarians; it is satisfactory.[1]

President Wilson. But they haven't yet halted hostilities.

M. Clemenceau. We must call their adversaries here and say to them: here is what we want. They will obey us, because if we don't go to their aid, they will be defeated.

Mr. Lloyd George. Unless we act promptly, we will stop nothing at all.

M. Clemenceau. I propose to see M. Brătianu and M. Beneš this afternoon.

Mr. Lloyd George. M. Kramář will have to be summoned; he is the Prime Minister.

M. Clemenceau. Even so, I will invite M. Beneš, because he is a conciliatory spirit.

Mr. Lloyd George. I would also like you to invite M. Mişu at the same time as M. Brătianu.

M. Clemenceau. You received M. Orlando's note.[2] We must speak about it as soon as possible.

*H., PPC, VI, 272ff. M. Orlando is not present at the beginning of the session.

[1] B. Kun to G. Clemenceau, June 9, 1919, Wilson Papers, Library of Congress. Kun stated that the Hungarian government had taken note of the intention of the Allied and Associated Powers to invite Hungary to the peace conference. Hungary, he went on, had only friendly designs toward her neighbors, had, in fact, not attacked Czechoslovakia, and had always respected the demarcation lines drawn by the Allies. However, Czech, Yugoslav, and Rumanian troops had launched offensives against Hungary, and, as a consequence, her people had been forced to take up arms. Kun maintained that Hungary was ready to cease all hostilities at once if the Allies were able to cause Czechoslovakia, Yugoslavia, and Rumania to lay down their arms and obey the clauses of the military convention of November 13, 1918. The best solution, Kun concluded, would be to convoke the immediate meeting of a conference of delegates from the interested states under the presidency of a representative of one of the Allied powers.

[2] V. E. Orlando to WW, June 9, 1919, with memorandum dated June 7, 1919, printed in PWW, Vol. 60, pp. 307-11. The memorandum reviewed all major stages of the negotiations between the British, French, and American delegations and the Italians on the Adriatic questions. It then compared Wilson's latest proposal (for a discussion of which, see CXIV) with the Tardieu plan (about which,

Mr. Lloyd George. I want that, as you do. I would like to speak to M. Orlando about it now; but I haven't yet had time to think about it. Can't we ourselves propose a solution?

President Wilson. M. Clemenceau could prepare a memorandum for us.

M. Clemenceau. I am not very good at memoranda. If you wish, I will make a proposal for a settlement.

President Wilson. Are we ready on reparations?[3]

Mr. Lloyd George. I think we must make haste. The press is agitated at home as well as in France, and our newspapers are exaggerating the concessions they think they foresee. If that should continue, it would result in difficulties of all kinds.

My proposal is very simple.[4] Immediately after the signing of the peace, the Germans will be invited to prepare their estimate for reparations. They will have four months to present it to us and we to consider the best means of payment.

One can think of this in three different ways. Germany can make a lump-sum offer for all that she is to pay. Germany can offer, for everything not susceptible to an immediate numerical determination, reparation in kind. Finally, the Germans can offer reparation in kind for one part only of the damages. The Allies will reply without being committed in advance to accept the German offer, and they will fix the details of execution. The required work of preparation will be assisted by the presence of the German experts. If we treat the question of reparation proper in this way, the figures for the rest are easy to determine.

M. Clemenceau. I accept this suggestion in principle. But I ask to see a text.

President Wilson. This is your reply to the American proposal about fixing the figure. Have you read the rest of the American report?

---

see C, n. 1), which Italy had earlier accepted. Among other things, the memorandum pointed out that, in Wilson's proposal, Italy was to be deprived of the integral possession of the Istrian peninsula and would have to accept provisions for Fiume that were less favorable to her than those of the Tardieu plan. In addition, Italy would lose the island of Cherso, the city of Sebenico and the islands around it, and the Assling triangle. In all, the memorandum concluded, these new provisions were so much to the detriment of Italy that it was an "absolute impossibility" for her to accept them.

[3] The council had before it the document printed as an appendix to these notes.

[4] Lloyd George here begins to paraphrase a document prepared by Lord Sumner. Its main portions are printed in PWW, Vol. 60, pp. 336-37, 338-39, 342-43.

Mr. Lloyd George. I think that the first four pages are perfect.

M. Clemenceau. Remind me of the main points.

President Wilson. I will reread this document.

Mr. Lloyd George. At the beginning, I would repeat the definition of reparation as it was given in our correspondence before the conclusion of the Armistice. Moreover, instead of indicating only the numbers of the articles quoted, I would recall their meaning and, if necessary, I would quote the complete text in a note.

Perhaps there is reason to insert some of the explanations that Lord Sumner, in the draft text that he prepared, gives about the powers of the Reparation Commission.[5] That draft of Lord Sumner is very well written and very precise in its terms.

—Mr. Lloyd George reads this text aloud.

M. Clemenceau. I favor inserting that page into our text.

President Wilson. We could put it at the end of the second paragraph on page 2.

Mr. Lloyd George. I would leave aside the entire second paragraph in order to avoid repetition. I would keep the lines where it is said that the Allied and Associated Governments have rejected any proposal tending to compel the Germans to divulge their industrial secrets.

President Wilson. You would eliminate the part of the American text relative to the fixing of the total sum?

Mr. Lloyd George. I propose to put there instead an invitation to Germany to make an offer after the necessary study.

I must observe in passing that, on the question of German manpower, I just received a protest from the representatives of British workers against the plan to require payments from Germany in manpower. They say that it is slavery. We must undeceive them by indicating clearly the nature of the assistance we are asking for. One important point is that the Germans must accept the categories of reparation without any discussion. What they have the right to do is to discuss such and such a figure for a given category; but they can dispute none of the categories.

---

[5] In this portion of his memorandum, Sumner said that the German observations on the commission were "so distorted and so inexact, that it is impossible to believe that the clauses of the Treaty have been calmly or carefully examined." The Reparation Commission was not an "engine of oppression" or a device for interfering with German sovereignty. It would simply fix what Germany should pay, try to satisfy itself that Germany could pay, and report if Germany defaulted. The commission would study the German systems of taxation as much for the protection of the German people as for the protection of its own peoples.

President Wilson. I would like to connect to that the question of leaving Germany the capital and tonnage necessary for her economic needs. You recall that the American delegation proposes to leave her 30 per cent of her tonnage for two years and to exempt her, until further notice, from all payments in gold.

Mr. Lloyd George. Do you want to discuss this point immediately?

M. Clemenceau. I think we should see the experts again.

Mr. Lloyd George. Let us speak frankly. The United States, Brazil, and Portugal hold today more German tonnage than they themselves lost due to the war. Brazil, which lost some thousands of tons, holds in her ports 250,000 tons of German ships. The United States has 650,000 tons of them, and its losses don't surpass 280,000. France lost nearly a million tons, and she has taken 40,000; Great Britain lost eight to nine million tons and she has taken less than a million and a half. We suffered enormous losses, and in great part while our merchant marine was working for other countries, including the United States of America.

What I am asking is not special protection for British interests. If we decide to leave the Germans 30 per cent of their tonnage, very well. But it must be done on a basis of complete equality amongst us, each taking equal part in the losses suffered. Thirty per cent which would burden England and France—that is what our public opinion could not accept. It would accept it if we were all placed on an equal footing. But it is not the same if a friendly power gains 400,000 tons of the best German vessels that it holds only because they were chased into American ports by English cruisers, which would have taken them if America had not given them refuge before its entry into the war. English public opinion is aroused about that.

President Wilson. That emotion is not justified. America asks nothing by way of reparation.

Mr. Lloyd George. What damages did she suffer?

President Wilson. She spent millions of dollars and thousands of lives.

Mr. Lloyd George. In lives, America lost a little less than Australia. At present, tonnage represents much more than money. Obviously, there will be immediate efforts to secure trade in different parts of the world; the first to arrive will make themselves masters of it.

President Wilson. Let us return to the point under discussion. If Germany doesn't have the tonnage and the capital that she needs immediately, she won't be able to put her business to work.

Mr. Lloyd George. I don't deny it. But I ask that the contribution be equal. If you did not ask for the equivalent of pensions which you will have to pay, it is you who did not want it. It would have been much easier to get the House of Commons to accept that than what you ask as regards tonnage. If something must be done for Germany, let us not do it at the expense of the nations that suffered most.

M. Clemenceau. In my opinion, this question of knowing what must be left to the Germans for their immediate needs should not be discussed with them. It must be settled amongst us. I am prepared to do what is necessary for them, but not to promise them anything. Must they be left gold? My right is to obtain for my country the reparations which are due her. It goes without saying that, in our own interest, as well as in that of Germany, I would leave her what would put her back on her feet. But I would not speak of it in the document here.

President Wilson. The paragraph we have just discussed recalls Germany's duty to replace sunken ships, ton for ton.

Mr. Lloyd George. I would confine myself to saying that the Allies will take into consideration the means of providing Germany what is absolutely necessary for her maritime commerce and imports.

M. Clemenceau. We have no more tonnage because our ships were sunk. I am ready to help Germany; but I won't take a specific commitment regarding tonnage.

Mr. Lloyd George. Be assured, Mr. President, that we shall do what is necessary towards Germany. I am convinced that the largest part of the tonnage that will be provided to her will come from Great Britain. The real shortage of ships that we suffer is the result of the crimes of the submarine war.

President Wilson. This discussion underestimates the efforts of the United States in the war in such a way that I don't care to continue to participate in it.

Mr. Lloyd George. We don't wish to belittle the efforts of anyone. Great Britain has done just as much.

President Wilson. Right now, we aren't working on a practical basis, and, in these circumstances, I have nothing more to propose to you. We have talked for months, and for months the points of view of the American and British experts have never come closer.

I believe that it is very helpful to give the Germans the assurance that they will have what is necessary to resume their economic activity. If, from the French point of view, it is possible to give it to them, that will be for the best. The only goal of this statement is to make the signing of the treaty easier. Lord Sumner's plan only allows the Germans to make proposals.

Mr. Lloyd George. I believe that responds to the greatest concern of the Germans. They say that they don't know what they will have to pay and want to be enlightened on this point as soon as possible.

M. Clemenceau. Here, there must be neither Frenchman, nor Englishman, nor American, nor Italian. We have to make peace in a common spirit. The question which arises at this time is that of knowing if we must now fix the figure of what the Germans will pay, or if we should accept Mr. Lloyd George's proposal, which delays the announcement of this figure for a few months. I accept Mr. Lloyd George's proposal. There is no offense to America in it. What I say is that the proposal of the American experts is the complete reversal of the peace treaty. After long and difficult discussions, we arrived at conclusions; this document asks us to abandon them.

At the head of the chapter on reparation, we set forth this principle: damages will be repaired. If we fix a figure today, do we know if this figure will be large enough to pay us? I don't need to recall what France has suffered. She has also suffered at sea and lacks more tonnage than any other country. As for myself—I state it clearly—I am not for a policy which aims at making the Germans forgive us for our victory; I have known them too well, too long.

The entire world knows today what our proposals are, on what principles they rest. Because the Germans make objections—which is not surprising—should we abandon our principles? I cannot do it. We are asked, in order to coax them, to admit them tomorrow to the League of Nations, to commit ourselves to abolishing compulsory military service at home, to give them all the gold and ships they will need. This is a world turned upside down, it is the Germans who lay down their terms to us, or very nearly so. If we are now asked, at the last moment, to upset the terms of peace, I cannot consent to it.

I accept Mr. Lloyd George's proposition. To believe, however, that, because one will make such or such concession to them, the Germans will sign, is an error. We must render this justice to Germany; she is a strong nation, powerful, which knows what she wants. From today on, she is thinking about her recovery. Are you certain that, if you yield on all points, you will have peace?

When England abandoned her "splendid isolation" to enter the war, when the United States came so far to contribute to the final victory of the right, they began a struggle which must be pursued to the end. If the Germans feel that the peace is a peace imposed by the strongest, which has justice on its side, they will resign themselves to it. Otherwise, they will use your concessions to ask you for others. The conversation will drag on, the confidence of our peoples will fall, it will be a public misfortune.

I am ready, like you, for concessions, but *not* concessions which can compromise the peace. I repeat that it is not a matter of thinking as Frenchmen, as Americans, as Italians, or as Englishmen, but of thinking and acting in the interest of all. I conclude by remarking that we would be committing ourselves to the Germans by these propositions; now the Germans themselves would not be committed. We offer them ships, gold, admission to the League of Nations: these are promises which, once made, we cannot withdraw. The Germans will have made none. Thus, the day after tomorrow, they can present new requests. If they should come today to say to me: "Grant me such or such thing, and we will sign," I would see what I have to do. But such is not the situation.

President Wilson. I will remind you again that the United States has proposed no concession. We have simply wished to cooperate in a common work and to assist in the signing. If the proposals made displease you, they will be withdrawn.

M. Clemenceau. I thought that you were complaining that we didn't have the regard for the United States which is its due.

President Wilson. I only said that, for a long time, we have expressed views which, on the whole, were not accepted.

Mr. Lloyd George. I approve of the spirit of the American document. The fundamental idea is good. It is right to wish to show Germany that we don't want to annihilate her economic life; but I would like to change the wording. What the Germans need is not assurances on points of detail, it is to know in what spirit we will apply the treaty. Obviously, if we begin by making them promises, they will ask for everything that seems to be missing on the list. All that needs to be written is a general assurance that they will have the right to appeal later. Can one say that it is too vague? I believe it will satisfy the Germans.

President Wilson. The only difference between us relates to the question of knowing whether our offers should or should not be clearly defined.

Mr. Lloyd George. If you begin to define them, you will never get out of it. The Germans need our tungsten, our wool, your cotton, etc. Why give guarantees on particular points, since you can't mention all? There is no doubt that we will provide them with all the raw materials they need. It is enough today to say to them: "Our interest, like yours, is to allow you to resume your economic activity."

—Mr. Lloyd George reads aloud the draft proposed by Lord Sumner.[6]

M. Clemenceau. I accept that draft.
President Wilson. Must we not add the word "cooperation?"
Mr. Lloyd George. Our people wouldn't like it very much.
M. Clemenceau. We must be careful about words, especially in a country like ours, where the Germans systematically destroyed factories in order to wipe out certain industries.
Mr. Lloyd George. I am not saying that, after having read that, they will sign. But a statement of this kind will have an effect on the German commercial world and will make it understand that its interest lies in signing.

I just read a document written by two Alsatians, who recently traveled through Germany. They say that the desire for peace is paramount throughout the country. What especially disturbs German public opinion is the question of the eastern frontier; I have this information from Mr. Zaharoff.
M. Clemenceau. The desire for peace amongst the German people is undeniable. If the delegates at Versailles refuse to sign, I am convinced we will have peace two weeks later; others will sign.
Mr. Lloyd George. If, in the heat of debate, I have said anything which might have displeased you, I apologize. You know the Celtic temperament.
President Wilson. And the expenses of the occupation army?
M. Clemenceau. That is a matter to be settled amongst ourselves. I will fall in with any reasonable solution.
Mr. Lloyd George. We must tell the Germans.
M. Clemenceau. The expenses of the occupation army don't concern them at all.
Mr. Lloyd George. It is they who will pay.
M. Clemenceau. They will pay neither more nor less. It is impor-

---

[6] Actually, Lloyd George read a paragraph from the Sumner memorandum. It assured the Germans that the Allied and Associated Powers stood ready to give Germany all access to the raw materials and provision for their transport to German factories, that the resumption of German industry was in their own interest as well as Germany's, and that they were ready to afford Germany "facilities in these directions for the common good."

As will be seen, these and other changes were incorporated in the American draft, and the revised version was then incorporated in the general reply sent to the German delegation on June 16, 1919. This document is printed in PPC, VI, 926-96. We will print the most important portions of this document as they were worked over and approved by the Council of Four because, we think, they reveal an earnest and serious effort to respond to the German observations on and protests against various portions of the preliminary peace treaty. As will become evident, Philip Kerr, Lloyd George's Private Secretary, was general editor of the long single reply of June 16 and in fact wrote important sections of it.

tant for us to know what the expenses of the occupation army will cost us, for they will be taken out of reparations. Don't be afraid of me; on this question, I think exactly as you do, and I won't leave it to my generals to do all they want.

President Wilson. So you would say nothing in this document about the occupation army?

M. Clemenceau. To you, I will say all that you want, but not to the Germans. I don't see how we could put that in writing.

Mr. Lloyd George. I want them to sign.

M. Clemenceau. So do I; it isn't that that will make them sign.

Mr. Lloyd George. We can tell them first that we have no intention of interfering in their civil administration, I could recall the precedent of Marshal Manteuffel in France, after 1871.

M. Clemenceau. I haven't the least intention of interfering in their civil life.

Mr. Lloyd George. At this time, your generals are working to create a Rhenish republic.[7] That is the real way to keep it from existing. I saw Sir William Robertson, and I spoke to him about it; he understood the thing very well.

M. Clemenceau. In this I am entirely with you. For five or six days, I have been enjoining my representatives to observe the same attitude that you have indicated to Sir William Robertson.

Mr. Lloyd George. It is useful to make the Germans understand that we have no intention of interfering in their civil administration.

M. Clemenceau. I am ready to do it.

Mr. Lloyd George. And about the occupation costs?

M. Clemenceau. I would go as far as to say that it is in our interest to reduce the occupation costs as much as possible.

Mr. Lloyd George. You know that frightened people always exaggerate the danger. The Germans already think that they see the expenses of the occupation army imposing a crushing burden upon them—fifty million pounds sterling or more. If we could indicate a moderate figure to them, that would help us.

M. Clemenceau. In any event, they will owe us all that they can pay. The expenses of the occupation army will be taken from what we will receive.

---

[7] About which, see *PWW*, Vol. 59, p. 402, n. 4, and numerous documents printed in Vols. 59 and 60. See the index reference "Rhineland" in those volumes.

{ A P P E N D I X }[8]

REPARATION.
U. S. PROJECT FOR REPLY TO GERMAN COUNTER-PROPOSALS.

The Allied and Associated Governments, consistent to their policy already enunciated, decline to enter into a discussion of the principles underlying the Reparation Clauses of the Conditions of Peace, which have been prepared with scrupulous regard for the correspondence leading up to the Armistice of November 11, 1918.

To the extent that your reply deals with practical phases of the execution of the principles enunciated in the Conditions of Peace, you appear to proceed on the basis of a complete misapprehension, which is more difficult to understand as the inferences you draw and the statements which you make are wholly at variance with both the letter and with the spirit of the Treaty Clauses. In order, however, that there may be no possible excuse for misunderstanding, and for purposes of clarification, the Allied and Associated Governments submit the following observations:

The vast extent and manifold character of the damage caused to the Allied and Associated Governments in consequence of the war, has created a reparation problem of extraordinary magnitude and complexity, only to be solved by a continuing body, limited in personnel and invested with broad powers to deal with the problem in relation to the general economic situation. The Allied and Associated Powers recognising this situation, themselves propose to delegate power and authority to the Reparation Commission. The Reparation Commission is, however, instructed by the Treaty itself so to exercise and interpret its powers as to insure in the interest of all, as early and complete discharge by Germany of her reparation obligations as is consistent with the due maintenance of the social, economic and financial structure of a Germany earnestly striving to exercise her full power to repair the loss and damage she has caused.

The provisions of Article 241 are not to be misconstrued as giving the Commission power to dictate the domestic legislation of Germany. Nor does Paragraph 12(b), of Annex II, give the Commission power to prescribe or enforce taxes or to dictate the character of the German budget. The Commission is required to in-

[8] Printed in PPC, VI, 267-71.

form itself as to the German system of taxation and of the character of the German budget, only in order that it may intelligently and constructively exercise the discretion accorded it in Germany's interest particularly by Article 234. The provisions of Article 240 are similar in character and purpose and there should be no occasion for the exercise of these powers after May 1, 1921, if Germany is in a position to, and does, comply with the schedule of payments which then will have been notified to her and with the specific provisions of the several Annexes relative to reparation in kind. It is further to be observed that the power of modification accorded by the said Article 236 is expressly designed to permit of a modification in Germany's interest of a schedule of payments which events may demonstrate to be beyond Germany's reasonable capacity.

The purposes for which the powers granted to the Commission are to be utilised are plainly indicated on the face of the Treaty, and the Allied and Associated Powers vigorously reject the suggestion that the Commission, in exercising the power conferred by Article 240 and by Paragraphs 2, 3 and 4 or Annex IV, might require the divulgence of trade secrets and similar confidential data.

It is understood that the action necessary to give effect to the provisions of Annex IV, relative to reparation in kind, will be taken by Germany on its own initiative, after receipt of notification from the Reparation Commission.

The provisions of the Treaty are in no wise incompatible with the creation by Germany of a commission which will represent Germany in dealings with the Reparation Commission and which will constitute an instrumentality for such co-operation as may be necessary. The Treaty specifically and repeatedly provides opportunities for the German Government to present facts and arguments with respect to claims and modes of payments, within the limits of the principles and express provisions of the Treaty. This may be done through a commission and no reason is perceived as to why such a commission could not work in harmony with the Reparation Commission. Certainly this is greatly to be desired.

The Allied and Associated Governments, after examining the considerable data which are available, have unanimously reached the conclusion that the total damage under Annex I, when estimated on a gold basis, will approximate the principal sum of one hundred and twenty milliards of marks gold. These Governments recognise the desirability from every aspect that Germany's liability be rendered as precise as circumstances will permit and that the benefits to follow from any reasonable and prompt decision in this respect will greatly outweigh any loss consequent upon a possible error in estimation. Accordingly the sum of 120 milliards* of marks gold may be regarded as an accepted maximum of the damage for which Germany is liable in accordance with Article 232. Inasmuch as the damage specified in Annex I includes damage caused by the former Allies of Germany, any sums received from Germany's former allies will be credited against Germany's liability. Further while not recognizing any right of contribution as between Germany and her former allies, the Reparation Commission will give to the Government of Germany an opportunity to present such facts as that Government deems relevant as to the capacity of payment of Germany's former allies.

Germany proposes to assist in the restoration of the devastated areas by supplying labour and material. The Allied and Associated Governments had not desired to stipulate for German labour lest they be charged with demanding forced labour. The principle, however, of the general application of Germany's entire economic resources to reparation is consecrated by Article 236 and the provisions of Paragraph 19 of Annex II authorise the Reparation Commission to accept payment in various forms. It is thus within the plain contemplation of the Conditions of Peace that Germany may address direct proposals to the Reparation Commission for the supplying of German labour for reparation purposes.

The Allied and Associated Governments do not ignore the economic needs of Germany. To do so would be contrary not only to their own material interests but to the spirit which has animated them in the preparation of the Conditions of Peace and of which ample evidence is to be found. The Commission is instructed in all its activities to take into account the social and economic requirements of Germany. In furtherance of such general instructions specific instructions are now in preparation directing the Commission to permit the retention by Germany for two years of ships, designated by the Commission, representing 30 per cent in tonnage of the total amount of ships referred to in Paragraph I of Annex III. These ships, the delivery of which is to

---

*This sum might be still further increased were Germany given credit for various property to be taken from her without payment (e.g., in the Colonies) and were Germany further given credit for portions of war debt attaching to ceded territory. To give such credits appears just in principle. [The "increased," which appears in all transcripts, must have been a typographical error. "Decreased" only makes sense in the context. Ed.'s note.]

be deferred, will be available for use by Germany to meet her economic needs and to assist in the fulfillment of Germany's external obligations. The Commission will similarly receive detailed instructions to apply the provisions of Article 235 so as to permit the retention by Germany at home and abroad of certain amounts of working capital and so that for the present no gold will be required to be delivered by Germany for reparations purposes.

With reference to the provisions of Annexes V and VI, it is, of course, understood that the options therein referred to will be exercised exclusively to meet the domestic requirements of the country exercising the option. In further precision of the general principle above referred to enunciated by the Allied and Associated Governments for the guidance of the Commission, additional detailed instructions are in preparation, advising the Commission that to avoid any possibility of interference with the economic and industrial life of Germany the option for delivery of coal to France will, for the first year be exercised as to 50% only of the maximum amount mentioned, and that deliveries should commence with small monthly amounts, gradually increasing.

The Government of France has always contemplated that an arrangement would be made for the exchange of minette ore on mutually acceptable conditions.

With reference to the cost of maintaining the Army of Occupation, it is impossible for obvious reasons for the Allied and Associated Governments to make any commitment which would operate to limit the size of each army. The Allied and Associated Governments, however, perceive no reason for not advising the German Government that it is their hope and expectation that it will be unnecessary for such army to be of a size such that the cost of maintenance would exceed 240 millions of marks per annum.

The foregoing should suffice to demonstrate the reasonableness of the conditions under which Germany is to discharge her reparation obligations, and how utterly unfounded are the criticisms of the German reply. These are, indeed, explicable only on the theory that the German plenipotentiaries have read into the Conditions of Peace, in clear defiance of their express terms, an intent which it would be not unnatural to see evidenced by victorious nations which have been the victims of cruelty and devastation on a vast and premeditated scale. The burdens of Germany undeniably are heavy, but they are imposed under

conditions of justice by peoples whose social well-being and economic prosperity have been gravely impaired by wrongs which it is beyond the utmost power of Germany to repair.
Paris. 9th May [June], 1919.

CXVII

Conversation among President Wilson and MM. Clemenceau, Lloyd George, Orlando, Brătianu, Mişu, Kramář, and Beneš*

JUNE 10, 1919, 4 P.M.

President Wilson. We summoned you, gentlemen, because we are very concerned about the military situation in and around Hungary. At present, the Hungarian army is driving back the Czechoslovak troops. According to the more or less accurate information that we are receiving, this movement of the Hungarian army was provoked by an advance of Czech forces, which appeared to threaten the mining basin. But I am going to tell you the facts which rule the situation.

You remember that General Franchet d'Esperey, at the time of the armistice, drew a line at which the Rumanian army was to halt. The Rumanians crossed that line. Later, a second line was drawn; it was also crossed, contrary to the orders of the commander in chief. That second offensive caused the fall of Károlyi, whose attitude towards the Entente was more friendly than that of any other Hungarian statesman. It was then that Béla Kun seized power.

His government was not of the kind to be accepted by the most established classes of the population. But when the Czechs, in their turn, attacked Hungarian territory, it was reported to us that the officers of the old Hungarian army themselves rallied around the government of Béla Kun. Thus, the latter came to power as a consequence of the Rumanian offensive, and his power was consolidated by the Czech offensive.

Nothing can be more fatal to our policy. We are trying to reach a just division of territories and a lasting agreement amongst peoples; hence our great desire to remove all causes of irritation and

*H., PPC, VI, 281ff.

mutual aggression. I have explained to you the situation such as we see it. I beg M. Brătianu to inform us of his views.

M. Brătianu. I fear that you are not perfectly informed about the role of the Rumanian army and the Hungarian provocations. At the time of the proclamation of the armistice, General Franchet d'Esperey, with whom I had it out a short time afterwards, knew nothing about the military and political situation in that region. He drew an absolutely arbitrary line, which left the most Rumanian parts of Transylvania and of Hungary to the Hungarians. The result was as follows: behind the Rumanian front, order was immediately established, and the Saxon peoples of Transylvania themselves not only accepted Rumanian administration but publicly proclaimed their adhesion to Rumania.

During this time, Károlyi was organizing, under the color of Bolshevism, the devastation of Rumanian lands located across from us. At that time, I sent you Hungarian proclamations whose object was to provoke Bolshevik agitation. It was then that we obtained the drawing of another line. The Hungarians immediately proceeded to their work of destruction. Rumanian troops moved ahead, in order to occupy the line which had been determined by the Supreme War Council. There was armed conflict, and the Rumanians stopped on the bank of the Theiss. We have proof that the Bolshevik movement was organized and paid for by Károlyi. We possess proclamations printed in Pest when his government was still established there.

After Károlyi's retreat and the establishment of a Bolshevik government, we wanted, in a spirit of solidarity with the Entente, to march on Pest in order to help in the reestablishment of order. The Allied governments demanded that we stop; we did, and we haven't budged since. Yet, several days ago, I received a communication from M. Pichon which expressed to me the fear of the great powers at seeing the Rumanian army marching on Pest. I replied to him that, if the Allies preferred to allow Bolshevism to ferment in Pest until it destroyed itself, I had nothing to say. I repeat that Bolshevism was organized by the Hungarian government, as much under Károlyi as under Béla Kun.

You have received incorrect information on the attitude of the peoples during the advance of the Rumanian troops. In the purely Hungarian city of Debreczen, we saw the mayor and bishop come to thank the commander of the Rumanian army for having come to guarantee order in the country. The King of Rumania, who recently inspected that region, everywhere received the thanks of representatives of all social classes, who congratulated the Rumanians for having preserved them from anarchy.

Hungary was not sufficiently given the impression that she is defeated. If that had been done, we would be at peace with her today. But if the Hungarians don't understand their true situation and don't renounce their former pretensions, peace will become more and more difficult. At the present time, strong words will be understood, and they won't be able to resist. Any other attitude would make the situation more delicate and put off the solution.

As for us, if we must give you more proof of the attitude that Rumania takes today, we have recently received emissaries from all the anti-Bolshevik parties of Hungary, asking us to march on Pest, and we have refused.

Mr. Lloyd George. Hasn't the commission instructed by the conference to determine Hungary's boundaries finished its work?

M. Beneš. In fact, it has just determined our boundary and Rumania's.

M. Brătianu. I have no knowledge of it. I still know only the line of the armistice and what our claims are.

Mr. Lloyd George. How can that be?

Sir Maurice Hankey. The decisions of the commission were submitted to the Council of Foreign Ministers.

Mr. Lloyd George. How is it that they were not communicated to the Rumanian government?

M. Mişu. We only heard about them indirectly.

M. Brătianu. All that I have ever known about the decisions you have taken in this regard comes from the newspapers.

Mr. Lloyd George. In any case, according to what I just heard, Rumania is not demanding Debreczen.

M. Brătianu. Certainly not.

M. Mişu. If we are on the Theiss, it is because of a strategic necessity.

Mr. Lloyd George. You are on purely Magyar territory, halfway from Pest; that is what creates Bolshevism.

M. Brătianu. We had halted on another line drawn earlier. There, we were attacked by the Bolsheviks. It was then we marched up to the present line.

Mr. Lloyd George. You will be hard put to make me believe that it was Károlyi who created Bolshevism in Hungary.

M. Brătianu. There are matters that we know better than you, because we are closer. The Bolshevik movement in that region was from the outset set in motion by the Germans under the direction of Marshal Mackensen. The pieces of the machine that he erected are still in place. Hungarian Bolshevism was prepared for a long time. If I cannot convince you of the reality of these facts, I regret it.

President Wilson. I have no doubt that intrigues of this kind took place at the instigation of the Germans who, when their position became desperate, tried to create an impossible situation for everybody. But propaganda is one thing, and aggression is another. We ourselves must avoid creating Bolshevism by giving peoples of enemy countries just reasons for discontent.

In America, we had to put up with the agitation created by an organization of anarchistic tendencies, the "Independent [Industrial] Workers of the World." In order to combat it, we sought as far as possible to remove the subjects of legitimate complaint. It is the true way to combat Bolshevism.

Whatever the strategic reasons, the Rumanian armies have no right today to be on the Theiss. That is contrary to the terms of the armistice, and the present state of things is a provocation to Hungary.

I have been very astonished to learn that the representatives of Rumania had not been informed of deliberations relating to the Rumanian boundaries. I am convinced that it is necessary to fix these boundaries and to cause them to be respected, otherwise we will never arrive at a solution. When we have convinced the Hungarians that the boundary, once fixed, won't be violated, Bolshevism will weaken and approach its end. What we want is to be in the right. The Rumanian army has no right to be on purely Hungarian territory. If I were a Hungarian—and I am happy not to be one—I would be the first to take up arms to defend my country.

Mr. Lloyd George. We were told that Béla Kun was close to falling when the Czech offensive rallied round him the Hungarian officers and a large number of enemies of the Bolsheviks.

M. Kramář. I am astonished to learn that it is the Czechs who provoked the Hungarians. I know there was a great discussion amongst us whether we should advance or not. Some wanted to prevent Hungarian aggression by marching at the moment when the Rumanians were advancing on their side to stamp out Bolshevism. But a lively opposition manifested itself amongst the democratic elements who are dominant in our republic, and particularly in the Socialist party, and all plans of this kind were condemned. Was there some movement of troops near Miskolcz?

I know nothing precise. What I know is that General Piccioni, when leaving us, asked for guns and munitions for us, and I would be astonished if he had done it if he had ascribed aggressive designs to us. I understand still less the intentions that you attribute to us when I look at the Hungarian side. The Hungarian army is very well organized: it numbers more than 100,000 men, very well armed with what remains of the equipment of Marshal Mackensen's army; it includes a certain number of Germans and Bolsheviks from Russia. It is not an army improvised for defense.

I know nothing about a Czech offensive. All I know relates to the advance of Hungarian Bolshevism, mixed and confused with Magyar chauvinism.

My duty is to support, on another point, what was said by M. Brătianu. He and I know Count Károlyi well; his friendship for the Allies was not what you imagine. His relations with the Bolsheviks are perfectly well known to us; we even know who the person was who negotiated in his name with Béla Kun.

If we had wanted to cross the armistice line and make conquests, we would have prepared ourselves. We were not even organized to defend ourselves; that was because we believed we were secure behind the line drawn by the conference. We did not lack the temptation to advance; the entire Magyar bourgeoisie asked us to come to its help. It is necessary to see reality such as it is.

The Hungarians have assembled a great army. It was given the equipment left by Marshal Mackensen, and they attacked us. We are the weaker. What we are waiting for is for the Entente to stop them and, if they don't obey its injunctions, to come to our aid.

At this time, an extraordinary enthusiasm manifests itself in the Czechoslovak Republic to defend our threatened soil. Many people who thought themselves Bolsheviks are marching with the patriots. We lack only arms. We have no desire to cross the line drawn; but we don't know whether the danger is going to increase. From the side of Vienna also, we are menaced by Bolshevism. We know that 20,000 Bavarians are concentrated at Furth-im-Wald. Our geographical position isolates us. We have the full right to ask the Allies for their assistance and the armament we need. We are ready to commit ourselves to using the arms they give us only to defend ourselves against the Bolsheviks united with Magyar chauvinists.

As for a compromise with Hungary, at the very moment when her soldiers are advancing in Slovakia and committing atrocities, we would consider it a political mistake and a crying injustice.

President Wilson. I should already have told you that, forty-eight hours ago, we ordered the Hungarians to halt immediately, warning them that, if they didn't, we would take the most drastic measures. They replied that they will halt if they are not attacked.

M. Beneš. I want to add a few words to what M. Kramář said, recalling the historical facts of the demarcation line between us and Hungary. That line was notified to us last November. It was fixed in such a way that communications were cut between Bohemia and Slovakia; for that reason, we asked that it be changed, and that change wouldn't even have brought the line up to the border claimed by us and accepted today by your commission.

In the meantime, we remained on the line that had been drawn for us. But since our communications with Slovakia remained very precarious, we told Marshal Foch and the high command that a change was absolutely essential. After having repeated that request three or four times, we succeeded in getting the demarcation line shifted a little towards the south. Our troops were then sent to occupy the new temporary line, under the command of General Piccioni, then of Generals Mittelhauser and Hennocque, both French.

Mr. Lloyd George. Was that change of the line notified to the Hungarians?

M. Beneš. I know nothing about it. I will observe that the change was also asked by Mr. Hoover because famine was spreading in Slovakia due to lack of means of communication.

All was quiet at home; we were busy with our domestic reforms and forthcoming elections. Our forces were assembled on the German border because of the concentration of German troops which threatened Poland, and also because Marshal Foch had asked us to be prepared in case of need to move on Bavaria, in the event the peace treaty was not signed. It was then that the Magyars, seeing Slovakia completely defenseless, advanced.

Mr. Lloyd George. Didn't you have your troops advance on the Hungarian mines?

M. Beneš. Our troops advanced in the area of Salgótarján. The Quai d'Orsay made an observation on this subject to us, and we immediately gave the troops the order to retreat.

Mr. Lloyd George. What General Cavallero told us the other day is that you had crossed the line and threatened the only important coal mine remaining in Hungary. The Hungarians defended themselves and then invaded you.

M. Beneš. The Hungarians advanced in another direction, in the area of Kaschau.

M. Brătianu. I will remind you that we are still in a state of war with Hungary, and that it is necessary for us to keep our positions as long as the state of war lasts.

M. Clemenceau. At this time, General Pellé asks us to send troops to Bohemia; we cannot do it. The Rumanians have twice crossed the line drawn for them. We are determined to stop the Hungarians; you must also stop.

—The Four withdraw to deliberate.

Mr. Lloyd George. Concerning the Czechs, I notice that a change of the line was made by Marshal Foch without consulting us.

M. Clemenceau. Mustn't we now send to Budapest two or three officers with some Czechs and Rumanians, in order to fix a line?

President Wilson. What is clear is that the Rumanians must evacuate Hungary proper. The danger of that evacuation is that it will have the appearance of a retreat. But if, as we said a short time ago, the territorial commission has determined the boundary, it is easy for us to tell the Hungarians: "Here is your boundary; we will show our good faith by making the troops of our allies withdraw behind this border. If you cross it, we will no longer negotiate with you."

We will make this decision known to the governments of Bohemia and Rumania. It appears to me to be the only practical one.

Mr. Lloyd George. They will accept the boundary we will offer them. You will notice that M. Brătianu, when we asked him a short time ago if he wanted Debreczen, answered no.

President Wilson. These gentlemen will see the Foreign Ministers. The boundary will be fixed, we will tell Hungary: "We won't negotiate with you if you cross that line." At the same time, we will tell our allies of Bohemia and Rumania: "We will send you nothing you ask us for if you violate the boundary drawn."

—The discussion is resumed with the ministers of Czechoslovakia and Rumania.

President Wilson. We wanted to agree amongst ourselves with a view to a practical solution, and here are our conclusions.

The armistice lines and all the temporary conventions have not worked out. We are going to ask our Foreign Ministers to receive you as soon as possible and to arrive at a final decision about the boundaries between the Czechoslovak state and Hungary on the one hand, and between Hungary and Rumania on the other hand. Immediately afterwards, we will say to Hungary: "Here are your boundaries; if you cross them, we refuse to negotiate with you."

We hope you will respect these boundaries and withdraw your troops behind them. On that will depend the assistance which the Allied and Associated Powers will give you.

M. Clemenceau. Does this suit you?

M. Beneš. It is precisely what I asked you for in a letter written two or three days ago.

M. Brătianu. This solution appears reasonable to me; we will have to see how its execution will be guaranteed.

M. Clemenceau. This concerns us. Can't we conclude in twenty-four hours? It is important to send a message to Budapest soon.

CXVIII

Conversation between President Wilson and MM. Clemenceau, Lloyd George, and Orlando*

JUNE 11, 1919, 11 A.M.

Mr. Lloyd George. We are taking up again the text of our reply to the Germans on reparation.[1] I have an addition to propose. To the statement that we will not refuse Germany the means to revive her industry must be added the indication of the priority owed to the reconstruction of industries in the devastated regions. It is obvious, for example, that the industry of Roubaix must have the right to supply itself with Australian wool before German looms do.

President Wilson. Must the entire text be reread?

M. Clemenceau. This text is so important that it is better to reread it entirely. I will indicate some changes of detail proposed by M. Loucheur.

—President Wilson reads aloud the text of the reply on reparation.

President Wilson. I would add a few words to the preamble in order to say that, according to our own definition of damages, we would have been able to ask much more and that we haven't done it.

*H., PPC, VI, 290ff.

[1] This draft, printed in PWW, Vol. 60, pp. 394-99, is not reproduced here. The text as approved at the next meeting is printed as an appendix to the notes of that meeting.

M. Clemenceau. I don't know if it is to our advantage to say that, because our peoples would say to us: "In that case, why haven't you asked for more?" The estimate of damages must be made in each case in agreement with the power concerned. That is necessary in order to avoid having the Germans make proposals that would have no chance of being accepted.

Mr. Lloyd George. I agree with the idea; it all depends on the way in which it is expressed. But isn't it necessary to speak first of the study of the devastations on the spot?

President Wilson. I would rather indicate it amongst the terms imposed on any offer the Germans might make.

M. Clemenceau. Further on, I read that the Allied Powers will not deprive Germany of "the commercial relations and assistance" necessary to her. I would prefer to write "commercial facilities"; this phrase covers everything.

—(Assent.)

Mr. Lloyd George. I propose to decide that these facilities will be subordinated to the necessities of the economic situation created in various countries by German aggression and the consequences of the war.

President Wilson. I would prefer to put: "in certain countries." It is a matter of providing for the special needs of France and Belgium after the devastations.

Mr. Lloyd George. It is not only that. Although only a small part of her territory was devastated, Italy suffered very much economically. Great Britain can in certain cases find herself in a difficult situation which would not allow her to give priority to Germany's needs. I would rather say "in Allied and Associated countries."

President Wilson. In that case, you are making no concession. You are saying to the Germans: "We will give you something if we don't need it."

M. Clemenceau. That is the truth. For, if we need it, that is because the Germans took it from us. In the case of France, you know the systematic destruction they wrought on our factories and our mines in order to destroy our competition.

Mr. Lloyd George. Let us say: "It will be necessary to take into account the special economic situation created by German aggression and the war for the Allied and Associated Powers."

President Wilson. Shall we move on to the question of the occupation?

M. Clemenceau. The text which I have is very complicated. I wrote a dozen lines, which are much clearer and which suffice.

Mr. Lloyd George. Up to now, I have received only a French text,[2] and I haven't yet had time to read it.

M. Clemenceau. You know that I have no objection to your ideas and that they are my own. I simply want to express them clearly and briefly.

Mr. Lloyd George. Wouldn't it be better to begin by seeing the reply to Count Brockdorff-Rantzau's letter?[3] I have it at your disposal.[4]

President Wilson. Mustn't we distribute it amongst us?

M. Clemenceau. It is a long document. We must be able to read it at our leisure.

Mr. Lloyd George. Lord Sumner has written a text[5] on the subject of the offer made by the Germans of five billion pounds; he shows that this offer is illusory, since these five billion pounds would be paid without interest, payments would be spread out over an indefinite period of time, and the Germans want the value of the guns that they handed over to us to be included in the total.

M. Clemenceau. M. Paderewski asked that the Polish army be placed under the command of Marshal Foch. I favor accepting it; it is the way to keep the Poles in hand.

Mr. Lloyd George. Do we have Marshal Foch himself in hand?

M. Clemenceau. If we don't, it is our fault.

[2] *Rapport Présenté au Conseil des Principales Puissances Alliées et Associées par la Commission Interalliée de la Rive Gauche du Rhin*, dated June 9, 1919, Wilson Papers, Library of Congress. For a detailed discussion of this report, see CXXII.

[3] For which, see the appendix to CIII.

[4] That is, Kerr's draft of the general reply, about which, see CXVI, n. 6.

[5] Printed in *PWW*, Vol. 60, pp. 391-92.

[6] Printed in *ibid.*, pp. 406-11.

CXIX

Conversation between President Wilson and MM. Clemenceau, Lloyd George, and Orlando*

JUNE 11, 1919, 4 P.M.

Mr. Lloyd George. Our commercial advisers are a bit frightened about a few words in the text[1] we read this morning concerning the "commercial facilities" we will grant to German commerce. Sir Hubert Llewellyn Smith proposes a changed text which would prevent the Germans from claiming what we couldn't grant them. His formula gives our statement a rather negative form: it is restricted to saying that we don't want to place any obstacles in the way of German commerce.

President Wilson. It is indeed a purely negative formula.

Mr. Lloyd George. Llewellyn Smith says to us: "We must avoid promising what we cannot deliver. All nations will have arrears to recover, which will compel them to defend their own interests."

President Wilson. I believe he did not see our final draft: in the note you give me, he quotes the previous version.

Mr. Lloyd George. I will show him our latest text.

President Wilson. I prefer our draft with the word "commercial facilities," which we have put in this morning. We are doing nothing but saying: "We won't deprive Germany of certain commercial facilities."

Mr. Lloyd George. Lord Sumner says: "The Germans might believe, for example, that we will protect their commercial travelers against the poor welcome awaiting them." This won't be easy.

M. Clemenceau. Nor amongst us.

President Wilson. The question will solve itself in time.

Mr. Lloyd George. If the Germans are wise, they will not send their commercial travelers amongst us for some time.

President Wilson. That is true even in the United States.

Mr. Lloyd George. It is true that we passed a law that will prevent them from visiting England for some years.

*H., PPC, VI, 301ff.

[1] The council had before it a redraft of the document cited in n. 1 to the previous meeting. It is printed in PPC, VI, 305-10. Again, we do not reproduce this draft but print the text as adopted as an appendix below.

President Wilson. In my opinion, that is a debatable measure, unless it is required for reasons of public order.

—Mr. Lloyd George rereads the text of the note.

M. Clemenceau. We can say no less. I think the text must be left as it is.

Mr. Lloyd George. I think we can and must run this risk.

M. Clemenceau. We cannot demand that the Germans give us money whilst refusing them the means to earn it.

President Wilson. In the passage which indicates that the Allies are prepared to consider all evidence, estimates, etc., presented in writing by the Germans, I propose to omit the words "in writing," which would make them think that we will continue, after the signing of the peace, the procedure presently followed regarding the German plenipotentiaries.

—(Assent.)

I will also point out that the supply of foodstuffs to Germany is not mentioned. I would indicate it in the same place as the providing of raw materials.

—(Assent.)

M. Clemenceau. Do you wish to hear the committee[2] on the question of the boundary of Silesia?

Mr. Lloyd George. The members of the Commission on Polish Affairs are very biased in favor of Poland. I prefer not to talk with them.

M. Clemenceau. We must hear them, ask them questions; we will argue only amongst ourselves. For my part, I am against the plebiscite in Upper Silesia. I accept it so as not to create difficulties. In any case, there are areas where the population, having elected Polish delegates, has already made its opinion known.

President Wilson. There might be reason to consider whether the plebiscite should be limited to a part of the province. Mr. Lloyd George distrusts the impartiality of the Commission on Polish Affairs. Mr. Henry White, my colleague, has himself just brought me evidence of systematic action on the part of the German clergy in Silesia in favor of the German cause.

Mr. Lloyd George. That is what the Poles, who are excellent propagandists say; they resemble the Irish in that regard. We are hearing only what comes from a single side; if we listened to the Ger-

[2] The Committee on the Eastern Frontiers of Germany, a sub-committee of the Commission on Polish Affairs. About its report, see *PWW*, Vol. 60, p. 411, n. 2.

mans, they would say the same thing about their adversaries. What is the source of Mr. White's information? I am sure it comes exclusively from a Polish source. Look at what the Poles are saying about the Jews: to hear them, one might believe that they treat them like angels. Everyone knows it is a lie. That is what they say to M. Paderewski.

If we provide a waiting period before the plebiscite, with occupation by Allied troops, I am certain that, to the extent that you can have free elections in any country, you will have them in Silesia. If there should be no plebiscite, I would not myself acknowledge the right to send British troops to get themselves killed for the solution of that question.

President Wilson. Then try also to see the other side of the question. Mr. White did not receive his information from Poles, but from Americans who visited the country. You speak of propagandists: do you know any people more skilled than the Germans in the matter of propaganda? We saw them at work in America; I would never have been able to believe in advance what I saw them do, and let us not forget that, in German Silesia, they are the masters, politically and economically. I beg you not to forget that there are two sides to the question: compared with the Germans, I confess that I am on the side of the Poles.

Mr. Lloyd George. What I fear is that they will fight about that eastern border of Germany, and our troops won't fight for that, if they know that the plebiscite was rejected against the advice of a great power.

President Wilson. Let us be careful, after having vainly sought sacrifices that we ourselves could make, not to make them at the expense of Poland, which is weaker.

Mr. Lloyd George. All I want, as you know, is to avoid having Poland receive territories inhabited by peoples who don't want to be Polish. If that was the case, we certainly couldn't fight to give them to her.

President Wilson. I regret that my words have provoked such a strong reaction from you. I acknowledge, moreover, that you have always taken the same position.

Mr. Lloyd George. I fear a conflict in that region. In the eyes of the Germans, the Poles are an inferior and despised people. To put Germans under the domination of a people whom they regard as inferior is to create the most dangerous source of irritation and trouble.

M. Clemenceau. Never fear; you will have troubles from this source whether or not there is a plebiscite.

Mr. Lloyd George. Really? I don't believe it. Of course, the Germans must withdraw their troops.

M. Clemenceau. Remember what I tell you today.

President Wilson. The experts are of opinion that, in any case, we ourselves must put troops in the country to guarantee a free vote. But won't the Germans object to that?

M. Clemenceau. The Germans have 350,000 men in Silesia; they even bring some from Danzig. I don't believe it is in order to fight, but to say to us: "We are there, and we will stay there."

Mr. Lloyd George. Even if one offers them the plebiscite?

President Wilson. Will your soldiers fight to insure the plebiscite?

Mr. Lloyd George. I believe so, because it is a fair solution. Will French soldiers fight for Upper Silesia to be Polish?

M. Clemenceau. Yes, because that is not the real issue. The question is whether the Germans will or will not sign the treaty.

President Wilson. As for American soldiers, they would support any people against the Germans.

Mr. Lloyd George. I don't know how it is with your soldiers, but I know mine. You know that Lord Northcliffe attacked me in his newspaper for the planned concessions which he ascribes to us. But he came out in favor of the plan for a plebiscite in Silesia; that shows you the unanimity on this point in English public opinion.

—M. Jules Cambon, General Le Rond, Mr. Headlam-Morley, and Dr. Lord are introduced.*

President Wilson. I ask General Le Rond to tell us, concerning Upper Silesia, on what points the experts agree and on what points they differ in opinion.

General Le Rond. Four questions were raised: the territorial question, the one of the plebiscite in Upper Silesia, the question of coal, the financial clauses. There is agreement on the first, the third, and the fourth. Is there any point in talking about them?

M. Clemenceau. What have you decided about coal?

General Le Rond. That the Germans will be able to purchase at the same prices and under the same conditions as the Poles.

M. Clemenceau. There is no mention of quantity?

General Le Rond. No. Concern was shown about preventing the Germans, by their purchases, from causing prices to rise. The experts, being consulted, told us that was an excessive fear. During

---

*H., *PPC*, VI, 311ff.

the first years, Germany won't have means to buy much, and afterwards, the danger will disappear.

President Wilson. Why do you provide a period of fifteen years on this point?

General Le Rond. In the question of the Saar, the period is the same as that which must precede the plebiscite. Here, there is no connection of this kind, but it is preferable to indicate the same period in both cases because of possible repercussions on the coal market.

Mr. Lloyd George. We agree.

General Le Rond. As for the plebiscite, we received instructions from the Four on this subject which were confirmed by President Wilson two days ago. We have two plans to present to you, one in which the plebiscite would take place at the end of a relatively long period of time, the other in which it would take place almost immediately.

The problem must be considered from two points of view: from the point of view of equity and from the practical point of view. From the point of view of equity, it must be said first that the Poles in Upper Silesia are not free. The land belongs to great landowners. The German statistics, the German book by Partsch,[3] show that the greatest part of the country belongs to thirty or forty people; they are veritable feudal lords, more powerful than those of the thirteenth century, for they possess, not only the land, but the subsoil, factories, and capital—such power as was unknown in the Middle Ages.

M. Clemenceau. Is the Prince-Bishop of Breslau not one of these great landowners?

General Le Rond. I don't think that his influence is exercised in that way. I will soon speak of the action of the clergy. The great landowners, by their action of every kind, cover the country like a web. No one is free to express his opinion; this applies, not only to the countryside, but to the industrial centers, where everything belongs to these great landlords.

On the other hand, the clergy has a very considerable influence. Its role has become much more active during the past few years, through the initiative of the Bishop of Breslau, and his effort goes entirely in the German direction.

Since the Armistice, the Germans have done everything possi-

---

[3] Josef Franz Maria Partsch, *Landeskunde der Provinz Schlesien* (Breslau, 1898), or *Schlesien: Eine Landeskunde für das deutsche Volk auf wissenschaftlicher Grundlage*, 2 vols. (Breslau, 1896-1911).

ble to keep Polish opinion in check. The Polish press has been suppressed. Polish priests have been sent to other dioceses. The Germans of Upper Silesia have been organized into a kind of militia, which includes not only residents but Germans from other provinces. At present, the inhabitants are unable to express their feelings freely. Besides, everything is being done to persuade them that separation from Germany would be a disaster for them. For example, they are told that, if Upper Silesia should become Polish, the money in savings banks would be lost.

On all these points—this involves questions of facts—all the members of your committee agree. If the powers wish to hold a plebiscite in Upper Silesia, it is necessary to take measures to be sure that it is genuine. The majority of the committee thinks that this is possibly only after a rather long interval. Time is needed to change a regime so strongly established and to allow the inhabitants to emerge from their prostration. The period that we propose would be a year at the least and two at the most; it is impossible to determine it exactly at present. It should belong to either the great powers or the League of Nations to fix the final date of the plebiscite after a period of one year and before the end of two years.

Mr. Lloyd George. I readily accept that.

General Le Rond. There are eight electoral districts in Upper Silesia. Five were represented in the Reichstag by deputies of the National Polish party.

M. Clemenceau. Did their program include the independence of Poland?

General Le Rond. Under the German regime, it was impossible to make this aspiration the avowed basis of political action.

President Wilson. In any case, there was an openly Polish party in Silesia?

General Le Rond. Yes. Perhaps it would be better if I allowed the arguments in favor of an early plebiscite to be explained by a committee member who was in favor of this method.

Mr. Lloyd George. I believe it is useless to raise the question.

General Le Rond. I am going to indicate how the preparation of the plebiscite is contemplated.

Mr. Lloyd George. Have you something to add to your written report on this subject?

General Le Rond. Naturally, if the plebiscite takes place only after a rather long period of time, the commission established in Silesia to prepare it will have more extended powers.

Mr. Lloyd George. I consider the question settled.

General Le Rond. Then there remains the question of deciding if the date of the plebiscite will be set by the Allied and Associated Powers or by the League of Nations.

Mr. Lloyd George. Either would be equally satisfactory to me.

President Wilson. Can you tell us about the National Polish party of Upper Silesia?

Dr. Lord. Properly speaking, there are two Polish parties in Upper Silesia, one Socialist, the other non-Socialist. Under the German regime, both were working for a united Poland, but one which could only be realized in the indefinite future. The Poles of Silesia were as devoted to the Polish cause as the Poles residing in every other part of the German Empire.

Mr. Lloyd George. But can't their role in German politics be compared to that of the Irish, or even the Welsh, in English politics? These are very attached to their nationality, but even the Irish, until recently, had never seriously thought about separation.

Dr. Lord. The parties just mentioned never put the separation of Upper Silesia in their program; perhaps it was because they didn't believe it possible.

General Le Rond. Since the war, there has been a very marked movement in these areas in favor of union with Poland.

Mr. Lloyd George. I haven't the least doubt about the feeling of that population. The only question before us is to know the strength of this feeling.

Dr. Lord. The two Polish parties in Silesia were affiliated with parties existing in other Polish regions of the German Empire. The Polish Socialists had the unity of Poland in their program, and it is the same with the National Democrats. Naturally, it was impossible, under the Prussian regime, to make statements of this kind in public meetings.

Mr. Lloyd George. We are used to these national movements. In the United Kingdom, they go to a certain point which generally they don't dare pass. Italy might have the same experience with the Yugoslavs.

—The members of the committee withdraw.

President Wilson (*after study of the map*).* I consider it settled that we adopt the plan providing for the plebiscite after a period of one year at least and two years at most. Dr. Lord has just told me that he had recently received a report from an American who visited Upper Silesia. This witness says that all classes of the pop-

---

*H., *PPC*, VI, 316ff.

ulation want the plebiscite. Since Dr. Lord personally opposes it, it is in a spirit of objectivity that he transmitted this information to me. He says that he has confidence in the witness in question.

M. Clemenceau. I have nothing to say in reply. I believe we will have great difficulties in this area. It seemed to me that the more quickly the question was settled the better it would be.

President Wilson. Dr. Lord tells me also that the text prepared by Mr. Headlam-Morley[4] to define the powers of the commission in case of an early plebiscite was, in his opinion, the best, even for a longer period.

—*Reading of the [Headlam-Morley] plan, which is adopted.*

M. Orlando. I suppose that Japan would not have to participate in this affair. In the resolution we just adopted, it is said that the commission will be appointed by the five great powers, which includes Japan.

President Wilson. We can write: "By the principal European powers."

Mr. Lloyd George. You are forgetting America. The simplest thing is to name in the text the powers which will designate the members of the commission.

M. Clemenceau. Is the occupation provided for?

President Wilson. Yes, as well as the right of passage for occupation troops across German territory.

M. Clemenceau. And the evacuation of the German troops?

President Wilson. It is scheduled for the two weeks after the signing of the peace treaty.

There remains a small territorial question to be settled, that of the Ratibor district. When we decided to assign Upper Silesia to Poland outright, the small district of Ratibor was attached to the Czechoslovak state. The establishment of the plebiscite leaves the question of Upper Silesia in suspense, but can't we take Ratibor back from the Czechoslovaks?

M. Clemenceau. We can't go back on a decision of this kind.

President Wilson. Here is another point. Articles 296 and 297 provide that, if Poland takes possession of the property of German citizens who keep their nationality, she will have to indemnify

---

[4] Headlam-Morley's substitute for the original article of the report granted all powers of government, except those of taxation and legislation, to the inter-Allied commission. This commission would replace the government of the province and its administrative units. Moreover, changes in existing law and taxation could only be put into effect with the consent of the commission. See *PWW*, Vol. 60, p. 416, n. 2.

them, subject to reciprocity for Polish citizens who remain in Germany. This arrangement, provided for other provinces, must be applied to Upper Silesia as well.

Mr. Lloyd George. Obviously.

M. Clemenceau. How long a period do you anticipate before the plebiscite?

Mr. Lloyd George. The commission that we are going to set up in Silesia will itself recommend a date after the end of the first year.

M. Clemenceau. And the occupation troops? Who will occupy Upper Silesia?

Mr. Lloyd George. I believe we must all participate in this occupation. I would prefer to see Americans there.

President Wilson. That is a question of whether it is possible. I will consult our military authorities.

M. Clemenceau. Who will pay the costs of the occupation?

M. Orlando. Isn't it the country that will hold sovereignty after the plebiscite?

President Wilson. And in the meantime?

Mr. Lloyd George. Each of us will pay. This is a small thing. But why not make Upper Silesia itself pay, in the end?

President Wilson. That would seem fair to me. But in that case, we must indicate in the text that the expenses of the military occupation and of the commission—which mustn't be forgotten—will be borne by the occupied region.

President Wilson. What is the state of the question of the boundary between Hungary, the Czechoslovaks, and the Rumanians?

M. Clemenceau. M. Brătianu replied that he was compelled to consult the King, and he asked for ten or twelve days, during which M. Mişu has to go to Bucharest and return. I remind you that, when we saw him, he said that he was very satisfied with our solution.

President Wilson. Undoubtedly, he would have been less satisfied seeing the line on the map. But we can't wait ten or twelve days; it is urgent to take a decision.

—Reading of the report of the Ministers of Foreign Affairs on their discussion with the representatives of Rumania and the Czechoslovak state:[5] M. Brătianu was very surprised and said that he could not accept

---

[5] The Council of Foreign Ministers informed Brătianu and Alexandru Vaida-Voevod, a member of the Rumanian delegation, and Kramář and Beneš of the Rumanian-Hungarian and Czechoslovak-Hungarian boundaries which had been agreed upon by the Supreme Council. Brătianu remarked that this was the first time that the decision concerning the Rumanian-Hungarian boundary had been

the decisions taken without referring them to the King of Rumania. M. Kramář accepted the decisions taken, asking only for two small changes, one which would give the Czechoslovaks the central part of the Csatad-Losoncz railroad, the other a territory opposite Pressburg, on the other side of the Danube, in order to avoid having that city itself be on the frontier.

Mr. Lloyd George. The Ministers of Foreign Affairs are making no precise recommendation.

M. Clemenceau. They are only sending back to us the question we sent them; we must ask them for conclusions.

—(*Assent.*)

President Wilson. We will also ask them to remind us if the drawing of these boundaries, where there is no special comment, has already been approved by us.

Mr. Lloyd George. They don't say, moreover, if it is true that M. Brătianu had not been informed of the delimitation that had been decided for the borders of Rumania.

M. Clemenceau. That is the first question I'll ask them.

Sir Maurice Hankey. I must ask you if Admiral Kolchak's reply[6] should be published.

Mr. Lloyd George. My opinion is that must be done.

President Wilson. It is better to reread the text, now that we have it complete.

—Admiral Kolchak's telegram is read.

M. Clemenceau. I favor publishing this text immediately.

Mr. Lloyd George. A copy would have to be sent to the Japanese delegates, and they would have to be asked if they agree with us on publication.

Sir Maurice Hankey. Do you also want to publish your correspondence with Béla Kun?

President Wilson. It is still incomplete.

Sir Maurice Hankey. On the question of minorities, M. Paderewski was to write a letter that the Commission on Minorities is still waiting for.

---

brought to his notice and that he would have to refer the council's decision to the Bucharest government. Kramář said that his delegation accepted the decision concerning the Czechoslovak-Hungarian boundaries on the whole but asked that two slight changes in that boundary line be made. See *PPC*, VI, 320-21.

[6] About which, see CXII, n. 6.

M. Clemenceau. It is on my desk, along with M. Vesnić's letter. I'll bring it tomorrow.

Sir Maurice Hankey. On the question of Klagenfurt, the committee asks that the time of the plebiscite be set by the Council of Four. M. Vesnić, when asked, presented certain observations on this subject; he asks that the plebiscite take place in zone A in one month, and, in zone B, three weeks after the announcement of the results of the plebiscite in zone A.

President Wilson. The best thing is to send this letter back to the commission and to decide only after receiving its advice.

Sir Maurice Hankey. M. Hymans asks that a provision be placed in the treaty regarding German munitions depots, whose presence constitutes a danger in many areas of Belgium. He wants the Germans to be compelled to assist in the removal of these munitions.

M. Clemenceau. This problem arises for all of us. I don't think it necessary to put a special provision in the treaty.

{ A P P E N D I X }[7]

SECRET. W.C.P. 950
1st Revise 11.6.19 (Morning)
2nd Revise 11.6.19. (Afternoon)

REPARATION.
REPLY TO GERMAN COUNTER PROPOSALS.

(Finally approved by the Council of the Principal Allied and Associated Powers on afternoon of June 11th, 1919.)

The Allied and Associated Governments, consistently with their policy already expressed, decline to enter into a discussion of the principles underlying the Reparation Clauses of the Conditions of Peace, which have been prepared with scrupulous regard for the correspondence leading up the Armistice of November 11th, 1918, the final memorandum of which, dated 5th November, 1918, contains the following words:

"Further, in the conditions of Peace laid down in his address to Congress of the 8th January, 1918, the President declared that the invaded territories must be restored as well as evacuated and freed, and the Allied Governments feel that no doubt

---

[7] Printed in *PWW*, Vol. 60, pp 406-11.

ought to be allowed to exist as to what this provision implies. By it they understand that compensation will be made by Germany for all damage done to the civilian population of the Allies and their property by the aggression of Germany by land, by sea, and from the air."

To the extent that your reply deals with practical phases of the execution of the principles enunciated in the Conditions of Peace, you appear to proceed on the basis of a complete misapprehension, which is the more difficult to understand as the inferences you draw and the statements which you make are wholly at variance with both the letter and the spirit of the Treaty Clauses. For purposes of clarification, however, and in order that there may be no possible ground for misunderstanding, the Allied and Associated Governments submit the following observations:

The vast extent and manifold character of the damage caused to the Allied and Associated Governments in consequence of the war, has created a reparation problem of extraordinary magnitude and complexity, only to be solved by a continuing body, limited in personnel and invested with broad powers to deal with the problem in relation to the general economic situation. The Allied and Associated Powers, recognising this situation, themselves delegate power and authority to a Reparation Commission. This Reparation Commission is, however, instructed by the Treaty itself so to exercise and interpret its powers as to ensure in the interest of all, as early and complete a discharge by Germany of her reparation obligations as is consistent with the true maintenance of the social, economic and financial structure of a Germany earnestly striving to exercise her full power to repair the loss and damage she has caused.

The provisions of Article 241, by which the German Government is to invest itself with such powers as may be needed to carry out its obligations, are not to be misconstrued as giving the Commission power to dictate the domestic legislation of Germany. Nor does Paragraph 12 (b), of Annex II, give the Commission power to prescribe or enforce taxes or to dictate the character of the German budget, but it is to examine the latter for two specified purposes. This is necessary in order that it may intelligently and constructively exercise the discretion accorded to it in Germany's interest particularly by Article 234, with regard to extending the date and modifying the form of payments. The provisions of Article 240 with regard to the supply of information are similar in character and purpose and there should be little occasion for the exercise of these powers when once the amount of the liability of Germany is fixed, if Germany is in a position to, and does, comply with the schedule of payments which then will have been notified to her and with the specific provisions of the several Annexes relative to reparation in kind. It is further to be observed that the power of modification accorded by the said Article 236 is expressly designed to permit of a modification *in Germany's interest* of a schedule of payments which events may demonstrate to be beyond Germany's reasonable capacity. The Allied and Associated Powers vigorously reject the suggestion that the Commission, in exercising the power conferred by Article 240 and by Paragraphs 2, 3 and 4 of Annex IV, might require the divulgence of trade secrets and similar confidential data.

The observations of the German Delegation present a view of this Commission so distorted and so inexact, that it is difficult to believe that the clauses of the Treaty have been calmly or carefully examined. It is not an engine of oppression or a device for interfering with German Sovereignty. It has no forces, which it commands; it has no executive powers within the territory of Germany; it cannot, as is suggested, direct or control the educational or other systems of the country. Its business is to fix what is to be paid; to satisfy itself that Germany can pay; and to report to the Powers, whose Delegation it is, in case Germany makes default. If Germany raises the money required in her own way, the Commission cannot order that it shall be raised in some other way; if Germany offers payment in kind, the Commission may accept such payment, but, except as specified in the Treaty itself, the Commission cannot require such a payment. The German observations appear to miss the point that the Commission is directed to study the German system of taxation for the protection of the German people no less than for the protection of their own. Such study is not inquisitorial, for the German system of taxation is not an object of curiosity to other Powers, nor is a knowledge of it an end in itself. If any plea of inability which the German Government may advance, is to be properly considered, such a study is necessary. The Commission must test whether a sincere application is being given to the principle, accepted in the observations "that the German taxation system should impose in general on the taxpayer at least as great a burden as that prevailing in the most heavily burdened of the States represented on the Reparation Commission." If the German resources are to be properly weighed, the first subject of inquiry, and perhaps the first ground for relief, will be the German fiscal burden.

It is understood that the action necessary to give effect to the provisions of Annex IV, relative to reparation in kind, will be taken by Germany on its own initiative, after receipt of notification from the Reparation Commission.

The provisions of the Treaty are in no wise incompatible with the creation by Germany of a Commission which will represent Germany in dealings with the Reparation Commission and which will constitute an instrumentality for such co-operation as may be necessary. The Treaty specifically and repeatedly provides opportunities for the German Government to present facts and arguments with respect to claims and modes of payments, within the limits of the principles and express provisions of the Treaty. This may be done through a commission and no reason is perceived why such a commission could not work in harmony with the Reparation Commission. Certainly this is greatly to be desired. The Allied and Associated Powers are therefore ready to agree to such a procedure as the following:

Immediately after the Treaty is signed, Germany may present and the Allied and Associated Powers will receive and examine such evidence, estimates and arguments (in writing), as she may think fit to present. Such documents need not be final but may be presented subject to corrections and additions.

At any time within four months of the signature of the Treaty, Germany shall be at liberty to submit, and the Allied and Associated Powers will receive and consider, such proposals as Germany may choose to make. In particular, proposals will be acceptable on the following subjects and for the following purposes: Germany may offer a lump sum in settlement of her whole liability, or in settlement of her liability under any of the particular categories which have been decided upon and laid down. Germany may offer to undertake to repair and reconstruct part of the whole of any damaged district, or certain classes of damage in each country or in all the countries which have suffered. Germany may offer labour, materials or technical service for use in such work, even though she does not undertake to do the work herself. She may suggest any practicable plan, category by category, or for the reparations as a whole, which will tend to shorten the period of enquiry and to bring about a prompt and effectual conclusion. Without making further specifications, it may be said in a word that Germany is at liberty to make any suggestion or offer of a practical and reasonable character for the purposes of simplifying the assessment of the damage, eliminating any question or questions from the scope of the detailed enquiry, promoting the performance of the work and accelerating the definition of the ultimate amount to be paid. Suitable facilities for inspecting the damage done will be afforded to Germany's agents at reasonable times. Three conditions and three only are imposed upon the tender of these proposals. Firstly, the German authorities will be expected before making such proposals to confer with the representatives of the Powers directly concerned. Secondly, such offers must be unambiguous, and must be precise and clear. Thirdly, they must accept the categories and the reparation clauses as matters settled beyond discussion. The Allied and Associated Powers will not entertain arguments or appeals directed to any alteration. The Allied and Associated Powers have to remark that in the Observations submitted the German Delegation has made no definite offer at all but only vague expressions of willingness to do something undefined. A sum of £5,000,000,000 is indeed mentioned, and this is calculated to give the impression of an extensive offer, which upon examination it proves not to be. No interest is to be paid at all. It is evident that till 1927 there is no substantial payment but only the surrender of military material and the devolution upon other Powers of large portions of Germany's own debt. Thereafter a series of undefined instalments is to be agreed, which are not to be completed for nearly half a century. The present value of this distant prospect is small, but it is all that Germany tenders to the victims of her aggression in satisfaction of their past sufferings and their permanent burthens.

Within two months thereafter the Allied and Associated Powers will so far as may be possible, return their answer to any proposals that may be made. It is impossible to declare in advance that they will be accepted, and if accepted, they may be subject to conditions, which can be discussed and arranged. The Allied and Associated Powers, however, declare that such proposals will be seriously and fairly considered; no one could be better pleased than they, if, in the result, a fair, a speedy, and a practical settlement were arrived at. The questions are bare questions of fact, namely, the amount of the liabilities, and they are susceptible of being treated in this way. Beyond this, the Powers cannot be asked to go.

The Powers will, however, make a declaration on another point, as follows: The resumption of German industry involves access by the German people to food supplies and by the German manufacturers to the necessary raw materials and provision for their transport to Germany from overseas. The resumption of

German industry is an interest of the Allied and Associated Powers as well as an interest of Germany. They are fully alive to this fact and therefore declare that they will not withhold from Germany (the) commercial facilities without which this resumption cannot take place, but that, subject to conditions and within limits, which cannot be laid down in advance, and, subject also to the necessity for having due regard to the special economic situation created for Allied and Associated countries by German aggression and the war, they are prepared to afford to Germany facilities in these directions for the common good.

Even if no settlement were arrived at, it must be evident that the early production of the German evidence would greatly abbreviate the enquiry, and accelerate the decisions. The information at present at hand comes from one side only. The German Authorities have had long occupation of a large part of the damaged areas and have been over the ground, forwards and backwards, within the last twelve or fifteen months. Their information must be extensive and exact. The Allied and Associated Powers have as yet had no access to this mass of material. The mere comparison of the evidence forthcoming on the one side and the other must greatly narrow the field of dispute and may eliminate dispute altogether. It is obvious that, if the class of damages done in the devastated areas can be dealt with in this fashion, the liability under the other categories can be quickly established, for it depends on statistics and particulars of a far simpler character. By giving a satisfactory covenant to execute the work of rebuilding themselves, the Germans could at once dispose of the only difficult or long subject of inquiry.

Meanwhile, the draft Treaty must be accepted as definitive and must be signed. The Allied and Associated Powers cannot any longer delay to assure their security. Germany cannot afford to deny to her populations the peace which is offered to them. The Reparation Commission must be constituted and must commence its task. The only question open will be how best to execute the provisions of the Treaty.

The foregoing should suffice to demonstrate the reasonableness of the conditions under which Germany is to discharge her reparation obligations, and how utterly unfounded are the criticisms of the German reply. These are, indeed, explicable only on the theory that the German plenipotentiaries have read into the Conditions of Peace, in clear defiance of their express terms, an intent which it would be not unnatural to see evidenced by victorious nations which have been the victims of cruelty and dev-

astation on a vast and premeditated scale. The burdens of Germany undeniably are heavy, but they are imposed under conditions of justice by peoples whose social well-being and economic prosperity have been gravely impaired by wrongs which it is beyond the utmost power of Germany to repair.
Paris.
11th June, 1919.

CXX

Conversation between President Wilson, MM. Clemenceau and Lloyd George, and Baron Makino*

JUNE 12, 1919, 11 A.M.

M. Clemenceau. I have a word to say on the Hungarian question. I saw M. Pichon yesterday; he reminded me that we had in fact taken a decision on the subject of the Rumanian frontier in a session of the Council of Ten, and it is true that M. Brătianu had not been officially informed of that decision. But he has undoubtedly known it for a long time.

The question of the small rectifications of the border requested by the Czechoslovaks presents no difficulties and will be settled this afternoon. This evening, we will send a telegram to Béla Kun on this latter question. It is urgent to send a note to Béla Kun; in the meantime, the Hungarians continue to advance on Czechoslovak territory.

I call to your attention a telegram from Count Brockdorff-Rantzau, which we intercepted. He tells his government to prepare the German press to make the public understand that the small concessions we might make are not worth much; it is on the treaty as a whole that a decision will have to be taken.

Mr. Lloyd George. Good, we'll see.

—Study of the reply drafted by Mr. Philip Kerr to the cover letter of the German counterproposals.[1] *The text of that reply is approved.*

*H., *PPC*, VI, 334ff.

[1] It is printed as Appendix I to these notes. It was later sent as the cover letter to the general note to the Germans of June 16.

Mr. Lloyd George. After the reply given by Admiral Kolchak, we decided to support him.

Baron Makino. We must leave no doubt that we acknowledge the satisfactory character of this reply.

M. Clemenceau. It is best to express this satisfaction. In our correspondence with Admiral Kolchak, what have we promised to send him by way of support?

Mr. Lloyd George. We did not promise to send him men. You will recall that there was a sentence in our first draft about the volunteers who might leave for Russia; we omitted it.

M. Clemenceau. From my point of view, that is better.

Mr. Lloyd George. What is curious is that, at this time, one would find in England as many volunteers as one might want.

Baron Makino. Then the Allied and Associated governments will reply to Admiral Kolchak that his assurances satisfy them?

M. Clemenceau. I will do it in your name.

Mr. Lloyd George. Won't we be compelled to guarantee the boundaries of Germany?

M. Clemenceau. What? We recognize them, that is enough.

Mr. Lloyd George. I am thinking of the danger that a weakened Germany might be attacked by her neighbors; these little peoples have their freedom, but that doesn't satisfy them, they only think about aggrandizement.

M. Clemenceau. For the moment, all we have to do is to fix their boundaries.

M. Clemenceau. The German White Book on war responsibilities,[2] which has just appeared, seems tied to the German counterproposals to which we are preparing our reply.[3] Would it not be necessary to answer it specifically?

President Wilson. We can't enter now into a great historical debate.

Mr. Lloyd George. On the other hand, we cannot leave unanswered the note from the Germans about their responsibility.

M. Clemenceau. I don't believe you could do it without having examined their White Book. I add that, as far as French public opinion is concerned, it is pointless, because our minds are made up.

---

[2] [German Foreign Office] *Is Germany guilty? German White-book concerning the Responsibilities of the Authors of the War* (Berlin, 1919). This was the first of a myriad of such "revisionist" treatises.

[3] The council had before it a draft, also prepared by Philip Kerr, on the responsibility of Germany for the war and the legal basis of the peace negotiations. It is printed in *PWW*, Vol. 60, pp. 451-59. A slightly revised and enlarged version of the first part of Kerr's memorandum was incorporated in the general reply to the Germans on June 16 and is printed in *PPC*, VI, 957-61.

President Wilson. All that we need to do is to reject the German affirmation that Germany is not responsible for the war. It is enough to reply that we don't believe a word of what the German government says.

M. Clemenceau. I will see if the Quai d'Orsay can send you the translation of the White Book.

Mr. Lloyd George. Do you accept the text prepared for the reply to the preamble of the counterproposals?

M. Clemenceau. In my opinion, this text will weaken the effect of the reply to the cover letter with the German counterproposals. It is not bad in itself, but it resembles a review article more than a political manifesto.

Mr. Lloyd George. This text can be helpful if we are later compelled to resume hostilities because the Germans refuse to sign. Then it will be necessary to remind our peoples of the responsibility of the Germans, the teaching of their universities for fifty years, the preparation of the entire nation for war.

Sir Maurice Hankey. What time limit do the governments provide for Germany's final reply? Seven days?

M. Clemenceau. I propose five days; that is what the members of the German delegation themselves have asked for.

—(Assent.)

Present Wilson. The next question to which we are replying to the Germans is that of the League of Nations. I have the modified text of Colonel House and Lord Robert Cecil and a new text by M. Clemenceau.[4]

—Reading of M. Clemenceau's text on the possible admission of Germany into the League of Nations.

Mr. Lloyd George. It is an excellent paragraph, and I propose to substitute it for the prepared text.

—(Adopted.)

M. Clemenceau. In the paragraph on disarmament, I propose to omit the last lines and to conclude by saying simply that the reduction of armaments in the entire world will depend above all on the faithful execution of the treaty by the Germans.

President Wilson. The difference between Lord Robert Cecil's modified text and M. Clemenceau's is that the first offers the Germans hope of early admission into the League of Nations.

[4] The council had before it a revised version of the text discussed in CXIII. It is printed in PPC, VI, 339-40. Clemenceau's text is missing.

M. Clemenceau. I will do all that I can towards that end; but what I cannot do is to say it today to the French people.

Mr. Lloyd George. It is a matter of obtaining the signature of the Germans.

M. Clemenceau. Don't believe it will change anything.

President Wilson. We are told from all sides that admission into the League of Nations is one of the questions which most concerns them.[5]

Mr. Lloyd George. Concerning the question of the occupation,[6] the regime to be established in the occupied territories depends on the duration of the occupation itself. If the period of occupation is long, the regime must be as lenient as possible. For my part, I would prefer a short occupation, even if the regime has to be more severe.

M. Clemenceau. Don't ask me to shorten the duration of the occupation.

President Wilson. Wouldn't you agree to reexamine that question of the duration of the occupation after a certain date?

M. Clemenceau. I am prepared to commit myself, just amongst ourselves, to come back to this question if we see that the Germans are doing all they can to carry out the treaty.

Mr. Lloyd George. I must speak to Mr. Bonar Law about it. But if I encounter difficulties in Parliament in winning acceptance of the military guarantee that I promised you, will I be able to say that, for your part, you have promised possibly to reconsider the clauses relating to the period of occupation?

M. Clemenceau. I see great difficulties in that.

Mr. Lloyd George. I shall tell you why. This question causes me great difficulties. I could provoke a crisis in my government and in the Labour party. Mr. Barnes, who represents the working class in our delegation, threatens to leave if no change is made. I ask you to help me.

M. Clemenceau. I believe it can be arranged. We can draft something that will satisfy you and that you can quote. Whatever we do, I am of opinion that we shouldn't hide it.

---

[5] The text of the council's reply on the League of Nations as finally approved is printed as Appendix II to these notes.

[6] They had before them the text of a French-language draft, cited in CXVIII, n. 2, of an Anglo-French-American draft agreement on the occupation of the left bank. Since Lloyd George had only the French-language version available, the Four agreed to postpone consideration of the document. They came back to it on June 13 at 12 noon, when they all had an English-language version in hand. For the text of this document, see the appendix to CXXII.

Mr. Lloyd George. This occupation has no other aim than to protect the French government against the opposition. In my opinion, it will serve no use, for it will only last during the period when Germany is weakest; it will be a danger for France and for the peace of Europe. All we can do is to try to make it as inoffensive as possible.

M. Clemenceau. That's a point of view I can't accept. We need a guarantee for the execution of the financial clauses. Please believe that military considerations have nothing to do with this question. In 1871, the German army occupied French territory until payment of that indemnity, and it did not leave before the last sou had been paid. The situation is the same, on a larger scale. It is a matter of reminding Germany that she owes us money and must pay it. I don't see the danger for Europe. The French army is disciplined, and we are keeping it in hand. I am determined to keep our commitments, I am determined to do nothing that could compromise the peace. Without agreeing with you on your premises, I agree with your conclusions.

As for the occupation arrangement, I accept completely what satisfies President Wilson. I don't see the advantage of having certain questions treated by civilian commissions and others by military authorities. I would combine everything, except the command of troops, in the hands of the civilian commission.

—President Wilson reads aloud the reply to the German counterproposals on the Saar Basin.[7]

Mr. Lloyd George. I have only one observation to make: we must recall at the end that the contemplated arrangement is purely temporary.

{ A P P E N D I X   I }[8]

Confidential
M. 256.   DRAFT LETTER

The Allied and Associated Powers have given the most earnest consideration to the observations of the German Delegation on the draft Treaty of Peace. The reply protests against the peace both on the ground that it conflicts with the terms upon which the Armistice of November 11th, 1918, was signed, and that it is

---

[7] It is printed in *PWW*, Vol. 60, pp. 460-62.
[8] Printed in *ibid.*, pp. 442-51.

a peace of violence and not of justice. The protest of the German Delegation shows that they utterly fail to understand the position in which Germany stands to-day. They seem to think that Germany has only to "make sacrifices in order to attain peace," as if this were but the end of some mere struggle for territory and power. The Allied and Associated Powers therefore feel it necessary to begin their reply by a clear statement of the judgment of the war which has been formed by practically the whole of civilised mankind.

In the view of the Allied and Associated Powers the war which began on August 1st, 1914, was the greatest crime against humanity and the freedom of peoples that any nation, calling itself civilised, has ever consciously committed. For many years the rulers of Germany, true to the Prussian tradition, strove for a position of dominance in Europe. They were not satisfied with that growing prosperity and influence to which Germany was entitled, and which all other nations were willing to accord her, in the society of free and equal peoples. They required that they should be able to dictate and tyrannise to a subservient Europe, as they dictated and tyrannised over a subservient Germany. In order to attain their ends they used every channel with which to educate their own subjects in the doctrine that might was right in international affairs. They never ceased to expand German armaments by land and sea, and to propagate the falsehood that it was necessary because Germany's neighbours were jealous of her prosperity and power. They sought to show hostility and suspicion instead of friendship between nations. They even developed a system of espionage and intrigue which enabled them to stir up internal rebellion and unrest and even to make secret offensive preparations, within the territory of their neighbours, whereby they might, when the moment came, strike them down with greater certainty and ease. They kept Europe in a ferment by threats of violence and when they found that their neighbours were resolved to resist their arrogant will, they determined to assist their predominance in Europe by force. As soon as their preparations were complete, they decided, in conjunction with a subservient colleague, to declare war at 48 hours' notice over a matter which could not be localised and had long been a subject of European concern, knowing perfectly well that this almost certainly meant a general war. In order to make doubly sure, they refused every attempt at conciliation and conference until it was too late, and the world war was inevitable for which they had plotted, and for which alone among the nations they were adequately equipped and prepared.

Germany's responsibility, however, is not confined to having planned and started the war. She is no less responsible for the savage and inhuman manner in which it was conducted. Though Germany was itself the guarantor of Belgium, the rulers of Germany violated, after the solemn promise to respect it, the neutrality of this unoffending people. Not content with this they deliberately carried out a series of promiscuous shootings and burnings with the sole object of terrifying the inhabitants into submission by the very frightfulness of their action. Their conduct of the war was animated by exactly the same disregard for humanity or law. They were the first to use poisonous gas, notwithstanding the appalling suffering it entailed. They began the bombing and long distance shelling of towns for no military object, but solely for the purpose of reducing the morale of their opponents by striking at their women and children. They commenced the submarine campaign with its piratical challenge to international law, and its destruction of great numbers of innocent passengers and sailors, in mid-ocean, far from succour, at the mercy of the winds and the waves, and the yet more ruthless submarine crews. They drove thousands of men and women and children with brutal savagery into slavery in foreign lands. They allowed barbarities to be practised against their prisoners of war from which the most uncivilised peoples would have recoiled. The conduct of Germany is almost unexampled in human history. The terrible responsibility which lies at her doors can be seen in the fact that not less than seven million dead lie buried in Europe, while more than twenty million others carry upon them the evidence of wounds and sufferings, because Germany saw fit to gratify her lust for tyranny by resort to war.

The Allied and Associated Powers believe that they will be false to those who have given their all to save the freedom of the world if they consent to treat this war on any other basis than as a crime against humanity and right.

This attitude of the Allied and Associated Powers was made perfectly clear to Germany during the war by their principal statesmen. It was defined by President Wilson in his speech of September 27th, 1918, and explicitly and categorically accepted by the German people as a principle governing the peace:

"If it be in truth," he said, "the common object of the Governments associated against Germany and of the nations whom they govern, as I believe it to be, to achieve by the coming settlement a secure and lasting peace, it will be necessary that all who sit down at the peace table shall come ready and willing to pay the price, the only price, that will procure it, and ready and willing also to create in some virile fashion the only instrumentality by which it can be made certain that the agreement of the peace will be honoured and fulfilled. That price is impartial justice in every item of the settlement, no matter whose interest is crossed; and not only impartial justice, but also the satisfaction of the several peoples whose fortunes are dealt with."

It was set forth clearly in a speech of the Prime Minister of Great Britain dated 14th December 1917:

"There is no security in any land without certainty of punishment. There is no protection for life, property or money in a State where the criminal is more powerful than the law. The law of nations is no exception, and, until it has been vindicated, the peace of the world will always be at the mercy of any nation whose professors have assiduously taught it to believe that no crime is wrong so long as it leads to the aggrandisement and enrichment of the country to which they owe allegiance. There have been many times in the history of the world criminal States. We are dealing with one of them now. And there will always be criminal states until the reward of international crime becomes too precarious to make it profitable, and the punishment of international crime becomes too sure to make it attractive."

It was made clear also in an address of Monsieur Clemenceau of September 1918:

"What do they (the French soldiers) want? What do we ourselves want? To fight, to fight victoriously and unceasingly, until the hour when the enemy shall understand that no compromise is possible between such crime and 'justice.' "

Similarly, Signor Orlando, speaking on October 3rd, 1918, declared—

"We shall obtain Peace when our enemies recognise that humanity has the right and duty to safeguard itself against a continuation of such causes as have brought about this terrible slaughter; and that the blood of millions of men calls not for vengeance but for the realisation of those high ideals for which it has been so generously shed. Nobody thinks of employing— even by way of legitimate retaliation—methods of brutal violence or of overbearing domination or of suffocation of the freedom of any people—methods and policies which made the whole world rise against the Central Powers. But nobody will contend that the moral order can be restored simply because he who falls in his iniquitous endeavour declares that he has renounced his aim. Questions intimately affecting the peaceful life of Nations, once raised, must obtain the solution which Justice requires."

Justice, therefore, is the only possible basis for the settlement of the accounts of this terrible war. Justice is what the German Delegation asks for and says that Germany had been promised. Justice is what Germany shall have. But it must be justice for all. There must be justice for the dead and wounded and for those who have been orphaned and bereaved that Europe might be freed from Prussian despotism. There must be justice for the peoples who now stagger under war debts which exceed £30,000,000,000 that liberty might be saved. There must be justice for those millions whose homes and land, ships and property German savagery has spoliated and destroyed.

That is why the Allied and Associated Powers have insisted as a cardinal feature of the Treaty that Germany must undertake to make reparation to the very uttermost of her power, for reparation for wrongs inflicted is of the essence of justice. That is why they insist that those individuals who are most clearly responsible for German aggression and for those acts of barbarism and inhumanity which have disgraced the German conduct of the war must be handed over to a justice which has not been meted out to them at home. That, too, is why Germany must submit for a few years to certain special disabilities and arrangements. Germany has ruined the industries, the mines and the machinery of Belgium, Northern France, and Poland, not during battle, but with the deliberate and calculated purpose of enabling her own industries to seize her neighbour's markets before their own industries could recover from the devastation thus wantonly inflicted upon them. Germany has despoiled her neighbours of everything she could make use of or carry away. Germany has destroyed the shipping of all nations in the high seas, where there was no chance of rescue for their passengers and crews. It is only justice that restitution should be made and that these wronged peoples should be protected for a time from the competition of a nation whose industries are intact and have even been fortified by machinery stolen from occupied territories. If these things are hardships for Germany, they are hardships which Germany has brought upon herself. Somebody must suffer for the consequences of the war. Is it to be Germany or the peoples she has wronged?

Not to do justice to all concerned would only leave the world open to fresh calamities. If the German people themselves, or any other nation, are to be deterred from following the footsteps of Prussia; if mankind is to be lifted out of the belief that war for selfish ends is legitimate to any State; if the old era is to be left behind and nations as well as individuals are to be brought beneath the reign of law, even if there is to be early reconciliation and appeasement, it will be because those responsible for concluding the war have had the courage to see that justice is not deflected for the sake of convenient peace.

It is said that the German Revolution ought to make a difference and that the German people are not responsible for the policy of the rulers whom they have thrown from power. The Allied and Associated Powers recognise and welcome the change. It represents a great hope for peace, and a new European order in the future. But it cannot affect the settlement of the war itself. The German Revolution was stayed until the German armies had been defeated in the field, and all hope of profiting by a war of conquest had vanished. Throughout the war, as before the war, the German people and their representatives supported the war, voted the credits, subscribed to the war loans, obeyed every order, however savage, of their government. They shared the responsibility for the policy of their government, for at any moment, had they willed it, they could have reversed it. Had that policy succeeded they would have acclaimed it with the same enthusiasm with which they welcomed the outbreak of the war. They cannot now pretend, having changed their rulers after the war was lost, that it is justice that they should escape the consequences of their deeds.

II.

The Allied and Associated Powers therefore believe that the peace they have proposed is fundamentally a peace of justice. They are no less certain that it is a peace of right on the terms agreed. There can be no doubt as to the intentions of the Allied and Associated Powers to base the settlement of Europe on the principle of freeing oppressed peoples and re-drawing national boundaries as far as possible in accordance with the will of the peoples concerned, while giving to each facilities for living an independent national and economic life. If there is any doubt upon this point they would refer to the section of the attached Memorandum which deals with the legal basis of the peace.

Accordingly the Allied and Associated Powers have provided for the reconstitution of Poland as an independent state with "free and secure access to the sea." All "territories inhabited by indubitably Polish populations" have been accorded to Poland.

All territory inhabited by German majorities, save for a few isolated towns and for colonies established on land recently forcibly expropriated and situated in the midst of indubitably Polish territory, have been left to Germany. Wherever the will of the people is in doubt a plebiscite has been provided for. The town of Danzig has been constituted as a free city, so that the inhabitants are autonomous and do not come under Polish rule and form no part of the Polish State. Poland has been given certain economic rights in Danzig and the city itself has been severed from Germany because in no other way was it possible to provide for that "free and secure access to the sea" which Germany has promised to concede. The justification for the proposals can be seen from the following table:
[Blank]
The German counter-proposals entirely conflict with the agreed basis of peace. They provide that great majorities of indisputably Polish population shall be kept under German rule. They deny secure access to the sea to a nation of over twenty million people (whose nationals are in the majority all the way to the coast), in order to maintain territorial connection between East and West Prussia, whose trade has always been mainly seaborne. They cannot, therefore, be accepted by the Allied and Associated Powers. At the same time in certain cases the German Note has established a case for rectification which will be made (see Appendix) and in view of the German contention that Upper Silesia though inhabited by a two to one majority of Poles (1,250,000 to 650,000, 1910 German census) wishes to remain a part of Germany they are willing that the question of whether or not Upper Silesia should form part of Germany or of Poland, should be determined by the vote of the inhabitants themselves.

In regard to the Saar basin the régime proposed by the Allied and Associated Powers is to continue for fifteen years; this arrangement they considered necessary both to the general scheme for reparation, and in order that France may have immediate and certain compensation for the wanton destruction of her Northern coal mines. The district has been transferred not to French sovereignty, but to the control of the Society of the League of Nations. This method has the double advantage that it involves no annexation, while it gives possession of the coal field to France and maintains the economic unity of the district, so important to the interests of the inhabitants. At the end of fifteen years the mixed population which in the meanwhile will have had control of its own local affairs under the governing supervision of the League of Nations, will have complete freedom to decide whether it wishes union with Germany, union with France, or the continuance of the régime provided for in the Treaty.

As to the territories which it is proposed to transfer from Germany to Denmark and Belgium, some of these were robbed by Prussia by force, and in every case the transfer will only take place as the result of a decision of the inhabitants themselves taken under conditions which will ensure complete freedom to vote.

Finally, the Allied and Associated Powers are satisfied that the native inhabitants of the German colonies are strongly opposed to being again brought under Germany's sway, and the record of German rule, the traditions of the German Government and the use to which these colonies were put as bases from which to prey upon the commerce of the world, make it impossible for the Allied and Associated Powers to return them to Germany, or to entrust to her the responsibility for the training and education of their inhabitants.

For these reasons the Allied and Associated Powers are satisfied that their territorial proposals are in accord both with the agreed basis of peace and are necessary to the future peace of Europe. They are therefore not prepared to modify them except in the respects laid down.

III.

Arising out of the territorial settlement are the proposals in regard to international control of rivers. It is clearly in accord with the agreed basis of the peace that inland states should have secure access to the sea along rivers which are navigable to their territory. In the case therefore of four international rivers, the Allied and Associated Powers propose to place those waterways under control of international boards. They believe that this arrangement is vital to the free life of the inland states. They do not think that it is any derogation of the rights of the other riparian states. If viewed according to the discredited doctrine that every state is engaged in a desperate struggle for ascendancy over its neighbours, no doubt such an arrangement may be an impediment to the artificial strangling of a rival. But if it be the ideal that nations are to co-operate in the ways of commerce and peace, it is natural and right. The provisions for the presence of representatives of the League of Nations on the boards is security that the river boards will consider the interests of all. A number of modifications however have been made in the original proposals, the details of which will be found in the attached memorandum.

IV. Economic and Financial.

Under the heading of economic and financial clauses the German Delegation appear to have seriously misinterpreted the proposals of the Allied and Associated Powers. There is no intention on the part of the Allied and Associated Powers to strangle Germany or to prevent her from resuming her proper place in international trade and commerce. Provided that she abides by the Treaty of Peace, and provided also that she abandons those aggressive and exclusive traditions which have been apparent in her business no less than her political methods the Allied and Associated Powers intend that Germany shall have fair treatment in the purchase of raw materials and the sale of goods, subject to those temporary provisions already mentioned in the interests of the nations ravaged and artificially weakened by German action. It is their desire that the passions engendered by the war should die as soon as possible, and that all nations should share equally in the prosperity which comes from the honest supply of each others needs. They wish that Germany shall enjoy their prosperity like the rest, though much of the fruit of it must necessarily go for many years to come, in making reparation to her neighbours for the damage she has done. In order to make their intention clear, a number of modifications have been made in the financial and economic clauses of the Treaty, details of which will be found in the memorandum attached. But the principles upon which the Treaty is drawn must stand.

REPARATION.

The German Delegation have greatly misinterpreted the Reparation proposal of the Treaty. They confine the amounts payable by Germany to certain specific categories clearly justified by the terms of the armistice. They do not provide for that interference in the internal life of Germany by the Reparation Commission which is alleged. They are designed to make the payment of that reparation which Germany must make as easy and convenient to both parties as possible and they will be interpreted in that sense. The Allied and Associated Powers therefore are not prepared to modify them.

But they recognise with the German Delegation, the advantage of arriving as soon as possible at the fixed and definite sum which shall be payable by Germany and accepted by the Allies. It is not possible to fix this sum to-day, for the extent of damage and the cost of repair has not yet been ascertained. They are therefore willing to accord to Germany all necessary and reasonable facilities to enable her to survey the devastated and damaged regions, and to make proposals thereafter within four months of the signing of the Treaty for a settlement of the claims under each of the categories of damage for which she is liable. If within the following two months an agreement can be reached, the exact liability of Germany will have been ascertained. If agreement has not been reached by then, the arrangement as provided in the Treaty will be executed. Full details will be found in the annexed memorandum.

LEAGUE OF NATIONS.

The Allied and Associated Powers have given careful consideration to the request of the German Delegation that Germany should be admitted to the League of Nations as one of the conditions of peace. They regret that they cannot accede to this request. The German revolution was postponed to the last moments of the war and there is as yet no guarantee that it represents a permanent change. In the present temper of international feeling, it is impossible to expect the free nations of the world to sit down immediately in equal association with those by whom they have been so grievously wronged. To attempt this too soon would delay and not hasten that process of appeasement which all desire. But the Allied and Associated Powers believe that if the German people prove by their acts that they intend to fulfil the conditions of the peace, and that they have abandoned forever those aggressive and estranging policies which caused the war, and have now become a people with whom it is possible to live in neighbourly good fellowship, the memories of the past years will speedily fade, and it will be possible within a reasonable time to complete the League of Nations by the admission of Germany thereto. It is their earnest hope that this may be the case. They believe that the prospects of the world depend upon the close and friendly co-operation of all nations in adjusting international questions and promoting the welfare and progress of mankind. But the early entry of Germany into the League must depend principally upon the action of the German people themselves.

CONCLUSION.

In conclusion the Allied and Associated Powers must make it clear that this letter and the memorandum attached constitute their last word. They have examined the German observations and counter proposals with earnest attention and care. They have, in consequence, made important modifications in the Draft Treaty. But in its fundamental outlines they stand by the Treaty. They believe that it is not only a just settlement of the great war, but that it provides the basis upon which the peoples of Europe can live together in friendship and equality. At the same time it creates the machinery for the peaceful adjustment of all international problems by discussion and consent, and whereby the settlement of 1919 itself can be modified from time to time to suit new facts and new conditions as they arise. It is frankly not based upon a general condonation of the events of 1914-1918. It would not be a peace of justice if it were. But it represents a sincere and deliberate attempt to establish "that reign of law, based upon the consent of the governed, and sustained by the organised opinion of mankind" which was the agreed basis of the peace.

As such it must be accepted or rejected as it now stands. The Allied and Associated Powers therefore require a declaration from the German Delegation within five days as to whether they are prepared to sign the Treaty as now amended. If they are willing to do so, arrangements will be made for the immediate signature of the Peace of Versailles. If they refuse the armistice will terminate and the Allied and Associated Powers will take such steps as they think needful to enforce their terms.

Villa Majestic, Paris. June 12th, 1919.

{ APPENDIX II }[9]

(Revised) THE LEAGUE OF NATIONS.
REPLY TO THE GERMAN PROPOSALS.

(Approved by the Council of the Principal Allied and Associated Powers on 12th June, 1919.)

1. The pact of the League of Nations constitutes for the Allied and Associated Powers the base of the Treaty of Peace. They have weighed with care all its terms. They are convinced that it brings into the relations of peoples, for the benefit of justice and of peace, an element of progress which the future will confirm and develop.

The Allied and Associated Powers have never, as the text itself of the Treaty proves, had the intention of indefinitely excluding Germany or any other power from the League. They have taken

[9] Printed in *ibid.*, pp. 459-60.

measures accordingly which apply as a whole to the states which are not members and which fix the conditions for their subsequent admission.

Every country whose government shall have clearly proved its stability, as well as its desire to observe its International obligations—particularly those obligations which result from the Treaty of Peace—will find the Principal Allied and Associated Powers disposed to support its demand for admission to the League.

In that which especially concerns Germany it goes without saying, that the events of the last five years are not of a nature to justify, at the present time, an exception to the general rule which has just been mentioned. Its case demands a definite test. The length of this delay will depend on the acts of the German Government, and it is within the choice of that Government, by its attitude towards the Treaty of Peace, to shorten the period of waiting which the Allied and Associated Governments may consider it necessary to fix, without any intention of prolonging it unduly.

They see no reason, provided these necessary conditions are assured, why Germany should not become a member of the League in the early future.

2. The Allied and Associated Powers do not consider that an addition to the Covenant in the sense of the German proposals regarding economic questions is necessary. They would point out that the Covenant already provides that "subject to and in accordance with the provisions of international conventions existing or hereafter to be agreed upon, the Members of the League * * * will make provision to secure and maintain freedom of communications and of transit, and equitable treatment for the commerce of all Members of the League," and that a General Convention with regard to Transit questions is now being prepared. So soon as Germany is admitted to the League, she will enjoy the benefits of those provisions.

3. The Allied and Associated Powers are prepared to accord to Germany guarantees, under the protection of the League of Nations, for the educational, religious and cultural rights of German Minorities in territories hitherto forming part of the German Empire. They take note of the statement of the German Delegates that Germany is determined to treat foreign minorities within her territory according to the same principles.

4. The Allied and Associated Powers have already pointed out to the German Delegates that the Covenant of the League of

Nations provides for "the reduction of national armaments to the lowest point consistent with national safety and the enforcement by common action of international obligations." They recognise that the acceptance by Germany of the terms laid down for her own disarmament will facilitate and hasten the accomplishment of a general reduction of armaments; they intend to open negotiations immediately with a view to the eventual adoption of a scheme of such general reduction. It goes without saying that the realisation of this programme will depend in large part on the satisfactory carrying out by Germany of its own engagements.
Villa Majestic, Paris, 12th June, 1919.

CXXI

Conversation between President Wilson, MM. Clemenceau, Lloyd George, and Orlando, and Baron Makino[*]

JUNE 12, 1919, 4 P.M.

—Mr. Lloyd George proposes a text for the reply to Admiral Kolchak[1] and adds:

We cannot do more than promise him our support. It is impossible to recognize his government as the one of all Russia. We don't know what will happen after the fall of the Bolsheviks. A new situation can arise, and all that we can do is to promise Admiral Kolchak to support him.

Baron Makino. It is not recognition, but it is a move in that direction.

M. Clemenceau. Shall we publish this reply?

Mr. Lloyd George. Certainly, along with all the correspondence of which it constitutes the conclusion.

[*] H., PPC, VI, 348ff.

[1] Printed in PPC, VI, 356, it reads as follows: "The Allied and Associated Powers wish to acknowledge receipt of Admiral Koltchak's reply to their note of May 26th. They welcome the tone of that reply, which seems to them to be in substantial agreement with the propositions which they had made, and to contain satisfactory assurances for the freedom, self-government, and peace of the Russian people and their neighbours. They are therefore willing to extend to Admiral Koltchak and his associates the support set forth in their original letter."

Baron Makino. It will certainly be an encouragement for Admiral Kolchak.

Mr. Lloyd George. I am pressed again to publish the text of the treaty. I have no strong feeling about that. Sir George Riddell tells me that the English press demands this text and will publish it if we see no objection to it.

M. Clemenceau. Obviously, it would be rather ridiculous to oppose it. You see what is happening in America, where texts have been published in spite of everything.

Mr. Lloyd George. The position of certain American senators is rather odd—if you allow this observation from a foreigner.

President Wilson. It doesn't seem to me necessary to publish today a text that doesn't conform precisely to the one which will be signed in a few days by the Germans.

Mr. Lloyd George. We can let it be published at the same time as our reply to the Germans.

M. Clemenceau. Upon reflection, I think we have gone too far in the other direction, and that it is now too late to change our position.

President Wilson. Believe me, it is better to publish the treaty only in its final form.

M. Orlando. Will it be made known to the parliaments as soon as it takes this final form?

M. Clemenceau. We have said nothing about the parliaments. The moment we make the treaty known to them will depend on the reply from the Germans.

Mr. Lloyd George. The reply to the German counterproposals is made up of a series of bits and pieces, which must then be coordinated, whilst making sure that nothing is missing. I propose to establish a small committee for that.

—(Assent.)

Mr. Lloyd George. That committee will be made up of Messrs. Tardieu, Philip Kerr, Manley Hudson, Saburi, and Count Vanutelli.

—President Wilson reads the reply to the German counterproposals on the clauses relating to Alsace-Lorraine.[2] *This text is approved.*

---

[2] "*Draft Reply*: Alsace Lorraine," June 8, 1919, printed in *ibid.*, pp. 356-58. This document stated that the clauses of the German treaty relating to Alsace and Lorraine were "but the application of the 8th of the 14 Points which Germany, at the time of the Armistice, accepted as the basis of Peace; 'the injustice committed by Prussia towards France in 1871, as regards Alsace and Lorraine ... must be repaired....'" This injustice consisted in "the annexation of a

President Wilson. The Commission on Czechoslovak Affairs calls our attention to the fact that the holding of a plebiscite in Upper Silesia requires that the border of the Czechoslovak state in the Ratibor district be defined. We must hear the experts on this matter.

—(*Assent.*)

—The report of the Council of Foreign Ministers on the meeting of June 12 at 10 a.m. is read aloud.[3]

1. It is true that the decision taken about the eastern boundary of Rumania was not officially communicated to M. Brătianu. But that was in conformity with precedents, since decisions of this kind have always been communicated to small powers only in secret plenary sessions which have preceded the communication of texts of treaties with the enemy powers.

President Wilson. That means that M. Brătianu knew nothing officially; but he was informed.

—Continuation of the reading.

2. M. Brătianu contests the delimitation of the boundary between Hungary and Rumania. M. Mişu was sent to Bucharest to consult the King and will not return for ten days. The Council of Foreign Ministers stands behind the conclusions of the commission.

3. Concerning the Czechoslovak boundary, the modification asked for around Pressburg is not granted since the Danube constitutes the best frontier. But a slight change of the line will give the Czechoslovaks the junction between the Karpona line and that from Komarom to Losonc.

4. General Pellé asks for the immediate fixing of an armistice line between the Czechoslovaks and the Hungarians, which could be different from the final boundary. The Foreign Ministers deem it preferable to fix the boundary immediately and to hold to it there.

President Wilson. What are we going to do after this report? I favor imposing the boundary that we have accepted on the Rumanians.

French country against the will of its inhabitants." "To repair an injustice," the document continued, "is to replace things, as far as possible, in the state in which they were before being upset by the injustice. All the Clauses of the Treaty concerning Alsace and Lorraine have this object in view." The Allied and Associated governments could not, therefore, agree to a plebiscite for these provinces. The inhabitants of these regions had long since made clear their desire to be reunited to France. Finally, France was not obliged to assume any part of the public debt of the two provinces, since Germany had assumed no part of their debt in 1871.

[3] The full text is printed in *ibid.*, pp. 358-60.

M. Clemenceau. They will scream.

Mr. Lloyd George. Most of the difficulties come from them.

M. Clemenceau. What are we going to do about Béla Kun? He asks that we send delegates to Vienna to talk with his representatives.

Mr. Lloyd George. Concerning the boundary, I favor taking our decision and compelling everyone to obey us. If the Rumanians resist, it will be necessary to refuse to send them munitions.

President Wilson. We will have to tell them that we will not recognize their frontier. What they want is to force our hand and compel us to sanction what they have done.

Mr. Lloyd George. We must impose our will now; we can no longer hurl vain orders.

President Wilson. Then it is necessary also to fix the boundary between Poland and the Ukraine.

Mr. Lloyd George. M. Paderewski says that a third of the inhabitants of Galicia are Polish, and that the other two thirds would prefer to be united to Poland than to another state.

President Wilson. I would hold a plebiscite to be sure of it.

Mr. Lloyd George. I agree. This plebiscite could take place in a short time.

President Wilson. Do you want to hold a plebiscite in all Galicia?

Mr. Lloyd George. No, only in eastern Galicia.

President Wilson. Would the demarcation be determined by our experts?

Mr. Lloyd George. Yes, there is no doubt about the western part, which is entirely Polish.

President Wilson. We must ask the Foreign Ministers, after having heard the experts, to draw the line which will delimit the zone of the plebiscite.

Mr. Lloyd George. That's it. Naturally, they will have to hear the Poles and the Ukrainians before taking their decision.

President Wilson. Shouldn't we have telegrams prepared to send immediately to the Hungarians, Czechoslovaks, and Rumanians?

I think Mr. Balfour would take care of it very well. It is necessary to employ a rather severe tone towards the Hungarians but a more friendly tone with the Rumanians and Czechs.

—(Assent.)

—The draft reply to the German counterproposals on the colonies is read aloud.[4]

---

[4] The section on "Colonies" and "Kiaochow" in the "Observations of the German Delegation on the Conditions of Peace," May 29, 1919, printed in *ibid.*, pp. 841-44. The German memorandum protested against Article 119 of the prelimi-

Mr. Lloyd George. One question that we must settle concerns the properties of the German Catholic missions. The Vatican represents to us that these properties actually belong to the Holy See; that is a most debatable proposition. In England, long before the Reformation, the Crown always rejected this pretension of the Holy See to be the owner of property of the Church on our territory.

M. Clemenceau. It has been the same in France; that is a pretension our kings never accepted.

Mr. Lloyd George. We can't agree to hand these properties over to the Holy See; but we can stipulate that they will be transferred to Catholic missions of other nationalities. None of us wants to keep them from their prime mission. What we can't accept is the doctrine of the right of the ownership of the Holy See.

President Wilson. In short, it is a matter simply of transferring these properties to non-German Catholic missions.

Mr. Lloyd George. Agreed. What we can't accept is that they be considered as property of the Vatican.

M. Clemenceau. You wouldn't accept that in America?

---

nary peace treaty which required Germany to renounce all rights and claims to her overseas possessions. This, the memorandum said, was a violation of Point 5 of the Fourteen Points, which called for "a free, open-minded and absolutely impartial adjustment of all colonial claims," since Germany had not even been consulted on the subject. It insisted that Germany's colonies were vital to her economic life as a source of raw materials, a market for her exports, and an outlet for her surplus population. It claimed that Germany had an excellent record of administering her colonies in the interest of their inhabitants. It also objected to the treaty provisions which required that all German public property in the colonies pass to the mandatory powers without compensation and which placed German private property under the discretion of the mandatory states. It did agree that Germany would renounce all rights and privileges in Kiaochow and Shantung but assumed that Germany would receive indemnification for all German public and private property in those areas.

The Allied reply was "GERMAN COUNTER-PROPOSALS, CONCLUSIONS OF THE COMMITTEE ON THE POLITICAL CLAUSES OF THE TREATY RELATING TO COUNTRIES OUTSIDE EUROPE," printed in *ibid.*, pp. 360-63. "No concessions," this document began, "can be made in regard to the Clauses of the Treaty which concern the former German Colonies and German rights outside Europe." It insisted that, even on the basis of German evidence, Germany's record as a colonial power was very poor. Moreover, the Allied and Associated Powers felt compelled to safeguard peace and their own security against "a military imperialism" which had established military bases in its colonies. They could not agree to compensation for German public property, and they felt obliged to have full liberty of action as to what influence and rights German private citizens might exercise in former German colonies. These same principles would apply in the case of Kiaochow.

President Wilson. No. The text that was drafted provides that the trustees charged with the administration of these properties will have to be Christians; it is this last word that has given rise to objections.

Mr. Lloyd George. I remind you that it is not the Germans who have raised the question, but the Vatican.

President Wilson. I favor stating that the act establishing a mandate over each of the German colonies will contain a special clause stipulating that the properties of missions be placed in the hands of missionaries of the same confession.

—(Assent.)

—Sir Eyre Crowe is introduced.

President Wilson. We ask you to tell us about the Ratibor district, which is assigned to the Czechoslovak state. It seems that our decision to hold a plebiscite in Upper Silesia somewhat changes our previous decision about this matter.

Sir Eyre Crowe. If Upper Silesia becomes part of Poland, the district concerned will be entirely cut off from Germany and must be assigned entirely to the Czechoslovak Republic. But if the plebiscite leaves Upper Silesia to Germany, there is no reason to place the territory north of Leobschütz, whose population is German, in the Czechoslovak Republic; it is the southern part of that region, where the population is Moravian, which alone would be assigned to Bohemia. The previous conclusions of the commission preceded your decision about the plebiscite.

President Wilson. In these circumstances, I think we can only adopt your recommendations.

Sir Eyre Crowe. It is what seems to me most fair. If Upper Silesia remains German, Leobschütz must share its fate; if Upper Silesia is Polish, Leobschütz will be isolated and can only go to the Czechoslovak state.

Mr. Lloyd George. How will you spell this out in the treaty?

Sir Eyre Crowe. It must be stipulated that one part of the territory in question will be immediately assigned to the Czechoslovaks, and that another part will be handed over to the Allied and Associated Powers which, according to the result of the plebiscite, will dispose of it either in favor of the Czechoslovak state or in favor of Germany.

—This proposal is adopted.

—Sir Eyre Crowe withdraws.

President Wilson reads aloud the text of the reply to the German counterproposals on the military clauses.[5]

Mr. Lloyd George. I would strengthen the beginning of this text; it is important to recall that is was Prussian militarism which imposed the crushing weight of armaments on the entire world.

—(*Assent.*)

M. Clemenceau. I have another observation to make. This text would allow the Germans 300,000 men during the three months which follow the signing. This figure seems too high to me; we don't know exactly how many men they have under arms, but they have about 300,000 men on the Polish frontier. The complete demobilization of Germany is a great problem. I believe they will try passive resistance, notably in Poland. If you allow them right away to keep 300,000 men, that will help them to do so. Two hundred thousand men should be enough. The Allied commission charged with overseeing the execution of the military clauses could grant them the right to delay their disarmament if that should seem necessary.

President Wilson. Why not simply remind the Germans that they have to reduce their forces to 100,000 men, and that the commission will have complete discretion to settle the means and determine the periods of time?

Mr. Lloyd George. It seems useful to me to fix an intermediate figure during this period of three months.

M. Clemenceau. Then I propose 200,000 men.

Mr. Lloyd George. That is quite enough. It is the figure that Marshal Foch proposed for the permanent strength of the German army.

President Wilson. The last lines of this text indicate that the members of the League of Nations might rule on the admission of Germany to the League when the military terms of the treaty have been carried out; this statement has no place in this document. We have already studied the reply that is to be made to Germany on the subject of her admission to the League of Nations.

M. Clemenceau. I agree; we must omit these last lines.

—*This proposal is adopted.*

—President Wilson reads the text of the reply to the German counterproposals concerning the naval clauses.[6]

[5] The draft reply is printed in *ibid.*, pp. 363-65.
[6] Printed in *ibid.*, pp. 367-68. This document declared that Germany had to accept unconditionally all of the naval articles of the treaty.

—No observation is presented.

—Reading of the reply regarding prisoners of war; *this reply is omitted as pointless.*

M. Orlando. I must warn you that I am expecting an important communication from Rome at 7 o'clock. There are strikes in Italy that worry me, and I also have to replace two ministers who have resigned–those of food supplies and of industry. The news that I receive might compel me to leave for Rome this evening.

Mr. Lloyd George. I have some information about what happened in Rome during the visit of Ramsay MacDonald. The Italian Socialists favored a coup, in agreement with the workers' groups in France and England. But Ramsay MacDonald, taking account of public opinion in Great Britain, has probably discouraged them.

M. Orlando. The agitation now taking place in Italy is directed especially against the rise in prices. There were some serious incidents in La Spezia; one person was killed and two wounded.

Mr. Lloyd George. This question of prices concerns me very much, and I believe we will soon have to make a common effort to settle it. In my opinion, we will have to establish a system of inter-Allied purchases; otherwise, we run the risk of a revolution in all of Europe.

—Mr. Philip Kerr is introduced and reads aloud the new draft of the text relating to armaments. *This text is adopted.*[7]

—President Wilson reads aloud a report from the Supreme War Council on the situation in Estonia.[8] All the military experts ask that the powers order the Germans to halt their offensive and evacuate Estonia. But the English delegates ask only for the immediate evacuation of Libau and Windau, with preparation for a general evacuation. The French, the Americans, and the Italians designate a much larger number of localities to be evacuated immediately.

[7] This reply, printed in *ibid.*, pp. 365-67, said that the Allied and Associated Powers wished to make it clear that their proposals in regard to German armaments were not made solely with the object of making it impossible for Germany to resume her policy of military aggression. "It is also the first step towards that general reduction and limitation of armaments which they seek to bring about as one of the most fruitful preventives of war, and which it will be one of the first duties of the League of Nations to promote." The colossal growth in armaments of the last few decades had been forced upon the nations of Europe by Germany, and the Allied and Associated Powers could not agree to any changes in the basic provisions of the treaty concerning German military forces. However, the Allied and Associated Powers were willing to allow Germany to reduce her army gradually and in stages.

[8] It was E. E. Belin *et al.*, "Report to the Supreme War Council by its Military and Naval Representatives," about which, see *PWW*, Vol. 60, p. 474, n. 21.

Mr. Lloyd George. What is not in doubt is that the Germans must leave this country. They are in the midst of installing themselves there and treat the whole region as if it belonged to them. They speak to us of the "German" railroads of Estonia and Livonia. An end must be put to it.

President Wilson. Agreed. But in case they resist, I don't know how we would chase them out of these areas. Local forces are insufficient, and we can't send troops there.

M. Clemenceau. The Armistice gave us the right to leave the Germans there as long as we like and to make them leave when we deemed it appropriate.

Mr. Lloyd George. It is very dangerous to leave them there. At this very moment, they are sending German colonists to settle in the Baltic provinces. They haven't renounced the idea of making it into a land for the expansion of their people.

CXXII

Conversation between President Wilson, MM. Clemenceau and Lloyd George, and Barons Sonnino and Makino*

JUNE 13, 1919, 11 A.M.

Mr. Lloyd George. The military means to be used if the Germans refuse to sign have been studied. But in my opinion, the best way to obtain the signing is to announce now that we are preparing to resume the blockade in case of refusal.[1]

*H., PPC, VI, 370ff.

[1] The council had before it "SUPERIOR BLOCKADE COUNCIL: NOTE to be transmitted to the Council of Heads of State," June 11, 1919, printed in PPC, VI, 374. The note reminded the Council of Four that no decision had yet been made as to the application of "further economic pressure"on Germany should she refuse to sign the peace treaty. The Superior Blockade Council had endeavored to bring the blockade system to "the most advanced state of readiness," but it was so complex that it would require some time to set it in motion. The Blockade Council believed that it could go no further in preparation so long as it remained doubtful whether the blockade would be used "in case of necessity." "The Council," the note concluded, "therefore submit as a matter of urgency that the time has now come when the Council of Heads of State should arrive at a definite decision as to whether it is the intention to make use of a reinforced Blockade as a measure of pressure upon Germany in the event of a refusal to sign the Peace Terms."

President Wilson. I must tell you that I am opposed to that statement. We don't have the right to threaten an entire population with famine if its government doesn't sign the treaty. I prefer military action, and I would keep the blockade as a supreme weapon and last resort.

M. Clemenceau. Don't you fear the blockade will not work since the frontiers are open?

Mr. Lloyd George. As of now, Germany can import nothing from neighboring countries.

President Wilson. The immediate renewal of the blockade would create a painful impression on the entire world. Military occupation is a regular and legitimate means of action according to the laws of war, which have been forgotten in the course of the present war.

M. Clemenceau. We used the blockade during the war.

Mr. Lloyd George. And without the blockade, the war would have lasted much longer. The Germans were still on conquered territory. Germany was defeated because the morale of her people, undermined by the blockade, collapsed at the time of her military reverses. In times almost as critical, our peoples held on because they were not suffering from hunger.

President Wilson. You are reasoning now as if war had to begin again; I hope it is not so.

M. Clemenceau. Have no fear about that. I am convinced our demonstration will suffice.

President Wilson. You will only produce Bolshevism with the blockade.

Mr. Lloyd George. The blockade is the only weapon that reaches all Germans, whilst there are many whom an occupation frightens not at all. The owning classes, in particular, prefer occupation to a social revolution.

President Wilson. The threat of the blockade will be nothing if the thing itself does not follow. I do not believe we should act through a blockade.

Mr. Lloyd George. I would return to it, however, if it was necessary. What I want is to shorten this dreadful period of waiting. Mr. President, your feeling does you honor. The blockade is indeed a horrible weapon, but it can't be compared to asphyxiating gases.

President Wilson. I would refuse, in any case, to take part in the blockade if it should precede occupation. I will never hesitate to punish those who bear responsibility for the war; but I recoil before the idea of making innocent people suffer.

M. Clemenceau. In any case, do you see a difficulty in allowing the newspapers to say that we are preparing a possible resumption of the blockade? That can make a useful impression, without causing anyone to suffer.

Mr. Lloyd George. What I want is to hasten the conclusion of peace. If peace doesn't come promptly, I fear chaos, which would be much worse than anything years of blockade could do.

President Wilson. Famine has produced chaos elsewhere, and I fear it will also produce it in Germany.

Sir Maurice Hankey. The naval authorities say they need to be informed of the possible resumption of the blockade in order to prepare ships for sea duty. To do that, it is also necessary to commit certain funds.

President Wilson. It seems to me the blockade can be executed without so many preparations, since Germany has no fleet left today.

Mr. Lloyd George. We have the Baltic to watch. I propose that you authorize us to display our destroyers there now.

M. Clemenceau. Danzig would be a good place to send them.

Mr. Lloyd George. We will also send them off Stettin and the surrounding area. We will also send them off Stockholm to show that we are making preparations. The best thing would be to lead the Germans to sign without having to raise a finger. What I fear most is passive resistance.

M. Clemenceau. Do you see any problem in allowing the newspapers to say that we are making preparations to resume the blockade?

President Wilson. No, but what I wish to avoid is a threat which might be carried out.

Mr. Lloyd George. However, there is danger in allowing our countries to believe that the peace will be signed without difficulty in three or four days. It is better, whilst announcing our preparations, to make them understand that we consider resistance possible.

You have seen that our military experts are not completely in agreement about the evacuation of Estonia. But, in reality, the divergence of their views is not great. General Sackville-West, like the French, American, and Italian experts, wants the total evacuation of Estonia. If he prefers to ask the Germans for the immediate evacuation of only two important points, it is in order to avoid complications and gross errors, for the positions occupied by German troops are not perfectly well known. All our experts agree with yours to ask the Germans to withdraw inside their frontiers.

President Wilson. Then we will limit ourselves to saying that the Germans must, in a very short time, evacuate all the territories which made up part of the former Russian Empire, beginning with the evacuation of Libau and Windau.

Should we send munitions to the local forces?

Mr. Lloyd George. We have done it already.

President Wilson. We must continue. And the money requested?

Mr. Lloyd George. We are sending them all they need; I don't know why they are asking for money.

Baron Makino. They don't make it clear precisely why. Their request for ten million pounds sterling was made some time ago.

Mr. Lloyd George. I propose to leave aside for the moment the question of subsidies and to refer the one of military supplies to Versailles [the Supreme War Council], to see what proportion each of us has to contribute.

(*To M. Clemenceau*) Have you seen M. Loucheur about the occupation of the left bank of the Rhine?

M. Clemenceau. Yes.

Mr. Lloyd George. Are we agreed?

M. Clemenceau. I can't change the text I showed you.[2]

Mr. Lloyd George. What do you mean by these "guarantees" that the Germans will have to give you before we end the occupation?

M. Clemenceau. By that I mean bonds or financial securities.

Mr. Lloyd George. It is better to indicate it explicitly. But you will know shortly whether the Germans will or will not give you the bonds provided for by the treaty.

M. Clemenceau. I will say to you frankly that I don't want to fix a shorter time limit to the occupation now.

Mr. Lloyd George. I am not asking you for that; but I am asking you to fix a date on which we could take up the question.

M. Clemenceau. I am willing to study that with you.

Mr. Lloyd George. I will see you with Mr. Bonar Law and Mr. Barnes; both insist that we indicate a date, and they represent very different political points of view. I prefer that you speak to them. If you satisfy them, you will have no difficulty satisfying me.

President Wilson. In any case, we must now study the agreement concerning the occupation arrangements.[3]

[2] See n. 1 to the notes of the next meeting.

[3] The council now had before it an English-language version of the Rhineland

—M. Loucheur and Mr. Wise are introduced.*

Mr. Lloyd George. At home, they fear this occupation of fifteen years as a permanent cause of conflict in Europe.

—The agreement concerning the occupation arrangement is read aloud.

President Wilson. I read in Article 3 that the civilian commission can promulgate ordinances to assure the upkeep and safety of the occupation troops. That clause is worded in terms much too broad, and I think it is dangerous. I propose to omit it.

—(Assent.)

Mr. Lloyd George. Let us not go too fast. Aren't there questions on which this commission must be able to act at its discretion, for example, concerning the dismantling of German fortresses?

M. Clemenceau. This concerns Marshal Foch and the commission that will assure the execution of the military clauses during the three months following the signing. The commission we are concerned with now is only there to facilitate relations between the occupation army and the local authorities. Marshal Foch's objection to the arrangement spelled out in this agreement is that certain military authorities, especially the commissariat, will have economic duties and that conflict could occur between them and the civilian commission.

Mr. Lloyd George. I don't think so. We can say that it is the civilian commission which, in all cases, will interpret the clauses.

M. Loucheur. This question must be considered apropos the document concerning relations between the commission and the military authorities.

President Wilson. Article 5 says nothing about the freedom of relations between local German authorities and the central government of the German state. Some lines must be added to indicate clearly that we don't want to cut this region off from the rest of Germany.

—President Wilson proposes a text which is adopted.

President Wilson. In Article 8[b], it is said that the troops will be lodged in barracks "except in case of necessity." I should like to see more precision here.

*H., PPC, VI, 577ff [377ff].

---

convention. It is printed as adopted as an appendix to these notes. The draft, with Wilson's extensive changes, is printed camera copy in PWW Vol. 60, pp. 504-10.

Mr. Wise. Marshal Foch wanted to anticipate a case in which it would be necessary to move troops or to concentrate them at a certain point.

President Wilson. Then I would write: "in cases of exceptional necessity."

—(Assent.)

Mr. Wise. In Paragraph 9, which aims at exempting all supplies for the Allied armies from all German taxes and duties, it is necessary to make a small change. An Allied soldier, buying merchandise in a shop, must not be able to ask to buy it duty free.

—(Assent.)

—*Thus, the text will be written:* "Will be free of all direct duties and all taxes.* * *"

M. Clemenceau. Does the text on a state of siege, which can be proclaimed by the civilian commission, mean that the military authorities don't have the right to do it?

President Wilson. Military authorities might act too hastily.

M. Clemenceau. Very well, but they must be allowed to take temporary measures in case of emergency.

President Wilson. The text provides for that: "In case of emergency, if public order is threatened, the military authorities have the right to take temporary measures."

M. Clemenceau. All right.

—Reading of the memorandum on the relations between the civilian commission and the military authorities.

President Wilson. The economic questions will be referred to the Supreme Economic Council. What does that mean?

M. Loucheur. We thought that, since the Supreme Economic Council exists, it is better not to impose this task on the governments.

President Wilson. In what case would that apply?

M. Loucheur. If, for example, there is a decision to be taken for victualing the civilian population on the left bank of the Rhine, it must be anticipated; in case of disturbances, we might have to feed that population.

Mr. Lloyd George. It is better to refer that to the governments, which will turn it over to the Supreme Economic Council if they deem it wise.

Mr. Wise. Under the Armistice arrangements, we were responsible for provisioning the entire left bank of the Rhine.

Mr. Lloyd George. After all, since the agreement is one amongst us,

I see no objection to referring the question to the Supreme Economic Council. If it was a question of dealing with the Germans, I would not want to give them the impression that the commission is more or less independent of the governments.

M. Loucheur. It would be dangerous to encourage the commission to involve itself in all the economic and financial affairs of the left bank of the Rhine. The difficulty lies in making a distinction between what should belong to the civilian authorities and what should belong to the military authorities. In the matter of victualing, things would have to be arranged so that the commissariat could act without going to the civilian commission.

M. Mantoux. Where it is written that the commission will deal with questions affecting economic life, why not add "of the civilian population"?

—*This wording is adopted.*

Mr. Lloyd George. The president of the commission will be a Frenchman. But I ask that he be named with the assent of the governments concerned.

M. Clemenceau. That is perfectly fair.

President Wilson. I propose that that stipulation be the same for all members of the commission.

—(*Assent.*)

{ A P P E N D I X }[4]

Confidential. W.C.P.993.

CONVENTION REGARDING THE MILITARY OCCUPATION OF THE TERRITORIES OF THE RHINE.

Approved by the Council of the Principal Allied and Associated Powers on June 13th, 1919.

(Note: The use of the terms "Allies" and "Allied" throughout this document must be interpreted to mean "the Allied and Associated Powers.")

I. As provided by Section XIV, (Articles 428 et seq.) of the Treaty dated [blank], armed forces of the Allies will continue in occupation of German territory (as defined by Article 5 of the Armistice Convention of 11th November, 1918, as extended by Ar-

---

[4] Printed in *ibid.*, pp. 513-18.

ticle 7 of the Convention of 16th January 1919), as a guarantee of the execution by Germany of the Treaty.

No German troops, except prisoners of war in process of repatriation, shall be admitted to the occupied territories, even in transit; but police forces of a strength to be determined by the Allied Powers may be maintained in these territories for the purpose of maintaining order.

II. There shall be constituted a civilian body styled the Inter-Allied Rhineland High Commission, and hereinafter called "the High Commission" which, except in so far as the Treaty may otherwise provide, shall be the supreme representative of the Allies within the occupied territory. It shall consist of four members representing Belgium, France, Great Britain and the United States.

III. (a) So far as may be necessary for securing the maintenance, safety and requirements of the Allied forces, the High Commission shall have the power to issue ordinances for that purpose. Such ordinances shall be published under the authority of the High Commission, and copies thereof shall be sent to each of the Allied and Associated Governments and also to the German Government. When so published they shall have the force of law and shall be recognised as such by all the Allied military authorities and by the German civil authorities.

(b) The members of the High Commission shall enjoy diplomatic privileges and immunities.

(c) The German courts shall continue to exercise civil and criminal jurisdiction subject to the exceptions contained in paragraphs (d) and (e) below.

(d) The armed forces of the Allies and the persons accompanying them, to whom the General Officers Commanding the Armies of Occupation shall have issued a pass revokable at their pleasure, and any persons employed by, or in the service of such troops, shall be exclusively subject to the military law and jurisdiction of such forces.

(e) Any person who commits any offence against the persons or property of the armed forces of the Allies, may be made amenable to the military jurisdiction of the said forces.

IV. The German authorities, both in the occupied and in the unoccupied territories, shall, on the demand of any duly authorised military officer of the occupying forces, arrest and hand over to the nearest commander of Allied troops any person charged with an offence who is amenable under Clause (d) or Clause (e) of Article III above to the military jurisdiction of the Allied Forces.

V. The civil administration of the provinces (Provinzen), Government Departments (Regierungsbezirke), Urban Circles (Stadtkreise), Rural Circles (Landkreise), and Communes (Gemeinde), shall remain in the hands of the German authorities, and the civil administration of these areas shall continue under German Law and under the authority of the Central German Government except in so far as it may be necessary for the High Commission by Ordinance under Article III to accommodate that administration to the needs and circumstances of military occupation. It is understood that the German authorities shall be obliged, under penalty of removal, to conform to the ordinances issued in virtue of Article III above.

VI. Subject to the conditions laid down in the Hague Convention, 1907, the right to requisition in kind and to demand services shall be exercised by the Allied Armies of Occupation.

The charges for the requisitions effected in the zone of each allied army, and the estimate of damage caused by the troops of occupation, shall be determined by local Commissions composed in equal representation of both German civilians appointed by the German civil authorities and Allied military officers and presided over by some person appointed by the High Commission.

The German Government shall also continue to be responsible for the cost of maintenance of the troops of occupation under the conditions fixed by the Treaty.

The German Government shall also be responsible for the costs and expenses of the High Commission and for its housing. Suitable premises for the housing of the High Commission shall be selected in consultation with the German Government.

VII. The Allied troops shall continue undisturbed in possession of any premise at present occupied by them, subject to the provision of Art. VIII (b) below.

VIII. (a) The German Government shall undertake, moreover, to place at the disposal of the Allied troops and to maintain in good state of repair, all the military establishments required for the said troops, with the necessary furniture, heating and lighting, in accordance with the regulations concerning these matters in force in the various armies concerned. These shall include accommodation for officers and men, guard-rooms, offices, administrative, regimental and staff headquarters, workshops, store-rooms, hospitals, laundries, regimental schools, riding schools, stables, training grounds and rifle and artillery ranges, aviation grounds, grazing grounds, warehouses for supplies and grounds for military manoeuvres, also theatre and cinema premises, and reasonable facilities for sport and for recreation grounds for the troops.

(b) Private soldiers and non-commissioned officers shall be accommodated in barracks, and shall not be billeted on the inhabitants, except in cases of exceptional emergency.

In the event of the existing military establishments being insufficient or not being considered suitable, the Allied troops may take possession of any other public or private establishment with its personnel, suitable for those purposes, or, if there are no such suitable premises, they may require the construction of new barracks.

Civilian and military officers and their families may be billeted on the inhabitants in accordance with the billeting regulations in force in each army.

IX. No German direct taxes or duties will be payable by the High Commission, the Allied armies or their personnel.

Food supplies, arms, clothing, equipment and provisions of all kinds for the use of the Allied armies, or addressed to the military authorities, or to the High Commission, or to canteens and officers' messes, shall be transported free of charge and free of all import duties of any kind.

X. The personnel employed on all means of communication (railways, railroads and tramways of all kinds, waterways (including the Rhine), roads and rivers, shall obey any orders given by, or on behalf of, the Commander-in-Chief of the Allied armies for military purposes.

All the material and all the civil personnel necessary for the maintenance and working of all means of communication must be kept in its entirety on all such means of communication in the occupied territory.

The transport on the railways of Allied troops or individual soldiers or officers, on duty or furnished with a warrant, will be effected without payment.

XI. The Armies of Occupation may continue to use for military purposes all existing telegraphic and telephonic installations.

The Armies of Occupation shall also have the right to continue to instal and use military telegraph and telephone lines, wireless stations and all other similar means of communication which may appear to them expedient; for this purpose, subject to the approval of the High Commission, they may enter upon and occupy any land, whether public or private.

The personnel of the public telegraph and telephone services shall continue to obey the orders of the Commander-in-Chief of the Allied Armies given for military purposes.

Allied telegrams and messages of an official nature shall be entitled to priority over all other communications and shall be despatched free of charge. The Allied military authorities shall have the right to supervise the order in which such communications are transmitted.

No wireless telegraphy installations shall be allowed to be erected by the authorities or by the inhabitants of the occupied territory without previous authorisation by the Allied military authorities.

XII. The personnel of the postal service shall obey any orders given by or on behalf of the Commander-in-Chief of the Allied Armies for military purposes. The public postal service shall continue to be carried out by the German authorities, but this shall not in any way affect the retention of the military postal services organised by the Armies of Occupation, who shall have the right to use all existing postal routes for military requirements.

The said armies shall have the right to run postal wagons with all necessary personnel on all existing postal routes.

The German Government shall transmit free of charge and without examination letters and parcels which may be entrusted to its post-offices by, or on behalf of the Armies of Occupation or of the High Commission; and shall be responsible for the value of any letters or parcels lost.

XIII. The High Commission shall have the power, whenever they think it necessary, to declare a state of siege in any part of the territory or in the whole of it. Upon such declaration the military authorities shall have the powers provided in the German Imperial Law of May 30th, 1892. In case of emergency, where public order is disturbed or threatened in any district, the local military authorities shall have the power to take such temporary measures as may be necessary for restoring order. In such case the military authorities shall report the facts to the High Commission.

MEMORANDUM
DEFINING THE RELATIONS BETWEEN THE ALLIED MILITARY AUTHORITIES AND THE INTER-ALLIED RHINELAND HIGH COMMISSION.

Approved by the Council of the Principal Allied and Associated Powers on 13th June, 1919.

1. Each High Commissioner is directly responsible to his Government, economic questions being first referred by the High Commissioner to the Supreme Economic Council as long as that body exists.

2. The ordinances of the High Commission are to be communicated to the Commanders of Armies by, or on behalf of, the Allied High Command.

3. Whenever the High Commission has occasion to publish ordinances affecting the interests of the occupying armies, in respect of which the initiative does not come from the military authorities, the High Commission shall consult the military authorities beforehand.

4. Communications between the High Commission and the various military authorities will always take place through the channel of the Allied High Command.

5. All civil commissions or officials already appointed or to be appointed by any one or more of the Allied and Associated Powers who deal with matters affecting the civil administration or the economic life of the civilian population in the occupied territory shall, if they are retained, be placed under the authority of the High Commission.

6. (a) The appointment of each High Commissioner shall be subject to the approval of all the Allied and Associated Governments represented.

(b) The French member of the High Commission shall be president thereof.

(c) The decisions of the High Commission shall be reached by a majority of votes.

(d) Each High Commissioner shall have one vote. But in case of an equality of votes the President shall have the right to give a casting vote.

(e) In either of these two cases the dissenting High Commissioner, or High Commissioners, may appeal to their Governments. But such an appeal shall not, in cases of urgency, delay the putting into execution of the decisions taken, which shall then be carried out under the responsibility of the members voting for the decisions.

CXXIII

Conversation between MM. Clemenceau, Lloyd George, Bonar Law, Barnes, and Loucheur*

JUNE 13, 1919, 4 P.M.

M. Clemenceau. What do you think of my plan for the agreement on the occupation?[1]

Mr. Bonar Law. The occupation can have only two aims: either to

*H., PPC, VI, 395ff, bearing the same date, contains nothing of the discussion reported here.

[1] A special protocol concerning the duration and payment of the costs of the inter-Allied occupation of the Rhineland. We have not found a copy of Clemenceau's draft of this document. However, the text of the protocol as signed by Clemenceau, Wilson, and Lloyd George on June 16, printed in PWW, Vol. 60, pp. 575-76, reads as follows:

16th June 1919.
DECLARATION BY THE GOVERNMENTS OF THE UNITED STATES OF AMERICA, GREAT BRITAIN AND FRANCE IN REGARD TO THE OCCUPATION OF THE RHINE PROVINCES.

The Allied and Associated Powers did not insist on making the period of occupation last until the Reparation Clauses were completely executed, because they assumed that Germany would be obliged to give every proof of her goodwill and every necessary guarantee before the end of the fifteen years' time.

As the cost of occupation involves an equivalent reduction of the amount available for reparations, the Allied and Associated Powers stipulated, by Article 431 of the Treaty, that if, before the end of the fifteen years' period, Germany had fulfilled all her obligations under the Treaty, the troops of occupation should be immediately withdrawn.

If Germany, at an earlier date, has given proofs of her goodwill and satisfactory guarantees to assure the fulfilment of her obligations the Allied and Associated Powers concerned will be ready to come to an agreement between themselves for the earlier termination of the period of occupation.

Now and henceforward, in order to alleviate the burden on the reparations bill, they agree that as soon as the Allied and Associated Powers concerned are convinced that the conditions of disarmament by Germany are being satisfactorily fulfilled, the annual amount of the sums to be paid by Germany to

protect France or to guarantee the execution of the treaty. In both cases, I don't see why a period of fifteen years should be adopted. We could just as well say five years. The occupation troops will leave German territory precisely at the moment when Germany becomes strong again. The British people do not understand the *raison d'être* of the occupation. I believe that, unless it is absolutely necessary, it can only be a cause of difficulties and dangers. It is natural that we should take all measures to insure the immediate execution of certain clauses of the treaty. As for those whose execution will unfortunately extend over a great number of years, an occupation of fifteen years will be of no help.

Mr. Barnes. This occupation can have an effect absolutely contrary to what you want. It could create a feeling of sympathy for the Germans; it is what we want to avoid.

—Mr. Bonar Law proposes a text stipulating a re-examination of the question after a period of three years.

M. Clemenceau. It is better to be frank amongst ourselves. It is completely impossible for me to accept this. You have said that the occupation could have two fundamental reasons: either to protect France against unprovoked aggression or to insure payment of what is owed us. But in fact that doesn't say enough. The present treaty is the most extensive that has ever been written. It touches a number of questions that Germany will try to exploit in order to create difficulties for us. No other peace treaty has ever imposed so many terms to be fulfilled, and, consequently, no other has left so many risks of not being carried out.

To put an end to the occupation, we have to consider two things: the good will of Germany and the guarantees she can give. Those are the two points upon which I insist. Proofs of good will are something rather difficult to refine. But we mean by that more or less important actions by which a man or a country demonstrates that his intentions are good. Unfortunately, a war like this doesn't end instantly, and I see many signs in Germany which don't reassure me about the good intentions of that country.

This very morning, I received from Berlin a letter from General Dupont, who tells me that the Germans will not sign, and the letter ends with these words: "As for the question of knowing

---

cover the cost of occupation shall not exceed 240 million marks (gold). This provision can be modified if the Allied and Associated Powers agree as to the necessity of such modification.   Woodrow Wilson
G Clemenceau
D Lloyd George

what will happen in Poland, the unanimous opinion is that the Germans will resist." Consequently, in a few days, the Germans will have given you proof of their ill will.

Mr. Bonar Law. I don't contest that.

M. Clemenceau. What I am trying to do is to make you understand my state of mind, whether you agree with me or not. Against this ill will, I see no other means of action except occupation. If you had foreign troops in a single county of England, I believe that would so offend you that you would do anything to rid yourself of them.

I come to the guarantees. I recall that I had first asked that the length of occupation be prolonged the entire length of the period of payments. Mr. Lloyd George, and then President Wilson, offered me the military guarantee of Great Britain and the United States against German aggression if I consented to reduce the length of the occupation. So I renounced an occupation of thirty years and satisfied myself with fifteen years. You tell me today: "These fifteen years represent the period during which there will be no danger." I don't claim that this figure is sacred. But the reason we chose it is that we thought this period would suffice to obtain from Germany all proofs of good will and all the guarantees we need.

Then you told me: "It would be absurd to stipulate the period of fifteen years, whatever might happen; if all goes well, why not reduce it?" I answered: certainly; and we placed an article along these lines in the treaty.

I am ready to make a further effort. It is obvious that Germany can't fulfill her commitments in fifteen years. But when she has convinced us that she is truly disposed to fulfill them, and when she has given us the necessary guarantees, I will be ready to evacuate the left bank of the Rhine. You are asking me what I mean by this word "guarantees." If Germany gives us bonds bearing her signature, if she remits financial securities—whether from banks, customs, railroads—I don't see why we should leave soldiers there unnecessarily.

You will ask me: "Why this obstinacy?" I cannot act otherwise. Our birth rate is low. We lost 1,500,000 men. France's first need is security. Our people need to know that there is somewhere a barrier behind which they can begin to work and rebuild their ruins. I am not free as I would be in ordinary circumstances. I ask Mr. Lloyd George not to compel me to take commitments towards Germany. Between us, I state that, if proofs of good will and the guarantees furnished by Germany satisfy us, I will be ready to resume this conversation with you. I have to reckon with national feeling. That doesn't mean I fear being overthrown; that doesn't matter to me at all. I don't want to do something that would break down the vital resilience of our people.

Marshal Foch has taken the attitude you know. You said to me, Mr. Bonar Law, that in England you wouldn't have tolerated it for ten minutes if a general had taken that position. If I acted as you perhaps would have done, I would, you know, have created a dangerous situation. I know that he spreads recriminations against me; I intend to ignore him. On two different occasions, we might have dismissed him; we refrained from doing so. You are not unaware that he has support in very high places. I held on, and I supported our common policy without hesitation.

My generals on the left bank of the Rhine followed a policy which displeased us. I stopped them. Don't believe that, if I take the position I am defending now about the occupation, it is for reasons of political opportunism. In the union between France, England, and America, France herself is absolutely essential. As for myself, I am prepared to look at the question, as far as I can, as you do. Do the same for me.

Mr. Bonar Law. There is not such a great difference of views between us. The only question that remains in suspense is whether we mustn't now fix the date on which we will re-examine the problem of the occupation.

M. Clemenceau. Don't ask me to do that.

Mr. Bonar Law. Wouldn't you accept a period of five years?

M. Clemenceau. I cannot do it, because the French would believe we tried to deceive them by announcing first a period of fifteen years, to replace it almost immediately by another.

Mr. Lloyd George. But if the Germans should give you all the guarantees you want in five years, you wouldn't remain in Germany?

M. Clemenceau. No.

Mr. Lloyd George. But we can't legislate for madmen. In England, we also have irrational people.

M. Clemenceau. It is not that. There is a difference of psychology between your people and ours: you are on your island, behind the rampart of the sea; we are on the Continent, with a bad frontier.

Mr. Barnes. Your text says that, by a later agreement, the end of the occupation can be set at an earlier date: why not specify that date?

M. Clemenceau. I will point out that an earlier date could mean four years. What I cannot do is set that figure today.

Mr. Lloyd George. Here is what I propose. "If, at an earlier date, Germany has given proofs of her good will by fulfilling her obligations and has furnished satisfactory guarantees, the Allied and Associated Powers will be ready to agree to end the period of occupation before the stipulated time."

M. Clemenceau. I accept this; I am granting you everything I can.

Mr. Barnes. I would have preferred a definite indication of a period of five years.

Mr. Lloyd George. What you want is to give the Germans reasons to satisfy us. This text encourages them to show their good faith and to make offers of acceptable guarantees.

M. Clemenceau. If you set a date today, the French will be against this treaty. If there is no date, they will think that Germany will be judged according to her merits.

Mr. Lloyd George. When must the annual payment of 240 million gold marks to cover the occupation costs begin? The text says: "when disarmament is an accomplished fact." What does that mean?

M. Clemenceau. That means: when the German forces have been reduced to 100,000 men.

Mr. Bonar Law. You might find yourselves compelled, all things considered, to leave them more than 100,000 men; what would happen in this case?

M. Loucheur. We can write: "Beginning on a date set by common agreement by the Allies."

Mr. Bonar Law. I would write instead: "The expense, unless the Allies decide otherwise, will be 240 million gold marks." That leaves us the possibility to determine the time when we can accept a different arrangement.

M. Clemenceau. That is too vague. We can and must reduce the sum within a short time. I would insert: "After the execution of the military clauses of the treaty."

Mr. Lloyd George. M. Loucheur and Mr. Bonar Law together can find the best wording.

—(Assent.)

CXXIV

Conversation between President Wilson,
MM. Clemenceau and Lloyd George,
and Barons Sonnino and Makino*

JUNE 13, 1919, 5 P.M.

Mr. Lloyd George. Once more, I must ask you a question concerning the publication of the treaty. My attention has been called to the fact that, if the summary of the German counterproposals and that of the reply of the Allies arrive at the same time in the press, this mass of copy will overwhelm the newspapers.

President Wilson. Our replies are shorter than the German counterproposals.

Mr. Lloyd George. I believe they will nevertheless make up a rather voluminous collection. Moreover, it doesn't seem to me that we can make them known to the Germans before Monday.

President Wilson. We could allow the newspapers to publish the German counterproposals on Monday and a summary of our reply on Tuesday morning.

Sir Maurice Hankey. I sent the various replies, insofar as they were ready, to those who have already prepared the resumé of the treaty. Their work must already be rather advanced.

—Reading of the reply on the question of responsibilities.[1]

—(Approved.)

—Reading of the text about ways of communication.[2]

President Wilson. The American delegation requests omission of Article 325, forbidding Germany to take measures on its railway network which could have the effect of turning trade away from certain ports.

Mr. Lloyd George. In reality, such a clause is against the interest of states like the Czechoslovak Republic, which might profit if competition between Hamburg, Antwerp, and Trieste remained free.

*H., PPC, VI, 395ff.

[1] Drafted by Philip Kerr. It is printed as an appendix to these notes.

[2] This was a reply to the German counterproposal on international waterways. As approved at this meeting, it is printed in PPC, VI, 401-405. As a section of the long Allied note of June 16, it is printed in ibid., pp. 992-96.

President Wilson. Even if this was inserted in the treaty, you couldn't insure its execution.

Baron Sonnino. In certain cases, couldn't the reduction of rates be likened to "dumping"? The Germans could, by this means, divert commerce from certain routes and ruin some of our ports.

Mr. Lloyd George. How could you manage to prevent that?

President Wilson. I agree with you. I don't believe that clause can be justified; above all, I don't believe it is possible to insure its execution.

Baron Sonnino. That latter objection could be applied as well to many other clauses of the treaty.

Mr. Lloyd George. Nothing prevents your railway companies from lowering their rates between Trieste and Prague. If German railroads sell cheap tickets between Prague and Hamburg, will you go to war because of that?

President Wilson. Doesn't Baron Sonnino believe with us that the proposed arrangement couldn't work?

Baron Sonnino. It could serve to prevent extreme abuses. It is possible that the Germans might try to divert the trade of the Adriatic completely to their benefit.

Mr. Lloyd George. In any case, the consent of a state like Bohemia would be necessary. That country has the right to benefit from competition amongst lines. In reality, the omission of such a clause is much more in the interest of Czechoslovakia than in Germany's interest.

Baron Sonnino. The Belgian delegation insisted on this clause. Indeed, Belgium has reason to fear that the Germans might try to ruin Antwerp to the profit of Bremen or Hamburg.

Mr. Lloyd George. In short, that would amount to insuring protection to companies which would impose less favorable conditions on travelers or merchandise. We didn't do it when it was a matter of protecting the interests of Southampton or Liverpool, which suffered indeed from German competition.

President Wilson. I hope you will accept the omission of this article, because, in my opinion, it would have no practical effect.

—*Article 325 is eliminated.*

—Reading of the observations of the labor commission,[3] which objects to the use of German manpower in the devastated regions, because a

[3] It is printed in *ibid.*, pp. 407-11. This was a report that was intended to serve as the basis for the section on labor in the Allied reply of June 16, which is printed in *ibid.*, p. 996.

provision of this kind would seem contrary to the freedom of workers. In any case, German workers must only be used under the same conditions and at the same wages as those of the countries where they will work.

The labor commission also requests the insertion of a clause by which German workers in foreign countries would benefit from local labor laws, subject to reciprocity.

Mr. Lloyd George. Does that mean that German workers in England would straightaway be able to benefit from our pension system? I refuse to consider the question.

—Reading of the conclusions of the Committee on the Eastern Frontiers of Germany.[4] *These conclusions are adopted.*
—Reading of the text of the reply on prisoners of war.[5] *This reply is definitely discarded.*
—Mr. Balfour is introduced.

Mr. Balfour. You have instructed me to draft telegrams addressed to the Hungarians, Rumanians, and Czechs in order to halt hostilities and settle the boundaries. I think we must begin with a preamble explaining the policy of the Allies in Central Europe; this preamble would be the same for all three telegrams.

What creates the immediate difficulty is that, if the boundaries fixed are good boundaries for peacetime, they are not so good from the strategic point of view. For example, there are certain railway lines that cross these boundaries several times; it is easy to settle their status in peacetime, but much less easy to insure their operation as long as the present situation lasts. There are also some points which can only be settled on the spot.

But, above all, here is what I must consult you about. We say to Hungary: "You must get out of Czechoslovak territory." We say to the Czechoslovaks: "You will remain on the other side of the boundary drawn for you." We say to the Rumanians: "You will withdraw behind your final boundary." It doesn't seem to be possible to ask the Rumanians to withdraw before the Hungarians have evacuated Czechoslovak territory.

It remains to be seen how our orders will be carried out. The greatest difficulty could come from Rumania. But I don't believe she dares put herself in opposition to the western powers.

President Wilson. We can say to the Rumanians: "If you don't obey

---

[4] We have not found this report. However, it was incorporated in the sections on Poland in *ibid.*, pp. 945-46.
[5] Not found.

our decisions, we will stop supporting your claims, and you will remain outside the peace treaty."

Mr. Balfour. You can say that, but in fact, you won't put Rumanian populations back under Hungarian domination.

Mr. Lloyd George. No, but, in doubtful cases, we have always decided in favor of our friends; modifications of that policy are possible.

—Mr. Balfour reads aloud the text of the telegrams, *which is approved.*[6]

{ A P P E N D I X }[7]

THE RESPONSIBILITY OF GERMANY FOR THE WAR

The German Delegation have submitted a lengthy Memorandum in regard to the responsibility of Germany for the initiation of the war. The burden of the argument in this document is that at the very last moment of the crisis the German Government endeavoured to induce moderation on the part of an Ally to whom she had previously given complete liberty of action, and that it was the mobilisation of the Russian army which finally made inevitable the outbreak of the general war.

The Allied and Associated Powers, however, wish to make it clear that their view as to the responsibility for the war is not based merely upon an analysis of the events which took place in the last critical hours of the crisis which preceded the actual outbreak of hostilities. There is nothing in the German Memoran-

---

[6] These were telegrams to each to the governments of Hungary, Czechoslovakia, and Rumania. The "preamble," which constituted the first part of each telegram, said that these governments seemed to believe that they could determine their future boundaries by "the temporary accidents of military occupation." This was not so; no state would be rewarded by any increase of territory for prolonging the horrors of war. All states involved had to respect the boundaries described in the accompanying telegram, cease hostilities forthwith, and immediately withdraw their troops to within the defined boundaries. The telegram to Hungary ordered the Hungarian army to withdraw within the assigned frontier of Hungary. If it did not so withdraw, the Allied and Associated governments would hold themselves free to advance on Budapest. Rumanian troops would be withdrawn from Hungarian territory as soon as Hungarian troops had evacuated Czechoslovakia. The message to Czechoslovakia informed Prague of the telegram to Budapest. The message to Bucharest also informed the Rumanians about the order to Budapest and said that, once the Hungarian army had withdrawn from Czechoslovakia, the Rumanian army would in turn withdraw within the new Rumanian borders. PPC, VI, 411-13.

[7] Printed in *PWW*, Vol. 60, pp. 451-55.

dum which shakes their conviction that the immediate cause of the war was the decision, deliberately taken, of those responsible for German policy in Berlin and their confederates in Vienna and Budapest to impose a solution of a European question upon the nations of Europe and, if the other members of the concert refused this dictation, by war itself instantly declared. The German Memorandum indeed admits without reserve the accuracy of this view. The Serbian question was not, and never could have been, purely an Austro-Hungarian question. It affected Germany. It affected all the Great Powers. It was essentially a European question, and concerned the peace, not only of the Balkans, but of the whole of Europe. It was impossible to isolate it and the authors of the ultimatum of July 21st knew that it could not be isolated. If, therefore, the German and Austro-Hungarian Governments had desired a pacific settlement they would have consulted with the other Powers whose interests were vitally affected, and only taken action after making the utmost endeavour to arrive at an agreed solution. Yet the Memorandum of the German Delegation explicitly admits that the German Government authorised its Ally to endeavour to solve the Austro-Serbian question on its own initiative and by war. "On the strength," it says, "of statements received from the Cabinet in Vienna, the German Government considered an Austrian military expedition against Serbia essential for the preservation of peace. The German Government considered itself obliged to take the risk of Russian intervention with the resultant *casus foederis*. She gave her Ally Austria a completely free hand as to the nature of the demands to be made by her on Serbia. When the ultimatum was to be made by an answer which appeared to Germany herself sufficient to justify the abandonment of the expedition after all, she indicated this view to Vienna."

The later action of the German Government was perfectly consistent with this initial policy. It supported the rejection, without consideration, of the extraordinary concessions made by Serbia in response to the insolent and intolerable demands of the Austro-Hungarian Government. It supported the mobilisation of the Austro-Hungarian army, and the initiation of hostilities and steadily rejected every proposal for conference, conciliation or mediation, though it knew that once mobilisation and military action were undertaken by any of the Great Powers, it inevitably compelled a response from all the rest and so hourly reduced the chances of pacific settlement. Only at the eleventh hour, when all chance of avoiding war had practically vanished, did the German Government counsel moderation on her Ally. Even on this single point in Germany's favour, the Memorandum of the German Delegates is forced to admit a doubt. "The reason," they say, "for the delay in the reply of the Cabinet at Vienna to this proposal is not known to us," and then they go on to say in words which are underlined, "This is one of the most vital points which still require elucidation." May it not be that, as was not uncommon with the German Foreign Office, unofficial communications or a previous understanding between those who had the real power, differed somewhat from the messages which travelled over the official wires?

After reading what the German Delegation has to say in self-defence, the Allied and Associated Powers are satisified that the series of events which caused the outbreak of the war was deliberately plotted and executed by those who wielded the supreme power in Vienna, Budapest and Berlin.

The history of the critical days of July 1914, however, is not the sole ground upon which the Allied and Associated Powers consider that the responsibility of Germany for the war must be tried. The outbreak of the war was no sudden decision taken in a difficult crisis. It was the logical outcome of the policy which had been pursued for decades by Germany under the inspiration of the Prussian system.

The whole history of Prussia has been one of domination, aggression and war. Hypnotised by the success with which Bismarck, following the tradition of Frederick the Great, robbed the neighbours of Prussia and forged the unity of Germany through blood and iron, the German people after 1871 submitted practically without reserve to the inspiration and the leadership of their Prussian rulers. The Prussian spirit was not content that Germany should occupy a great and influential place in a Council of equal nations to which she was entitled, and which she had secured. It could be satisfied with nothing less than supreme and autocratic power. At a time, therefore, when the Western nations were seriously endeavouring to limit armaments, to substitute friendship for rivalry in international affairs, and to lay the foundation of a new era in which all nations should cooperate in amity in the conduct of the world's affairs, the rulers of Germany were restlessly sowing suspicion and hostility among all her neighbours, were conspiring with every element of unrest in every land, and were steadily increasing Germany's armaments and consolidating her military and naval power. They mobilised all the resources at their command, the universities, the press, the pulpit, the whole machinery of governmental authority to indoctrinate their gospel of hatred and force, so that when the time came, the German people might respond to their call. As a result in the later years of the 19th century, and during the 20th century, the whole policy of Germany was bent towards securing for herself a position from which she could dominate and dictate.

It is said that Germany developed her armaments in order to save herself from Russian aggression. Yet it is significant that no sooner was Russia defeated by Japan in the Far East and almost paralysed by the subsequent internal revolution than the German Government immediately re-doubled its attempts to increase its armaments and to domineer over its neighbours under the threat of war. To them the collapse of Russia was not an occasion to try to reduce armaments and bring peace to the world in concert with the Western Powers. It was the opportunity to extend their own power. Further the whole point of German organisation was aggressive. Their railways, both east and west, their schemes of mobilisation, their long concocted plan to turn the flank of France by invading Belgium, the elaborate preparation and subsequent equipment, both within and beyond her borders, as revealed on the outbreak of the war—all had aggression in view, so that when the time came, all resistance might be overcome, and Germany might be left the master both in the East and in the West. The whole thought of Germany was bent towards the settlement of every problem, not by reason or justice, but by the enforcement of her own will by blood and iron.

It is not the purpose of this Memorandum to traverse the diplomatic history of the years preceding the war, or to show how it was that the peace-loving nations of Western Europe were gradually driven, under a series of crises provoked from Berlin, to come together in self-defence. Autocratic Germany, under the inspiration of her rulers, was bent on domination. The nations of Europe were determined to preserve their liberty. It was the fear of the rulers of Germany lest their plans for universal domination should be brought to nought by the rising tide of democracy, that drove them to endeavour to overcome all resistance at one stroke by plunging Europe in universal war. The view of the Allied and Associated Powers could not indeed be better expressed than in the words of the German Memorandum itself: "The real mistakes of German policy lay much further back. The German Chancellor who was in office in 1914 had taken over a political inheritance which either condemned as hopeless from the start his unreservedly honest attempt to relieve the tension of the internal situation, or else demanded therefor a degree of statesmanship, and above all a strength of decision which on the one hand he did not sufficiently possess, and on the other, could not make effective in the then existing conditions of German polity."

In the view, therefore, of the Allied and Associated Powers Germany's responsibility is far wider and far more terrible than that to which the Memorandum of the German Delegation would seek to confine it. Germany, under the inspiration of Prussia has been the champion of force and violence, deception, intrigue and cruelty in the conduct of international affairs. Germany for decades has steadily pursued a policy of inspiring jealousies and hatred and of dividing nation from nation in order that she might gratify her own selfish passion for power. Germany has stood athwart the whole current of democratic progress and international friendships throughout the world. Germany has been the principal mainstay of autocracy in Europe. And in the end, seeing that she could attain her ends, in no other way, she planned and started the war which caused the massacre and mutilation of millions and the ravaging of Europe from end to end.

The truth of the charges thus brought against them the German people have admitted by their own revolution. They have overturned their Government because they have discovered that it is the enemy of freedom, justice and equality at home. That same Government was no less the enemy of freedom, justice and equality abroad. It is useless to attempt to prove that it was less violent and arrogant and tyrannical in its foreign than it was in its internal policy, or that the responsibility for the terrible events of the last five years does not lie at its doors.

CXXIVA

Conversation between President Wilson, MM. Clemenceau and Lloyd George, and Baron Sonnino*

JUNE 14, 1919, 11 A.M.

—Reading of the reply to the German counterproposals on the economic clauses.[1] *This document is approved.*

*H., *PPC*, VI, 417ff.

[1] Printed in *PPC*, VI, 422-45. As incorporated in the memorandum of June 16, it is printed in *ibid.*, pp. 972-91.

—Reading of the reply to the German counterproposals on the air clauses.² *This reply is eliminated.*

² This document is missing in all collections.

CXXV

Conference among President Wilson, MM. Clemenceau and Lloyd George, Barons Sonnino and Makino, and MM. Kramář, Beneš, Hymans, Van den Heuvel, Paderewski, and Dmowski*

JUNE 14, 1919, 4:30 P.M.

President Wilson. We are in a hurry to finish our reply to the German counterproposals, and we thought that, in order to avoid the delay that might be caused by the convocation of a Plenary Session, it would be better to inform the powers directly concerned about the contemplated changes.

We favor eliminating Article 373.¹ The original text of this article gave the states neighboring Germany the right to compel her to construct certain connecting railway lines at the expense of the interested states. The commission has proposed a change in this text, specifying a certain number of works to be executed, at the request of Belgium and the Czechoslovak state, within a period of five years after the signing of the treaty. A special agreement would settle the division of expenses, instead of these being at the exclusive expense of the states concerned, as in the earlier text. The second text seems to us to constitute an extension of the first, and we thought it preferable to delete this clause completely. Germany herself has an interest in the development of communications across her territory. Should we impose on her specific obligations in favor of certain states? Isn't it better to allow the question to solve itself through the competition of in-

*H., *PPC*, VI, 446ff.

¹ It is printed in *PPC*, VI, 407.

terests? Nevertheless, we didn't want to make this change without consulting the interested parties.

—President Wilson reads aloud from the text referred to and adds:

The text as it was first drafted is so qualified by reservations and conditions that its value is almost nil. It seemed to us that there was no reason to adopt a new draft, imposing new obligations on Germany.

M. **Kramář.** I can explain what happened, because I am a member of the commission. Italy asked for a connecting line towards the Tauern, the Belgians were interested in certain communications towards the Rhine. The Germans protested, because the text written in general terms, which was first adopted, could have compelled them to construct new lines or to build connecting lines from whatever point from Germany. In my opinion, their protests were justified. It is impossible to impose on them a stipulation of this kind, formulated in general terms. The amendment which was submitted to you is precisely aimed at removing that objection. It shows the Germans that we don't intend to deprive them of their right to construct their domestic railways as they wish, and, in the second place, it limits our claim by precise stipulations. In fact, it reduces our request to a connecting line that involves the port of Antwerp and, concerning the Czechoslovaks, to two small connecting lines important for the transport of coal from Upper Silesia to Bohemia, whilst on a third point, between Schwandorf and Furth-im-Wald, the creation of a double track would allow great international trains between Paris and Warsaw to pass by way of Prague.

In short, the aim of this amendment is to reassure the Germans by showing that it involves solely small changes that are important for us; for example, concerning Antwerp, the Belgians, before the war, often asked for that connecting line, and the Germans refused it to them.

The American delegation declared itself against the amendment. The British delegation stated reservations. I stress the importance that this text has for us. Will we obtain this construction from the Germans by mutual agreement? We would hope to be able to obtain it with the support of the Allies. The Czechoslovak state will always be in the position of a small power towards the Germans. So I insist that the amendment proposed by the commission be kept. The Germans won't see in it the danger that the more general terms of the text previously adopted made them fear.

M. Hymans. I must thank M. Kramář for having pleaded our case better than we could have done ourselves, because he is a member of the Commission on Ports and Railroads. I see what the Belgian delegates have aimed at: the latter, who first asked for two lines, have afterwards been content with only one. I am convinced that this last line is of real importance to us. I think the Germans are alarmed by the general obligation that we seemed to want to impose on them. I favor keeping the commission's amendment, which stipulated work limited to a very few short lines. In reality, this is a reduction of the burden first imposed on Germany.

President Wilson. Thank you for your statements. What we wanted was to understand how the matter stood.

Mr. Lloyd George. If you were told that the expense will devolve on the country that demands the work, would it be in your interest to maintain the clause? The entire question rests on that. The best thing would be to ask this question of the experts, who could give us their reply this afternoon.

—The Belgian and Czechoslovak delegates withdraw.

President Wilson.* We have brought back for discussion two questions of direct interest to Poland. The first is that of the revision of the eastern frontier of the Polish state, in order to make it coincide more rigorously with the line of ethnographic demarcation. The changes contemplated would leave to Germany certain German territories and assign to Poland several territories inhabited by Poles.

The second question is the holding of a plebiscite in Upper Silesia; I think you have already been informed.

In addition, there a general clause in the treaty, which was not written especially for Poland, about the expropriation of enemy properties. France, England, and the United States have the right to expropriate enemy properties on their territory, the value having to be assigned to the credit of Germany in the reparation account, with Germany being responsible for indemnifying her expropriated nationals. For Poland, the case seemed different to us. Neither does the arrangement seem applicable to the Czechoslovak state or Transylvania. The principle that we will apply is thus the following: the Polish state has the right to expropriate a German subject, but there must be liquidation, and the product of this liquidation will be handed over to the person expropri-

*H., *PPC*, VI, 449ff.

ated. In case the settlement should be contested, the question would be brought before a joint court of arbitration; in short, that amounts to the normal system of expropriation. Do you have any objection to this solution?

M. Dmowski. Is it said clearly that this arrangement will apply only to German properties situated in Polish territories retaken from Germany?

President Wilson. We first contemplated this arrangement for Upper Silesia. Then it seemed to us necessary to make it general.

Mr. Lloyd George. The same arrangement has been recommended to us by the Economic Commission for all the new states.

M. Paderewski. The Polish government doesn't intend to expropriate anyone without fair compensation.

President Wilson. We thought as much; but we didn't want to take this decision without having talked to you about it. The plebiscite we want to hold in Upper Silesia aims at removing any pretext for a German irredentist movement in the future. The Germans don't contest the fact that the great majority of the population in Upper Silesia is Polish. What they contest is the wish of that population to be reunited to the Polish homeland. When we consulted him earlier about this, M. Paderewski distinguished between two regions: the eastern region—the mining area—where a favorable result in the plebiscite seems certain to him, and the agricultural region of the West, about which he made certain reservations. What we have in mind is a plebiscite by commune. It would only take place after a rather long period, to permit the populations to free themselves from any influence able to corrupt the expression of their opinion. The evacuation of Upper Silesia by German troops is scheduled within a period of three weeks.

M. Paderewski. I cannot hide from you the fact that this decision will be a cruel blow for our people. It is a blow to the feeling the Poles have towards you; for they believe in the new principles articulated by President Wilson as in a new Gospel. Moreover, I will remind you that, if the results of the plebiscite are not what you want, the victims will not be Polish nobles, the middle class, or businessmen, but poor peasants, workers. For it is they who constitute the Polish element in Upper Silesia. For centuries they have suffered oppression in all forms. They hoped finally to live freely in their homeland. If the results of the plebiscite go against us, it will be a veritable calamity for our people.

Moreover, the waiting will prolong intolerable tension. I hope the plebiscite will take place in a short time—three months for example, six months at most. In the meantime, the struggle will be terrible. It is not a matter of an election that will assign seats for a few years, but of a vote that will decide the fate of the country for all centuries to come. If this waiting period is prolonged, I fear that the morale of our population will be more agitated than during the war itself.

Our delegation doesn't dream of opposing your decision. It is compelled to accept it with the respect we owe you, whilst expressing its profound regret.

President Wilson. Don't think that your words haven't moved me. I confess to you that I did not arrive at the conclusions you just discussed without doubts and scruples.

Mr. Lloyd George. I was moved by what M. Paderewski told us the other day. We did not take our final decision without long reflection. I am certain that Poland has nothing to fear from the plebiscite in the great mining region of Silesia. There, it is a question of a working population, rather independent in expressing its true feeling, which undoubtedly will attach itself to the Polish Republic.

President Wilson. We are told that, in the elections of 1907, Upper Silesia, with eight districts, elected five Polish deputies. It seems that their party had secret relations with Polish political groups in other parts of Prussian Poland. We are assured that Polish feeling in Upper Silesia has grown strongly since the beginning of the war. An American, whose testimony I recently heard, informed me that he found a desire for union with Poland everywhere in that region. These different facts reassure me about the probable result of the plebiscite.

M. Dmowski. Altogether, I believe in the good results of the plebiscite. The Germans say: this population does not want to be Polish. It is true that, forty or fifty years ago, it was no longer Polish in anything but language; but since then, Polish consciousness has reappeared and grown. This movement will continue. There may be districts which, having hesitated in 1919 to declare themselves Polish, will revolt later against German domination. What will you do then?

President Wilson. One of the duties of the League of Nations will be precisely to resolve problems of this kind.

Mr. Lloyd George. That is what I said recently to the House of Commons; we know very well that we can't settle all problems in the peace treaty. We have established the League of Nations as a permanent organ of reorganization and conciliation.

M. Dmowski. When do the German troops have to evacuate Upper Silesia?
President Wilson. Immediately after the signing of the treaty.
M. Dmowski. And the German civil servants?
President Wilson. The inter-Allied commission charged with preparing the plebiscite will have full powers to expel any person whose influence might prejudice a free vote.
M. Dmowski. In that case, I will request that the commission be assisted by both Germans and Poles in its work.
President Wilson. We thought it best to leave discretionary powers to this commission, which will judge on the spot.
M. Dmowski. We accept the changes in the boundary line. We would only like to draw your attention to a few points where Polish groups remain on German territory. This particularly concerns Bomst and Meseritz.

—*M. Paderewski and M. Dmowski withdraw.*

Mr. Lloyd George.* What we have just heard shows how difficult it is to make laws for peoples other than one's own. All the friends of Poland have come to tell us that it was important to allow a long period of time to elapse before the plebiscite. Poland's representatives come here to ask us to shorten this period as much as possible.
President Wilson. I thought the period of one to two years had the best chance of allowing Polish opinion to express itself freely.
M. Clemenceau. Paderewski tells you that his compatriots would go crazy in the meantime.
President Wilson. I propose a change which will make it possible, if it is right, to shorten the period, and, if it is discovered that it is wrong, to prolong it as much as necessary. Instead of "from one to two years," we should write "from six to eighteen months."

—*This proposal is adopted.*
—*Reading of the reply on the financial clauses, which is adopted.*[2]

President Wilson. I see nothing here about the expenses of the occupation.
M. Clemenceau. We agreed that we would not put them in the treaty but in a convention signed amongst ourselves.

*H., *PPC*, VI, 453ff.

[2] Printed in *ibid.*, pp. 457-63; in the reply of June 16, *ibid.*, pp. 967-72.

Mr. Lloyd George. We have to reply to the Czechoslovaks and the Belgians on the question of the railways.

President Wilson. I must say that their arguments seemed quite strong to me.

Mr. Lloyd George. It seems to me that the Czechoslovaks were right. It is a matter of insuring the transport of the coal absolutely essential to their industries. I am less convinced that the Belgian request is justified; it seems to me that the Belgians want to give an advantage to Antwerp to the detriment of German ports.

President Wilson. I understand the interest there might be in establishing rapid communications between Prague and Paris.

—Reading of the reply to the German counterproposals on the Belgian and Danish frontiers.[3]

President Wilson. I must say that we just sent a new American Minister to Denmark.[4] The Danes immediately expressed to him their anxieties abut the plebiscite in southern Schleswig, which they say goes beyond what they ask.

Mr. Lloyd George. I admit that the decision taken gives us the appearance of having been more concerned with taking territories away from Germany than with redressing an obvious wrong. The Danes beg us not to give them this southern part of Schleswig. I propose to omit the third zone of the plebiscite.

President Wilson. I am also in favor of omitting the plebiscite in the southernmost region of Schleswig.

Mr. Lloyd George. I think we must abide by the two zones claimed by the Danish government. The best thing is to send this decision to the Tardieu commission,[5] which is charged with putting our reply to the German counterproposals into shape.

Baron Sonnino. It may become necessary to change the southern limit of the second zone. I don't know if certain indisputably Danish elements were not included deliberately in the southernmost zone.

—M. Fromageot and Mr. James Brown Scott are introduced.

President Wilson. A question is raised about the part of Schleswig which might become Danish again; it involves the financial set-

---

[3] Printed in *ibid.*, pp. 464-65; in the reply of June 16, *ibid.*, pp. 941-42, 950-51.

[4] Norman Hapgood, a progressive publicist and writer.

[5] There was no "Tardieu commission." The council said that the Drafting Committee should confer with Tardieu, who had special knowledge about them, before making these changes.

tlement. In particular, shouldn't the value of public properties which would be acquired by the Danish government be deposited into the reparation fund?

Mr. Lloyd George. This raises a much more general and very important issue, for it affects all the territories we are detaching from Germany. For instance, Upper Silesia is an area of very great economic value; if it becomes Polish, will it bear no part of the financial burden of Germany? It is the same for the free city of Danzig. Should the fact that it will form a free state have the consequence of freeing it from all obligation towards us?

Mr. Brown Scott. As drafted, the text of the treaty imposes no part of the reparation debt on new states.

President Wilson. In the case of Poland, it is true that many of her inhabitants fought against us, but that was against their will, and the country, trampled in all directions by Russian and German armies, suffered enormously. From the beginning of this war, the Allies declared their intention to liberate Poland; must we, as a gift of happy accession, impose that heavy charge upon her?

Mr. Lloyd George. In any case, Danzig will not be part of Poland.

President Wilson. Financially, it comes to the same thing; if you burden Danzig, Poland will suffer from it.

Mr. Lloyd George. Undoubtedly; but do you want to burden France, England, and Italy instead?

President Wilson. We have already tried to settle this question for the Austrian states. You remember the idea set forth by M. Orlando of balancing assets and liabilities against each other. We have always come to an impasse, and we have been compelled to give it up.

Mr. Lloyd George. No. For Austria, we said that the different territories which will be detached will pay, as a contribution to the cost of the war of liberation, 25 per cent of the value of the war loans within their respective borders. Isn't it inadmissible to allow the rich German landowners of Silesia to escape without paying a penny?

President Wilson. It is much more important to know whether we will or will not have peace at the end of next week.

Mr. Lloyd George. I don't recall whether the arrangement contemplated for the different parts of the Austrian Empire must or must not apply to Poland. In any case, the Czechoslovaks have accepted it. Why should Poland not submit herself to it? Concerning Upper Silesia, this money will be paid not by Poles, but by Germans.

President Wilson. We are establishing a Poland almost without capital. Are we going to take from her what little she has? Bohemia is not in the condition of Poland, trampled by the successive sweeps of armies.

Mr. Lloyd George. Upper Silesia is a great industrial region where the capital is German. As for Danzig, it is a German city, and a rich city. It is as much responsible for the damages we suffered as any other city of Germany.

President Wilson. It has been understood up to now that, in revising the treaty, we shouldn't impose new burdens on Germany.

Mr. Lloyd George. What I propose would alleviate the burdens of the German state; what won't be paid by Upper Silesia and Danzig will be paid by the rest of Germany.

President Wilson. What you will take from Danzig is relatively little. But, above all, in my opinion, it is too late to concern ourselves with it; we mustn't delay the signing of the treaty.

Mr. Lloyd George. Can't we write that, if after the plebiscite, part of Upper Silesia returns to Poland, there will be ground for taking a decision about the participation of this territory in the reparation debt?

President Wilson. This will act against the union with Poland.

M. Clemenceau. That argument moves me.

Mr. Lloyd George. If you don't do it, that will cost us hundreds of millions. It is not the Poles you will exonerate, but the great landowners of Silesia. As for your last argument, it doesn't seem fair to me to tell the Poles that they will be assured of a pecuniary advantage if they vote in the way we wish; that amounts to loading the dice.

President Wilson. I call to your attention that, according to the thirteenth of the Fourteen Points, concerning Poland, I did not commit myself to holding a plebiscite in Upper Silesia.

Mr. Lloyd George. As for us, we never understood, when the right of peoples to self-determination was mentioned, that it meant we could dispose of them without consulting them.

President Wilson. All I said was that the thirteenth of my Fourteen Points doesn't obligate me to the Germans to hold a plebiscite. I don't believe it would be cheating to take away from those who oppressed a country for a long time an argument that they could use to maintain their domination.

Mr. Lloyd George. I can't take back what I have said; that is called loading the dice.

President Wilson. I hope that you do not hold to that expression.

Mr. Lloyd George. Yet it expresses the fact.

M. Clemenceau. You are right in principle, concerning the responsibility of the German territories which are going to be detached from Germany. But it is too late to think about it, and I believe it could create serious difficulties.

Mr. Lloyd George. That is going to compel us to abandon the plan we had prepared for Austria. For my country and France, the result will be a loss of hundreds of millions. If it is in the interest of the plebiscite that it be done, I can't call this procedure anything but what I have just called it.

Mr. Brown Scott. The question arises whether the five days which will be given the Germans to make known their final reply include the three days of warning before the renewal of hostilities provided by the Armistice Agreement. This must be indicated clearly.

M. Clemenceau. Indicate it clearly: these three days are included. On the sixth day, the Armistice is over, hostilities are resumed.

President Wilson. Of course, it will suffice if the Germans declare themselves prepared to sign before the end of the fifth day. The date of the signing can be set later.

M. Clemenceau. Certainly. What must be said is that hostilities will be resumed immediately if we have not received an affirmative answer from them before the end of the fifth day.

CXXVI

Conversation between President Wilson, Mr. Lloyd George, and Barons Sonnino and Makino*

JUNE 16, 1919, 11 A.M.

—President Wilson reads aloud the text of a note on the question of the properties of German religious missions outside Europe.

—*The text of this note is approved.*[1]

Mr. Lloyd George. A telegram I received from Berlin reveals that

*H., *PPC*, VI, 470ff.

[1] It is printed in *PPC*, VI, 478-79. This was a declaration to be sent to the Vatican. It placed the German Catholic missions at the disposal of properly authorized persons of the Roman Catholic faith.

the domestic situation is serious and that it is thought everywhere that the German government won't sign.

Baron Makino. Rumors of that kind can be spread intentionally.

Mr. Lloyd George. I think so.

Sir Maurice Hankey. A brief reply to the German delegation has been prepared about Memel:[2]

> The mass of the population in the area around Memel is Lithuanian. Memel is a German city. But that is no reason to leave this entire district to Germany, even more so since the port of Memel is the only maritime outlet of Lithuania. This territory will be transferred temporarily to the Allied and Associated Powers, because the Lithuanian state has not yet been finally constituted.

Baron Sonnino. I must convey to you a letter from Prime Minister Orlando.[3] It expresses the reservation that the Italian government must make, before the signing of the peace treaty, concerning the Covenant of the League of Nations incorporated in that treaty. The Covenant indeed stipulates the mutual guarantee of their territories for the members of the League. Now, the territorial questions concerning Italy are not yet settled, and, consequently, we can only guarantee the frontiers of other states without reciprocity. M. Orlando hoped that the solution of our territorial questions would precede the signing of the treaty with Germany; since that is not possible, he is compelled to make this reservation today.

President Wilson. I will observe that your territorial questions lie outside the German treaty. The Covenant of the League of Nations, which has been incorporated in the text of this treaty, is also in the treaty with Austria; it is there that the mutual commitment of League members to guarantee their respective boundaries will apply to the boundaries of the old Austria-Hungary. It is obvious that this guarantee cannot be applied to boundaries still undetermined.

Baron Sonnino. I can present a reservation to the Four which you will put on record.

President Wilson. I think that is the best way to proceed.

—Reading of a plan relating to the military occupation of Bulgaria.

—*This plan is approved.*

---

[2] Printed in *ibid.*, p. 479; in the letter of June 16, *ibid.*, pp. 949-50.
[3] Printed in *ibid.*, pp. 485-86.

Baron Sonnino. Italy must participate in the agreement concerning the occupation of the left bank of the Rhine.

M. Clemenceau. But you are not one of the powers that will occupy.

Baron Sonnino. We have an interest in having a liaison officer there, if only in order to be informed about what is happening. For instance, there can be economic questions that concern us.

President Wilson. According to the prepared text, the commission will have no power over the left bank of the Rhine except to control the relations between the occupation army and the local authorities.

M. Clemenceau. You can send whom you want to see what is happening on the left bank of the Rhine. But a liaison officer can only be named to establish communications between two services cooperating with one another. Here, these services don't exist. The occupation army will do nothing but mount guard, and the commission nothing but maintain contact with the military authorities, on the one hand, and the local authorities, on the other.

CXXVII

Conversation between President Wilson, MM. Clemenceau and Lloyd George, and Baron Sonnino*

JUNE 16, 1919, 4 P.M.

—Marshal Foch and General Weygand are introduced.

President Wilson. We have summoned you, Marshal, to ask you what your plans are if Germany refuses to sign the treaty. We would like to know what you have contemplated. We are responsible for the political direction of affairs; you have the responsibility for military operations. It is absolutely necessary for our common action that we understand each other perfectly.

Marshal Foch. The military action we will undertake must have a goal. I will ask the governments: what goal will you set for it? We have no enemy army before us. But we have the German govern-

*H., PPC, VI, 501ff.

ment before us. What result do you want to obtain? Do you want to overthrow a government that resists you? We will see if we have the means to do it. Do you want to obtain more immediate and more limited results, for example, by the occupation of a productive region like the Ruhr Basin? Do you want an economic result or a political result? Military action depends on the goal you pursue. Once this goal is set, we will see if the military means at our disposal allow us to attain it.

M. Clemenceau. I thought we had already agreed about that. We don't seek an economic result, no more than we seek conquests. What we want is a political result—the signing of the peace treaty.

Germany is vanquished; she is so weak that Marshal Foch tells us: "I have no enemy army before me." In these circumstances, there are two ways to proceed—the mild way and the strong way. For myself, I favor the strong way. There must be a resolute, brutal advance to obtain a decisive effect. A slow advance, which would have the appearance of hesitation, could give the Germans the impression that demobilization has weakened us and that we ourselves don't know if we have the means to go further. It could encourage resistance and prolong the period of uncertainty in which we find ourselves. So I am for the strong way. In my opinion, we should question the Marshal about this.

To my mind, there is no other operation to have in mind than a direct march on Berlin. That is what will be understood by everyone, and the immediate effect of it will be unquestionable. It is probable that, before our armies get that far, the German government will have changed and the treaty will be signed. Moreover, the intentions of those who will sign in Germany's name will remain doubtful. We mustn't give them the impression at any moment that we have become incapable of vigorous action. A limited action would be fatal. If Germany refuses, I favor a vigorous and unremitting military blow that will force the signing.

President Wilson. I agree with you.
Mr. Lloyd George. We agree completely.
Baron Sonnino. There is no possible doubt.
Marshal Foch. Then I am asked to use the strong way. That doesn't displease me. The result in view is to compel the German government to sign the peace. Thus, it must be sought where it is and be destroyed, until we find ourselves dealing with another government that will sign the peace. In the realm of facts, everything depends on the means at our disposal. It is June 16, 1919. Since November 11, we have demobilized, and, today, we have on the

left bank of the Rhine thirty-nine divisions: eighteen French, ten English, five American, and six Belgian. On November 11 last, we had 198. So we must not expect the same effort today that we would have been able to make in November.

As for the German army, it has been reduced to very little in western Germany. The military resistance we might meet is not of a kind to stop thirty-nine divisions. But we are faced with a large population. Germany still has sixty-five million inhabitants. This population is not under arms; but it includes a great number of men who were soldiers yesterday—noncommissioned officers, officers, experienced in war and capable of improvised organization. The regions crossed could present difficulties of a particular nature. The more extensive our advance, the more we have to leave behind us occupation troops strong enough to keep the population—that is to say, sixty-five million men—at a respectful distance. It is unlikely we would meet organized armies; consequently a striking force is useless. But we must have occupation forces, because of the danger which comes from the military valor of the German people, if they should ever be stirred by patriotic sentiment or by an organizing activity.

Let's not forget that these people have a powerful and unique central organization behind them, which could work towards stirring them up and creating special difficulties for our passage. We are still faced with a single force, driven from above, over a very vast territory.

To smash the head of this government in Berlin, we have to pass through 480 kilometers across northern Germany, that is, across the most populated, best organized, most militaristic region of Germany. Moreover, this region has the support of the states of the South—Bavaria, Württemberg, the Grand Duchy of Baden. This powerful whole could be difficult to handle with only thirty-nine divisions if the German government arouses the population.

On the other hand, from this same statement follow the means we have to weaken German resistance. If, through our maneuvers, we can detach southern Germany from northern Germany at the same time that our troops are marching in the Main Valley, we will have only forty-five million men before us, instead of sixty-five million. A strategy of separation, aided by a separatist policy, would allow us to get at the head of the German organization in Berlin.

The question in this: are we inclined to deal separately with the separated states—the Grand Duchy of Baden, Württemberg,

Bavaria? This separate peace would immediately detach from the rest of Germany twelve or fifteen million men, and this solution would allow our troops to march on Berlin. Conversely, if we march right on Berlin in a straight line, leaving southern Germany on our right flank in a state of war against us, with the possible support that might come from Austria, we can quickly find ourselves faced with a more or less formidable opposition and threat on our southern front. To march on Berlin with thirty-nine divisions, part of which would be necessarily employed to guard lines of communication, can bring us before Berlin in a very weakened state, threatened on our right flank. We will avoid this threat only by putting southern Germany out of commission by special treatment and a final peace.

President Wilson. What do you mean by "special treatment"?

Marshal Foch. The states of the South are the first we will meet on our passage, and we would treat with them.

Mr. Lloyd George. Would you cancel for them part of the debt for reparation that encumbers them?

Marshal Foch. I would impose a down payment on them immediately; then you could calculate the total of their contribution.

Mr. Lloyd George. I don't believe that could induce them to sign. We must choose: either we will deprive ourselves of what they owe us as an integral part of Germany, or, if we treat them like the rest of Germany, I don't see why they should come over to us.

M. Clemenceau. Politics must not be mixed with strategy. As far as politics are concerned, their part is nearly over. Politics should not be mixed up with military forecasts, any more than strategy has arisen in our councils here.

Marshal Foch is right, if he foresees difficulties, to inform us about them. But we must look at the other side of the picture. Germany has sixty-five million inhabitants, it is true. But she is conquered, and the reaction of a German to defeat is completely different from that of a Frenchman. In Germany, there are many men who have been good soldiers, but they are conquered; the Germans only resist if they are organized.

It is not fair to compare the thirty-nine divisions we have at our disposal today on the left bank of the Rhine with the 198 divisions of November 11. The military problem that exists is no longer the same.

For all these reasons, I would like for the Marshal, after having shown the shadows in the picture, not to forget to show the lights in it. Nothing is comparable between our military situation and the Germans'. It is said the the Germans have manufactured much war matériel; according to our latest information, these are only rumors. On the other hand, we know that the Germans have tried to sell war materials abroad, and sometimes succeeded. In contrast, our war supplies are overflowing. In heavy artillery, machine guns, tanks, we are as abundantly supplied as is possible. According to our military, our superiority is absolute, crushing.

It is obvious that if lines of supply are established, the Main line seems excellent. It must be secured; but will this necessity weaken the advancing forces as much as the Marshal says? I doubt it. Let us not forget that these thirty-nine divisions in reality equal forty-four, because American divisions are much stronger than ours.

One of the objectives we must aim at immediately is junction with the Czech army, which has ten divisions of first-rate soldiers. It lacks matériel; we will give it to them. It is true that the Czechs are still fighting against the Hungarians; but besides concerning ourselves actively with halting the conflict, it will be enough, if necessary, to send a few air squadrons to the Hungarian front to stop it all. In Poland, the information I have makes me believe the Germans are determined to resist whatever might take place. The Poles have twenty divisions to hold them back. Therefore, I don't put credence in the weakness that could be hastily inferred.

Marshal Foch speaks of detaching Bavaria and Württemberg from Germany. By the sole fact of cutting southern Germany off from northern Germany and by an attack of the Italian army against Bavaria, which would be easy, resistance on the part of the Bavarians becomes impossible, and they will be quickly reduced to impotence. This will insure the security of our flank. We can then march on Berlin with the aid of the Poles, who will hold back the Germans of Upper Silesia during this time. We have nothing much to fear from the population, if it is not organized. Remember the wars of Napoleon.

If the Marshal thinks this march too hazardous, let him explain. If he thinks we must use the mild way, let him say so also. We have only a few days to decide and prepare our program.

President Wilson. I will remind Marshal Foch that we have already studied this question with him on the map; he explained to us his plan for the advance, his system of communications. It would thus seem obvious that the Marshal had no doubt then about the possibility of a march on Berlin. Has something happened meanwhile which has changed his views?

Marshal Foch. Since then, time has gone by. German organizations are unknown to us; there could be some. The Germans could have manufactured war materials. German morale has certainly stiffened.

But to return. I have difficulty explaining myself. I have not been understood. I will say: we have all the forces required to break the military resistance of the enemy. But as we advance, we will need increasing numbers of occupation troops, all the more important because we will have all of Germany on our hands. In order to avoid this ruinous occupation, which can take us to Berlin too anemic to deliver the decisive blow, I say: the only way is to put southern Germany out of action, that is, to think about a separatist strategy. But in order for this separatist strategy to obtain results, it must be completed by a separatist policy, which imposes a separate peace and disarmament on the states of the South. I ask the governments not to pursue only one signing for all of Germany, but to have the treaty signed along the way and thus to weaken the final resistance, which will be that of Prussia.

President Wilson. This would be worth considering during the advance of the armies. What we are asking Marshal Foch today is if he is ready to carry out the planned march on Berlin which he has already explained to us.

Marshal Foch. I am obliged to make reservations. I will not go further if I am not assured either of the execution of the plan I just explained or of forces other than those I now have at my disposal.

M. Clemenceau. I must say I am unfavorably impressed by the plan we have just heard explained. The situation is too serious for any one of us to hide his feelings. Several weeks ago, Marshal Foch explained a plan to us without any reservations. He seemed to us full of confidence. What strikes us today is that he is asking us for a political action without which, he says, he cannot advance. We must come to an agreement. We are ready to do anything to weaken the enemy. We summoned the Marshal here to hear him on a military question. He replies to us: "Make good policy, and I will make good strategy." Good policy—does that mean negotiations with Bavaria, sending high commissioners, I don't know what? In my opinion, that will only diminish our prestige. I cannot agree to that. If the march on Berlin is impossible, we will have to talk about it amongst ourselves and see what can be done.

I must say I was not prepared for what we have just heard. Marshal Foch tells us: "I make reservations." If, afterwards, our policy doesn't yield what he expects, the responsibility will be thrown on us. Conversely, we could say that our policy did not succeed because it was not sufficiently supported by his strategy. But it is not a question of throwing responsibility on one or the other. The Marshal never feared responsibilities; he has shown that well during the war. Let him tell us frankly what he thinks, and we will see what we can do.

About what he has just said, I, too, am compelled to make reservations. To encircle Bavaria with the aid of the Czechs and, at the same time, to pursue an unknown policy—I cannot commit myself to that. During this time, the Poles will be crushed in Upper Silesia. I am not prepared to go that way. I don't know strategy, it is not my profession. But if the situation is truly as Marshal Foch describes it, we will have to take decisions in consequence.

I had thought an action by Italy against Bavaria could produce interesting results. I thought everything was settled. Marshal Foch has anxieties; his duty is to make them known; but time presses. If in five days we can only undertake a hesitant march along the Main Valley, that won't give the results we want. The Germans will quickly see that these are feints, and their resistance will grow from the weakness they will attribute to us.

Mr. Lloyd George. I have a few words to say from the British point of view. Marshal Foch is the Commander in Chief of the Allied armies. Three weeks ago, we asked him for his opinion about the military means to force the signing. At the same time, we consulted our naval advisers. The Marshal gave us a report on the situation. He brought a carefully prepared plan, anticipating an advance between the two valleys of the Lippe and the Main, which were to cover both flanks of his army. He told us what forces were at his disposal; he didn't complain of not having enough. He told President Wilson that it seemed to him necessary to delay the departure of two American divisions; the President gave the required orders. He informed us that the French were ready to advance, but the English were not completely ready; I asked him to see Mr. Winston Churchill who was in Paris, straightaway, and he met him the same day. The British War Secretary promised to take the necessary measures without delay; I suppose they have been taken.

Today, three weeks later, Marshal Foch seems to have doubts, he brings us a different plan. When President Wilson tells him: "We prefer your earlier plan," the Marshal replies: "I make my reservations." If there are changes in Germany that have made you change your opinion, you should have informed us about them. You say Germany's morale has stiffened; Germany has manufactured war materials. In that case, you should ask us for more divisions and more complete armaments. But the Marshal did not hurry from Luxembourg to tell us about his anxieties. If he is here today, it is at our invitation. If he thinks there has been such a change in Germany that a plan that was excellent three weeks ago has become insufficient, at what moment did he realize this? We were ready at any time to receive him and listen to him.

Speaking in the name of the governments whose armies are under Marshal Foch's command, and proud to obey him, I think we have the right to complain: we heard nothing before the Marshal came here today at our appeal, and we are hearing him at a time when it is too late to send him new divisions if he needs them.

I fear the Marshal is mixing policy with strategy and allowing his judgment about political matters to create doubts in his mind about purely military questions. The events of the last year showed that our confidence in his great military capabilities was entirely justified. We ask him to give us his opinion about the march on Berlin, and I would prefer to have it in writing. We must be prepared to advance rapidly, resolutely, in such a way as not to give the impression that we are too weak to obtain decisive results. If, indeed, we have become too weak, it must be said; I'll go to London and ask that I be given the necessary troops. But the Marshal must say so.

President Wilson. In case of need, I will bring back troops from the United States. But I would be compelled to tell Congress that I had not sent home any divisions without Marshal Foch having been informed, and that I had kept in Europe the forces he had asked of me.

—Mr. Lloyd George reads aloud the report of the statements made by Marshal Foch on May 10 and 19, and he adds:

Here is what Marshal Foch told us then; since then, we have not heard a word from him.

Marshal Foch. You have made me say many things I haven't said, undoubtedly because you have spoken longer than I. The plans decided upon on April 25 continue to serve as the basis for our offensive. But our bow is slackening. We can certainly go in the direction of Weimar. If we want to go all the way to Berlin, we will leave behind us territories whose watch will be a heavy burden to us. The maneuver indicated on May 10 becomes more difficult to the degree that we advance—granting that our anemia doesn't prevent us from going all the way to Berlin; moreover, I never said we could go that far. The march in the Main Valley becomes more interesting, provided policy enters into that plan. I said only this: we will go no further if we are not aided by a separatist policy. Our march on Berlin will have all the more force as this separatist policy clearly succeeds. If the governments don't want to contemplate this policy, we can be compelled to halt earlier. This separatist strategy is, moreover, the one that leads us most directly to the junction with the Czechs and the Poles. We can have results before arriving at the end, if, by a rational strategy, we cut Germany in two. I ask the governments to anticipate this contingency.

Mr. Lloyd George. Shouldn't this question be studied amongst the heads of governments?

President Wilson. Like you, I think we must ask the Marshal for a written report.

Marshal Foch. You have spoken of responsibilities, of the mild way. I have already shown what I understood by the mild way. As for responsibilities, I am ready to assume them. If I am asked to indicate my views in writing, I am ready to do it.

—Marshal Foch and General Weygand withdraw.
—The members of the commission entrusted with studying the economic and financial clauses of the treaty with Austria are introduced.*

President Wilson. If I am not mistaken, the experts agree on the financial and economic clauses; the only remaining difficulty relates to the distribution of the costs amongst the different states which share the territories of the former Austria-Hungary.

Mr. Davis. Exactly. Several points concerning private property also remain to be settled.

President Wilson. The text now submitted to us leaves aside the question about the contribution to be provided by states other than Austria proper. It is indeed impossible to stipulate anything in this regard before having concluded agreements with those states themselves. M. Loucheur will no doubt inform us about the state of the negotiations.

Mr. Lloyd George. I must inform you of a communication I received from our representative in Vienna. He observes that Vienna was and undoubtedly will remain the financial center of the entire group of states we are concerned with. If the financial

*H., PPC, VI, 510-11.

clauses of the treaty remain as they are, all the banks in Vienna will collapse, and I am assured that, at least financially, Vienna is an absolutely necessary center. If it disappeared, it would perhaps be replaced by Berlin, which is neither in our interest nor in that of the Czechoslovaks or the Yugoslavs. It seems necessary to change our provisions in such a way as to avoid what our advisers consider to be a catastrophe.

President Wilson. I propose that the study of this question be referred to a special committee.

—This proposal is adopted, and the members of this subcommittee are designated.[1]

President Wilson. I will now ask M. Loucheur about the status of the question of the contribution of the new states.

M. Loucheur. There are two problems mingled here. Some of these states have the right to reparation. On the other hand, all must bear part of the burden of the Austro-Hungarian prewar debt and of the debt contracted during the war, and they must also contribute to the expenses of the war of liberation. After a study of the credits and debits, I proposed to Rumania that she renounce her part of the reparations and that she be discharged from all debt. I hope she will accept this settlement. The case of Serbia is different: there will remain a credit in her favor under the heading of reparation. Italy is also studying the settlement of this question concerning her liberated provinces. I hope to be able to bring you firm proposals the day after tomorrow.

I haven't yet seen the Poles about their contribution to the costs of the war of liberation. I thought it was better that the question be first settled for Rumania, Serbia, and Italy.

Mr. Lloyd George. That is very well.

Baron Sonnino. I have a question to ask: if you free Poland and Czechoslovakia from their debts, who will pay us?

M. Loucheur. We do not anticipate this exemption either for Poland or Bohemia. As for Austria, she will perhaps go bankrupt; but I must point out that her domestic debt is payable in crowns.

Mr. Davis. I thought each of the new states would relieve Austria of part of her debt.

Mr. Lloyd George. I didn't realize that all this would fall to that extent on Austria and Hungary, which will be two small states without great resources. That seems impossible to me.

M. Loucheur. What I am asked to establish is the balance of each

---

[1] Baruch, Crespi, Loucheur, and Col. Sidney Cornwallis Peel.

state. Take Rumania: we place to her debit part of the prewar debts of Austria-Hungary, part of the war debt, and the repurchase of state properties. We place to her credit reparations, whose total is, moreover, strictly speaking, higher than the total of the other column. All my work has consisted of balancing the two figures.

Mr. Lloyd George. Indeed, I didn't think the war debt of Austria would ever be paid by anyone.

President Wilson. Even if that is true, it is not we who can annul the Austrian debt by the treaty.

—*It is decided that the question will be sent back for study. The experts withdraw.*

—Reading of a telegram from Béla Kun,* announcing that he has given the order to halt hostilities against the Czechoslovaks,² and asking the Allies to make the latter also stop them. The Hungarian government complains about the boundaries whose outline has been indicated to it. It expresses the wish that a meeting of the representatives of the different states of former Austria-Hungary be convened in Vienna for a common study of the liquidation of the monarchy.

Mr. Lloyd George. That's not a bad reply.

President Wilson. The telegrams prepared by Mr. Balfour say nothing about this question of a meeting between the representatives of these different states. Hadn't the idea of that meeting already been formulated by General Smuts at the time of his mission to Budapest? I don't believe, moreover, that this meeting is possible if there isn't some external authority to keep order in the discussion amongst these states.

Mr. Lloyd George. Perhaps it is better to summon them here, under the auspices of the conference.

Baron Sonnino. I fear that the impression produced will be that of another Prinkipo.³

*H., *PPC*, VI, 513ff.

² B. Kun to G. Clemenceau, June 16, 1919, printed in *PWW*, Vol. 60, pp. 596-98.

³ The heads of the Allied and Associated Powers, on January 22, 1919, had invited the warring factions in Russia to send representatives to Prinkipo, an island in the Sea of Marmara, to confer and negotiate, under Allied auspices, for an end to the Russian Civil War and the establishment of an all-Russian government that the powers could recognize. This initiative was totally unsuccessful. About this matter, see the index references to Prinkipo Declaration and Russia in *PWW*, Vols. 54 and 55. For a detailed discussion, see Thompson, *Russia, Bolshevism, and the Versailles Peace*, pp. 82-130.

President Wilson. Indeed, it is possible that some of these governments won't want to meet with the government of the Hungarian soviets.

M. Clemenceau. As for the military side of the question, I propose to refer it to the Supreme War Council.

Mr. Lloyd George. General Bliss could manage it alone.

M. Clemenceau. I have confidence in his judgment.

President Wilson. He has indeed a good mind, even beyond purely military questions. He should be told to confer with the Rumanians and Czechoslovaks.

President Wilson. You remember that, on the question of who would have the right to put before the League of Nations infractions of the article on national or religious minorities in the new states, we hesitated between two solutions; should this right be given to all members of the League, or only to members of the Council? I spoke to M. Vénisélos and M. Beneš about that question; both support the second solution. In my opinion, it is the best.

—(Assent.)

CXXVIII

Conversation between President Wilson and MM. Clemenceau and Lloyd George*

JUNE 16, 1919, 6:30 P.M.

President Wilson. I don't know what to think about what Marshal Foch just told us. I can't imagine what happened since we last heard him.

M. Clemenceau. Nothing at all happened.

President Wilson. Marshal Foch said to us: "The morale of the enemy is slightly improved; but I know of no new organization, I know nothing precise about the production of munitions." What has happened?

Mr. Lloyd George. Marshal Foch seems to me to be dominated by purely political considerations. He wants to resume the policy of the past, of the time when France aspired to the conquest of the left bank of the Rhine. He first brought plans of this kind to Lon-

*H., PPC, VI, 521ff.

don; we rejected them, and you, too, M. Clemenceau, you rejected them.

I fear that General Weygand's influence over him is considerable. I saw him speaking nonstop into the ear of the Marshal, indicating to him what he should say. I find Marshal Foch changed; his face has an inscrutable expression.

President Wilson. He has seen his plans collapse and doesn't want to help in the execution of ours.

Mr. Lloyd George. In the Plenary Session which preceded the delivery of the treaty to the Germans, he made a quasi-public protest.[1] Then he gave a resounding interview to an English newspaper.[2] All that didn't have the effect he anticipated. France

---

[1] "In the afternoon [of May 6] a secret Plenary Session was held at which the context of the Peace Treaty was communicated to the smaller nations and a general debate took place which was marked by sharp exchanges. There was quite a tilt between Foch and Clemenceau over military questions. There is a clique between Poincaré, the President of the French Republic, and Marshal Foch against Premier Clemenceau. While Foch was on the floor Clemenceau came over and said to the President [Wilson]: 'You must save me from these two fools.' The President asked Foch some very pointed questions and Foch was unable to answer them; the only way he answered them was by shrugging his shoulders and saying that he was unable to reply. This was concerning the creation of a buffer state in the Rhine and in connection with military reenforcements there. He (Foch) wanted to put there what seemed to be an excessively large number of troops. The President said to me: 'Foch may be a great soldier but he appeared to be very simple and seemed to have no ideas for planning. He either did not know how to answer questions or did not seem to know what he was talking about. I was very much disappointed in him.'" From the Diary of Dr. Grayson, printed in *PWW*, Vol. 58, p. 462. The exchange between Foch and Clemenceau is not recorded in the minutes of the Plenary Session of May 6.

For the background of the Poincaré-Foch "clique" against Clemenceau on the subject of Rhineland policy, see Jere Clemens King, *Foch versus Clemenceau: France and German Dismemberment, 1918-1919* (Cambridge, Mass., 1960), pp. 60-70, and Duroselle, *Clemenceau*, pp. 756-58.

[2] Foch does not seem to have given this interview following the Plenary Session of May 6, 1919. Lloyd George was probably referring to an interview that the Marshal gave to the Paris correspondent of the London *Daily Mail*, which appeared in that newspaper on April 18, 1919. Foch declared that the peace had to be "a peace of victors and not of vanquished" for the Allies, and that the safety of both France and Great Britain required that Allied troops stay on the Rhine to "double lock the door." He said that the Germans were an "envious and warlike people," who would always remain a menace, and that it would be possible to stop another German attack only on the Rhine. Foch concluded: "The next time, remember, the Germans will make no mistake. They will break through into Northern France and seize the Channel ports as a base of operations against England. . . . You think the Germans will have no arms for another attack. Ho! Ho! How do you know? By the time you found out that they had got them it would be too late." *New York Times*, April 19, 1919.

knew little of the thing and was not concerned with it. Even *Le Matin* stated then that it was satisfied with the treaty.

President Wilson. General Bliss tells me that he doesn't see what could make a march on Berlin dangerous. What Marshal Foch can justifiably say is that he had already spoken to us about cutting southern Germany off from northern Germany by means of a strategic maneuver; but he hadn't spoken about political separation.

M. Clemenceau. It is Mangin's policy, expanded. When we asked Marshal Foch questions about his military plans, he replied to us: "Carry out a policy of separation." What does that mean? We know very well that the true way to succeed in Germany, if it is possible, is not to meddle with her.

I deeply regret the attitude taken by Marshal Foch; I believe, like you, in the influence of General Weygand, but I must say in his favor that he is a first-rate staff officer.

Mr. Lloyd George. Probably the best we have.

President Wilson. We asked Marshal Foch for a written statement; won't it be a repetition, pure and simple, of what we have just heard?

M. Clemenceau. That's not certain. I noticed that the Marshal was in no hurry to end the conversation.

President Wilson. After we receive the memorandum he is going to send to us, shall we leave the execution of the operation to him?

M. Clemenceau. That would be no problem without General Weygand. I intend to consult Marshal Pétain about all this.

Mr. Lloyd George. I called Robertson in order to speak to him about it; but Robertson is a man full of caution, who never advances except after having taken every safeguard. From this perspective, I regret that Haig did not remain at the head of the army.

M. Clemenceau. What strikes me is that, when you asked Marshal Foch: "Do you need a larger number of divisions?," he gave no reply. I must consult Marshal Pétain.

President Wilson. If operations begin and General Weygand pushes the Marshal into the policy he indicated, we will be committed ourselves, and we'll no longer be able to get out of it.

Mr. Lloyd George. I fear a repetition of what happened with the Poles in Lemberg; all our injunctions changed nothing there.

M. Clemenceau. If he has it in his head not to go to Berlin, he won't go. What troubles me is that, in our last meetings, Marshal Foch has not always proved entirely frank. I recently spoke to him about a newspaper article that I knew was inspired by him; he denied it. Then I said to him: "Do you want me to give you the name of the officer on your general staff who corrected the proofs?" He couldn't reply.

President Wilson. What solution do you see?

M. Clemenceau. I ask you for twenty-four hours.

Mr. Lloyd George. If Marshal Foch is no longer there, the Germans will soon say: "He left because he judged the thing impossible."

M. Clemenceau. True. On the other hand, it is dangerous to allow him to return to the field if it is to carry out a policy in Germany which is not our own.

President Wilson. The danger is to leave the fate of Europe in the hands of General Weygand; that is what, for my part, I could not agree to.

Mr. Lloyd George. As you know, I have always supported Marshal Foch; I, more than anyone, contributed to placing him at the head of the Allied armies. Do you want me to see him personally?

M. Clemenceau. I fear that wouldn't help at all.

Mr. Lloyd George. Can't you remove General Weygand?

M. Clemenceau. Without Weygand, I must say that Foch would no longer be himself.

Mr. Lloyd George. Yes, but it is a matter of a simple operation, and everything is ready.

M. Clemenceau. The Marshal placed two generals in Mainz and Cologne, of whom one—Mangin—is a good soldier but a bad politician, whilst the other—Gérard—is both a mediocre soldier and an execrable politician. He placed them there with a political intention. The policy of dismemberment, that is what he offers us. The only way to obtain that dismemberment is to remain quiet.

President Wilson. Obviously, if you involve yourself in it you will make the thing impossible.

M. Clemenceau. I need twenty-four hours. I will see Pétain and perhaps see Foch again. This crisis is serious from a general point of view; but beyond that, it greatly saddens me personally.

Mr. Lloyd George. It is especially important to let nothing leak to the press.

M. Clemenceau. Very important, but news can percolate from General Weygand's quarter.

Mr. Lloyd George. This is the time to use the censor.

CXXIX

Conversation among President Wilson, MM. Lansing, Clemenceau, Pichon, Lloyd George, and Balfour, Marquis Imperiali, Baron Makino, and Viscount Chinda*

JUNE 17, 1919, NOON.

(After the hearing of the representatives of the Ottoman Empire by the Council of Ten.)[1]

Mr. Lloyd George. What are we going to do now? Are we going to say to these gentlemen: "We have heard you, return home"—or "Stay, and we will negotiate the peace with you"?

Mr. Lansing. In my opinion, they must be asked for a more precise presentation.

President Wilson. A sort of general protest, like the one we have just heard, has absolutely no value. The Turkish delegates say: "Don't judge on a basis of what has happened these last years, but on the whole history of the Ottoman Empire." I believe that would be worse still. They also say: "It is the tyrannical government of one party which is responsible for the errors and crimes committed; we are innocent." We didn't accept that manner of discussion in matters concerning Germany.

Mr. Lloyd George. You noticed that they appealed to Wilsonian principles, but adding, "Beyond the Taurus,[2] there is something stronger than the principle of nationality, than even the will of peoples if it was expressed by a plebiscite." I understand very well that they don't want a plebiscite; they know too well what the result would be.

President Wilson. They have done nothing but wail. It was they who asked to come here to explain their case, and here is all they said. That amounts to nothing.

Mr. Lloyd George. We must answer them.

M. Clemenceau. I propose to do it in writing.

Mr. Lloyd George. The question is whether we should say to them: "Good, return home"—or: "Stay, and we'll negotiate with you."

M. Clemenceau. First we must answer in writing to the statement

---

*Does not appear in H.

[1] The minutes of this meeting are printed in PPC, IV, 508-12.

[2] A mountain range in southern Turkey.

they brought us. I favor telling them to stay here for the negotiations that will follow.

President Wilson. In that case, it would be wise to warn them that they may be compelled to wait.

Mr. Lloyd George. They have to be told that we haven't yet signed the treaty with Germany, that the treaty with Austria isn't finished, and give them the choice of returning to Constantinople or staying, if they have time to waste.

What strikes me most in the document which they read a short time ago is that it reveals a much more dreadful situation even in Asia Minor than we had imagined. According to them, three million Mohammedans have been chased from their homes and are in the most precarious situation.

Mr. Balfour. The latest information I have on Asia Minor surpasses in horror all one can believe; in some places, the people are reduced to cannibalism.

M. Clemenceau. In view of public opinion, we must reply to their document as it is, remembering that they came here on their own initiative.

Mr. Lloyd George. We have to tell them that we are not ready, and that we need time. If they can't stay, we'll call them back when we are ready.

M. Clemenceau. In any case, they must take with them a reply to their document, which is a veritable confession. I will tell them that they will get an answer on Saturday.

Mr. Balfour. Don't you believe it is better to send them back to Constantinople than to keep them here unnecessarily? Their statement ends with a kind of appeal to the three hundred million Mohammedans. Paris is probably now the most favorable center for all kinds of propaganda.

President Wilson. I propose that the reply to the statement of the Ottomans be prepared by Mr. Balfour.

—Mr. Balfour accepts.

CXXX

Conversation between President Wilson and MM. Clemenceau and Lloyd George*

JUNE 17, 1919, 3 P.M.

—Reading of a note from Marshal Foch in reply to the question asked him by the heads of governments.[1]

President Wilson. That note leaves us where we were. The only difference I see between this written document and the Marshal's oral statement is that here it is a question of "separate armistice" instead of "policy of separation."

M. Clemenceau. It is probably a smart move to lead us to his views. The fact remains that the Marshal says today that he can't push toward Berlin for lack of troops; and he hasn't asked for reinforcements.

Mr. Lloyd George. Yesterday, you noticed that, when I said to him: "I can go to London to ask for divisions if you don't have enough," he said nothing in reply.

M. Clemenceau. Nor did he take up what I said about the possibility of cooperation of the Italian army against Bavaria; in the document which he sends today he takes care of that.

Mr. Lloyd George. Mustn't we see him now?

M. Clemenceau. Let's not be in a hurry. On the whole, things are better. I sent General Mordacq to speak to Marshal Pétain in Chantilly. In the meantime, can we make an effort off Danzig?

Mr. Lloyd George. Our battleships can do nothing if land batteries fire on them. The inferiority of an attack by sea is obvious today after our unfortunate experience in the Dardanelles. Concerning Danzig, we have already asked our naval officers the question when it was a matter of sending Polish troops by that way; we were compelled to give it up.

M. Clemenceau. That settles the question.

If Marshal Foch doesn't have enough men, why hasn't he said so? It is best not to hurry. I will let you go for two days;[2] I will inform the Marshal that you have left. During that time, I will

*H., PPC, VI, 523-24, contains almost nothing of this conversation.

[1] It is printed in PPC, VI, 525-26. In this note, Foch simply repeated the plans and problems that he had presented to the council at its meeting at 4 p.m. on June 16. He presents them again in CXXXII.

[2] Lloyd George was going to London, Wilson, to Brussels for a two-day tour of Belgium.

prepare a letter saying that we don't understand very well what he wrote about the armistices to be concluded; for the armistice is not our business, but his. I won't say a word on the policy of separation; the best thing is to let that drop.

Mr. Lloyd George. It really seems as if he still had the thing in his head.

M. Clemenceau. I will especially ask him if he doesn't have enough troops, and if he thinks not, why he didn't ask for them earlier.

President Wilson. If you ask him that question, he can use it to say later that it was asked of him too late.

Mr. Lloyd George. Yesterday, I proposed to him to ask for other divisions in England; he said nothing in reply. I wouldn't have to apply to Parliament to have them come here; the King's consent would be enough.

M. Clemenceau. I will ask him: "If you need stronger forces, why didn't you say so earlier?"

President Wilson. I see a danger in that question. If he answers you: "Indeed, I need troops," that can delay the offensive.

M. Clemenceau. That is right, and that is what must be avoided above all. What I ask you for is authority to write to him, in a friendly tone, a letter in which I will ask him what he means when he speaks of an armistice, adding that this isn't our business, but his.

Mr. Lloyd George. We must be careful; he is an obstinate man, and I fear that, instead of going directly to Berlin, he is pursuing a policy of the dismemberment of the German Empire that would throw us into infinite difficulties. I would prefer to see a man like Pétain there, although I don't propose to replace Marshal Foch.

M. Clemenceau. After the letter he just wrote us, we can't do that. We'll watch him and judge him by his acts. He has all the prestige of victory on his side today.

Mr. Lloyd George. It is necessary to send him over there, but under very clear instructions: he must march on Berlin in order to compel Germany to sign the treaty. We should send a copy of these instructions to General Robertson and to General Pershing.

President Wilson. Getting the treaty signed—that is politics.

Mr. Lloyd George. He must be reminded simply, in a written document taking the form of an order, of what he himself has said about the necessity of striking at the head of the German government. The best thing would be to entrust the drafting to someone who has a military mind.

President Wilson. He shouldn't have too much of one.

Mr. Lloyd George. What I mean is someone who can give these instructions the form of an order.

M. Clemenceau. I can show you a document of this kind on your return.

President Wilson. I will be here Friday morning around nine o'clock.

Mr. Lloyd George. I will return on Thursday evening.

M. Clemenceau. This morning I asked M. Sonnino if Italy could participate in an operation in southern Germany; he seemed rather inclined towards it.

President Wilson. Without Italian cooperation, one part of Marshal Foch's plan would fail.

M. Clemenceau. I am going to prepare a reply, and if you agree, I will make no allusion to the past; I won't say a word about our conversation of yesterday.

Mr. Lloyd George. Mr. President, may I ask you when you intend to return to the United States?

President Wilson. As soon as the treaty is signed, I must leave and get into intimate contact with the Senate. As you know, it has taken the bit between its teeth.[3] Fortunately, it is not the same with the country.

Mr. Lloyd George. I must say that a party that behaved at home like your opposition would be absolutely discredited.

President Wilson. If the Germans accept our last proposals, the treaty could be signed Tuesday or Wednesday, and I would leave immediately; naturally, my colleagues will remain here to continue the negotiations with Austria.

Mr. Lloyd George. Concerning the Austrians, I wonder if we wouldn't have to make an effort to show them we are treating them differently from the Germans, in order to detach them from Germany. Wouldn't it be advantageous to see them and talk directly with them?

President Wilson. For the moment, the most pressing matter is to conclude with Germany.

Sir Maurice Hankey. Mr. McCormick and the Economic Council are asking for a decision concerning the blockade against Russia and Hungary. They point out that the blockade will necessarily disappear when the peace with Germany has been signed.

President Wilson. You know that, if it was up to me alone, I would have lifted the blockade a long time ago.

[3] About the buildup of opposition to the League of Nations in the United States, see Lloyd E. Ambrosius, *Woodrow Wilson and the American Diplomatic Tradition: The Treaty Fight in Perspective* (Cambridge, etc., 1987), pp. 136-51, and Thomas A. Bailey, *Woodrow Wilson and the Great Betrayal* (New York, 1945), pp. 16-37.

CXXXI

Conversation between President Wilson, MM. Clemenceau and Lloyd George, and Barons Sonnino and Makino*

JUNE 17, 1919, 4 P.M.

Mr. Lloyd George. We received a letter from M. Paderewski on the question of national and religious minorities.[1] M. Paderewski makes objections and reservations. We must take the time to examine this document, which is rather important.

President Wilson. I don't think we can delay discussing it, for this question must be settled at the time of the signing of the treaty.

On the question of who has the right to appeal to the League of Nations when the article on minorities is violated, it will, I believe, be easy to agree amongst ourselves. As I have already told you, I consulted M. Beneš and M. Vénisélos on this subject. They think, like me, that it would be dangerous to give this right of intervention to all nations which are members of the League, and that it is better to reserve it to members of the Council.

Another question remains to be settled: who will have the right to appeal to the international tribunal charged with deciding on questions of fact and on the interpretation of the treaty? Should this right be reserved to governments or can one extend it to groups of individuals inside each country?

Mr. Lloyd George. It is better to begin by reading M. Paderewski's letter, which touches on all these questions.

—Reading of M. Paderewski's letter.

Mr. Lloyd George. That letter is a general critique of the entire order of things we had wanted to establish; it is, moreover, a serious critique. We can't answer it without having devoted the greatest attention to it. Wouldn't it be best to entrust the study to the committee which prepared the text relating to minorities? At first glance, it seems to me that some of M. Paderewski's arguments are not without weight.

President Wilson. There is one point on which he is certainly right: the treaty assures the protection of Germans in Poland much

*H., PPC, VI, 529ff.

[1] It is printed as an appendix to these notes.

more completely than of Poles in Germany. As for the rest of his arguments, it all boils down to the question I'm going to ask.

Some years ago, we abrogated a treaty with Russia, which gave us important economic advantages, and we did that because of the treatment of Jews in the Russian Empire who were American citizens. We denounced the treaty, basing ourselves not on the injustice of the situation of the Jews in Russia, but on the fact that the Russians were practicing a discrimination between American citizens that we ourselves did not practice, whilst they had taken certain commitments towards American citizens in general. The danger of our provisions on behalf of minorities is that they would constitute the Jewish minority into a kind of entity.

Mr. Lloyd George. Moreover, it must be acknowledged that it is legitimate for all states to try to strengthen national consciousness through the schools. If you accept the existence of a special organization to create and direct the Jewish schools, there is no doubt that will strike at the national character of the schools. One might also fear that a center of German intrigues could form there.

President Wilson. On the other hand, let's recall the dishonest manner in which Rumania violated or circumvented the obligations which were imposed on her by the Treaty of Berlin. If we should ask the new states to commit themselves purely and simply to grant equal treatment to all their citizens, without providing a right of appeal to the League of Nations, exactly what happened in Rumania after 1878 would happen in Poland.

Mr. Lloyd George. I propose that M. Paderewski's letter be referred to the Commission on Minorities [Committee on New States], which will present a report to us.

President Wilson. What all those countries fear is the intervention of the great powers in their internal affairs. It is certain that the great powers are the ones which best treat the Jews domiciled on their territories.

Mr. Lloyd George. The committee must be informed of M. Paderewski's objections and asked to see how they should be answered. It seems to me that, on certain points, we have gone perhaps a bit far. But if Poland was resurrected, if Rumania today sees her territory doubled, it is thanks to the effort and the victory of the great powers; we have the right to call them to account.

As for the right of appeal to the League of Nations, I believe it would be dangerous to give it to groups of individuals within each state. Nothing could be more dangerous for the League itself.

President Wilson. I agree. There will always be people in our countries who will draw our attention to the abuses committed, and it will be up to us to decide if we wish to intervene or not.

Mr. Lloyd George. The Economic Council asks us whether we should not lift the blockade of Bolshevik Russia and Hungary at the time of the signing of the treaty with Germany. The question, in reality, amounts to whether the Germans will be the only ones to have the right to trade with Russia.

President Wilson. That is an excellent argument, and, moreover, it is impossible from the legal point of view to maintain the blockade after the signing of peace. I don't see how we could do it. We fought for international law; it is not for us to violate it.

Mr. Lloyd George. If I believed we could crush the Bolsheviks this year, I would favor making a great effort in which the English and French fleets would participate. But Admiral Kolchak has just been pushed back 300 kilometers. One of his armies is destroyed. In this strange war taking place in Russia, each time one of the two adversaries is defeated, part of his troops goes over to the other side.

President Wilson. Undoubtedly, the people don't have much faith either in one party or in the other.

Mr. Lloyd George. There are a number of people in Moscow who are ranged closely around Lenin; but it really seems that the mass of the people wants tranquility and peace above all.

—President Wilson reads aloud a report from General Bliss:

Admiral Kolchak's armies have retreated towards the Urals. The last information about Petrograd shows that the fall of that city is not near. A revolt took place on the road to Tomsk and has not yet been completely put down. In eastern Siberia, Admiral Kolchak's power rests on the reactionary General Horvat and Hetman Semenov.

Mr. Lloyd George. General Janin just sent us a report almost identical to this one.

To my mind, Admiral Kolchak will not beat Lenin. Instead, there will come a time when the adversaries will get together to put an end to the anarchy. It seems that the military affairs of the Bolsheviks are well managed. But the observers who keep us informed say that pure Bolshevik doctrine is being increasingly abandoned, and that what is being established over there is a state that doesn't differ noticeably from a bourgeois state.

M. Clemenceau. Are you sure of the fact?

President Wilson. It is perhaps too early to believe it. But that is bound to happen.

Mr. Lloyd George. I am told the Bolsheviks have given up paying the same salary to a bootblack and a first-class engineer.

Baron Sonnino. The Germans are helping them a great deal.

Mr. Lloyd George. Certainly; they are infiltrating everywhere in Russia.

M. Clemenceau. In any case, we must keep the commitment we just took towards Admiral Kolchak.

Mr. Lloyd George. Certainly.

President Wilson. But we committed ourselves only to help him by providing war materials.

Baron Sonnino. Don't you fear the resumption of commercial relations with Bolshevik Russia, on the day following the commitment we have taken towards Admiral Kolchak, may produce a deplorable effect on the others?

President Wilson. In my opinion, there is no cause to make a statement on this subject.

Mr. Lloyd George. We will be asked questions in Parliament, and we'll have to answer them.

President Wilson. The question is this: are we at war with Bolshevik Russia?

Mr. Lloyd George. British troops are in Archangel.

President Wilson. What I mean is that the operations in which Allied troops participated in Russia don't constitute a state of war in the legal sense of the word. There has been no declaration of war.

Mr. Lloyd George. That recalls a bit our battles with Spain on the sea and in the colonies, which took place often in time of peace, whilst our ambassadors were in Madrid and Spanish ambassadors were in London. It has sometimes been the same between England and France, notably during our battles for possession of the Indies.

President Wilson. The signing of the peace with Germany will remove all legal basis for the blockade established in the Baltic.

Mr. Lloyd George. The question also arises from the practical point of view. If English merchants ask me: "Do we have the right to buy linen in Russia?" and I refuse, there are Germans who will buy this linen.

President Wilson. What must be said to our merchants is: "You can go to Russia at your risk and peril."

Mr. Lloyd George. As merchants went to central Africa fifty years ago. But there is one trade we cannot allow: it is the one in war materials.

Sir Maurice Hankey. What reply should be transmitted to the Supreme Economic Council?

Mr. Lloyd George. A decision must be taken. In any case, we will certainly have to watch the Baltic coast in order to prevent the Germans from sending war materials into Russia.

President Wilson. I point out to you that the Inter-Allied Council on Maritime Transport gave the order yesterday to stop ships carrying food destined for the Baltic ports. There is an immediate danger there for the Poles and the Czechoslovaks, for whom these food supplies were destined.

Mr. Lloyd George. If hostilities are resumed with Germany next week, these food supplies will be retained by Germany.

President Wilson. At this very moment, there are two or three American ships, which were transporting food supplies destined for the Poles and Czechoslovaks, held up in English ports.

M. Clemenceau. I am thinking about the effect of an immediate statement on the subject of the blockade; it could help in the signing of the treaty.

President Wilson. In any case, it would be disastrous to begin by starving the Poles and the Czechs. The Inter-Allied Maritime Council has no right to establish this blockade today, or, in any case, to stop American ships.

Mr. Lloyd George. It is a matter, not of a British organization, but of an inter-Allied organization on which America is represented; the representatives of the United States took part in the decision.

President Wilson. That is wrong. The American delegate said he couldn't give his consent without referring the matter to Mr. Hoover.[2] The argument advanced by the Maritime Transport Council is that it took that decision so that the cargoes wouldn't run the risk of falling into the hands of the Germans. That is well enough. But does one have the right to do that one week before the date provided for the affirmative or negative reply of the Germans?

Mr. Lloyd George. The time of the voyage and unloading must be taken into account. What they wanted to avoid was having this wheat arrive in German ports at the precise moment when the Germans would be breaking with us.

---

[2] Wilson based this statement on H. C. Hoover to WW, June 16, 1919, *PWW*, Vol. 60, p. 606.

President Wilson. I have always declared myself against the prolongation of the blockade, and today I see that organization instituting the blockade on its own authority.

Mr. Lloyd George. That organization is presided over by Lord Robert Cecil, whose spirit of moderation and humanity you know.

Sir Maurice Hankey. It was the executive which acted in an emergency.

President Wilson. It is unfortunate that that organization took a decision of this kind at the moment we were discussing this same question here.

Mr. Lloyd George. You know that Lord Robert Cecil would be the last person to adopt a brutal policy. The executive has undoubtedly done nothing but interpret our general instruction to prepare for the resumption of the blockade. The ships concerned are rather slow. The transport executive thought it would be vain to proclaim the blockade at the very moment when ships sent by us would be unloading thousands of tons of food supplies in Hamburg or Stettin.

President Wilson. I recall that I strongly insisted that we begin with military action and have recourse to the blockade only as a last resort. I insist on protesting formally against this procedure. I have already protested against the stopping of American ships.

Mr. Lloyd George. It is obvious that this decision is not valid if the American representative opposed it.

President Wilson. I am not in favor of reducing the population of a large country to famine, unless it is the last means of action available, and the food supplies concerned are destined for Poland and Bohemia.

Sir Maurice Hankey. What is your decision about the resumption of trade with Russia?

Mr. Lloyd George. I will accept it, but whilst maintaining our right to prevent the importation of arms. That is what we have done in countries like Afghanistan and Abyssinia.

President Wilson. We must reply to the question asked by the Supreme Economic Council by saying that trade with Russia resumes automatically at the time of the signing of the peace, since there is no reason to make any statement on this subject. At the same time, the council must be asked if it sees a means to prevent the traffic in arms.

Baron Sonnino. I draw your attention to the situation of the Allied officers whom we sent to Klagenfurt. They find themselves there in the presence of an accomplished fact and don't know what to do. Either they must be given the means to make both adversaries leave the Klagenfurt Basin, or they'll remain reduced to impotence.

President Wilson. My personal opinion is that the Austrians and the Yugoslavs must alike withdraw from the Klagenfurt Basin. We can give no instructions to these officers before we have sent a summons to the two governments involved.

Mr. Lloyd George. Where are the Yugoslavs now?

Baron Sonnino. In Klagenfurt, and they are threatening to advance if the present armistice is denounced.

Mr. Lloyd George. It is difficult for us to act directly. If we send Italian troops, the Yugoslavs will believe it is a maneuver directed especially against them, and I don't see any other troops to send there.

M. Clemenceau. They must withdraw from the Klagenfurt Basin.

President Wilson. We must invite both governments to withdraw their troops beyond the two lines drawn in the North and in the South.

We can instruct our Foreign Ministers to send that order to them, and our military representatives on the spot will tell us if it has been carried out or not.

{ A P P E N D I X }[3]

MEMORANDUM BY M. PADEREWSKI.

The Polish Delegation to the Peace Conference appreciates the high importance of the confirmation of the sovereignty and independence of the Polish State through a treaty between the principal Powers and Poland. But precisely from the point of view of the sovereign rights of Poland, the Delegation considers it to be a duty to present its objections to the introduction, in the Treaty with Germany, of article 93, according to which Poland should admit the intervention of the Chief Powers in her internal affairs. Poland has already experienced the nefarious consequences which may result from the protection exercised by foreign Powers over ethnical and religious minorities. The Polish Nation has not forgotten that the dismemberment of Poland was the consequence of the intervention of foreign powers in affairs concerning her religious minorities, and this painful memory makes Po-

---

[3] Printed in *ibid.*, pp. 629-34.

land fear the external interference into internal matters of State more than anything.

This fear has been recently once more confirmed by the unanimous vote of the Polish Diet. Whilst requiring the Government to prepare without delay the schemes of laws respecting the rights of the minorities, the Diet has, at the same time, finally declared its opposition to any foreign intervention.

Poland will grant full rights of citizenship to all her subjects, but will demand in return that all citizens should develop a consciousness of their duties towards the State. This, however, cannot be attained should the rights granted to minorities be imposed on the Polish State, and if those minorities, feeling themselves under external protection, were thus encouraged to lodge their complaints against the State, to which they belong, before a foreign court of appeal. This would fatally provoke excitement against the minorities and would become the cause of incessant unrest.

Polish-Jewish relations.

We have to note with regret that the relations between the Jewish and Christian population in Poland have lately become strained. To those who are acquainted with the evolution of the Jewish question in Poland, this is a surprising phenomenon. The Polish nation with whom the Jews, chased from Germany, had found refuge for several centuries and all facilities for organizing their religious life, wished towards the end of the 18th Century to emancipate these Jews, relegated to their ghettos, and even after the loss of its independence attempted to grant them the full measure of civic rights. The Polish-Jewish relations during the whole of the 19th Century were distinguished by good understanding. The present discord is caused by the attitude adopted by the Jews who, considering the Polish cause as being a lost one, on many occasions sided with Poland's enemies.

This policy of the Jews called forth a change of public opinion against them. However, the reconstruction of the Polish State, which must be admitted by the Jews as an established fact, will allow the Polish nation, whose existence will no longer be imperilled by their hostility, to return to her ancient principles respecting the Jewish question. The relations between Jews and Poles will be automatically established, within a short time, in a normal way, to the satisfaction of both parties; whereas protection granted to the Jewish population in Poland, through transferring the question on to international ground, can but create difficulties.

The representatives of Poland admit equal rights, based on the principles of freedom, to all citizens, without distinction of origin, creed or language, admitting at the same time the necessity of guaranteeing these principles by the Polish Constitution. The representatives of Poland must however firmly stipulate against any clauses of the Treaty which would cause prejudice to the sovereignty of the Polish State, by imposing one-sided obligations concerning the essence and form of the Polish Constitution and which would submit for approval to the Council of the League of Nations the eventual modifications of the said constitution.

To place one special part of the Polish Constitution under the protection of the League of Nations and demand the consent of its Council (para. 13 to 14 of the scheme of the Treaty) is equivalent to regarding the Polish nation as a nation of inferior standard of civilisation, incapable of ensuring to all its citizens the rights and civic liberties and ignorant of the conception of the duties of a modern State. The Polish State, sovereign in principle, would thus be permanently placed under the control of the Powers: every modification of the Constitution which is the expression of the sovereign will of the people would be submitted, in as far as concerns the obligations stipulated in the scheme of the Treaty, to the examination and approval of the Council of the League.

In reality, the will of one member of the Council could hamper any development of the Polish Constitution, which the vital needs of the country might require.

The constitutional principles, stipulating the rights of minorities, as well as the Constitution, as a whole, will contain in Poland alike to other States guarantees of inviolability. Laws, decrees, and administrative acts which are contrary to the Constitution will have no validity. The organisation of the political authorities and the corresponding political and judicial guarantees will constitute a sufficient safeguard of inviolability of the fundamental laws.

Art. 14 of the scheme of the Treaty concerning the approval of Constitutional modifications by the Council of the League of Nations, as well as the clause of Art. 1, according to which the stipulations of the Treaty, which are to form part of the Constitution, fall under the jurisdiction of the League, must accordingly be struck out as being prejudicial to the sovereignty of Poland.

While all the schemes of Constitution laid before the Diet, and all declarations voted as well as all special laws passed originate from the idea of equal rights of all citizens; while legislative motions concerning national minorities who form the bulk of the population of a given territory guarantee to these minorities an extensive autonomy; the scheme of the treaty puts to doubt the value of the leading ideas which have hitherto directed the Polish State. This scheme appears to aim at depriving the principles of equality, stated in the Constitution, of their character of free expression of national will, tending to represent them as the result of the imposed demands of Foreign Powers, who retain for themselves the right of control. Art. 1 refers to: "the desire (of Poland) to conform her institutions to the principles of liberty and justice, also to give a sure guarantee to all the inhabitants of the territories over which she has assumed the sovereignty," as if Poland were a state without a past or constitutional traditions for the first time aware of the principles of justice and freedom. Precisely the living traditions of the former Polish State, which had outdistanced others in the matter of assuring equality of political rights to all its citizens, without distinction of origin, language, or creed, and had opened its doors for the sects persecuted in the neighbouring states and assured a refuge to the Jews banished from the West,—these traditions have helped to sustain amongst the Poles the consciousness of their nationality. Poland expresses the ardent desire that the principles of freedom should be universally applied to the minorities. Poland promises to realise the stipulations concerning their rights which the League of Nations will recognise as being obligatory for all States belonging to the League, in the same way as with regard to the protection of labour.

The regulation, by the Treaty, of details concerning Jewish schools and the right of use [of] the Jewish language in the Courts of Justice, seems to be especially inappropriate, considering that, at the present time, the Jewish question in Poland is a question of violent dissention among the Jewish population itself. One part of the Jewish population only demands complete equality of rights for people of Jewish origin. This has been granted them. The others demand a separate religious organisation, endowed by the State with political, national, social, economic, cultural and linguistic attributions, which would transform the Jews into an autonomous Nation. Some Jews consider the Jewish dialect used by the majority of Jews in Poland and which is a corrupted German as spoken in the middle ages, as inadequate to modern intellectual requirements, and merely adaptable to the germanisation of Jews, when cultivated in schools. Others, on the contrary, wish to regard it as their national language, whereas a part of the Jewish population tends to revive the ancient Hebrew tongue. The actual State of transitions of the Jewish question scarcely allows the national and linguistic rights of the Jews in Poland to be determined. There is no doubt that the stipulations proposed with regard to the rights of the Jewish population will call forth a deep resentment on that part of the Jewish population, which whilst attached to its religion, considers itself as being of Polish nationality and is anxious to avoid a conflict with the Poles about national and linguistic rights.

The fact that the proposed stipulations may in future have a fatal influence on Polish internal relations cannot be sufficiently emphasized. The school authorities for the whole population are controlled by the Polish Government. In the meantime, Article 10 of the Treaty creates one or several special school committees for the Jewish population, as strictly religious institutions, to be appointed by the Jewish communities, independently of the Government and recognizes their right to organise and manage the Jewish schools. Such a privilege must needs call forth analogous demands on the part of organisations of other creeds and may lead to the establishment of schools, specially reserved to scholars of a given faith, and tend to the creation of strictly religious education,—which would contribute to deepen religious divergencies in Poland. This article is inadmissible, as it would bring about the breaking up of the political organisation, into religious organisations, having public rights, privileged from an administrative point of view, as was the case in the middle ages. It is also contrary to the modern tendency of all States of using schools as a means of producing citizens brought up in a certain spirit of unity and social solidarity. This tendency must be specially adopted by the Polish State, which is being formed by the reunion of regions having been for over a century under foreign and decidedly hostile influences.

Article 9 is no less likely to cause general discontentment, as it creates a certain privilege in favour of the ethnical, linguistic and religious minorities, assuring them "an equitable part in the revenues and attribution of sums which could originate from public funds, ministry departments, municipal, or other budgets having educational, religious or charitable aims." Considering that the above-mentioned minorities will at the same time have the right of taking the advantage of educational or charitable institutions destined to the population as a whole and kept up on the State communal or other funds, a privileged minority would in this way get more advantage out of public funds than the generality of the inhabitants. In the same way Article 12 justly assuring to the Jews the right to celebrate their Sabbath can become a cause of conflict between them and the Polish population, as the clause, according to which: "Jews will not be obliged to accomplish any acts constituting a violation of their Sabbath" can authorise them to refuse public service as civil officials (State service, railways or commons) or in the Army.

The Great Powers, by refusing to grant to the Polish State the necessary time to experience in the Jewish question the methods of civic equality—the efficiency of which have been recognised by the United States, Great Britain, France and Italy, and by distinguishing with the aid of special privileges the Jewish population from their fellow-citizens—create a new Jewish problem assuming thereby before humanity a heavy responsibility instead of contributing to solve the problem peacefully, they complicate it in an unforeseen way. It is to be feared that the Great Powers may be preparing for themselves unwelcome surprises, for, taking into consideration the migratory capacities of the Jewish population, which so readily transports itself from one State to another, it is certain that the Jews, basing themselves on precedent thus established, will claim elsewhere the national principles which they would enjoy in Poland.

The motives for which clauses concerning Polish nationalities (Art. 2-5) should be inserted in a special Treaty between the Great Powers and Poland, and in the fundamental laws of the Polish Constitution are not clear. The Treaty with Germany (Art. 90-91) solves the question in as far as the population of Polish territories acquired by Prussia is concerned. This question is to be solved in the same way in the Treaties with Austria-Hungary and Russia. All questions concerning Polish nationality will then be avoided and the stipulations of the present Treaty will be superfluous.

The Treaty of the Principal Powers with Poland stipulates, as far as we understand, the general directing principles of the relation to national minorities, it being the tendency of the scheme to create fundamental laws of these principles, laws which would be an immutable part of the Constitution, a declaration of rights (paragr. 13). The Treaty, however, places amongst these fundamental principles such administrative and Government details as, for instance, the organisation of the school system, the re-partition of education and charity funds (paras. 9-10) which cannot be entered as the fundamental laws of a Constitution.

Finally, we trust that the stipulations of the scheme of the

Treaty do not embrace the German population in Poland. After the conclusion of Peace, a large proportion of Polish population will remain within the German Empire. Formerly, the Polish population in Germany was not only deprived of equality of rights, but was submitted to a rigorous system of exceptional laws and administrative decrees, aiming at the extermination of the Polish element. The Peace Treaty does not impose on the Germans any obligation of granting equality of rights to the Poles of the Empire. The linguistic rights of the Poles in the Courts of Justice, the possibility of keeping Polish schools with the aid of State and Communal funds, are not guaranteed therein. The treatment of the Polish minorities in Germany and of the German minorities in Poland cannot therefore be considered on the basis of reciprocity. As the Peace Treaty with Germany does not contain any clauses guaranteeing the rights of Polish minorities, it would be unjust that the Treaty of the Principal Powers with Poland should ensure to the Germans in Poland, in addition to an equality of rights, the privilege of making use of the German language in the Polish Courts of Justice, as well as of keeping up schools of German language out of public funds.

Whilst handing in the present answer to the scheme of the Treaty, the Polish Delegation points out that in this matter, wherein the internal legislation of Poland is concerned, the Diet and the Government of Poland are in the first place entitled to express their opinion.

The scheme of the Treaty has been sent to them.
Paris, June 15th, 1919.

CXXXII

SUPREME WAR COUNCIL

JUNE 20, 1919, 5 P.M.

Present are: President Wilson, MM. Clemenceau and Balfour, Baron Sonnino, Marshals Foch and Pétain, and Generals Robertson, Bliss, Cavallero, Weygand, and Sir Henry Wilson*

M. Clemenceau. The heads of governments have summoned their military advisers to hear them explain their plan of action in the

*H., *PPC*, VI, 543ff.

event the treaty is not signed within the stipulated period. We have already heard Marshal Foch, who, at our request, has provided a written memorandum about the line of action that he proposes to follow. Before the time of action, we wanted to summon him once more, and to hear the heads of the Allied armies along with him, to see if everyone is in firm agreement.

Marshal Foch. The offensive has been prepared in conformity with the plan decided upon with agreement of the heads of the armies and approved by the governments on May 20 last. Everything is ready for immediate execution, this very evening if necessary.

We leave from the Rhine, that is to say, from Cologne, Koblenz, Mainz, and a bit further south, in the direction of Weimar and Berlin, with the view to reducing, if necessary, the resistance of the German government. The departure will be made without any difficulty. Everything is prepared, and the troops are ready to march.

The question that arises is this: how far can we go? Berlin is 450 kilometers from the Rhine. Our offensive capacity depends on the obstacles we might meet en route. The populations we will pass through will be more or less hostile. The military elements amongst them can be used against us. Our lines of communication can be threatened or cut, or more simply, strikes can deprive us of absolutely necessary manpower. To guard itself against all these dangers or risks, the army must then grow weaker as it advances. Since this weakness will result essentially from the need to maintain its communications behind the lines across hostile areas, what would make things easiest for us would be the ability to disarm the populations and put an end to the war in the territories that we cross. We will pass through, successively, the Grand Duchy of Baden, Württemberg, and Bavaria. If, by successive armistices, we could put an end to hostilities in these different areas, that would assure us entirely of the line of the Main and permit our march on Berlin. The result would be, in fact, a considerable economy of forces. Our maneuver in the Main Valley lends itself to this separation of the areas of southern Germany. Moreover, it is the most direct route to effect a junction with the Czechs and the Poles. In joining hands with the latter, we surround Germany and its redoubt, Berlin.

Germany can be reduced to impotence if we have the right to conclude successive armistices with the Grand Duchy of Baden, Württemberg, and Bavaria. In order to do that, the possibility must be anticipated of negotiating with the governments of those states. Without this cutting up of Germany, and if we are obliged to maintain our position towards southern Germany at the same time that we aim at Berlin, our forces will not be sufficient and our anemic offensive will be forced to stop halfway.

In that case, in order to disarm the German government, it would undoubtedly be necessary to reinforce the armies in a proportion that is not yet possible to anticipate. If, on the other hand, a lateral offensive takes place towards Bavaria, it could be important to obtain on that side the cooperation of an Italian army which, with the means at its disposal, could march on Munich without difficulty.

This is how the problem of the western front between the Rhine and Berlin presents itself. In a short time, I will tell you about the junction with the Czechoslovaks and the Poles. We are in communication with their armies; they have received our instructions and can act with us against Berlin.

As for the duration of the operation, here is what I can say at present. On leaving the Rhine, we anticipate two rapid moves of one hundred kilometers each. The second carries us to the banks of the Weser, which constitutes an excellent stopping line, analogous, if not equivalent to, that of the Rhine. These two successive advances, combined with our march in the Main Valley, should take twelve to fourteen days. During that short period, we could finish with southern Germany, and, if we were set free from that side, we could then resume the march on Berlin.

M. Clemenceau. Do you have in mind entering Bavaria?

Marshal Foch. Yes. Here is the question that I ask the governments: is the General in Chief allowed to consider the possibility of special treatment that could be applied successively to the governments of southern Germany?

M. Clemenceau. What do you mean by special treatment?

Marshal Foch. An immediate armistice. If, for example, the government of Baden tells me: "Stop the war," I must be able to agree to it on prearranged conditions.

That is what I had to say about the offensive starting from the Rhine. At the same time, we could contemplate an offensive starting from Prague, which is much closer to Berlin, and from Posen, which is even closer. On the day when our union with the Czechs and Poles takes place, the concentric march on Berlin would become easy. But for that, I must know your intentions regarding the Czechoslovaks. Will the Hungarian offensive against them be halted? For that, will recourse to military action be necessary? Assuredly, Bohemia will be able to act on the northern side only when she is set free on the southern side. As for Poland, she is free for the moment; she disposes a total of twenty-one divisions.

General Weygand. Twelve Polish divisions face the Germans.

M. Clemenceau. Do they have enough munitions?

General Weygand. We have done a great deal to supply them.

Marshal Foch. General Haller left for Poland with 2,000 rounds per gun. We had only 700 at the beginning of the war.

President Wilson. What is the strength of a Polish division?

General Weygand. Fifteen thousand men for the divisions coming from France. For the others, the numbers vary.

General Sir W. Robertson. Marshal Foch sent me his instructions to march on the Weser in two rapid moves. I have nothing to say about this. How far can we go? That depends on the attitude of the populations, on the resistance of the Germans, both civilians and the military, and on the way we can operate the railroads and the telegraphic and telephone lines along the length of which we will be compelled to use German personnel.

In my opinion, nothing can stop us before the Weser. The question of a march beyond that line is a problem of high strategy, about which I have no opinion, because I don't know enough about what we can expect from the Poles and the Czechs. But as the chief responsible for the British army, 200,000 men strong, I would like to explain myself on several points.

It is necessary that the governments consider the results that can be expected, from the political point of view, of a march on the Weser. For, concerning the British army, I don't see the possibility of sending troops beyond the Weser; unless the country behind us is completely pacified, all the men at my disposal won't be numerous enough to assure the occupation of the region crossed. What we will have to do will depend on Germany's position. If Germany is obstinate in not wanting to sign, we must see where that can lead. I don't see the possibility of the British army, as it is now constituted, going beyond the Weser. If that became necessary, new forces would have to be added to it. On the Weser, we will be 200 miles from the German border and 200 miles from Berlin.

Can the desired goal be attained by taking our armies to the Weser? That is for the governments to worry about. If the Germans continue to refuse peace, they have numbers of trained men—hundreds of thousands in the areas we will occupy. This is the time to think about it and to make advance plans in consequence.

President Wilson. Do the Germans have war materials?

General Sir Henry Wilson. Without being able to guarantee the figures, I think they have about 2,000 pieces of heavy artillery and 7,000 field guns. The question is whether one wishes to push beyond the Weser.

General Bliss. I have little to add. General Robertson put his finger on the essential point of the problem. Something must be done if Germany refuses to sign, and I don't see anything other than an immediate military action, for it is important to avoid any impression of weakness or hesitation.

If our armies reach the Weser, they will separate a population of twenty million inhabitants from the rest of Germany. If the plan consisting of concluding separate armistices with the states of the South is followed and gives good results, that means another twelve million Germans who will be detached from the mass. Moreover, the industrial system of Germany will be completely disorganized. It is up to the governments to see day by day the conclusions that can be drawn appropriately from events. In any case, it is impossible to anticipate anything beyond the Weser.

First, we must see if southern Germany is inclined to negotiate separately. How can it be induced to do so? Is there reason to make it special offers and to discharge part of the burden that will fall on the rest of Germany? This concerns the governments. If we treat southern Germany exactly like the rest of Germany, there is no reason for that region not to take the same position of passive resistance. It is impossible to guess whether or not there will be a surge of German national sentiment if German troops will be more or less held back by the Poles and the Czechs. We can't know now if our forces will be sufficient for the task or if it will be necessary to increase them. Perhaps we will meet no resistance and march on Berlin without firing a shot; in that case, moreover, we don't know if we will be closer to the signing than we are today. In any event, what is incontestable is that we must act, and act immediately.

The situation that will result is impossible to foresee today. It will be up to the high command and the governments to follow events and to search gradually for the means to face them.

General Cavallero. The question of Italy's cooperation in southern Germany was only asked of us yesterday by Marshal Foch. I immediately telegraphed General Diaz; I hope to be able to tell you tomorrow what we will be in a position to do. However, I can indicate now that our contribution will be relatively modest because of the precautions we have to take for the maintenance of order at home, and also because of the uncertainty of the situation on our eastern frontier. As soon as we receive General Diaz's reply, we will communicate it to Marshal Foch.

Marshal Pétain. I have no objection to make to the initial arrangements explained by Marshal Foch. We debouch from the Rhine. The principal mass marches along the Main Valley, separating southern Germany from northern Germany. We advance in two rapid moves to the Weser. Barring unforeseen events, this plan will be carried out. But as General Robertson and General Bliss have said, it is a new war that begins beyond the Weser. I don't think that, with the present numbers, and given the necessity of guarding our communications and holding the people at a respectful distance, we are strong enough to continue our march.

Here is the situation concerning the French armies. The army groups of Generals Mangin and Gérard, under the command of General Fayolle, have everything required for a long-distance campaign and are abundantly provided with materials for railroads, telegraphs and telephones, and so on. It is not the same with the Fourth Army, located further south. It would be an illusion to believe it could advance far into the interior of Bavaria, for it lacks depth and doesn't have the means necessary to protect long lines of communication. The center, constituted of the Army of the Main, is thus very powerful. The right, that is the Fourth Army, is relatively weak. The left, which will advance along the Lippe Valley, won't be very well protected and would run risks in advancing beyond the Weser.

As for the cooperation of the Poles, Czechs, and Italians, it is a bit late to organize it. It would have to have been arranged much longer in advance. As far as they are concerned, we have only intentions.

M. Clemenceau. The Polish army is under the supreme command of Marshal Foch.

Marshal Pétain. That is true, but only for the past two or three days.

Marshal Foch. The Poles have a plan for systematic defense. I asked them to dig themselves in and not to budge.

M. Clemenceau. Do you know the forces the Germans could oppose to our offensive?

Marshal Pétain. This morning, we received an important communication on the German forces and their defensive plan. These forces form three groups, one in Hannover, another west of Weimar, and the third in Bavaria.

M. Clemenceau. What is the strength of these groups?

Marshal Pétain. We don't know exactly. But all three together can be estimated at 80,000 men, with 120,000 volunteers in reserve; these are at present the best troops in Germany. In total, that makes 200,000 men west of Berlin. To the east, facing Poland, the Germans have around 350,000 men. If we add to that 200,000 armed police, it can be said that Germany has at her disposal a total of 750,000 men.

President Wilson. Why send troops to Bavaria, if your intention is to conclude an immediate armistice with that state?

Marshal Foch. To obtain the armistice.

President Wilson. Isn't there a disadvantage in developing your movement fan-wise?

Marshal Foch. It wouldn't last long.

M. Clemenceau. What I understand is that the march on Berlin is conditioned on the conclusion of a series of successive armistices in southern Germany. I don't complain about this change in the original plan, as I had understood it. I believe it is prudent. A failure must be avoided at all costs. What strikes me is the agreement amongst all the heads of the Allied armies; everyone thinks the operation is easy as far as the Weser, but, beyond that, that we could only advance with considerably more men. I want that to be clearly understood. If we are lucky, it won't be necessary to think about it; but if we meet resistance, we will have to contemplate an increase in our forces. I ask the Commander in Chief of the Allied armies to inform us in advance of his needs as soon as he can foresee them; for, as he knows, time is needed to carry out things.

So we cross the Rhine; we march along the line of the Main. Perhaps we will have Italian cooperation on the southern side; but we have just been warned that it could only be modest. We will try to put southern Germany out of commission. If it is not clearly detached, we won't cross the Weser without having reinforced our armies. I renew my request of Marshal Foch to inform us, as soon as he can, about what additional forces he will need.

Mr. Balfour. My opinion has little weight when it comes to military questions. I can only express my agreement with M. Clemenceau. All our generals have declared themselves along the same line: a march on Berlin now presents too many difficulties and risks to be undertaken; our first effort must be to aim at putting southern Germany out of commission. I believe that is indeed extremely desirable. I venture to have doubts about the possibility of managing it. Marshal Foch did not tell us what his hope of having the states of southern Germany sign separate armistices is based on. To go beyond the Weser, either southern Germany must be detached or our armies must be reinforced. So it is important not to announce loudly that we are going beyond the Weser and as far as Berlin. Anything that could later give us the appearance of having suffered a defeat must be avoided. But that is a purely political question and a question of public opinion.

M. Clemenceau. The less the press speaks of it, the better. But you won't prevent our journalists and yours from saying we are marching on Berlin, nor the Germans, in case we should stop en route, from declaring that we couldn't have done otherwise.

Before breaking up, I would like to return to the question of our intervention to halt the hostilities between the Hungarians and the Czechoslovaks. I have General Bliss' report[1] before me; I approve the conclusions; it is obvious that we cannot leave this situation as it is, for the Czechs would be crushed. Our telegram to Béla Kun received a rather satisfactory reply. It is completely impossible to know who launched the first offensive. General Bliss' proposal seems to indicate the best way to settle the situation. Afterwards, it will be up to Marshal Foch to see if the stated terms are carried out, and, if necessary, to resort to force.

President Wilson. In General Bliss' report, the instructions that would guide Marshal Foch are included in Paragraph B. The next paragraph rather concerns the peace conference. It must address itself to the Rumanians in order to make them withdraw when the Hungarians have evacuated Czechoslovak territory.

Mr. Balfour. I don't really see the difference between General Bliss' report and the telegrams we have already sent to those involved.

General Bliss. The boundary between Hungary and the Czechoslovak state has been fixed. Now, the Hungarians are today forty or fifty kilometers north of that frontier. The Rumanians, as you know, are considerably to the west of theirs. When I saw the representatives of the Czechoslovaks in Paris, the difficulty was making them agree to talks with the Hungarians. They refused that. What I propose and what they accept is that, the Czechoslovak arms being under the supreme command of Marshal Foch, whatever is necessary be done by military means, that is, by an order from Marshal Foch to General Pellé, who is at the head of the Czechoslovak troops.

Mr. Balfour. We haven't asked the Czechoslovaks to negotiate directly with the Hungarians.

General Bliss. I tried to obtain a practical solution, and I hope we will arrive at one.

---

[1] It is printed in *PPC*, VI, 552-55.

M. Clemenceau. A question of capital importance remains—that of the terms of the armistice which might be negotiated with such or such of the states of southern Germany. Marshal Foch says to us: "What will I reply to the states which come to ask me for an armistice?" In my opinion, we must demand of each of these states, in the first place, that they lay down their arms, and, in the second place, that they send three delegates to Versailles. But must more be done? Must they be told: "We are ready to sign a separate peace with you under such and such conditions?" I spoke to Mr. Balfour and President Wilson about it this morning. Marshal Foch has to receive our instructions on this subject before beginning the march.

Mr. Balfour. Suppose that Württemberg asks you for an armistice and you reply: "Come and sign a peace with the Allies." What will you make it sign? Can the treaty we have prepared be thus cut into pieces for the different states of Germany?

M. Clemenceau. I understand the objection. It is certain that the entire treaty would then have to be rewritten. That is why I would confine myself to replying: "Come to Versailles, and we will make peace with you." But Marshal Foch finds that that is a bit brief and that he must be in a position to say more.

Baron Sonnino. It is possible that these states are ready to make an armistice separately without daring to make a separate peace, and it could suit us to take advantage of that if we can't obtain more.

Mr. Balfour. Does Württemberg have its own government in the new German state?

M. Clemenceau. Yes.

Mr. Balfour. The question which arises is in part a legal question. I will ask the lawyers on our Drafting Committee if they see the possibility of detaching a piece from their text in order to negotiate with Württemberg, for example.

Marshal Foch. The most difficult question being that of reparation, couldn't we, for example, say to each state that it will bear that part of Germany's total debt that is proportionate to its population?

President Wilson. That is an idea which at least has the merit of clarity.

M. Clemenceau. Marshal Foch has only to stop hostilities and to indicate the general lines on which we are inclined to enter into talks with each of these states.

Marshal Foch. I will tell them, for example: "Lay down your arms and you will have peace on the basis of a proportionate division of the charges."

Baron Sonnino. They won't enjoy much advantage in making peace on these terms. Isn't it necessary for them to have the impression of gaining something by signing a separate peace?

M. Clemenceau. They will gain immediate peace.

Baron Sonnino. If they oppose you only with passive resistance, you can't fight them.

Marshal Foch. I will tell the government of Württemberg, for example: "Hostilities will cease if you lay down your arms and send plenipotentiaries to Versailles to sign a treaty by which Württemberg will have to pay her proportionate share of the damages."

Baron Sonnino. But won't it be to their advantage to lay down their arms and not to send anyone to Versailles?

Marshal Foch. I will have the rights of war against them. For example, I can impose an immediate tax on their capital.

Mr. Balfour. In any case, it is a question that must be studied. The division of charges based solely on the number of the population could be very unjust and not give the results we expect. We must take into account the relative economic value of each of the parts of Germany.

M. Clemenceau. We will consult our experts and give Marshal Foch a formula before his departure.

General Weygand. In any case, we can make the burden of occupation felt enough so that the states of southern Germany will want to be delivered from it.

M. Clemenceau. Our formula cannot be improvised. We will prepare it, and we'll agree with President Wilson on this subject.

Marshal Foch. Today is June 20. If, on the twenty-third, at 7 p.m., there is no reply from the Germans, do I have the full right to begin to advance? It is very important for the success of a military operation to start immediately. That shows that one is prepared and there is no hesitation.

—(Assent.)

Marshal Pétain. I must inform you of the wish of the French army, which is: no new delay for the Germans. Indeed, our troops are concentrated on their starting positions in uncomfortable conditions, and they would become irritable if they remained there much longer.

Mr. Balfour. I ask that everything be provided to make the movements of the fleet coincide with those of the army.

M. Clemenceau. That goes without saying.

CXXXIII

Conversation between President Wilson, MM. Clemenceau and Balfour, and Barons Sonnino and Makino*

JUNE 21, 1919, 11 A.M.

—The members of the Reparation Commission and the Drafting Committee are introduced.

President Wilson. We have asked the Reparation Commission to bring us its reply to the supplementary note from the German delegation.[1]

M. Klotz. Our reply is directed at observations 8, 9, and 10 of the last German note. Here is the text we drafted.[2]

—Reading of the proposed text.

President Wilson. You write: "The provisions of the 'Terms of Peace' remain, with regard to reparation, the only charter of the contracting parties." That is not correct, since we are bound by commitments taken in writing in the course of our negotiations since May 7.

M. Loucheur. That is true.

—The draft is modified in this respect.

Mr. Balfour. One of the principal observations made by the Germans is this: "We are faced with two texts, between which there

*H., PPC, VI, 558ff.

[1] Edgar K. A. Haniel von Haimhausen to G. Clemenceau, June 20, 1919, printed in PPC, VI, 561-64. Haniel acknowledged receipt of the cover letter and the comprehensive letter of June 16, a copy of the peace treaty with changes in red ink, and a copy of the declaration of the Big Three printed in CXXIII, n. 1. Haniel pointed out that there were a number of concessions to Germany in the comprehensive letter that had not been incorporated in the text as modified by hand. He then listed twelve such concessions and asked that the German delegation receive definitive assurances that the changes were authoritative.

[2] Clemenceau, the day before, had instructed the various commissions to prepare draft replies on the points raised in Haniel's note. Klotz was replying for the Reparation Commission. His draft as approved and initialed said that it was only in the instructions that would eventually be addressed to that commission that the assurances given by the Allied and Associated governments would be expressed. It would not be necessary to add a protocol to the treaty of peace since the council's letter to the German delegation of June 16 fully bound the Allied and Associated Governments. *Ibid.*, pp. 564-65.

are differences; which is authoritative?" It is very easy to reply to that.

The Germans also say that our letter doesn't commit us sufficiently. On this point, we must consult the legal experts. In reality, it could be said that a letter—signed in our name by M. Clemenceau, it is true—doesn't commit us in the same way as the articles of a treaty.

M. Clemenceau. By writing: "In the name of the Allied and Associated Powers," the President of the Conference commits those powers.

Mr. Balfour. The Germans ask that a protocol attached to the treaty establish the legal status of the letter; it is about this that we must consult the legal advisers.

President Wilson. I have just asked them for their opinion; they think that M. Clemenceau's letter would be enough to bind the parties before a court of arbitration; but if that letter limits the powers the treaty gives us, it is through a kind of commitment of honor. If we want to satisfy the Germans by transforming this commitment of honor into a legal commitment, it is easy to add a protocol to the text of the treaty.

M. Clemenceau. Can't we simply say that our last reply will be annexed to the treaty?

President Wilson. That would also apply to the cover letter.

M. Clemenceau. Can our legal advisers tell us if there is an objection to this procedure?

M. Fromageot. In that case, the letter would have to be endorsed by an article of the treaty. Without that, it would be only an annexed document.

President Wilson. The Germans could say that the letter, on certain points, takes precedence over the treaty. I think it would be safer to annex all our correspondence to the treaty.

M. Clemenceau. I agree.

Mr. Balfour. That would lengthen the treaty remarkably. I think it would be much better to synthesize these documents in a protocol.

M. Clemenceau. So you want to make a new text? I fear this will take much time and make us run risks in drafting.

—Reading of the reply to the German observations on the financial clauses.[3]

---

[3] This draft, prepared by the Financial Commission, said that France would assume the public debt of Alsace-Lorraine and that the Reparation Commission could authorize the Reichsbank to export gold. *Ibid.*, pp. 567-68.

President Wilson. The divergences which the Germans think they perceive between the treaty and the memorandum of the Allies don't exist.[4]

M. Clémentel. On the subject of the five-year period when, according to the treaty, the economic clauses will be applied to Germany without reciprocity, our reply is that the right to prolong it assigned to the League of Nations aims at taking into account the needs of the countries that have suffered most.[5] Prolongation would take place only through a formal decision of the League Council.

President Wilson. That is the point that must be emphasized, for that is what answers the objection of the Germans. It must be said clearly that the period stipulated terminates automatically at the end of five years, unless a formal decision of the Council of the League of Nations prolongs the special arrangement instituted by the treaty in favor of such and such a country.

M. Clemenceau. I still believe that the best way to satisfy the Germans without running the risk of a new draft is to add our letters as they are to the treaty.

President Wilson. What I propose is not to make a new draft, but to extract from our letters everything that constitutes commitments, in the legal sense of the word, eliminating from them arguments and rhetoric and the mention of mere intentions on our part, which bind us morally but not legally.

M. Clemenceau. How can we make these extracts without danger?

President Wilson. In any case, you will be compelled to do the same work when you have to reply to Parliament. You'll be asked what parts of these letters are enforceable at law.

M. Clemenceau. We lack time. I would hand over the document as it is.

President Wilson. What we can do is to send the Germans a letter today saying that the commitments taken in our previous letters bind us. Later, we will make an extract of these commitments.[6]

---

[4] Wilson was referring to the first discrepancy mentioned in Haniel's note. As Haniel pointed out, the Allied letter of June 16 said that, once Germany was admitted to the League, she would enjoy the advantages resulting from the Covenant's provisions relative to the freedom of commerce and transit. On the other hand, the letter also stated that certain restrictions on German commerce would be imposed for at least five years.

[5] This portion of the note to be sent to the German delegation was approved to this effect. It is printed in *PPC*, VI, 567-68.

[6] The Council of Four, in a brief meeting at 6 p.m. on June 21, which Mantoux does not record, approved a letter and protocol which was sent to the German delegation, probably on June 22. The letter took note of the discrepancies be-

—The experts withdraw.
—Mr. Headlam-Morley is introduced.*

President Wilson. We asked a special committee to prepare a reply to M. Paderewski's letter about the treatment of minorities. To satisfy M. Paderewski, the committee proposes that the clauses of the treaty relating to minorities may be changed by a majority vote of the Council of the League of Nations, instead of a unanimous one. Then again, it will be indicated that the articles protecting German minorities will only apply in territories that were part of the German Empire.[7]

Mr. Balfour. Is that what M. Paderewski requested?

Mr. Headlam-Morley. M. Paderewski says that if it was otherwise an obligation would be imposed on Poland without reciprocity, for nothing protects Polish minorities inside Germany.

President Wilson. Concerning the observance of the Sabbath, the committee proposes not to allow it to stand in the way of the obligations of military service. Undoubtedly, it is desirable that these clauses be applicable in a general manner in all new states where there are grounds for providing for the protection of minorities.

Mr. Headlam-Morley. There remains one point to be settled. If it is desirable to allow Jews to have their schools, we cannot fail to recognize that there is a risk that the privileges granted to these schools might encourage and perpetuate the use of Yiddish. You might want to consider whether something can't be done to avoid this danger; in any case, they could demand that use of the Polish language be compulsory in the upper classes of Jewish schools.

—*The amendments presented are adopted. The question of Polish schools is referred to study by the committee.*

*H., *PPC*, VI, 569ff.

---

tween the text of the treaty and the council's letter to the German delegation of June 16. The "explanations" in the council's letter were to be "regarded as constituting a binding engagement," and they were embodied in a protocol to the treaty, which was annexed to it by its formal signing on June 28. The letter and the protocol are printed in *PPC*, VI, 601-604.

[7] Actually, the Committee on New States prepared the letter to Paderewski. It is printed in *PWW*, Vol. 61, pp. 47-50, as P. J. L. Berthelot to I. J. Paderewski, June 19, 1919.

CXXXIV

Conversation between President Wilson, MM. Clemenceau and Balfour, and Barons Sonnino and Makino*

JUNE 21, 1919, 4 P.M.

—Reading of a letter from Marshal Foch asking the governments to designate their representatives on the supervisory commission charged with overseeing the execution of the military clauses of the treaty with Germany.

President Wilson. I am embarrassed to designate my representative on account of the position taken by the United States Senate. I am certain it will ratify the treaty, but many of its members are looking for a pretext to refuse ratification. If I named a member of the commission for the execution of the treaty today—before the text itself had been ratified in America—I would be reproached for having anticipated the vote in some way.

M. Clemenceau. You can wait without great inconvenience.

President Wilson. My embarrassment is greater than you think; for the period of execution is only three months, and if the United States Senate gives in to its taste for prolonged controversies, it is possible that the commission will accomplish the greater part of its task before we have a chance to participate.

Mr. Balfour. In any case, you could have a liaison officer there, who could keep you in touch with everything.

President Wilson. Indeed, it is a difficulty of form rather than of content.

M. Clemenceau. Belgium has to be invited to designate her representatives on this commission.

Sir Maurice Hankey. Who should issue this invitation? Should it be Marshall Foch or the President of the Conference?

President Wilson. The President of the Conference.

—Reading of the reply written by Mr. Balfour to the statement of the plenipotentiaries of the Ottoman Empire.[1]

*H., PPC, VI, 575ff.

[1] A. J. Balfour, "Draft Answer To The Turks," June 19, 1919, printed in PPC, VI, 557-80. Balfour's draft flatly denied the contention of the Turkish delegation that the Ottoman Empire should be preserved in its territorial integrity, both because the Turkish people should not be blamed for the sins of their wartime

President Wilson. Excellent; it is just what they deserve.

Mr. Balfour. Mr. Lloyd George hasn't yet seen this text; but Mr. Montagu, to whom I showed it, made vehement objections.[2] He says that such a statement will make a bad impression amongst the Mohammedans of India. For my part, I cannot accept this view. I took care to show that we cannot be accused of any feeling of hostility against Islam.

President Wilson. Your entire indictment—which is hard, it must be admitted—is against the bad government of the Turks. Moreover, according to the facts that they themselves reported, they have been as cruel to Mohammedans as to Christians. I accept your text, which satisfies me completely.

Mr. Balfour. This text is thus approved by M. Clemenceau, President Wilson, and Baron Sonnino. On this subject, I will see Mr. Lloyd George, who has to speak to Mr. Montagu about the question.

—M. Tardieu and the members of the committee[3] charged with studying the question of the plebiscite in the Klagenfurt Basin are introduced.*

President Wilson. Because of the troubled situation in the Klagenfurt Basin, the new proposal[4] made to us is that the Yugoslavs occupy zone A, south of Klagenfurt, and the Austrians, zone B. This proposal is the committee's, with the exception of the Italian delegation. The same dissent shows itself about the period that is to precede the vote; the majority of the committee proposes three months; the Italian delegation requests six to eighteen months. Likewise, for the length of residence conferring the right to vote on inhabitants, the committee proposes to give this right to all residents since 1905; Italy asks that this date be substituted by that of August 1914. I must say that my personal opinion agrees with that of the majority of the committee, but we must hear the arguments of the Italian delegation.

Baron Sonnino. The occupation of both zones of the Klagenfurt Ba-

*H., *PPC*, VI, 581ff.

---

government and because of the alleged good record of Turkish rule over subject peoples. Every nation, Balfour replied, had to be judged by the government which ruled over it at a given time. Moreover, history proved conclusively that Turks were totally unfit to rule over subject peoples, whether Christian or Moslem. In fact the subject peoples would do much better both culturally and economically if freed from the burden of Turkish rule.

[2] "MR MONTAGU'S COMMENTS ON MR BALFOUR'S REPLY TO THE TURKS AND MR BALFOUR'S REMARKS THEREON," about which, see *PWW*, Vol. 61, p. 60, n. 5.

[3] That is, the Committee on Rumanian and Yugoslav Affairs.

[4] The committee's recommendations are printed in *PWW*, Vol. 61, pp. 57-59.

sin by those concerned can only have the effect of compromising or even making impossible a free vote. That is what I have already said to the Council of Four. It would be much better to institute an occupation there by Allied troops or to send a commission exercising temporary authority there with the help of the local police. The presence of Yugoslav troops on one side and Austrians on the other can only suppress freedom of opinion.

Despite an initial telegram from the Four, which arrived in Belgrade on June 3, the Yugoslavs have continued to fight and to advance northwards. An Italian officer sent from Vienna tried to establish relations with both belligerents to bring about a truce. He got as far as the Yugoslavs; but they prevented him from communicating with the Austrians. A sort of armistice was later concluded in Klagenfurt, but it hasn't been ratified by the Austrian government.

I thought the Four would renew their order and compel the Austrians and the Yugoslavs to evacuate the basin. If it is really thought preferable, for the goal proposed, to leave the country occupied, I have nothing more to say.

President Wilson. Our guarantee consists of the presence of a commission named by us, which, if there is undue pressure on public opinion, will inform us and, if necessary, bring about the annulment of the plebiscite.

M. Clemenceau. The commission can see what happens at the time of the plebiscite itself; but what it can't control is what will happen during the months of the occupation, with troops dispersed throughout the area.

President Wilson. However, I think that it is not difficult to obtain the required information in so restricted an area as the Klagenfurt Basin.

Baron Sonnino. You could leave the area in the hands of the local police.

I thought our military representatives sent to the spot would settle the question. President Wilson seems to be of opinion that they must simply report to us.

President Wilson. What I had in mind concerning the powers of these officers was simply the suspension of hostilities between the Austrians and the Yugoslavs.

Baron Sonnino. It would at least be necessary to hear the officers who have been on the spot before finally settling the occupation of the different parts of the region.

President Wilson. Italian troops marching on Klagenfurt were mentioned to us.

Baron Sonnino. I know nothing about that.

President Wilson. Can you find out?

Baron Sonnino. If that is correct, it is possible that these troops were called by our military representative who is down there.

President Wilson. We never intended to give this power to the military representatives whom we sent to the Klagenfurt Basin. If they have called in Allied troops without consulting us, I consider that serious.

M. Tardieu. What influenced the conclusion of the majority of the committee are the recent decisions taken by the Council of Four about the differences amongst Yugoslavs, Hungarians, and Rumanians. The council concluded that the best thing was to draw the final boundaries and compel the belligerents to withdraw their troops behind those boundaries. We tried to proceed in the same way here; the committee believed that was better than fixing a new line.

Baron Sonnino. I have already made the following objection to M. Tardieu: in the case involved, it is dangerous to apply the same rule as between Bohemia and Hungary, because here it is impossible to say what the final boundary will be before the plebiscite has taken place.

President Wilson. The committee assumes that it is dangerous to leave that area without occupation troops. If we admit this first point, we must acknowledge that it is impossible to have troops there other than Austrians in the German-speaking region and Yugoslavs in the southern zone. Indeed, there are no Allied troops nearby, except Italian troops. But the latter's presence, on account of the difference between the Italians and the Yugoslavs, could only be dangerous.

Baron Sonnino. It is not a matter of sending large forces there. Very few are needed to maintain order in such a small zone. A few Englishmen and Americans would suffice.

President Wilson. We have no troops nearby.

Baron Sonnino. You have a battalion in Fiume.

M. Tardieu. We have found no reason to discard the lines fixed for the plebiscite.

Baron Sonnino. To install Yugoslavs in zone A and Austrians in zone B is to prejudge the result.

Mr. Balfour. In any case, is it not necessary that our committee be entrusted with the distribution of the troops?

M. Tardieu. That is one point on which we agree.

President Wilson. Is it not better to state it expressly? I propose to authorize the committee to add this provision to its text.

—(*Adopted.*)

President Wilson. The question remains of the length of residence that will confer the right to vote. What are the arguments of the Italian delegation in favor of the date of 1914?

Baron Sonnino. Our principal argument is that there is no reason to adopt the date of 1905 rather than another. The simplest thing is to move it to the eve of the war, when the question to be settled had not even been raised.

President Wilson. Isn't there reason to be guided by the precedent created by our decision on the Saar Basin.

M. Tardieu. What led us to fix this date of 1905 is that M. Vesnić told us that, since 1905, there has been systematic German immigration in this region. The Italian delegation says it finds no proof of this. This is a question of fact, which is rather difficult to settle out of hand.

Baron Sonnino. There may have been German immigration; but I don't think a date like 1905 can be taken arbitrarily as the beginning of this immigration. The population in 1914 was the population of the district as it was before the war. I don't see how another date can be chosen without some tendentious intention. If we can arrive at a certain result, why not obtain it by an immediate decision, and what good is it to have recourse to a plebiscite?

President Wilson. The fact has been pointed out to me that the opening of a railroad in 1907 brought in a rather large number of new inhabitants, that a change in the administration of the schools took place around the same time and changed the spirit of these schools.

M. Tardieu. Without any doubt there has been a determined effort to Germanize the Slovenes since the annexation of Bosnia-Herzegovina. Perhaps the date of 1905 could be replaced by 1908.

Baron Sonnino. All these dates are arbitrary. The population is what it is. If we want to prejudge the result, we could spare ourselves the trouble and disturbance of a plebiscite.

President Wilson. In the case of Poland, I recall that, in fixing the boundary, we took into account the systematic character of German immigration in certain districts.

Baron Sonnino. In Poland, you were faced with a truly organized immigration, the consequence of special legislation of expropriation and buying back of Polish lands. You will find nothing as clearly defined in the Slovene region. M. Vesnić's impression may be justified; but that should not be enough to make us take an arbitrary decision.

President Wilson. In America, we have as much experience as anyone with problems of immigration and naturalization. But we have never permitted naturalization after a period as short as four years. In the case of the Klagenfurt Basin, couldn't we choose a period of six or seven years? The important thing is to go far enough back to be sure that we are dealing with true inhabitants of the region. I propose the date of 1912.

(*Adopted.*)

President Wilson. There remains the question of the time that has to elapse before the plebiscite.

M. Tardieu. M. Vesnić asked that the plebiscite take place within a period of a month. We preferred three months.

Baron Sonnino. I go along with that opinion. There is no advantage in allowing the agitation to be prolonged in the plebiscite area.

CXXXV

Conversation between President Wilson and MM. Clemenceau and Lloyd George*

JUNE 22, 1919, 7:20 P.M.

The council takes cognizance of three notes from the German delegation dated June 22: (1) announcement of the resignation of the German government and the formation of a new government;[1] (2) replacement of the head of the delegation at Versailles, Count Brockdorff-Rantzau, by Herr von Haniel;[2] (3) reply[3] to the note of the Principal Allied and Associated Governments of June 16 by a long declaration ending as follows: "The government of the German Republic is ready to sign the peace treaty, without, however, acknowledging the German people as the author of the war, and without accepting the responsibility for delivering persons referred to in Articles 227 to 230 of the treaty."

President Wilson. Our reply must be immediate: we can no longer accept any reservation or evasion.

—(*Assent.*)

*H., *PPC*, VI, 605ff.

[1] The note is missing; however, the Scheidemann cabinet had resigned and been replaced on June 21 by one headed by Gustav Adolf Bauer, Social Democratic leader of a coalition of the Social Democratic and Center parties formed for the explicit purpose of obtaining the approval of the National Assembly for the signing of the peace treaty.

[2] It is printed in *PPC*, VI, 608.

[3] It is printed as an appendix to these notes.

President Wilson. Here is what I suggest for a reply: "The Allied and Associated Governments have replied completely and clearly to the observations of the German delegation, making all concessions acknowledged to be fair and possible. The note addressed to them today contains nothing that has not already been considered. They state that the time for discussion has passed, and they can accept no change or reservation. The German government must accept or refuse, without any possible equivocation, to sign the treaty within the fixed period of time."[4]

M. Clemenceau. I would add a sentence to say that, if Germany signs, we will hold her responsible for the total execution of the treaty—I mean by that, of each line of the treaty.

President Wilson. I already said we could accept no change or reservation before the signing.

—*The text proposed by President Wilson is approved, with the addition proposed by M. Clemenceau.*

M. Clemenceau. We also have something to say to the Germans about the ships sunk in the Orkney Islands.[5] But I think it must be done in a separate note.

Mr. Lloyd George. Mr. Balfour, who knows the facts, could draft that note.

President Wilson. It must be said that it is a violation of the Armistice Agreement.

Mr. Lloyd George. And a violation of their given word.

President Wilson. They must be informed that we are reserving our right to take all appropriate measures.

Mr. Lloyd George. In any case, this question has to be treated apart from the peace treaty. Otherwise, the Germans might think that once the treaty is signed, their responsibility ends.

[4] This is a good paraphrase. See *PWW*, Vol. 61, pp. 76-77.

[5] Following detailed plans made weeks in advance, Vice Adm. Ludwig von Reuter, commander of the German High Seas Fleet interned at Scapa Flow, a sea basin in the Orkney Islands off the northern coast of Scotland, at approximately 11:20 a.m. on June 21 gave a flag signal to the German crews maintaining the ships to scuttle them by opening their seacocks. Under the terms of the Armistice, no British guards had been placed on the vessels. Most of the British naval squadron assigned to guard the German fleet was on maneuvers in the North Sea. By the time the British ships were alerted and had returned to Scapa Flow in midafternoon, most of the German warships had sunk. Fifteen of the sixteen capital ships went down; one was beached by the British. Four light cruisers sank; four others were beached. Of fifty destroyers, thirty-two sank, fourteen were beached, and four were kept afloat. See Arthur J. Marder, *From the Dreadnought to Scapa Flow: The Royal Navy in the Fisher Era, 1904-1919*, 5 vols. (London, 1961-70), V, 270-93, and Dan van der Vat, *The Grand Scuttle: The Sinking of the German Fleet at Scapa Flow in 1919* (London, 1982).

Another violation of the Armistice is their presence and action in the Baltic provinces. All that could be indicated in Mr. Balfour's letter.

I would like to return to the question of military operations in case the Germans do not sign. I don't much like the idea of stopping halfway. You remember that what we wanted was to march right to the seat of the German government. Our generals tell us they don't have enough troops for that; it would be better to let them have them. As far as England is concerned, we can provide three divisions in a very short time, and we will find two more if necessary. I propose to ask Marshal Foch what he needs by way of divisions and to see if we can find them amongst ourselves.

M. Clemenceau. Isn't it a bit late?

Mr. Lloyd George. Yesterday, I saw Mr. Winston Churchill. He told me he could send three divisions in a fortnight.

M. Clemenceau. We will then be on the Weser.

Mr. Lloyd George. That will be just the moment.

M. Clemenceau. Perhaps President Wilson will find American troops in France?

President Wilson. Unfortunately, Marshal Foch told General Pershing some time ago that it wasn't necessary to retain here two divisions that we could have kept and which have left for America.

Mr. Lloyd George. Before sending the Germans the reply drafted by President Wilson, mustn't we see Baron Sonnino and Baron Makino?

M. Clemenceau. That is a matter of form.

Mr. Lloyd George. We could communicate this text to them straightaway. But perhaps it is better to summon them here.

—*It is agreed that Baron Sonnino and Baron Makino will be summoned for tomorrow morning at 9 a.m.*

Mr. Lloyd George. When do you think the Germans will sign?

M. Clemenceau. They'll agree tomorrow, around 5:30 or 6:00 p.m.

President Wilson. They waited to be forced; they will be.

{ A P P E N D I X }[6]

Confidential

W.C.P.1046   TRANSLATION OF GERMAN NOTE

No. 70.   GERMAN PEACE DELEGATION
Mr. President: Versailles. June 22nd. 1919.

The Imperial Minister of Foreign Affairs has instructed me to communicate the following to Your Excellency:

"The Government of the German Republic has, from the moment when the Peace Conditions of the Allied and Associated Governments were made known to it, left no doubt to subsist as to the fact that the Government, in harmony with the whole German people, must regard these conditions as being in sharp contrast with the principle which was accepted by the Allied and Associated Powers on the one hand, and Germany on the other hand, as being binding in accordance with the law of nations for the peace before the conclusion of the armistice.

"Relying upon this principle of justice which was agreed upon between the parties to the negotiations, and assisted by a clear exposition of conditions in Germany, the Government has left no stone unturned in order to arrive at direct verbal exchange of opinions, and thus to obtain some mitigation of the unbearably harsh conditions which might render it possible for the Government of the German Republic to sign the Treaty of Peace without reservations, and to guarantee its execution.

"These endeavours of the Government of the German Republic, which were undertaken in the interest of the peace of the world, and the reconciliation of peoples, have failed owing to rigorous insistence on the conditions of peace. Far-reaching counter-proposals of the German Delegation have only in certain points received any acceptance. The concessions made only reduce the severity of the conditions in a small degree. The Allied and Associated Governments have, in an ultimatum which expires on June 23rd, confronted the Government of the German Republic with the decision either to sign the Treaty of Peace presented by them or to refuse to sign. In the latter case a completely defenceless people has been threatened with the forcible imposition of the conditions of peace already presented and with the increase of the heavy burdens.

"The German people does not wish for the resumption of the

[6] Printed in *PWW*, Vol. 61, pp. 72-76.

bloody war, it honestly wishes for a lasting peace. In view of the attitude of the Allied and Associated Governments, the German people has no other force in its hands save to appeal to the eternally inalienable right to an independent life which belongs to the German people as to all peoples. The Government of the German Republic can lend no support to this sacred right of the German people by the application of force. The Government can only hope for support through the conscience of mankind. No people, including those of the Allied and Associated Powers, could expect the German people to agree with thorough conviction to an instrument of peace, whereby living members of the very body of the German people are to be cut off without consultation of the population concerned, whereby the dignity of the German State is to be permanently impaired, and whereby unendurable economic and financial burdens are to be laid upon the German people.

"The German Government has received passionate expressions of opinion from the population in the districts to be cut off in the East, to the effect that they (the population) will oppose themselves to the separation of these districts which have for the greater part been German for many centuries by all means they possess. The German Government therefore finds itself compelled to decline all responsibility for any difficulties which may arise from the resistance of the inhabitants against their separation from Germany.

"If the Government of the German Republic is nevertheless ready to sign the conditions of the Allies with the above-mentioned reservation, yet this is not done of its free will. The Government of the German Republic solemnly declares that its attitude is to be understood in the sense that it yields to force, being resolved to spare the German people, whose sufferings are unspeakable, a new war, the shattering of its national unity by further occupation of German territories, terrible famine for women and children, and mercilessly prolonged retention of the prisoners of war. The German people expects in view of the grievous burdens which it is to take upon itself that all German military and civilian prisoners beginning on July 1, and thereafter in uninterrupted succession, and within a short period shall be restored. Germany gave back her enemies' prisoners of war within two months.

"The Government of the German Republic engages to fulfil the conditions of peace imposed upon Germany. It desires, however, in this solemn moment to express itself with unreserved clearness, in order to meet in advance any accusation of untruthfulness that may now or later be made against Germany. The conditions imposed exceed the measure of that which Germany can in fact perform. The Government of the German Republic therefore feels itself bound to announce that it makes all reservations and declines all responsibility as regards the consequences which may be threatened against Germany when, as is bound to happen, the impossibility of carrying out the conditions comes to light even though German capacity to fulfil is stretched to the utmost.

"Germany further lays the greatest emphasis on the declaration that she cannot accept Article 231 of the Treaty of Peace which requires Germany to admit herself to be the sole and only author of the war, and does not cover this article by her signature. It consequently follows without further argument that Germany must also decline to recognise that the burdens should be placed upon her on the score of the responsibility for the war which has unjustly been laid at her door.

"Likewise, it is equally impossible for a German to reconcile it with his dignity and honour to accept and execute Articles 227 to 230, by which Germany is required to give up to the Allied and Associated Powers for trial individuals among the German people who are accused by the Allied and Associated Powers of the breach of international laws and of committing acts contrary to the customs of war.

"Further, the Government of the German Republic makes a distinct protest against the taking away of all the colonial possessions of Germany, and against the reasons given therefor which permanently deny to Germany fitness for colonial activity, although the contrary is clearly established and irrefutable evidence to this effect is contained in the Observations of the German Peace Delegation on the Conditions of Peace.

"The Government of the German Republic assumes that it is in accordance with the desires of the Allied and Associated Governments that it has spoken openly, both as regards what concerns its goodwill and also as regards its reservations. Therefore, in view of the condition of constraint into which the German people are forced by the requirements of the Allies—a condition of constraint such as has never been inflicted on any people in any manner more crushing and more disastrous in its consequences—and relying on the express undertaking of the Allied and Associated Governments in their memorandum of June 16, 1919, the German Government believes itself to be entitled to address the following modest request to the Allied and Associated Governments in the expectation that the Allied and Associated Governments will consider the following declaration as an integral portion of the Treaty:

> 'Within two years counting from the day when the Treaty is signed, the Allied and Associated Governments will submit the present Treaty to the High Council of the Powers, as constituted by the League of Nations according to Article 4, for the purpose of subsequent examination. Before this High Council the German plenipotentiaries are to enjoy the same rights and privileges as the representatives of the other contracting Powers of the present Treaty. This Council shall decide in regard to those conditions of the present Treaty which impair the rights of self-determination of the German people, and also in regard to the stipulation whereby the free economic development of Germany on a footing of equal rights is impeded.'

The government of the German Republic accordingly gives the declaration of its consent, as required by the Note of June 16th, 1919, in the following form:

'The Government of the German Republic is ready to sign the Treaty of Peace without, however, recognising thereby that the German people was the author of the War, and without undertaking any responsibility for delivering persons in accordance with Articles 227 to 230 of the Treaty of Peace.'

Weimar, June 21st, 1919.
(Signed) Bauer.
President of the
Imperial Ministry."

Accept, Mr. President, the expression of my distinguished consideration. (Signed) von Haniel.

CXXXVI

Conversation between President Wilson, MM. Clemenceau and Lloyd George, and Barons Sonnino and Makino*

JUNE 23, 1919, 9 A.M.

Mr. Lloyd George. The Germans again request a delay of forty-eight hours.[1] We are all in favor of not granting it to them.
Baron Makino. Our essential goal is to make them sign.
M. Clemenceau. It will be even more important to make them carry out the treaty.
Baron Sonnino. There is something Jesuitical in the way they are acting. They will tell you that they clearly warned you that they couldn't carry out the treaty.
President Wilson. Won't our refusal to grant them this final delay make their consent more difficult?
Mr. Lloyd George. All our military men agree in saying it would be a serious error to grant them another delay. It is impossible to have the least confidence in them. On the other hand, our soldiers have just slept for five nights out of doors, huddled like flocks.

—Mr. Balfour favors replying to the Germans that they have had plenty of time to study our terms, that nothing new has taken place since then, and that the only changes made in the original text have been concessions on our part.

President Wilson. The only reason the Germans can put forward is that their new government hasn't had time to make up its mind.
Mr. Lloyd George. What would we do if they told us today that this government is dissolved and if we found ourselves faced with a new German government tomorrow?
President Wilson. I favor saying only, in polite terms and as briefly as possible, that we refuse.
M. Clemenceau. I would say that, after complete consideration of their request, we regret that it is not possible to extend the period of time already granted.

*H., PPC, VI, 607ff.

[1] E. K. A. Haniel von Haimhausen to G. Clemenceau, June 23, 1919, printed in PWW, Vol. 61, pp. 81-82.

—*The text of the reply*[2] *is read and approved.*

[2] "The Allied and Associated Governments beg to acknowledge the receipt of your communication of June 23. After full consideration of your request they regret that it is not possible to extend the time already granted to your Excellency to make known your decision relative to the signature of the Treaty without any reservation." Clemenceau to Haniel, June 23, 1919, *ibid.*, p. 82.

CXXXVII

Conversation between President Wilson, MM. Clemenceau and Lloyd George, Barons Sonnino and Makino, and Mr. Balfour*

JUNE 23, 1919, 11 A.M.

Mr. Lloyd George. I had a talk with Mr. Montagu about Mr. Balfour's letter to the Ottoman delegates. We must be careful about the feeling of the Mohammedans of India.

President Wilson. I assure you that I had this same concern whilst hearing the letter read. But, in my opinion, there is nothing to be said with this in mind against the text as it has been drafted.

Mr. Lloyd George. That's my opinion also. But it is important to indicate clearly that we are not denying the Mohammedans the right to govern themselves. We are not denying this right to the Turks, and we'll give it to the Arabs. It must be acknowledged that, in the past, Mohammedan governments—I don't say Turkish governments—have done much for civilization. As for Constantinople, I favor saying nothing that commits us.

Mr. Balfour.** We have two notes to be addressed to the Germans; one, about the ships that have been scuttled; the second, about the evacuation of the Baltic provinces.

As for the sunken ships, I am told that it is not certain that their destruction was—legally speaking—a violation of the Armistice. But it would seem to be a violation of the customs of war. We must consult the navy on that question. The thing was done deliberately by the German admiral. He said he thought the Armistice had expired at noon and that hostilities would be resumed.

*H., *PPC*, VI, 617ff.
**H., *PPC*, VI, 623ff.

M. Clemenceau. What do you propose to do?
Mr. Balfour. First, to protest.
Mr. Lloyd George. It would be necessary to confirm if it is true, as we read in the *Daily Mail*, that the Germans had recently sent new crews to these ships.
Mr. Balfour. That doesn't seem correct. I propose to hear the admirals.

—Admirals Hope, Ronarc'h, and Grassi are introduced.

President Wilson. We ask you to give us the facts.
Admiral Hope. On Saturday, June 21, at noon, the Germans hoisted their colors and took to their boats. Believing it was an escape, our crews fired on some of these boats. During that time, the German ships were sinking. The German admiral went aboard a trawler. According to the newspapers, he said that he thought the Armistice expired at noon and that hostilities were being resumed.
President Wilson. What truth is there in the rumor that the German ships had received new crews?
Admiral Hope. That's not correct. The only change that took place in those crews was a reduction of their numbers.
  A German battleship of the most recent type and four destroyers are still afloat. Three light cruisers and eighteen destroyers are stranded and can be raised.
M. Clemenceau. We must hear our legal advisers.

—MM. James Brown Scott, Fromageot, Hurst, and Weiss are introduced.

Mr. Balfour. It seems there was no precise provision in the Armistice Agreement. But by sinking their ships, didn't the Germans violate the general principles they accepted by signing that agreement.
M. Fromageot. Article 23 of the Armistice Agreement—the naval clauses—says that interned German vessels must remain in the port where internment will take place. The obligation thus imposed on the Germans extended until the signing of the peace treaty. The destruction of the ships is thus an infraction of the Armistice. Moreover, only a custodial crew entrusted with the maintenance of these ships should have been on board.
M. Clemenceau. If the custodial crew entrusted with upkeep causes the destruction, that is an obvious violation of the agreement. It's a question of a custodial crew and not of a war crew.
Mr. Hurst. The French text had been adopted as the official text. It says: "Ils y demeureront." The fact that the German admiral

thought he had the right to act as he did because he thought the Armistice had expired is no justification. Moreover, the publication of a statement by the German government accepting or refusing to sign the treaty wouldn't suffice to end the Armistice.

Baron Sonnino. What the German admiral said shows that he himself did not believe he had the right to act as he did as long as the Armistice lasted.

Mr. Balfour. Undoubtedly, the admiral thought the signing would be refused and the war resumed.

M. Clemenceau. What the German admiral thinks doesn't interest us.

Mr. Balfour. I agree with you. But the question arises whether, apart from the reparation that we have the right to exact from Germany, we must not and cannot punish the German admiral. Wasn't he under the orders of the British Admiralty?

Mr. Lloyd George. No; the latter had only a right of surveillance.

Mr. Hurst. According to the laws of war, the matter is very clear; any violation committed by an individual leads to punishment and reparation.

M. Weiss. Article 3 of the Hague Convention of 1907 lays down the principle of the responsibility of the government when its soldiers or sailors violate international law. This responsibility doesn't seem in doubt here.

Mr. Balfour. But what is the competent tribunal?

M. Weiss. That can be the object of negotiation or arbitration.

Mr. Balfour. This isn't very satisfactory. But isn't there a contradiction between looking at it this way and what was said previously, namely, that the individual can be held personally responsible?

M. Clemenceau. That depends; either he received orders or he did not receive them. In the present case, we don't know if he received them. But I don't see a contradiction between the two principles which have been spelled out to us. If the admiral is personally at fault, he can be punished; but further, there is damage done and ground for indemnity. It is not the admiral whom we will ask for this indemnity, it is his government. Thus, the two principles complement each other; the man must be punished, and the government is responsible for reparation.

I ask that our legal experts give us a text that establishes the doctrine applicable to the act which has been committed.

Mr. Balfour. And what is the competent tribunal?

M. Clemenceau. As for fixing the amount and nature of reparation, and as to whether we judge it necessary and opportune to impose punishment, these are political questions that the governments will settle.

Mr. Balfour. Before tackling this subject, I will ask our admiralties the following question: since punishment is less important to us than reparation, and since it is pointless to ask Germany for more money than we already have asked for, is it possible to lay claim to ships from her?
Admiral Hope. We have left the Germans a certain number of warships.
Mr. Lloyd George. We must discuss this amongst ourselves.
M. Clemenceau. But I insist that we first have the conclusions of our legal advisers. We could hear them this afternoon.

—(Assent.)

Mr. Balfour. Now we are going to consider the presence of the Germans in the Baltic provinces.

—Mr. Hurst reads aloud a memorandum:

On June 10, General Gough ordered the German troops to withdraw from the Baltic provinces. General von der Goltz answered that he would take orders only from his German superiors. Then it was decided to call upon the Germans to evacuate the Baltic provinces according to the regular procedure provided by the Armistice Agreement. The communication arrived at Spa on June 18. The time that has passed since then is too short to accuse the Germans of having violated the Armistice.

President Wilson. A secondary question, but whose importance seems real for the people involved, is the following. When the Germans entered the Baltic provinces, they changed the gauges of the railways to make them coincide with those of the German network, and they brought in their rolling stock. If they withdraw this rolling stock today, it will become impossible to distribute foodstuffs in the Baltic provinces, and, according to Mr. Hoover, most of that region will be threatened with famine.
Mr. Balfour. Can this rolling stock be claimed from the Germans?
President Wilson. Beyond doubt it belongs to them.
Mr. Balfour. Can't it be claimed in compensation for the ships that they have just sunk?
M. Clemenceau. I will have something to say on this subject. Can't we have the Letts buy back this rolling stock?
President Wilson. The Germans won't agree to turn it over to them, and how can we force them to do it?
Mr. Balfour. This is the first time I have heard this problem mentioned.
Mr. Lloyd George. The inhabitants themselves must be asked for their opinion; do they prefer to see the country occupied by the

Germans or run the risk of being deprived of their rolling stock? They seem to insist that the Germans leave.

President Wilson. There is an article in the treaty which obliges the Germans to divide the rolling stock between themselves and the Lithuanians. This article undoubtedly applies to all the Baltic provinces. I propose to ask the commission that deals with Baltic affairs to give us its opinion on the consequences of the withdrawal of rolling stock, as far as victualing is concerned.

Mr. Lloyd George. If it was possible, we ought to ascertain the opinion of the inhabitants.

—The experts withdraw.

Mr. Lloyd George. I can't help thinking that the duty of surveillance incumbent on our Admiralty implied something more than precautions necessary to prevent German ships from escaping. I ordered an inquiry. I would like to have the opinion of the Allied admiralties on this point: if the surveillance of the German ships had been their responsibility, would they have placed a guard on board each of those ships?

President Wilson. We did it in the United States for interned German merchant ships.

M. Clemenceau. The best thing would be to ask this question of our naval people in writing.

President Wilson. You wish each of our admiralties to give you its opinion separately?

Mr. Lloyd George. Certainly.

—Mr. Headlam-Morley is introduced.*

President Wilson. One of our remaining difficulties is the resistance of the new states to the clauses for the protection of minorities. A reply to M. Paderewski's last letter has been prepared; today, we are brought the final draft,[1] which has been drawn up with much care.

Mr. Lloyd George. What are the concessions made to the Poles?

President Wilson: The first relates to military service. The clause relating to the observance of the Sabbath cannot be invoked by the Jews during their active service. The second deals with the use of Yiddish in the schools. Its use as a language of instruction in Jewish schools subsidized by the state will be limited to the elementary classes.

*H., *PPC*, VI, 624ff.

[1] It is printed in *PWW*, Vol. 61, pp. 93-99. At the end of the discussion it was agreed to send this letter subject to the changes made.

Mr. Lloyd George. Has nothing been done to avoid having these schools form an entirely separate organized body? M. Paderewski made an objection that seemed valid to me in pointing out the danger that such organized groups could pose to national unity.

M. Clemenceau. From the religious point of view, it is good that some schools be Jewish. But they certainly have to be incorporated in the national system of public instruction.

Mr. Lloyd George. The Jewish schools of the East End in London are established on this principle.

President Wilson. The most important thing is to calm the anxieties of the Jews. I always fear allowing a dangerous ferment to exist in that quarter.

Mr. Lloyd George. Our desire to protect the Jews doesn't have to go so far as to make them into a state within a state. In all our countries having a national system of education, we allow religious instruction for only a few hours a week. The right of the Jews to create schools founded on particularist principles and giving instruction absolutely different from that of Polish schools could constitute a real danger for the Polish state.

President Wilson. I will remind you that I have always been opposed to the formation of an autonomous Jewish community inside the Polish state. But the best thing is to ask Mr. Headlam-Morley about that question.

Mr. Headlam-Morley. The clause relating to Jewish schools authorizes their administration by Jewish committees.

Mr. Lloyd George. What must be granted to these schools is the treatment that we give in England to schools created and maintained by the different churches. But there must be a national authority above these Jewish administrative committees, in particular in matters concerning the curriculum.

Mr. Headlam-Morley. What we tried to do is precisely to institute a system for these schools like the one governing Catholic schools in England, with the general curriculum to be determined by the Polish authorities.

Mr. Lloyd George. That was not how M. Paderewski understood that clause. If it gives him the guarantees he wants, he must be made to understand them clearly, even if the wording has to be changed to do that. That is very important, so that the Jews can't claim what we no longer wanted to grant them.

Mr. Headlam-Morley. I had thought of substituting the word "persons" for the word "committees." The committee has already changed the original draft, which said: "These schools will be administered by a committee or committees." And it left only the words "by committees," in order to prevent the establishment of a central administration of Jewish schools.

Mr. Balfour. I don't think your text prevents that. Isn't it necessary to add a word or two and say "local committees"?

Mr. Lloyd George. I think that is very important.

President Wilson. It could be made even more precise by saying: "committees named by the local Jewish communities."

Mr. Lloyd George. On the other hand, we must avoid anything that might recognize Yiddish as the language of the Jews. We must see to it that Poland is not obliged officially to allow that language, which is only corrupt German.

Mr. Headlam-Morley. It must indeed be allowed in elementary schools; one couldn't make oneself understood amongst children by speaking another language. But I acknowledge that it would be serious to compel the Polish state to do more.

Mr. Lloyd George. What is being done in New York concerning the Jewish population, now very numerous, which has preserved the use of Yiddish?

President Wilson. We are compelled to appoint Yiddish-speaking teachers.

Mr. Lloyd George. Very good; but that is to teach something other than Yiddish. What must be avoided is that that language be considered as the very basis of instruction. Above all, we must have national unity in view.

President Wilson. We must always remember that we are dealing with states which, until now, have treated Jews in the spirit of the Middle Ages. Our goal must be to help to transform that state of mind.

Mr. Headlam-Morley. It would be dangerous to allow the use of Yiddish in the upper forms.

Mr. Balfour. We all agree on this point. What is important to indicate clearly is that, in the primary schools, where use of Yiddish is absolutely necessary, that language shall not be the subject of instruction, but only the language used for teaching.

Mr. Headlam-Morley. I propose to write: "Yiddish can be used as a vehicle of instruction in elementary schools and primary classes." The Polish state should not be compelled to subsidize schools where Yiddish was taught in the upper forms.

Baron Sonnino. How will you prevent Yiddish from being taught in the primary schools?

Mr. Headlam-Morley. We are at this time imposing no obligation or restriction on the Jews; we are limiting the terms imposed on the Polish state.

Baron Sonnino. Let us suppose that the Poles forbid the teaching of Yiddish in all schools; wouldn't that lead to serious difficulties?

Mr. Lloyd George. That risk must be accepted.

Mr. Headlam-Morley. The great danger would be doing what would, instead of only protecting the Jews, go beyond that by encouraging Jewish nationalism. It is essential that the Jews can have their separate schools because of the bad treatment that Jewish children suffer in Polish schools. But everything must be avoided that could serve an aggressive nationalism, which has only too great a tendency to develop.

President Wilson. We are dealing with Jews of the Middle Ages in a hostile environment.

Mr. Headlam-Morley. We must also think about the application of these clauses to other minorities. A number of cities contain a considerable proportion, and sometimes a majority, of German population.

President Wilson. In a city like Chicago, where Germans are very numerous, we don't allow German to be used otherwise than as a language of instruction for young children, and that out of toleration.

Mr. Headlam-Morley. The problem isn't the same. The Germans of Poland are attached to the land; most of them are not recent immigrants.

President Wilson. Yes, but their property will become part of Poland, and we don't want them to remain German forever.

Mr. Headlam-Morley. The question is to know the treatment that will most contribute to making them faithful citizens of the Polish state.

Mr. Balfour. What is the treatment of Poles in German schools?

Mr. Headlam-Morley. The use of Polish is forbidden, even for prayers.

President Wilson. The text must be drafted in such a way as to indicate that minorities, whatever they are, will have the right to use their language in primary schools, without their being able to change the curriculum.

Mr. Balfour. I greatly fear that the Jewish problem will become one of the most serious in the future. This idea of establishing a Jewish nation within Poland is very dangerous. We must not stipulate anything for Jews, but only for persons of the Jewish religion. It is dangerous to appear to legislate in favor of a single race.

President Wilson. On the other hand, the danger is to expose Jews, who won't be able to prove that they attend the synagogue, to being excluded from the benefit of these clauses.

CXXXVIII

Conversation between President Wilson, MM. Clemenceau, Lloyd George, and Balfour, and Barons Sonnino and Makino*

JUNE 23, 1919, 4 P.M.

—MM. Davis, Loucheur, Tardieu, and Taussig are introduced.
—Mr. Balfour reports:

1. A dispatch intercepted from the Weimar government to the German delegation in Versailles: the Allies having decided to employ the most extreme violence to force Germany to accept terms without material importance, but which tend to besmirch the honor of Germany, and since the German people no longer have the means to defend themselves, the government declares itself prepared to sign. The German delegation must await confirmation of this message before communicating it to the Allied and Associated Powers.

2. A telegram seized by the Polish authorities and addressed to two German generals, to organize local resistance against the cession of German territories to Poland. This resistance will be disavowed by the German government, but it will do what is necessary to support it.

3. A note from General Dupont, reporting that, in Berlin, French flags which, according to the treaty, had to be restored to France, were carried off and burned publicly.

Mr. Lloyd George. That is German honor; truly, this is not a civilized nation that we have to deal with.

Mr. Winston Churchill will come before long to speak to you about the repatriation of the Czechs by way of Archangel. In Bohemia, they are insistently demanding the return of the Czech troops from Russia. Mr. Winston Churchill is especially concerned to establish, if possible, communications between Admiral Kolchak and Archangel, and the Czech troops on the return route could help with that. But for that, they must be replaced, along the Trans-Siberian, by Japanese and American troops. I ask you to ponder this question.

Sir Maurice Hankey. I must point out to you that I have found in the naval clauses of the Armistice one article—Article 31—that forbids all destruction of ships or naval matériel by the Germans before evacuation, surrender, or restitution.

*H., *PPC*, VI, 635ff.

M. Clemenceau. Article 31 is magnificent; why didn't our lawyers spot it?

Mr. Lloyd George. When can we sign? Not tomorrow, in any case.

M. Clemenceau. It's impossible; Wednesday at the earliest.

Mr. Lloyd George. All our plenipotentiaries couldn't be in Paris for tomorrow.

President Wilson. I had hoped to leave tomorrow evening for Brest.

Mr. Lloyd George. The experts refer to us Article 41 [49] of the treaty with Austria, which relates to private property. I am told that this arrangement, as it has been drafted, constitutes an injustice.

Mr. Taussig. According to the first draft, all enemy property in the territories detached from Austria could be expropriated and liquidated. The new draft limits this arrangement to properties of the Crown and merchant tonnage.

Mr. Lloyd George. I thought we had already taken that decision.

President Wilson. Yes, but this is the draft which corresponds to the decision taken. It is only fair. This text has to be communicated to the powers concerned.

Mr. Davis. It should be done without delay, for the expropriations have already begun.

M. Loucheur.* I submit to you the report of the subcommission which you instructed to consider—along with the states whose territories, in whole or in part, belonged to the Austro-Hungarian monarchy—the distribution of war costs and reparations.

As far as reparations are concerned, the Yugoslav and Rumanian delegations don't seem inclined to accept our proposals. They prefer to await the estimate which will be made by the Reparation Commission.

As far as the contribution of these states to the expenses of the war of liberation is concerned, we proposed that each of them pay a sum equivalent to 20 per cent of the Austro-Hungarian war loans floated on its territory. There is no difficulty there. I hope an agreement will be reached on that basis today.

As far as reparations are concerned, must the solution we proposed be insisted upon? The states concerned are making extravagant demands. Serbia, for example, instead of the balance of 500 million francs which we offer her, is asking for five billion. For myself, I propose to leave the task of fixing the sum to the Reparation Commission: the difference between the sum thus determined and the 20 per cent of war loans that have to be paid to us

---

*H., *PPC*, VI, 638ff.

will be entered either to the debit or the credit of each of these states.

Mr. Lloyd George. Let us suppose that Serbia, on account of the acquisition of the territories forming, along with her, Yugoslavia, be debited with a sum of one hundred million pounds, and that, moreover, the Reparation Commission estimates that Serbia has the right to 150 million pounds; the difference, that is to say fifty million pounds, would be paid to Serbia. Is that right?

M. Loucheur. Not exactly. The question is more complicated, because the reparations will be payable in gold, whilst the amount of the contribution of each country will be calculated in the currency of that country.

Mr. Lloyd George. In short, they will pay almost nothing and receive everything.

M. Loucheur. That's what I think.

Mr. Lloyd George. That is what you recommend?

M. Loucheur. For Serbia and Rumania, I am compelled to do it. For the Poles and Czechoslovaks, the problem doesn't arise in the same terms, and in my opinion, it should have been treated differently; we should have imposed on them the payment of their contribution in certificates of external debt.

Mr. Lloyd George. Will you give the states you speak of all they ask without imposing on them charges on account of the territories they are acquiring?

M. Loucheur. In every case, they will carry the prewar debt and the war debt accruing to these territories.

Mr. Lloyd George. In any case, their debt to the Allies would have to come before their obligations towards bearers of certificates of the Austrian or Hungarian debt.

M. Loucheur. Take Serbia, for example. By virtue of the financial clauses of the treaty, she must take her part of the Austro-Hungarian prewar debt. She will also bear part of the war debt. If we ask her, in addition, to pay us a certain sum on account of the expenses we incurred for her liberation, she could answer that she has already paid her share of the costs of the war, and the only result we would obtain would be to crush her. The same reasoning applies to Rumania.

If I have a different opinion concerning Poland and Czechoslovakia, it is because for the one as for the other, the expenses of the war have been almost nil. As a consequence, they can make us a payment.

Mr. Lloyd George. What I can't understand is this. M. Loucheur considers it settled that Rumania and Yugoslavia must carry their part of the Austro-Hungarian war debt. If that is so, Poland should carry a part of Germany's war debt for the territories which she is acquiring. The situation would be exactly the same.

Mr. Davis. It was decided that Austria proper would be liberated from the part of her prewar debt corresponding to the detached territories, and moreover, that each of those countries would contribute to the cost of the war of liberation. It is in executing the second part of that decision that we are requesting of the states concerned a sum equivalent to 20 or 25 per cent of the war loans floated on their territory. We tried to balance, on the one hand, the contribution these states will owe us, and on the other, the reparation to which they will have a right. They are not prepared to accept it, because we can't reach an agreement with them on the figures.

Mr. Lloyd George. In any case, if the Reparation Commission is left with the task of determining what will be due to each of these states, it must hold out strongly for the 20 or 25 per cent contribution. I really hope we will deduct nothing from this. When the claims of each of these countries have been verified, this figure will be put on one side, and the 25 per cent they must pay us [will be put] on the other, and they will receive the difference, if any. I hope we will not budge from that conclusion.

—The experts withdraw.
—The members of the Drafting Committee are introduced.*

M. Clemenceau. Our attention has just been called to Article 31 of the Armistice Agreement, which forbids the Germans to destroy ships.

M. Fromageot. We know that article; but we didn't believe we had the power to invoke it, because, in our opinion, it applies to ships before they left German ports.

—Reading of a first draft of a note, drawn up by the Drafting Committee, to be addressed to Germany.

Mr. Lloyd George. What do you have to say about the application of Article 31?

Mr. Hurst. Your legal advisers don't believe Article 31 applies to the case at hand.[1] In any event, there is doubt, and we don't want to use an argument in the name of the Allied and Associated Governments which could appear doubtful. In fact, that article

*H., PPC, VI, 641ff.

[1] The written opinion of the legal advisers is printed in PPC, VI, 641-42.

appears to be attached to a group of stipulations different from those which concern us. The destruction in question took place after the surrender of the German ships. We believe this article applies to destructions which might have taken place before the execution of the Armistice Agreement.

Mr. Lloyd George. In my opinion, Article 31 responds to the present situation exactly. It is said there that any destruction is forbidden before evacuation, surrender, or restitution. After the end of the Armistice, we can only guard these ships—that's surrender—or give them up—that's restitution. Article 31 says: there will be no destruction before one or the other has taken place; the preceding article of the Armistice relates precisely to interned vessels.

President Wilson. I understand the argument of our legal advisers. The article says that no destruction must take place before evacuation, surrender, or restitution. The word "before" governs the entire sentence.

Mr. Lloyd George. The word "restitution" can't apply to anything at all in the Armistice; it can apply only to restitution in execution of the peace treaty.

M. Clemenceau. I can't accept the theory of the lawyers. No Frenchman will admit that one could make no use of Article 31. The experts in international law have given their opinion. That is well enough; the governments must consult them, but it is up to them to decide.

Mr. Balfour. In any case, if we have arguments which, in the opinion of the lawyers, are valid, can it do the least harm to add another which, according to them, is less conclusive?

Baron Sonnino. I believe that in that Article 31 it was not a matter of restitution of German ships to Germany, but, on the contrary, restitution by Germany of ships that had been taken from us and which they were forbidden to destroy.

M. Clemenceau. I don't agree. Three cases are anticipated. First evacuation, that is the departure of German ships for the place where they were to be interned. Then two eventualities can take place: surrender or restitution. In one case or the other, the Germans don't have the right to destroy their vessels. If the text doesn't mean that, I don't know what it means. Above the commentaries of the lawyers, there is a supreme authority—common sense.

President Wilson. The meaning of the word "evacuation" doesn't seem so clear to me.

M. Clemenceau. To evacuate is to empty a place. A ship that leaves a port evacuates it.

President Wilson. I will call to your attention that Article 31 applies to cases anticipated by the preceding articles, that is Articles 29 and 30.

Mr. Balfour. It is pointless to settle the question out of hand. All that matters is to punish the culprit and obtain the reparation due us. Our legal advisers tell us that, even without invoking Article 31, we have the right to take sanctions; as for reparation, it has already been indicated that the only thing possible is a new cession of enemy vessels.

—At 5:40 p.m., M. Dutasta, Secretary-General of the Conference, brings the note from the German delegation announcing the unconditional acceptance of the treaty by the German government.[2]

[2] Printed in PWW, Vol. 61, p. 79, n. 2.

CXXXIX

Conversation between President Wilson, MM. Clemenceau and Lloyd George, and Baron Sonnino*

JUNE 24, 1919, 11 A.M.

—Admiral Hope, Admiral Ronarc'h, and Admiral Grassi are introduced.

Mr. Lloyd George. I recall how it was decided last October, before the conclusion of the Armistice, to intern the German ships. You remember that the British and French admiralties were of opinion that the surrender of all these vessels should be required. Admiral Benson, representing the American navy, declared himself opposed. Marshal Foch spoke in the same way, saying: "I don't want to risk the lives of my soldiers for these miserable boats which have never been capable of fighting against ours on the high seas." So we adopted Admiral Benson's views, against the opinion of the French and British navies. We decided unanimously that the designated vessels would be interned in a neutral port.

*H., PPC, VI, 649ff.

We later stated that it was impossible to find a suitable neutral port. Then it was decided to send these vessels to Scapa Flow, under the surveillance of the British navy. Only watch and maintenance personnel were to remain aboard them. It was judged pointless to put English sailors aboard those ships. The opinion of our admirals, which is the same today, was that, short of placing a man behind each German, it was impossible to prevent acts of sabotage. The instructions given by the English admiral, of which I have a copy, show that he did not fail to anticipate the possibility of willful destruction of these vessels by the Germans.

I won't hark back to the facts. At present, one German battleship is intact. Another can be recovered without great difficulty, as well as a certain number of destroyers. The rest, as you know, are lost. The Japanese Admiralty, having been consulted, thinks no reproach can be made to the English admiral.

—Mr. Balfour reads aloud a letter from Admiral Ronarc'h;[1] the French navy thinks there should have been a guard of Allied sailors aboard the German vessels.

Mr. Lloyd George. I will remind you that that would have been impossible if these ships, as was first proposed, had been interned in a neutral port. Moreover, the precautions taken were all aimed at preventing these ships from resuming the offensive against us. We were mostly thinking about that.

President Wilson. The American navy thinks that, if it had been charged with guarding these ships, it would have thought it was authorized to place sailors aboard them, in view of the acts of sabotage of which the Germans had already been held guilty aboard merchant ships.

Admiral Hope. It seemed impossible to us to watch the Germans in such a way as to prevent acts of destruction. The only way would have been to disembark the German crews and replace them with Allied sailors.

President Wilson. We can hold the German government responsible. But what will it profit us? We don't want to begin the war again; what we want is reparation. I believe we will find enough ships in Germany to make possible the distribution we had in view, except as far as the British navy is concerned. Doesn't something remain to be given as appropriate compensation to the weakest navies, whilst the strongest navies renounce it?

Mr. Lloyd George. A battleship and a battle cruiser remain.

---

[1] It is printed in *PPC*, VI, 653.

M. Clemenceau. I think President Wilson puts the question very well. It is first a question of law. Has Germany violated the Armistice? We heard the legal experts; they are explicit. You remember our discussion of Article 31, which, as far as I am concerned, seems to me to apply to the present case. For the moment, we must mention this article in our letter to the German government, taking note of the violation committed. It is not only a violation of the Armistice; it is an anticipated violation of the peace treaty.

If there had been only this fact of the destruction of ships at Scapa Flow, it would have been very significant in itself. We may be told that the German admiral, after having read the newspaper, believed that the Armistice expired at noon; we know well enough the lies of the Germans, and I consider all that to equal zero. But another serious fact has just been reported to us, that is, the destruction of French flags which, according to the treaty, were to have been restored to France. That is an insult strongly felt by the French army, about which the French Parliament is aroused. That is also a violation of the Armistice and peace terms.

We also heard yesterday the reading of a dispatch seized by the Polish authorities, showing that insurrection is being organized in Upper Silesia; the German government is prepared to deny it officially and to support it unofficially. This time, it is a matter of a very serious violation. In the last message he addressed to us,[2] Von Haniel said: "There will be an insurrection in Silesia, and we won't be able to prevent it." During the fortnight following the signing, the treaty requires the evacuation of Upper Silesia by German troops; will it take place?

What we already know justifies what I have often repeated: it is difficult to make the Germans sign the treaty; but the greatest difficulty will be to make them carry it out.

All these facts must be grouped together. For myself, as soon as we have verified the authenticity of the document relating to Poland, I favor informing the Germans that we know about it and publishing it in the newspapers. That will show that we have our eyes open, and that they won't defy us so easily.

Reparation has just been mentioned; it is said it would be possible to find what would be necessary to assure compensation to the French navy; I hope so. The question of immediate respon-

---

[2] Actually not the "last message," but Haniel to Clemenceau, June 22, 1919, printed as an appendix to CXXXV.

sibility most especially concerns Mr. Lloyd George. But material reparation and a local sanction are not enough. I have the honor of formally demanding reparation for the burned French flags. I am convinced that this act took place by order of the German government, and that it is the same with the outrage at Scapa Flow.

I will be told: "You can't demand compensation in money." We know too well that that would only result in stealing from ourselves. Reparation in ships has been mentioned; we will see what it is possible to do in that regard. But the most important thing is to show that we will not tolerate acts like those at Scapa Flow and Berlin, and like those that are being prepared in Poland, where our direct intervention is so difficult.

All this proves that the Germans, even before having signed the treaty, are preparing to violate it. We are warned. President Wilson has serious reasons for wishing to leave as soon as possible, but, even after his departure, our flags remain together and committed. I request a military act that demonstrates our will to make the treaty be respected; we must not allow it to be thought that violations will meet no resistance.

I don't hide from myself the danger of what can appear as an act of violence on our part, at the very moment when we are going to sign the peace. In addition, what I ask today is only to send the German government a document that will recall what happened at Scapa Flow and the flag incident in Berlin, and that will indicate what we have good reason to believe the Germans are preparing to do in Poland. This document will conclude by affirming our right to reparation and guarantees. I would say nothing more. The signing must not be compromised. The essential thing is to establish our right.

But amongst us, I will tell you frankly what must follow: we must take possession of Essen. That's the reason why I asked M. Loucheur to come here; he will tell you that Essen is still today the great manufacturing center of German artillery; he will tell you that, until a short time ago, the production of artillery parts has continued in Essen. You know well that my intention is not to keep Essen but to remove immediately a powerful means of military resistance from the Germans, and above all, to affirm the sovereign will of the Allies. In that way, we will prevent Germany from supporting her military operations in Poland. Seeing how we act, the Germans will have only one idea—to give in. At the same time, we will satisfy public opinion which, throughout the most serious crises of this war, has supported us with its perseverance and constancy.

The danger is that Germany is trying to take back, bit by bit, everything the treaty gives us. If we don't act today, we risk being compelled to recall men to arms and to commit acts of war tomorrow. That's why I ask that we act with caution, but in such a manner as to impose the execution of the treaty on Germany.

President Wilson. Do you want to postpone discussion of this question until this afternoon? It is a serious question, and I would like to be able to think about it.

Mr. Lloyd George. I must also consult my colleagues.

Mr. Balfour. According to M. Clemenceau, the first thing to do is to address a formal letter of protest to the Germans, both on the destruction of the vessels at Scapa Flow and the burned flags, whilst mentioning the information we have about the attitude of the Germans in Silesia.

Mr. Lloyd George. Are you certain of the authenticity of the document relating to Poland?

M. Clemenceau. It is very important; I'll speak to you again about it this afternoon. In any case, this dispatch coincides with all our other information.

Mr. Balfour. You propose to conclude our message to the German government by demanding reparation, but without indicating anything more?

M. Clemenceau. I will say nothing more for the present. Moreover, it is important not to rank the three incidents equally.

Mr. Balfour. You would just as soon that the treaty be signed before the Germans have replied to this communication?

M. Clemenceau. Certainly.

Mr. Balfour. And in case the German reply would not appear sufficient to us, you would go further by demanding definite reparation?

M. Clemenceau. The most important thing is not material reparation.

Mr. Balfour. Do you propose the permanent occupation of Essen?

M. Clemenceau. You know very well that I don't want annexation. But I consider it important that the Germans be deprived of this incomparable source of war materials during the acute period of the Polish affair.

Mr. Balfour. The latter is the most serious of all.

CXL

Conversation between President Wilson, MM. Clemenceau and Lloyd George, and Barons Sonnino and Makino*

JUNE 25, 1919, 11 A.M.

—M. Dutasta is introduced.

M. Clemenceau. M. Dutasta asks us for authorization to send immediately a reply to the Germans to the question they have just raised about the occupation.[1] They ask when the agreement provided by the treaty will be presented to them. In the treaty, there is a very important paragraph, in which it is said that the Germans will have to accept all agreements we might make on this subject.

—Reading of Article 432 of the treaty with Germany.

Mr. Lloyd George. The word "accord"—*agreement* in the English text—can be understood in the sense of a convention between us and the Germans.

M. Clemenceau. Why? It is a matter of an agreement between us. The only question is whether this convention on which we agree must or must not bear the signature of the Germans.

Mr. Lloyd George. It is preferable to risk nothing; I would make them sign it. The best thing is to send them the text of the agreement immediately.

—Reading of the reply to the German communication:[2]

There is no reason for negotiation about the occupation arrangement since this arrangement is the subject of a conversation already concluded amongst the Allies. The Germans will have to sign this convention under the same conditions as the peace treaty.

President Wilson. So that there be no ambiguity, I would prefer to write: "At the same time as the peace treaty."

—(Adopted.)

M. Clemenceau. Another point relating to the signing: I favor mak-

*H., PPC, VI, 655ff.

[1] Haniel to Clemenceau, June 24, 1919, printed in *PWW*, Vol. 61, p. 139.
[2] See *ibid.*, p. 140.

ing the Germans sign first. This seems contrary to precedent; but that doesn't bother me, and I think you will agree with me about the advantages of this procedure.

—M. Clemenceau's proposal is adopted.

—Reading of the report of the admirals on the reparations to be demanded for the destruction of the German fleet at Scapa Flow;[3] they must include delivery of floating docks, of a certain proportion of the merchant fleet left to Germany. Beyond that, Germany can be compelled to construct a certain additional quantity of merchant tonnage for the Allies.

M. Clemenceau. This deals only with the naval question. In our letter, we must take into account the incident of the flags and the information relating to the situation in Poland.
Mr. Lloyd George. Have you inquired about the authenticity of the Polish document?
M. Clemenceau. There isn't the slightest doubt.
Mr. Lloyd George. What I find odd is that that document appeared in the newspapers without being accompanied by our protest.
M. Clemenceau. I would not like to do anything today that could compromise the signing of the treaty. Moreover, rest assured that, whatever the authenticity of the document, the Germans will deny it.
Mr. Lloyd George. In my opinion, we must not lose an instant in acting. If possible, we must immediately stop what is being prepared on the Polish side.
M. Clemenceau. I don't know if we can, but we can try.
President Wilson. We must be careful. You remember a letter from Erzberger, which appeared some time ago in the newspapers.[4] It was acknowledged to be not genuine; it came from a Polish source. I must say I distrust Polish sources of information.
M. Clemenceau. We have the same information from General Dupont. But it is true that that doesn't remove all kind of doubt from the document itself. My idea is to send someone to Warsaw to see this document, and, if necessary, to photograph it.
Mr. Lloyd George. In any case, there is a document that announces the intention of the German government to violate the treaty,[5] and all we do is to publish it in *Le Matin*? That's not enough. If we can, we must stop the fight in Poland.

[3] It is printed in *PPC*, VI, 664-68.
[4] See CV, n. 4.
[5] That is, Haniel's letter of June 22.

Baron Sonnino. I understand M. Clemenceau's worry about not compromising the signing of the treaty by announcing very drastic measures.

M. Clemenceau. If we take the necessary position, I believe there will be local disturbances in Poland, but not armed struggle. In any case, this movement must not be allowed to grow.

President Wilson. I have thought much about the Scapa Flow affair, and, the more I think of it, the more I doubt what it is appropriate to do. I went to the Hôtel Crillon to consult my colleagues of the American delegation. Mr. Lansing, who is almost without exception the most competent man in the United States in the field of international law, is not sure we can hold the German government responsible for an event that did not take place under its jurisdiction. If the thing had happened on the high seas or in a German port, there would be no doubt; but it seems to him that, in the case before us, the German admiral alone is responsible.

We are on the point of making peace. We are dealing with a people whose character does not appear to us in a new light. I fear—and M. Clemenceau, I acknowledge, has often warned us about it—that incidents of this kind will recur frequently. The Germans will destroy what they must hand over and will say that the destruction was done by such and such an irresponsible person. But we must face the question. If such is the case, will we go to war to prevent them from doing it?

The deed at Scapa Flow is undoubtedly a violation of the Armistice. A violation of the Armistice is the renewal of hostilities. Now, the Armistice must last until the treaty has been ratified by Germany and by three of the Principal Allied and Associated Powers. If we declare today that there has been a violation of the Armistice on the part of the Germans, we say thereby that the war has begun again, and this at the precise moment when we are going to place our signatures at the bottom of the peace treaty.

M. Clemenceau. It is not we who have violated the Armistice.

President Wilson. No, but if we take note of the violation committed and we act, it is war.

M. Clemenceau. After the violation of the Armistice Agreement by the Germans, we have the right to resume hostilities.

Mr. Lloyd George. There is no doubt that to take a city by force is to commit an act of war.

M. Clemenceau. If we look at it that way, I fear we would appear to be capitulating, purely and simply, before the insolence of the Germans.

Baron Sonnino. If, after having signed the peace treaty, we do something contrary to the Armistice, the Germans will be able to say that it is we who are breaking the peace.

M. Clemenceau. Two questions arise: one is a question of international law; the other is a political question.

On the point of international law, here is what I have to say: yesterday, we all agreed that the acts committed by the Germans are violations of the Armistice. I have not changed my opinion. Whatever the consequences, the fact is there. We are free to say nothing, or even to say that it pleases us enormously. But that will change nothing about the fact. For myself, if it was to be decided that we do nothing, I would have to find out in what form the protest of the French government should be presented. A French Parliament would never accept it if I acted otherwise.

President Wilson begs us not to begin the war again. I should think so! My country suffered more than any other. A universal cry for demobilization is rising in France; in the corridors of the Senate, where I went yesterday, they could speak of nothing else. Nevertheless, there is a supreme interest that rises above the legitimate desire to be done with the war; we must not let the outcome of the war escape us by our weakness.

Germany has given every proof of her bad faith. It is certain that we are faced with anticipated violations of the peace treaty. Today, Germany isn't prepared to resist if we take a forceful posture. But if we allow her to commit one violation of the treaty, than another, then another still, the moment will come when we will have parted company, or will have no more soldiers, and Germany will do what she wants.

This is the moment to act. If we don't, I beg President Wilson to consider that tomorrow the entire treaty will be imperiled.

Mr. Lloyd George. I feel embarrassed to come into the discussion; for, although the British Admiralty, at the time of the conclusion of the Armistice, declared itself against the internment of German ships and in favor of their surrender pure and simple, it is a fact that these ships were under our guard when they were sunk.

I consulted my colleagues about the measures to be taken. The question is not whether we can allow a flagrant violation of the Armistice to pass without protest, punishment, and compensation; it is simply a matter of making the punishment and the compensation fit the crime. What must be known is whether, because the Germans sank their vessels in the roadsteads of Scapa Flow, we have the right ourselves to seize an important German city and occupy it after having signed the peace treaty.

The act we are complaining about took place on Saturday. The treaty isn't yet signed. We are saying nothing. We sign the treaty; we make the Germans countersign the convention that fixes the clear geographical lines of the occupation, and later we say: "We are compelled to occupy Essen." That wouldn't be honest. In any event, it is thus that British public opinion would take it. Today, whilst not revealing our intentions out of fear that the Germans won't sign the treaty, we lead them to sign, and later we act beyond what the treaty has provided.

At present, the sentiment of the entire world is arrayed against Germany; nothing must be done that can change it to our detriment. British public opinion is as agitated by the incident of the French flags burned in Berlin as by the destruction of the German ships in Scapa Flow. As far as the destruction of the ships is concerned, we don't know if our sailors, had they been in the place of the German sailors, wouldn't have done as much. On the other hand, to burn French flags is a gratuitous and intolerable insult. But to make the Germans sign a treaty that fixes a certain boundary line to the occupation with the mental reservation to advance as soon as they have signed and to pass that boundary line—that would give birth, amongst many honorable people, to a feeling that would be unfavorable to us.

Perhaps it would not be quite the same in France; France has been invaded and devastated; she has suffered terribly, and Germany is her old enemy, all of whose heinous crimes she knows. Amongst the English people, there is no sentiment favorable to the Germans. But you have seen the position taken by those whom I will call the intellectuals, who are rather well represented by Lord Robert Cecil, by the Archbishops of York and Canterbury, whose letters I quoted to you not long ago. That must be taken into account. We must avoid creating the impression that it is not justice we want, but the crushing of a defeated enemy. If you want to occupy Essen, that is well and good; but the Germans must be told about it today.

M. Clemenceau. You well know that I will do absolutely nothing without your consent. All I am doing here is to ask you the question in order to settle it amongst ourselves.

Mr. Lloyd George. We are not saying that violations committed must be allowed to pass, but that there must be no dissimulation in our conduct. I would prefer to risk having the Germans refuse their signature to the treaty. The culprits must be punished, and by that I mean not only those responsible for the destruction of the ships, but those who burned the French flags.

On the other hand, we are claiming appropriate compensation. If the violation of the Armistice had taken place on land, the idea of asking for compensation in ships would never have occurred to you. The punishment must fit the crime.

Two of the best ships in the German fleet were saved; these are first-rate vessels. As far as we are concerned, we renounce all claims to them. All that can be had today, France will have. Our feeling is that, since it is in one of our ports that the German fleet was sunk, all that remains must go to France.

That is not to be scorned. You have no battle cruisers. When the war ended, we had only one more than Germany. In 1921, Germany would have surpassed us, and that would have placed us in a dangerous situation; for, because of the superior speed of her vessels, it would have been impossible for us to give battle to the German fleet. You will have these battle cruisers, and the light cruisers that remain, if they interest you. It is up to the French navy to say what it wants, and it will receive it.

It is the same with what remains of the German fleet in German ports. Our admirals say: "That is worth nothing." In fact, several of the vessels left to the Germans are as good or better than the best in our fleet. Their light cruisers are the best ever made. I am prepared to ask for them to be handed over. If France requests them, we will support her.

As for the flags, the only thing that can be asked is punishment of the culprits. But I hope, in any case, that France will not act alone.

M. Clemenceau. Never fear; you know well that I am not the man to break our alliance.

Mr. Lloyd George. The serious difficulties won't occur in the fifteen years which lie ahead.

M. Clemenceau. I regret that I'm not of your opinion; I fear they will begin immediately.

Mr. Lloyd George. It is all the more important to remain united.

In a way, I am here in the position of a man who has to justify himself, since it was in a British port that the German ships were sunk. But I beg M. Clemenceau to be content with a sanction appropriate to the crime, and not to occupy a part of German territory after the signing of the peace.

President Wilson. The anxiety that has haunted me for weeks is this: if the Germans don't carry out the treaty, what means do we have to compel them to do it? From the moment we use force and begin the war again, the treaty itself disappears. Any military action after the signing of the treaty renews the war.

Mr. Lloyd George. The sanction for the Scapa Flow affair must be naval.

President Wilson. The only sanction provided by the treaty is the right that the Council of the League of Nations possesses to extend the period of occupation if Germany doesn't keep her commitments.

Mr. Lloyd George. If France also wants the German destroyers, of which there remain a rather large number, we ask nothing for ourselves.

President Wilson. What does M. Clemenceau think about the question I have just asked? I assume that Germany, whilst protesting her good faith, will do everything in order not to carry out the treaty. What can we do? It seems to me that any use of force on our part would be an act of war, and the first effect of war would be the abrogation of the entire treaty. The difficulty we find ourselves faced with now is part of this more general problem. We have told Germany: "If the treaty is not signed on Monday at 7 P.M., the Armistice is terminated and the war begins again." It will be the same on the day we decide on military action.

Mr. Lloyd George. We would sign the treaty Saturday, and the next day commit an act of war!

President Wilson. We agree to declare that the German admiral violated the terms of the Armistice, that we hold him responsible for the act committed, and that we will ask the German government for reparation in kind.

Mr. Lloyd George. According to the information we have, there is no doubt that the German government knew everything.

President Wilson. An appropriate sanction is necessary, but we must avoid giving the world the impression that war is beginning again. I insist on telling my friends frankly what is at the bottom of my thoughts.

M. Clemenceau. I am doing my best to put myself in your place; I ask the same effort of you. I don't want to do anything that can complicate things. I consulted M. Fromageot, and I asked him this question: "In the conditions that we foresee, will the occupation of Essen be a renewal of the war?" He answered me that, from the legal point of view, one could doubt it. An act of reprisal is not necessarily the beginning of a new period of hostilities. But he called to my attention that it would be an act of war in the eyes of the world. So I am inclined to renounce it, although obviously it would be the best way of depriving Germany of her means of action in Poland.

I agree with you concerning the protest and the sanctions we must demand, as well as the material reparation to which we have a right. I recognize that, if we can receive complete reparation in kind, the rest will be easy to arrange. We can demand merchant tonnage in addition to the military vessels which undoubtedly will not suffice to replace those which were destroyed.

M. Mantoux. It is mentioned in the report of the admirals.

M. Clemenceau. I would perhaps specify the delivery of tankers that we need, according to what M. Bérenger told me again yesterday. My idea is to send a letter to the Germans today. I bring you a text drafted by our legal experts. It seems good to me; but something must be added to it. About the flags, it says that we will ask for reparation after an inquiry; for today, I don't want to do more. But what I want to add is a few lines indicating clearly that we will take sanctions and warn the Germans that, if they act in this way, we will be compelled to consider whether there are grounds for extending the occupation period. I would tell them simply that we would be forced to think about it if such conduct continued; that will make them reflect and will satisfy public opinion in France. We'll ask our experts for information about merchant tonnage and tankers that the Germans can give us in addition to available warships.

As you see, I am going a long way to meet you. I ask you only to take a step in my direction.

Mr. Lloyd George. I would like to see your proposals in writing.

—Reading of the text prepared by the legal experts.[6]

M. Clemenceau. I favor mentioning Article 31. We could write, for example: "According to the principle acknowledged in Article 31 * * *"

President Wilson. You know my doubts about that article.

Mr. Lloyd George. What we must do is simply to recall it as supporting one of our counts of indictment.

M. Clemenceau. That is all I wish.

President Wilson. I read further on: "Sanctions, reparations, and other measures that * * * *" I propose to eliminate these last words.

—(Adopted.)

—It is decided that the final draft will be prepared by MM. Balfour and Loucheur.

President Wilson. It is important to tell the Germans that their con-

[6] That is, the report cited in CXXXVIII, n. 1.

duct throws doubt on their willingness to carry out the treaty as a whole, and that it might compel us to confer about the necessary sanctions.

M. Clemenceau. I insist that the possibility of an extension of the occupation period be indicated clearly.

Mr. Lloyd George. I would prefer not to specify this.

M. Clemenceau. I still insist, because our only means of action comes from that quarter.

Mr. Lloyd George. I don't believe it. Can't we refuse raw materials to the Germans, for example?

M. Clemenceau. You won't be able to do it. I repeat that I have gone far enough to meet you so that you should take a step towards me.

Mr. Lloyd George. Do you have news about the time of the signing?

M. Clemenceau. What we know is that the German plenipotentiaries will arrive on Friday. But we don't know who these plenipotentiaries will be.

Mr. Lloyd George. We have the right to know. I am told that, when the Germans at Versailles received the message announcing the arrival of that delegation, they began to laugh. We don't know what they were laughing at. But are we sure that the German government won't send subordinates of the lowest rank here to sign the treaty? We mustn't tolerate that. We must warn the Germans, all the more since at the time we communicated the preliminary treaty to them, they manifested the intention to send mere messengers to Versailles to receive it from us and we refused.

CXLI

Conversation between President Wilson, MM. Clemenceau and Lloyd George, and Barons Sonnino and Makino*

JUNE 25, 1919, 4 P.M.

—M. Dutasta, Secretary-General of the Conference, is introduced.

M. Dutasta. Von Haniel telephoned Berlin twice to ask for the names of the delegates and the precise time they will arrive. He hasn't yet received a reply. He told me the new German govern-

*H., *PPC*, VI, 669ff.

ment has just moved from Weimar to Berlin, and that its first meeting is to take place this morning.

Mr. Lloyd George. If there is a delay owing to acceptable causes, we haven't much to say. But we won't tolerate being made fun of.

M. Dutasta. According to remarks made by Von Haniel's entourage, the German government is encountering a real difficulty in finding men who will agree to come to sign the treaty. I told Von Haniel that you were waiting for a reply this evening or tomorrow morning at the latest.

M. Clemenceau. Very good.

—M. Dutasta withdraws.
—Mr. Lloyd George reads aloud the final draft of the note to the German government on the violations of the Armistice at Scapa Flow and Berlin.[1]

Mr. Lloyd George. The time of the evacuation of Upper Silesia by the Germans is tied to that of the ratification of the treaty; when will we have ratified the treaty?

President Wilson. If I leave France on Sunday, that is June 29, I can't present the treaty to Congress before July 10.

M. Clemenceau. In France, it is necessary to take into account the time for the work of the parliamentary commissions. I intend to submit the treaty soon after the signing, but to accompany this submission only with a few words and a welcome to recovered Alsace and Lorraine. Isn't it better for us in France and England not to speak before the President of the United States?

Mr. Lloyd George. I'll do what you like. I intend simply to submit the treaty and to speak only later.

President Wilson. I cannot deliver a speech to Congress; I can only read a written message.

M. Clemenceau. How long might the debates in the American Congress last?

President Wilson. I anticipate a month. The Senate has no set rules for such a matter; each of its members can speak as long as he wishes.

M. Clemenceau. It will also take a month for us.

President Wilson. According to the treaty, the evacuation of Upper Silesia must take place only two weeks after it goes into effect, and its going into effect will begin only when the treaty has been ratified by Germany and three of us.

Mr. Lloyd George. This shows the importance of not delaying the

---

[1] It is printed in *PWW*, Vol 61, pp. 168-70.

ratification of the treaty. We must anticipate opposition from the Germans when it comes to delivering persons indicted in conformity with the clauses on responsibility. The opinion of Sir Ernest Pollock, our Attorney General, is that a warning must be given to the Germans on this point.[2] What will we do about Holland when it comes to obtaining the extradition of the Kaiser? Shouldn't we address her as soon as possible?

President Wilson. We can't do it before the treaty goes into effect.

M. Clemenceau. In Germany, there is a good deal of indifference about this matter.

President Wilson. We have no means to compel Holland to give us satisfaction.

Mr. Lloyd George. I believe we can find some. What do you think of the trial itself?

M. Clemenceau. I hardly know where it is to take place.

Mr. Lloyd George. In any case, it is impossible for it to take place in a neutral country.

President Wilson. The judges must be very carefully chosen.

Mr. Lloyd George. Obviously, we must send our most eminent judges there. In my opinion, the trial must take place either in England or in America. In France or in Belgium, the memories of the invasion are too recent and the violence of feeling is too strong.

M. Clemenceau. How would this be thought of in the United States?

President Wilson. The Americans would not like that very much.

Mr. Lloyd George. The best thing would probably be to have the trial in England. Feeling is really too strong in France and Belgium. Do we agree that the trial should take place in England?

—(Assent.)

Mr. Lloyd George. I return to the question of the destruction of the enemy warships. I propose to send the representatives of our admiralties the question of how the German ships remaining at Scapa Flow, those of the Austrian fleet, and the submarines already delivered to us will be distributed. The question has already been studied a long time ago, without a decision having been taken. Some of the powers represented were in favor of the destruction of all these ships, others for keeping them. I am of opinion that France should receive what she asks for.

M. Clemenceau. How do we settle the question of the merchant

---

[2] Pollock also suggested linking the repatriation of German prisoners of war to the delivery of Germans indicted for war crimes. PPC, VI, 679.

ships we are demanding from Germany, in addition to the war vessels still available?

Mr. Lloyd George. A special commission must be named for that, for this question is not within the competence of our admirals.

—*Mr. Lloyd George's proposal is adopted. A commission is named: England will be represented by Mr. Hipwood; the United States, by Mr. Gordon; France, by M. Monnet; Italy, by M. Crespi; Japan by an expert to be designated.*

President Wilson. The Blockade Council asks if the blockade has to be lifted immediately after the signing of the peace treaty.

M. Clemenceau. On my instructions, M. Mantoux prepared a report[3] that will be read to you.

—(*Summary*). To prevent the Germans from delaying ratification, and according to the precedent provided by Article 3 of the preliminaries of peace of February 26, 1871, the Allied and Associated Powers have to remind the German government that the blockade is to end at the same time as the state of war. However, the latter will only end by the exchange of ratifications. Nevertheless, out of humanitarian concern, the Allied and Associated Powers can consent to lift the blockade as soon as they have received official notification of the ratification of the treaty by the German National Assembly.

Mr. Lloyd George. That seems perfectly reasonable to me.

President Wilson. I agree, although you know how hostile I have always been to the prolongation of the blockade.

M. Clemenceau. Germany is not dying of hunger now.

Sir Maurice Hankey. Should a statement about this be drafted?

M. Clemenceau. In any case, the Germans must be notified.

—*The conclusions of the report are adopted. A text will be drafted to be communicated to the Germans.*

Mr. Lloyd George. I ask that we be presented with a list of everything that must be done for the execution of the treaty during a period of one, two, and three months. I propose to create a commission that will see to the execution of the treaty.

President Wilson. It can't begin to concern itself with the execution before ratification.

Mr. Lloyd George. No, but it is a matter of preparing for it. The members of this commission must be named without delay, and they must get to work now.

—Reading of the report of the Commission on Baltic Affairs about the

[3] It is printed in *PWW*, Vol. 61, p. 152.

German rolling stock that is now located in the Baltic provinces;[4] the commission recommends claiming this rolling stock by virtue of the Armistice Agreement, since the deliveries prescribed by this agreement have not been completely carried out.

President Wilson. That seems to be a practical solution. Thus, in the East, the Germans would give what they didn't hand over in the West. In that case, it is the Armistice Commission that would claim this rolling stock.

—*The conclusions of the report are adopted.*

—Reading of a second report from the Commission on Baltic Affairs[5] about the German advance, which is being systematically pressed. The danger from the side of the Bolsheviks is no less serious. The commission proposes that the Allied and Associated Governments give immediate financial assistance to the populations of the Baltic provinces.

—An annexed report originating from the agents of the Allied and Associated Powers in the Baltic[6] asks for the dispatch of an inter-Allied military mission under the command of an English general. It also asks for the dispatch of instructors and arms for local forces, with the money required to pay them, as well as an advance of funds to Lithuania, Estonia, and Latvia.

President Wilson. Unfortunately, that is impossible; we have no money to send them.

Mr. Lloyd George. Here are men who are fighting for their freedom and who can't go on if we send them no money. As far as providing them with foodstuffs and munitions is concerned, I am completely ready to do it, and I favor sending them the mission requested.

Sir Maurice Hankey. General Gough is already there.

Mr. Lloyd George. Yes, but he is staying in Helsinki. The reports that he sends us show, moreover, a terribly complicated situation. The Estonians are at this moment being attacked by the Latvians, and behind the latter, General Gough tells us there are Germans. It is a frightful confusion.

The news that we receive from Russia is a mixture of good and bad. The good on the whole outweighs the bad. You remember the defeat and retreat of Admiral Kolchak; he lost 300 kilometers of ground. But, at the same time, Denikin is advancing from the southern side, and the Don Cossacks are rallying to his support.

[4] Printed in *ibid.*, pp. 160-61.
[5] Printed in *ibid.*, pp. 161-62.
[6] Printed in *ibid.*, pp. 162-63.

They fought the Bolsheviks, took 50,000 men and 300 guns. The last telegram about Kolchak is bad; the last telegram about Denikin is excellent. It is a kind of seesaw.

—Reading of the letter addressed to the German government[7] to warn it that it will be held strictly responsible for all disturbances that might take place in western Poland in case agitation by the German elements of the population should be supported by Germany.

Mr. Lloyd George. They must be reminded that, at the time fixed by the treaty, evacuation of German troops must take place as provided.
Baron Sonnino. But the treaty says it expressly.
President Wilson. It is important to emphasize this point.

—*The text is changed accordingly.*

Mr. Lloyd George. I have proposals from Mr. Winston Churchill on the subject of the Czech troops in Russia.[8] Isn't it better to submit them first to the Supreme War Council?
M. Clemenceau. Indeed, that is best.
Mr. Lloyd George. According to this report, it is obvious that, even if the Bolshevik front was breached, the Czechoslovaks would not reach Archangel in time to be embarked before the winter. We can offer to make an effort to hasten their liberation; but we run some risk if the effort doesn't succeed.
M. Clemenceau. I received a letter from the Chinese delegation warning me that it could sign the treaty only with reservations. I propose to reply that, if it makes reservations, that delegation cannot be admitted to the signing.
President Wilson. I believe sovereign states have this right in signing a treaty.
M. Clemenceau. We have granted it neither to Rumania nor Serbia.
President Wilson. Mr. Lansing says that this procedure is allowed by international custom.

[7] Printed in *ibid.*, pp. 163-64.
[8] Printed in *ibid.*, pp. 164-66. Churchill reported that he and Beneš had agreed to the following proposals: (1) the Allies would guarantee to repatriate the Czech troops now in Siberia; (2) thirty thousand Czech troops would join Kolchak's right wing with a view to establishing a junction with the Archangel forces by way of Viatka to Kotlas and would be repatriated from Archangel before the end of the year; and (3) the remainder of the Czech forces in Siberia would be evacuated by way of Vladivostok. Churchill then went on to explain what he said were the great advantages of this plan which would, of course have to be worked out in cooperation with the Czech government, Kolchak, etc. The Four did not consider this report any more seriously than is indicated in Mantoux's notes.

Mr. Lloyd George. However, the treaty must be signed or not signed. What does the signature mean if, at the same time, the signatory declares that he rejects the clause that particularly concerns him?

Baron Makino. We would have to know exactly the meaning and scope of this reservation. If it was accepted, we would be compelled to make a corresponding reservation.

President Wilson. It is a protest against our solution of the Shantung question.

Baron Makino. If it is only a protest, I have nothing to say. But it might mean something more.

President Wilson. The Chinese delegation must be asked the question. But it is acting on the instructions of its government.

Mr. Lloyd George. If this reservation means that China does not accept the only articles of the treaty that concern her, what use is her signature?

President Wilson. We could ask M. Pichon to question the Chinese delegation in our name.

—(Assent.)

Mr. Lloyd George. When will we discuss Turkish affairs?

M. Clemenceau. We have received a memorandum from the Turks, in which they say they will apprise you of what you must do in Egypt and Cyprus.[9]

Mr. Lloyd George. Their advice will be welcome; we have the greatest need of it!

What I mean is that the President of the United States is leaving, and we can't allow the state of war with Turkey to last two more months, or longer. Can we agree on the terms we must impose on Turkey, reserving entirely the question of apportioning the territories of the Ottoman Empire until the time when we know what mandates the United States can assume? We can't wait until the decision of the American Senate to make peace with Turkey.

M. Clemenceau. If you think you can do it, I am ready.

President Wilson. I think we can confine ourselves for the moment to taking everything from Turkey that must no longer belong to her: Armenia, the Arab countries, etc., and compelling her to accept in advance our decisions about the future fate of these territories.

[9] Printed in *PPC*, VI, 691-94. It is summarized in detail later on in these notes.

M. Clemenceau. What are you doing about Constantinople?

Mr. Lloyd George. You cut off the limbs; but are you going to cut off the head?

President Wilson. You can tell the Turks now: "Armenia, Mesopotamia, Smyrna, Syria, etc., will no longer belong to you." And you can proceed to the occupation of these regions.

Mr. Lloyd George. We have no more troops in Armenia. If we tell the Turks: "From July 1 onwards, Armenia ceases to belong to you," they will straightaway send people there to resume the massacres.

M. Clemenceau. As for the way we will dispose of the territories of the Turkish Empire, after our last conversations, I must say I no longer know where we are.

President Wilson. Without settling this question, can't we finish with the Turks?

M. Clemenceau. I don't believe so; we can try.

Mr. Lloyd George. We can't determine the future of Anatolia without settling the question of the Italian occupation. If the Turks ask us: "Why are the Italians in our country?", the only response we can give is that they are there against our will and despite our protests.

President Wilson. I can tell you in a few words what I anticipate. Turkey, reduced to Anatolia, would accept terms for the administration of that country that would be fixed later. I believe it would be an error from the psychological point of view to establish a mandate over Turkey, but that the Allied and Associated Powers must have the right, through one of them, to aid and oversee Turkish administration. A neutral zone would be drawn around the Straits; the Sultan would leave Constantinople, which, together with the area of the Straits, would be ceded to the Allied and Associated Powers.

All that can be drafted in the form of a treaty. The Turks have nothing to do with the settlement that will follow, no more so than Austria has in the solution of the question raised today between the Italians and the Yugoslavs.

Mr. Lloyd George. This assumes that the Turks will leave Constantinople.

President Wilson. Yes.

M. Clemenceau. That is a big decision to take.

President Wilson. It is the only possible one, in my opinion.

Mr. Lloyd George. Mr. Balfour has come to the same conclusion, after having defended the opposite policy all his life.

President Wilson. I have studied the Turkish problem very closely and for a long time, and I arrive at the conclusion that the only possible solution is to get the Turks out of Constantinople.

Mr. Lloyd George. I must also inform you that Emir Faisal sent a telegram[10] to General Allenby, who transmitted it to us, in which he complains that the mission that arrived in Syria is an American mission and not an inter-Allied mission. He asked General Allenby if the mandate established in Syria would be conferred on Great Britain. General Allenby answered no. The Emir asked then if Great Britain would not accept that mandate in case the conference should insist that she be entrusted with it. I instructed General Allenby to reply that in no event would Great Britain assume the mandate for Syria.

President Wilson. I come to a question that is rather delicate from the point of view of international law; how are we going to approach Holland about the extradition of the Kaiser?

Mr. Lloyd George. Holland must be told that Germany signed a treaty by the terms of which the Kaiser has to be handed over to us, and that we are addressing her since he is on her territory.

President Wilson. It must be done in such a way that Holland is discharged of all responsibility. She gave the Kaiser asylum at a time when there was no legal obstacle to it. She might not like handing him over when no treaty of extradition compels her to do it.

Can't we say: "Germany signed a treaty that would force her to hand over the Kaiser if he was on her territory. He is on Dutch territory; as a consequence, you have the duty, finding yourself accidentally in the place of Germany, to do what is imposed on her by the treaty." This would relieve Holland of all responsibility.

Baron Sonnino. Is the case of the Kaiser a case of extradition? I don't think so.

President Wilson. That is only a proposal that doesn't have to be taken literally.

Mr. Lloyd George. The truth is that we are faced with an unprecedented situation. We want to punish a crime committed against the entire world. The principal culprit has taken refuge in a neutral country. We can't allow that country to protect him against all punitive action.

President Wilson. That's all very well. But what are our means of constraint?

[10] About which, see PWW, Vol. 61, p. 157.

M. Clemenceau. I would be surprised if Holland resisted. I saw the minister of the Netherlands the other day; he referred rather obscurely to this question, and it seemed to me—as far as I could understand him—that we would not meet strong opposition on the part of his government.

President Wilson. Can we designate someone to draft our request in such a way as to make it difficult for Holland to refuse? I could ask Mr. Lansing to draft a text.

Mr. Lloyd George. I believe Mr. Lansing will draft that text very well, undoubtedly better than our Attorney General.

M. Clemenceau. What do we decide?

Mr. Lloyd George. To entrust this draft to Mr. Lansing.

—(*Assent.*)

—Reading of the memorandum from the Turkish delegation "on the new organization of the Ottoman Empire":

(*Summary.*) Despite the interests and traditions of friendship which carry it towards the western powers, Turkey was dragged into a disastrous war. Memory glorifies Turkey's past, recalls that she knew how to create and administer a great empire, that in it she respected the existence of all religious communities, and that she entered on the path of reform as soon as she came into contact with the West. Turkey desires only to continue her advance towards progress.

The problems of the Ottoman Empire divide themselves into three parts: (1) in Thrace; (2) in Asia Minor; (3) in Arabia.

1. Thrace. To assume a lasting peace, it is important that Adrianople be better protected against possible attacks. The Turks are, moreover, in the majority in western Thrace—today Bulgarian. Turkey requests that her boundary be moved forward up to the Kara-Su, which flows into the sea across from the Island of Thasos.

2. All of Asia Minor, as well as the neighboring islands of the coast, must remain Turkish. If the Armenian Republic of Erivan—former Russian Armenia—is recognized by the Allied and Associated Powers, its boundary can be determined by common agreement, and all facilities will be given to the Armenians of the Ottoman Empire who wish to settle in its territory. Just and equitable treatment will be assured to all minorities inside the Ottoman Empire.

3. The Arab countries will receive large administrative autonomy, under the sovereignty of the Sultan, who will name their governors, a special arrangement being provided for Mecca. The Turkish flag will fly over all these areas, justice will be rendered in the name of the Sultan, and currency printed with his effigy.

From the time of the signing of the treaty, the Allied troops will be withdrawn from Ottoman territories, except where, by common agreement, it would be agreed that their presence is necessary to maintain order. Further, the Ottoman government declares itself ready to settle finally, in the most friendly spirit, the legal status of Egypt and the island of Cyprus.

The people of the Ottoman Empire will not accept the division of their territories nor the establishment of a system of mandates. All are attached to the Ottoman government, and the latter receives protests from everywhere in favor of the unity and independence of the empire.

Mr. Lloyd George. That delegation and its memorandum are good jokes.

President Wilson. I have never seen anything more stupid.

Mr. Lloyd George. It is the best proof of the complete political incapacity of the Turks. They have always placed men of other races at the head of their government.

President Wilson. Is it necessary to reply to a document of this kind?

Mr. Lloyd George. Our reply is already made by Mr. Balfour's letter.[11] I propose to acknowledge receipt of this memorandum and to tell the Turkish delegation: "You can go home."

President Wilson. Besides, the Turks only came here to explain their views. We are not bound to answer them.

M. Clemenceau. We must reply for form's sake. Is it necessary to see them?

Mr. Lloyd George. In any case, they must be dismissed in one way or another. I propose to devote a morning in the near future to the discussion of the Turkish question. We will see if we can arrive at a solution, and, in that case, there could be reason to inform the Turkish delegates.

President Wilson. The solution we will reach has nothing to do with these three wan characters.

Mr. Lloyd George. If we could only make peace summarily and finish with it.

M. Clemenceau. I fear that is not possible.

—MM. Loucheur, Fromageot, and Hurst are introduced.

—Reading of the note addressed to the Germans on the violation of the Armistice by the destruction of the ships interned at Scapa Flow.[12]

—*This note is approved.*

M. Clemenceau. Can I give this to the press?

[11] About which, see CXXXIV, n. 1.
[12] Printed in *PWW*, Vol. 61, pp. 168-70.

Mr. Lloyd George. Certainly. We will do the same.

—The experts withdraw.

Mr. Lloyd George. When will we consider the mandate system?

M. Clemenceau. When you wish. But I believe the question of Constantinople won't be settled in a day.

CXLII

Conversation between President Wilson, MM. Clemenceau and Lloyd George, and Barons Sonnino and Makino*

JUNE 26, 1919, 11 A.M.

—M. Dutasta is introduced.

M. Dutasta. I have just seen Von Haniel; the German government has named its plenipotentiaries, the list will be completed today. The two names communicated to me are those of Herr Hermann Müller, Minister of Foreign Affairs, and Herr Giesberts, Minister of Posts and Telegraphs. A third delegate will no doubt join them: that will be Herr Leinert, President of the Prussian Assembly.

These delegates are to arrive Saturday at dawn, by ordinary train. Von Haniel questioned me about the verification of the credentials. I told him that, in my opinion, that could be done Saturday morning at 10 o'clock. He telegraphed accordingly to Berlin. Under these conditions, the signing could take place Saturday afternoon, at 3 o'clock.

Von Haniel said to me again: "We want to verify the text of the copy which the German plenipotentiaries will sign." I answered him that that would be a very long operation. He told me that he had thought of that, and that the Germans were prepared to renounce this right if the Allied and Associated Governments will give them a declaration attesting that the text of the authentic copy of the treaty is indeed identical on every point to that of the 200 copies which were sent to Germany. That declaration would have to be made by a letter from the President of the Conference.

*H., *PPC*, VI, 697ff.

M. Clemenceau. Do you agree?

Baron Sonnino. Couldn't we give the Germans two copies of the treaty today?

M. Dutasta. There is only one diplomatic instrument, and it would take two days to collate it.

M. Clemenceau. Do you agree to send the letter in question?

—(*Assent.*)

M. Dutasta. Von Haniel asked if the President of the Conference would make a speech. I told him that I could not reply officially, but that, unofficially, I could tell him no.

I must draw your attention to the question of the seals, which will take much time to affix. Since the Germans are only three in number, I would propose that their seals be affixed by them at the very moment of the signing.

M. Clemenceau. For the other seals, the best thing is to have them affixed in advance.

President Wilson. We only have to give the seals to the secretaries of our respective delegations.

M. Clemenceau. We could proceed to that operation tomorrow at 2 o'clock. But couldn't the seals of the Germans be affixed Saturday morning? The presence of ours will reassure them.

M. Dutasta. Von Haniel delivered to me, moreover, a note about Poland. I transmit it to you.[1]

—M. Dutasta withdraws.

M. Clemenceau. On July 14, we will have a state parade of the troops. We intend to invite General Robertson, Marshal Haig, General Pershing, and General Diaz to participate in it. We would like to see as many English and American soldiers there as you can send, and also, naturally, Italian soldiers. I believe Japan can only send us officers. Of course, the sailors must not be forgotten.

—(*Assent.*)

Mr. Lloyd George. I have interesting news from Holland. The Crown Prince[2] has fled eastwards by automobile with a staff officer. That bodes no good.

---

[1] Printed in *PWW*, Vol. 61, pp. 193-94. It is paraphrased below. Haniel also said that the German government had already taken action to calm Germans on both sides of the new German-Polish frontiers.

[2] Friedrich Wilhelm Viktor August Ernst. The newspapers reported on June 26 and 27 that he had escaped from Holland into Germany. These reports were inaccurate.

M. Clemenceau. He didn't leave without a purpose.

Mr. Lloyd George. I am told that he is not as stupid as he looks, and that he is even rather crafty.

President Wilson. From the military point of view, he played a ludicrous role.

—Reading of the German note concerning Poland, brought by M. Dutasta:

The German government asks that the peoples on both sides of the line of demarcation be warned by Germany and by the Allies, respectively, of the moment when the cession of territories will be made. In any case, the latter can only take place after the ratifications of the treaty.

Mr. Lloyd George. This is not too bad. It seems the German government is rather striving to prevent misunderstandings. But attention must be paid to the manner in which we reply to them, and I propose to send this question to our committee of legal experts.

—(*Assent.*)

President Wilson. Since we are speaking of legal experts, I must tell you that I consulted Mr. Lansing on the subject of Holland. In his opinion, we must notify her of our intention to claim the Kaiser, indicating that he is sought for a moral crime rather than a political one. The place and time when he will be handed over will be fixed only after ratification of the treaty. This notification must be addressed to Holland by France in the name of the conference. I submit to you the draft of the letter that Mr. Lansing has drawn up.[3]

Mr. Lloyd George (*after reading*). I think that's an excellent draft.

M. Clemenceau. I agree.

Mr. Lloyd George. But can we really wait to send this letter to Holland? The crown Prince has already fled, not because he fears being indicted by us, but undoubtedly because he wants to attempt some political venture. He left with a staff officer, and, at this very moment, appeals are being launched in Berlin and in different parts of Prussia for the army to revolt against the treaty. The Crown Prince is rather dangerous; but the Emperor would be much more so because of the prestige he had in Germany.

President Wilson. You can't address Holland before the treaty is signed.

Mr. Lloyd George. We can invoke reasons of international public

[3] Printed in *PWW*, Vol. 61, pp. 200-201.

safety. Here is a man who was a kind of demigod in his country; we mustn't forget the power he can still exert over the imagination of his people.

President Wilson. At bottom, I agree with you. I think Holland will find no excuse to refuse to hand over the Kaiser after the signing of the treaty. But today, she can oppose you.

Mr. Lloyd George. I think the Kaiser and his son are preparing a dirty trick against us.

President Wilson. Then we must address Holland now, representing to her that she must not allow the Kaiser to cross the border. From the strictly legal point of view, he has the right to go where he wishes.

Mr. Lloyd George. I would indicate clearly the political reason for our action, the signs that disturb us, and the danger of a civil war in Germany, which could be the prologue to a resumption of hostilities. The Dutch must commit themselves either to keeping the Kaiser or to delivering him without delay.

—*The drafting of a note along these lines is decided.*

President Wilson. M. Beneš announces to us that hostilities between Czechoslovak and Hungarian troops were halted on June 24. Mr. McCormick calls to my attention that, from the moment of the cessation of hostilities, the blockade must be lifted for Hungary, or at least relaxed, as for Germany after the Armistice.

M. Clemenceau. I received a telegram from Béla Kun a few days ago;[4] he asked for guarantees, the first of which was the recognition of his Republic of Soviets. I did not reply. Today, he complains that the Rumanians are renewing hostilities after they were stopped on the Hungarian side.

—*Reading of the telegram from Béla Kun.*[5]

M. Clemenceau. I propose to send this to General Bliss for verification of the facts.

President Wilson. What the Hungarian government says does not seem unreasonable.

M. Clemenceau. No, but the facts must be verified.

Mr. Lloyd George. On the other hand, we can't say that we will never recognize a government of soviets. However defective this kind of government may be, it is, all in all, more representative than the Czar's

---

[4] See CXXVII, n. 2.
[5] B. Kun to G. Clemenceau, June 26, 1919, printed in *PPC*, VI, 706-707.

M. Clemenceau. That recognition would present real dangers here.

Mr. Lloyd George. Our justice must be impartial. We have taken a decision; if the Rumanians violate it, we must hold them responsible.

M. Clemenceau. The Hungarians complain about the Rumanians; but if we listen to the Rumanians, we will conclude that it is the Hungarians who are violating the agreement.

—Reading of a note from General Pešić, in which the Yugoslavs complain of a movement of Italian troops on Tarvis.

President Wilson. Is Baron Sonnino informed?

Baron Sonnino. I know nothing; I didn't know that there was fighting on that side. I will find out.

Mr. Lloyd George. I received a letter from M. Beneš[6] about the plan relating to the Czechoslovak troops in Russia. M. Beneš is not very keen for Mr. Winston Churchill's plan; he says that if we can give him a firm promise to bring back these troops, he will submit the plan to his parliament. One part of the Czechoslovak troops will have to be embarked at Vladivostok; but only America could take charge of them. Does she have the necessary tonnage?

President Wilson. I don't think so. According to the last news, we had very few ships in the Pacific.

Mr. Lloyd George. See if you can transport twenty or thirty thousand Czechs.

President Wilson. I fear this is impossible.

Baron Makino. Where are these Czech troops at present?

Mr. Lloyd George. In Siberia. If we don't evacuate them, we will have great difficulties with the Czechs. Could Japan undertake to transport them?

Baron Makino. I'll find out. We have already received a request from the Transylvanian prisoners in Siberia, who also want us to help repatriate them.

Mr. Lloyd George. Then we will ask President Wilson and Baron Makino to inform us about the tonnage which their countries could provide respectively.

---

[6] E. Beneš to D. Lloyd George, June 23, 1919, *PWW*, Vol. 61. pp. 201-202. Beneš certainly was not keen about the prospect of 30,000 Czech troops supporting Kolchak and fighting their way to Archangel. He said that, in any event, such a maneuver would have to have the strong support of public opinion in Bohemia, and that there had to be very certain guarantees for the evacuation of all Czech troops before the end of the year.

—Appointment of the members of the committee charged with preparing the execution of the treaty of peace with Germany: Mr. Clement Jones (British Empire) and M. Tardieu (France) are designated; the American and Italian members will be named later.

Sir Maurice Hankey. Your military advisers ask to be authorized to continue the preparatory work of the commission for the control of armaments in Germany.

—Reading of a draft decision: *Marshal Foch will be instructed to form a commission to prepare in detail the organization of the permanent commission which is to control the execution of the military clauses of the treaty.*

Mr. Lloyd George. Why Marshal Foch? Should this business not belong to the Supreme War Council?

M. Clemenceau. Certainly.

Mr. Lloyd George. I prefer the Supreme War Council because civilian control makes itself better felt there.

M. Clemenceau. This task must be entrusted to the organization in Versailles.

Sir Maurice Hankey. There is also the question of the measures to be taken for the execution of the treaty where Heligoland is concerned.

Mr. Lloyd George. Let us refer that also to the Supreme War Council.

Sir Maurice Hankey. I have to submit to you yet another note on the subject of the release of German prisoners.

M. Clemenceau. I propose to wait for a while before putting the treaty into execution. In a telegram about Poland, General Dupont warned me that the German prisoners of war that we send back to Germany will be immediately employed in fighting the Poles.

Mr. Lloyd George. There is much to be said in favor of a suggestion of Sir Ernest Pollock, consisting of tying the liberation of German prisoners of war to the handing over of the culprits we intend to put on trial.

M. Clemenceau. According to certain information, we also know that the Germans are still holding prisoner two or three hundred French, English, and others. I think the Germans should begin by returning them to us.

Mr. Lloyd George. Couldn't we take up the question of the mandate system?

President Wilson. The only plan which has been given to me was drafted by Lord Robert Cecil, with amendments presented by the American experts;[7] he proposes a provisional understanding on the different kinds of mandates. After our provisional decision, the plan would be published, and we would see what criticism would be made of it.

Mr. Lloyd George. Lord Milner has prepared a text[8] which I haven't yet read.

President Wilson. I would like to get it and to have the time to study it. Did Lord Milner prepare this plan alone?

Mr. Lloyd George. No, with the representatives of the dominions.

President Wilson. I will remind you that the preparation of this plan belongs to the League of Nations.

Mr. Lloyd George. All we are doing is presenting proposals. We couldn't have them drafted by a man more competent than our Colonial Secretary. Lord Robert Cecil has no definite ideas on that question. The ministers of the dominions and their advisers are precisely the men most capable of anticipating difficulties and advising on the means of getting around them.

Sir Maurice Hankey. I have M. Paderewski's letter and your reply. Their publication has been decided; is it not your intention that it take place only after the publication of the treaty?

—(Assent.)

—Presentation of a report of the Supreme War Council on the strength of the army of occupation.

M. Clemenceau. I must consult Marshal Pétain about that. I therefore request postponement.

Mr. Lloyd George. Do you want to take up the Turkish question this afternoon? We could take an overall glance at it?

President Wilson. Agreed.

M. Clemenceau. There is one point on which I believe Marshal Foch must be questioned; what will we do if something happens on the Polish side?

Mr. Lloyd George. If only small local movements develop in Poland, we should do nothing. But I believe that can't fail to happen, even without any outside encouragement from Germany.

M. Clemenceau. I don't believe these encouragements will be lacking.

President Wilson. What exactly is your worry?

[7] See ibid., Vol. 59, pp. 475-76.
[8] It is printed, along with an American counterdraft, in ibid., Vol. 61, pp. 260-70.

M. Clemenceau. It is a matter of knowing how we will help the Poles if they are attacked by the Germans.

Mr. Lloyd George. Of course we must stand by the treaty.

President Wilson. Then we should ask Marshal Foch: "In case of a conflict in the western part of Poland, what help can we bring to the Poles?"

Mr. Lloyd George. In my opinion, unless the Poles are attacked from the outside, they must begin by defending their liberty themselves.

M. Clemenceau. In what way can we help them? The other day you acknowledged that we couldn't go through Danzig.

Mr. Lloyd George. I beg your pardon: once the peace is signed, we have the right to demand passage through Danzig to help the Poles. If Germany prevented us from doing it, we would find ourselves again in a state of war with her.

I propose to put the question first to the Supreme War Council and to formulate it in the following terms: "If there is a conflict in the territories ceded to Poland by the treaty, how does the council think we should help the Poles to establish their authority over those areas?"

This first question is completely different from the one which would arise for the area of the plebiscite; there, if Germany refuses to withdraw her troops in conformity with the treaty, that means war. The question I would ask would be the following: "What measures are proposed to us for the occupation of the area where the plebiscite is to take place? What forces should we employ there? What should their strength be? What should be the occupation arrangement?"

M. Clemenceau. But we must anticipate what might happen before the occupation begins.

Mr. Lloyd George. If the Germans refuse to evacuate the territories they must evacuate according to the treaty, it means war. Then we have the right to advance our troops from the Rhine. What we must avoid is committing ourselves to acts of war if Germany doesn't violate her commitments.

CXLIII

Conversation between President Wilson and MM. Clemenceau and Lloyd George*

JUNE 26, 1919, 4 P.M.

M. Clemenceau. M. Wellington Koo has informed me that the Chinese delegation will raise a protest, which is necessary to satisfy public opinion in China, but only in the hope of a later revision of the clauses of the treaty relating to Shantung. Must this letter of protest be written before or after the signing of the treaty? For myself, I would prefer that it be written after.

Mr. Lloyd George. Certainly

M. Clemenceau. Otherwise, that could encourage Rumania to do the same.

Mr. Lloyd George. We must also be on guard against the Germans.

President Wilson. We have M. Tittoni's first statements and the letter that he addressed to Mr. Lloyd George.[1] If he comes here in the frame of mind that he indicates, he would do as well to remain in Rome.

Mr. Lloyd George. He won't begin by tackling the Adriatic question. He will first try to obtain a solution favorable to Italy in the colonial field, and, once satisfied from that quarter, he will present us with his bill for the Adriatic.

Mr. Lloyd George. What do we reply to the Turks?

President Wilson. Mr. Balfour has already replied.

Mr. Lloyd George. Yes, but that's not what I mean. Do we allow the Turks to leave? Do we summon them? Or send them a letter to tell them: "Go home, you will return when we summon you"?

President Wilson. It is better to let them leave. They have given proof of an absolute lack of common sense or a complete misun-

---

*H., PPC, VI, 710ff.

[1] Orlando's government had fallen on June 19 and was succeeded on June 23 by one headed by Francesco Saverio Nitti, with Tommaso Tittoni as Foreign Minister. Sonnino stayed on in Paris as a plenipotentiary delegate. We can find no references to Tittoni's letter to Lloyd George; perhaps Mantoux misheard at this point. Tittoni made his "first statements" to the Italian Senate on June 25. After a few banalities, he then became specific about Italian grievances and unsettled claims regarding the Adriatic, Albania, Asia Minor, particularly Smyrna, and the colonial settlement in Africa. Albrecht-Carrié, *Italy at the Paris Peace Conference*, pp. 235-36.

derstanding of the West. They thought we didn't know a word of history, and they have presented us with enormous lies.

Mr. Lloyd George. That is Turkish diplomacy.

President Wilson. We didn't promise to reply to what they might say to us.

M. Clemenceau. In fact, they only asked to be heard.

President Wilson. I think we have given them enough attention. We have treated them courteously. We have invited them to come to see us, and we have listened to all they wanted to tell us. We didn't do as much for the Austrians.

Mr. Lloyd George. The question I already asked yesterday is this: would it be best not to try to make peace with Turkey without settling the question of the mandates now?

President Wilson. I have thought about that. We could say to them: "You are abandoning your possessions in Europe and such and such territories in Asia." Or better still: "Your territory will be delimited as follows, and Turkey renounces all rights over territories located outside that limit, accepting in advance the disposition of it which will be made by the Allied and Associated Powers. In addition, Turkey accepts, for certain departments of her administration—finances, police, coastal surveillance—the assistance of a power which will be designated later."

This seems practicable to me and postpones the settlement of all the other questions.

Mr. Lloyd George. It is practicable, if you decide now to take Constantinople from the Turks.

President Wilson. In fact, Constantinople is not a Turkish city; the other peoples are in a majority there.

Mr. Lloyd George. That means expelling the Turks from Europe once and for all.

M. Clemenceau. Here is my objection. If we put the question to them, they will answer no and remain where they are. Now, we have nothing ready for immediate execution. What will we do? You can settle all these questions only at the same time.

For my part, I am of opinion that it is not necessary for Constantinople to remain with the Turks. The capture of Constantinople by the Turks was in its time a very great event that shook all of Europe. Since then, Europe has done all it could to leave the Turks in Constantinople.

President Wilson. That was no doubt because they did not know how to replace them.

Mr. Lloyd George. It was above all because they feared Russia then.

M. Clemenceau. What settlement do you have for tomorrow? Constantinople has been offered to President Wilson; he doesn't seem decided to accept it.

President Wilson. I will submit the proposal to the Senate of the United States.

M. Clemenceau. With the chance that it will be accepted?

President Wilson. I think it will be.

M. Clemenceau. I would like that. The presence of America in Constantinople would have a calming effect on the entire situation in the Near East.

President Wilson. What will help to get this proposal accepted in America is that it is not a matter of business, in the financial and commercial sense of the word. Constantinople ceases to be the center of a great empire. Its only importance is that it commands the Straits, and we would go there only to guard them in the interest of all nations. That won't involve us in European politics—that would be alarming to most Americans.

M. Clemenceau. Would you occupy Constantinople only?

President Wilson. No, but the Straits, with a strip of territory all around.

M. Clemenceau. Would the forts be occupied by American soldiers?

President Wilson. The Straits must be fortified in such a way as to make an attack on them impossible.

M. Clemenceau. That solution satisfies me. But it doesn't solve the other questions, and you know that some of them are very delicate. I sense around me feelings that could become dangerous if they were not treated with caution.

President Wilson. I saw M. Vénisélos this morning. I told him that the difficulties which embarrass us in Asia Minor don't stem from a divergence of opinion amongst our three countries, but from the situation created by Italy's action; she hasn't ceased to make landings and to send troops to Asia Minor. M. Tittoni will no doubt push his troops forward. A collision is to be feared. What Italy wants is to entrench herself so that we won't be able to chase her out without opening hostilities. If she pursues this policy, she will put herself beyond the law. A great nation which acts in this way loses all its rights. The problem of Asia Minor would be easy to settle if Italy was not involved.

Mr. Lloyd George. Say: "Would be *easier* to settle."

M. Clemenceau. That is the word; delicate problems would still remain. Didn't the Mohammedans of India, when they came here, protest against any division of Asiatic Turkey?

Mr. Lloyd George. Only against the division of Anatolia.

M. Clemenceau. The Greeks are in Smyrna and spread out as far as Aydin; it is a part of Anatolia. Even in Smyrna, there is a large Turkish population. I don't protest, but I state the fact.

As for the Italians, they have seized ports; they have remained there despite our formal warnings; they have pushed into the interior and don't stop penetrating it. I don't believe they will get out at a word from us. M. Tittoni says today: "You promised us Smyrna." That means: "We are a great nation, and we can perhaps make concessions; but we will leave Smyrna to others only with compensation." What shall we do?

President Wilson. This government will not last; for, it will come here to present unacceptable claims to which we can only answer no. Then it will be compelled to resign.

M. Clemenceau. I favor refusing to discuss the questions of Asia with the Italians at present. I would say to them: "We are making peace with Austria, and we cannot leave that negotiation in suspense. The first question to settle is that of the Adriatic."

President Wilson. I agree with you.

M. Clemenceau. Moreover, I believe it is dangerous to hurry concerning the Turkish question. Let's look at it from the French point of view. We have a difference with England. I don't want to raise the question as long as the peace treaty with Germany isn't signed. Most fortunately, public opinion is not pressing us; we are offered a rare opportunity. If, unfortunately, this question came to be mixed up with European questions, I greatly fear what some people who lack a cool head might say and do. If we have reached satisfactory solutions for other more important problems, that will bring great satisfaction to public opinion and make the discussions which will follow much easier.

President Wilson. I am only proposing for the moment to fix the boundaries of Turkey.

M. Clemenceau. We will be forced to leave it at that without means of immediate execution, and the result will be deplorable.

Mr. Lloyd George. The Italian danger in Asia Minor concerns me greatly. The Italians are advancing straight ahead, seizing everything in the interior of the country that pleases them. England has no design on that region; but I fear the repercussions in the Mohammedan countries. That concerns us in Egypt and India, and that concerns France in North Africa.

M. Tittoni says that what Italy desires in Asia is, above all, mining concessions. But the Italians are now grabbing everything of value to them.

President Wilson. They want what it would be impossible for them to obtain under the mandate system.

Mr. Lloyd George. I will remind you that Italy, alone amongst us, has not demobilized. She fears doing it, because her government fears domestic disorder. So she has troops, and she is sending them to Asia Minor, to the Caucasus, everywhere she wishes.

President Wilson. When the English troops are relieved in the Caucasus, I fear a famine caused by the sudden accession of mouths to feed. This is a problem pointed out to me, and which we must beware of. As for the Italians, they must be told clearly: "Are you in the Entente or not? If you are, you must participate at the same time as the Allies in the negotiations with Turkey and do nothing apart from them."

Mr. Lloyd George. Even according to the agreement of Saint-Jean de Maurienne, they would not have the right to occupy in force all these localities, as they are doing.

President Wilson. I can't go and say to the Senate of the United States: "Here is a treaty which reestablishes peace" if we leave Italy a free hand. On the contrary, it would be a treaty preparing for war, and we could not give it our guarantee.

M. Clemenceau. For myself, I would ask them the question as frankly as possible. Do you know that Fiume is today administered in the name of the King of Italy? The local government recently asked our general to expel the Serbs. He refused twice. Then the Italians expelled them themselves. The city is surrounded by barbed wire; it is in a state of war. Is that what is called the execution of the Treaty of London? The Italians are violating their word there, and everywhere else besides.

President Wilson. The pretext they invoke to justify their presence in Fiume is the right which the armistice gave them to advance in order to restore order.

M. Clemenceau. Do you know that during these last few days they have gone so far as to ask us for a small piece of French territory in the County of Nice to improve the border which, it seems, is poorly drawn?

Mr. Lloyd George. It is madness.

—Reading of the telegram addressed by the British government to Emir Faisal.[2]

—Reading of the letter addressed to the government of the Netherlands[3] to protest against the departure of the Crown Prince, and to ask that government to prevent the German Emperor from leaving its territory; the return of the Kaiser to Germany could only aid the recovery of the

---

[2] That is, the telegram cited in CXLI, n. 10. It said, "in the most specific terms," that in no circumstances would Great Britain take a mandate over Syria.

[3] It is printed in *PPC*, VI, 714-15.

military party which ruined that country and put Europe in danger. To allow the Kaiser to return to Germany would be an outrage against all nations.

M. Clemenceau. I think that letter should be published.

Mr. Lloyd George. Yes, but not before the Dutch government has had time to take its precautionary measures. The Kaiser doesn't have to be warned before it. I propose that publication take place only on Saturday.

—(Assent.)

Mr. Lloyd George. Will you see M. Pichon about the telegram to be sent to M. Tittoni?

M. Clemenceau. Yes.

President Wilson. Do we agree on speaking very frankly to the Italians?

Mr. Lloyd George. The unfortunate thing is that neither you nor I will be still here when M. Tittoni arrives.

President Wilson. What we can do is to prepare a note now in which I would say, first, that, by their action in Fiume, the Italians have violated the Treaty of London and that they cannot invoke it hereafter.

Mr. Lloyd George. I thought we would only speak to them of Asia Minor.

President Wilson. In Asia, they have acted without taking account of the very clear protests and formal warnings given their government. They must act with the Entente or against it. If they stay with us, they must evacuate Asia Minor and Fiume. Before talking with them, we must receive positive proof of their good will.

M. Clemenceau. What they will do is to go back directly towards Vienna and Berlin.

President Wilson. Then they would give us the right to do what we like towards them.

Mr. Lloyd George. The Germans will no longer have confidence in Italy, given the manner in which she abandoned them.

President Wilson. An Italian statesman said to me: "We were in the Triple Alliance when, in 1914, we heard vague rumors about the conflict between Austria and Serbia. We asked our allies questions. They denied having any intention to resort to force and were still denying it two hours before the accomplished fact." This shows the lack of respect with which the Germans were already treating Italy at that time, when they were powerful and victorious.

Mr. Lloyd George. Italy is at the mercy of the maritime powers.

President Wilson. Yes, but none of us dreams of attacking her.

Mr. Lloyd George. The two main railway lines of the peninsula run along the coast. Any threat from the sea would be serious for Italy.

President Wilson. What is tragic in the situation is that we are friends of Italy, we want to be such, and it is she who is making that friendship impossible. It is a miserable tragedy.

M. Clemenceau. For myself, I can't say that the Treaty of London no longer exists. I can say: "You are now violating it yourselves in Fiume, and you are threatening the very existence of the treaty."

Mr. Lloyd George. England's position is the same as France's. Mr. Balfour could draft our common note.

President Wilson. I hope you will seize the favorable opportunity to rid yourselves of a treaty which, speaking in all conscience, I have never thought continued to bind you.

Mr. Lloyd George. We must take into account the critical moment when Italy joined us and the 500,000 dead which the war cost her.

M. Clemenceau. Don't take that figure too literally.

President Wilson. The truth is that Italy went to the highest bidder.

Mr. Lloyd George. That is a harsh thing to say; but I fear there is some truth in it.

President Wilson. During this conference, Italy had no interest in anything that did not directly affect her. She took no active part in our deliberations.

Mr. Lloyd George. I went through the entire war, and, unfortunately, I always saw Italy trying to do as little as possible. France, England—and the United States, when she joined us later—threw themselves into the battle without reserve and with all their hearts. Italy always carefully measured what she gave.

President Wilson. The problem, today, is to know how to save Italy from those who are leading her and driving her to ruin.

M. Clemenceau. I greatly fear they represent the Italian people fairly well.

Mr. Lloyd George. Our Ambassador, Sir Rennell Rodd, wrote us that M. Tittoni, in a conversation, said to him that "the question of Fiume would be easier to settle if Italy could obtain satisfaction in other directions. The new government can't go to Paris only for a renunciation. That could only force it to resign, with the most serious consequences." The best way to prevent Italy from going back to Germany is to show the Italian people that the Allies are their best friends.

M. Clemenceau. Thiers anticipated all that. He made I don't know how many speeches on the dangers which would result from Italian unification.

Mr. Lloyd George. Can't Mr. Balfour take charge of drafting the note?

M. Clemenceau. Let him write it very bluntly.

Mr. Lloyd George. He will be sarcastic, in his usual way.

M. Clemenceau. That's not enough, he must appear very forceful.

—Mr. Balfour is introduced.
—Sir Maurice Hankey reads aloud the protest made by the American, English, and French governments on May 17, 1919, against the Italian landings in Asia Minor.[4] In the same meeting, to Baron Sonnino, who asked if the *status quo* could be accepted, President Wilson replied that he could not sanction the maintenance of Italian troops at points where they ought not to be.

President Wilson. If Italy continues to advance in Asia, we could only ask her the question clearly: are you with us or against us?

Mr. Balfour. Don't you believe the new government will try to turn over a new leaf?

Mr. Lloyd George. You see the first manifestation of its sentiment.

Mr. Balfour. Baron Sonnino is an honest man, but extremely obstinate, and his head is full of imperialistic ideas. He believes in nearly all the principles that we reject, and it is impossible to make him abandon positions which he has taken. M. Tittoni is a much less reliable man, but more flexible.

Mr. Lloyd George. Read the telegram from Sir Rennell Rodd; you will see there that the Italians want mines in Asia Minor.

Mr. Balfour. Without encroaching upon Turkish sovereignty, we can acknowledge the right of the Italians to priority for concessions in such or such a region. If they accept that, we can say to them: "Are you going to break with us to obtain in the Adriatic what has no true value?" I think we could come to terms then.

M. Clemenceau. I don't believe it. According to my information, M. Tittoni will come to say to us: "Here are my proposals; if you don't accept them, I return to Rome."

President Wilson. M. Tittoni is inclined to take up questions at the point where M. Orlando left off, and, if we don't accept what he demands, he will leave. I remember that M. Orlando told me that Italian soldiers in Fiume would not withdraw, even if one gave them the order to do so. He added that his son, who is in Fiume amongst these soldiers, would stand by them.

[4] For which, see LXXXII, n. 1.

Mr. Lloyd George. I don't envision things that way. M. Tittoni will purr like a cat. He will carefully avoid everything that could cause conflict and will compel us to admit him into our councils without abandoning any of his pretensions. The best thing is to ask the question quickly, without beating around the bush.

President Wilson. He has shown his hand. He has said that, if concessions are made to him in other regions, he won't insist as much on the Adriatic. But in any case he will demand Fiume. I don't see what rights the Italians have in Asia.

Mr. Balfour. The unfortunate thing is that the Treaty of London, in fact, recognizes certain rights of the Italians in Asia and Africa. For it promises them compensation if England and France make acquisitions in the Mediterranean region.

Mr. Lloyd George. That doesn't give them the right to occupy the province of Adalia before the distribution of mandates has taken place.

—Mr. Balfour reads aloud the article referred to in the Treaty of London.[5]

President Wilson. The case anticipated is that of a partition of the Ottoman Empire.

M. Clemenceau. This partition hasn't taken place yet.

President Wilson. There will be no partition. The territories of the Ottoman Empire will not be distributed amongst us like properties; they will be administered, for the good of their peoples, according to the mandate system. This is not partition. In addition, it is not a matter of a partition between France and England; these territories will be placed by the treaty at the disposal of the Principal Allied and Associated Powers. No solution is possible

---

[5] Article 9, which said that, "generally speaking," France, Great Britain, and Russia recognized that Italy was interested in the maintenance of the balance of power in the Mediterranean and that, "in the event of the total or partial partition of Turkey in Asia, she [Italy] ought to obtain a just share of the Mediterranean region adjacent to the province of Adalia, where Italy has already acquired rights and interests which formed the subject of an Italo-British convention. The zone which shall eventually be allotted to Italy shall be delimited, at the proper time, due account being taken of the existing interests of France and Great Britain.

"The interests of Italy shall also be taken into consideration in the event of the territorial integrity of the Turkish Empire being maintained and of alterations being made in the zones of interest of the Powers.

"If France, Great Britain and Russia occupy any territories in Turkey in Asia during the course of the war, the Mediterranean region bordering on the Province of Adalia within the limits indicated above shall be reserved to Italy, who shall be entitled to occupy it."

without an agreement amongst ourselves. Under these conditions, Italy must agree that the entire question be re-examined.

Mr. Balfour. The Italians will say: "If France's influence increases in the Mediterranean, by whatever means, our influence must increase proportionately." If any of us takes possession of territories, Italy will demand that she be given a sphere of influence, such as France will have in Syria.

M. Clemenceau. But France doesn't have one now.

Mr. Balfour. I am speaking of the final solution.

Mr. Lloyd George. The question is what we will say immediately to M. Tittoni. I propose to say: "Even if you have the right to a sphere of influence, that does not mean that you have the right to occupy territories militarily. You have not waited for the discussion of the fate of the Ottoman territories, nor for the settling of boundaries of regions put under mandate; you have sent troops wherever you pleased, not when it was a matter of fighting the Turks, but to occupy ports and mines. We must protest against this attempt to force our hand."

President Wilson. If we want to settle the affairs of Asia today, we will be forced to make Italian troops evacuate the territories. It is an unbelievable situation.

Mr. Balfour. If you begin to enumerate what the Italians can be reproached for, their present conduct in Hungary must not be forgotten.[6] There is much to be said about that.

Mr. Lloyd George. I'm not proposing to go into all these questions, but to tell them that they must not be in Asia Minor or Fiume today, contrary to our decisions.

President Wilson. Their presence in Fiume is contrary to the Treaty of London.

Mr. Balfour. Let us say to them: "You must withdraw your troops from all localities to which they have been sent in spite of our protest."

President Wilson. Their presence in Fiume and in Asia Minor makes the settlement of the Asiatic questions impossible.

M. Clemenceau. I have a reservation to make about Fiume. For, if there are Italian troops there, they are alongside French and British troops. It is true we have only sent our soldiers there because the Italians were already there.

President Wilson. Are you sure that royal decrees have been promulgated in Fiume?

M. Clemenceau. That is a certain fact.

[6] A mysterious reference.

Mr. Balfour. I don't want to speak about the Treaty of London any more than absolutely necessary. I have every possible aversion to this treaty. But if we reproach the Italians too much for not conforming to it, they will say to us: "Very well! In that case, we demand of you nothing more or less than the execution of the Treaty of London."

M. Clemenceau. Then they would have to abandon Fiume, and they know that, for his own part, President Wilson would not accept the application of the Treaty of London.

Mr. Balfour. Yes, but that would be a way of casting responsibility on us—on the signatory powers of this treaty.

President Wilson. It is necessary to refuse to talk with them so long as their troops remain where they don't have the right to be.

Mr. Balfour. In the letter we addressed to the Rumanians and the Serbs about Hungary, we told them that "occupation is nine points of the law." Baron Sonnino was there, and he said "ditto."

—*Mr. Balfour is instructed to draft the note to be presented to the Italian government.*

CXLIV

Conversation between President Wilson, MM. Clemenceau and Lloyd George, and Barons Sonnino and Makino*

JUNE 27, 1919, 11 A.M.

—MM. Crespi, Davis, Loucheur, and McCormick are introduced and communicate[1] the result of studies on the distribution of charges amongst the states detached from the former Austro-Hungarian monarchy.

M. Loucheur. I must express my thoughts frankly. We will succeed in extracting from all these small powers together only a sum of one billion or one and a half billion in gold. To require this sum of them is to expose ourselves to serious discontent for a relatively insignificant advantage. Consider, for example, the cases

*H., PPC, VI, 716ff.

[1] Orally.

of Serbia and Rumania, already loaded with the burden of their devastation and their war expenditures, and whom we are asking to assume their part of ours. One will give us 200 million, the other 400 million francs gold; what is that compared to the figures we contemplated? If we could obtain very large sums from these states, we would be in a position to face objections. But in reality, we will have all the odium of this policy, without deriving any truly useful result from it.

If, however, we persist on the same road, I agree with Mr. Dulles about the sums to be fixed. In a conversation I just had with the Rumanian delegation, the latter seemed inclined to accept the figure of one and a half billion francs for the total of the payments of these different states. We can ask for it. But, in my opinion, it would be better to ask for nothing at all, because the share for each of us will be relatively insignificant, and because the critical financial situation of each of these new states has to be taken into account.

M. Clemenceau. I support the observations just presented by M. Loucheur.

Mr. Lloyd George. I would like this to be very clear. Is it proposed that Rumania and Serbia have the right to assert all their claims against Germany, without offering any counterpart for the acquisitions they will make of half of the Austro-Hungarian Empire?

M. Loucheur. Yes; according to the treaty with Germany, these states have the right to their part of reparations.

M. Clemenceau. If that is the case, I cannot accept your proposal.

Mr. Lloyd George. If M. Loucheur confines himself to saying: "It is hardly worthwhile, at the price of greater difficulties, trying to collect this relatively small sum from these different states," I am entirely in agreement with him. But the problem does not arise in that way. Rumania and Serbia, together, are acquiring half of the Austro-Hungarian Empire, which, if it was still intact, would owe us reparations amounting to a considerable sum. On the other hand, these two states retain their right to present their reparations bill to Germany, which can only be paid by reducing by the same amount what is owed us. Is it fair for them to acquire all these territories without any financial obligation towards us?

M. Loucheur. The observation is right; but, now, we can no longer change anything in the provisions of the treaty with Germany. When the principle of the interdependence of debts was included in it, I, for my part, opposed it. But that principle was admitted.

Mr. Lloyd George. I don't propose to revise the treaty with Germany and to go back on the principle of interdependence. All I ask is that we accept the proposal of Mr. Dulles and Mr. Davis;[2] it is a matter of making a debit and credit calculation. Let's suppose that the countries we have just mentioned have a right to 200 million pounds sterling under the heading of reparation, and that, on the other hand, we charge 150 million to their debit, representing their contribution to the costs of the war because of the acquisitions they are making at the expense of Austria: what they will receive at the final accounting will equal the difference, that is, fifty million pounds sterling, instead of the 200 million they claim.

M. Loucheur. It was indeed on that basis that we worked. But I warned you that the sum we can claim from them is so insignificant in comparison to the damages they suffered that the result will be negligible. We concluded that the maximum of what we can claim amounts to two billion francs. Now, in my opinion, the total of damages amounts to twenty billion.

Mr. Lloyd George. We must not think only about states, but also about individuals, and about the comparisons that could be made between these individuals and those who live in our respective countries. In these new states there are rich men, who would come out of this without having to make the least sacrifice. I don't propose to treat these countries harshly. But if we renounce all claims against them, that can cost France a billion francs, and there are very rich Germans in Bohemia who can and should pay.

M. Loucheur. Then a figure must be fixed. Will we say two billion francs?

Mr. Lloyd George. It is not my intention to impose any figure on you. It is better to leave the task of fixing one to the Reparation Commission.

Mr. Davis. These small powers protest precisely against the uncertainty in which this procedure would leave them. They want to know now what will be asked of them.

Mr. Lloyd George. Yes, but on the other hand, they reject all your figures when you announce them.

Mr. Davis. The only question that remains to be settled is between the two billions we are asking and the one and a half billion that these powers agree to pay now.

Mr. Lloyd George. It is not up to the heads of governments to calculate the figures.

[2] It is summarized in Burnett, *Reparation at the Paris Peace Conference*, I, 311-12.

President Wilson. All we want to do is to agree here on the method. You will tell these states, as Mr. Dulles proposes: "Do you accept the settlement we are proposing to you? If not, you will be placed under the normal operation of the treaty with Austria."

—(Assent.)

Sir Maurice Hankey. What are the consequences of the decision that has just been taken in relation to the completion of the treaty with Austria?

M. Loucheur. With this question settled, all the financial and economic clauses of the treaty will be ready.

CXLV

Conversation between President Wilson, MM. Clemenceau and Lloyd George, and Barons Sonnino and Makino*

JUNE 27, 1919, 4 P.M.

—MM. Paderewski and Hurst are introduced.

M. Paderewski. I have proposed a slight change in the convention between Poland and the Allied and Associated Powers. We are ready to sign this convention; but we beg you to provide for the Polish populations that will remain under German domination the same rights concerning their language and culture that will be granted to the Germans becoming citizens of the Republic of Poland.

President Wilson. This claim is perfectly justified. I will only observe that, if we write it into the convention, it won't bind Germany, since Germany won't be amongst the signatories of this convention.

M. Paderewski. If that is so, I hope that Article 93 of the peace treaty[1] with Germany is enough to bind the Germans.

—Reading of Article 93.

*H., PPC, VI, 723ff.

[1] In which Poland agreed to sign a treaty with the Allied and Associated Powers for the protection of the rights of ethnic and religious minorities in Poland.

President Wilson. That article only mentions the convention that Poland will have to sign.

Mr. Hurst. The clauses protecting the Germans of Poland will only be applicable in the territories detached from the German Empire. It is difficult to extend them, by applying them to the Poles, to territories that will remain inside the German boundaries.

Mr. Lloyd George. Wouldn't what M. Paderewski asks have the effect of making conditional the application to the Germans of the arrangement provided by the treaty? There would be a condition of reciprocity between the treatment that would be granted to them and that granted to the Poles in Germany; but controversies could occur unceasingly over the question of whether Germany has really kept her promises. On both sides, the application could remain in doubt.

President Wilson. Article 93 says: "Later agreements will be concluded." Between whom?

Mr. Hurst. We were thinking of agreements between Germany and Poland.

Mr. Lloyd George. Isn't it in Poland's interest to treat her citizens of German origin in such a way as to win them over? In all countries, people who are treated generously end up accommodating themselves to the regime that grants them that treatment. Isn't it better for Poland to carry out the treaty as it is and to appeal to the League of Nations if the Germans don't behave as they should towards her nationals? That appeal will be all the more irresistible if Poland has shown herself more liberal towards the Germans. That would be much better than making that liberality conditional in some way.

M. Paderewski. I agree with you; but how can the League of Nations act in Germany?

President Wilson. It can act only by external pressure so long as Germany is not one of its members. When will Germany enter the League of Nations? We have already said that she can only do it when she has furnished proof of her good faith and her willingness to keep her commitments.

Mr. Lloyd George. The goal that Poland must have in view is to make the Germans of Poland satisfied and faithful citizens.

M. Paderewski. For the moment, you know that the Germans are arresting Poles in Silesia en masse; we are told that there have been 12,000 arrests.

Mr. Lloyd George. I am not surprised, and even more serious incidents might occur. But these are temporary difficulties; time will put things in order, little by little.

President Wilson. I will remind you that, from the moment of the signing of the peace treaty, it is we who are responsible for order in Upper Silesia.

Mr. Lloyd George. We asked the Supreme War Council what measures we have to take for the occupation.

In your place, I would place no condition on the treatment that you are to grant the German minority in Poland; to obtain reciprocity, I would rely on the support of the League of Nations.

M. Paderewski. That would be enough for me, if I was always sure that I was dealing with men like you.

President Wilson. The first task of the League of Nations will be to see if the Germans are behaving as they should. They will indeed need to prove that they are worthy of being admitted to the League, and they know very well that they will be in a very disadvantageous situation as long as they are not admitted. I regret that we didn't think, when we drafted the treaty with Germany, about the question which M. Paderewski has just raised. But since we haven't done it, the best thing is to refer it to us in case of need—to the League of Nations.

M. Clemenceau. I will remind M. Paderewski that the League of Nations are the countries and men who are before him today: we are the state. You will appeal to us in circumstances that don't differ much from today's.

M. Paderewski. I have another word to say about the articles relating to the status of the Jews in Poland. We have never persecuted any nation. I asked President Wilson to send a commission of inquiry to Poland. I don't deny that there have been deeply regrettable acts of violence. But they took place at a time when the state of war had not truly ceased. In fact, the Jews came to Poland from all sides—from Russia and the Ukraine; that is proof that Poland wasn't the country where they were the worst off. To grant them a special administration of public instruction would be dangerous. It is also important that the use of Yiddish be very strictly limited; I have an amendment[2] on this subject to our con-

---

[2] Proposed by Paderewski. It read: "In the towns and districts where a considerable proportion of Polish subjects of Jewish faith reside, there shall be assured to this minority an equitable part in the division of the sums which shall be raised from public funds, municipal or otherwise, for the object of education, religion or charity. These sums shall be employed for the establishment, under the control of the Polish State, of primary schools, in which the needs of the Jewish faith shall be duly respected and in which the popular Jewish language (Yiddish) should be considered as an alternative language." *PWW*, Vol. 61, pp. 272-73.

vention to propose to you, with the approval, moreover, of the Jewish committees which came to see me.

—Reading of the amendment.

Mr. Lloyd George. It seems to me your amendment grants the Jews more than our text.

President Wilson. In our last draft, it is said that Yiddish will be used only as the language of instruction in elementary classes, but not as the subject of instruction. So we thought about the danger you point out.

—Reading of a note from M. Fromageot:

Article 93 of the treaty with Germany provides for the conclusion between the Allies and Poland of a convention determining the status of the Polish state. But the latter could benefit from the provisions of the peace treaty with Germany, even if the Polish Diet refused to ratify the clauses of the convention relating to German minorities.

President Wilson. The Polish Diet will surely ratify the convention.

M. Paderewski. There isn't the least doubt.

President Wilson. Then there is no reason to insist.

M. Paderewski. We also enter an objection to the article that provides for the internationalization of our rivers. Germany has so penetrated our country, and will seek so much to penetrate it economically, that we don't want to be bound by a provision of this kind. We read every day in the German newspapers sentences like this one: "The treaty will bind us legally, but not morally." The Poles have no confidence in the Germans and don't want to see the German flag fly over their rivers.

—M. Paderewski reads aloud the provisions relating to the internationalization of the Vistula.

President Wilson. It is merely a matter of applying to the Vistula the same arrangement that we have provided for all the rivers serving several countries. Our intention is to establish a system of river navigation for all of Europe, and this provision is part of it.

Mr. Lloyd George. Won't the course of the Vistula be in part German?

M. Paderewski. No, it becomes completely Polish.

Mr. Lloyd George. And the tributary rivers?

M. Paderewski. Some of them flow on Ruthenian territory.

President Wilson. Our sole intention in drafting this article was to include the Vistula in a general system of international navigation that should extend all over Europe.

M. Paderewski. I fear the consequences of this clause for Poland.

Before withdrawing, I would like to express once more my gratitude to President Wilson for all he has done for my country.

—M. Paderewski withdraws.

Mr. Lloyd George. When will we take up the mandate system?

M. Clemenceau. M. Henry Simon will be ready tomorrow morning.

President Wilson. I propose to submit Lord Milner's plan, or any other plan that could be presented, to a special commission.

Mr. Lloyd George. I will call your attention to the fact that Lord Milner goes further, in the same direction, than the Covenant of the League of Nations.

President Wilson. In certain respects. But in my opinion, his plan is not complete enough concerning the protection of native populations, and I don't find it explicit enough on the freedom of commerce.

Mr. Lloyd George. On this last point, I believe on the contrary that this text is very complete. It even goes beyond what we had contemplated.

President Wilson. I propose to submit this plan to a commission and to publish it later, so as to provoke and hear criticism.

—*Lord Milner, Colonel House, M. Henry Simon, M. Crespi, and Viscount Chinda are appointed to participate in the commission.*

Mr. Lloyd George. This commission could meet in London; that is where the provisional secretariat of the League of Nations is being organized. If M. Henry Simon can't go to London, couldn't he delegate someone?

President Wilson. These gentlemen could have a preliminary conference today or tomorrow and determine their procedure themselves.

Mr. Lloyd George. I would like for this study to be somewhat hastened to allow me to say something definite to the House of Commons next week.

M. Clemenceau. When do you leave for London?

Mr. Lloyd George. Tomorrow evening or the following morning. I propose that we meet tomorrow, after the signing of the treaty, to consider amongst ourselves the questions of Togoland and the Cameroons and the Belgian claims in the Congo. This last question is difficult; we have protests from societies representing native interests because of the treatment they say natives have suffered in the areas already administered by the Belgians.

Concerning the assignment of the territories in question, Lord Milner is ready to recommend that we approve it.

President Wilson. Where are these natives or those who speak for them?

Mr. Lloyd George. They are at this moment in London.

Sir Maurice Hankey. If the question of East Africa is raised, M. Alfonso Costa must be summoned.

M. Clemenceau. Why?

Mr. Lloyd George. Because if Belgium made acquisitions, Portugal could claim an increase of territory. But I am not in favor of granting it to her; her colonies are already more than she can administer.

President Wilson. After my departure and Mr. Lloyd George's, what will take our council's place? I suppose that it will meet at the Quai d'Orsay and that the Council of Ten will begin to function again. What are the questions that remain to be settled?

M. Clemenceau. The Bulgarian questions, the Adriatic questions.

Mr. Lloyd George. I propose to postpone the Turkish questions. I will be represented on the Council of Ten by Mr. Balfour.

President Wilson. And I by Mr. Lansing. But we will need him in America, and he will soon be replaced by Mr. Polk, whom I can recommend to you warmly.

M. Clemenceau. What do we reply to the Turks?

Mr. Lloyd George. We must thank them for having come to visit us and wish them a pleasant journey.

President Wilson. I remember what Mr. Balfour said about the coalition of Protestant Germany, Catholic Austria, Orthodox Bulgaria, and Muslim Turkey with the aim of plundering their neighbors.

Mr. Lloyd George. Indeed, that proves their impartiality from the religious point of view; they have destroyed impartially on all sides.

Mr. Lloyd George. A report of the Inter-Allied Council on Maritime Transport, submitted to us, proposes to place temporarily a certain number of German liners at the disposal of France, which is deprived of 60 per cent of her means of normal communication with her colonies. I am not discussing the question in depth; but I will remind you that England was represented on the Council on Maritime Transport, not by an expert on the matter, but only by a naval officer. I am ready to consider this question when it has been studied, insofar as we are concerned, by a competent man.

Besides, it is pointed out to me that France is not the only one involved; Italy also has claims to present that will have to be considered, and I believe there is also reason to take into account the pressing needs of Great Britain.

—M. Tardieu is introduced.

Mr. Lloyd George. I can say neither yes nor no to the proposal that M. Tardieu has transmitted to us[3] so long as the expert whom I summoned has not spoken. I had a wire sent to him yesterday, and I am waiting for him. These questions of tonnage, about which British public opinion is very sensitive, must be treated with caution. I only ask you to leave things as they are until our representative arrives.

—M. Dutasta is introduced.

M. Dutasta. I bring you two communications from the German delegation. The first is a reply to your note of June 21 instant, and hardly does more than acknowledge receipt of the cover letter.[4] The second relates to the occupation convention.[5]

—Reading of the German note relating to this convention:

The Germans maintain that the arrangement provided by the treaty must be made between themselves and the Allies, and, consequently, the text of the convention should have been discussed with them. If the Allied and Associated Powers require that the signing of this convention take place at the same time as that of the treaty, the German delegation will sign. But it requests that a conference take place later between the representatives of Germany and the representatives of the Allies, to study the text of the convention and see what changes could be made in it from the practical point of view, whilst taking into account the administrative government of the provinces involved and the present situation in Germany, known better by the German delegates than by the Allies.

M. Clemenceau. I propose to reply that the Germans must sign, and

---

[3] Tardieu had just submitted a report of a subcommittee which recommended that, in view of France's critical lack of passenger tonnage, the Reparation Commission should report to the council on the possibility of placing at France's disposal the passenger ships used for the transportation of American troops, as soon as those ships became available. See *ibid.*, p. 278.

[4] This note agreed that the long Allied memorandum of June 16 should be considered as binding. The note said also that the German delegation had no objection to some of the promises in the memorandum being laid down in a final protocol, as the council had proposed on June 21. PPC, VI, 734.

[5] This note is printed in *ibid.*, pp. 733-34.

that we will agree to send our representatives to study the details of application with them.

Mr. Lloyd George. If the Germans really suggest changes of a practical character, we will see what we can do about them.

—M. Claveille and General Mance are introduced.

General Mance. We come to meet with you about a question which has its place in the Austrian treaty—that of the Southern Austrian Railroads. One of the effects of the peace treaty is to cut this network, which ties Budapest and Vienna to Trieste, Fiume, and Trento, into four distinct parts. The bonds of this company are for the most part in the hands of French bearers. Before the war, the Austro-Hungarian government had the right to expropriate this system. It never used it. Now, four different governments inherit this right, and if one of them wanted to take advantage of it, that would be enough to imperil the functioning of the entire network. What your commission proposes is to bring about an agreement amongst the four governments concerned—Austria, Hungary, Yugoslavia, and Italy—about the future administration of this railroad and the right of expropriation. If their discussions have no result, then they will have recourse to arbitration.

Mr. Lloyd George. Who would do the arbitrating? The League of Nations?

General Mance. The Council of the League of Nations.

Mr. Lloyd George. That seems fair to me.

M. Clemenceau. Excellent.

Mr. Lloyd George. What do the Italians think?

General Mance. They say that this question is part of the financial questions and recall that, as such, it has been referred to our Reparation Commission. But the latter has never acted on it.

Mr. Lloyd George. I see no objection to your conclusions.

President Wilson. They seem perfectly reasonable to me.

Mr. Lloyd George. I don't see why this question should be handled by the Reparation Commission. It is a matter of private property whose owners, moreover, are for the most part French. The proposed solution seems satisfactory to me.

General Mance. In that case, a clause of the treaty with Austria must specify the acceptance of this procedure by Austria.

Baron Sonnino. Our representative on the commission had a different opinion. You should know his reasons.

President Wilson. I will point out that the proposed procedure is only a method of discussion, with arbitration as the last resort if those concerned can't agree.

Baron Sonnino. All I am asking you to do is to hear the experts.

M. Clemenceau. In this affair, do you fear for Italian interests? We could see the experts tomorrow morning.

Mr. Lloyd George. We can't carry out the plan relating to the Czechoslovaks, of which I have already spoken to you, without questioning Admiral Kolchak. I propose to send him a telegram on this subject.

Baron Makino. If the Czechs have to be replaced along the Trans-Siberian line, we will have to consult our government.

Mr. Lloyd George. It goes without saying that we can't take it for granted, without having consulted them, that Japan and the United States will agree to shoulder the burden of the occupation of the line.

Mr. Lloyd George. We have in hand the report of our special commission about the strength of the army of the Rhine. I don't know what should be done. This document recommends a figure of 150,000 men; it is pure Foch. Moreover, it was he who signed the document. This study should have been made by the Supreme War Council.

President Wilson. As far as the United States is concerned, it was agreed that we would leave a contingent on the left bank of the Rhine sufficient to show our flag. I can announce to you today that we will send a regiment with its auxiliary services.

M. Clemenceau. I agree with Mr. Lloyd George, and I propose that the question be referred to the Supreme War Council.

CXLVI

Conversation between President Wilson and MM. Clemenceau and Lloyd George*

JUNE 28, 1919, 10:30 A.M.

—President Wilson reads the text of a note which will be presented in the name of the United States to M. Tittoni upon his arrival.[1]

President Wilson. Concerning Asia Minor, I favor saying clearly that in no case will we admit Italian claims to the Dodecanese,

*H., PPC, VI, 738ff.

[1] It is printed as Appendix I to these notes.

and that, for the rest, no solution will be possible so long as Italy hasn't given proof of her willingness to act in accord with the Entente, and not outside it. That is the essential point; Italy must be with us or outside us. If she is with us, she must evacuate the regions she occupies despite our protests, that is, Asia Minor and Fiume. If she doesn't do it, she must give up counting on our assistance, and I must say, in particular, that the financial assistance of the United States to her can be continued only if she abandons the conduct of which we are complaining.

I have an observation to make concerning Fiume. We can't ask the Italians to evacuate it, in view of the fact that we also have troops there. What we have the right to ask is for Italy not to exercise sovereignty there. As for evacuation, no Italian government could consent to it.

Mr. Lloyd George. In any case, the Italians don't have the right to promulgate decrees in Fiume in the name of the King of Italy, no more so than we in the name of King George or President Poincaré.

President Wilson. The Italians will claim they have done no such thing, and that the King's name is only found at the bottom of manifestos and other acts which don't have the character of sovereign acts.

M. Clemenceau. It is necessary to indicate France and England's position frankly.

President Wilson. The text I have just read to you is that of my instructions to Mr. Lansing.

Mr. Lloyd George. I thought we would send a common note.

President Wilson. No; you yourself said that, because of the treaty that binds you to Italy, you would write a separate note.

Mr. Lloyd George. In Asia, I reckon we must stand on the same ground as you.

President Wilson. Mr. Lansing will be able to say: "Here are my instructions." That commits you to nothing. What is obviously to be feared is that Italy will publish this document, directly or indirectly, to inflame public opinion by saying that we want to exclude Italy.

—Reading of a text prepared by Mr. Balfour to be presented to M. Tittoni in the name of the French and English governments.[2]

Mr. Lloyd George. The conclusion is missing. In my opinion, we must say that we judge it pointless to talk so long as Italian troops

[2] The final version of this document is printed as an appendix to CXLVIIIA.

are in Asia Minor; they have stayed there only against our repeated protests.

M. Clemenceau. I ask that this text be reread. I notice that it mentions the Sykes-Picot agreement; it would be more correct to designate it under the name of "the agreement between M. Paul Cambon and the Foreign Secretary of Great Britain."

Mr. Lloyd George. Why mention it?

Sir Maurice Hankey. The text speaks of different agreements which, like that of Saint-Jean de Maurienne, must today be called into question.

Mr. Lloyd George. That seems pointless to me. I don't recognize the validity of the convention of Saint-Jean de Maurienne, since it was concluded subject to Russia's approval.

Mr. Lloyd George. Lord Robert Cecil came to Paris to present to you a recommendation of the Supreme Economic Council.[3] During the period of transition between the state of war and the establishment of the League of Nations, it is a matter of continuing, under a form to be determined, the cooperative work undertaken by the Economic Council in order to avoid the serious consequences that an abrupt halt of this cooperation could not fail to cause in the present situation of the world.

President Wilson. The difficulty for the government of the United States is of a legal kind. The signing of the peace makes it impossible for us to continue to collaborate with you on the same basis as before. Once peace is re-established, we can consider under what form and to what extent that collaboration might be resumed.

Mr. Lloyd George. Lord Robert Cecil proposes to establish a provisional organization until the effective establishment of the League of Nations.

President Wilson. I will see what it is possible to do from the legal point of view.

Mr. Lloyd George. Lord Robert Cecil is very concerned about this question, and he came expressly to submit it to you.

President Wilson. What I want is to avoid giving the impression that we are creating a economic bloc, a sort of coalition which would last after the war. That is the objection the Germans wouldn't fail to make, and it would be justified. At the same time, I admit the necessity of averting the danger that the abrupt halting of the system that functioned during the war could create.

---

[3] Cecil made his presentation at the following meeting.

—At 11 a.m. takes place the signing of the two treaties intended to insure to France the assistance of the United States and Great Britain in case of unprovoked aggression by Germany.[4]

{ A P P E N D I X I }[5]

PARIS, 27 JUNE, 1919.

MEMORANDUM OF ADDITIONAL SUGGESTIONS CONCERNING CONFERENCES WITH ITALIAN DELEGATION

In regard to Asia Minor, I think it ought to be made clearly evident to the Italians that we can in no case entertain their claim to the Dodecannesos, and that it is impossible to consider the wishes of Italy with regard to any other claims in Asia Minor until they have shown by action their wish and intention absolutely to cooperate upon equal terms with the United States and the Entente. The question, I suggest, should be put to them somewhat in this way. Either they do or they do not desire to act with the Entente. If they do desire to act with it, they must withdraw their armed forces from all parts of Asia Minor ⟨and also from Fiume⟩. If they retain their armed forces in these places, we will understand that they desire to be left to their own resources and to a forcible assertion of right wherever they choose to assert it, action which would clearly make it impossible for us to cooperate with or assist them in any way.

It ought to be made plain to them that the cooperation and assistance of the United States, including material and financial assistance of all kinds, is dependent upon her accepting as completely as the other powers have accepted the principles upon which the settlements of this peace have been made in respect of all other questions than those affecting Italy. We desire to be the friends of Italy and to render her every kind of assistance that it is in our power to render, but we cannot do so at the sacrifice of any of the principles upon which we have taken our unalterable stand in these negotiations.

Woodrow Wilson

---

[4] The treaties were identical, *mutatis mutandis*. The treaty between France and the United States is printed as Appendix II to these notes.

[5] Printed in *PWW*, Vol. 61, p. 307. Words in brackets deleted by Wilson.

{ A P P E N D I X I I }

AGREEMENT BETWEEN THE UNITED STATES AND FRANCE, SIGNED AT VERSAILLES JUNE 28, 1919.

Whereas the United States of America and the French Republic are equally animated by the desire to maintain the Peace of the World so happily restored by the Treaty of Peace signed at Versailles the 28th day of June, 1919, putting an end to the war begun by the aggression of the German Empire and ended by the defeat of that Power; and,

Whereas the United States of America and the French Republic are fully persuaded that an unprovoked movement of aggression by Germany against France would not only violate both the letter and the spirit of the Treaty of Versailles to which the United States of America and the French Republic are parties, thus exposing France anew to the intolerable burdens of an unprovoked war, but that such aggression on the part of Germany would be and is so regarded by the Treaty of Versailles as a hostile act against all the Powers signatory to that Treaty and as calculated to disturb the Peace of the world by involving inevitably and directly the States of Europe and indirectly, as experience has amply and unfortunately demonstrated, the world at large; and,

Whereas the United States of America and the French Republic fear that the stipulations relating to the left bank of the Rhine contained in said Treaty of Versailles may not at first provide adequate security and protection to France on the one hand and the United States of America as one of the signatories of the Treaty of Versailles on the other;

Therefore, the United States of America and the French Republic having decided to conclude a treaty to effect these necessary purposes, Woodrow Wilson, President of the United States of America, and Robert Lansing, Secretary of State of the United States, specially authorized thereto by the President of the United States, and Georges Clemenceau, President of the Council, Minister of War, and Stéphen Pichon, Minister of Foreign Affairs, specially authorized thereto by Raymond Poincaré, President of the French Republic, have agreed upon the following articles:

---

[6] Printed in *ibid.*, pp. 311-13.

ARTICLE I.

In case the following stipulations relating to the Left Bank of the Rhine contained in the Treaty of Peace with Germany signed at Versailles the 28th day of June, 1919, by the United States of America, the French Republic and the British Empire among other Powers:

"ARTICLE 42. Germany is forbidden to maintain or construct any fortifications either on the left bank of the Rhine or on the right bank to the west of a line drawn 50 kilometres to the East of the Rhine.

"ARTICLE 43. In the area defined above the maintenance and assembly of armed forces, either permanently or temporarily, and military manoeuvres of any kind, as well as the upkeep of all permanent works for mobilization are in the same way forbidden.

"ARTICLE 44. In case Germany violates in any manner whatever the provisions of Articles 42 and 43, she shall be regarded as committing a hostile act against the Powers signatory of the present Treaty and as calculated to disturb the peace of the world.",

may not at first provide adequate security and protection to France, the United States of America shall be bound to come immediately to her assistance in the event of any unprovoked movement of aggression against her being made by Germany.

ARTICLE II.

The present Treaty, in similar terms with the Treaty of even date for the same purpose concluded between Great Britain and the French Republic, a copy of which Treaty is annexed hereto, will only come into force when the latter is ratified.

ARTICLE III.

The present Treaty must be submitted to the Council of the League of Nations, and must be recognized by the Council, acting if need be by a majority, as an engagement which is consistent with the Covenant of the League. It will continue in force until on the application of one of the Parties to it the Council, acting if need be by a majority, agrees that the League itself affords sufficient protection.

ARTICLE IV

The Present Treaty will be submitted to the Senate of the United States at the same time as the Treaty of Versailles is submitted to the Senate for its advice and consent to ratification. It will be submitted before ratification to the French Chambers of Deputies for approval. The ratifications thereof will be exchanged on the deposit of ratifications of the Treaty of Versailles at Paris or as soon thereafter as shall be possible.

In faith whereof the respective Plenipotentiaries, to wit: On the part of the United States of America, Woodrow Wilson, President, and Robert Lansing, Secretary of State, of the United States; and on the part of the French Republic, Georges Clemenceau, President of the Council of Ministers, Minister of War, and Stéphen Pichon, Minister of Foreign Affairs, have signed the above articles both in the English and French languages, and they have hereunto affixed their seals.

Done in duplicate at the City of Versailles, on the twenty-eighth day of June, in the year of our Lord one thousand nine hundred and nineteen, and the one hundred and forty-third of the Independence of the United States of America.

[SEAL.] WOODROW WILSON
[SEAL.] ROBERT LANSING
[SEAL.] G. CLEMENCEAU
[SEAL.] S. PICHON

CXLVII

Conversation between President Wilson, MM. Clemenceau and Lloyd George, and Barons Sonnino and Makino*

JUNE 28, 1919, 11:15 A.M.

—MM. Claveille and Crespi, General Mance, and several members of the commission on ways of communication are introduced.

M. Crespi. The question for which we have sought a solution relates to the Southern Austrian Railways. The objection of the Ital-

*H., PPC, VI, 740ff.

ian delegation to the proposition submitted by the French delegation is that a question that concerns only one private company and the states served by its network could not be the subject of a provision written into the Austrian treaty. This question has already been raised before the Council of Four, and it was along these lines that the majority had decided. I recall that Mr. Lloyd George said on that occasion that he could not agree to the insertion in the treaty of a clause protecting special interests. We believe that a compromise text leaving the principle intact could be agreed upon.

—Reading of the text proposed by the Italian delegation:
Any change in the status of the company can take place only after agreement between the company and the states territorially concerned. In the event this agreement cannot be arrived at, the question would be brought before an arbitrator appointed by the Council of the League of Nations.

M. Crespi. The legal cases we have in mind include the expropriation and repurchase of these lines.

M. Claveille. We can accept this text, but with one addition. It is not only the states territorially concerned which must have the right to participate in the discussions, but also France and Great Britain. The capital of the company in question is three-quarters French, in the form of bonds chiefly in the hands of our peasants, which represent a value of one and a half billion francs. At the time when the network concerned is going to be cut by four different boundaries, when her interests will run the greatest risks, it is impossible for France not to be represented in the meetings that will decide its future.

So, we accept the clause proposed by the Italian delegation, but on condition that it be changed in such a way as to insure our presence. It would be impossible for us to accept another arrangement, when it is a matter of a network belonging, in fact, to French investors.

President Wilson. The text speaks of "contracts" presently in existence. These contracts have existed up to now only between the railroad company and the Austro-Hungarian state. Does the treaty oblige the new states to succeed Austria-Hungary in this respect? Unless the treaty indicates clearly that these states assume the existing contractual obligations, your text would introduce new participants into a contract without anything binding them legally.

Mr. Lloyd George. It seems to me that the text as it stands settles the question from the legal point of view. But I don't feel competent to speak with certainty.

President Wilson. Does Italy accept the French proposal?

M. Crespi. No, because in the anticipated meetings, the company will be already represented by its board of directors. There is no reason to give it another representative. It would be unprecedented to grant bondholders special representation and to confer it on a foreign power.

M. Claveille. In fact, there is a board of directors, but it is purely Austro-Hungarian and has always been a hotbed of Germanization. It used the money of French bondholders, but did everything against French interests. At this very time, the paper remaining in the hands of that board of directors is worthless. It is only our bonds that represent real value, and at the time when what constitutes the very security for these bonds is divided, you would exclude us from the deliberations.

M. Clemenceau. It is a billion and a half that you are taking from our pockets.

M. Crespi. The interests of the bondholders are protected by the financial clauses of the treaty.

M. Clemenceau. I tell you we won't agree under these conditions.

Baron Sonnino. The question has already been discussed here, and nothing was said about that.

Mr. Lloyd George. We mustn't go too fast. We have obviously less interest than France in this question. But I find that it is a very unreasonable demand to ask that France and England have a say when it comes to determining the future of Austrian, Hungarian, Yugoslav, and Italian railroads. M. Claveille tells us that the board of directors is under German influence. French bondholders were very well aware of this before the war. They bought Austro-Hungarian securities with full knowledge of the facts. To my mind, the Italian delegation has gone rather far in the direction of concessions, and that is the opinion of our experts. It is asking too much for France and England to insist on their right to interfere in questions that will be raised on the territory of four foreign states. I believe M. Crespi's text gives you satisfaction.

M. Clemenceau. How?

Mr. Lloyd George. By accepting the principle of arbitration.

M. Crespi. That covers just the case of expropriation.

M. Claveille. For myself, this question is one of justice. That network of 2,000 kilometers is French, as far as the capital is concerned. It is going to be divided amongst four powers, and we have grounds to fear its complete destruction. The country that provided the capital can't even participate in the discussions; we don't ask that it have the power to decide, but that it may be heard. The questions that will be raised are very complicated. In my entire career, I have never seen any question that presented such difficulties, and France would be excluded from their discussion? I have the feeling that it would be a profound injustice, and that it would be strongly resented in France.

M. Clemenceau. Our money is literally being taken from our pocket. France could never forget it.

M. Crespi. There is a misunderstanding, since, in the case of expropriation—the only one that can threaten the bondholders—the question can be taken before an arbitrator named by the Council of the League of Nations.

M. Clemenceau. But who can bring the question before the League of Nations? Not we. I won't sign a text of this kind; the French Parliament would not accept it.

President Wilson. The important thing is that, if this question remains in suspense, it will be impossible for us to draft one of the articles that must appear in the treaty with Austria.

Mr. Lloyd George. I assure you that I am not insensitive to French interests in this business. General Mance made me well understand the weight of your arguments. But, after all, before the war the Austrian government could have expropriated the company; what recourse would you have had then? Today, you are faced with four governments, and the danger of expropriation has become much less probable because of this fact.

M. Clemenceau. We won't accept a provision that we consider unjust.

Mr. Lloyd George. I myself believe it fair.

M. Clemenceau. You have the right to judge it thus; but I hold to my opinion.

M. Claveille. As it is presented to us, the clause is unacceptable in form and in substance. The four states which will decide have no capital in the business, and it will be enough for them to agree amongst themselves so that there will be no arbitration. This network of 2,200 kilometers is very important from the economic point of view; it is the one which, notably, gives the Czechoslovaks access to the Mediterranean. The four states are perfectly free to expropriate or not to expropriate; if they do, they must divide the rolling stock amongst themselves. France absolutely must have a say in all this. After the fifteen billion that we have already lost in Russia, this new loss, which would be inflicted on us by a treaty established in agreement with our allies, would be understood by no one at home and would cause a veritable explosion of indignation in Parliament.

President Wilson. Isn't it obvious that the states in question have no interest in destroying a network they all greatly need?

M. Claveille. When I say "destroy," I mean they can appropriate it for nothing.

Mr. Lloyd George. But what difference is there between the situation that would exist after the treaty and the one that existed before the war? Austria could also have expropriated. Now you are faced with four states which must begin by agreeing amongst themselves.

M. Claveille. This question presents another aspect. The company involved originally had part of its network in northern Italy. This part was expropriated in 1878, and Italy, for this part, had to pay a sum of twenty-nine million francs a year until the expiration of the concession. This sum was paid regularly in Paris every year. The peace treaty transfers this obligation to the Austrians, who won't pay. If Italy agreed to continue the payments until the end of the concession, the entire question would appear to us in a different light.

M. Crespi. That sum was not payable in Paris, but in Rome.

—An Italian expert explains that the sum was payable in gold in Rome, or, if gold was lacking, in drafts on London or Paris.

M. Clemenceau. We will take money in Rome if you wish; but we are sent back to the Austrians, who won't pay.

M. Crespi. This question has nothing to do with the clause that we are discussing at this time.

Mr. Lloyd George. There is no doubt that, when this business previously came before the Council of Four, we decided against the French proposition.

M. Clemenceau. I can't accept that, that's all.

Mr. Lloyd George. Then we can't sign the peace treaty with Austria, and it will be known that it is because we couldn't agree on a question concerning the bondholders of a railway company! For myself, I declare that the British government is not inclined to continue any war for bondholders, even English ones.

—The members of the commission on ways of communication withdraw.

—Lord Robert Cecil is introduced.[1]

[1] Actually, Hoover, Cecil, Edward Frank Wise of the Supreme Economic

—Lord Robert Cecil reads aloud a plan for a resolution providing for a provisional organization instructed to maintain the cooperation guaranteed up to now by the Supreme Economic Council, until the League of Nations can take over the tasks conferred on that council.

President Wilson. That presents no difficulty until the ratification of the peace treaty. But what must be avoided is the appearance of creating an economic bloc for the exclusive benefit of the Allied and Associated Powers. Germany complains about her exclusion, economically speaking. She would say, with some appearance of justification, that we are exploiting the difficulties of the situation to our advantage. A form of consultation must be found amongst our governments that will not lend itself to that criticism. That is why we cannot extend the existence of the Supreme Economic Council, whose powers are too extensive to be compatible with American peacetime legislation.

I will have to concern myself with this question on my return to America, and, if necessary, I will initiate appropriate legislative measures. I favor authorizing the Supreme Economic Council to present us with a plan. I ask only that this plan be drawn up in such a way as to avoid the criticism I have just pointed out.

Lord Robert Cecil. You fear that might be considered a new threat of the Allied and Associated Powers against Germany. But I remind you that it was the Supreme Economic Council which, several months ago, fed Germany, and that she couldn't have been provisioned without it. The economc questions of the entire world are today so complex, and our interests so entangled, that it is absolutely necessary to have a system of mutual consultation, and this in the interest of neutral and enemy countries as much as in our own interest.

President Wilson. Then I propose to draft the end of your text as follows: "The Supreme Economic Council is invited to submit to the different governments a plan indicating the most appropriate methods of mutual consultation for the goal in view."

Council, Clémentel, and Crespi appeared before the Council of Four at this point. Cecil spoke for them along the lines indicated in this paragraph of Mantoux's notes. Cecil also offered a formal proposal for the consideration of the council to the effect that international consultation on economic matters should be continued until the League Council had an opportunity to consider the acute international economic situation and that the Supreme Economic Council should be instructed to establish the necessary machinery for the purpose. The council approved a resolution along these lines. *PWW,* Vol. 61, pp. 314-16.

CXLVIII

Conversation between President Wilson, MM. Clemenceau and Lloyd George, and Barons Sonnino and Makino*

VERSAILLES, JUNE 28, 1919, 4:15 P.M.

—M. Clemenceau reads aloud a letter from Herr Bethmann Hollweg,[1] who asks, in his capacity as Chancellor of the German Empire in 1914, to be put on trial in the place of the Emperor as being responsible for all the acts committed in the name of the sovereign. He puts himself at the disposal of the Allied and Associated Powers.

President Wilson. It is the best thing he has ever done in his life.

Mr. Lloyd George. He was never one of the worst.

M. Clemenceau. Will we say that the tribunal must reply?

Mr. Lloyd George. No, it is a question of an indictment, which comes up prior to the establishment of the tribunal.

M. Clemenceau. Bethmann Hollweg is undoubtedly on the list of those who will be indicted.

President Wilson. I don't think so; for he doesn't fall into either of the two categories of the accused whom we want to put on trial. There is indeed, on one side, the Kaiser, who is accused of the violation of Belgium's neutrality, and, on the other, the men who were guilty of violations of the laws of war. Neither of these two counts applies to Bethmann Hollweg.

M. Clemenceau. In any case, a reply is necessary.

President Wilson. Bethmann Hollweg relies upon the letter of the Imperial constitution.

Mr. Lloyd George. His proposal would be correct if it was invoked by an English minister; it was Lord Grey, not the King, who was responsible for the actions of our Foreign Office at the beginning of the war.

President Wilson. Unfortunately for that argument, we know how the German constitution functioned.

M. Clemenceau. The German Emperor said often enough that he was the master and his will ruled all.

President Wilson. We can write that we render homage to Herr

---

*H., PPC, VI, 751ff. This meeting was held in the foyer of the Court Opera, at Versailles, after the signing of the treaty.

[1] It is printed in PWW, Vol. 61, p. 340.

Bethmann Hollweg's intention, but that we can't accept his interpretation of the German constitution. For myself, I once studied that constitution very closely, and I know it well.

Mr. Lloyd George. Shouldn't we instruct the Commission on Responsibilities to draft the reply?

President Wilson. I suggest instructing Mr. Lansing to do it.

M. Clemenceau. Very well.

Baron Makino. According to the letter of the German constitution, isn't the Chancellor responsible for the sovereign?

President Wilson. That is not my memory of it.

President Wilson. Mr. Hoover informs me that two of his agents have been arrested in Libau by the Germans. What must be done? I think we must remonstrate through Marshal Foch's intermediary.

Mr. Lloyd George. We have already remonstrated in that way about the treatment suffered by some of our officers, and we haven't yet had a reply.

Sir Maurice Hankey. The question is before us of whether, after the departure of President Wilson and Mr. Lloyd George, the minutes of the Council of Four have to be sent to Mr. Balfour and Mr. Lansing.

M. Clemenceau. It isn't a matter of submitting them to the House of Commons?

Mr. Lloyd George. No.

President Wilson. I remind you that our deliberations have had the character of private conversations.

M. Clemenceau. Assuredly, to publish these minutes would be the most dangerous thing possible.

President Wilson. But Colonel Hankey asks only if they have to be sent to Mr. Balfour and Mr. Lansing.

M. Clemenceau. In my opinion, these minutes must be in no one's hands. No one must be able to quote the remarks we have made in conversations as free as ours have been or be able to say: "On such a day, this one spoke against France; on such and such a day, that one spoke against England."

Baron Sonnino. Isn't it necessary to communicate these minutes to the new Italian delegation?

President Wilson. That is not my opinion; this is a matter of private conversations, and we weren't an official body.

M. Clemenceau. I must say that, if I leave office tomorrow, I would not be able to refuse to communicate these minutes to my successor. After all, if we met, it was as heads of governments.

President Wilson. When it was agreed to abandon our regular sessions at the Quai d'Orsay and you accepted my invitation to come to my house to talk more freely there, I, for my part, understood it was a matter of conversations of a confidential character. We can have successors very different from ourselves, and I must say I am very much opposed to the idea of revealing intimate conversations in which we expressed ourselves as freely as possible.

M. Clemenceau. In this country, it would be impossible for me to refuse this communication to my successor.

President Wilson. If I had thought this question would arise, I would never have consented to having notes taken. Our decisions have been recorded; they are what our successors have the right to know. What I don't want to be divulged is our conversations.

Baron Sonnino. How will new negotiators be able to do without knowledge of preceding negotiations?

President Wilson. They can have all the documents and all the resolutions. As for the rest, it can be transmitted by each of us to someone he has confidence in, and whom he entrusts with replacing him. But I will not make an official communication of it. Mr. Lansing is not only a member of my government, but he has my complete confidence; I can share my knowledge with him, but I must say that, if my government was replaced by another, I would not transmit these documents to it.

Baron Sonnino. We couldn't act that way in Italy.

Mr. Lloyd George. Are there precedents to go by? In fact, these minutes have never been officially noted. To mention them or quote them would be going back on one's word.

M. Clemenceau. We can see if there are precedents. But, in any case, the fact remains that our political system is different from that of the United States.

Mr. Lloyd George. Weren't there official minutes at the Congress of Berlin in 1878?

President Wilson. It is possible to have official minutes when it is a matter of regular deliberations like those of the Council of Ten. But when you agreed to come here to talk with me at my residence, that was for conversations of a confidential character. I have, moreover, never looked at Colonel Hankey's minutes more than once or twice, and they seemed to me perfectly faithful.

Mr. Lloyd George. And yet, we were glad to find the trail of the opinion expressed by Marshal Foch on the internment of German ships at the time of the discussion of the Armistice.

Baron Sonnino. That applies equally to the discussions that took place later, and for which it is very useful to remember what was said.

President Wilson. You will find contradictory things, for we have often used our right to change our minds. I repeat that, in my opinion, each of us has only the right to communicate these minutes to a colleague or a deputy in whom he has confidence. But that would be a very different thing from leaving them, like official documents, in the hands of civil servants in case of a change of government.

M. Clemenceau. For the present, I think, like you, that it is impossible to communicate these minutes to the parliaments. But I am not free to refuse them to the government that will replace me; I think that they don't belong to me.

Baron Sonnino. By refusing them, moreover, we could provoke the most dangerous debate.

M. Clemenceau. As for myself, I cannot treat these documents as my property; they belong to the state. If they were drafted, it was in order that useful information might be found there.

President Wilson. The Congress of Berlin of 1878 was mentioned; I am convinced that there were very important conversations there, which, having a confidential character, have left no trail. Moreover, if this question was ever discussed publicly, all I could be reproached for in the United States would be not having brought an American secretary to these meetings. I admit that each of us will have to act according to the tradition of his country. It is enough that it be understood that these documents are not to be published.

Mr. Lloyd George. That goes without saying; it would be a serious violation of one's word.

President Wilson. I don't mean only "published as a whole," I mean "quoted."

Mr. Lloyd George. However, if the British government is attacked on the question of the sunken German vessels and the conditions of their internment at Scapa Flow, if politicians are accused of having compromised everything by opposing their judgment to that of the naval people, I will be indeed obliged to reveal the opinions that were expressed.

M. Clemenceau. If you quote a document, you will be asked to transmit it. Marshal Foch will say: "But that is not what I said," and will himself ask to see the text.

Sir Maurice Hankey. Every time Marshal Foch was present, a regular record was kept, which can be quoted.

President Wilson. However, we can't return to the method of my predecessor, Theodore Roosevelt, who received journalists, poured out indiscretions, and ended by saying: "If you quote me, I'll deny it."

—Reading of a letter drafted by Mr. Balfour[2] and addressed to the Turkish delegation to inform it that its presence in France is no longer necessary.

—*The text of this letter is approved.*

—Reading of a report from M. Larnaude[3] on the connection that might be established between the repatriation of German prisoners of war and the handing over of persons accused of crimes against international law; it would seem preferable to consider all these clauses of the treaty as interdependent. Any delay in the execution by Germany of one of the clauses would give the Allies the right to delay the execution of another clause of their choice.

President Wilson. It is a bit draconian.
Baron Sonnino. It involves a more limited practical question.
Mr. Lloyd George. I favor restricting ourselves to the case that concerns us.
M. Clemenceau. How will we force the Germans to deliver the culprits to us?
Mr. Lloyd George. The best thing is not to take too high a stand about the question, but to find the specific means to get what we want. If Germany refuses to hand over the men whose names we provide to her, we have the right to say: "In that case, we won't return your prisoners to you."
M. Clemenceau. By that time, most of them will have already returned to Germany.
President Wilson. You forget that the prisoners will be returned only after ratification of the treaty; that gives us a bit of time. Don't we already have indications?
M. Clemenceau. Perhaps you are right.

Von Haniel asked for the opening of conversations on the execution of the treaty. In my opinion, we can't refuse.
Mr. Lloyd George. We have already decided to create a commission charged with preparing for the execution of the treaty.

What do we decide concerning the Germans guilty of crimes against international law?

[2] Printed in *PPC*, VI, 757-58.
[3] That is, the document prepared by Sir Ernest Pollock, about which, see CXLI, n. 2.

M. Clemenceau. We will tell the Germans that the liberation of their prisoners will depend on the delivery of the accused incriminated persons.

—(Assent.)

—Reading of a letter from General Bliss on Hungarian affairs; what was reported about an attack by the Rumanians against the Hungarians has not been confirmed.[4]

[4] Printed in PPC, VI, 758.

CXLVIIIA

Conversation between President Wilson and MM. Clemenceau and Lloyd George*

VERSAILLES, JUNE 28, 1919, 5:30 P.M.

—Reading of a note that will be sent to the new Italian delegation in the name of the French and British governments.[1]

Mr. Lloyd George. The sentence on the Dodecanese doesn't take into account the fact that we promised possession of them to Italy by the Treaty of London. We mustn't allow ourselves to be reproached for having gone back on our obligations. The Dodecanese can only be the subject of a friendly negotiation. I propose to eliminate that sentence.

—The text of the letter is approved with this correction.

{ A P P E N D I X }[2]

28 JUNE, 1919

The change in the Italian Delegation has occurred at a moment in which the associates of Italy were feeling considerable anxiety with regard to the part she was playing in the common cause. While nothing could be more friendly than the personal relations

*H., PPC, VI, 759ff.

[1] It is printed below.
[2] Printed in PPC, VI, 760-62. This was of course Balfour's redraft.

which have united the representatives of the Five Powers through many months of anxious discussion, and while we gladly recognise the aid and cooperation which the Italian Delegation have rendered in the framing of the peace with Germany, we feel less happy about the general course of the negotiations affecting other aspects of the world settlement.

There is no doubt that the present uncomfortable condition of affairs is largely due to the complications which the development of political and military events has brought about since the Treaty of London was signed in 1915. Since then the aspect of the world has changed. The Treaty was contracted with Russia, France and Britain, but Russia is no longer in the war. It contemplated a victorious peace with the Austro-Hungarian Empire; but while victory of the completest kind has been achieved, the Austro-Hungarian Empire has ceased to exist. It assumed that if Turkey was completely defeated, fragments of the Turkish Empire might be assigned to the victors; but while Turkey has indeed been completely defeated, and the alien peoples which she misgoverned are to be separated from her Empire, they are not to be handed over in possession to the conquerors, while any spheres of influence which the latter may acquire will be held by them not independently, but as Trustees or mandatories of the League of Nations. In 1915 America was neutral; but in 1917 she entered the war unhampered by any Treaty, and at a period when the development of this order of political ideas, to which she gave a most powerful impulse was in process of rapid accomplishment.

It is not surprising that the situation thus created presents complexities which only the utmost good-will and the most transparent loyalty can successfully deal with. The Treaty of London with which the history may be said to open was from the very beginning not strictly observed. Italy had undertaken to employ all her resources in prosecuting the war in common with her Allies against all their enemies. But she did not declare war on Germany for more than a year, and she took no part in the war against Turkey. By the Treaty of London, the central portion of Albania was to be made into an autonomous State under Italian protection; while northern and southern Albania were under certain circumstances to fall respectively to Serbia and Greece. But in 1917 Italy declared a Protectorate over the whole country—a Protectorate which she seems to have exercised ever since. By the Treaty of London Fiume was, with Italy's consent, assigned to Croatia. But since the armistice, Italy has been accumulating troops in that neighbourhood and local laws appear to have been promulgated in the name of the Italian King. Meanwhile America, which, unlike France and Britain, was not a party to the Treaty of London, has, in conformity with the general principles of settlement on which all the Allied and Associated Powers, including Italy, are agreed, declined to hand over reluctant Slav majorities in the Eastern Adriatic to Italian rule; and no arrangement on this vexed question has been arrived at.

Evidently the situation thus described is one of peculiar difficulty; but we feel bound to add that the difficulties have been greatly augmented by the policy pursued in Asia Minor by the Italian Government and Italian troops. This matter, as perhaps Your Excellency is aware, was the subject of warm debate in the Council of Four. President Wilson, Monsieur Clemenceau and Mr. Lloyd George complained in the strongest terms of the proceedings at Scala Nuova and elsewhere in South-Western Anatolia. They drew the sharpest contrast between the policy of the Greek Government, which moved no troops except with the cognisance, and usually at the request of the Allied and Associated Powers, including, of course, Italy herself, while Italy, which was one of those Powers, and as such cognisant of all that was being done by her friends, landed troops and occupied important positions without giving the least inkling of her proceedings to those whose counsels she shared, whose general policy she professed to support, but whose remonstrances on this point she persistently ignored.

We find it difficult fully to understand this action on the part of a friendly Power. At first sight it might seem to be animated by the idea that territories occupied by troops of a given nationality would be assigned to that nationality by the final terms of Peace. But this has never been the view of the other Allied and Associated Powers, and we had the best reason for supposing that it was not the view of Italy. We venture to quote a paragraph on the subject to which the Italian Representative gave his adhesion:

"No State will be rewarded for prolonging the horrors of war by any increase of territory; nor will the Allied and Associated Powers be induced to alter decisions made in the interests of Peace and justice by the unscrupulous use of military methods."

It is needless to say that we have not made the recital of our common difficulties for any other purpose than to contribute to their removal. The Treaty of London, the Anglo-French Declaration of November, 1918, President Wilson's fourteen points all bear on the situation, all have in different ways to be considered when Italy is discussing with her Allies and Associates the aspects of the final settlements which most nearly concern her. But they cannot be debated as contracts susceptible only of a strict legal interpretation. Italy herself has not so treated them; and if her partners attempted the task an amicable settlement would seem beyond the wit of man. For, as has been pointed out, they were framed in different periods in a rapidly changing world and under the stress of widely different motives. They could not be and are not in all respects consistent. They are in part obsolete or obsolescent, and cannot in their entirety be carried out. What in these circumstances seems to be required is a re-survey of the whole situation. Let the four Great Powers of the West, America, France, Britain and Italy, consider together with a fresh mind and perfect frankness, whether some solution cannot be found which is consistent both with the material interests of Italy, her enduring aspirations and the rights and susceptibilities of her neighbours. The difficulties in the way of such a solution may be great. But they should not be insuperable. We feel, however, compelled to add that it is wholly useless in our judgment to discuss Peace Terms in Paris as friends and associates, while one of our number is elsewhere pursuing an independent and even antagonistic course of action. If, for example, Italy insists, after our earnest protests, on maintaining troops in Anatolia, it can only be because she intends to obtain by force all she claims to be hers by right. This is quite inconsistent with genuine alliance; its inevitable end is complete isolation. It is for Italian statesmen to say whether or not this is in Italy's interests. To us and the world the loss will be immense, for the aid which Italy can render to mankind by helping in the establishment of a durable Peace through international co-operation is beyond price. To Italy it will mean the loss of all claim to further assistance or aid from those who were once proud to be her associates. To us such a consummation seems to be disastrous, but if Italian policy runs its course unchanged it seems also to be inevitable.

Dramatis Personae

Abdul Medjed, Crown Prince of Turkey.

Adenauer, Konrad (1876-1967). Lord Mayor of Cologne, 1917-1919; first Chancellor of the Federal Republic of Germany, 1949-1963.

Aga Khan III (Aga Sultan Sir Mohammed Shah) (1877-1957). Indian Muslim leader.

Aharonian, Avetis (1866-1948). Representative at the peace conference of the Armenian Republic in the Caucasus.

d'Aigremont, Lt. Gen. Baron Augustin-Michel Du Faing. Commander in Chief of the Belgian Army.

Albert I (1875-1934). Albert-Léopold-Clément-Marie Meinrad, King of the Belgians, 1909-1934; member of the Belgian Senate, 1893-1898; in exile in France during the war; led Belgian forces in final general Allied offensive through Belgium; guided Belgium's postwar economic recovery.

Alby, Gen. Henri-Marie-Camille-Édouard. Chief of the General Staff of the French army and military adviser in the French delegation to the peace conference.

Aldrovandi Marescotti, Luigi, Count of Viano (1876-1945). Chief of the office of the Italian Minister of Foreign Affairs and Secretary General of the Italian delegation to the peace conference.

Allenby, Sir Edmund Henry Hynman, 1st Viscount Allenby of Megiddo and Felixstowe (1861-1936). British Field Marshal; commander of the Third Army in France, 1915-1917; as commander in chief of the Egyptian Expeditionary Force, 1917-1919, he captured Jerusalem and won a decisive victory over the Turks.

Allizé, Henry (1860-1930). Career diplomat and head of the French mission in Vienna in 1919.

Alphand, Charles. Chief of section of the French Foreign Ministry and technical adviser on economic questions in the French delegation to the peace conference.

d'Amelio, Mariano (1871-1943). Counselor to the Italian High Court of Appeals and adviser on legal, economic, and financial questions in the Italian delegation to the peace conference.

Amet, Vice Adm. Jean-François-Charles. French High Commissioner at Constantinople.

Andrews, Rear Adm. Philip (1866-1945). American naval commander in the Mediterranean.

d'Anselme, Philippe-Henri-Joseph. Commander of Allied forces operating near Odessa, 1919.

Antonescu, Victor. Rumanian delegate to the peace conference; former Minister of Finance.

DRAMATIS PERSONAE

Asquith, Herbert Henry, 1st Earl of Oxford and Asquith (1852-1928). Liberal M.P., 1886-1918, 1920-1924; Prime Minister, 1908-1916.

Attolico, Bernardo (1880-1942). Adviser on economic and financial questions in the Italian delegation to the peace conference.

Auchincloss, Gordon (1886-1943). Special Assistant in the U. S. Department of State and secretary in the American delegation to the peace conference; son-in-law of Col. House and head of his secretariat in Paris.

Avksent'ev, Nikolai Dmitrievich (1878-1943). Leader of the right-wing faction of the Russian Social Revolutionary party and a former member of the Ufa Directorate.

Baker, Ray Stannard (1870-1946). Journalist, popular essayist, and authorized biographer of Woodrow Wilson; head of the American Press Bureau at the peace conference.

Balfour, Arthur James, 1st Earl of Balfour (1848-1930). Conservative M.P., 1874-1885, 1886-1905, 1906-1911; Prime Minister, 1902-1905; Foreign Secretary, 1916-1919; author of the so-called Balfour Declaration (1917) promising a homeland in Palestine for the Jewish people; plenipotentiary delegate to the peace conference.

Bark, Petr L'vovich (1869-1937). Statesman and prominent figure in Russian financial affairs on the eve of the Bolshevik Revolution.

Barnes, George Nicoll (1859-1940). One of the founders and chairman of the British Labour party; M.P., 1906-1922; Minister of Pensions, 1916-1917; member of the War Cabinet, 1917-1919; Minister without Portfolio, 1917-1920; plenipotentiary delegate to the peace conference and member of the Commission on International Labor Legislation.

Barrère, Camille-Eugène-Pierre (1851-1940). French Ambassador to Italy.

Baruch, Bernard Mannes (1870-1965). Chairman of the War Industries Board, 1918, and of the Supreme Economic Council at the peace conference; personal adviser to Wilson and economic and commercial adviser in the American delegation.

Barzilai, Salvatore (1860-1939). Trieste-born irredentist leader and member of the Italian Parliament; Minister without Portfolio for the Liberated Territories, 1915-1916; plenipotentiary delegate to the peace conference.

Bauer, Gustav Adolf (1870-1944). Chancellor in the new coalition government of the Social Democratic and Center parties, formed on June 21, 1919, to replace the Scheidemann cabinet.

Beer, George Louis (1872-1920). Technical adviser on colonial questions in the American delegation to the peace conference; distinguished scholar of eighteenth-century British policies toward the American colonies.

Belin, Gen. Émile-Eugène. French military representative on the Supreme War Council and adviser on military questions in the French delegation to the peace conference.

Beneš, Edvard (Eduard) (1884-1948). One of the founders of modern Czechoslovakia; Foreign Minister, 1918-1935; Prime Minister, 1921-1922; President, 1935-1938; plenipotentiary delegate to the peace conference.

Benson, Vice Adm. William Shepherd (1855-1932). Chief of U. S. Naval Operations, 1915-1919; appointed by Wilson to confer with Allied powers

in Europe, 1917; participated in drawing up naval terms of the Armistice with Germany; naval adviser to the American Commission to Negotiate Peace.
Bérenger, Victor-Henry. French author, politician, and diplomat.
Bernstein, Eduard (1850-1932). Socialist propagandist and political theorist opposed to the German war effort.
Bernstorff, Johann Heinrich, Count von (1862-1939). German diplomat; Ambassador at Washington, 1908-1917.
Berthelot, Gen. Henri-Mathias (1861-1931). Chief of the French military mission in Rumania.
Berthelot, Philippe-Joseph-Louis (1866-1934). French diplomat in the Ministry of Foreign Affairs; political and diplomatic adviser in the French delegation to the peace conference.
Bertram, Adolf Cardinal (1859-1945). Archbishop of Breslau.
Bethmann Hollweg, Theobald von (1856-1921). Chancellor of the German Empire, 1909-1917.
Bikaner, Maharaja of (Maharaja Shri Sir Ganga Singh Bahadur) (1880-1943). Indian soldier and statesman; plenipotentiary delegate to the peace conference.
Birkenhead, Frederick Edwin Smith, 1st Earl of Birkenhead (1872-1930). Lord Chancellor, 1919-1922.
Bliss, Howard Sweetser (1860-1920). Pioneer Protestant missionary in the Near East, President of Syrian Protestant College (now the American University of Beirut).
Bliss, Gen. Tasker Howard (1853-1930). General and Chief of Staff, U. S. Army, 1917; member of the Supreme War Council, 1917-1918; plenipotentiary delegate to the peace conference.
Blücher von Wahlstatt, Gebhard Leberecht, Prince (1742-1819). Prussian field marshal and commander during the Napoleonic Wars.
Böhm, Vilmos (1880-1949). People's Commissar for Defense in the Hungarian Soviet Republic of 1919.
Bon, Ferdinand-Jean-Jacques de (1861-1923). Chief of the French Naval General Staff and naval adviser in the French delegation to the peace conference.
Bonar Law, Andrew: see Law, Andrew Bonar.
Borden, Sir Robert Laird (1854-1937). Leader of Canada's Conservative party, 1902-1920; Prime Minister, 1911-1920; plenipotentiary delegate to the peace conference.
Borghese, Prince Luca Livio. Italian Minister to Serbia in 1919; the Belgrade government refused to accept his credentials.
Botha, Gen. Louis (1862-1919). First Prime Minister of the Union of South Africa, 1910-1919; plenpotentiary delegate to the peace conference.
Bottomley, Horatio William (1860-1933). Independent M.P. and a leader in the clamor for making Germany pay the full cost of the war.
Bourgeois, Léon-Victor-Auguste (1851-1925). Prime Minister of France, 1896; held numerous other cabinet posts; member of the League of Nations Commission and adviser on questions pertaining to the League

of Nations in the French delegation to the peace conference; winner of the Nobel Peace Prize for 1920.
Brambilla, Giuseppe. Technical expert on political and diplomatic questions in the Italian delegation to the peace conference.
Brătianu, Ion I. C. (Ionel) (1864-1927). Five times Prime Minister of Rumania; responsible for Rumania siding with the Allies in 1916; resigned from office in 1919 rather than accept a compromise on disputed territory with Yugoslavia; Rumanian plenipotentiary delegate to the peace conference.
Breslau, Archbishop of: see Adolf Cardinal Bertram.
Briand, Aristide (1862-1932). Eleven times Prime Minister of France.
Brockdorff-Rantzau, Ulrich Karl Christian, Count von (1869-1928). German Foreign Minister and head of the German peace delegation, 1919; resigned rather than sign the peace treaty.
Bullard, Rear Adm. William Hannum Brubb (1866-1927). Director of U. S. Naval Communications.
Bullitt, William Christian (1891-1967). U. S. diplomat; attaché to the American Commission to Negotiate Peace; sent by Col. House on special mission to Russia, 1919.
Cabrini, Angiolo (1869-1937). Adviser on economic and financial questions in the Italian delegation to the peace conference.
Cahen-Salvador, Georges-Joseph-Ernest. Director of the General Services of Prisoners of War in the French War Ministry.
Calthorpe, Adm. Sir Somerset Arthur Gough: see Gough-Calthorpe, Adm. Sir Somerset Arthur.
Cambon, Jules-Martin (1845-1935). French diplomat; Ambassador to the United States, 1897; Secretary-General of the French Foreign Ministry, 1915; chairman of the commissions for Greek, Czech, and Polish matters at the peace conference and plenipotentiary delegate.
Canterbury, Archbishop of: see Randall Thomas Davidson.
Cartier de Marchienne, Émile-Ernest, Baron de (1871-1946). Belgian Minister to the United States.
Castlereagh, Robert Stewart, 2nd Marquess of Londonderry (1769-1822). British Foreign Secretary, 1812-1822; guided Grand Alliance against Napoleon and was a major participant in the Congress of Vienna.
Cavallero, Gen. Ugo (1880-1943). Italian military representative on the Supreme War Council and adviser on military questions in the Italian delegation to the peace conference.
Cecil, Lord Robert (Edgar Algernon Robert Gascoyne-Cecil), 1st Viscount Cecil of Chelwood (1864-1958). One of the principal architects of the League of Nations Covenant; League of Nations adviser in the British delegation to the peace conference; winner of the Nobel Peace Prize, 1937.
Cellere, Count Vincenzo Macchi di. Italian Ambassador at Washington and political and diplomatic adviser in the Italian delegation to the peace conference.
Chaikovskii, Nikolai Vasil'evich (1850-1926). Member of the Russian Polit-

DRAMATIS PERSONAE

ical Council; his aims in Paris were to persuade the western Allies to aid the anti-Bolshevik forces in Russia.

Chamberlain, (Joseph) Austen (1863-1937). British statesman; member of the War Cabinet and Chancellor of the Exchequer.

Charles I, Karl Franz Josef (1887-1922). Emperor of Austria and, as Charles IV, King of Hungary, 1916-1918; the last monarch of the Austro-Hungarian Empire.

Chaume, Thion de la. Former French Inspector of Finance and technical expert on financial questions in the French delegation to the peace conference.

Chiesa, Eugenio (1863-1930). Technical adviser on reparation in the Italian delegation to the peace conference.

Chinda, Viscount Sutemi (1856-1929). Japanese Ambassador at London and plenipotentiary delegate to the peace conference.

Churchill, Winston Leonard Spencer (1874-1965). British statesman; First Lord of the Admiralty, 1911-1915; active military officer, 1915-1916; Minister of Munitions, 1917-1918; Secretary of State for War, 1918-1921; M.P. and plenipotentiary delegate to the peace conference, 1919; Prime Minister, 1940-1945 and 1951-1955.

Claveille, Albert (1865-1921). French Minister of Public Works and of Transport and a technical adviser on communications questions in the French delegation to the peace conference.

Clemenceau, Georges (1841-1929). French statesman and journalist. War correspondent in U. S. with Grant's army, 1865; member of the Chamber of Deputies, 1876-1893; senator, 1902-1920; French Prime Minister, 1906-1909 and 1917-1920; head of the French delegation to the peace conference.

Clémentel, Étienne (1864-1936). French Minister of Commerce, Industry, Posts, etc. and an economic adviser in the French delegation to the peace conference.

Colliard, Pierre. Minister of Labor and Social Security and adviser on labor questions in the French delegation to the peace conference.

Conger, Col. Arthur Latham. Assistant Chief of Staff to General Pershing; in charge of confidential work in Germany for the United States, 1918-1919.

Costa, Afonso Augusto da. Portuguese statesman; plenipotentiary delegate to the peace conference.

Cowan, Rear Adm. Sir Walter Henry (1871-1956). British commander of the Baltic Fleet.

Crane, Charles Richard (1858-1939). Member of special diplomatic mission to Russia, 1917; with Henry Churchill King, led the so-called King-Crane Mission to the Middle East in 1919.

Crespi, Silvio Benigno (1868-1944). Economic and financial adviser in the Italian delegation to the peace conference.

Crowe, Sir Eyre Alexander Barby Wichart (1864-1925). British Assistant Undersecretary of State for Foreign Affairs and plenipotentiary delegate to the peace conference.

Culme-Seymour, Rear Adm. Michael (1867-1925). Commander of the Black Sea and Caspian Squadron of the Royal Navy.

Cunliffe, Walter, 1st Baron of Headley (1855-1920). Adviser on financial questions in the British delegation to the peace conference and member of the Reparation Commission.

Curzon, George Nathaniel, 1st Marquess Curzon of Kedleston (1859-1925). British Secretary of State for War, later Foreign Secretary.

Damad Ferid Paşa (1850-1923). Turkish statesman of Albanian descent; Grand Vizier, 1919-1920.

Davidson, the Most Rev. Randall Thomas (1848-1930). Archbishop of Canterbury.

Davis, Norman Hezekiah (1878-1944). American financier and diplomat. Adviser on financial questions in the American delegation to the peace conference; member of the Reparation Commission.

Day, Clive (1871-1951). Chief technical adviser on questions relating to the Balkans in the American delegation to the peace conference.

Degoutte, Gen. Jean-Marie-Joseph (1866-1938). Commander of the French Sixth Army; military adviser in the French delegation to the peace conference.

Delacroix, Léon (1865-1929). Belgian lawyer and statesman; Prime Minister, 1919-1921.

Denikin, Gen. Anton Ivanovich (1872-1947). Anti-Bolshevik commander of the White forces in southern Russia, 1918-1919; controlled northern Caucasus in early 1919; was defeated by Red Army in October 1919 and fled to France in 1920.

Dernburg, Bernhard Jakob Ludwig (1865-1937). Former German Colonial Secretary, German Minister of Finance.

Despret. Adviser on economic questions in the Belgian delegation to the peace conference and inactive member of the Reparation Commission.

Desticker, Gen. Pierre-Henri (1866-1928). Assistant Chief of Staff to Marshal Foch.

Diaz, Gen. Armando (1861-1928). Italian Army Chief of Staff during the war and military adviser in the Italian delegation to the peace conference.

Dmowski, Román (1864-1939). President of the Polish National Committee and plenipotentiary delegate to the peace conference.

Donnersmarck, Count Henckel (Guidotto Karl Lazarus), Prince von. Son of Guido Georg Friedrich Erdmann Heinrich Adelbert, Count Henckel, Prince von Donnersmarck, who had developed the mineral resources of the approximately 50,000 acres of his estates in Silesia, and whose wealth was estimated in 1913 at $65,000,000.

Dresel, Ellis Loring (1865-1925). Head of the U. S. intelligence mission in Berlin.

Drummond, Sir James Eric (1876-1951). Private Secretary to Arthur Balfour and British Minister Plenipotentiary in the Secretariat of the delegation to the peace conference; first Secretary General of the League of Nations, 1919-1933.

DRAMATIS PERSONAE

Dulles, John Foster (1888-1959). Counsel to the American Commission to Negotiate Peace, 1918-1919; member of the Reparation Commission and Supreme Economic Council, 1919; Secretary of State, 1953-1959.

Dupont, Gen. Charles-Joseph (1863-1933). President of the Inter-Allied Commission at Berlin.

Dutasta, Paul-Eugène (1873-1925). French Minister at Bern and Secretary General of the peace conference.

Ebert, Friedrich (1871-1925). German Social Democratic leader and first President of the German Republic, 1919-1925.

Eyschen, Paul (1841-1915). Prime Minister of Luxembourg, 1889-1915.

Eisner, Kurt (1867-1919). Minister President of the first Bavarian Soviet Republic.

Erskine, William Augustus Forbes (1871-1952). Counselor of the British embassy in Rome.

Erzberger, Matthias (1875-1921). German statesman; leader of the Center (Catholic) party.

Faisal I (1885-1933). Arab leader and statesman; cooperated with Gen. Allenby in campaign which captured Jerusalem in 1917 and Damascus in 1918; was proclaimed King of Syria by Syrian National Congress in 1920 but was deposed by the French; placed on throne of Iraq in 1921 by the British.

Falk, Oswald Toynbee (1879-1972). Technical expert on financial questions in the British delegation to the peace conference.

Fayolle, Gen. Marie-Émile (1852-1928). French military commander prominent in several major battles during the war.

Fehrenbach, Konstantin (1852-1926). President of the German National Assembly, 1919; Chancellor of the German Republic, 1920-1921.

Fisher, Herbert Albert Laurens (1865-1940). M.P., historian, biographer; President of the Board of Education.

Foch, Marshal Ferdinand (1851-1929). Commander in Chief of the Allied Armies from 1918 until the end of the war; plenipotentiary delegate to the peace conference.

Fogazzaro, Antonio (1842-1911). Italian novelist.

Foster, Sir George Eulas (1847-1931). Canadian educator and statesman; Minister of Commerce and plenipotentiary delegate to the peace conference.

Franchet d'Esperey, Louis-Félix-Marie-François (1856-1942). Commander of the Army of the East based in Saloniki, Greece.

French, Field Marshal John Denton Pinkstone, 1st Viscount of Ypres (1852-1925). Commander in Chief of troops in the United Kingdom, 1915-1918; Lord Lieutenant of Ireland, 1918-1921.

Friedrich Wilhelm Viktor August Ernst (1882-1951). Crown Prince of Germany and of Prussia.

Fromageot, Henri-Auguste (1864-1949). Legal adviser to the French Ministry of Foreign Affairs and adviser in the French delegation to the peace conference.

DRAMATIS PERSONAE

Fryatt, Charles Algernon (1872-1916). British captain in the merchant marine; captured by Germans in 1916 and accused of attempting to ram a German submarine; condemned to death and shot the same year.

George V (George Frederick Ernest Albert) (1865-1936). King of England and Emperor of India, 1910-1936.

Gérard, Gen. Augustin-Grégoire Arthur (1857-1926). Commander of the French Eighth Army, with headquarters at Landau.

Gibson, Hugh Simons (1883-1954). American diplomat; United States Minister to Poland.

Gibson, Capt. Thomas. British military intelligence officer in Berlin.

Giesberts, Johann. Postmaster-General in the new coalition government formed on June 21 to replace the Scheidemann cabinet.

Giolitti, Giovanni (1842-1928). As Prime Minister of Italy during 1911-1914, he opposed Italy's entry into the war; Prime Minister, 1920-1921.

Gordon, Gen. Charles George (1833-1885). British soldier of fortune referred to as "Chinese Gordon"; led "Ever Victorious Army," a Chinese force, in suppressing the Taiping rebellion; killed at Khartoum.

Gordon, John R. U. S. member of the Inter-Allied Maritime Council, or Executive.

Gough, Lt. Gen. Sir Hubert de la Poer (1870-1963). Member of the Inter-Allied military mission to the Baltic region.

Gough-Calthorpe, Adm. Sir Somerset Arthur (1864-1937). Commander in Chief of Allied naval forces in the eastern Mediterranean and British High Commissioner at Constantinople.

Gounaris, Demetrios (1866-1922). Greek statesman; Prime Minister, 1915-1917 and 1920-1922; was court-martialed and shot after revolution following Greece's defeats by Turks in Asia Minor.

Gouraud, Gen. Henri-Joseph-Eugène (1867-1946). French High Commissioner in Syria.

Gout, Jean-Étienne-Paul. Chief of the Asiatic Section in the French Ministry of Foreign Affairs and technical adviser on political and diplomatic questions in the French delegation to the peace conference.

Grassi, Rear Adm. Adviser on naval questions in the Italian delegation to the peace conference.

Graves, Maj. Gen. William Sidney (1865-1940). Commander of the American Expeditionary Force in Siberia, 1918-1920.

Grayson, Rear Adm. Cary Travers (1878-1938). American naval physician; close friend of and physician to Woodrow Wilson; accompanied Wilson to Paris during peace conference.

Grey, Sir Edward, Viscount Grey of Fallodon (1862-1933). Secretary of State for Foreign Affairs, 1905-1916; Ambassador to the United States, 1919.

Guillaumat, Gen. Marie-Louis-Adolphe (1863-1940). Commander of Allied Army of the East, 1917; member of War Ministry in 1919.

Haase, Hugo (1863-1919). Leader of the German Independent Social Democratic party.

Haguenin, Émile. Head of the team of French observers in Berlin in 1919.

DRAMATIS PERSONAE

Haig, Field Marshal Douglas, 1st Earl Haig (1861-1928). Commander in Chief of the British forces in France during most of the war.

Haking, Lt. Gen. Sir Richard Cyril Byrne (1862-1945). British commander of XI Corps during the war.

Haller, Gen. Józef (1873-1960). Commander of the Polish National Army.

Haniel von Haimhausen, Edgar Karl Alfons (1870-1935). Member of the German diplomatic service; head of the German delegation during the final stage of the peace conference.

Hankey, Lt. Col. Sir Maurice Pascal Alers, 1st Baron Hankey (1877-1963). Secretary, Committee of Imperial Defence, 1912-1914, of War Cabinet, 1916-1918; head of the British secretariat at the peace conference; secretary of the Council of Four.

Hapgood, Norman (1868-1937). American editor and writer; Minister to Denmark.

Hapsburg, Archduke Joseph Ferdinand of (1872-1942). Austrian Archduke and general; commander of Austrian armies on the eastern front, 1914-1916.

Hardinge, Charles, 1st Baron Hardinge of Penshurst (1858-1944). Technical adviser on political and diplomatic questions in the British delegation to the peace conference.

Harries, Brig. Gen. George Herbert (1860-1934). Chief of the United States military mission in Berlin.

Harris, Ernest Lloyd (1870-1946). American Consul General at Irkutsk and Omsk, 1918-1921.

Haskins, Charles Homer (1870-1937). American medievalist; chief technical adviser on questions relating to western Europe in the American delegation to the peace conference.

Hawkins, Captain William (fl. 1595). One of the first English envoys to visit Jahangir, Mogul Emperor of India.

Headlam-Morley, James Wycliffe (1863-1929). English historian; secretary in the Foreign Office and technical adviser on political and diplomatic questions in the British delegation to the peace conference.

Hearst, William Randolph (1863-1951). American newspaper publisher and putative politician.

Heath, Maj. Ferry Kimball (1876-1939). Chief of the food commission of the American Relief Administration in Finland.

Heim, Georg (1865-1938). Head of the Bavarian Peasants' League.

Helfferich, Karl Theodor (1872-1924). Former Imperial Secretary of the Treasury and of the Interior.

Henderson, Arthur (1863-1935). Chief organizer of the British Labour party; Secretary of State for Foreign Affairs, 1929-1931; winner of the Nobel Peace Prize, 1934.

Hennocque, Gen. Edmond-Charles-Adolphe (1860-1933). Head of the French military mission in Prague.

Henry, Lt. Col. Marie-Joseph. Member of the French General Staff and head of the liaison group with enemy peace delegations.

Henrys, Gen. Paul-Prosper (1862-1943). Head of the French military mission in Poland.

Hindenburg, Paul Ludwig Hans Anton von Beneckendorff und von (1847-1934). Head of the German General Staff during the war; President of the German Republic, 1925-1932.

Hipwood, Charles (1869-1946). Assistant Secretary of the Board of Trade and an adviser on economic questions in the British delegation to the peace conference.

Hohenlohe-Schillingsfürst, Chlodwig Karl Viktor von (1819-1901). Chancellor of the German Empire, 1894-1900.

Hoover, Herbert Clark (1874-1964). Chairman of the American Relief Commission in London, 1914-1915, and of the Commission for Relief in Belgium, 1915-1917; U. S. Food Administrator, 1917-1919; Secretary of Commerce, 1921-1928; President of the United States, 1929-1933.

Hope, Rear Adm. George Price Webley (1869-1959). Technical adviser on naval questions in the British delegation to the peace conference.

House, Edward Mandell (1858-1938). Counselor and confidant of President Wilson; plenipotentiary delegate to the peace conference and member of the League of Nations Commission.

Horvat (Horvath), Gen. Dmitrii Leonidovich (1858-1937). Kolchak's commander of military operations in eastern Siberia.

Howard, Sir Esme William (1863-1928). Adviser on political and diplomatic questions in the British delegation to the peace conference; British civil commissioner on the Inter-Allied Special Commission to Poland.

Hudson, Manley Ottmer (1886-1960). International law expert; adviser on legal questions in the American delegation to the peace conference.

Hughes, William Morris (1864-1952). Prime Minister of Australia, 1915-1923; plenipotentiary delegate to the peace conference.

Humbert, Gen. Georges-Louis (1862-1921). Recently commander of the French Third Army.

Hurst, Cecil James Barrington (1870-1963). Legal adviser to the British Foreign Office, 1918-1929, and adviser in the British delegation to the peace conference; one of the authors of the League of Nations Covenant.

Hymans, Paul (1865-1941). Belgian Minister of Foreign Affairs, 1918-1920; plenipotentiary delegate to the peace conference.

Imperiali, Marquis Guglielmo. Italian Ambassador at London.

Ionescu, Take (1858-1922). Rumanian politician; founder and leader of the Conservative Democratic party and strong supporter of the Allies.

István, Count: see Tisza, István, Count.

Iudenich: see Yudenich, Gen. Nikolai Nikolaevich.

Ivanov-Rinov, Gen. Pavel Pavolich. Former czarist officer, nominal leader of anti-Bolshevik forces in eastern Siberia in late 1918 and early 1919.

Jahangir (1569-1627). Mogul Emperor of India.

Janin, Gen. Maurice-Pierre-Thiébaut-Charles. Head of the French military mission in Siberia.

Johnson, Douglas Wilson (1878-1944). Chief technical adviser on Adriatic questions in the American delegation to the peace conference; Professor of Geology, Columbia University; geographer.

Johnson, Lt. Col. Robert Arthur (1874-1938). Commander of a battalion of the Hampshire Regiment of the British army which had been sent to Siberia from India to assist in the training of anti-Bolshevik troops.

Jones, Capt. Clement Wakefield (1880-1963). Assistant Secretary of the War Cabinet and secretary in the British delegation to the peace conference.

Kaiser: see William II.

Kanellopoulos, Efthymios. Greek agent in Constantinople.

Károlyi, Count Mihály (1875-1955). Prime Minister and President of Hungary, 1918-1919; replaced by Béla Kun in March 1919.

Keller, Friedrich von. Member of the German diplomatic service.

Kerenskii, Aleksandr Feodorovich (1881-1970). Socialist Revolutionary who served as head of the Russian provisional government from July to October 1917.

Kernan, Maj. Gen. Francis Joseph (1859-1945). Technical adviser on military questions in the American delegation to the peace conference.

Kerr, Philip Henry, 11th Marquess of Lothian (1882-1940). Private Secretary to Lloyd George, 1916-1921; member of the secretariat of the British delegation to the peace conference.

Keynes, John Maynard, 1st Baron Keynes (1883-1946). Principal representative of the Treasury and adviser on financial questions in the British delegation to the peace conference.

King, Henry Churchill (1854-1934). President of Oberlin College, 1902-1927; with Charles Richard Crane, led the so-called King-Crane Commission to the Middle East in 1919.

Kisch, Lt. Col. Frederick Hermann (1888-1943). Technical expert on Russian, Chinese, and Japanese military questions in the British delegation to the peace conference.

Kitchener, Horatio Herbert, 1st Earl Kitchener of Khartoum and of Broome (1850-1916). British soldier; Secretary of State for War, 1914-1916.

Klein, Franz (1854-1926). Representative of the Foreign Ministry in the Austrian delegation to the peace conference.

Klofáč, Václav Jaroslav (1868-1942). Minister of National Defense of the Czechoslovak Republic.

Klotz, Louis-Lucien (1868-1930). French Minister of Finance and plenipotentiary delegate to the peace conference; member of the Reparation Commission.

Knox, Gen. Alfred William Fortescue (1870-1964). Chief of the British military mission to Siberia.

Kolchak, Adm. Aleksandr Vasil'evich (1873-1920). Recognized by White Russians as supreme ruler of Russia, 1918-1920; shot by the Bolsheviks in 1920.

Koo, Vi Kyuin Wellington (1887-1986). Chinese statesman and diplomat; Minister to Mexico, the United States, and Great Britain, 1915-1922; plenipotentiary delegate to the peace conference.

Kramář, Karel (1860-1937). First Prime Minister of Czechoslovakia, 1918-1919; plenipotentiary delegate to the peace conference.

Krüger, Stephanus Johannes Paulus (1825-1904). President of the South African Republic (Transvaal), 1883-1899.

Kun, Béla (1886-1939). Leader of the Hungarian Soviet Republic of 1919; assumed power in mid-March but his regime collapsed in August of that year.

Lamont, Thomas William (1870-1948). Partner in J. P. Morgan & Co.; financial adviser in the American delegation to the peace conference; member of the Reparation Commission.

Landru, Henri-Désiré (1869-1922). French criminal charged in April 1919 with committing several murders; he was convicted in 1922 and guillotined.

Landsberg, Otto (1869-1957). German Minister of Justice and member of the German delegation to the peace conference.

Lang, the Most Rev. Cosmo Gordon (1864-1945). Archbishop of York.

Lansbury, George (1859-1940). British Labour party leader, publicist, and pacifist.

Lansing, Robert (1864-1928). United States Secretary of State, 1915-1920, and plenipotentiary delegate to the peace conference.

Larnaude, Fernand. Dean of the Faculty of Law of the University of Paris and adviser on legal questions in the French delegation to the peace conference.

Lasteyrie, Charles, Comte de (1877-1936). Technical expert on financial questions in the French delegation to the peace conference.

Law, Andrew Bonar (1858-1923). Lord Privy Seal, leader of the House of Commons, and plenipotentiary delegate to the peace conference; Prime Minister, 1922-1923.

Layton, Walter Thomas (1884-1966). An economist and official of the British Ministry of Munitions; technical adviser to the British delegation at the peace conference.

Lebrun, Albert-François (1871-1950). French Minister for the Liberated Areas and a technical adviser on economic questions in the French delegation to the peace conference.

Leeper, Alexander Wigram Allen (1887-1935). Secretary in the British Foreign Office and a technical adviser on political and diplomatic questions in the British delegation to the peace conference.

Leinert, Robert. Leader of the German Social Democratic party; member of the German delegation to the peace conference.

Lenin, Vladimir Ilich Ul'anov (1870-1924). Founder of the Russian Communist party and leader of the Bolshevik revolution; first head of the Soviet state.

Le Rond, Gen. Henri-Louis-Édouard. Adjutant General to Marshal Foch.

Lersner, Baron Kurt von (1883-1954). Representative of the German Foreign Office and member of the German delegation to the peace conference.

Leygues, Georges-Jean-Claude (1857-1933). French Minister of the Navy.

Liebknecht, Karl (1871-1919). Spartacist leader and the foremost opponent

DRAMATIS PERSONAE 619

of the German war effort; main organizer of the German Communist party; shot during the Spartacist insurrection of January 1919.

Lloyd George, David, 1st Earl of Dwyfor (1863-1945). M.P., 1890-1922; Prime Minister, 1916-1922; head of the British delegation to the peace conference.

Long, Walter Hume (1854-1924). First Lord of the Admiralty.

Longare, Count Lelio Bonin. Italian Ambassador to France.

Lord, Robert Howard (1885-1954). Historian at Harvard University; adviser on questions relating to Russia and Poland in the American delegation to the peace conference.

Loucheur, Louis (1872-1931). French Minister of Industrial Reconstruction and technical adviser on economic questions in the French delegation to the peace conference; member of the Reparation Commission.

Ludendorff, Gen. Erich Friedrich Wilhelm (1865-1937). Chief aide to Hindenburg during the war.

Lukomskii, Aleksandr Serge'vich (1868-1939). Head of the War Department and president of the Special Council in Denikin's government.

Luxemburg, Rosa (1871-1919). Spartacist leader; a founder of the Polish Social Democratic party and of the German Communist party; shot during the Spartacist insurrection in January 1919.

Luzzatti, Luigi (1841-1927). Former Prime Minister and Treasury Minister of Italy; at this time, a spokesman for Orlando in the Chamber of Deputies.

L'vov, Georgii Evgen'evich, Prince (1861-1925). First premier in the Russian Provisional government; chairman of the Russian Political Conference, a group of anti-Bolshevik Russian political leaders whose aim, in part, was to represent the interests of Russia at the peace conference.

McCormick, Vance Criswell (1872-1946). Chairman of the U. S. War Trade Board and technical adviser on economic and commercial questions in the American delegation to the peace conference.

MacDonald, James Ramsay (1866-1937). A founder of the Labour party; Prime Minister, 1924, 1929-1931, 1931-1935.

Mackensen, Field Marshal August von (1849-1945). Led victorious German campaign in Rumania, 1916-1917.

Maclay, Sir Joseph Paton. British Shipping Controller.

Macleay, James William Ronald (1870-1943). Member of the British diplomatic service and a technical expert in the British delegation to the peace conference.

Mair, George Herbert (1887-1926). Director of the press section of the British delegation at the peace conference.

Makino, Baron Nobuaki (1861-1949). Japanese Minister of Education, Agriculture, Commerce, and Foreign Affairs prior to 1919; plenipotentiary delegate to the peace conference.

Maklakov, Vasilii Alekseevich (1869-1957). One of the organizers of the Russian Political Conference, a group of anti-Bolshevik Russian political leaders at Paris whose aim, in part, was to represent the interests of Russia at the peace conference.

Mance, Brig. Gen. Harry Osborne (1875-1966). Technical adviser on military questions in the British delegation to the peace conference.

Mangin, Gen. Charles-Marie-Emmanuel (1866-1925). French soldier who halted the German advance at Villers-Cotterêts in 1918.

Manteuffel, Baron Edwin Hans Karl von (1809-1885). Distinguished Prussian general, commander of the Prussian occupation forces in France, 1871-1873; noted for his tact in dealing with French civilian officials.

Marinelli, Olinto (1874-1926). Italian ethnographer and geographer.

Marshall-Cornwall, Lt. Col. Sir James Handyside. Technical expert on military questions relating to Austria, Czechoslovakia, and Hungary in the British delegation to the peace conference.

Martino, Giacomo de (1868-1957). Italian diplomat; adviser on political and diplomatic questions in the Italian delegation to the peace conference.

Masaryk, Thomas Garrigue (1850-1937). First President of Czechoslovakia, 1918-1935.

Massey, William Ferguson (1856-1925). Prime Minister of New Zealand and plenipotentiary delegate to the peace conference.

Matsui, Baron Keishiro (1868-1946). Japanese Ambassador at Paris and plenipotentiary delegate to the peace conference.

Melchior, Carl Joseph (1871-1933). Banker and representative of German financial interests; head of the German financial commission at the peace conference.

Memalek-el-Mochaverol. Persian Minister of Foreign Affairs.

Mercier, Désiré-Félicien-François-Joseph, Cardinal Mercier (1851-1926). Spiritual leader and spokesman of the Belgians during the German occupation of Belgium.

Mezes, Sidney Edward (1863-1931). Director of the staff of technical experts (The Inquiry) in the American delegation to the peace conference; President of the College of the City of New York; brother-in-law by marriage of Col. House.

Michitch: see Mišíc.

Miles, Lt. Col. Sherman (1882-1966). American observer stationed in various parts of present-day Yugoslavia, including Fiume.

Miller, David Hunter (1875-1961). International lawyer; collaborated in drawing up final draft of Covenant of League of Nations; technical adviser on legal questions in the American delegation to the peace conference.

Milliès-Lacroix, Raphaël. Member of the French Senate.

Milne, Lt. Gen. Sir George Francis, 1st Baron Milne (1866-1948). Commander of the Army of the Black Sea, active at this time in the Ukraine.

Milner, Alfred, 1st Viscount Milner (1854-1925). British Secretary of State for War, 1918-1919; Colonial Secretary, 1919-1921; plenipotentiary delegate to the peace conference.

Mišíc, Field Marshal Zivojin (1855-1921). Chief of Staff of the Serbian army.

Mişu, Nicolae. Rumanian Minister to Great Britain and a plenipotentiary delegate to the peace conference.

DRAMATIS PERSONAE 621

Mittelhauser, Gen. Eugène-Désiré-Antoine (1873-1949). Head of the French military mission in Czechoslovakia.

Moltke, Field Marshal Count Helmuth von (1800-1891). Prussian soldier who, under Bismarck, directed strategy in the war against France, 1870-1871.

Monnet, Jean-Omer-Marie-Gabriel (1888-1979). Adviser to the French delegation on economic questions; later leading advocate of western European unity.

Montagu, Edwin Samuel (1879-1924). Secretary of State for India and plenipotentiary delegate to the peace conference.

Montenegro, King of: see Nicholas I.

Mordacq, Gen. Jean-Jules-Henri (1868-1943). Clemenceau's principal Private Secretary at the Ministry of War.

Morel, Jean-Paul. Adviser on economic questions in the French delegation to the peace conference.

Morison, Samuel Eliot (1887-1976). American historian; assistant to R. H. Lord on questions relating to Russia, Poland, and the Baltic countries in the American delegation to the peace conference.

Morris, Roland Sletor (1874-1945). U. S. Ambassador to Japan, 1917-1921; on special mission to Siberia in 1918 and 1919.

Muehlon, Wilhelm von. Former official in the German Foreign Office who had been one of the leading opponents of the German war effort.

Müller, Hermann (1876-1931). German Minister of Foreign Affairs and delegate to the peace conference.

Nabokov, Konstantin Dmitrievich. Russian Chargé d'Affaires at London.

Namier, Lewis Bernstein (1888-1960). Polish-born naturalized British subject, historian; at this time, a member of the Political Intelligence Department of the Foreign Office.

Nansen, Fridtjof (1861-1930). Norwegian Arctic explorer and oceanographer who, after 1918, directed his efforts toward the repatriation of war prisoners and famine relief for Russia.

Neratov, Anatolii Anatolievich. Deputy Foreign Minister of Russia, 1910-1917; foreign-policy adviser to Gen. Denikin, 1919.

Nevin, John Edwin. Reporter for the International News Service, a Hearst organization.

Nicholas I (1841-1921). King of Montenegro.

Nicolson, Harold George (1886-1968). Staff member of the British Foreign Office and technical adviser on political and diplomatic questions in the British delegation to the peace conference.

Niederle, Lubor (1865-1944). Professor of Ethnography and Prehistorical Archeology at the University of Prague and a technical expert on geographic, ethnographic, and statistical questions in the Czechoslovak delegation to the peace conference.

Nitti, Francesco Saverio (1868-1953). Italian Prime Minister, 1919-1920.

Nolan, Brig. Gen. Dennis Edward (1872-1953). Chief of the Intelligence Department of the American Expeditionary Force.

DRAMATIS PERSONAE

Northcliffe, Alfred Charles William Harmsworth, 1st Viscount Northcliffe, (1865-1922). British newspaper proprietor, sometime diplomat and politician.

Noulens, Joseph. French politician and diplomat, head of the Inter-Allied mission to Poland in 1919.

Noyes, Pierrepont Burt (1870-1959). American representative on the Inter-Allied Rhineland Commission.

Nudant, Gen. Alphonse-Pierre (1861-1952). President of the Inter-Allied Armistice Commission at Spa.

Omelianovych-Pavlenko, Mykhailo. Commander of the Ukranian Galician army.

Orlando, Vittorio Emanuele (1860-1952). Italian Prime Minister, 1917-1919; head of the Italian delegation to the peace conference; resigned June 19, 1919.

Ossoinack, Andrea. Former member for Fiume of the Hungarian Parliament.

Paderewski, Ignace Jan (1860-1941). Polish pianist, composer, and statesman; Prime Minister and Minister of Foreign Affairs, 1919; plenipotentiary delegate to the peace conference.

Page, Thomas Nelson (1853-1922). American novelist; U. S. Ambassador to Italy, 1913-1919.

Paneyko, Vasil. Secretary of State for Foreign Affairs in the Western Ukrainian (Galician) government and head of its diplomatic delegation in Paris; also a member of the delegation of the Ukrainian National Republic.

Partsch, Joseph Franz Maria. German historian of Silesia.

Pašíc, Nikola P. (1845-1926). Serbian Foreign Minister and Prime Minister, one of the founders of the Kingdom of the Serbs, Croats and Slovenes (Yugoslavia); plenipotentiary delegate to the peace conference.

Pavlenko: see Omelianovych-Pavlenko.

Peel, Lt. Col. Sidney Cornwallis (1870-1938). Technical expert on financial questions in the British delegation to the peace conference.

Pellé, Gen. Maurice-César-Joseph (1863-1924). Head of the French military mission in Czechoslovakia and Commander in Chief of the Czechoslovak army.

Pershing, Gen. John Joseph (1860-1948). Commander in Chief of the American Expeditionary Force.

Pétain, Marshal Henri Philippe (1856-1951). Commander in Chief of the French armies at Verdun; Marshal of France, 1918.

Piccioni, Gen. Luigi. Head of the Italian military mission in Prague.

Pichon, Stéphen-Jean-Marie (1857-1933). French Minister of Foreign Affairs and plenipotentiary delegate to the peace conference.

Piip, Ants. Representative of the provisional government of Estonia to the peace conference.

Piłsudski, Gen. Józef Klemens (1867-1935). Polish Chief of State, 1918-1922.

Plamenac: see Plamenatz.

Plamenatz, Jovan S. (1873-?) Montenegrin Minister of Foreign Affairs and representative of King Nicholas to the peace conference.

DRAMATIS PERSONAE 623

Pless, Hans Heinrich XV, Prince of (1861-1938). Member of an ancient princely family of Silesia.

Poincaré, Raymond (1860-1934). French statesman, President of the French Republic, 1913-1920.

Pollock, Sir Ernest Murray (1861-1936). M.P., Solcitor-General, and adviser on legal questions in British delegation to the peace conference.

Pollock, Sir Frederick (1845-1937). British legal expert; former Corpus Professor of Jurisprudence at Oxford University, at this time Judge of the Admiralty Court of Cinque Ports.

Poska, Jaan. Estonian Foreign Minister and representative of the Estonian provisional government to the peace conference.

Pralon, Eugène-Léon. French Minister at Warsaw.

Pupin, Michael Idvorsky (1858-1935). Professor of Electro-mechanics at Columbia University; adviser to the Yugoslav delegation to the peace conference.

Raggi, Marquis Salvago. Italian plenipotentiary delegate to the peace conference.

Reading, Rufus Daniel Isaacs, 1st Marquess of Reading (1860-1935). British statesman; Lord Chief Justice of England, 1913-1921; special envoy to the U. S., 1918-1919.

Reboul, Col. French liaison officer with Polish troops.

Renner, Karl (1870-1950). Chancellor of the new Austrian state and head of its delegation to the peace conference.

Reuter, Émile. Prime Minister of Luxembourg at this time.

Reuter, Vice Adm. Ludwig von (1869-1943). Commander of the German High Seas Fleet interned at Scapa Flow.

Revel, Adm. Paolo Thaon di. Chief of the Naval General Staff and adviser in the Italian delegation to the peace conference.

Revelstoke, John Baring, 2nd Baron Revelstoke (1863-1929). Partner in Baring Brothers and Co., Ltd., London merchant bankers.

Ribot, Alexandre-Félix-Joseph (1842-1923). French statesman; Finance Minister, 1914-1917; Prime Minister, 1917.

Rinov: see Ivanov-Rinov.

Robertson, Gen. Sir William Robert (1860-1933). Chief of the British Imperial General Staff, 1915-1919; Commander in Chief of the British Army of the Rhine.

Robinson, Henry Mauris. Adviser on labor and shipping questions in the American delegation to the peace conference.

Rodd, Sir James Rennell, 1st Baron Rennell Rodd (1858-1941). British career diplomat and writer; Ambassador to Italy.

Rogers, Walter Stowell (1877-1965). Adviser on communications in the American delegation to the peace conference.

Ronarc'h, Vice Adm. Pierre-Alexis-Marie-Antoine. Chief of the French Naval General Staff.

Rothschild, Lionel Walter, 2nd Baron Rothschild (1868-1937). Zoologist and founder of the Rothschild Natural History Museum; conservative M.P., 1899-1910; active in the British Zionist movement.

Roussos, Paris. Member of the delegation representing the inhabitants of the Dodecanese Islands to the peace conference.
Saburi, Sadao. Secretary of the Japanese delegation to the peace conference.
Sackville-West, Maj. Gen. Charles John (1870-1962). Member of the Supreme War Council and adviser on military questions in the British delegation to the peace conference.
Saint-Aulaire, Auguste-Félix-Charles de Beaupoil, Comte de (1866-1954). French Minister to Rumania.
Saionji, Marquis Kimmochi (1849-1940). Japanese plenipotentiary delegate to the peace conference.
Salisbury, Robert Arthur Talbot Gascoyne-Cecil, 3d Marquess of Salisbury (1830-1903). British Prime Minister, 1885-1886, 1886-1892, 1895-1900, 1900-1902.
Samuel, Herbert Louis, 1st Viscount Samuel (1870-1963). British Liberal leader; Home Secretary, 1916; Special Commissioner to Belgium, 1919.
Sazanov, Sergei Dmitrievich (1866-1927). Minister of Foreign Affairs in the last czarist government and for Kolchak; member of the Russian Political Conference, a group of anti-Bolshevik Russian political leaders whose aim, in part, was to represent the interests of Russia to the peace conference.
Scheidemann, Philipp (1865-1939). German Social Democratic leader; first Chancellor of the German Republic.
Schmidt: see Schmidtt
Schmidtt, Ernst. Member of the German diplomatic service.
Schücking, Walther Max Adrian (1875-1935). Professor of International Law, member of the Reichstag and of the German delegation to the peace conference.
Scialoja, Vittorio (1856-1933). Adviser on legal questions in the Italian delegation to the peace conference.
Scott, James Brown (1866-1943). Authority on international law; technical adviser on legal questions in the American delegation to the peace conference and member of the Drafting Committee.
Segre, Gen. Roberto. Italian military leader; head of the Inter-Allied Armistice Commission at Vienna.
Semenov, Hetman Grigorii Mikhailovich (1890-1946). Anti-Bolshevik general in Siberia; head of the Ussuri Cossacks with the reputation of a cutthroat and a brigand.
Sergent, Charles. Under Secretary of State for Finance and technical adviser on financial questions in the French delegation to the peace conference.
Seymour, Adm.: see Culme-Seymour.
Seymour, Charles (1885-1963). Historian; chief technical adviser on questions relating to Austria-Hungary in the American delegation to the peace conference; President of Yale University, 1937-1950.
Simon, Henry-Louis. Minister for the Colonies and technical adviser on colonial questions in the French delegation to the peace conference.
Sinha, Satyendra Prasanno, 1st Baron Sinha of Raipur (1864-1928). Parlia-

mentary Under Secretary of State for India and plenipotentiary delegate to the peace conference.

Sixtus of Bourbon-Parma, Prince (1886-1934). Of French nationality; fought in the Belgian army; brother of Empress Zita; was used by Charles of Austria-Hungary as chief emissary to feel out the French government on prospects for a peace settlement in 1917.

Skoropadskii, Hetman Pavel Petrovich (1873-1945). Commander in Chief of Ukrainian forces after the Bolshevik seizure of power; overthrown by Ukrainian democratic coalition, 1918, and fled to Germany.

Smillie, Robert (1859-1940). President of the Miners' Federation of Great Britain, 1912-1921.

Smith, Sir Hubert Llewellyn (1864-1945). Permanent Secretary of the Board of Trade, 1907-1919, and Director General of the economic section in the British delegation to the peace conference.

Smuts, Gen. Jan Christiaan (1870-1950). South African statesman and soldier; plenipotentiary delegate to the peace conference; Prime Minister of the Union of South Africa, 1919-1924, 1939.

Sonnino, Baron Sidney (1847-1921). Italian statesman; Minister of Foreign Affairs, 1914-1919; plenipotentiary delegate to the peace conference.

Sookine, Jean (John, Ivan). Foreign Minister in Kolchak's government.

Spier, Gen. With the French military mission in Warsaw.

Stevens, John Frank (1853-1943). American engineer, president of the Inter-Allied Technical Board supervising the Trans-Siberian Railway.

Strandmann, Otto. Prime Minister of Estonia.

Strauss, Albert (1864-1929). Technical adviser on financial questions in the American delegation to the peace conference; member of the Financial Commission.

Sumner, John Andrew Hamilton, Baron Sumner of Ibstone (1857-1934), life peer. Adviser on legal questions in the British delegation to the peace conference and member of the Reparation Commission.

Sydorenko, Gregory. Head of the delegation of the Ukrainian Republic in Paris.

Sykes, Sir Mark (1879-1919). British Foreign Office adviser; advocate of Arab independence and pro-Zionist; instrumental in concluding the Sykes-Picot Agreement in 1916.

Tardieu, André-Pierre-Gabriel-Amédée (1876-1945). Member of Chamber of Deputies, 1914-1924; High Commissioner of France in U. S., 1917-1918; plenipotentiary delegate to the peace conference; Clemenceau's principal adviser.

Taussig, Frank William (1859-1940). Instructor, etc., of Political Economy at Harvard University, 1882-1935; chairman, U. S. Tariff Commission, 1917-1919; economic adviser in the American delegation to the peace conference.

Taylor, Alonzo Englebert (1871-1949). Pathologist and physiologist, member of the U. S. War Trade Board, 1917-1919; specialist in nutritional science.

Théry, Edmond-Amédée (1854-1925). French economist and sometime diplomat.
Thwaites, Maj. Gen. William (1868-1947). Director of Military Intelligence in the War Office and technical expert on military questions in the British delegation to the peace conference.
Tirpitz, Grand Adm. Alfred von (1849-1930). Founder of the Imperial German navy; Navy Secretary, 1897-1916.
Tisza, István, Count (1861-1918). Prime Minister of Hungary, 1913-1918; assassinated by terrorists who charged him with responsibility for bringing on the war.
Tittoni, Tommaso (1855-1931). Italian statesman; Minister of Foreign Affairs, June-November 1919.
Treitschke, Heinrich von (1834-1896). German historian and political writer.
Trumbić, Ante (1864-1938). Croatian nationalist who played a leading role in the founding of Yugoslavia. Minister of Foreign Affairs and plenipotentiary delegate to the peace conference.
Tseng-tsiang, Lou. Chinese Minister of Foreign Affairs and plenipotentiary delegate to the peace conference.
Tumulty, Joseph Patrick (1879-1954). Secretary to Woodrow Wilson, 1911-1921.
Uchida, Viscount Yasuya (or Kosai) (1865-1936). Japanese Minister of Foreign Affairs.
Vaida-Voevod, Alexandru (1871-1950). Rumanian plenipotentiary delegate to the peace conference.
Van den Heuvel, Jules-Norbert-Marie (1854-1926). Belgian Minister of State and plenipotentiary delegate to the peace conference.
Vandervelde, Émile (1866-1938). Belgian Minister of Justice and plenipotentiary delegate to the peace conference.
Vannutelli-Rey, Count Luigi. Counselor of Legation and technical expert on political and diplomatic questions in the Italian delegation to the peace conference.
Vénisélos, Eleutherios Kyrios (1864-1936). Greek Prime Minister, 1917-1920; plenipotentiary delegate to the peace conference.
Vesnić, Milenko R. (1862-1921). Yugoslav plenipotentiary delegate to the peace conference.
Vio, Antonio. Mayor of Fiume.
Vix, Lt. Col. Ferdinand. French soldier, representative of the Allied powers in Budapest in 1919.
Voldemaras, Augustinas (1883-1946). Lithuanian Minister of Foreign Affairs and head of the Lithuanian delegation to the peace conference.
Von der Goltz, Gen. Gustav Adolf Joachim Rüdiger, Count (1865-1930). Commander of German troops in the Baltic region.
Warburg, Max Moritz (1867-1946). German banker, financial adviser to the German delegation to the peace conference.
Ward, Col. John (1866-1934). Labour party M.P.; served in Siberia in the 25th Middlesex Regiment, 1918-1919.

Weiss, André (1858-1928). Legal adviser to the French Ministry of Foreign Affairs and a technical adviser in the French delegation to the peace conference.
Wemyss, Adm. of the Fleet Rosslyn Erskine, 1st Baron of Wemyss (1864-1933). First Sea Lord, 1917-1919.
Weygand, Gen. Maxime (1867-1965). Marshal Foch's chief of staff; French representative on the Supreme War Council.
White, Henry (1850-1927). Former U. S. Ambassador to Italy and France; plenipotentiary delegate to the peace conference.
William II, Friedrich Wilhelm Viktor Albert (1859-1941). German Emperor and King of Prussia, 1888-1918.
Williams, Edward Thomas (1854-1944). Former chief of Far Eastern Division, Department of State, and technical adviser on far eastern questions in the American delegation to the peace conference.
Wilson, Capt. Arnold Talbot (1884-1940). British Political Resident in the Persian Gulf and Civil Commissioner in Mesopotamia.
Wilson, Field Marshal Sir Henry Hughes (1864-1922). Member of the Supreme War Council, 1917; Chief of the British General Staff, 1918-1922; Field Marshal, 1919; technical adviser on military questions in the British delegation to the peace conference.
Wilson, (Thomas) Woodrow (1856-1924). President of Princeton University, 1902-1910; Governor of New Jersey, 1911-1913; President of the United States, 1913-1921. Nobel Peace Prize, 1919; President of the American Historical Association, 1924.
Wise, Edward Frank (1885-1933). British member of the Supreme Economic Council and chairman of its sub-committee on Germany.
Wise, Stephen Samuel (1874-1949). President of the delegation of the American Jewish Congress at the peace conference; Zionist leader; founder of the Free Synagogue of New York.
Wolf, Lucien (1857-1930). English writer, editor, and historian of Jewish subjects, an authority on anti-Semitism; president of the National Union for Jewish rights.
Wolff, Theodor. Editor of the *Berliner Tageblatt* and German moderate spokesman.
Yamagata, Prince Aritomo (1838-1922). Leading figure of the Genrō, or Elder Statesmen.
York, Archbishop of: see Cosmo Gordon Lang.
Yudenich, Gen. Nikolai Nikolaevich (1862-1933). Commander of the Russian Army of the Caucasus, 1915-1917; at this time, commander of the Anti-Bolshevik Northern Corps, operating in the Baltic region.
Zaharoff, Sir Basil (1849-1936). International armaments dealer and financier; founder of various chairs in aviation and of the Marshal Foch professorship of French literature at Oxford University.
Zervos, Skevos. Member of the delegation representing the inhabitants of the Dodecanese Islands to the peace conference.

Sources and Works Cited

Adams, Arthur E., *Bolsheviks in the Ukraine: The Second Campaign, 1918-1919* (New Haven and London, 1963).
Adler, Cyrus, and Aaron M. Margalith, *With Firmness in the Right: American Diplomatic Action Affecting Jews, 1840-1945* (New York, 1946).
Albrecht-Carrié, René, *Italy at the Paris Peace Conference* (New York, 1938).
Aldrovandi Marescotti, Luigi, *Guerra Diplomatica, Ricordi Framenti di Diario (1914-1919)* (Milan, 1936).
Aldrovandi Marescotti, Luigi, *Nuovi Ricordi e Frammenti di Diario* (Milan, 1938).
Ambrosius, Lloyd E., *Woodrow Wilson and the American Diplomatic Tradition: The Treaty Fight in Perspective* (Cambridge, New York, etc., 1987).
Bailey, Thomas A., *Woodrow Wilson and the Great Betrayal* (New York, 1945).
Baker, Ray Stannard, *Woodrow Wilson and World Settlement*, 3 vols. (New York, 1922-23).
Bardens, Dennis, *The Ladykiller: The Life of Landru, the French Bluebeard* (London, 1972).
Baruch, Bernard M., *The Making of the Reparation and Economic Sections of the Treaty* (New York and London, 1920).
Birdsall, Paul, *Versailles Twenty Years After* (New York, 1941).
Burnett, Philip M., *Reparation at the Paris Peace Conference: From the Standpoint of the American Delegation*, 2 vols. (New York, 1940).
Chi, Madeleine, *China Diplomacy, 1914-1918* (Cambridge, Mass., 1982).
Deák, Francis, *Hungary at the Paris Peace Conference: The Diplomatic History of the Treaty of Trianon* (New York, 1942).
Dockrill, M., *British Documents on Foreign Affairs: Reports and Papers from the Foreign Office Confidential Print*, Kenneth Bourne and D. Cameron Watt, general eds., Part II, Series I, Vol. 4 [Frederick, Md., 1989].
Duroselle, Jean-Baptiste, *Clemenceau* (Paris, 1988).
Earle, Edward Mead, *Turkey, the Great Powers, and the Bagdad Railway: A Study in Imperialism* (New York, 1923).
Epstein, Fritz T., "Zwischen Compiègne und Versailles: Geheime amerikanische Militärdiplomatie in der Periode des Waffenstillstandes 1918/19: Die Rolle des Obersten Arthur L. Conger," *Vierteljahrshefte für Zeitgeschichte*, III (Oct. 1955), 412-24.
Evans, Sir Arthur John, "Diagrammatic Map of a Future South Slav State," *The New Europe: A Weekly Review of Foreign Politics*, IV (Oct. 11, 1917), 415-16.

Fifield, Russell H., *Woodrow Wilson and the Far East: The Diplomacy of the Shantung Question* (New York, 1952).
Fogazzaro, Antonio, *Picolo Mundo Antico: Romanza* (Milan, 1895).
German Foreign Office, *Is Germany guilty? German White-book concerning the Responsibilities of the Authors of the War* (Berlin, 1919).
Germany, National Assembly, *Verhandlungen der Verfassunggebenden Deutschen Nationalversammlung, Stenographische Berichte*, Vol. 327 (Berlin, 1920).
Gerson, Louis L., *Woodrow Wilson and the Rebirth of Poland, 1914-1920* (New Haven, Conn., 1953).
Hale, Robert, *The Baltic Provinces: Report of Mission to Finland, Esthonia, Latvia, and Lithuania on the Situation in the Baltic Provinces*, 66th Cong., 1st sess., Sen. Doc. No. 105 (Washington, 1919).
Hancock, William Keith and Jean van der Poel, eds., *Selections from the Smuts Papers*, 7 vols (Cambridge, 1966-1973).
Haskins, Charles Homer and Robert Howard Lord, *Some Problems of the Peace Conference* (Cambridge, Mass., 1920).
Headlam-Morley, James W., *A Memoir of the Paris Peace Conference 1919*, Agnes Headlam-Morley, Russell Bryant, and Anna Cienciala, eds. (London, 1972).
House, Edward M. and Charles Seymour, eds., *What Really Happened at Paris* (New York, 1921).
Howard, Harry Nicholas, *The King-Crane Commission: An American Inquiry in the Middle East* (Beirut, 1963).
Italy, Ministry of Foreign Affairs, *Diplomatic Documents Submitted to the Italian Parliament by the Minister for Foreign Affairs (Sonnino), Austria-Hungary, Session of the 20th May, 1915* (London, 1915).
Janowsky, Oscar I., *The Jews and Minority Rights, 1898-1919* (New York, 1933).
Kernek, Sterling J., *Distractions of Peace during War: The Lloyd George Government's Reaction to Woodrow Wilson, December, 1916-November, 1918* (Philadelphia, 1975).
Kernek, Sterling J., "Woodrow Wilson and National Self-determination along Italy's Frontier: A Study of the Manipulation of Principles in the Pursuit of Political Interests," *Proceedings of the American Philosophical Society*, CXXVI (Aug. 1982), 243-300.
Keynes, John Maynard, *The Economic Consequences of the Peace* (London, etc., 1919).
King, Jere Clemens, *Foch versus Clemenceau: France and German Dismemberment, 1918-1919* (Cambridge, Mass., 1960).
Király, Bela et al., eds., *War and Society in East Central Europe*, Vol. VI, *Essays on World War I: Total War and Peacemaking, A Study on Trianon* (Brooklyn, N. Y., 1982).
Langer, William L., *European Alliances and Alignments, 1871-1890* (New York, 1931).

Lehovich, Dimitry V., *White against Red: The Life of General Anton Denikin* (New York, 1974).
Lentin, A[ntony]., *Lloyd George, Woodrow Wilson and the Guilt of Germany: An Essay in the Pre-History of Appeasement* (Baton Rouge, La., 1984).
Leverkuhn, P., ed., *Wirtschaftliche Bestimmungen in Friedesverträgen* (Hamburg, 1948).
Link, Arthur S. et al., eds., *The Papers of Woodrow Wilson*, 65 vols. to date (Princeton, N. J., 1966-).
Link, Arthur S., *Wilson: The Struggle for Neutrality, 1914-1915* (Princeton, N. J., 1960).
Lloyd George, David, *The Truth About the Peace Treaties*, 2 vols. (London, etc., 1938).
Lloyd George, David, *War Memoirs of David Lloyd George*, 6 vols. (Boston, 1933-37).
Luckau, Alma, *The German Delegation at the Paris Peace Conference* (New York, 1941).
Lundgreen-Nielsen, Kay, *The Polish Problem at the Paris Peace Conference: A Study of the Policies of the Great Powers and the Poles, 1918-1919* (Odense, Denmark, 1979).
McDougall, Walter A., *France's Rhineland Diplomacy, 1914-1924: The Last Bid for a Balance of Power in Europe* (Princeton, N. J., 1978).
Mantoux, Étienne, *The Carthaginian Peace or the Economic Consequences of Mr. Keynes* (London, New York, and Toronto, 1946).
Marder, Arthur J., *From the Dreadnought to Scapa Flow: The Royal Navy in the Fisher Era, 1904-1919*, 5 vols. (London, 1961-1970).
Marks, Sally, *Innocent Abroad: Belgium at the Paris Peace Conference of 1919* (Chapel Hill, N. C., 1981).
May, Arthur J., *The Passing of the Hapsburg Monarchy, 1914-1918*, 2 vols. (Philadelphia, 1966).
Mayer, Arno J., *Politics and Diplomacy of Peacemaking: Containment and Counterrevolution at Versailles, 1918-1919* (New York, 1967).
Medlicott, W. N., *The Congress of Berlin and After: A Diplomatic History of Near Eastern Settlement, 1878-1880*, 2d edn. (London, 1963).
Miller, David Hunter, *My Diary at the Conference of Paris, with Documents*, 21 vols. (New York, 1924).
Mitchell, Allan, *Revolution in Bavaria, 1918-1919: The Eisner Regime and the Soviet Republic* (Princeton, N. J., 1965).
Nash, George H., *The Life of Herbert Hoover: The Humanitarian, 1914-1917* (New York and London, 1988).
Nelson, Harold I., *Land and Power: British and Allied Policy on Germany's Frontiers, 1916-1919* (London and Toronto, 1963).
Noble, George Bernard, *Policies and Opinions at Paris, 1919: Wilsonian Diplomacy, the Versailles Peace, and French Public Opinion* (New York, 1935).
Page, Stanley W., *The Formation of the Baltic States: A Study of the Effect*

of Great Power Politics upon the Emergence of Lithuania, Latvia, and Estonia (Cambridge, Mass., 1959).

Partsch, Josef Franz Maria, *Landeskunde der Provinz Schlesien* (Breslau, 1898).

Partsch, Josef Franz Maria, *Schlesien: Eine Landeskunde für das deutsche Volk auf Wissenschaftlicher Grundlage*, 2 vols. (Breslau, 1896-1911).

Pastor, Peter, *Hungary Between Wilson and Lenin: The Hungarian Revolution of 1918-1919 and the Big Three* (Boulder, Colo., 1976).

Perman, Dagmar, *The Shaping of the Czechoslovak State: Diplomatic History of the Boundaries of Czechoslovakia, 1914-1920* (Leiden, 1962).

Poincaré, Raymond, *Au Service de la France*, 11 vols. (Paris, 1926-1974).

Rauch, Georg von, *The Baltic States — The Years of Independence: Estonia, Latvia, Lithuania, 1917-1940* (London, 1970).

Reshetar, John S., Jr., *The Ukrainian Revolution, 1917-1920: A Study in Nationalism* (Princeton, N. J., 1952).

Roskill, Stephen, *Hankey: Man of Secrets*, 3 vols. (London, 1970-1974).

Rudin, Harry R., *Armistice, 1918* (New Haven, Conn., 1944).

Schwabe, Klaus, *Deutsche Revolution und Wilson-Frieden: Die amerikanische und deutsche Friedensstrategie zwischen Ideologie und Machtpolitik 1918-19* (Düsseldorf, 1971).

Schwabe, Klaus, *Woodrow Wilson, Revolutionary Germany, and Peacemaking, 1918-1919: Missionary Diplomacy and the Realities of Power* (Chapel Hill, N. C., and London, 1985).

Senn, Alfred E., *The Emergence of Modern Lithuania* (Westport, Conn., 1975).

Shotwell, James T., *The Origins of the International Labor Organization*, 2 vols. (New York, 1934).

Spector, Sherman D., *Rumania at the Paris Peace Conference: A Study of the Diplomacy of Ioan I. C. Brătianu* (New York, 1962).

Tansill, Charles Callan, *America and the Fight for Irish Freedom, 1866-1922* (New York, 1967).

Tardieu, André, *The Truth About the Treaty* (London, 1921).

Taylor, Allan, *Prelude to Israel: An Analysis of Zionist Diplomacy, 1897-1947* (New York, 1959).

Temperley, Harold W. V., ed., *A History of the Peace Conference of Paris*, 6 vols. (London, 1920-1924).

Thadée, Ann-Yuen Yong, *Chine & Japon à la Conférence de la Paix* (Abaye de Saint-André, 1934).

Théry, Édmond Amédée, *La fortune publique de la France* (Paris, 1911).

Thompson, John M., *Russia, Bolshevism, and the Versailles Peace* (Princeton, N. J., 1966).

Tillman, Seth P., *Anglo-American Relations at the Paris Peace Conference of 1919* (Princeton, N. J., 1961).

Tökés, Rudolf L., *Béla Kun and the Hungarian Soviet Republic: The Origins and Role of the Communist Party of Hungary in the Revolutions of 1918-1919* (New York, 1967).

Trachtenberg, Marc, *Reparation in World Politics: France and European Economic Diplomacy, 1916-1923* (New York, 1980).
Trask, David F., *The United States in the Supreme War Council: American War Aims and Inter-Allied Strategy, 1917-1918* (Middletown, Conn., 1961).
U. S., Department of State, *Papers Relating to the Foreign Relations of the United States 1919: Russia* (Washington, 1937).
U. S., Department of State, *Papers Relating to the Foreign Relations of the United States 1919: The Paris Peace Conference*, 13 vols. (Washington, 1942-1947).
Unterberger, Betty Miller, *America's Siberian Expedition, 1918-1920: A Study of National Policy* (Durham, N. C., 1956).
Urofsky, Melvin I., *American Zionism from Herzl to the Holocaust* (Garden City, N. Y., 1975).
Van der Vat, Dan, *The Grand Scuttle: The Sinking of the German Fleet at Scapa Flow in 1919* (London, 1982).
Viefhaus, Erwin, *Die Minderheitenfrage und die Entstehung der Minderheiten-Schutzverträge auf der Pariser Friedens-Konferenz 1919* (Würzburg, 1960).
Völgyes, Iván, *Hungary in Revolution, 1918-19: Nine Essays* (Lincoln, Neb., 1971).
Waldman, Eric, *The Spartacist Uprising of 1919 and the Crisis of the German Socialist Movement* (Milwaukee, Wisc., 1958).
Walworth, Arthur, *Wilson and His Peacemakers: American Diplomacy at the Paris Peace Conference, 1919* (New York and London, 1986).
Wandycz, Piotr S., *France and her Eastern Allies, 1919-1925: French-Czechoslovak-Polish Relations from the Paris Peace Conference to Locarno* (Minneapolis, Minn., 1962).
Ward, Alan J., *Ireland and Anglo-American Relations, 1899-1921* (London, 1969).
Williams, Warren E., "Die Politik der Alliierten gegenüber den Freikorps in Baltikum 1918-1919," *Vierteljahrshefte für Zeitgeschichte*, XII (April 1964), 147-69.
Wilson, Woodrow, the Papers of, the Library of Congress.
Yates, Louis A. R., *The United States and French Security, 1917-1921* (New York, 1957).

Index

Abyssinia, II: 112, 486
Adalia (now Antalya), Turkey, II: 37, 38, 58, 84n1, 112-13; Italian landing at, I: 454, 480n3; II: 39, 92, 110n1, 573,n5
Adams, Arthur E., I: 9n1
Adana (Seyhan), Turkey, I: 480n3
Aden, II: 59
Adenauer, Konrad, II: 187,n3
Adler, Cyrus, I: 473n7
Adlon Hotel (Berlin), II: 103
Adria Company, I: 132
Adrianople, Turkey, II: 555
Adriatic question, I: xxii, xxvi, 275-89, 290-96, 297-304, 304-11, 336-39, 342-50, 350-54, 358-69, 448-55; II: 50-59, 108, 127-30, 214-28, 340-42, 362-63n2, 568, 583; Orlando presents Italy's claims to Council of Four, I: 125-28, 276; WW's statement on, I: 307-308, 314-17,n5; issue of publication of WW's statement on, I: 311, 312, 329, 338; Big Three meet on, I: 342-45; and Orlando's reply to WW's statement, I: 351n1; T. N. Page on reaction to WW's statement on, I: 385n2, 466, 479; Balfour's draft letter to Italy on Treaty of London and, I: 342, 356; Lloyd George and Clemenceau sign and send Balfour letter, I: 346-50; WW on Lloyd George-Clemenceau letter, I: 342, 343, 344; Tardieu plan, II: 138-40; Miller-House initiative, II: 109n7, 222; and Yugoslavia, I: 67n11, 304; II: 53, 108-109, 241; map of, I: xlv, xlvi; *see also* Treaty of London; Fiume; Dalmatia
Aegean Sea, II: 30, 69, 116, 298
Afghanistan, I: 36; II: 54, 99, 128, 486
Aga Khan III (Aga Sultan Sir Mohammed Shah), on Turkish question, II: 53-54, 95-96, 99
Agram (now Zagreb, Yugoslavia), II: 220
Agreement of Saint-Jean de Maurienne, I: 480n3; II: 36, 37, 38, 111, 112, 113, 114, 569, 588
Aharonion, Avetis, II: 57n4
Aidin, Turkey, II: 57, 58, 70, 112, 114, 116, 117, 118, 568
Aigremont, Gen. Baron Augustin-Michel De Faing d', II: 20n4
Aisne River, I: 25n1
Aix-la-Chapelle (Aachen, Germany), I: 259
Albania, I: xxii, 495; II: 4, 236n1
Albanian Colony of Rumania, I: 495n4
Albanian Colony of Turkey, I: 495n4
Albanian Political Party of America, I: 495n4
Albert, King of the Belgians, I: 124,n3, 129, 154; meets Council of Four on Belgian claims, I: 135-44; on Luxembourg, I: 142
Albrecht-Carrié, René, I: xlvi, xlix, 125n4, 285n6, 293n3, 343n7; II: 106n5, 236n1, 323n1, 565n1
Alby, Gen. Henri-Marie-Camille-Edouard, I: 10-11, 12, 39, 231; II: 85n2, 125, 148, 339,n4
Aldrovandi Marescotti, Count Luigi, I: xivn3, xxxvn6, 276, 358; II: 106, 188, 323
Aleppo, Syria, II: 162, 163
Alexandretta (now Iskenderun), Turkey, II: 136,n5, 162
Alfassa, Maurice, I: vii
Ali, Yusuf, II: 97-98, 100
Allenby, Gen. Sir Edmund Henry Hynman, 1st Viscount Allenby of Megiddo and Felixstone, I: 506; II: 138, 165, 265,n1, 266,n2, 267, 554
Allenstein (now Olsztyn, Poland), II: 282
Allgemeiner Deutscher Schulverein, II: 299,n2
Allizé, Henry, I: 503; II: 351
Alto-Adige, Italy, I: 298, 339
Alphand, Charles, II: 198

634   INDEX

Alsace-Lorraine, I: 28, 185, 186, 247, 250, 430-34; II: 196, 198, 270, 280; map of, I: xliii; coal production and consumption, I: 227; and reparation, I: 390, 431, 432; II: 199; payment of civil service pensions, I: 430; provision for damages suffered by inhabitants of, I: 431; question of Germany buying back marks from, I: 432-34; reply to German counterproposals on, II: 418,n2

Ambrosius, Lloyd E., II: 480n3

Amelio, Mariano d', I: 29

America and the Fight for Irish Freedom, 1866-1922 (Tansill), I: 500n1

American Commission for Irish Independence, I: 500n1

American Epoch: A History of the United States Since the 1890's (Link), I: liii

American Expeditionary Force, I: 100n1

American Historical Review, I: viiin2

American Line: *see* Wilson Line

American Zionism from Herzl to the Holocaust (Urofsky), I: 440n5

America's Siberian Expedition, 1918-1920: A Study of National Policy (Unterberger), II: 14n1

Amet, Vice Adm. Jean-François-Charles, II: 32

Anatolia, I: 494; II: 98, 128, 136, 553, 567, 568; mandates in, I: 483; II: 39, 55, 57-58, 70, 71, 84n1, 107; possible U.S. mandate of, II: 130

Andrews, Rear Adm. Philip, I: 385n3

Anglo-American Relations at the Paris Peace Conference of 1919 (Tillman), I: 6n2, 105n1

Anglo-Japanese secret treaty of 1917, I: 251n3, 321-22

Anselme, Gen. Philippe-Henri-Joseph d', I: 115

anti-Semitism: in Poland, I: 439-40, 472; II: 88, 89, 90, 91; in Rumania, II: 90

Antonescu, Victor, I: 11,n3

Antwerp, Belgium, I: 91n6, 139, 140, 262; II: 442, 443, 451, 456

Arabs, I: 231; II: 162

Arad, Rumania, II: 254

Archangel, Russia, I: 501; II: 484; government of, I: 429; II: 119, 200; repatriation of Czech troops via, II: 528, 551

Armenia, I: 111, 483; II: 57, 70, 95, 128, 133, 555; possible mandate over, II: 55, 129, 130, 132, 552, 553; Turkish abuses in, II: 57

Armistice of *Nov. 11, 1918* [Compiègne Forest with Germany]: xxx; WW on occupation of territories and, I: 45; and occupation of Vienna, I: 47; and reparation, I: 49, 50, 52, 53; and issue of transport of Haller's troops, I: 69-70, 70n3, 101n4, 113-15, 166,n4; and German troops in Baltic provinces, I: 72n5; duration of, I: 97,n9; extension of, I: 116,n1; and sinking of German fleet at Scapa Flow, II: 540

Armistice of *Nov. 3, 1918* [Armistice of Villa Giusti with Austria-Hungary]: xxx; I: 45, 97, 299,n1; WW on Italy's occupation of Fiume and, I: 485

Armistice: Commission at Spa, I: 42

Armistice, 1918 (Rudin), I: 97n9

Armistice of Belgrade (Nov. 13, 1918), I: 10n2

Army of Occupation of Germany: *see* Rhineland

Army of the East, II: 320

Arras, France, II: 339

Ashton, T. S., I: viii

Asquith, Herbert Henry, I: 120, 344, 477

Assling Triangle: map of, I: xlix; II: 51, 219n6, 236n1, 343

Atlantica Company, I: 132

atrocities, I: 33, 122, 414

Attolico, Bernardo, II: 122n4

Auchincloss, Gordon, I: 208n2

Au Service de la France (Poincaré), I: 437n2

Australia: opposes inclusion of principle of racial equality in League of Nations Convenant, I: 399-400n7

Austria, II: 205-209, 249; and Armistice of Nov. 3, 1918, I: 45; representatives summoned to Chantilly, I: 429; Clemenceau changes venue to Saint-Germain, I: 446; border questions, II: 3, 5, 33, 73, 219, 220, 234; Southern Austrian Railways (Südbahn), II: 60, 61, 62, 63, 232,n3, 585, 593-97; treaty

provisions for, II: 61, 214,n1, 218n3, 228, 229, 230, 231, 238, 329; size of future military forces of, II: 73-74n1, 76, 180-85, 191, 229, 304, 306,n7, 314, 315, 316, 317; distribution of fleet of, II: 175-77; armaments manufacture by, II: 185; note from delegation, II: 206; question of protection of minorities in, II: 214, 215; credentials of plenipotentiaries, II: 230-31, 235; Orlando's objections to preamble of treaty, II: 264
Austria-Hungary, I: 245; debt of, II: 529; successor states, I: 8, 422; II: 575
Autobiography, An (Flexner), I: xn7
Avksentiev, Nikolai Dmitrievich, II: 123
aviation, I: 255; airfields in Germany, I: xiii, 420,n1; II: 185
Ayasalouk, Turkey, II: 116, 117
Ayvalik, Turkey, II: 116
Aydin, Turkey: see Aidin
Azores, I: 438

Backa, Yugoslavia, I: 133
Baden, Grand Duchy of, II: 463, 494
Baghdad Railroad, II: 136
Bailey, Thomas A., II: 480n3
Baker, Ray Stannard, I: xxxvn4; diary of, I: 54n3
Balfour, Arthur James, I: 129, 424, 478; II: 272, 583; on Hungary and Rumania, I: 95; on discussion of peace preliminaries, I: 236; on Luxembourg, I: 248; on Heligoland, I: 249, 252-53, 254; on Danish border, I: 249, 256-57; on Belgian-German border, I: 249, 259; on rectification of Dutch-German border, I: 249, 257, 258-64; on situation in Baltic states, I: 258; on requiring Germany to reveal production secrets of gas and chemicals, I: 267; opposed to Persian representation at peace conference, I: 341; letter to Italian government, I: 342, 356; interview with Japanese representative, I: 396,n4, 399-400; on extraterritoriality for Japanese-held railroad in China, I: 404; draft declaration on Shantung, I: 406; on submarine cables, I: 438,n3, 462-63; opposed to compensating Italy with Smyrna, II: 37; on Sonnino, II: 40; reply to German labor proposals, II: 43; calls for a single mandate over Turkish territory, II: 84n1; on establishing Hungarian, Rumanian, and Czechoslovak frontiers, II: 420, 444, 445,n6; on possibility of separate peace with several German states; drafts reply to Turks, II: 477; on Allied advance on Germany in event of German failure to sign treaty, II: 499-500; statement to Ottoman representatives, II: 507,n1, 520, 602; on sinking of German fleet at Scapa Flow, II: 520, 521, 522, 532, 545; on possible French occupation of Essen, II: 537; on demanding withdrawal of Italian troops from Asia Minor and Fiume, II: 574, 575, 587,n2
Balfour Declaration, I: 480n2
Balfour Mission, II: 37n2
Balkans, Balkan peninsula: WW's interest in keeping great powers out of, I: 283
Balkan War, II: 336
The Baltic Provinces: Report of Mission to Finland, Esthonia, Latvia, and Lithuania on the Situation in the Baltic Provinces (Hale), I: 73n5
Baltic Sea, I: 20; II: 145
Baltic states, I: 72-73n5; II: 124, 427, 485; anti-Bolshevik forces in, I: 72,n5, 167n4; continued German presence in, I: 72n5; II: 344, 425, 514, 523, 550; R. H. Lord on creating commission to study, I: 258, 399; borders of, II: 3; H. Hoover recommends aid to, II: 124,n6, 203,n3, 204; relations with Russia, II: 203; assistance to, II: 204n3; German invasion of Estonia, II: 343, 344; and ending blockade, II: 484, 485; and rolling stock, II: 523-24, 549-50; proposed Inter-Allied military mission, II: 550
Baltic States—The Years of Independence: Estonia, Latvia, Lithuania, 1917-1940, The (von Rauch), I: 73n5
Baltische Landeswehr, I: 72
Baluchistan, II: 95
Banat, The, I: 133; II: 66
Banca Commerciale di Fiume, I: 134
Bardens, Dennis, II: 52n2

Bark, Petr L'vovich, II: 5, 15
Barnes, George Nicoll, I: 424; II: 46, 67, 269, 404, 428, 438, 440
Barrère, Camille-Eugène-Pierre, I: 466; II: 187, 188, 208-209
Baruch, Bernard Mannes, I: 6n2, 80, 85,n3, 370n1; II: 270, 271n3, 287, 470n1
Barzilai, Salvatore, I: 286, 341
Basel, Switzerland, I: 382, 383
Bauer, Gustav Adolf, II: 512n1
Bavaria, II: 187, 217, 298; victualing of, I: 103,n5, 104, 183; declaration of soviet republic in, I: 183,n5, 234-35; question of presentation of credentials, I: 408, 420; possible occupation of, II: 22, 463, 464, 494, 498
Bavarian Peasants' League, I: 183n5, 234
Bedford College, I: ix
Beer, George Louis, II: 106n5
Béla Kun and the Hungarian Soviet Republic: The Origins and Role of the Communist Party of Hungary in the Revolutions of 1918-1919 (Tökés), I: 10n2
Belgian Relief Commission, I: 208n2
Belgian Socialist party, I: 415
Belgium, I: 370, 427n1, 435, 461; II: 293; and revision of Treaty of 1839, I: 91; presents claims to Council of Ten, I: 91n6; and Luxembourg, I: 91n6, 239, 247, 410, 415, 459; II: 179; and request for priority in reparation, I: 135, 411; and reparation, I: 173, 174, 175, 176, 177, 411-19, 427, 456; as possible prosecutor of William II, I: 191, 239; borders of, I: 249, 257, 258-64; II: 3; Declaration of Sainte-Adresse, I: 411-12; possibility of absence from meeting with German delegates, I: 416; on question of railroads, II: 451, 456; to participate in commission to oversee execution of military clauses, II: 507
Belgrade, I: 74
Belin, Gen. Emile-Eugène, II: 350
Belsk (now Bielsk, Poland), II: 148
Beneš, Eduard, I: 386; II: 88, 207, 362, 393n5, 481, 560; on assumption of war costs by Czechoslovakia and new states, II: 231; wishes universal discussion of disarmament, II: 317-18; on Hungarian aggression against Czechoslovakia, II: 320, 322, 339, 362n1, 445n6; proposed withdrawal of Czechs from Russia, II: 551n8, 561,n6
Benson, Adm. William Shepherd, I: 182n4, 375, 377, 385n3; II: 80-81; on Heligoland, I: 253, 255; on destruction of German ships, I: 376
Berbera, British Somaliland, II: 55, 59
Bérenger, Victor-Henry, II: 161, 545
Berlin, I: 116, 141; situation in, II: 103, 459-60; possible Allied march on should Germany fail to sign treaty, II: 20, 21, 270, 464, 494; burning of French flags in, II: 528
Berliner Tageblatt, I: 32, 342; II: 349
Bern, Switzerland, II: 43
Bernard, Georges-François, I: viii
Bernstorff, Johann Heinrich Count von, I: 32, 446
Berthelot, Gen. Philippe-Joseph-Louis, I: 10, 11; II: 214-15
Bertram, Adolf Cardinal, II: 308,n4
Bessarabia, Rumania, I: 505; II: 333
Bethmann Hollweg, Theobald von, I: 416; requests to be tried for war crimes in place of Kaiser, I: xxxiv; II: 598, 599
Bikaner, Maharaja Shri Sir Ganga Singh Bahadur, II: 59, 98
Birdsall, Paul M., I: 6n2, 55n1, 105n1
Birkenhead, Frederick Edwin Smith, 1st Earl of, II: 275,n6
Bismarck-Schoenhausen, Otto Eduard Leopold von, Prince, I: 36, 101
Black Sea, I: 9n1; II: 31, 58n5, 145
Bliss, Howard Sweetser, I: 39
Bliss, Gen. Tasker Howard, I: 249, 271, 429n2, 430, 446; II: 309, 354, 472; on Bolshevism, I: 46; on size of German and Austrian armies, II: 183-84, 191; reservations to Supreme War Council Note No. 43, II: 338,n2; on situation in Russia, II: 483; on military action in event of German failure to sign treaty, II: 474, 497; proposal to secure Hungarian and Rumanian withdrawal from Czechoslovakia, II: 500,n1; on Hungarian affairs, II: 603

INDEX 637

blockade: R. Cecil recommends lifting, II: 9-10; will be lifted upon signing of treaty, II: 11; Lloyd George wishes to resume if Germany refuses to sign treaty, II: 425,n1, 426; *see also* Inter-Allied Blockade Council
Blücher von Wahlstatt, Gebhard Leberecht, Prince, I: 31, 36
Board of Trade (Great Britain), II: 176, 177
Boers, I: 487
Boer War, I: 298
Bohemia: *see* Czechoslovakia
Böhm, Vilmos, I: 503n4
Bolsheviks, Bolshevism, I: 501; and Hungary, I: 74n9, 75; and Baltic states, I: 167n4; Kolchak and, II: 15, 123, 484; reply to Nansen's proposal, II: 104,n3, 122,n3; Hoover on Baltic states and, II: 124,n6, 203,n3, 204; and Polish-Ukrainian situation, II: 125, 144, 147; and Ukrainians, II: 205; Kramář on, II: 379; and Czech troops in Siberia, II: 528, 551, 561; *see also* Russia; Prinkipo Declaration
Bolsheviks in the Ukraine: The Second Campaign, 1918-1919 (Adams), I: 9n1
Bomst, II: 455
Bon, Adm. Ferdinand-Jean-Jacques de, I: 357, 375, 376, 377, 438, 464, 485; II: 31, 81; on Heligoland, I: 253-56
Bonar Law, Andrew: *see* Law, Andrew Bonar
Bonin Longare, Count Lelio, I: 427, 444,n1, 474, 475, 478, 482, 485
Borden, Sir Robert (Laird), I: 371, 372, 373, 381, 382, 490-91
Borel, Eugene, I: xn8
Borghese, Prince Luca Livio, I: 73, 74,n7,8, 75, 92, 93
Bosnia-Herzegovina, I: 133
Bosporus, II: 58n5
Botha, Gen. Louis, I: 487; II: 86, 104, 126, 269; on Poland, II: 147, 148, 149, 150
Bottomley, Horatio William, I: 226
Bourgeois, Léon-Victor-Auguste, II: 348
Bowman, Isaiah, I: xliii, xliv, xlvii, xlviii, xlix, l, lii
Boxer Rebellion: and indemnity, I: 326
Brambilla, Guiseppe, II: 203n2

Brătianu, Ion I. C., I: 12-13; II: 332,n5, 362, 393,n5, 401, 419; and minorities rights, II: 291n6, 335, 341; on arms limitation, II: 316-17; and hostilities with Hungary, II: 320n3, 352, 376-77, 377-78
Brazil, I: 370, 395, 398
Brazza (now Brac Island, Yugoslavia), II: 240
Bremen, Germany, I: 203; II: 443
Breslau, II: 311
Brest, France, I: 182n4, 453, 529
Brest-Litovsk, Treaty of, I: 165; possible annulment of by Germany, I: 459, 460
Briand, Aristide, I: 344, 437n2
British Documents on Foreign Affairs: Reports and Papers from the Foreign Office Confidential Print (Dockrill), II: 269n1
British Somaliland, II: 55
Brockdorff-Rantzau, Ulrich Karl Christian, Count von, I: xxii, 33,n4, 296, 317n1, 424, 443, 445, 477, 478; II: 3,n1, 7, 17, 67n2, 141, 167n3, 300,n5, 384,n3, 401; attitudes toward treaty provisions, I: 354; notes on treaty provisions, II: 18n1, 85,n3, 116-17,n3, 128,n3, 178,n1,2; draft of international agreement on labor law, II: 42,n1; approves speeches by P. Scheidemann and K. Fehrenbach, II: 69,n1; "Observations of the German Delegation on the Conditions of Peace," II: 256,n2, 258-63, 300n5; replaced as head of delegation by Von Haniel, II: 512
Brown, Philip Marshal, II: 104n4
Brusa, Turkey (now Bursa, Turkey), II: 72,n4, 84n1, 129
Brussels, Belgium, I: 136
Brussels Agreement, I: 104n6
Bryant, Russell, I: 55n1
Buccari (now Bakar, Yugoslavia), I: 127; II: 51, 53, 109,n7, 131
Bucharest, Rumania, I: 165
Budapest, Hungary: possible Allied occupation of, I: 45; II: 105
Budrum (Bodrum), Turkey, II: 48, 92
Bukovina, Rumania, II: 144, 145, 238
Buldur, Turkey, I: 482
Bulgaria, I: 477, 483; II: 191, 336, 583;

Bulgaria (cont.)
　Italian occupation of, I: 482, 484; disarmament of, I: 483, 484; borders of, II: 3; size of future military establishment, II: 314n1
Bullard, Rear Adm. William Nannum Brubb, II: 53
Bullitt, William Christian, I: 208n2
Bülow, Bernhard von, Prince, I: 294
Burnett, Philip M., I: xix, 6n2, 50n1, 111n7; II: 577n2

cables: see submarine cables
Cabrini, Angiolo, II: 47
Cadets: see Russian Constitutional Democrats
Cahen-Salvador, Georges-Joseph-Ernest, II: 181; wishes to coordinate repatriation of prisoners with that of German workers and accused prisoners of war, I: 409, 410
Caliphate: see Ottoman Empire
Calthorpe, Adm. Sir Somerset Arthur Gough-, II: 30-31,n1, 39, 40, 41, 47, 115
Cambon, Jules-Martin, II: 231; on first meeting with German delegation, I: 419, 424, 443; language to be used at conference, I: 443
Cambon, Paul, I: 42,n2; II: 37, 588
Cameroons, I: 313, 496, 508; II: 130, 275, 582
Canada, I: 42, 382; II: 275; and submarine cables, I: 464; and membership in labor organization, I: 490-91
Canal des Houillères, I: 59
Canton, China: British claims concerning, I: 423
Caporetto, Battle of, I: 209,n3, 253n1, 301
Carinthia, Italy, II: 218,n4, 219, 254, 255, 307, 336
Carnegie Endowment for International Peace, I: xi
Carniola, Italy, I: 132
Carpathian Mountains, I: 44n5
Carthaginian Peace or the Economic Consequences of Mr. Keynes, The (E. Mantoux), I: xi, xix
Cartier de Marchienne, Émile-Ernest, Baron de, I: 435

Castlereagh, Robert Stewart, I: 56
Cattaro (now Kotor, Yugoslavia), I: 127, 280
Caucasus, I: 483, 484,n3; II: 95
Cavallero, Gen. Ugo, II: 17, 75, 253, 351, 380; on military action in event of German failure to sign treaty, II: 497-98
Cecil, Lord Robert (Edgar Algernon Robert Gascoyne-Cecil), II: 64-65, 122,n4, 126,n1, 253, 270, 271, 331, 347n10,11, 348, 403, 486, 542, 588,n3, 596n1; opposes inclusion of principle of racial equality in League of Nations Covenant, I: 399n7; wishes to establish form of mandates, I: 479; on European unemployment, II: 9; raw materials and credits, II: 9-10; discusses difficulties faced by Polish economy, II: 9; wishes blockade to be lifted, II: 9-10; drafts plan for mandate system, II: 563; on transition from Supreme Economic Council to League of Nations, II: 597
Cellere, Count Vincenzo Macchi di, I: 475-76,n1; II: 106n5
Centenaire Woodrow Wilson, I: xi
Chaikovskii, Nikolai Vasil'evich, I: 429, 502; on Kolchak government, I: 501; II: 25-26,n7,8, 27, 28, 189, 205
Chamberlain, (Joseph) Austen, II: 270, 275, 287
Chantilly, France, I: 429; II: 478
Charles I (of Austria-Hungary): and question of responsibilities, I: 110; II: 6
Charles I (of England), I: 192
Château de Villette, France, I: 116, 145; II: 154
Chemin des Dames, France, I: 25,n1
Cherso (now Cres, Yugoslavia), I: 279, 304, 337; II: 51, 240, 241, 323-24, 328
Chi, Madeleine, I: 251n5
Chicago Tribune, II: 273,n4
China, Chinese: treaties with Japan regarding Kiaochow, I: 251n4, 320; Sino-Japanese Treaty of 1915, I: 273, 320, 329; and Tsingtao Railroad, I: 312-13, 320, 323, 401, 401-402, 406, 425n4; negotiations with Japan on Kiaochow and Shantung Province, I:

320; places loan with Japan, I: 320; Sino-Japanese convention of 1918, I: 320, 329, 333, 334, 405; question of extraterritoriality for commercial enterprises, I: 325, 401, 406; Makino on difficulties caused by extraterritoriality in, I: 326; Balfour's draft declaration on Shantung, I: 406; laborers on western front, I: 493; communications with Wilson, II: 67; wishes to sign treaty with reservations, II: 551, 552

Chinese Eastern Railway, II: 14n1

China Diplomacy, 1914-1918 (Chi), I: 251n5

Chinda, Viscount Sutemi: on Japanese treaties with China, I: 322; on merger of mining company with Tsingtao Railroad, I: 323, 324; on Japanese control of railroad in China, I: 402, 403, 425,n4; proposal for *de facto* recognition of Omsk government, II: 201-202

Chine & Japon à le Conférence de Paix (Thaddée), I: 251n3

Chios, Greece, II: 41, 116

Churchill, Winston Leonard Spencer, II: 101, 275, 467, 528; proposed withdrawal of Czechs from Russia, II: 551,n8, 561

Ciencials, Anna, I: 55n1

Cilicia, Turkey, II: 133, 161, 266

Claveille, Albert: on proposed Rhineland Convention, I: 382, 384; on provisions on railroads serving Adriatic ports in Austrian treaty, II: 62-63; on Southern Austrian Railways, II: 593, 594, 594-95, 595–96, 596

Clemenceau, Georges, I: xiii, xxvii, xxviii, 473; on admission of Germany to League of Nations, I: 4, 33; on basis of reparation, I: 5n2; suggests arbitration commission for reparation distribution, I: 21; on Allied approach to Germany, I: 32; on German Social Democrats, I: 33, 34; and disarmament, I: 34; on Bolshevism, I: 35; on opinions of military, I: 35; and Klotz plan for reparation, I: 49; and Saar Valley, I: 54n3, 62, 84, 210, 212; II: 165, 166, 167; on sending commission to Hungary, I: 75, 76, 97-98; on Haller's Army passing through Danzig, I: 102; victualing of Bavaria, I: 104, 183; on Luxembourg, I: 142, 247-48; II: 179, 242-43, 246-47; and issue of specifying amount of reparation, I: 155; and duration of German reparation payment, I: 156; on trying William II, I: 189, 193, 194, 269; II: 548; on responsibility for war, I: 197n1; on bonds issued by Germany, I: 237; on summoning German plenipotentiaries, I: 238, 242-43; on Heligoland, I: 254; on Kiel Canal, I: 268; notes that Treaty of London gives Fiume to Croatia, I: 286; France bound by Treaty of London, I: 297-98, 302; II: 52, 571; on Italian claims, I: 298-99; meets with Wilson on Adriatic question, I: 298; implores Sonnino to compromise on Adriatic question, I: 299; opposed to Haller's Army proceeding to Lemberg, I: 309; may force Germany to accept peace by occupying territory of, I: 310; on Wilson publishing statement on American position on Adriatic question, I: 311; on restrictions on German delegates, I: 317-18; submits final text on disarmament and occupation of left bank of Rhine, I: 318,n2; drafts of French security treaties, I: 319,n3; II: 439; submits texts on Austrian boundaries, I: 319,n4; opposed to German journalists at Versailles, I: 340, 423; on publication of preliminaries, I: 342; suggests Italian departure from conference would break Pact of London, I: 344, 351, 454, 467-68,n3; memorandum with Lloyd George on Adriatic question, I: 345, 346-50; on publishing summary of preliminaries, I: 345, 486; on question of Fiume, I: 345; on period allowed for German review of treaty, I: 387; on provision forbidding Germany from providing instructors to foreign armies or enlisting in them, I: 392-93; on credentials of Serbs, Croats and Slovenes, I: 393-94, 410-11; wishes to wait to recognize Yugoslavia, I: 394; questions credentials to be presented for Bavaria and Saxony, I: 408, 420; on prisoners of war, I: 408, 409, 562;

640 INDEX

Clemenceau, Georges (cont.)
on summoning Austrians and Hungarians, I: 428, 429; on absence of Italian representative at presentation of peace preliminaries to German delegation, I: 436; annoyed by Poincaré's letter to Italy, I: 437; changes venue for Austrians to Saint-Germain, I: 446, 447; on issue of publication of Lloyd George-Clemenceau letter on Italian question, I: 448; on German-Russian relations, I: 459, 460; conversation with Bonin Longare on Adriatic question, I: 475; on landings in Smyrna, I: 505; II: 37-38, 212; on decision to use only written documents for discussion of treaty provisions with German delegation, II: 3; insists upon fulfillment of provisions of Armistice Agreement, II: 8; on lifting blockade upon signing of treaty, II: 11; receives notes from Brockdorff-Rantzau, II: 18,n1, 20,n3, 85,n3, 120n1, 178,n1,2; on condition of Greece, I: 56; on future Austrian military forces, II: 77, 180, 184, 185, 230, 306; on Hungary, II: 79; discusses limiting armaments of eastern European nations, II: 79, 87, 180, 192; armaments manufacture by Austria, II: 82; on publication of treaties, II: 84; and clothing for German prisoners, II: 85; note on Italian landing at Scala Nuova, II: 92-93,n1; on possible Allied occupation of Budapest, II: 105; justifies French landing at Heraclea, II: 111; discusses Lenin's reply to Nansen proposal, II: 122; on German request for extension, II: 125; on French position in Syria, II: 132, 133-34, 162; on sending commission to Syria, II: 135, 137-38, 162, 266; on warning to Poland to cease hostilities with Ukraine, II: 152-53; discusses Sykes-Picot Treaty, II: 160-62, 163, 164; on Italian public opinion toward France, II: 187-88; on possible withdrawal of French troops from Italy, II: 188, 189; on annulment of contracts by mixed tribunals, II: 199; dealing with Austria differently from Germany, II: 208-209; Italian insistence on Fiume will abrogate Treaty of London, II: 212; on summoning nations involved to reading of summary of Austrian treaty, II: 239; on relations with Luxembourg, II: 246-47; on army of occupation and its costs, II: 252, 274, 275, 437,n1, 455; on French public opinion and provisions of treaty, II: 272-73; on plebiscite in Klagenfurt Basin, II: 304; on plebiscite in Upper Silesia, II: 313, 386; on disarmament, II: 320-21; on Hungarian aggression against Czechoslovakia, II: 320, 322, 339; on Hungarian-Rumanian frontier, II: 338; and support of Kolchak, II: 402, 417; requests guarantee for financial clauses of German treaty, II: 405; on publication of treaty, II: 418; on reply to German counterproposal on military clauses, II: 423; discusses occupation of Rhineland, II: 429, 430, 438, 440; on military action should Germany not sign treaty, II: 462, 472, 473, 474, 475; comments upon shift in Foch's position, II: 464-65, 466-67, 472, 478-79; on possibility of separate peace with several German states, II: 499, 501; on scuttling of German fleet at Scapa Flow, II: 513, 522, 535-36, 541; refuses to grant Germans further delay, II: 519, 520,n2; wishes to occupy Essen, II: 536-37, 544-45; suggests Germans sign treaty first, II: 538-39; on Italian presence in Fiume, II: 569; and seals for treaty, II: 585; on Southern Austrian Railways, II: 585, 594, 595, 596; on Bethmann Hollweg's request to be tried for war crimes in place of Kaiser, II: 598; on transmitting minutes of meetings of Council of Four, II: 599, 600, 601
Clemenceau (Duroselle), I: 437n2; II: 473n1
Clémentel, Étienne, I: 370n1; II: 196, 271, 597n1; on tariff rates, I: 371, 373; on foreigners located inside Allied countries, I: 371-72; on merchant ships, I: 371; on mixed tribunals determining annulment of contracts in Alsace-Lorraine, II: 196, 197, 198
coal, II: 388; production of Saar Valley,

INDEX   **641**

I: 56, 58, 227, 228, 229; ownership of Saar mines, II: 165, 166, 167
Collège Chaptel, I: viii
Colliard, Pierre, II: 46
Collonges, France, II: 290n5
Cologne, Germany, II: 20, 22, 101, 475, 494
Commercial Bank of Budapest, I: 134
Commission on Baltic Affairs, II: 203; report on rolling stock, II: 549-50; report on German advance, II: 550
Commission on Belgian and Danish Affairs, I: 91,n6; presents report to Council of Foreign Ministers, I: 139n2, 256n2
Commission on Czechoslovak Affairs, II: 419
Commission on International Labor Legislation: report of, I: 123,n1; II: 443-44,n3
Commission on Polish Affairs, I: 65n8, 272; II: 126, 257, 352, 386,n2; report of printed in newspapers, I: 69,n2; message to Poland insisting upon end to hostilities with Ukraine, I: 501; Report (with Appendixes) presented to the Supreme Council of the Peace Conference for the Negotiation of an Armistice between Poland and the Ukraine, II: 147n2
Commission on Prisoners of War, I: 408n1
Commission on Reparation of Damage: see Reparation Commission
Commission on Rumanian and Yugoslav Affairs, I: 181
Commission on the International Regime of Ports, Waterways, and Railways, I: 140, 343n7, 381-85; II: 6; subcommission on Kiel Canal, I: 250, 356n5, 357; and "Recommendations Regarding the Kiel Canal," I: 257,n1; on provisions on Austrian railroads, II: 61-62, 592-95; on railroad construction and competition, II: 452
Commission on the League of Nations: see League of Nations Commission
Commission on the Responsibility of the Authors of the War and the Enforcement of Penalties, II: 599; report of, I: 110n6, 118,n2

Committee on New States, II: 482, 506n7; report of, II: 88n5, 214,n2, 331,n2
Committee on Rumanian and Yugoslav Affairs, II: 508-12; report of on plebiscite in Klagenfurt Basin, II: 341,n6
Committee on the Eastern Frontiers of Germany, II: 386,n2, 444
Committee on the Verification of Powers, I: 424, 444; II: 230-31
Comte, Auguste, I: vii
Conger, Col. Arthur Latham, I: 445,n2
Congo River, I: 499n1
Congress of Berlin, II: 600, 601
The Congress of Berlin and After: A Diplomatic History of Near Eastern Settlement, 1878-1880 (Medlicott), I: 473n7
Congress of Vienna (1814-1815), I: xix
Constitutional Democrats (Russian), II: 29
Conservatoire des Arts et Métiers, I: xn9
Constantinople, II: 107, 128, 129, 132, 557; and Straits, I: 111; II: 32, 36, 70, 553; possible American occupation of, I: 483; II: 56, 130; Islamic leaders of India on, II: 95-100; see also Ottoman Empire
Contemporary Review, II: 54
"Contribution to the History of the Lost Opportunities of the League of Nations, A" (Mantoux), I: ixn6
Convention Regarding the Military Occupation of the Territories of the Rhine, II: 428,n3, 429, 431-35
Cooperative Bank (of Fiume), I: 134
cordon sanitaire, I: xx-xxi, xxxvi, 45, 46
Corfu: evacuation of, II: 19, 24
Cossacks, II: 14; Don Cossacks support Denikin, II: 550-51
Costa, Alfonso, II: 583
Council of Foreign Ministers (Council of Five), I: 265; on Allied plans for Bavaria, I: 103n5; on prisoners of war, I: 408n1; to discuss question of boundaries of Austria and successor states, II: 5, 6; approves plebiscite for Klagenfurt Basin, II: 218n4
Council of Four, I: xiii, xx, xxxiii, 265, 484n3; Mantoux interprets for, I: ix, xiv; Sir Maurice Hankey becomes sec-

Council of Four (*cont.*)
retary to, I: xiv; on secrecy of proceedings, 599-602
Council of Ten, I: xiii, xxxiii, 484n3; II: 401; Mantoux interprets for, I: ix; appoints Reparation Commission, I: 5n2; on German forces in Baltic, I: 72n5; approves limitation of German army, I: 87,n3; Belgium presents claims to, I: 91n6; requests Polish-Ukrainian truce in Galicia, I: 118n1; discusses report on Polish-German boundaries, I: 199-203; approves plebiscite for Klagenfurt Basin, II: 219; meets with Ottoman representatives, II: 476
Covenant of the League of Nations: see League of Nations
Cowan, Rear Adm. Sir Walter Henry, II: 342,n7
Cracow, Poland, II: 257
Crane, Charles Richard, I: 231n3; II: 132n4
Craonne, France, I: 25n1
Crespi, Silvio Benigno, I: 362, 370, 388n2, 427, 449, 450; II: 214n1, 231,n1, 470n1, 549, 597n1; on Austrian treaty provisions on railroads serving Adriatic ports for Austrian treaty, II: 61; on reparation owed by successor states of Austria-Hungary, I: 492; principle of interdependence of debt, II: 174; on Southern Austrian Railways, II: 592-93, 594
Crete, II: 59
Crimea, I: 9n1
Crimean War, I: 57
Crise du Trade-Unionisme, La (Alfasa and Mantoux), I: vii
Croatia, Croats: Treaty of London gives Fiume to, I: xxii, 125,n4, 303, 308, 315
Cromwell, Oliver, I: 440
Crowe, Sir Eyre (Alexander Barby Wichart), II: 292, 422
Cunliffe, Walter, 1st Baron of Headley, I: 5-6n2, 22; II: 34, 35, 287
Curzola (now Korcula Island, Yugoslavia), II: 240
Curzon, George Nathaniel, 1st Marquis Curzon of Kedleston, II: 108, 133, 134, 136; drafts reply to German delegation's note on economic consequences of the peace, II: redrafts reply, 121, 153,n4, 156-60
Cyprus, II: 56, 552, 556
Czechoslovakia, Czechs, I: 503,n4; II: 21, 91, 231, 238, 314n1, 350,n2, 375-82, 445n6; borders of, I: 144; accepts war costs under a name other than reparations, II: 231; requests return of national monuments, II: 267, 294, 295; amendments proposed by, II: 291,n7; incursions by Hungary, II: 320, 322, 339; on question of railroads, II: 443, 456; repatriation of troops from Russia, II: 528, 551, 561

Dahomey, I: 498
Dalmatia, I: 245n2, 328, 421, 448, 475, 482; II: 236,n1, 240, 281, 324, 328, 340; Italian claims to, I: xxii, 279; II: 51; Treaty of London gives to Italy, I: 125n4, 485, 486; II: 109
Damascus, Syria, I: 231; II: 162, 163, 266
Damascus-Aleppo railroad, II: 163n1
Danzig (now Gdansk, Poland), I: 199, 270, 271; II: 200, 241, 257, 388, 427, 457, 478; map of, I: xliv; aiding Poland through, I: 9; transport of Polish troops through, I: 43,n3, 68-72, 100, 101n4, 102, 113-15; disposition of, I: 18, 20,n4, 101, 102, 106,n3, 107, 108, 123, 199-200,n3; plebiscite in, I: 201-203; II: 281; see also Poland
Danzig-Mława-Warsaw Railway, I: 106n3, 124, 200, 201, 271
Dardenelles, II: 478
Davidson, Most Rev. Randall Thomas, II: 270,n2, 542
Davis, Norman Hezekiah, I: xxxix, 6n2, 80, 109, 236, 388n2; II: 271n3, 337; on amount of reparation, I: 5n2, 16, 157; on proportional distribution of reparations, I: 26, 27; on duration of German reparation payment, I: 149
Day, Clive, II: 218n1
Deák, Francis, I: 10n2
De Bon, Adm. Ferdinand-Jean-Jacques: see Bon, Adm. Ferdinand-Jean-Jacques de

Debreczen, Hungary, II: 376, 377, 381
Declaration of Sainte-Adresse, I: 411-12, 415
Defence of the Realm Act (Great Britain), I: 232
Degoutte, Gen. Joseph, I: 15
Delacroix, Léon, I: 269n1
Délibérations du Conseil des Quatres, Les (Mantoux), I: xviii
Denikin, Anton Ivanovich, I: 12, 15, 484, 501, 502; II: 15, 27, 33, 34, 119, 123, 124, 189, 200, 204, 205; promises democratic reforms, II: 25,n7; troops accused of atrocities, II: 104; progress of forces, II: 204, 550, 551
Denmark, II: 456; and Schleswig, I: 92; II: 456
Dernburg, Bernhard Jakob Ludwig, II: 121
Despret, M., I: 415
Desticker, Gen. Pierre-Henri, II: 186
Deutsche Revolution und wilson-Frieden: Die amerikanische und deutsche Friedensstrategie zwischen Ideologie und Machpolitik 1918/19 (Schwabe), I: 104n5
"Diagrammatic Map of a Future South Slav State" (Evans), I: 301n3
Diaz, Gen. Armando, I: 46; II: 558
Die Pariser Friedenskonferenz 1919 und die Friedensverträge 1919-1920: Literaturbericht und Bibliographie (Guzenhäuser), I: xxx
"Die Politik der Alliierten gegenuber den Freikorps in Baltikum 1918-1919" (Williams), I: 72n5
Dinant, Belgium, I: 190
Diplomatic Documents Submitted to the Italian Parliament by the Minister for Foreign Affairs (Sonnino), Austria-Hungary, Session of the 20th May, 1915, I: 305n1
disarmamant, II: 79-83, 192, 305-306, 317-18, 403; of small powers, II: 79, 87,n4, 88, 180
Disraeli, Benjamin, 1st Earl of Beaconsfield, I: 36; II: 326
Distractions of Peace during War: The Lloyd George Government's Reaction to Woodrow Wilson, December, 1916-November, 1918 (Kernek), I: 66n9

Djibouti, French Somaliland, II: 55
Dmowski, Román, I: 107,n4, 108, 472; II: 90, 151, 234, 285, 453, 454
Dniester River, I: 115
Dobruja, Bulgaria, II: 79
Dockrill, M., II: 269n1
Dodecanese Islands, I: xxiv, 125n4, 480n3, 482, 494; II: 39, 131, 137, 586-87, 603; Austria-Hungary renounces claims to, I: 285n6
Don: government of the, II: 119
Donnersmarck, Count Henckel von (Guidotto Karl Lazarus), II: 280
Drafting Committee, I: 110, 258, 383, 451, 461; II: 24, 71, 456n5; phrasing treaty articles, I: 388,n1, 449, 457; question of prosecution of war criminals no longer nationals of Austria-Hungary, II: 66; and articles on responsibilities and sanctions, II: 255-56; clauses of Austrian treaty, II: 228, 251, 292, 329; on naval provisions of Armistice (Art. 31), II: 531-32
Drava River, II: 219, 268
dreadnoughts, I: 495
Drummond, Sir (James) Eric, I: 488
Druse Mountains, II: 161-62
Dulles, John Foster, II: 122, 576, 578
Dunne, Edward Fitzsimons, I: 500n1
Dupont, Gen. Charles-Joseph, II: 186, 438, 528, 539, 562
Duroselle, Jean-Baptiste, I: 437n2; II: 473n1
Dutasta, Paul-Eugène, I: 487, 493; II: 210, 239, 538

Earle, Edward Meade, I: 336n3
East Prussia, I: xxiv, xxv, 124, 199; II: 309, 311n7, 341
Eastman, Mark, I: x
Ebert, Friedrich, I: 445; II: 329, 349
Echo de Paris, I: 69n2
École des Hautes Études Commerciales, I: viii
École des Hautes Études Sociales, I: vii-viii
École Normale Superieure, I: vii
Economic Commission: *see* Supreme Economic Commission
Economic Consequences of the Peace (Keynes), I: xi, xxxviiin9, 6n2

Egypt, II: 99, 128, 552, 556, 568
Eisner, Kurt: assassination of, I: 183n5
Elbe River, I: 374
Emden, Germany, I: 203
Emergence of Modern Lithuania, The (Senn), II: 27n11
English Historical Review, I: viiin2
Entente cordiale, I: 42
Epstein, Fritz T., I: 445n2
Erivan, U.S.S.R., II: 555
Erskine, William Augustus Forbes, I: 466
Erzberger, Matthias, I: 184; II: 273,n4; on Haller's Army transiting Danzig, I: 166-67n4; Germany will sign if Fourteen Points are respected, I: 445-46
Essen, Germany, II: 141; Clemenceau wishes to occupy, II: 536-37
Estonia, II: 26-27,n10, 204n3, 424, 425, 550; German troops in, I: 72n5; attacking Petrograd, II: 342; Adm. Hope on situation in, II: 344
Eupen, Germany, I: 91n6, 138, 259; and Hertogenwald Forest, I: 259; map of, I: xliv
Eupen-Malmédy Railroad, I: 139, 259
Evans, Sir Arthur John, I: 301n3
Eyschen, Paul, I: 143

Fabian Society, I: vii, ix
Faisal I (Emir), I: 39, 231, 380; II: 132, 266, 267, 554, 569-70,n2
Falk, Oswald Toynbee, I: 430,n5
Fayolle, Gen. Marie-Émile, II: 498
Fehrenbach, Konstantin, II: 69,n1
Ferid Paşa, Damad, II: 255,n1
Fifield, Russell H., I: 251n5
Financial Commission, I: 125; II: 295, 504n3; report of, I: 388-92,n1; II: 231n2
Finland, I: 258; Hoover recommends recognition of, I: 399; German-Finnish Army, I: 399
First Savings Bank of Zagreb, I: 134
Fisher, Herbert Albert Laurens, II: 270
Fiume (now Rijeka, Yugoslavia), I: xxii, 125,n4, 126, 277-79, 337, 343,n7, 421n2, 428, 448, 466, 470, 475, 479, 482, 485, 486, 494; II: 51, 52, 106, 131, 212, 236n1, 240-42, 323, 569, 571, 587; nationalities in, I: 126-27; possibility of free city status, I: 127; II: 328, 340; Trumbić on, I: 129-35; Sušak, I: 130, 131; II: 323,n2; and shipping, I: 133; banking in, I: 134; Orlando discusses Polish precedents for Italian claim to, I: 278; historic background of Italian claim to, I: 279; memorandum by Lloyd George and Clemenceau on, I: 346-50; Sonnino on, I: 369; Italy sending vessels to, I: 385, 453; Italian Council of the City of, II: 53; Miller-House proposal, II: 109n7; plebiscite in, II: 131, 281; and railroads, II: 341
Fiume, Gulf of, I: 304
Flensburg, Schleswig-Holstein: city of, I: 256
Flexner, Abraham, M.D., I: x,n7
Foch, Ferdinand, I: 437n2; II: 4, 234, 257, 473n1,2; wishes to create *cordon sanitaire* to contain Bolshevism, I: xxi, 45; on occupation of left bank of the Rhine, I: xxxvi, 86,n1, 89; II: 253, 271; on situation in Rumania, I: 14, 15; on Odessa, I: 14; and transport of Polish troops through Danzig, I: 43,n3, 70, 101n4, 113-15; plans to aid Rumania, I: 44; limit on time for discussion with Germany on transit of Danzig by Haller's Army, I: 72; discusses transit of Haller's Army through Germany at Spa, I: 72, 113-14, 115; report on negotiations at Spa, I: 166,n4; on action should Germany not sign treaty, I: 184n6; II: 20-22, 210-11, 461-62, 462-64, 494-95; reports on Army of Occupation, II: 20, 100-101, 101-102, 103; report on situation between Rumania and Hungary, II: 307,n1; on possibility of separate peace with various German states, II: 464, 466, 468-69, 478,n1, 494-95, 495-96; interview with London *Daily Mail*, II: 473n2
Foch versus Clemenceau: France and German Dismemberment 1918-1919 (King), II: 473n1
Fogazzaro, Antonio, II: 299,n3
Fontainebleau Memorandum, I: xxxvi, 31n1
Food Commission: and Odessa, I: 11

Formation of the Baltic States: A Study of the Effect of Great Power Politics upon the Emergence of Lithuania, Latvia, and Estonia (Page), I: 73n5
Fortnightly Review, II: 54
Fortune publique de la France, La (Théry), I: 24n1
Fosdick, Raymond Blaine, I: x
Foster, Sir George Eulas, I: 370n1
Fourteen Points, I: 28, 29, 30, 138, 415; II: 95, 106, 107, 458; address, I: 66n9; Wilson on, I: 181-82,n4, 245n2, 291,n1; Wilson says spirit of supersedes Treaty of London, II: 223
France: desire for Rhenish Republic, I: xx, 39,n1; demands of concerning the Saar Valley, I: xx, 54,n3; and trial of William II and others for war crimes, I: xx, 189; security treaties, I: xxxiii,n1, 39n1, 319,n3, 488, 489,n1; II: 439, 589,n4, 590-92; national wealth of, I: 24, 25; public reaction to Wilson's threatened departure, I: 182n4; Franco-Japanese treaty, I: 320; Declaration of Sainte-Adresse, I: 411-12, 415; participation in landing at Smyrna, II: 29; possibility of mandate over Turkey, II: 55, 70; on reaffirming unity of purpose with Italy, II: 212n1; burning of French flags in Berlin, II: 528; major shareholder in Southern Austrian Railways, II: 594, 596
France and her Eastern Allies, 1919-1925: French-Czechoslovak-Polish Relations from the Paris Peace Conference to Locarno (Wandycz), I: 61n6
France-Italie, I: 437,n2
France's Rhineland Diplomacy, 1914-1924: The Last Bid for a Balance of Power in Europe (McDougall), I: 40n1
Franchet d'Esperey, Gen. Louis-Félix-Marie-François, I: 15, 483, 505, 506,n1; II: 83, 105, 350, 351, 353, 375, 376; on situation in Odessa, I: 10; on Bulgarian boundary, I: 69; on Army of the East and situation in Rumania, II: 320n2
Frankfurter Zeitung, I: 137
French, Field Marshal Sir John, I: 501
French Congo, I: 499n1

Friedrich Wilhelm Viktor August Ernst, Crown Prince of Prussia and of Germany, II: 558,n2, 559, 569
Friesland, I: 263
Fromageot, Henri-Auguste, I: 449, 451, 454, 457, 481; II: 265, 521, 531, 581
From the Dreadnought to Scapa Flow: The Royal Navy in the Fisher Era, 1904-1919 (Marder), II: 513n5
Fryatt, Capt. Charles Algernon, I: 121,n3
Furth-im-Wald, Germany, II: 379, 451

Galbraith, John Kenneth, I: viiin4
Galicia, II: 145, 217, 234; Polish-Ukrainian conflict over, I: 44,n4, 118,n1, 144; II: 238; Ukrainian atrocities in, II: 312; plebiscite in, II: 420
gas and gas warfare, I: 185, 198, 255; German manufacturing secrets, I: 266-67, 393
Gelderland, I: 91n6, 263
General Confederation of Labor of Luxembourg, II: 244
George V (of Great Britain), I: 42n2, 97,n8, 120
George Washington, U.S.S., I: 182n4, 453,n3
Georgia (Russian), I: 484
Gérard, Gen. Augustin-Grégoire-Arthur, II: 475
The German Delegation at the Paris Peace Conference (Luckau), I: 318
German East Africa: to be administered as mandate of the League of Nations, I: 479
German High Seas Fleet: see Scapa Flow
Germany, I: xxiv; map of, I: liii; admission to League of Nations, I: 4; II: 403; and ability to pay reparation, I: 5-9; loses highly productive areas, I: 17, 18; Weimar government lacks credit, I: 20; and transport of Polish troops through Danzig, I: 70n3, 113-15; troops in Lithuania, Latvia, and Estonia, I: 72n5; occupation of, I: 84; size of future military forces of, I: 87n3; II: 80, 82, 183, 191, 315; would allow Polish troops to transit by rail, I: 100, 115; and Brussels Agreement, I: 104n6; and border with Czechoslovakia, I: 144; issuance of bonds, I:

Germany (cont.)
171, 172, 218, 221, 224, 236; and imposition of mark in occupied territories, I: 176, 176-77; Polish border, I: 199-203; border with Belgium, I: 258-63; right to raise and use cables cut during the war, I: 275; disposition of Kiaochow, I: 313, 397; delegates to leave for Paris on April 28, I: 317,n1; on destruction of ships under provisions of treaty, I: 377-78; Financial Commission on, I: 388-92; provision for construction of airfields in, I: 420,n1; proposed text of renunciation of Chinese concession in Canton, I: 423n3; question of buying back marks from Alsace-Lorraine, I: 432-34; disposition of merchant ships, I: 442; colonies of to become mandates under League of Nations, I: 479; failure to deliver ships in Spanish ports as provided for in Armistice Agreement, II: 8; requisitioning securities, II: 10; note on labor legislation, II: 42,n1; P. Scheidemann's speech on preliminary peace terms in National Assembly, II: 49-50,n1; note on Saar Basin, II: 85,n3, 165n1, 167n3; requests delay in delivery of observations on treaty, II: 125; distribution of merchant fleet of, II: 175-77; distribution of captured shipping of, II: 176; "Observations of the German Delegation on the Conditions of Peace," II: 256,n2, 258-63; attacks Estonia, II: 342, 344; to make estimate of reparation, II: 363; border with Lithuania, II: 460; resignation of Scheidemann cabinet, II: 512,n1; and formation of new government, II: 512,n1; prepared to sign treaty with reservations, II: 512, 515-18; Allied reply to request for extension prior to signing treaty, II: 520,n2; burning French flags in Berlin, II: 528, 539; continued presence in Baltic provinces, II: 550; note on violation of Armistice by scuttling of warships at Scapa Flow, II: 556; wishes to inform residents on both sides of new Polish border of precise time of change, II: 559

Gerson, Louis L., I: 107n4
Gex, French territory: neutral zone and free zone in, I: 493; II: 290,n5
Ghent, Belgium, I: 91n6
Gibson, Hugh Simons, I: 355, 358; II: 103
Gibson, Capt. Thomas, I: 297
Giesberts, Johann, I: 317n1, 557
Giolitti, Giovanni, II: 329
Gladstone, William Ewart, II: 326
Glogau, Poland, I: 341
Gold Coast, I: 498, 499
Gordon, Gen. Charles G. (Chinese), I: 406,n1
Gordon, John R., II: 549
Gough, Lt. Gen. Sir Hubert de la Poer, II: 344, 523, 550
Gounaris, Demetrios, II: 114
Gouraud, Gen. Henri-Joseph-Eugène, II: 266
Gout, Jean-Étienne-Paul, I: 378
Graduate Institute of International Studies (Institut Universitaire des Hautes Études Internationales Geneve), I: ix,n6, x, xi
Grant Scuttle: The Sinking of the German Fleet at Scapa Flow in 1919, The (Van der Vat), II: 513n5
Grassi, Rear Adm., II: 533
Graves, Maj. Gen. William Sidney, II: 14n2
Grayson, Rear Adm. Cary Travers: diary of, I: 3n1, 181n4, 234n2, 294n4; II: 291n6, 473n1
Graz, Austria, II: 298
Great Britain, I: 438; and trial of William II and others for war crimes, I: xx, 189, 191, 193, 194, 269; II: 548; security treaty with France, I: 39n1, 319, 488, 489,n1; II: 439, 589,n4, 590-92; on French demands on Saar Valley, I: 54n3, 65, 84, 165, 166, 167, 211, 212; Archduke Joseph proposes alliance with, I: 97,n8; attitude of Parliament on reparation, I: 147,n3; public opinion in, I: 169; II: 271, 274, 542; secret agreement with Japan regarding German territories in the Pacific, I: 215n3, 321-22; Declaration of Sainte-Adresse, I: 411-12, 415; claims concerning Canton, I: 423

INDEX

"Great Britain and the Making of the Treaty of Trianon" (Sakmyster), I: 97n8

Greece, Greeks, I: 63; II: 314n1; possibility of landing troops in Smyrna, I: 505, 506; II: 38, 109n1; requests Allied evacuation of Corfu, II: 19; threat of massacre of in Smyrna, II: 41, 47, 111; condition of, II: 56; negotiates with Entente to aid Serbia in return for concessions in Asia Minor, II: 114; refugees, II: 116; landing in Smyrna, II: 212, 568; and losses of merchant shipping, II: 583-84

Grey, Edward, Viscount Grey of Fallodon, I: 42,n2, 344; II: 114, 598; protested Twenty-One Demands, I: 332

Gross Wartenberg (now Sycow, Poland), II: 308,n4

Guerra Diplomatica, Ricordi e Frammenti di Diario (1914-1919) (Aldrovandi Marescotti), I: xvn3, xxxvn6

Guhrau (now Gora, Poland), II: 270

Gulf of Kiaochow, I: 397, 426

Guillaumat, Gen. Marie-Louis-Adolphe, I: 15

Gurk River, II: 302

Guzenhäuser, Max, I: xxx

Haase, Hugo, II: 65, 290,n4
Haguenin, Émile, II: 238
Haifa, Palestine, II: 161
Haig, Field Marshal Douglas, 1st Earl Haig, II: 88, 474, 558
Haking, Lt. Gen. Sir Richard Cyril Byrne, I: 183
Hale, Robert, I: 73n5
Haller, Gen. Józef, II: 234, 257, 309, 322-23; troops of sent to Poland, I: 43n3, 68, 100, 101n4, 113-15, 166n4; II: 102; army to proceed to Lemberg, I: 309; II: 86; Council of Four warns to cease hostilities in Ukraine, II: 153, 154,n5, 155-56, 233
Hamburg, Germany, I: 203; II: 442, 443, 486
Hamburg-Baghdad Plan, I: 325,n3
Hancock, William Keith, I: 36n6
Haniel von Haimhausen, Edgar Karl Alfons, I: 296; II: 546-47, 547, 557, 558; note pointing out inconsistencies between treaty text and Clemenceau letter, II: 503,n1, 505n4; becomes head of German delegation, II: 512

Hankey, Lt. Col. Sir Maurice (Pascal Alers), I: 450, 501; II: 32n1, 60, 109n7, 154, 286, 395, 427, 599; becomes Secretary to Council of Four, I: xiv, xxxiv; workload of Drafting Committee, I: 270; delivers Lloyd George's proposal on Adriatic question to Orlando and Sonnino, I: 307; reports Italian Ministers inflexible on Adriatic question, I: 310; on recognition of Yugoslavia, I: 394; Allied protest against Italian landings in Asia Minor, II: 572

Hankey: Man of Secrets (Roskill), I: xvin4, 294n4

Hannover, Germany, II: 217, 498
Hanseatic League, I: 106
Hapgood, Norman, II: 456,n4
Hapsburg, Archduke Joseph Ferdinand of: requests alliance with Great Britain, I: 97,n8
Hardinge, Charles, 1st Baron Hardinge of Penshurst, I: 420
Harris, Ernest Lloyd, II: 334n7
Haskins, Charles Homer, I: xlv, 55n1, 83n1, 91n6, 109, 123, 185, 195, 199n3, 204, 207, 214n2, 230, 260, 357,n6
Hauser, Henri, I: viii, xn8
Hawkins, Capt. William, II: 97
Headlam-Morley, Agnes, I: 55n1
Headlam-Morley, James Wycliffe: on various treaty provisions, I: 55n1, 83n1, 106, 123, 185, 199n3, 207, 214n2, 230, 357n6; II: 90, 166, 214, 215, 229, 286, 392,n4, 506, 525-26
Hearst, William Randolph: press, I: 232, 453
Hedjaz, The, II: 266
Heim, Georg, I: 234, 235; II: 102; suggests partition of Germany, II: 186-87
Heligoland: dismantling of naval facilities at, I: 252-56; II: 562
Helvetic Confederation, I: 493
Henderson, Arthur, II: 68
Hennocque, Gen. Edmond-Charles-Adolphe, II: 351, 380
Henry, Lt. Col. Marie-Joseph, II: 125; on German threat to leave Paris, I: 481

Henrys, Gen. Paul-Prosper, I: 96, 483; II: 234
Heraclea Pontica, II: 57, 58,n5, 83, 109n1; Clemenceau justifies French landing at, II: 111
Hertogenwald Forest, I: 259, 260, 261
Hesse, II: 288
Hindenburg, Paul Ludwig Hans Anton von Beneckendorff und von, I: 70
Hipwood, Charles, II: 549
History of the Peace Conference of Paris (Temperley), I: li, 55n1, 61n6
Hohenlohe-Schillingsfürst, Chlodwig Karl Viktor von, I: 57
Holland: *see* The Netherlands
Homs, Syria, II: 162
Hoover, Herbert Clark, II: 88, 122n4, 485, 523, 596n1, 599; victualing of Bavaria, I: 103n5, 104,n6; victualing of Russia, I: 208n2; on Hungary, I: 257, 386; recommends lifting German blockade, I: 340; recommends recognition of Finland, I: 399; recommends aid to Baltic states, II: 203,n3, 204
Hope, Adm. George Price: on Heligoland, I: 253, 254-55; on destruction of German ships, I: 376; on Estonian situation, II: 344; on scuttling of German fleet at Scapa Flow, II: 521, 534
Horvat (Horvath), Gen. Dmitrii Leonidovich, II: 14n1, 483
Hôtel Crillon, I: 40n1; II: 277
Hôtel Edouard VII, I: 307
Hôtel Majestic, II: 269
House, Edward Mandell, I: xiii, 6n2, 55n1, 145, 429n2, 440n5; II: 106n5, 210, 347,n10,11, 403; diary of, I:16n1, 54n3, 182n4; II: 347n11; and formation of Rhenish Republic, I: 39n1; and duration of German reparation payment, I: 150; and reparation for Belgium, I: 154; victualing of Russia, I: 208n2; prevents Orlando from adding reservations to Points 9, 10, 11, 12, I: 293,n3; Tardieu plan, II: 236,n1; on summoning nations involved to reading of summary of Austrian treaty, II: 239
Howard, Sir Esme (William), II: 125-26, 203n2,3
Howard, Harry N., I: 231n3

Hudson, Manley Ottmer, I: 440n5; II: 418
Hughes, William Morris, I: 314; II: 275
Humbert, Gen. Georges-Louis, II: 92-93, 208, 237
Hungarian-Croatian Company for Coastwise Trade, I: 132
Hungarian-Croatian Company for Free Shipping, I: 132
Hungarian-Croatian Convention (forged), I: 130
Hungarian Discount Bank, I: 134
Hungarian Realty Bank, I: 134
Hungary and Hungarians, II: 78, 307,n1, 317, 339,n4, 349,n1, 350; and Rumanian occupation of Transylvania, I: xxiv; map of, I: li; fall of Károlyi government, I: 9n2, 74; formation of Hungarian Soviet Republic, I: 74n9; Archduke Joseph requests alliance with Great Britain, I: 97,n8; representatives summoned to Chantilly, I: 429; Clemenceau changes venue to St.-Germain, I: 446; Rumanian and Czech incursions into, I: 503n4; borders of, II: 3, 419, 471; size of future military establishment, II: 74n1, 314n1; question of protection of minorities in, II: 218,n3; aggression against Czechoslovakia, II: 320,322, 339; Allied call for end to advances into Czechoslovakia, II: 362,n1, 445n6; reply to Allied demand, II: 349,n1, 362,n1
Hungary at the Paris Peace Conference: The Diplomatic History of the Treaty of Trianon (Deák), I: 10n2
Hungary Between Wilson and Lenin: The Hungarian Revolution of 1918-1919 and the Big Three (Pastor), I: 10n2
Hungary in Revolution, 1918-1919: Nine Essays (Völgyes, ed.), I: 10n2
Hurst, Cecil James Barrington, I: 270; II: 229, 521-22, 523, 531-32, 579
Hymans, Paul, I: 129, 239, 248; and reparation for Belgium, I: 89-90, 411, 417, 418, 419, 435; and Belgian-German border, I: 89, 259; and Eupen, I: 138, 260; question of Dutch-German border, I: 92; requests priority for Belgian reparation, I: 411; letter about co-

lonial territories conquered by Belgium, I: 457, 479

Illustration, I: xxxvn4
Imperiali, Marquis Guglielmo, I: 181,n2, 444, 466, 478; II: 37, 253; conversation with Lloyd George, I: 448, 473-75, 476; recalls proposal for Italian mandate for Zara and Sebenico, I: 476
India, II: 128, 568; leaders of and status of Constantinople, I: 503; II: 57, 59, 94-100, 128, 520, 567
Industrial Revolution, The . . . (Bernard), I: viii,n4
Industrial Workers of the World, II: 378
Innocent Abroad: Belgium at the Paris Peace Conference (Marks), I: 91n6
Inquiry, The, I: 39n1
Inter-Allied Blockade Council, II: 549
Inter-Allied Commission for the Negotiation of an Armistice between Poland and the Ukraine, II: 104n2
Inter-Allied Commission on Reparation: see Reparation Commission
Inter-Allied Commission on Teschen, I: 61n6
Inter-Allied Council on Maritime Transport: and blockade, II: 485; report of, II: 583
Inter-Allied Military Council, II: 180, 350,n2; and repatriation of prisoners of war, II: 180-81,n4
Inter-Allied Rhineland High Commission, II: 251n1; Memorandum Defining the Relations between the Allied Military Authorities and the Inter-Allied Rhineland High Commission, II: 436-37
International Armistice Commission, I: 97n9
International Court of Justice: proposed, II: 127, 331
International Labour Organization, I: xxiv, 123n1; II: 91,n7, 178, 288
International Trades Unions Conference (Bern Conference), II: 42n1, 43
Ionescu, Take, II: 333
Iraq, I: 39
Ireland, I: 500, 501
Ireland and Anglo-American Relations, 1899-1921 (Ward), I: 500n1

Irish Americans, I: 501,n1
Irish Race Convention: third, I: 500n1; selects American Commission for Irish Independence, I: 500n1
Irkutsk, Russia, II: 13
Is Germany guilty? German White-book concerning the Responsibilities of the Authors of the War (German Foreign Office), II: 402,n2, 403
Isonzo Valley, I: 299
Istria, I: xxii, 125n4; II: 225, 240; Italian claim to, I: 277, 299, 366; II: 51, 241, 346
István, Count: see Tisza, István, Count
Italian Council of the City of Fiume: see Fiume
Italy, I: 415; war debt of, I: 8; possible occupation of Budapest, I: 45; and Yugoslavia and determination of frontiers of, I: 67n11; mission to Laibach, I: 98; proposals for settlement of Adriatic question, I: 109n7, 138-40, 222, 346-50; and Treaty of London, I: 125,n4, 227, 276,n1; II: 212; claims annexation of all territory within natural boundaries, I: 276-77; Wilson Line, I: 277; II: 328; public opinion, I: 299; II: 210, 277, 325; and relations with Balkans, I: 284-85; "Green Book," I: 305; sends ships to Smyrna, I: 422; absence from presentation of peace preliminaries to German delegation, I: 435-36; failure to participate in negotiations will abrogate Treaty of London, I: 467,n2,3, 468; delegation plans to return to Paris, I: 482; far-flung occupations, I: 482; landing at Marmaris, I: 482; mandates in Asia Minor, I: 484,n3; II: 55; landing at Scala Nuova, II: 38, 47; possibility of constructing port for Yugoslavia in return for possession of Fiume, II: 53; takes possession of Fiume, II: 237; and Tardieu Plan, II: 323,n1, 327; Alpine frontier of, II: 326; rolling stock of, II: 330-31; fall of Orlando government, II: 565; desire for mines in Asia Minor, II: 574; memorandum to new Italian delegation, II: 603-606; see also Adriatic Question
Italy at the Paris Peace Conference (Al-

Italy at the Peace Conference (cont.)
　brecht-Carrié), **I**: xlvi, xlix, 125n4, 285n6, 293n3, 343n7; **II**: 106n5, 236n1, 323n1, 565n1
Iudenich: *see* Yudenich, Gen. Nikolai Nikolaevich
Ivanov-Rinov, Gen. Pavel Pavlovich, **II**: 27,n13

Jäckh, Ernst, **I**: xn8
Jahangir, **II**: 97
James II (of England), **I**: 190
Janin, Gen. Maurice-Pierre-Thiébaut-Charles, **II**: 483
Janowsky, Oscar I., **I**: 440n5
Japan, **I**: xxii, 113; and issue of responsibilities, **I**: 119, 191; and Tsingtao Railroad, **I**: 312, 320, 425n4; Franco-Japanese Treaty, **I**: 319-20,n5; secret exchange with Great Britain on division of German possessions in Pacific, **I**: 320; negotiations and treaties with China regarding Kiaochow and Shantung, **I**: 320; ultimatum to Germany demanding Kiaochow, **I**: 320; Sino-Japanese Treaty of 1915, **I**: 320, 329, 407; Sino-Japanese Convention of 1918, **I**: 320, 329, 333, 334; interest in mines in China, **I**: 323, 324; Balfour meets with representatives of, **I**: 396; question of racial equality, **I**: 399-400,n7; Balfour's draft declaration on Shantung, **I**: 406, 407; requests seat on Reparation Commission, **I**: 420, 426; will give interview on question of Chinese concession, **I**: 425,n4; statement on special police force used by owners of railway, **I**: 425n4; on German prisoners of war, **I**: 426; recommends *de facto* recognition of Omsk government, **II**: 178, 179, 202; on assisting in repatriation of Czech troops from Siberia, **II**: 561
Jaurès, Jean, **I**: vii
Jews, **I**: 439-41; **II**: 148; in Poland, **I**: 440,n4,5, 473,n7, 480; **II**: 88-89, 90-91, 332; question of protection in Austria and Hungary, **II**: 214; guarantee of observation of Sabbath, **II**: 88-89n6; guarantee of schools and use of Yiddish in Poland, **II**: 524-27, 580

Jews and Minority Rights, 1898-1919, The (Janowsky), **I**: 440n5
Jèze, Gaston, **I**: xn, 8
Johnson, Douglas Wilson, **II**: 34, 106n5, 340n5
Jones, Capt. Clement Wakefield, **II**: 121, 562
Journal des Débats, **I**: 69n2

Kanellopoulos, Efthymios, **II**: 30n2
Karawanken Mountains, **II**: 342
Karlsbad (now Karlovy Vary, Czechoslovakia), **I**: 63
Karlsruhe, Germany, **I**: 55n2
Kara-Su River, **II**: 555
Károlyi, Count Mihály: fall of government of, **I**: 9-10n2, 12, 74n8; **II**: 375, 376, 377, 379
Karpona Line, **II**: 419
Kaschau (now Kosice, Czechoslovakia), **II**: 380
Kavalla, Greece, **I**: 506; **II**: 47
Kehl, Germany, **I**: 430, 432, 457
Keller, Friedrich von, **I**: 296
Kerenskii, Aleksandr Feodorovich, **II**: 119, 123, 201, 202
Kernan, Maj. Gen. Francis Joseph, **I**: 248; mediates between Poles and Ruthenians, **I**: 249
Kernek, Sterling J., **I**: 66n9, 125n4
Kerr, Philip Henry, **II**: 255, 369n6, 401, 418; drafts letter to Italy informing of decisions taken after Italian departure, **I**: 451; draft of message to Russian governments, **II**: 124, 179, 189,n4, 193-95; draft of text on armaments, **II**: 424
Keynes, John Maynard, **I**: xi, xxxvii,n9, 5n2, 51, 85, 168n5, 388n2, 435, 456, 478; **II**: 287, 353n5; on proportional distribution of reparation, **I**: 27; on ability of Germany to pay reparation, **I**: 51; on disposition of German shipping, **I**: 442
Khan, Aftab Ahmed, **II**: 96-97
Kiaochow, **I**: 273-75, 312, 319-28, 378-80, 396-97, 401-408, 426; treaties between China and Japan on, **I**: 320; Germany on rights to, **II**: 420n4
Kiel Canal, **I**: 250; discussed, **I**: 257,n1, 356, 374-78

King, Henry Churchill, I: 231n3; II: 132n4
King, Jere Clemens, II: 473n1
King-Crane Commission: An American Inquiry in the Middle East, The (Howard), I: 231n3
Kingdom of the Serbs, Croats and Slovenes: see Yugoslavia
Király, Béla, I: 97n8
Kisch, Lt. Col. Frederick Hermann, I: 13; II: 118, 147, 204-205
Kitchener, Horatio Herbert, 1st Earl Kitchener of Khartoum, I: 487
Klagenfurt Basin, II: 235, 272, 298-304, 335,n2; map of, I: xlix, 1; plebiscite in, II: 218n4, 268, 281, 341-42,n1, 508; need to stop hostilities in, II: 219-20, 254; occupation by Yugoslavs and Austrians, II: 487
Klein, Franz, I: 504
Klofáč, Václav Jaroslav, II: 351,n3
Klotz, Louis-Lucien, I: 109, 388n2, 449, 450, 451,n2; reparation plan, I: 49-50,n1; wishes to avoid exact accounting of reparation owed, I: 50, 51, 85; II: 171; on Lloyd George memorandum, I: 80, 81, 82, 83, 146; on duration of German reparation payments, I: 148, 150, 151; redraft of reparation plan, I: 157-58n5, 159; on issue of German bonds to finance part of reparation, I: 171, 172, 220-21; on distribution of German and Austrian merchant marine, II: 175; on Germany buying back marks in reconquered territories, I: 176, 176-77, 433; on policy of restitution, I: 389; on payment of debt assigned to former German colonies, I: 390; question of interdependence of claims, I: 434
Knox, Gen. Alfred William Fortescue, II: 34
Koblenz, Germany, II: 101, 494
Kolchak, Adm. Aleksandr Vasil'evich, I: 13, 502; II: 15, 33, 104, 119, 123, 124, 189, 193-95, 200, 204, 205, 334,n7, 342, 402, 417,n1, 484, 551n8, 561; forces advancing, I: 429, 501; II: 204; promises democratic reforms, II: 25,n8, 333; offers to recognize Russian debt, II: 190, 201, 333; replies to Allies' demand for guarantees, II: 333; proclamation of, II: 335; reply to be published, II: 335, 394,n6; setbacks of, II: 289, 483, 550, 551
Komarom, Hungary, II: 419
Königsberg (now Kaliningrad, U.S.S.R.), I: 203; II: 186; passage of Haller's army through, I: 70, 113
Konya (Konia), Turkey, II: 39, 84n1, 129
Koo, Vi Kyuin Wellington: appears before Council of Four, I: 329-36; on Twenty-One Demands of Japan, I: 331; on second Sino-Japanese treaty, I: 333; on treaty provisions relating to Shantung, II: 565
Korea, I: 380
Kossuth, Louis, I: 135
Kotlas, Russia, II: 34, 205, 551n8
Kowno (now Kaunas, Lithuania), I: 73
Kramář, Karel, I: 386; II: 88, 362, 394,n5; note on political clauses of Austrian treaty, II: 250, 251; on Hungarian aggression against Czechoslovakia, II: 378-79; on railways, II: 451
Krupp (arms manufacturer), I: 103n5
Kun, Béla, I: 9n2, 503n4; II: 350, 375, 378, 379, 401, 500, 560; aide mémoire for Prince Borghese explaining position toward Russia, I: 74n9; orders halt to hostilities against Czechoslovakia, II: 362,n1, 471,n2

Ladykiller: The Life of Landru, the French Blue-beard, The (Bardens), II: 52n2
Lagosta Island (now Lastovo Island, Yugoslavia), II: 340
Laibach (now Ljubljana, Yugoslavia), I: 98
Lamont, Thomas William, I: 5n2, 80, 151, 168n5, 222, 370n1, 427; II: 214, 231,n1; explains formula by which small states will pay war costs, II: 168, 296; on establishing amount of reparation, II: 175
Land and Power: British and Allied Policy on Germany's Frontiers, 1916-1919 (Nelson), I: xix, 40n1, 55n1, 199n3
Landau, Germany, I: 55,n2, 57, 60, 65, 210

Landeskunde der Provinz Schlesien (Partsch), II: 389n3
Landru, Henri-Désiré, II: 52,n2
Landsberg, Otto, I: 317n1
Lang, The Most Rev. Cosmo Gordon, II: 270,n2
Lansbury, George, I: 38
Lansing, Robert, I: 94, 187, 188, 429n2; II: 238, 256, 358, 583, 587, 599; opposes prosecution of William II, I: 118-19n2; on publicity of peace preliminaries, I: 235, 236; on compelling Germany to reveal production secrets of gas and chemical agents, I: 266-67; questions disposition of Dobruja and the granting most-favored-nations status to Italians in Austria, II: 239; on requesting The Netherlands to turn over the Kaiser, II: 555, 559
Larnaude, Fernand, II: 602
Lasteyrie, Charles, Comte de, I: 433
Latvia, I: 258; II: 203n3, 550; German troops in, I: 72; II: 344
Lavisse, Ernest, I: ix
Law, Andrew Bonar, I: 147, 220; II: 84, 287, 355, 428; discusses occupation of Rhineland, II: 404, 437-38, 440
Layton, Walter Thomas, II: 87,n4
Le Rond, Gen. Henri-Louis-Édouard, II: 388-89
League of Nations, II: 403; Mantoux becomes Director of Political Section, I: ix; Covenant of, I: 4n1, 364, 388; II: 71; Council of, I: 42; and sovereignty over the Saar, I: 204, 205, 207, 211; will give powers the right to intervene in Far East if necessary, I: 333; and limiting period of special tariff rates, I: 371, 372, 373; amended to allow investigation of German failure to meet her commitments upon a majority vote, I: 398; and provision for equality of the races, I: 399; Japanese propose including principle of racial equality in Covenant, I: 399n7; on right of a nation to bring questions concerning national or religious minorities before, II: 90-91, 331,n2, 341; Tardieu plan to make Fiume a state under authority of, II: 236n1, 340; and arms reduction, II: 305; and disarmament of small powers, II: 316-17; may establish Court of International Justice, II: 331; reply to German proposals on, II: 415-17
League of Nations Commission, I: 4
Lehovich, Dimitry V., I: 9n1
Leinert, Robert, I: 317n1; II: 557
Lemberg (now L'vov, U.S.S.R.), I: 44,n4, 48, 248-49; II: 66, 126, 257,n4, 310; Haller's army to proceed to, I: 309; II: 86, 234
Lenin, Vladimir Ilich Ul'anov, I: xx, 430; II: 189-90, 483; and Nansen plan, I: 208n2; replies to Nansen plan, II: 104,n3, 122,n3; progress of Red forces, II: 204, 483
Lentin, Antony, I: 6n2; II: 269
Leobschutz (now Glubczyce, Poland), II: 308, 422
Lersner, Baron Kurt von, I: 481; II: 141
Les Amis de Georges Clemenceau, I: xi
Lesina (now Hvar, Yugoslavia), II: 240
Levant Company, I: 132
Leygues, Georges-Jean-Claude, I: 264
Libau (now Liepaja, Latvia), I: 72,n5; II: 204n3, 424, 428, 599
Libya, I: 482n2, 509
Liebknecht, Karl, I: 166n3
Liège, Belgium, I: 138
Life of Herbert Hoover: The Humanitarian, 1914-1917 (Nash), I: 413n4
Lille, France, I: 8
Limburg, Netherlands, I: 91n6, 140
Link, Arthur Stanley, I: liii, 251n5
Lippe Valley, II: 21, 467, 498
Lissa (now Vis, Yugoslavia), I: 295; II: 131, 324, 340
Lithuania, II: 27,n11, 103, 203n3, 308-309, 313, 550; German troops in, I: 72-73,n5; border with Germany, II: 460; and rolling stock, II: 524
Livonia, II: 425
Lloyd George, David, I: xiii, xxiv-xxvii, 6n2, 40n1, 66n9; Mantoux works with, I: ix; on admission of Germany to League of Nations, I: 4; and basis for reparation, I: 5n2; on distribution of reparation, I: 7; defines reparation, I: 7-8; on situation in Odessa, I: 11; on supplying Rumania, I: 14; on calculation of reparation, I: 17, 18, 19, 22, 24;

seeks compensation for sunken ships, I: 25; seeks compensation for pensions, I: 25, 26; on moderation toward Germany, I: 31-32n1; and Bolshevism, I: 35; on opinions of military, I: 36; on Polish-German boundary, I: 37; on making Danzig a free port, I: 38, 106-107, 108; on sending a commission to the Near East, I: 39; and French security treaty, I: 39n1; on Klotz plan for reparation, I: 52, 76; plans for disposition of Saar Valley, I: 54n3, 66, 67, 107, 186,n7, 233-34; II: 165, 270; on statement of British war aims, I: 66, 291,n1, 414; speech to Trades Union Congress, I: 66n9; on Haller's army passing through Danzig, I: 68, 69-70, 71; protests leak of report of Commission on Polish Affairs, I: 69,n2; on sending commission to Hungary, I: 75, 76, 98; memorandum on Klotz plan, I: 78, 109, 146; on question of responsibilities and war crimes trials, I: 110, 118-19,n2, 120, 121, 187, 188, 197n1, 486-87; "moderation interview," I: 147n3; Fountainebleau Memorandum, I: 147n3; on duration of reparation payments, I: 148, 151; on pensions and reparation, I: 173-74; on action should Germany not sign treaty, I: 184,n6; on submarines, I: 188; on trying William II, I: 189, 191, 239; II: 548, 554; on possible plebiscite in Saar, I: 212; on German issuance of bonds, I: 218, 224-25, 225; on establishing amount of reparation, I: 222-23; II: 355-56; on Teschen Basin, I: 229, 233; on publication of preliminaries of peace, I: 232, 235, 342; on delay in summoning German plenipotentiaries until Adriatic question is resolved, I: 240-41, 243; workload of Drafting Committee, I: 270; provisions for occupation of left bank of the Rhine, I: 270,n1; clarifies provision of Polish sovereignty over the Vistula, I: 271-72; on Kiaochow controversy, I: 273, 378, 379, 380; wishes Open Door to continue in China, I: 273, 274; on reparation and successor states of Austria-Hungary, I: 274; II: 206; on Italian claims, I: 287-88, 298, 300, 301; Great Britain is bound by Treaty of London on Adriatic question, I: 287-88, 302, 343-44, 469; II: 213, 571; prevents Orlando from adding reservations to Points 9, 10, 11, and 12, I: 293n3; Council of Four demands Germany send plenipotentiaries to Paris, I: 297; on necessity of American credit for European reconstruction, I: 298; proposes Italian occupation of coastal islands and resettlement of Slavic residents, I: 300, 304; II: 221, 222; opposed to Haller's army proceeding to Lemberg, I: 309; possibility of resuming hostilities should Germany refuse to sign the peace, I: 310; speculates that Japan wishes to escape control of League of Nations, I: 313; objects to lengthy occupation of left bank of Rhine, I: 318; government must honor Treaty of 1917 with Japan, I: 322; mandates for Australia and New Zealand, I: 322, 497; informs Makino and Chinda of settlements regarding Danzig and the Saar, I: 327; on making Zara and Sebenico free cities, I: 328; II: 236; on British dilemma regarding Japan and China, I: 330, 335; concerned over Italian Tyrol, I: 339; on result of Italian absence during discussion of reparation, I: 339; memorandum with Clemenceau on Fiume, I: 346-50, 365; on Fiume, I: 350; asks Orlando not to withdraw from conference, I: 350; on fortification of Kiel Canal, I: 374, 375; on Syria, I: 380, 381; on proposed Rhineland convention, I: 382, 383, 384; on recognition of Yugoslavia, I: 387; suggests period allowed for German review of Treaty, I: 387, 388; accepts policy of restitution, I: 389; on payment of debt assigned to former German colonies, I: 390; on disclosure of German trade secrets regarding gases and explosives, I: 393; II: 364; on Japanese policing of railroad in China, I: 402, 402-403, 405; rejects proposal to hold prisoners hostage until Germany turns over alleged criminals, I: 409;

Lloyd George, David (cont.)
on Belgian request for priority of reparation, I: 412-13; on provision for construction of airfields in Germany, I: 420; opposes Japanese seat on Reparation Commission, I: 420; discusses possible presence of journalists at presentation of peace terms to German delegation, I: 424; suggests Japan be represented on Reparation Commission whenever questions on Article 13 of financial clauses are discussed, I: 426; on summoning Austrians and Hungarians, I: 428, 429; on reparation for Alsace-Lorraine, I: 431, 432; on Germany buying back marks from Alsace-Lorraine, I: 433; on financial interdependence, I: 434; II: 35, 576; on question of publication of Balfour letter on Italian question, I: 356; on submarine cables, I: 438, 462, 463, 464; on protection of minority rights, I: 439, 440; on mandates, I: 439, 441; II: 54, 55, 556, 582; conversation with G. Imperiali, I: 448, 473-75, 476; on Italian incursions in Balkans, I: 454; question of publication of treaty, I: 486; on Canadian representation in labor organization of League of Nations, I: 490-91; wishes to allow Greek landing at Smyrna, I: 495-96; II: 29; and exclusion of photographers at meeting with German delegation, I: 500; position on Irish-Americans, I: 500-501; on landing at Smyrna, I: 505; II: 30; on decision to use only written documents for discussion of treaty provisions with German delegation, II: 3; suggests military representatives at Versailles study question of Austrian disarmament, II: 4; issue of credits held by U.S., II: 7; wishes to support Kolchak government in Russia, II: 15; calls for common policy on Russia, II: 44; on disposition of Austrian vessels, II: 44; on labor legislation and Germany, II: 46; on P. Scheidemann's speech to German National Assembly, II: 49-50; on Wilson's Adriatic proposal, II: 51, 52; wishes to give Cyprus to Greece, II: 56; on provisions concerning railroads serving Adriatic in Austrian Treaty, II: 61; on timing of lifting of German blockade, II: 65; on lifting blockade of Germany, II: 65; on future Austrian military forces, II: 74, 77; on troop strengths of Germany and Austria, II: 76, 77; on troop strength of German and eastern European armies, II: 79, 184-85, 191-92, 206; on weapons manufacture by Austria, II: 81; on Italian landing at Scala Nuova, II: 83, 92, 93, 94; on publication of treaty provisions, II: 84; and clothing for German prisoners, II: 85, 118; on Polish-Ukrainian situation, II: 86, 104, 126, 151-52; on possible occupation of Budapest, II: 105; discusses Lenin's reply to Nansen proposal, II: 122, 123-24; presents plan for Adriatic and Asia Minor including U.S. mandate for Anatolia, II: 127; on French position in Syria, II: 132, 133; wishes implementation of Sykes-Picot Treaty, II: 135, 162-63; on financial burden of new states, II: 169-70; recommends that right to reparation be limited to period during which each state was belligerent, II: 173, 174; on distribution of Austrian and German fleets, II: 176; on mixed tribunals, II: 196; on possible loan to Kolchak, II: 204; on dealing with Austria differently from Germany, II: 206, 207; on payment of war costs by small states, II: 232, 296; summary of Austrian treaty, II: 238, 239; on occupation of Rhineland, II: 251, 252, 270-71; on sending commissioners to Syria, II: 266,n2; on plebiscite in Klagenfurt Basin, II: 268, 343; discusses British desire for peace and summarizes various issues discussed by Big Four, II: 268-69,n1; on army of occupation and its costs, II: 271, 275; on Allied right of expropriation as means of compensation, II: 279; disposition of Upper Silesia, II: 280, 281, 283, 284, 352, 386-87, 454, 547; on ethnic divisions in Poland, II: 280, 311, 312-13; "Observations of the Ger-

man Delegation . . . ," II: 289; on disarmament, II: 319-20; on Italian public opinion, II: 326; Germany to prepare estimate of reparation, II: 339, 363; German assault on Estonia, II: 342, 427-28; on distribution of captured German shipping, II: 365; on Rumanian-Hungarian situation, II: 377; decision to support Kolchak, II: 402, 417,n1, 483; on publication of treaty, II: 418, 442; on plebiscite in Galicia, II: 420; on reply to German counterproposals on military clauses, II: 423; wishes to resume blockade if Germany will not sign treaty, II: 425,n1, 426; discusses occupation of left bank of Rhine, II: 429, 437n1, 440, 441; on railroad competition, II: 442, 443; comments upon Foch's shift in position, II: 467-68, 472-73, 478; on scuttling of German fleet at Scapa Flow, II: 513, 534, 541-42, 542-43, 544, 548; refuses to grant Germans further delay, II: 519; on naval terms, II: 532, 533-34; on possible occupation of Essen, II: 543; reads draft of note to Germany on action at Scapa Flow, II: 547; on Italian behavior in Anatolia, II: 553; on draft of plan for mandate system, II: 562, 563; on demanding withdrawal of Italian troops from Asia Minor and Fiume, II: 574, 587; on Southern Austrian Railways, II: 594, 595; on Bethmann Hollweg's request to be tried for war crimes in place of Kaiser, II: 598; on transmitting minutes of meetings of Council of Four, II: 600, 602

Lloyd George, Woodrow Wilson and the Guilt of Germany (Lentin), I: 6n2; II: 269n1

London School of Economics, I: ix

London *Daily Mail*, II: 473n2, 521

London *Times*, I: 421n2, 453

London *Westminster Gazette*, I: 147n3; II: 34

Long, Walter, II: 163

Lord, Robert Howard, I: xlv, 55n1, 91n6; II: 281, 286, 391; on Polish-Ukrainian truce, I: 118; II: 150-51; recommends formation of commission to study questions relating to Baltic nations, I: 258, 399

Lorraine, I: 214

Losonc (now Lucenec, Czechoslovakia), II: 419

Loucheur, Louis, I: xn8, 168n5, 230, 236, 250; II: 87, 253, 271, 337, 428, 470n1, 545; on amount of German reparation, I: 5n2; II: 287, 339,n3; and ability of Germany to pay reparation, I: 16; on action should Germany refuse to sign treaty, I: 19; on calculation of reparation, I: 17, 18, 22; on calculation of pensions, I: 26; on proportional distribution, I: 26, 27; on duration of reparation payments, I: 149; on Saar Valley and Lorraine, I: 227, 357; on small powers and reparation, I: 370, 396; II: 575-76; on reparation for Belgium, I, 176; on Southern Austrian Railways, II: 232,n3

Louis XVI, I: 56, 192, 210

Lou Tseng Tsiang, I: 329

Louvain, Belgium, I: 190

Luckau, Alma, I: 318n1

Lukovsky, Gen. Aleksandr Serge'vich, II: 205

Lundgreen-Nielsen, Kay, I: xix, 43n3, 44n4, 61n6, 100n2, 440n5

Lusitania, II: 122

Lussino [or Lussin] (now Losinj, Yugoslavia): Italian claims to, I: 279; II: 241, 324

Luxembourg, I: 65,n7, 91n6, 239, 247-48, 459; II: 179; Albert, King of the Belgians on, I: 142; text regarding, I: 410; negotiations with Belgium, I: 415; wishes to remain independent, II: 243; to conduct plebiscite on form of government and dynasty, II: 243; calls for economic alliance with Belgium and France, II: 244, 248; requests reparation from Germany, II: 246

Luxemburg, Rosa, I: 166n3

Luzzatti, Luigi, I: 444

L'vov, Georgii Evgen'evich, Prince, II: 25n8, 27

Lycée Condorcet, I: vii

McCormick, Vance Criswell, I: 174, 175, 427n1, 435; II: 65, 480
MacDonald, (James) Ramsay, II: 424
McDougall, Walter A., I: 40n1
Macedonia, I: 505; II: 41, 100, 116
Mackensen, Field Marshal August von, II: 378, 379
McKinley, William, I: 119
Maclay, Sir Joseph Paton, I: 100
Macleay, James William Ronald, I: 378
Magnesia (now Manisa, Turkey), II: 254
Main River Valley, II: 21, 463, 467, 469, 494, 498
Mainz, Germany, I: 137, 234, 235; II: 20, 22, 100, 475
Mair, George Herbert, I: 486
Making of the Reparation and Economic Sections of the Treaty (Baruch), I: 5n2, 370n1
Makino, Baron Nobuaki, I: 399; on Japanese treaty with China, I: 320-21; on extraterritoriality in China, I: 326; on question of provision for equality of races, I: 399; decision to support Kolchak, II: 402, 418; refuses to grant Germans further delay, II: 519; on Bethmann Hollweg's request to be tried for war crimes in place of Kaiser, II: 599
Makri (now Fethiye, Turkey), II: 56, 58, 70, 93, 112
Maklakov, Vasilii Alekseevich, II: 25n8
Malmédy, Belgium, I: 91n6, 138, 259, 260; map of, I: xliv
Mance, Brig. Gen. Harry Osborne, I: 382, II: 585, 595
Manchuria, I: 332, 380
mandates: system of, I: 231, 314, 381, 390, 439, 441, 461, 496, 497, 502; II: 54-55, 69, 582; Lloyd George on Japan and, I: 322; in Africa and the Pacific, I: 322, 497, 498, 499; in Asia Minor, II: 58, 70, 556, 573,n5
Mangin, Gen. Charles-Marie-Emmanuel, I: 15; II: 474, 475, 498
Mannheim Convention (1868), I: 384
Manteuffel, Baron Edwin Hans Karl von, II: 370

Mantoux, Adrien, I: vii
Mantoux, Esther Berthe, I: vii
Mantoux, Étienne-Gabriel, I: xi, xii, xix, 6n2
Mantoux, Jacques-Adrien, I: xii
Mantoux, Mathilde Babette (Mme. Paul), I: xi, xii, xviii
Mantoux, Paul-Joseph, I: vii, x, xii, xvii; education of, I: vii; studies at Passmore Edwards Settlement, I: vii; and *La Crise du Trade-Unionisme*, I: vii; Secretary of École des Hautes Études Sociales, I: vii-viii; teaches at Collège Chaptel, I: viii; receives doctorate, I: viii; teaches at École des Hautes Études Commerciales, I: viii; and *Á Travers l'Angleterre Contemporaine*, I: viii-ix; teaches at University of London, I: ix; joins French Army, I: ix; works with Lloyd George, I: ix; interpreter to Supreme War Council, I: ix; interpreter to Council of Four, I: ix; interpreter to Council of Ten and Council of Heads of Delegations, I: ix; Director of Political Section of League of Nations, I: ix; Director of Graduate Institute of International Studies, I: x; becomes head of British Section of French Ministry of Information, I: xi; prepares manuscript by E. Mantoux, I: xi; prepares notes of discussions of Council of Four, I: xi; keeps record of discussions of Council of Four, I: xv; fate of manuscript, I: xvii; note to German delegation linking lifting of blockade to signing treaty, II: 549
Mantoux, Philippe-Roger, I: xii
Marder, Arthur J., II: 513n5
Margalith, Aaron M., I: 473n7
Marienwerder (now Kwidzyn, Poland), I: 106n3, 107, 108, 124, 199-200,n3, 201, 233, 250, 271
Marks, Sally, I: 91n6, 419n5
Marinelli, Olinto, II: 240,n1, 324
maritime prizes, I: 268-69
Marmara, Sea of, II: 471n3
Marmaris, Turkey: Italian landing at, I: 482; II: 39, 48, 58, 69, 70, 92,n1, 93, 112, 113
Marne, 1st Battle of, I: ix

Martino, Giacomo de, II: 61, 292
Masaryk, Thomas Garrigue, I: 301n3; II: 350
Massey, William Ferguson, II: 272
Masuria (formerly East Prussia, now Poland), II: 311,n7
Matra Mountains, II: 351n4
Le Matin, I: 493; II: 474
Maximalists: *see* Bolsheviks
May, Arthur J., II: 38n3
Mayer, Arno J., I: 9n1, 10n2, 503n4
Mayflower (presidential yacht), I: 495
Meanderes River, II: 69, 70
Medjid Effendi, Abdul, II: 329,n4, 334
Medlicott, W. N., I: 473n7
Melchior, Carl, I: 116, 317n1, 478; II: 154, 337
Meleda (now Mljet Island, Yugoslavia), II: 240, 241
Memel, Germany (now Klaipeda, U.S.S.R.), I: 272; II: 270, 308-309, 460
Memoir of the Paris Peace Conference 1919, A (Headlam-Morley, Bryant, and Cienciala, eds.), I: 55n1
Mercier, Désiré-Félicien-François-Joseph, Cardinal, I: 136
Mersina (now Mersin, Turkey), II: 56, 58, 69
Meseritz (now Miedzyrdecz, Poland), II: 455
Mesopotamia, I: 39; II: 98, 129, 135, 553; railroad to Syrian coast, II: 135-36, 161
Mezes, Sidney Edward, I: 39n1; II: 200,n3
Mikhailov, M., II: 28
Miles, Lt. Col. Sherman, I: 127n5; II: 219n7
Militsch (now Milicz, Poland), II: 270, 310
Miller, David Hunter, I: 5n2, 39n1, 55n1, 59n1, 61n6, 72n5, 91n6, 195, 208n2, 214n2, 256n2; II: 106n5, 210, 214, 215, 216, 292; presents conventions between Allies and Poland, I: 472,n6; on Adriatic question, II: 109n7
Miller-House initiative, II: 109n7, 222
Milliès-Lacroix, Raphaël, II: 273
Milne, Lt. Gen. Sir George Francis, II: 34

Milner, Alfred, 1st Viscount, I: 487, 498; II: 59, 132, 563, 582
Minderheitenfrage und die Entstenhung der Minderheiter-schutzverträge auf Pariser Friedenskonferenz 1919, Die (Viefhaus), I: 440n5
Miners' Federation of Great Britain, I: 35n1
Mišíc, Field Marshal Zivojin, I: 96
Miskolcz, Hungary, II: 378
missions, missionaries, II: 421, 459,n1
Mişu, Nicolae, II: 362, 393, 419
Mitchell, Allan, I: 183n5
Mitrovic (now Kosovska Mitrovica, Yugoslavia), I: 127
Mittelhauser, Gen. Eugène-Désiré-Antoine, II: 380
Mitylene, Greece, II: 116
Mochaverol-el-Memalek, I: 341,n3,n4
Monnet, Jean-Omer-Marie-Gabriel, II: 549
Montagu, Edwin Samuel, I: 29, 80, 148, 388n2; II: 94, 95, 98, 508,n2, 520; amount of reparation to be paid, I: 5-6n2
Montenegro, I: 127, 337,n4; relations with Serbia, I: 503; II: 91
Montejoie, I: 260
Mordacq, Gen. Jean-Jules-Henri, II: 233, 478
Morel, Jean, I: 370n1
Moresnet, Belgium, I: 91n6
Morison, Samuel Eliot, II: 203n2
Morocco, I: 499
Morris, Roland Sletor, II: 34; sent to Omsk to determine influence of Kolchak in, II: 119n5, 205
Moslem League of India, II: 95
Mosul, II: 132, 133, 161, 163, 164
Muehlon, Wilhelm von, I: 103-104,n5
Müller, Hermann, II: 557
My Diary at the Conference of Paris, with Documents (Miller), I: 5n2, 39n1, 55n1, 59n1, 61n6, 72n5, 91,n6, 256n2

Nabokov, Konstantin Dmitrievich, II: 37,n1
Namier, Lewis Bernstein, II: 89
Namslau (now Namyslow, Poland), II: 308,n3

Nancy, France, I: vii, 59
Nansen, Fridtjof: plan for supplying Russia, I: 208,n1; Lenin's reply to plan of, II: 104,n3, 122,n3
Narva, Russia, II: 344
Nash, George H., I: 413n4
National Albanian League of America, I: 495n4
National Center for Scientific Research, I: xi, xviii
Nauru: mandate for, I: 497
Nelson, Harold I., I: xix, 40n1, 55n1, 199n3
Neratov, Anatolii Anatolievich, II: 25n7
Netherlands, The, I: 383, 569; sheltering William II, I: 194, 197; II: 548, 554, 560, 570; borders of, II: 3
Nevin, John Edwin, I: 232n1
"New Boundaries of Germany" (Haskins), I: 55n1
New Europe: A Weekly Review of Foreign Politics, I: 301,n3
New Guinea, I: 313
New York Times, I: 421n2; II: 50n1, 212n1
New World: Problems in Political Geography, The (Bowman), I: xliii, xliv, xlvii, xlix, l, lii
New Zealand, I: 322, 497; II: 275
Nicaragua, II: 239
Nice, France, II: 569
Nicholas I (of Montenegro), I: 337n4, 503n3
Nicolson, Harold George, II: 59
Niederle, Lubor, II: 298,n1
Nieman River, I: 272
Nigeria, I: 499, 508
Nitti, Francisco Saverio, II: 565n1
Noble, George Bernard, I: 181n4
Nolan, Brig. Gen. Dennis Edward, I: 100n1
Northcliffe, Alfred Charles William Harmsworth, 1st Viscount, I: 226, II: 388
"Note on the Supply of Armaments to the New States of Central and Eastern Europe," II: 87n4
Noulens, Gen. Joseph: mission to Poland, I: 43n3, 116
Noyes, Pierrepont Burt, II: 251n1, 252n2, 253-54

Nudant, Gen. Alphonse-Pierre, I: 42

Odessa, Russia, I: 507; question of Allies supplying, I: 9,n1, 11, 13; and Bolshevism, I: 12; evacuation of, I: xxxvi, 45, 115; military situation in, I: 12, 14, 15
Omelianovych-Pavlenko, Mykhailo, I: 249,n2; II: 309-10
Omsk, Russia: government at, II: 119, 189, 334; Japan recommends *de facto* recognition of government at, II: 202
Open Door policy, I: 324
Ore Mountains, II: 351,n4
Oriental Company, I: 132
Origins of the International Labor Organization, The (Shotwell), I: 123n1
Orlando, Vittorio, I: xiii, xxvii, xxxiv,n3; II: 109n1; and inclusion of Covenant of League of Nations in peace treaty, I: 4; and interdependence of claims, I: 8; on Russian situation, I: 48; supports Klotz plan for reparation, I: 53; on Treaty of London, I: 125,n4; II: 224; discusses Italian claim to Fiume, I: 125-29, 277-79; presents Italy's Adriatic claims, I: 126, 127, 128; on nationalities in Fiume, I: 126-27; on possibility of making Fiume a free city, I: 127; on trying William II, I: 191; on responsibility of heads of state, I: 192, 197n1; and possible plebiscite in Saar, I: 212; on publication of preliminaries of the peace, I: 232; on not summoning German plenipotentiaries until Adriatic question is settled, I: 238, 240, 241-42, 243-44; on Italian public opinion, I: 244; II: 188; meets with Wilson on Adriatic question, I: 245,n2; publishes WW's memorandum on Adriatic question, I: 245n2; issue of the responsibility of Austro-Hungarian successor states for damages of, I: 274; explains claim for annexation of all territories within Italy's natural boundaries, I: 276-80; claims Istria for Italy, I: 277; invokes Polish precedents to back Italian territorial claims, I: 278; presents historic background of claim to Fiume, I: 279; discusses Italian claims

to Dalmatia, I: 279; and islands of Istria-Cherso and Lussino, I: 279; warns of serious repercussions if Italy does not receive Fiume, I: 287; on application of Fourteen Points with regard to Italy's Adriatic claims, I: 293; wishes to add reservations to Points 9, 10, 11, and 12, I: 293,n3; explains Italian intransigence, I: 301-302; publication of WW's statement on Adriatic, I: 358-59; leaves conference, I: 359; on Italian Parliament and Adriatic question, I: 360, 362, 364; can't negotiate with Germany until Adriatic question is settled, I: 363-64; on League of Nations, I: 364; speech to Italian Chamber of Deputies, I: 421n2; wishes to negotiate with Austro-Hungarian successor states simultaneously, I: 504, 505; on Adriatic shipping, II: 43-44, 45; on Austrian vessels, II: 43, 44; on landing at Smyrna, II: 47, 93; on provisions on railroads serving Adriatic in Austrian treaty, II: 61, 62; on troop strengths for Austria and Germany, II: 77-78; on limitation of arms of eastern European states, II: 78; requests Italian mandate for all Asia Minor, II: 106,n5; Miller-House Adriatic proposal, II: 106n5; and debt of successor states, II: 170-71; discusses distribution of Austrian and German merchant fleets, II: 173-74, 175-76; and repatriation of prisoners of war, II: 181-82; on possible withdrawal of French troops from Italy, II: 188, 189; and possible annulment of contracts by mixed tribunals, II: 197, 198; on dealing with Austrians differently from Germans, II: 206-207, 207-208; is unable to accept plebiscite in Adriatic areas, II: 225; on partial acceptance of Tardieu plan, II: 236,n1; concerned with provisions on war crimes in Austrian treaty, II: 258; objections to preamble of Austrian treaty, II: 264; on disarmament, II: 322; opposed to plebiscite for Klagenfurt Basin, II: 342, 343; note to WW on Adriatic situation, II: 362-63,n2; reservation concerning League Covenant incorporated into treaty, II: 460,n3; fall of government of, II: 565n1

Ottoman Empire, I: 231,n3; II: 556; representatives meet with Council of Ten, II: 476; Balfour drafts reply to, II: 507,n1, 520, 602; statement by plenipotentiaries of, II: 555-56

Pact of London, I: 302, 314, 315, 316, 345n8, 347, 349, 360, 364, 365, 436,n1, 454, 467,n2,3, 476
Paderewski, Ignace Jan, I: 501; II: 103, 309-10, 318-19, 420; return to Warsaw provokes revolt, I: 100,n2; meets with Wilson, I: 107n4, 108; on question of Polish boundaries, I: 200; II: 306, 310; on question of plebiscite to determine status of Danzig, I: 201-203; on armistice in Galicia, II: 44n4, 118n1; addresses Polish Diet, II: 103; on ethnic makeup of Upper Silesia, II: 308; reads declaration on self-determination, II: 313; on plebiscite in Upper Silesia, II: 308, 310-11, 453-54; opposes guarantee of use of Yiddish, II: 341; memorandum on minority rights, II: 481, 487-93, 524; requests guarantee of language and culture for Poles remaining in German territory, II: 578, 579; opposed to special language and educational privileges for Jews, II: 580,n2
Page, Stanley W., I: 73n5
Page, Thomas Nelson, I: 385n2, 466, 479
Pago (now Pag, Yugoslavia), II: 236n1, 240
Paix, La (Tardieu), I: xxxvn4
Palatinate, I: 55n2
Palestine, II: 93, 161; mandate in, I: 480n2
Paneyko, Vasil, II: 143n1, 144-45, 145-46, 147
Pan-Germanism, II: 298
Papers of Woodrow Wilson, The (Link, ed.), I: liii, 251n5
Papers Relating to the Foreign Relations of the United States, I: xvii-xviii, xxxv,n5
Partsch, Josef Franz Maria, II: 389,n3
Pašić, Nikola P., I: 52; II: 291; note on

Pašić, Nikola P. (cont.)
boundary between Austria and Yugoslavia, II: 251
Passing of the Hapsburg Monarchy, 1914-1918, The (May), II: 38n3
Passmore Edwards Settlement, I: vii
Pastor, Peter, I: 10n2
Pavlenko, Gen.: see Omelianovych-Pavlenko, Gen.
Peel, Col. Sidney Cornwallis, II: 470n1
Peking Railroad, I: 332
Pellé, Gen. Maurice-César-Joseph, II: 350, 380, 419, 500
Peloponnese, II: 56
Perman, Dagmar, I: 61n6, 144n1
Permanent Inter-Allied Armistice Commission at Spa, Belgium, I: 43n3
Pershing, Gen. John Joseph, II: 20n4, 479, 558
Persia: wishes to be represented at Peace Conference, I: 341
Pesić, Gen., II: 561
Pétain, Gen. Henri-Philippe, I: 17; II: 20n4, 163, 474, 475, 478, 479; on military action in event of German failure to sign treaty, II: 498, 499
Petliura, Symon Vacyl'ovich, II: 309
Petrograd, Russia, II: 205, 342, 344, 483
Philippines, II: 17
phosphates, I: 497
Piave River, I: 209n3
Piccioni, Gen. Luigi, II: 379, 380
Piccolo Mundo Antico (Fogazzaro), II: 299,n3
Pichon, Stéphen-Jean-Marie, I: 437, 439, 485, 552; situation in Hungary, I: 93-94, 98, 355; II: 376; victualing of Bavaria, I: 103,n5; discusses difficulties presented by absence of Italian delegation, I: 435-36
Piip, Ants (Antoine), II: 27n10
Piłsudski, Gen. Józef Klemens, II: 87, 148, 309,n6; Council of Four warns that hostilities with Ukraine must end, II: 154,n5, 155-56, 233
Plamenatz, Jovan S., I: 502,n2
Pless, Hans Heinrich, Prince of, II: 281
Poel, Jean van der, I: 36n3
Poincaré, Raymond, I: 31,n2, 40n1, 143; II: 329, 334, 473n1; statement appearing to favor Italy, I: 437,n2
Poland: troops in Ukraine, I: xxiv, xxvi; and Danzig, I: 106,n3; transport of troops through Danzig, I: 43, 68-72, 100-103, 113-15; Noulens mission to, I: 43n3, 116, 248n1; and Ukrainians, I: 118n1, 501; II: 143-53; and borders, I: 199-203; II: 3, 452; behavior in Lemberg, I: 48-49; II: 66; negotiations with Ruthenians, I: 44n5; II: 581-82; representatives to be present at negotiations with German plenipotentiaries, I: 271; anti-Semitism in, I: 439-40; lacks raw materials or credit to purchase them, II: 9; minority rights in, II: 88, 89, 90, 238, 279, 331-32; moving against Ukrainians, II: 125, 143-44; Paderewski addresses Diet, II: 103; public opinion in, II: 103-104; Council of Four warns to cease hostilities with Ukraine, II: 86, 148, 154,n5, 155-56; Le Rond on Bolshevik threat in Ukraine and Poland, II: 149-50; size of military forces, II: 191; requests return of national monuments, II: 267, 294, 295; German return of state forests to, II: 295; declaration on self-determination, II: 313; National Polish Party of Upper Silesia, II: 390, 391; Socialists, II: 391; National Democrats, II: 391; guarantee of Jewish schools and use of Yiddish, II: 506, 524; protection of Polish minorities within Germany, II: 578, 579; protection of German minority within Poland, II: 580
Policies and Opinions at Paris 1919: Wilsonian Diplomacy, the Versailles Peace, and French Public Opinion (Noble), I: 181n4
Polish National Committee, I: 100n2
Polish Problem at the Paris Peace Conference, The (Lundgreen-Nielsen), I: xix, 43n3, 61n6, 100n2, 440n5
Political Science Quarterly, I: viiin2
"Political Situation in India" (*Fortnightly Review*), II: 54
Politics and Diplomacy of Peacemaking: Containment and Counter-revolution at Versailles, 1918-1919 (Mayer), I: 9n1, 10n2, 503n4
"Politik der Alliierten gegenüber den Freikorps im Baltikum 1918-1919" (Williams), I: 73n5

Politis, Nicolas, I: xn8
Polk, Frank Lyon, II: 583
Pollock, Sir Ernest (Murray), I: 194, 548; suggests linking liberation of German prisoners of war to handing over war criminals, II: 548n2, 562, 602n3
Pomerania, I: xxv; II: 279, 310
Porto Re (now Kraljevica, Yugoslavia), I: 127
Portugal, I: 398; II: 583; and reparation, I: 370
Posen (Poznan), Poland, I: 116; II: 21, 495; return of Paderewski provokes revolt in, I: 100,n2
Poska, Jaan, II: 27n10
Prelude to Israel: An Analysis of Zionist Diplomacy 1897-1947 (Taylor), I: 440n5
"President Wilson au Conseil des Quatre" (Mantoux), I: xi
Pressburg (now Bratislava, Czechoslovakia), I: 133; II: 338, 350, 419
Prinkipo Declaration, II: 189n5, 471n3
Prinkipo Island, I: xx; II: 471,n3
prisoners of war, I: 168, 185, 188, 408,n1; II: 85, 424, 444; repatriation of, I: 409, II: 561, 562, 602,n3
"Protection of Minorities and Natives in Transferred Territories" (Hudson), I: 440n5
Przemysl, Poland: Polish advance toward, II: 125
Pupin, Michael Idvorsky, I: 340

Quarantième Anniversaire (Institut Universitaire des Hautes Études Internationales Genève), I: xn8

Raggi, Marquis Salvago, I: 424
Ragusa (now Dubrovnik, Yugoslavia), I: 280
railways, I: 390; II: 115, 116, 270, 330, 341, 425, 450, 523; between Mesopotamia and Syrian coast, II: 135-36, 161; of southern Austria (Südbahn), II: 61, 232,n3, 585, 592-97; competition among, II: 62, 442, 443, 456
Rapallo Agreement, I: 253n1
Rappard, William Emmanuel, I: x,n8
Rapport Présenté au Conseil des Principales Puissances Alliées et Associées par la Commission Interalliée de la Rive Gauche du Rhin, II: 384,n2
Ratibor (now Raciborz, Poland), I: 145; II: 392, 419
Reading, Rufus Daniel Isaacs, 1st Marquis of, I: 471
Reboul, Colonel, I: 73
Reichsbank, II: 504n3
Renner, Karl, II: 300,n4
reparation, I: xxiv, 5-6n2, 16-22, 49-54, 109, 154-64, 168-80, 218-25, 456; II: 274, 339,n3, 529-31, 584; question of German capacity to pay, I: 5-9; II: 270; basis of, I: 5n2; duration of, I: 7, 148-53, 156; defined, I: 50; and Third Revise, I: 5n2; property damage and, I: 23; and restitution of stolen objects, I: 82; Klotz plan for, I: 49-50, 80; reconstruction of buildings by Germany, I: 101; question of inclusion of pensions and separation allowances, I: 105,n1, 111-12,n7, 491,n2; and compensation for deportation of workers, I: 106; Anglo-American accord (April 1), I: 111,n7, 157n5; Belgian request for priority in, I: 135; Sumner draft, I: 153n4, 156n4; interdependence of debts, I: 209-10, 374; II: 576-78; subcommission on, I: 218; issuance of German bonds, I: 218, 220, 221, 222, 224, 225, 236, 237, 356-57, 373; responsibility of successor states for damages by Austria-Hungary, I: 274, 275; II: 34-35, 168-75, 457; and mandates, I: 390; and Alsace-Lorraine, I: 390, 431, 432; II: 199; right to reparation may be limited to period during which each state was belligerent, II: 173, 174; Czechoslovak acceptance of war costs under a name other than reparation, II: 231; reply to German counterproposals, II: 354-55, 357-58, 395-401, 405-15; Sumner memorandum on, II: 369,n6, 384,n5; U.S. Project for Reply to German Counter-Proposals, II: 371-74
Reparation at the Paris Peace Conference: From the Standpoint of the American Delegation (Burnett, ed.), I: xix, 6n2, 50n1, 111n7, 153n4; II: 577n2
Reparation Commission, I: xxi, xxvi, 5n2, 111n7, 153n4, 237, 423; II: 167,n3, 168, 169, 171-72, 336,n5, 529-

Reparation Commission (cont.)
30, 531; adopts U.S. figure, I: 5n2; Third Revise, I: 6n2; determination of final total, I: 153; and duration of German payment, I: 153; principle of unanimity, I: 218, 219; on issuance of German bonds, I: 220; Serbia requests voting delegate on, I: 396, 397; Japan requests seat on, I: 420, 426; discusses reparations owed by Austria and Hungary, II: 4; on provision for reoccupation of Germany, II: 24; right of each member to withdraw, II: 70; has power to grant reductions, II: 171; to refer Austro-Hungarian questions to subcommittee, II: 172; report to Supreme Council, II: 359-61; to determine debt of successor states, II: 577

Reparation in World Politics: France and European Economic Diplomacy, 1916-1923 (Trachtenberg), I: xix, 6n2, 105n1

Report on the Negotiations of April 3rd and 4th 1919 at Spa (Foch), I: 166,n4

Report of the Reparation Commission to the Supreme Council, II: 359-61

Report (With Appendices) Presented to the Supreme Council of the Peace Conference by the Inter-Allied Commission for the Negotiation of an Armistice between Poland and the Ukraine, II: 147n2

Reshetar, John S., Jr., I: 9n1

responsibility for war, I: 118-22, 187-95, 269; II: 6, 442,n1; Allied memorandum on, II: 445-49

Reuter, Émile, II: 243; on economic concerns of Luxembourg, II: 243-45; requests reparation from Germany, II: 248

Reuter, Vice Adm. Ludwig von, II: 513n5

Reval (now Tallin, Estonia), II: 26, 204n3

Revel, Adm. Paolo Thaon di, II: 81

Revelstoke, John Baring, 2nd Baron Revelstoke, II: 204

Revolution in Bavaria, 1918-1919: The Eisner Regime and the Soviet Republic (Mitchell), I: 183n5

Révolution Industrielle au Siècle XVIIIe:
Essai sur les Commencements de la Grande Industrie Moderne en Angleterre, La (Mantoux), I: viii,n4

Revue Historique, I: viii

Rheims, France, II: 339

Rhineland Commission, II: 252

Rhineland, I: xxv; II: 252, 370,n7, 404,n6, 437-41,n1; left bank of, I: xxxiii,n1, 18, 19, 39,n1, 318,n2, 381-85; II: 6; map of, I: lii; bridgeheads, I: 19; question of disarming right bank, I: 42, 318,n2; P. B. Noyes on occupation of, II: 253-54; Convention Regarding the Military Occupation of the Territories of, II: 428,n3, 429, 431-35

Rhodes, I: 482; II: 70, 113

Ribot, Alexandre-Félix-Joseph, I: 143; II: 38, 273,n5

Ricordi e Frammenti de Diario (Aldrovandi Marescotti), I: xvn3, xxxvn6

Riesenburg, Germany, I: 271

Riga, Latvia, I: 72,n5; II: 344

Robertson, Gen. Sir William Robert, II: 20n4, 162-63, 370, 474, 479, 558; on military action in event of German failure to sign treaty, II: 13, 496, 497

Robinson, Henry Mauris, II: 46

Rockefeller family, I: x

Rodd, Sir James Rennell, 1st Baron Rennell Rodd, I: 467; II: 571

Rogers, Walter Stowell, I: 464

Ronarc'h, Vice Adm. Pierre-Alexis-Marie-Antoine, II: 534,n1

Roosevelt, Theodore, II: 602

Roskill, Stephen, I: xvi,n4, 294n4

Rothschild, Lionel Walter, 2nd Baron Rothschild, I: 480n2

Roussos, Paris, I: 482n1

Rovno, Russia, II: 309

Rudin, Harry R., I: 97n9

Ruhr Basin, I: 19; II: 21, 22, 462

Rumania and Rumanians, I: 415, 439, 473,n7; II: 105, 238, 254, 291,n6, 350, 375, 419; carries out offensive in Hungary, I: xxiv, xxvi, 10n2, 386, 503n4; supplying army of, I: 9, 11, 44; Bolshevik threat to, I: 9, 44; troops in Ukraine, I: 9n1; size of future military establishment, II: 314n1, 317; borders of, II: 419-20; Allies demand cease

fire, II: 445n6
Rumania at the Paris Peace Conference: A Study of the Diplomacy of Ioan I. C. Brătianu (Spector), I: 10n2
Russia, I: 429-30, 460; II: 13-17; military intervention in, I: 48; prisoners of war of, I: 168; victualing of, I: 208-209,n2; borders of, II: 3, 4, 5; Unified Governments pledge democratic reforms, II: 25-26n8; Japan recommends de facto recognition of Omsk government, II: 178, 179, 202; Kolchak offers to recognize debt of, II: 190, 201, 333; successes of Red army, II: 204, 483; Declaration of Sainte-Adresse, II: 411-12, 415; repatriation of Czechs from, II: 561
Russia, Bolshevism, and the Versailles Peace (Thompson), I: 208n2; II: 189n5, 471n3
Russian Railway Service Corps, II: 13-14
Ruthenia: and controversy with Poland, I: 44,n5; II: 581-82
Ryan, Michael J., I: 500n1

Saar Basin, I: 28,n1, 83,n1, 195-97, 198-99, 204-208, 210-17, 227-30, 247, 357-58; II: 165-67, 240, 270, 273, 303-304; map of, I: xliii, 214; French demands for, I: 54; Tardieu on, I: 55-59n1; mines of, I: 56, 58, 84; ownership of mines of, I: 185; II: 167n3; British plans for, I: 186,n7; plebiscite in, I: 195-96, 204; II: 281, 342, 511; and League of Nations, I: 204; draft proposals for, I: 214-17; German notes on, II: 85,n3, 166n2, 167n3; repurchase of mines of, I: 195,n1; German renunciation of sovereignty over, II: 204
Saarbrücken, Germany, I: 56,n4, 57
Saarelouis, Germany, I: 56, 57, 210
Saburi, Sadao, II: 418
Sackville-West, Maj. Gen. Charles John, II: 354, 427; on troop strengths of Austria and Germany, II: 76, 77
Sadowa, Battle of, I: 130
Saint-Aulaire, Auguste-Félix-Charles de Beaupoli, II: 238
Saint-Germain, France, I: 446; II: 208, 300

Saint-Jean de Maurienne: see Agreement of Saint-Jean de Maurienne
St. Lawrence Seaway, I: 382
St. Sophia, Church of, II: 99
Saionji, Marquis Kimmochi, I: 197
Sakmyster, Thomas L., I: 97n8
Salisbury, Robert Arthur Talbot Gascoyne-Cecil, 3rd Marquis of Salisbury: and Heligoland, I: 254
Saloniki, I: 133; II: 58
Salzburg, Austria, II: 298
Samara (now Kuibyshev, U.S.S.R.), II: 204
Samoan Islands, I: 497
Samos, II: 116
Samuel, Herbert, I: 477
San Giorgio, I: 385
San Marino, Republic of, I: 278
Savoy: neutral zone and free zone in, I: 493; II: 290,n5
Saxony, II: 217; question of presentation of credentials for, I: 408, 420
Sazonov, Sergei Dmitrievich, II: 25,n7,8, 27n12, 289
Scala Nuova (now Kusadasi, Turkey), II: 58, 112-13, 114; Italian landing at, II: 38, 47, 48, 92,n1, 93, 94, 111
Scapa Flow: High Seas Fleet scuttled at, I: xxvi; II: 513, 520, 521, 522, 534-37, 539; Allied note to Germany on, II: 556
Scelle, Georges, I: xn8, xvii
Scheidemann, Philipp, I: xxvi, 20n3, 33; II: 65, 187, 238, 313-14, 349; hopes to be able to sign treaty, I: 446; protests against treaty provisions in speech to German National Assembly, II: 49-50,n1, 69; cabinet resigns, II: 512n1
Scheldt (Schelde) River, I: 262, 415
Schlesien: Eine Landeskunde fur das deutsche Volk auf wissenschaftlicher Grundlage (Partsch), II: 389n3
Schleswig, I: 256; II: 33, 290, 303, 341
Schmidtt, Ernst, I: 296
Schneidemühl (now Pila, Poland), II: 270, 279
Schücking, Walter Max Adrian, I: xn8, 317n1
Schwabe, Klaus, I: 104n5, 445n2
Schwandorf, Germany, II: 451
Scott, James Brown, I: 187, 490; II: 11,

Scott, James Brown (cont.)
265; opposes prosecution of William II, I: 118n2; on Austrian treaty provisions, II: 228, 229
Sebenico (now Sibenik, Yugoslavia), I: 328, 366, 367, 428, 476, 482; II: 52, 236,n1, 240, 241, 324, 327, 328, 340
Second Moroccan Crisis, I: 499n1
Segno (now Senj, Yugoslavia), I: 127
Segre, Gen. Roberto, II: 351
Selections from the Smuts Papers (Hancock and Poel, eds.), I: 36n1
Semenov, Hetman Grigorii Mikhailovich, II: 483
Senegal: troops in occupation of left bank of Rhine, II: 121
Senn, Alfred E., II: 27n11
Serbia, I: 63, 133; II: 335; and reparation, I: 370; requests voting delegate on Reparation Commission, I: 396, 397; requests two billion francs in reparation, II: 60, 124,n7
Seton-Watson, Robert William, I: 301n3
Sevastopol, Russia, I: 9n1; II: 28
Sexten Valley, II: 50-51
Seymour, Charles, I: 6n2, 55n1, 440n5; II: 218n1
Shantung question, I: xxxix, 319-28, 329-36, 331, 396-97, 401-408, 423,n3, 425-27; II: 98, 552; Japanese desire for concessions in, I: xxii; Sino-Japanese notes of Sept. 24, 1918, I: 251n4, 405; Balfour's draft declaration on, I: 406; Germany on, II: 420n4; map of, I: xlvii
Shaping of the Czechoslovak State (Perman), I: 61n6, 144n1
Shotwell, James T., I: 123n1
Siam: see Thailand
Siberia, II: 13, 551n8, 561
Silesia, II: 256, 278, 279, 314, 388
Simon, Henry, II: 582; on mandates in Africa and the Pacific, I: 498, 502, 508
Sinha, Satyendra Prasanno, 1st Baron Sinah of Raipur, II: 98
Sinn Fein, I: 501
Sixtus, Bourbon Parma, Prince, II: 38
Sixtus Affair, II: 38n3
Skoda: armament plant, II: 81
Skoropadskii, Hetman Pavel Petrovich, II: 145

Smillie, Robert, I: 35,n5
Smith, Sir Hubert Llewellyn, I: 370n1, 374, 383; II: 336, 385
Smuts, Gen. Jan Christiaan, I: 98; II: 105, 471; on severity of German treaty terms, I: 36,n6, 37; on Danzig, I: 37, 38; visits Hungary, I: 99,n10; on Hungarian situation, I: 165, 181; opposed to publishing text of treaty, I: 486
Smyrna (now Izmir, Turkey), I: 128, 480n3; II: 553; map of, I: xlvii; Italian ships sent to, I: 422, 450, 453, 483; II: 37, 47, 56, 70, 93, 114; landing Greek troops at, II: 29, 31, 36, 41, 48, 92, 109n1, 254; threat of massacre at, II: 47; massacres in, II: 49; refugees from, II: 116
Socialisme à l'Oeuvre, Le (Mantoux), I: viiin5
Socialist Conference of Bern: requests meeting with Big Four, II: 68
Sofia, Bulgaria, I: 483
Soissons, France, I: 3
Somaliland, II: 56, 59
Some Problems of the Peace Conference (Haskins and Lord), I: xlv, 55n1, 91n6
Sonnino, Sidney, II: 106n5; question of opium trade, I: 265; question of Suez Canal, I: 265; issue of German renunciation of non-European territories, I: 265; question of upkeep of occupation armies, I: 265; on requiring German revelation of production secrets on asphyxiating gas, I: 267; proposals on disposition of maritime prizes, I: 268; on Italy's claims to Dalmatia, Zara, and Spalato, I: 284-85, 299, 366; on Wilson's position on Adriatic question, I: 289,n7, 296; leaves conference, I: 364; on Italian Parliament and Adriatic question, I: 364; delivers reply to note on landing at Scala Nuova, II: 109,n1, 110; on Greek action at Smyrna, II: 118; on possibility of separate peace with several German states, II: 501; on plebiscite in Klagenfurt Basin, II: 508-509, 510; on period of residence required to participate in Klagenfurt plebiscite, II: 511; on naval terms, II: 532; refuses to grant Germans further delay, II: 519; on

INDEX

Southern Austrian Railways, II: 594; on transmitting minutes of meetings of Council of Four, II: 599, 600, 601
Sookine, Jean, II: 14n2
South Africa, II: 269
South Tyrol, I: 125n4
South-west Africa, I: 313, 497, 498
Sorbonne: see Université de Paris
Southern Austrian Railways: question of status of company in successor states, II: 232,n3, 585, 593-97
Souvenir de Albert Thomas, Le, I: xi
Spa, Belgium: discussions with Germans at, I: 43, 113, 114, 116, 266; II: 186, 344; see also Armistice Commission
Spain, I: 461
Spalato (now Split, Yugoslavia), I: 127, 133, 280, 328, 336
Spanish-American War, I: 119
Spartacists, I: 166
Spartacist Uprising of 1919 and the Crisis of the German Socialist Movement, The (Waldman), I: 166n3
Spector, Sherman D., I: 10n2
Spier, Gen., II: 233-34
Stanislau (now Stanislav, Poland), II: 309
Stettin (now Szczeciu, Poland), I: 203; II: 21, 427, 486; passage of Haller's army through, I: 68-69, 113, 114
Stevens, John Frank, II: 13-14,n1
Stockholm, Sweden, II: 427
Strandmann, Otto, II: 344,n9
Strasbourg, I: 59, 382
Strauss, Albert, I: 388n2
Stuhm (now Sztum, Poland), I: 201, 271
Styria, II: 298
submarine cables, I: 275, 438, 458, 462-65, 480-81; II: 366; Japan on, I: 321; and Yap Island, I: 250, 275; German right to raise and use cables cut during war, I: 275; Japanese claims to, I: 465
submarines, submarine warfare, I: 122, 188; destruction of, I: 378; German, I: 435; Austrian, II: 6
Südbahn: see Southern Austrian Railways
Suez Canal, I: 375, 376
Sumner, John Andrew Hamilton, Baron Sumner of Ibstone, I: 5-6n2, 16, 22, 80, 151, 153n4, 172, 218, 237; II: 177, 287, 363n4, 366, 385; on proportional distribution of reparations, I: 28-29, 30; on duration of reparation payments, I: 148; draft establishing commission, I: 153n4, 156n4, 172; on Reparation Commission, II: 364n5; memorandum on reparations, II: 369,n6, 384,n5
Superior Blockade Council: *Note to be transmitted to the Councils of Heads of State,* II: 425
Supreme Council of the Principal Allied and Associated Powers: see Council of Four
Supreme Economic Council, I: 104n7, 159, 185, 265, 370,n1; II: 64, 453, 486, 588; requests that Council of Four decide on question of raw materials, II: 7; and occupation of left bank of Rhine, II: 251; and plans for blockade if Germany refuses to sign treaty, II: 430; and blockade of Bolshevik Russia and Hungary, II: 480, 483; transition from to League of Nations, II: 596-97,n1
Supreme War Council, I: 424; II: 376, 472; P. Mantoux interprets for, I: ix; on Heligoland, I: 253; established by Rapallo Agreement, I: 253n1; plan for occupation of Turkey, I: 484n3; to study reduction of army of occupation, II: 7; to report on measures to be taken should Germany fail to sign treaty, II: 17,n3; response to German note concerning Saar Valley, II: 167n3; on troop strengths for small powers, II: 182n5, 314n1; military representatives redraft military terms of Austrian treaty, II: 306n7; Joint Note No. 43 on achieving immediate Hungarian cease-fire in Czechoslovakia, II: 338,n1; report on conditions in Estonia, II: 424; meeting to discuss action in event of German failure to sign treaty, II: 493-502; on strength of army of occupation, II: 563; question of aid to Poland in event of a conflict with Germany, II: 564
Sušak: see Fiume

Swem, Charles Lee, **I**: xv
Switzerland, **I**: 104,n5, 493; **II**: 33
Sydorenko, Gregory, **II**: 143n1, 146; on conflict with Poland, **II**: 143-44
Sykes, Sir Mark, **II**: 93
Sykes-Picot Treaty, **II**: 132, 135, 136, 160, 588
Syria, **I**: 231, 380-83; **II**: 132, 133, 134-35, 136, 160-65, 266, 553, 554; mandate over, **I**: 483; **II**: 129, 130, 569n2; railroad transiting, **II**: 135-36, 161

Taiping Rebellion, **I**: 406,n1
Tansill, Charles Callan, **I**: 500n1
Tardieu, André-Pierre-Gabriel-Amédée, **I**: xxxvn4, 6n2, 40n1, 55n1, 123, 132, 138, 230; **II**: 214, 231n2, 292, 418, 456,n5, 562; receives copy of Mantoux' manuscript, **I**: xvii; and French security, **I**: 42; on the Saar Valley, **I**: 55-59, 214n2; **II**: 166, 195,n1; on coal production of Saar Valley, **I**: 213; and establishment of Belgian-German border, **I**: 139, 259; on Eupen-Malmédy Railroad, **I**: 139, 259; on discussions on Dutch-German border, **I**: 261; workload of Drafting Committee, **I**: 270; presents articles on Alsace-Lorraine, **I**: 430-35; on Germany buying back marks from Alsace-Lorraine, **I**: 432-43; prepares summary of treaty for publication, **I**: 486; "Tardieu Plan" to settle Adriatic Question, **II**: 138-40; on Klagenfurt Basin, **II**: 510; on merchant shipping, **II**: 584,n3; *see also* Tardieu Memorandum, Tardieu Plan
Tardieu Memorandum: on Saar, **I**: 195-96, 198,n2, 205, 211
Tardieu Plan, **II**: 138-40, 236,n1, 241, 327; and Italy, **II**: 323,n1
tariffs: Clémentel on, **I**: 371, 373
Taurus River, **II**: 476
Tarvis (now Tarvisio, Italy), Tarvis Pass, **II**: 51, 219, 236n1, 324, 342, 561; map of, **I**: xlix
Tashkent, Russia, **II**: 98
Tauern River, **II**: 451
Taussig, Frank William, **I**: 374
Taylor, Allan, **I**: 440n5
Taylor, Alonzo Englebert, M.D., **II**: 294

Temperley, Harold William Vazeille, **I**: li, 55n1, 61n6
Temps, Le, **I**: 182n4; **II**: 136; prints report of Commission on Polish Affairs, **I**: 69n2
Teschen (now Tesin, Czechoslovakia, and Cieszyn, Poland): Teschen Basin, **I**: 61,n6, 98, 386; **II**: 3, 88; and supplying coal to Bohemia, **I**: 229; map of, **I**: xlix
Thaddée, Ann-Yuen Yong, **I**: 251n3
Thailand, **I**: 493
Thasos, **II**: 555
Theiss River, **II**: 376, 377, 378
Théry, Edmond Amédée, **I**: 24,n1
Thompson, John M., **I**: 208n2; **II**: 189n5, 471n3
Thorn (Toruń, Poland), **I**: 101n4, 126
Thrace, **I**: 505; **II**: 95, 98, 555
Thwaites, Maj. Gen. William: on aid to Denikin, **I**: 13
Tillman, Seth P., **I**: 6n2, 105n1
Tilsit (now Sovietsk), Russia, **II**: 309
Tiraspol, Russia, **I**: 9n1
Tirpitz, Grand Adm. Alfred von, **I**: 188
Tisza, István, Count, **I**: 12, 429
Tittoni, Tommaso, **I**: 444; **II**: 565,n1, 567, 568, 571, 572, 573, 574, 586
Togoland, **I**: 496, 499, 508; **II**: 130, 582
Tökés, Rudolf L., **I**: 10n2
Tomsk, Russia, **II**: 483
Toynbee, A. J., **I**: xn8
Trachtenberg, Marc, **I**: xix, 6n2, 105n5
Trades Union Congress, **I**: 66n9
Trans-Siberian Railway, **II**: 13-14,n1, 191, 203, 528, 586
Transylvania, **I**: xxiv, 9n2, 12; **II**: 376
Trask, David F., **I**: 253n1
Trau (now Trogir, Yugoslavia), **I**: 280
Travers l'Angleterre Contemporaine (Mantoux), **I**: viii-ix
treaties of guarantee: *see* France
Treaty of 1839, **I**: 91,n6, 92, 139, 188, 190, 262
Treaty of 1871: *see* Treaty of Frankfurt
Treaty of Algeciras, **II**: 215
Treaty of Berlin, 1878, **I**: 473n7; **II**: 56, 319
Treaty of Bucharest, **I**: 9n2
Treaty of Campo-Formio, **I**: 280

Treaty of Frankfurt, I: 342,n6; II: 252; and Alsace-Lorraine, I: 86,n2, 205,n1; II: 330

Treaty of London (1915), I: 125,n4, 227, 308, 421n2, 479, 480, 494; II: 37, 38, 52, 109, 240, 241, 326, 328, 340, 569, 573,n5; and Adriatic question, I: xxii, 280, 287, 290, 344, 345; II: 212; U.S. did not sign, I: 276,n1; dissolution of Austria-Hungary leaves obsolete, I: 292, 316, 482; meeting of signatories, I: 296, 299; possible abrogation of if Italy refuses to participate in negotiations, I: 344, 350; Italy may be compensated with Smyrna, II: 36, 109n1; Wilson suggests spirit of Fourteen Points had superseded, II: 223

Treaty of Vienna, I: 493
Trebizond, Turkey, I: 483
Treitschke, Heinrich von, I: 57
Trentino, I: 292, 299; II: 292
Trianon Palace, I: xxiii, 420
Trier, Germany, I: 445
Trieste, I: 125n4, 128, 277, 292, 299; II: 6, 44, 45, 46, 52, 292, 342, 343, 442, 443
Trieste-Villach Railway, II: 40, 51
Tripoli (Lebanon), II: 136,n6, 161
Tripoli expedition (Libya), I: 482
Trotsky, Leon, I: xx
Trumbić, Ante, II: 291; on Fiume, I: 129-36, 304; II: 52
Truth about the Peace Treaties, The (Lloyd George), I: 6n2, 40n1
Truth about the Treaty, The (Tardieu), I: 6n2, 40n1, 54n1
Tsaritsyn (now Volgograd, U.S.S.R.), I: 13; II: 204
Tsinan, China, I: 404
Tsingtao-Huang Ho Railroad, I: 321,n6, 330; Japanese to administer, I: 312-13, 425,n4; merger of railroad with coal mining company, I: 323, 330; and Sino-Japanese relations, I: 331; on Japanese policing of railroad in China, I: 402, 403, 404, 425n4; *see also* China
Tumulty, Joseph Patrick, I: 471,n5
Turco-Italian War, I: 482,n2
Turkey, I: 111; II: 57, 216, 255, 476-77, 507,n1, 508,n2, 552, 565, 566, 583, 602; possible landing in Smyrna, I: 506; informed of landing, I: 506; II: 29, 30, 36, 47; Moslems of India on, II: 95-100, 508, 520; memorandum from delegation on suggested reorganization of Ottoman Empire, II: 555-56, 573; map of, I: xlvii

Turkey, the Great Powers, and the Bagdad Railway: A Study in Imperialism (Earle), I: 336n3

Twenty-one demands, I: 403, 404; V. K. Wellington Koo on, I: 331; U.S. protested, I: 332, 333

Tyrol, I: xxii, 303, 447, 460; *see also* Austria

Ubangi River, I: 499n1
Uchida, Yasuya, I: 326n7
Ukraine, Ukrainians, I: xxiv, 44; II: 5, 238, 309, 310; and Poland, I: 118n1, 501; II: 125, 143, 144, 145, 147-48,n2, 149-53; on Poles in Lemberg, I: 248-49; II: 257-58; borders of, II: 3, 317; atrocities in Galicia, II: 103, 104, 146, 312; Bolsheviks in, II: 205

Ukrainian Revolution, 1917-1920: A Study in Nationalism, The (Reshetar), I: 9n1

Uniates, II: 145
United States and French Security, 1917-1921, The (Yates), I: 40n1
United States Department of State: publishes Hankey's Minutes of Council of Four meetings, I: xvii
United States in the Supreme War Council: American War Aims and Inter-Allied Strategy, The (Trask), I: 253n1
United States Senate, I: 4
United States Treasury, II: 7
Université de Paris, Sorbonne: Mantoux receives doctorate, I: vii
University College, London, I: ix
University of Geneva, I: x, xi
University of London, I: ix
University of Prague, II: 298
Unterberger, Betty Miller, II: 14n1
Upper Silesia, I: xxiv; II: 270, 451, 457, 458; possible plebiscite in, I: xxv, xxvi; II: 131, 280, 281, 282, 283, 284,

Upper Silesia (cont.)
285, 307, 308, 390, 393, 419, 422; German clergy in, II: 386; National Polish Party of, II: 390, 391; possible insurrection in, II: 535
Urofsky, Melvin I., I: 440n5

Vaide-Voevod, Alexandru, II: 393n5
Valenciennes, France, I: 8
Van den Heuvel, Jules-Norbert-Marie: discusses Belgium's reparation requests, I: 413-14
Van der Vat, Dan, II: 513n5
Vandervelde, Émile, I: 239, 415-16
Vannutelli-Rey, Count Luigi, II: 418
Vatican, I: 299; ownership of German Catholic missions, II: 421, 422, 459,n1
Veglia (now Krk Island, Yugoslavia), II: 241, 324, 328
Vénisélos, Eleutherios Kyrios, II: 110, 111, 112, 177, 341, 481, 567; requests Allied warship be sent to Smyrna, I: 454; possibility of landing troops in Smyrna, I: 505, 506; negotiations with Entente for Greek aid to Serbia in return for concessions in Asia Minor, II: 114; landing at Smyrna, II: 115, 212; and Greek cooperation with Adm. Calthorpe, II: 115; on Greek refugees, II: 116; on arms limitation, II: 316
Verhandlungen der Verfassunggebenden Deutschen Nationalversammlung, Stenographische Berichte (Germany. Nationalversammlung), II: 49n1
Vernon, Marjorie, I: viiin4
Versailles Twenty Years After (Birdsall), I: 6n2, 55n1, 105n1
Vesnić, Milenko R., I: 394, 503; on Klagenfurt Basin and plebiscite in, II: 298-301, 302-303, 304, 343, 511; on disarmament, II: 315-16, 320-22
Viatka (now Kirov, U.S.S.R.), II: 204, 205, 551n8
Vienna, Austria, I: 386, 439; II: 220, 294, 469; possible occupation of, I: 45-46, 48, 181; possible Bolshevik coup in, I: 45, 181
Viefhaus, Erwin, I: 440n5
Vierteljahrshefte für Zeitgeschichte, I: 73n5

Villach, Austria, II: 51, 343
Villemain, Gen., II: 155, 233
Villers-Cotterêts, II: 164,n2
Vistula River, I: 106, 124, 271, 581
Vix, Lt. Col. Ferdinand, I: 10n2, 74n9, 75,n10, 76, 95, 98
Vladivostok, Russia, II: 561
Voldemaras, Augustinas, II: 27n11
Völgyes, Ivan, I: 10n2
Vologda, Russia, II: 205
Volosca, I: 367
Von der Goltz, Maj. Gen. Gustav Adolf Joachim Rüdiger, I: 72n5, 523
Vorlarberg, Austria, II: 230,n1

Waldman, Eric, I: 166n3
Walsh, Francis Patrick, I: 500n1
Walworth, Arthur, I: xxx
Wandycz, Piotr S., I: 61n6
War and Society in East Central Europe, Vol. VI, Essays on World War I: Total War and Peacemaking, a Study on Trianon (Király), I: 97n8
Warburg, Max Moritz, II: 337, 352-53
Ward, Alan, I: 500n1
Ward, John, II: 33, 34
War Memoirs of David Lloyd George (Lloyd George), I: 66n9
Warsaw: Haller's troops sent to, I: 68-72
Weimar, Germany, II: 20, 468, 494, 498
Weimar Republic: see Germany
Wemyss, Adm. of the Fleet Rosslyn Erskine, 1st Baron of Wemyss, I: 184n6; II: 8
Weser River, II: 496, 498, 500
Western Ukrainian National Republic, II: 309n5
Weygand, Gen. Maxime, II: 474, 475; on transport of Haller's army, I: 102, 103, 113-15, 167-68, 265; on action should Germany refuse to sign treaty, II: 21, 496
What Really Happened at Paris: The Story of the Peace Conference, 1918-1919 (House and Seymour, eds.), I: 6n2, 55n1, 440n5
White, Henry, I: 424, 429n2; II: 386
White against Red: The Life of General Anton Denikin (Lehovich), I: 9n1
William II: discussion of possible prosecution of, I: 119n2, 189, 190; II: 554,

569, 598; Yellow Peril speech, I: 336
Williams, Edward Thomas, I: 378
Williams, Warren E., I: 72n5
Wilson, Field Marshal Sir Henry Hughes, I: 69, 89, 183, 446; II: 101, 132, 135, 138, 253, 350; on military action in event of German failure to sign treaty, II: 141
Wilson, Woodrow, I: xxvii-xxviii; tribute to by Mantoux, I: xi,n13; suggests Council of Four meet at his residence, I: xiv; visits battlefields, I: 3; on importance of including Covenant in peace treaty, I: 4; addresses Third Plenary Session, I: 4n1; on German ability to pay reparations, I: 5-6, 77-78; on duration of payment of reparation, I: 7, 22; and interdependence of claims, I: 8, 422; and Hungarian-Rumanian frontier, I: 12; on supplying Odessa or Rumania, I: 12, 44, 48; on state of German economy, I: 20; on showing moderation toward Germany, I: 20, 27; amount of reparation, I: 22, 85; II: 286; on sending commission to Near East, I: 39; and opposition to formation of Rhenish republic, I: 39n1; and French security treaties, I: 40n1; on aid to Rumania, I: 44; and specifying amount of reparation, I: 50, 105; and question of Saar Valley, I: 54n3, 60, 80, 195-96, 206, 228; II: 303-304; on uniform application of principle of justice to all states, I: 61-62; Fourteen Points of, I: 66n9, 206, 291,n1, II: 284,n2; on sending mission to Hungary, I: 75, 95-96; and Klotz plan for reparation, I: 80; returns to Paris from U.S., I: 92,n7; on Haller's army passing through Danzig, I: 100, 113-15; victualing of Bavaria, I: 103,n5; and reparation for deportation of workers, I: 106; on Danzig, I: 106, 107, 108, 124; II: 257; meets with R. Dmowski and I. Paderewski, I: 107,n4, 108; on responsibilities and possible war crimes trials, I: 110, 119, 120, 121, 188; on trying William II, I: 119, 189; II: 548, 554, 560; on status of Fiume, I: 127-28, 315; calls up *U.S.S. George Washington* in preparation to depart if there is no progress on question of France's eastern borders, I: 182n4; on responsibilities, I: 188, 197; on Polish-German border, I: 200; on issuance of German bonds, I: 220, 222, 224, 225; II: 7; on commission to Near East, I: 231,n3; on publication of preliminaries of the peace, I: 232, 235, 342; visited by Polish peasants, I: 234; on summoning German plenipotentiaries, I: 238, 239-40, 241, 243, 244; discusses Adriatic question with Orlando, I: 245,n2; on question of cables and internationalizing Yap Island, I: 250, 275, 463; on Sino-Japanese controversy over Kiaochow, I: 251, 273, 378, 379, 380; on Heligoland, I: 253, 254, 255; on Danish border, I: 257; on Kiel Canal, I: 257,n1, 264, 268, 374, 375; drawing of German-Belgian border, I: 257, 258, 260; compares Eupen-Malmédy Railroad to Danzig-Mława line, I: 261; question of rectifying Dutch-German border, I: 261; Wilson Line, I: 277n2; on uniform application of principles of peace, I: 281, 289, 294, 315; II: 106; agrees with Orlando on Italian territorial claims within her natural boundaries, I: 281; on Italian claims to Fiume and Dalmatia, I: 281-82, 283, 307-308, 345-46; interest in keeping great powers out of Balkans, I: 283; U.S. cannot abide by provisions of Treaty of London, I: 289, 290-91; II: 213; ready to concede island of Lissa to Italy, I: 295; message to the Italian people describing American position on Adriatic, I: 307-308, 311, 314-17,n5, 329, 338; opposed to Haller's army proceeding to Lemberg, I: 309; possible action should Germany refuse to sign the peace, I: 310; supports making Fiume a free city, I: 311, 364; on inflexibility of Japanese position, I: 312; and Tsingtao Railroad, I: 312; drafts formula for movements of German delegates, I: 316; questions Japanese representatives on mines in China, I: 323; on disposition of former German concession in China, I: 323-24; on meeting with Chinese delegates

Wilson, Woodrow (cont.)
without Japanese present, I: 327; on Anglo-Japanese treaty, I: 329; recommends placing former German concessions in China in hands of the five powers as trustees, I: 330; on Japanese Twenty-one demands of China, I: 331, 332, 333, 404, 425; on ending extraterritoriality in China, I: 333; on publishing summary of preliminaries, I: 355, 356; on Kiel Canal, I: 356,n5, 357; on destruction of German ships, I: 378; wishes to set date to open negotiations with Austrians, I: 386; on verification of German credentials, I: 386; and recognition of Kingdom of Serbs, Croats and Slovenes, I: 387, 394; on period allowed for German review of treaty, I: 387; remarks on differences between Alsace-Lorraine and former German colonies, I: 391; question of German disclosure of trade secrets regarding gases and explosives, I: 393; recommends inviting all nations which declared war on Germany to sign treaty, I: 395; American public opinion demands just settlement between China and Japan, I: 400, 403; on Japanese policing of railroad in China, I: 401-402; and extraterritoriality in China, I: 402, 406; on draft declaration on Shantung, I: 406, 407-408; rejects suggestion to hold prisoners hostage until Germany turns over alleged criminals, I: 409; has small stroke, I: 419n5; on provision for construction of airfields in Germany, I: 420; on makeup of Reparation Commission, I: 420-21; discusses possible presence of journalists at presentation of peace terms to German delegation, I: 423; on summoning Austrians and Hungarians to peace conference, I: 428, 429; on question of Germany buying back marks from Alsace-Lorraine, I: 432, 433; discusses difficulties presented by absence of Italian delegation, I: 436, 437, 438; annoyed with Poincaré's letter to Italy, I: 437, 451; opposed to monopoly of submarine cables, I: 438; insists upon guarantees for national and religious minorities, I: 439, 440; II: 8, 89, 90; question of blockade, I: 442; and publication of Balfour letter on Italian question, I: 448, 468-69; on notifying Italians of meeting with German delegation, I: 450, 451; Italian absence from meeting with German delegation will be an abrogation of the Pact of London, I: 454, 477; on Italian actions in Dodecanese Islands, I: 480n3, 494; and French security treaties, I: 489,n1, 490; II: 590-92; does not have constitutional authority to station troops in a country not at war with U.S., I: 494; on possible American mandate for Constantinople or Armenia, I: 494-95; on need to land Greek troops in Smyrna, I: 496; II: 38, 48; recommends treating question of borders of Austria and successor states together, II: 3, 5; on speed of evacuation of U.S. forces in Army of Occupation, II: 13; discusses American presence in Siberia and attitude of Kolchak and Cossacks, II: 13-14, 16; on German desire to join League of Nations, II: 19,n2, 404,n5; replies to German notes, II: 24-25,n6, 32n1, 118; on N. Chaikovskii, II: 25, 33; on determining fixed sum of reparation for successor states of Austria-Hungary, II: 35; opposed to cession of Smyrna to Italy, II: 37; on labor legislation and Germany, II: 46; plan for settlement of Adriatic question, II: 50-51, 53; believes Senate will accept mandate in Armenia, II: 55; on treatment of Greece, II: 56; obligation to Turkish population, II: 57; agrees to give Italy a mandate over Makri, II: 57; on provisions concerning railroads serving Adriatic in Austrian Treaty, II: 60, 62, 63; supports military occupation of Germany if refuses to sign treaty, II: 65; on Luxembourg, II: 68, 217-18; discusses mandates in Asia Minor, II: 70; wishes to limit armaments of all eastern European states, II: 79, 80, 81, 192-93, 239, 305-306, 314-15,n1; on armaments manufacture by Austria,

II: 81; on landing at Scala Nuova, II: 83, 117; on publication of treaty provision, II: 84; on Poland, II: 86; on Ukrainian atrocities in Galicia, II: 103; on possibility of Allied occupation of Budapest, II: 104-105; on Sultan residing in Constantinople, II: 107, 137; on Russian situation, II: 119; discusses Lenin's reply to Nansen proposal, II: 122; on German request for extension, II: 125; on use of plebiscite in Fiume and Upper Silesia, II: 131; suggests France send commission to Syria at once, II: 137; on Near Eastern situation, II: 137, 237; suggests acceptance of German request for delay, II: 141; on warning to Poland to stop hostilities with Ukraine, II: 148, 149, 150; reads reply to German delegation on economic consequences of the treaty, II: 153; on annulment of contracts by mixed tribunals, II: 199; informs Japanese delegation of message to Kolchak, II: 200; on dealing with Austria differently from Germany, II: 206, 207; concerned with protection of minorities in Austria and Hungary, II: 214; on Klagenfurt Basin, II: 219, 220, 234-35, 302, 304, 487, 508, 509, 510, 511; notes similarities between Fourteen Points and Lloyd George's speech, II: 222-23; spirit of Fourteen Points and League of Nations supercedes Treaty of London, II: 223; on summoning nations involved to reading of summary of Austrian treaty, II: 239; on army of occupation in the Rhineland, II: 252; reads reply to last German note on labor legislation, II: 257; on Allied right of expropriation as means of compensation, II: 278, 279; on question of plebiscite in Upper Silesia, II: 280, 282, 285, 303, 307, 310, 386, 391-92, 422, 452, 453, 454, 457, 458; on size of future Austrian Army, II: 304, 306, 314; reads Kolchak's reply to Allied demand for guarantees, II: 333; on German membership in League of Nations, II: 347; draft reply by American commissioners to German counterproposal on reparation, II: 354-55, 357-58; and expense of occupation army, II: 369, 370, 455; discusses Hungarian situation, II: 375-76, 378, 393; Foreign Ministers to determine Czechoslovak-Hungarian and Hungarian-Rumanian borders, II: 381-82, 393,n5; reads reply to German counterproposals on reparation, II: 382; reads reply to German counterproposals on Saar Basin, II: 405; on publication of treaty, II: 418, 442; reads text of reply to German counterproposals on Alsace-Lorraine, II: 418,n2; on fixing boundary between Poland and Ukraine, II: 420; and plebiscite in Galicia, II: 420; and reply to German counterproposals on military clauses, II: 423,n5; reads reply to German counterproposals on naval clauses, II: 423,n6; prefers military action to blockade in event of German failure to sign treaty, II: 426, 461, 462, 468; discusses arrangements for occupation of left bank of Rhine, II: 428,n3, 429, 437n1; on railways, II: 442, 443, 450-51; on expropriation of German property, II: 452-53; comments upon shift in Foch's position, II: 465, 466, 472, 473, 474, 475, 478; believes only members of Council of League of Nations should appeal to League when article on minorities is violated, II: 472; anticipates return to U.S. immediately upon signing of treaty, II: 480; and procedure of appeal to League of Nations for violation of minority rights, II: 481, 482-83; on possibility of separate peace with several German states, II: 499; drafts reply to Germans saying Germans must sign treaty without reservation, II: 513; on scuttling of German fleet at Scapa Flow, II: 513, 532, 533, 534, 539; refuses to grant Germans further delay, II: 519; on guaranteeing Jewish schools and use of Yiddish in Poland, II: 524, 525, 526, 527, 581; wishes Sultan removed from Constantinople, II: 553, 554; and seals for treaty, II: 558; on Italian presence in Fiume, I:

Wilson, Woodrow (*cont.*)
385, 453; on demanding withdrawal of Italian troops from Asia Minor and Fiume, II: 570, 572, 574, 575, 586-87; on Southern Austrian Railways, II: 593; Memorandum of Additional Suggestions Concerning Conferences with Italian Delegation, II: 589; on Bethmann Hollweg's request to be tried in lieu of William II, II: 598, 598-99; on transmitting minutes of meetings of Council of Four, II: 599, 600, 601

Wilson and His Peacemakers: American Diplomacy at the Paris Peace Conference 1919 (Walworth), I: xxx

Wilson Line (American Line): proposed northern and northeastern Italian borders, I: 277n2; II: 328, 340

Wilson: The Struggle for Neutrality, 1914-1915 (Link), I: 251n5

Windau (now Ventspils, Estonia), II: 424, 428

Wise, Edward Frank, II: 596n1; on arrangements for occupation of left bank of Rhine, II: 430

With Firmness in the Right: American Diplomatic Action Affecting Jews, 1840-1945 (Adler and Margalith), I: 473n7

Wolf, Lucien, II: 89

Wolff, Theodor, II: 349

Woodrow Wilson and the American Diplomatic Tradition: The Treaty Fight in Perspective (Ambrosius), II: 480n3

"Woodrow Wilson and National Self-determination along Italy's Frontier . . ." (Kernek), I: 125n4

Woodrow Wilson and the Far East: The Diplomacy of the Shantung Question (Fifield), I: 251n5

Woodrow Wilson and the Great Betrayal (Bailey), II: 480n3

Woodrow Wilson and the Rebirth of Poland, 1914-1920 (Gerson), I: 107n4

Woodrow Wilson and World Settlement (Baker), I: xxxvn4

Woodrow Wilson, Revolutionary Germany, and Peacemaking (Schwabe), I: 445n2

World Crisis (Professors of the Graduate Institute of International Affairs), I: xn6

Württemberg, II: 217, 298, 463, 494, 501

Yamagata, Marquis, I: 326

Yap: WW requests internationalization of because of position as juncture of cable lines, I: 250, 275

Yates, Louis A. R., I: 40n1

Yiddish, II: 506, 524-27

Yudenich, Gen. Nikolai Nikolaevich, II: 15, 28

Yugoslavia, II: 255, 291,n6, 314n1, 328; and determination of Italian frontiers and Fiume, I: 67n11; II: 241; will fight to keep Fiume, I: 304; conquest of Montenegro, I: 337n4; recognition of, I: 386, 387, 394; borders of, I: 387; II: 3, 5, 234, 298; possibility of Italian construction of new port for, II: 53, 108-109; requests return of materials from Austrian museums, libraries, and archives which relate to Yugoslavia, II: 177; and Klagenfurt Basin, II: 218n4, 254, 268, 353

Zagreb, Yugoslavia, I: 133, 134

Zaharoff, Sir Basil, II: 369

Zara (now Zadar, Yugoslavia), I: 280, 328, 336, 366, 367, 428, 476; II: 52, 236,n1, 240, 241, 324, 327, 328, 340

zemstvos, II: 27

Zervos, Skevos, I: 482n1

Zimmern, Alfred, I: xn8

"Zwischen Compiègne und Versailles: Geheime amerikanische Militärdiplomatie in der Periode des Waffenstillstandes 1918/19: Die Rolle des Obersten Arthur L. Conger" (Epstein), I: 445n2

DATE DUE

DEC 18 1992			
DEC 19 1992			
	JAN 1 8 2007		
MAR 2 2 2007			

Demco, Inc. 38-293